THE OPEN LEARNING FOUNDATION

An Active Learning Approach

MARKETING

Elizabeth Barnes, Richard Meyer,
Bob McClelland, Hildegard Wiesehöfer,
Mike Worsam

BLACKWELL
Business

Copyright © Open Learning Foundation Enterprises Ltd, 1997

First published 1997

Reprinted 1998

Blackwell Publishers Ltd
108 Cowley Road
Oxford OX4 1JF, UK

Blackwell Publishers Inc
350 Main Street
Malden, Massachusetts 02148, USA

British Library Cataloguing in Publication Data
A CIP catalogue record for this book is available from the British Library

Library of Congress Cataloging in Publication Data
Marketing: an active learning approach/Elizabeth Barnes ... [et al.].
p.   cm. — (BABS)
At head of title: Open Learning Foundation
Includes bibliographical references (p.   ).
ISBN 0–631–20183–1 (alk. paper)
1. Marketing. 2. Marketing—Management. I. Barnes, Elizabeth.
II. Open Learning Foundation. III. Series.
HF5415.M2949   1997   96—6590
658.8—dc21   CIP

Typeset in 10 on 12pt Times New Roman
Printed and bound in Great Britain
by T. J. International Limited, Padstow, Cornwall

This book is printed on acid-free paper

Copyright acknowledgments

Contents

Resources

GUIDE FOR STUDENTS

Course Introduction

Welcome to *Marketing*. The objectives of this guide are:

- to give you an outline of the subject of marketing;
- to explain why it is necessary for you to study marketing as part of your degree;
- to describe the nature of the material on which this workbook is based;
- to outline the programme which you will be following;
- to offer practical hints and advice on how to study marketing using the open learning approach;
- to point out some of the advantages to you of studying marketing by the method used in this book.

What is marketing?

Marketing is concerned with identifying and satisfying customers' and consumers' needs. Its aim is to ensure that the business is able to anticipate changes in these needs, and to gain and retain customers efficiently and profitably. Although marketing is concerned with satisfying these needs, its scope goes far beyond the process of selling goods and services. Indeed, to be truly effective, the marketing process needs to be present throughout the entire business process, building on a broad understanding of the markets which the business serves, designing into the product or service the characteristics which consumers and customers will find attractive and ensuring that the entire business adopts policies and strategies that cater for their needs.

Marketing is sometimes presented as a discrete, specialised function or as a set of techniques. But as this workbook will make clear, a more appropriate understanding of marketing only emerges when it is viewed as a business philosophy or as a principle around which the business can be organised and managed. Organisations which place an emphasis on production, with everything else as an afterthought, or which emphasise selling whatever is produced, may be able to survive and prosper in some limited markets. But increasingly it is those organisations which put consumer and customer considerations at the heart of their operations and which adopt a marketing orientation to their entire operations, which are the profitable survivors.

Ensuring that this is achieved can be a complex and challenging activity. Decisions must be implemented which affect:

- the **product** or **service**, ... ensuring that it has the qualities and features which consumers are willing to purchase, that it has a suitable 'image', that it has the appropriate bundle of service and warranties;
- the **price**, ... ensuring that the pricing enables new products to penetrate

the market and allows existing products to compete successfully;

- the **place**, ... locating products in the right outlets, selling through the most appropriate channels;

- **promotion**, ... choosing the most suitable set of market communication devices such as advertising, personal selling or sales promotion.

Why study marketing?

It should be clear from the above brief account that marketing is a crucial part of the study of business and not just a subject for those who wish to make a career in this particular field. In recent years, the significance of the marketing concept has become even more pronounced, with a far wider range of organisations accepting it as an approach to achieving their objectives. For example:

- Privatisation in a number of countries throughout the world has led to public utilities becoming more commercial in their activities by identifying consumer needs, considering different segments of the market and providing new products and services to meet their needs;

- Competition has been extended in such fields as health care and education, requiring medical practices, schools and universities to become to become more marketing minded;

- Political parties have turned to a marketing approach in a bid to build their memberships and to address the issues most likely to attract the voting public.

Though not without a considerable amount of controversy, this extension of the marketing approach means that there are few aspects of our daily lives which are not affected by it.

As the level of competition increases, in many industries on a global basis, the concept of a 'safe market' has begun to disappear. Unless the company can impress itself on the market place, can develop consumer loyalty and develop alternative marketing opportunities, it risks the danger of disappearance through merger, take-over or corporate collapse. Even in the small business, which may be without the resources to maintain a professional marketing specialist, the need for marketing understanding is still vital. The independent corner grocer and the privately-owned hotel need to develop a customer base and serve their customers' needs every bit as much as the nationwide supermarket chain or the multi-national hotel group.

But marketing is not simply a function which affects the relationship between the business and its external environment. The growth in the notion of the 'internal market', the idea that one's colleagues are also one's customers, means that a wide range of people in organisations require a grasp of marketing. Consider the following:

- a personnel manager attempting to define the kind of services that would best meet the needs of the user department;
- information systems designers aiming to produce a decision support system relevant to the needs of end users;
- a transport fleet manager who has to compete with external operators for the opportunity to carry the companys' products.

All have one thing in common, the need to apply a marketing orientation and the use of marketing techniques to service the needs of the internal market and to provide value to the organisation. Marketing can therefore be regarded as a key discipline for all who wish to operate successfully in business

What is in this workbook?

The core of the workbook is nine study units. These were written specifically for undergraduate business students by authors who are experienced in teaching such courses. The content has been revised as a result of comments from students and tutors who have worked through the material.

The units are particularly useful to students, like you, who may be following a course where an 'open learning' approach is being adopted. The features which make it particularly suitable for open learning include:

- Very careful sequencing of the materials so that there is a clear and logical progression;
- A step by step approach so that you will be able to understand each new point thoroughly before proceeding to the next one;
- A very clear layout with relatively short sections and paragraphs;
- Numerous short case studies and examples which help to illustrate the ideas and provide opportunities for analysis and developing understanding;
- Many worked examples, particularly on the computational areas, with an emphasis on understanding rather than on computation;
- Lots of opportunities for you to check that you understand what you have just read;
- Review activities for each unit which enable you to extend and apply your knowledge, as well as to test your understanding;
- Plenty of opportunities for you to test your progress through end-of-unit exercises to which solutions are provided.

Students on more conventional courses will also find that the workbook provides a useful supplement to other text books which they may have been recommended.

Reader

At the back of the book there is a resources section, a collection of journal articles and extracts from texts. This allows you the opportunity of wider reading but in a way which ensures that it is highly relevant and closely integrated with the material covered in the units. Many of the activities in the workbook relate to these readings. Particular features of the resources section are:

- A significant number of journal articles and extracts, each dealing with a significant issue in marketing;
- Up-to-date material, some of which deals with topical issues;
- Fairly short articles and extracts written in clear, non-technical language;
- Material particularly relevant to undergraduate business studies students.

Although the workbook is designed to be complete in itself, your understanding of Marketing will be improved by wider reading. Each unit therefore has a list of recommended reading to guide you towards the more important and useful literature.

Using the workbook

You will probably find it most effective to work through the units in sequence. You should begin by noting the points which the unit outlines identify as the crucial aspects of the material. This will put the contents of the units into context and guide you through them.

Each unit is interspersed with a number of 'activities' and review activities. All of these are intended to be attempted by you as they arise and completed before you move on. The suggested solutions to each activity are given immediately following the activity. The solutions to the review activities are given at the end of the relevant unit.

The activities are intended to be a combination of a check that you are following the unit and understanding it on the one hand, and a way of making your learning a more active experience for you, on the other. By working through the activities, you can effectively divide your study time between that necessary for taking on new ideas and that which is necessary to reinforce those ideas. The review activities allow you to consider larger sections of material, testing and extending your understanding, often by applying the ideas to case studies or to readings in the resource section.

The self-assessment questions are intended to give you the opportunity to see whether you have really grasped the content of the unit. The additional exercises are intended to give you further practice and the opportunity to reinforce your knowledge and understanding. Avoid the temptation to skip through the exercises quickly. They are there to assist you in developing your knowledge and understanding and your confidence with the material.

Typically, the activities will only take you a few minutes to deal with. By contrast, the review activities may take considerably longer to complete. It is important that you discipline yourself to complete each activity, self-assessment question or exercise before you refer to the answer provided.

You should read the items in the resources section when recommended.

Avoid rote learning

You should avoid any attempt at rote learning the material in this workbook. You should aim to understand the underlying 'logic' in the ideas being presented by working through all the activities. Simply trying to learn the theories or remember the techniques is inappropriate and insufficient. Rather, you should attempt to understand the principles behind the theoretical ideas and models and understand the thinking behind the particular marketing techniques presented.

Given the complexity of the subject matter which forms the focus of the study of marketing, it is rarely possible to present single solutions to marketing problems. By working with the ideas, thinking about their implications and how they can be applied, you will develop a deeper understanding of them than if you simply attempt to commit them to memory.

Set aside time for your studies

At the start of the study period you will not know how long it will take to do the necessary work. It is sensible therefore, to make a start on the work at an early stage in the study period. Try to discipline yourself to set aside particular times in the week to study, though not necessarily the same times each week. Experiment with different ways of studying the material to find the one which suits you. Try skimming each unit to get a grasp of the ideas covered before you go through it in detail. Alternatively, try reading the unit objectives and the summaries before you settle down to study the unit in any depth. Try to find the most suitable time to study when your concentration is at its highest and interruptions are at a minimum. And do set aside sufficient time to complete all the activities – they are a crucial part of the learning process.

UNIT 1

INTRODUCTION TO MARKETING MANAGEMENT

Introduction

MARKETING ORIENTATION

Marketing is a specialised management activity which only becomes needed when market places become competitive. Whilst demand exceeds supply there can appear to be little need for marketing since everything can be sold quite easily. There is a temptation to take a cavalier approach to customers when they have little choice but to buy what is available. This, however, generates negative attitudes in the market place that only become apparent when supply catches up with and exceeds demand. Much work, time and expense has then to be expended in attempts to repair the relationships.

Marketing is concerned with identifying and satisfying customer and consumer need. Thus a marketer should automatically look at every situation from the viewpoint of the customer – be 'customer oriented'. Profits come from long-term customer and consumer satisfaction. Organisations that are 'product oriented' make products which they believe will be acceptable and then go out to sell them. Given the same market conditions, a marketing-oriented firm will be the more secure and will generate larger profits.

Marketing has a key functional role as the only part of the organisation which has proactive contact with customers; it is the bridge to the customer and the consumer. This is the aspect of marketing which most people recognise, and which can be thought to be marketing's sole role. But unless marketers take an active part at corporate level it is unlikely that the organisation *as a whole* will have a customer focus. A major role for marketing management is therefore to encourage and reinforce a marketing orientation that permeates every sector of the organisation.

At corporate level any organisation has a relationship with its environment – the need to manage this relationship should be obvious, but unfortunately this realisation only came to many British firms in the take-over battles of the 1970s when they found that although their brands might be well known the organisation itself was not. Corporate managers quickly came to realise the need to use marketing's core skills to market the organisation as well as its products.

MARKETING'S CORPORATE ROLE

The role of the marketing department within any organisation is to help focus corporate thinking – to use its special skills for the overall benefit of the organisation. Proactive marketers will be aware that when relating to their colleagues they are dealing with internal customers/consumers, with people who have needs. They need to apply identical techniques *inside* the organisation as outside. There is the necessity to have one's plans 'bought' by senior management, for other functions to co-operate, for marketing to be seen as helpful and essential. All of this can be achieved, but only if marketers realise that they are dependent on internal goodwill just as much as on external trade.

Marketing, however, is essentially a mind set which anybody can adopt. Thus, senior managers from other functions are adding marketing qualifications to their major disciplines and professional marketers are in danger of being shut out of corporate level planning and restricted to their functional role. In particular, marketers face a serious threat from public relations practitioners who are brought in to advise the Chief Executive on corporate communications and therefore to establish the communications policy for the organisation. Communications policy is of key marketing importance and if control of this policy is lost then marketing is automatically relegated to a functional role.

The career potential of individual marketing managers is dependent upon the profession actively gearing its thinking to the corporate level in addition to retaining its vital role as a major functional discipline.

THE PURPOSE OF THE MODULE

This module as a whole is designed to provide you with more than simply an understanding of marketing's role. You will find a need for marketing in whatever form of organisation you join, whatever functional speciality you take up. You already are involved with marketing – without, perhaps, being aware – because you are actively relating to your environment. You will find that the practical marketing skills contained in this module will enhance your career prospects as well as helping any organisation you join to be more effective.

In this unit we shall introduce the concept of marketing, explain the key terms you will need, and help you to establish a foundation upon which to build as you progress.

Objectives

By the end of this unit you should be able to:

- determine the role and effectiveness of marketing in given circumstances
- identify the key stages in the corporate planning process
- establish management objectives
- use key marketing terms correctly
- approach the remainder of this course with confidence.

SECTION 1

Management

Introduction

This section introduces the issue of management structure as an essential background to the course and as a foundation for the detailed coverage which you will find in Unit 2: Approaches to Environmental Monitoring in Marketing. The aim of this section is to help you to:

- discover the need for corporate as well as functional management

- recognise the need for a management structure to be adapted to the needs of different organisations

- become familiar with the corporate planning process and its specialised terminology.

1.1 The role of managers

It is very easy to miss the point that managers of marketing, of production, of distribution, of finance *are* managers. Their role calls for them to manage within their speciality. Thus, they are first trained as functional specialists, and then add on the needed management skills.

To a great extent this addition of management is allowed to develop through experience – by osmosis – rather than as a result of a deliberate plan. In recent years, however, the ineffectiveness of allowing managers to 'learn on the job' has been recognised. We have seen the transition of Personnel into Human Resource Management, and the development of specific management development activities.

Management is now recognised as not only a vital need, but also as a specialised skill which transcends functional disciplines.

LEADERSHIP

It is now generally recognised that leadership is an essential part of a manager's job – more important, perhaps, than administering and controlling. The origin of the terms 'manager' and 'leader' are, however, very different, which gives a clue, perhaps, to why some have difficulty in reconciling the different roles. 'Manager' may be the term, but today's manager is required more to lead than to administer and control.

Manager comes from the Latin 'manus', a hand, which led to the Italian verb for handling or 'managing' a war horse. It entered the English language via the military, where it was used to describe the handling – the control – of troops. **Leader** comes from the old North European word 'laed', which means a road, a path, a journey. A leader is a guide, a knowledgeable person who helps travellers find and keep to the right route.

When the entrepreneurs of the eighteenth and nineteenth centuries were leading their companies they needed administrators to ensure the smooth operation of the organisation. Thus the term manager entered the commercial world, but the leaders (the entrepreneurs) took on the term 'director'. Over time, the leadership role became blurred and, especially under conditions of 'scientific management', workers were seen as subject to detailed control by managers, who were focused on objectives to be achieved, rather than upon the processes that underpin success.

Process can be thought of as a course of action, a series of operations which, taken in sequence, produce a desired result. It is a manager's task to ensure that existing processes are controlled efficiently. By contrast, a leader will be concerned with achieving the desired end result, but will be actively seeking the most effective way of achieving it.

Today's manager tends to be far more proactive than the manager of only a decade ago – but the actual role of the manager in today's organisations is still far from universally accepted, let alone defined. The distinction between manager and leader is a complex, on-going and fascinating topic, which merits coverage in greater depth than is possible in this marketing course. See the prolific writings of Peter Drucker for an enlightened approach to management, and John Adair, whose work on leadership has added greatly to today's thinking but has led the way to the current emphasis on management education and training.

For simplicity, we shall use the accepted term 'manager', but remember that we are using the term in its modern form to mean manager/leader.

1.2 Corporate *v* Functional Management

In any organisation there is need to ensure that the entity *as a whole* survives and, if possible, prospers. This can only be achieved if all elements within the organisation pull in the same direction because they share common objectives.

Objectives which concern the whole organisation are 'corporate'. Those which concern each discipline are 'functional'. Thus functional objectives apply within Marketing, Finance, Production, Procurement, Human Resource Management – whatever specialities the organisation needs in order to achieve its corporate objectives. A major problem can be created when managers focus on the function of their department, with little or no concern for corporate needs. This short-term view is likely to lead to damaging internal politics and organisational ineffectiveness.

If a separate cadre of corporate management is formed – as when a holding company co-ordinates a group – there is a danger that a rivalry may develop, with corporate management seen by managers of functions as interfering and, functional management seen by corporate managers as old-fashioned and self-centred.

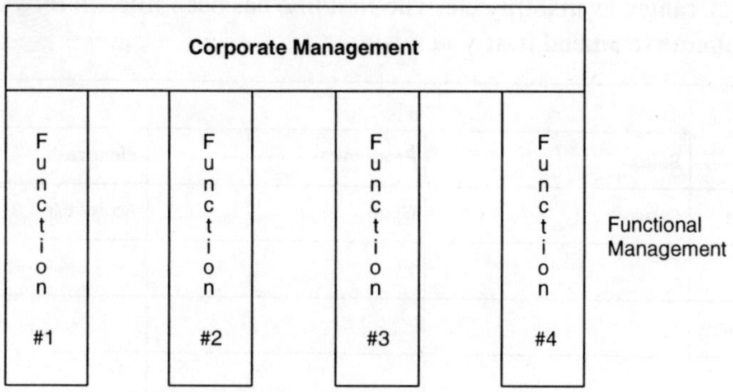

Figure 1: Corporate and functional management

DIRECTORS

Each function will be under the control of a senior manager, a Director. (Terminology will vary, especially between commercial, not-for-profit and public service organisations, but the principle holds true.)

Directors are, by legal definition, responsible for the whole organisation and they form the senior level of corporate management. Usually they are the only corporate management level, but may be joined by senior managers, such as the Marketing Manager, where the organisational structure makes this appropriate. They are (or should be) concerned with decisions that affect all the organisation's functions. They are charged with setting corporate objectives that provide a focus for the organisation as a whole. Each function is then responsible for setting its own objectives, subsidiary to the corporate objectives, which will assist the organisation as a whole to achieve its intentions.

The Marketing Director, therefore, is first a corporate manager, secondly a marketing specialist. It can be very difficult to make the transition from a functional to a corporate focus, and it requires a deliberate programme of education and training to help the young functional specialist acquire the necessary skills and experience as seniority develops.

Even junior functional specialists must be concerned with corporate issues, however. There is a need to work closely with the other functions, since without a congruence of purpose nothing meaningful can be achieved. If, for example, the production department does not produce to schedule, and/or the distribution department does not move the goods, there is little point in the marketing department securing orders from customers.

ACTIVITY 1

Fill in on the following table what managers of the various functions – Sales, Production, Finance etc – might use as their success criteria when judging a product, range, availability etc. The first line has been filled in for you, but you may of course amend it, if you wish.

	Sales	Production	Finance
Product	Quality	Good	Acceptable
Range			
Availability			
Stocks			
Price			
Credit			
Success			

Table 1: Success criteria

Then consider the effect on an organisation if any one of these functions is dominant.

There is no 'correct' answer to this exercise, but a possible answer is given below. The point is that the success criteria are likely to vary from function to function and might well be at odds with one another.

	Sales	Production	Finance
Product	Quality	Good	Acceptable
Range	Custom made to order	Long-run standard	Cost-efficiency
Availability	Fluctuates with season	Continuous level production	Minimum cost solution
Stocks	Ample – close to customers	Low – sales to match capacity	Minimum capital tied up
Price	Low, flexible	Little interest	Optimum price/volume solution
Credit	Long, flexible	Little interest	Short
Success	Order volume	Smooth production	High profits

Table 1: Success criteria

If Sales requires a better product than that produced by competitors, at lower price, available from stock in a range of custom designs and colours, it has major implications for production and finance.

If Production produces only one adequate product at lowest cost to facilitate continuous production runs, the unit costs will be very low but Sales will be forced into the mass market, with price as their only major selling point.

If Finance pursues a high profit/low risk policy, then few (if any) new products will meet their development criteria and of those that do it is likely that none will be sufficiently funded to achieve market penetration.

In short, if any single function dominates an organisation, the effects will be detrimental to the others. The marketing concept offers a solution to this dilemma by proposing an integrated approach based on external need rather than on an internal power struggle.

We shall return to corporate and functional issues as we consider the role of marketing in management in Section 3.

ACTIVITY 2

1 Indicate in the table below what functional disciplines are needed by different kinds of organisations: retail, manufacturing, charitable and educational. Show by the number of crosses you put in each box how important the function is to each type of organisation.

	Retail	Manufacture	Charity	Education
Finance				
Procurement				
Production				
Distribution				
Personnel				
Marketing				

Table 2: Functional disciplines by organisational type

A likely answer is given below:

	Retail	Manufacture	Charity	Education
Finance	XXXXX	XXXXX	XXXXX	XXX
Procurement	XXXXX	XXX	XX	
Production		XXXXX		
Distribution	XXXXX	XXXXX	XXX	X
Personnel	XXX	XXX	XXXXX	XXXXX
Marketing	XXXXX	XXX	XX	X

Table 2: Functional disciplines by organisational type

Note that within a generalised heading, such as 'Finance', there will be sub-specialities handling such issues as foreign exchange (Treasury), cost and price (Cost Accountants), credit (Credit Control). There will also be need for management and financial accounts to be prepared and corporate taxation to be handled.

There may also be a need for an Estates Management team – which in some organisations may be sufficiently important to justify a specialist function in its own right. Similar specialist sub-functions exist across the width and depth of an organisation.

The importance of any function is usually determined not only by the organisation's actual need, but also by the political skills of the functional managements. This is how it is – not how it should be – in many organisations. In such cases corporate management face a major task of organisational development involving attitude change.

Summary

The role of the manager as an administrator and controller is giving way to an understanding that management is concerned with leadership. The notion that functional focus is detrimental to overall corporate success is also gaining ground. Everybody in an organisation must have a shared view on purpose and objectives. Corporate objectives must be set if functional objectives are to have synergy, since without the guidance provided by corporate objectives each functional manager could, and probably would, set functional objectives without regard for their effect on other functions.

SECTION 2

Marketing

Introduction

This section examines what is meant by the term 'marketing' and looks at the philosophies underpinning it. The aim of this section is to help you to:

- assess a range of definitions of marketing
- create one or more definitions of marketing for yourself
- define key marketing terms
- begin an analysis of the effectiveness of the marketing concept in use.

2.1 Towards a definition

Marketing is a term which can arouse a surprising level of passion and hostility in those who equate it with hard selling, unacceptable techniques of persuasion and profligate spending on promotion in place of cost reduction. The marketer's response is that any tool can be misused, but misuse by some does not negate the benefits available to the many who use the tool properly.

That the value of marketing is becoming ever more widely appreciated is evidenced by its adoption by not-for-profit organisations, notably in the education world, where the most vociferous opponents of its adoption were (and still are) to be found.

ACTIVITY 3

1   Take 20 minutes to consider the definitions of marketing given in Resource Item 1.1.

2   Then turn the pages of a good newspaper and examine both the copy and the advertisements to identify organisations where marketing is being used well, and badly.

(You may find this slightly difficult at first since you will not know exactly what you are looking for. It is therefore good sense to make this media review a regular part of your daily routine as you are working through this course. As your skills and knowledge grow, so will your ability to penetrate deeper and understand more.)

You will have seen that marketing is very hard to define, even for academics who have made a lifetime study of the subject. It is apparent that the word 'marketing' is used in three different contexts:

1   The process of connecting the producing company with its market.

2   The concept that marketing is a social exchange process involving willing consumers and producers.

3   The orientation, present to some degree in both consumers and producers, which makes the process and the concept possible.

In the first of these contexts marketing differs very little from sales. This is not surprising since today's marketing has developed and extended from the sales and advertising functions. The second and third contexts, of willing exchange and shared orientation, underpin what we mean by marketing today. It is within these contexts that today's effective marketers operate.

In reviewing the media you will immediately see the advertising. Can you distinguish the one key feature which underpins all the adverts? It is an offer to exchange some benefit for a given return (usually but not always cash). The offer may appear to be simple – cleaner clothes if you use a particular detergent. But why should anyone want cleaner clothes? What is actually being offered? What does the potential buyer actually want, actually need to buy?

Organisations which appear to be using marketing well can be provisionally determined by the *style* (not the quality) of their advertising. If they show the benefits to be derived by the consumer, then they have a consumer focus. If they concentrate on what the product will do, they have a product orientation. Be careful, however, since this is only a superficial indication of the external face of the organisation. One needs a penetrating analysis to discover if the marketing concept is deeply rooted.

This is the area where marketing can be accused of manipulation, since it is a marketer's skill to identify actual or latent need and then to provide a product or service to meet that need. Marketers do not normally attempt to create a need. This is extremely hard to do and so many needs actually exist that it is far easier to identify and satisfy than attempt to create.

A typical detergent purchaser wants clean clothes, yes. But why are clean clothes important? Within the current social imperative to be clean (which is a modern phenomenon) he or she also wants one or a combination of the following:

- Less work – removal of the chore
- Time – freedom to do other things whilst washing is automatically taken care of
- Gratitude – substituting for affection in some cases
- Security – a specific role in the family group

- Pride – in the turnout of those for whom he or she washes in his or her appearance – no 'dishpan hands'
- Status – in the eyes of his or her peers, coupled with pride.

When next you see a detergent advertisement analyse it to discover at whom it is targeted, and what values the manufacturer thinks the typical targeted consumer will respond to.

2.2 Customers and consumers

We must distinguish customers from consumers. A **customer** is somebody who buys with the intention of reselling. A **consumer** uses up the worth of what is bought. Thus, a wholesaler is a customer, as is a retailer.

Individual purchasers can be customers and then consumers if they buy for their own use. They will first act in the role of consumer, determining what they need, then move on to become a customer when they actually buy the product. Finally, they revert to consumer mode and use up the benefits within the product.

People can be both customer and a consumer if buying for their own use, but a customer if buying for someone else.

This distinction is extremely important to understand, since the buying motivations differ if one is buying for one's own use – and the ability to take purchase decisions also changes. Marketers need to know who is buying and who is using. Examine Units 4 and 5 an example will make the distinction clear.

Situation 1
A person goes into a shop to buy a jar of Nescafé for her own use. The store is out of stock, but has a range of alternative instant coffees. The person has the ability to decide to buy an alternative, to visit another shop or to postpone purchase.

Situation 2
The same person is buying Nescafé for a neighbour. She doesn't have the authority to buy a substitute, and has the difficult task of deciding what her neighbour would want her to do. Any action may be wrong, how can she choose? If she selects wrongly (in the view of the neighbour) what unpleasantness may this cause?

Marketers devote a considerable proportion of their resources to understanding customer and consumer behaviour, as we shall see.

Used correctly, the terms customer and consumer are sufficient to describe every marketing transaction. There is no need for such terms as 'final consumer', which you will occasionally come across in the literature.

The terms 'buying' and 'selling' imply exchange, but not necessarily of money. A child exchanges gratitude for his mother's selection of food – or responds with a tantrum if she fails to buy what he prefers. When helping a charity one is exchanging time, effort and specialised skills for some form of satisfaction: the knowledge of doing good, status, enjoyment – something without monetary value. The point is that one chooses to 'spend' some resource that one controls in a given way when alternatives are available.

2.3 Wants and needs

We can and must distinguish want from need:

- A want is something that a person would like to have.
- A need is something that a person feels they must have.
- Basic needs, such as for food and shelter, are needs that must be satisfied.

Demand is experienced only when:

A need, want or desire...

The ability to pay, and...

The willingness to pay...

are present.

The willingness to pay comes only when wants are converted to needs; unless and until a want becomes a perceived need it will remain as an unfulfilled desire. Naturally a want may be prevented from becoming a need because there is no finance to allow the need to become tangible. Equally, what were wants become needs with changed circumstances, and perhaps then disappear. (New parents suddenly need lots of baby-centred information and products, but those needs pass as the child(ren) grow – to be replaced, of course, with other family-centred needs.)

Just as you can't sell baby products to those without babies, so you can't sell any products or services that are not perceived as needs. Marketing cannot equate with hard selling, since hard selling takes no account of a purchaser's long-term interests whereas marketing is concerned with an exchange that will continue over time. Marketers realise that their profits come from a long-term association, not from a one-off sale.

ACTIVITY 4

Take a few minutes to validate the truth of this last statement. List any organisation which is selling a product or service for which there is likely to be no long-term interest in the company or product by the customer – where there will be no possibility of a repeat sale. (Be careful. The marketing interest may be more subtle than it appears on the surface.)

Typically, these areas are among those where no repeat sales opportunities are obvious:

● Double-glazing

But:

Is the whole house glazed at the one time?

Will the householder not move to a single-glazed house in time?

– Are there no other products to offer – porches, greenhouses, etc?

● Weddings

But:

Caterers supply for all events. Even if there are no more weddings in this family there will be anniversaries, christenings, funerals.

● Funerals

But:

These are bought by the survivors, not the deceased. One person may have to organise funerals for several relatives.

Remember, also, the word-of-mouth recommendations to others who will need the product or service. This can be positive – leading to further business – or negative! It is therefore evident that almost no organisation can afford to make a quick sell and run for cover; they need to use the contact with their customer in a positive way to generate further business.

2.4 Marketing as a bridge

Marketing is often described as the 'bridge' between the consumer and the organisation providing the product or service which is being sold. This is because it is the only function within most organisations to be actively concerned with the exterior environment. It is part of marketing's role to monitor this environment and report back to those in other functions. This is necessitated by the requirement to identify customer and consumer need, and to alert the organisation to the opportunities that are – and will be – available in the market place.

Marketing's role extends beyond promotional activity (public relations, advertising, sales promotion and direct selling). It is concerned to research the needs of the customers and potential customers, but also has a concern for others who have a stake in the business. This concern extends from the financial community, through shareholders and out through lobbies and pressure groups to the general public. Much of this concern is with matters corporate rather than functional, which we shall return to in the next section.

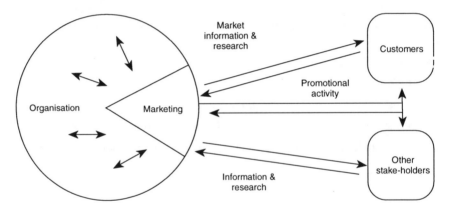

Figure 2: The marketing manager as a communication conduit between the organisation and its external audiences. (Hatton & Worsam, 1995)

ACTIVITY 5

Marketing has exchange as its central pillar. Without willing exchange there can be no true marketing. But what is offered as the exchange medium varies according to needs? Take sufficient time – probably spread over a period of days, even weeks – to create a series of marketing definitions with which you are comfortable. If you are happy with any of those given in this course, fine. If not, establish and validate your own.

Remember that you need either to have one definition that applies to all conceivable marketing circumstances or variations to suit particular needs. Consider such differing circumstances as: you marketing yourself to a prospective employer; a charity seeking volunteer support for local fund raising; a commercial enterprise selling in retail; another selling defence material to foreign buyers.

Summary

Marketing is a management discipline that is hard to define but is concerned with willing exchange relationships. The nature of the exchange is normally, but not exclusively, cash for a product or service, but no exchange is possible without actual need being perceived. The identification of such needs is a major functional task for the marketer.

Marketing is the bridge between an organisation and potential consumers. It also has a wider range of interests within the external environment, since a range of political, economic, social and technological factors impact upon organisations and their markets. There is also, of course, considerable interest in monitoring the activity of competitors.

SECTION 3

Marketing in Management

Introduction

As a manager it is necessary to understand how organisations are managed – and the contribution that functional specialisms can make to the overall success of the organisation. Marketing's role as a management discipline is vitally important because only if it is contributing fully to corporate decisions will it be empowered to operate effectively as a function.

This aim of this section is to help you to:

- distinguish the corporate and functional roles of management
- relate tactical activity to corporate need
- determine to what extent professional marketers are needed at corporate level
- assess the need for specialised training to be effective as a marketer.

3.1 Managing change

Change is an unavoidable part of everyday life. It impacts upon us all, and organisations are not excluded. An individual (or an organisation) can elect to make no proactive changes, but in the course of time there will be need to react to changes that occur in the environment. It is impossible to remain in a stable state for more than a brief time; generally speaking, organisms are either spiralling upwards through success or downwards through failure. Movement (action) is necessary to survival, let alone to progress.

Two ancient Chinese proverbs are appropriate to our understanding of the need to move:

- Every journey begins with a single step.
- He who hesitates will spend his entire life standing on one leg.

Managers, of course, need to evaluate the situation, since in certain circumstances the best policy is to keep still, to merge into the background. But this can only be a short-term action which is part of an overall plan designed to achieve specified corporate objectives.

Given that we have to move to survive and to prosper it seems obvious that we ought to know in which direction to move before taking that first step! There is not much point marching confidently to the south when our destination actually is in the far north west! Better, surely, to take the time to evaluate our environment, see what is possible, match that to our overall aims, and then establish short- and medium-term plans to help us achieve our long-term intentions.

The military have established that reconnaissance is an essential part of planning. Management has adopted the term 'auditing' – but the process is the same. The army drill into their officers that time spent in reconnaissance is seldom wasted. In exactly the same way time spent in auditing is a vital part of management planning.

3.2 Policies, strategies, tactics and controls

These key terms and the issues surrounding them will be covered in detail in the next unit. For now simply note that:

- Policies are concerned with overall direction
- Strategies express where an organisation plans to be at a given time
- Tactics are time-limited steps taken to achieve strategies
- Controls are the active steps of evaluation and judgement that monitor progress against objectives.

Each level of management is driven by the next senior. Thus one manager's policy is set by his or her senior's strategies and tactics. So, for example, corporate tactics are to hand down responsibility to functions. Marketing policy, therefore, is set as part of corporate planning. Marketing strategies are set within the function. The Marketing Director's tactics are to delegate to sub-specialists. Thus sales policy is set within marketing strategy, but sales strategies and tactics are set within sales.

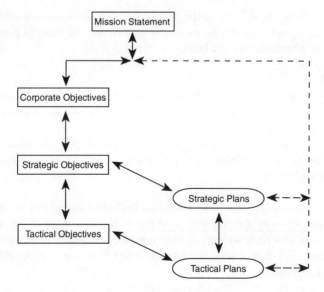

Figure 3: The planning hierarchy.

ACTIVITY 6

Classify, using the above terminology, the thought processes you would go through in the following circumstances:

a) You are about to leave university. How do you decide what role you want in life?

b) You have the offer of two widely different opportunities and can select only one. How do you choose?

c) Your car has broken down and you have an important meeting ten miles away in two hours. What decision-making process do you go through?

d) You are taken out to a restaurant of a kind you have never been to before. How do you assess the experience?

This activity shows how intrinsic the planning stages are to our everyday lives. We automatically apply policies, set strategies, carry out our tactical plans and then monitor how effective we have been.

POLICIES

When looking a long way into the future, in setting a pattern to follow, we are concerned with how we want to live our lives, how we want to behave, what quality of life we desire. This long-term **policy,** or series of policies, sets the background against which we shall operate. Policies establish the parameters of our behaviour, set the key overall criteria by which we shall judge our own and other's mode of behaviour.

Usually we do not consciously set policies – but when attempting to share our life with another we very quickly find that he or she has a set of behaviours and expectations with which we may or may not be compatible. Perhaps we can both adjust, perhaps not. Either way, our long-term life planning is affected by a change in our environment.

Naturally, long-term plans can be derailed by short-term environmental factors.

However we may desire a certain course, the job market, for example, may force us to adjust our plans. But, usually, these adjustments are intended to be short-term in nature. Just as we steer clear of a pothole on the road, so we cope with blockages on our chosen route.

Managers must set **corporate policies** that reflect the long-term aims of the organisation. Unless this is done there will be confusion in the organisation, with each manager acting in good faith but with no co-ordination, no synergy. Policies are needed to focus the efforts of each functional discipline within corporate need.

Thus we have corporate policies covering the organisation as a whole, and functional policies which drive each of the functions so that there is overall synergy.

The whole of the corporate purpose is encapsulated into a **Mission Statement,** which summarises overall policy crisply and unambiguously.

STRATEGIES

When one of several opportunities must be selected we have to discover all that we can about the positive and negative aspects of each in the short-, medium- and long-term. Thus we set out to research the information that we need.

When we have the information we can then apply criteria to help us determine which action(s) to initiate. Note that in every situation requiring choice, we have the option of taking no action at all. The 'remain unchanged' option should always be evaluated, along with the others.

We quickly find that there is a mass of data available – and that the information we need is hidden within the data. Usually we have to analyse the data, access and synthesise the information to transform it to a form that is useful to our specific need.

When we have the information we can then apply judgement criteria to help us determine which action(s) to initiate. Note that when faced with a choice, we usually have the option of doing nothing – of refusing to choose. This should always be evaluated as an opportunity.

> When it is necessary to do nothing...
>
> it is necessary to *decide* to do nothing.

In deciding on a course of action we have adopted the key management role. Decisions and leadership are two sides of the same manager/leader coin.

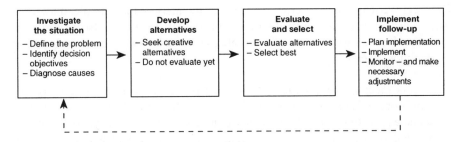

Figure 4: The Rational Decision-Making Process. (Stoner & Freeman, 1992)

We have also adopted a **strategy**. We have determined a broad course of action – what we want to achieve, where we want to be. Strategies are corporate when they drive the whole organisation, and functional when they relate to functional activities. Functional strategies should, of course, be derived from corporate strategies, so that synergy is maintained.

Helpful Hint

Refer to policies, strategies, etc, by their place in the organisation. Thus everybody will clearly understand that they are working with a corporate policy, a financial strategy, an advertising tactic, and so on.

TACTICS

When your car breaks down unexpectedly you are into 'transportation **tactics**'. Your transportation strategy was to buy/rent/borrow the car in the first place. Your tactics are to use it on short, cross-town journeys. Now you have an immediate problem that does not relate to your transportation strategy. Your problem will trigger an instant audit of the current situation which will identify a range of potential solutions (from postponing the meeting to renting a replacement car). You will decide and action a range of events such as calling out a breakdown service and phoning for a taxi.

In due course you will evaluate your actions against your success criteria. This will lead you to further actions – perhaps to consider that it is now time to replace your car – in which case your tactical need will have forced a reappraisal of your Transportation Strategy.

This **strategy review** may well spread out from transportation and you may consider your base location, alternative forms of transport, etc.

CONTROL

In a strange town you will not be able to contribute much to the decision since your friend has the necessary knowledge and experience. He or she will, hopefully, be interested in your policies on food and drink and take them into account when determining where to eat.

You will certainly evaluate the experience, and you may revise your 'restaurant strategies and tactics' by adding a new ethnic cuisine to your list of preferred eating experiences.

It should be obvious that there are active links between what you choose to do short-term (tactics) and with the progression of your overall life plan. We are very familiar with the temptations to do something tactically that will impinge on our strategic decisions – breaking a diet is a good example.

Why have we decided to slim? Without sufficient motivation – a need – we are unlikely to rank slimming as a high priority and will be easily tempted to that biscuit with our coffee, to the single spoon of sugar in our tea. When we weigh ourselves at the end of the week (running a check, a **control**, on our progress) we shall see that we haven't achieved our strategic weight loss objective, and so we shall fail in our declared health policy.

In just the same way, an organisation must ensure that its tactics are consonant with its functional and corporate strategic needs. If they are not, then strategies cannot be achieved.

3.3 Objectives

Clarity of purpose is essential. Managers at every level must be guided by specific objectives. These should be put into writing to enable effective control. The whole point of setting objectives and controlling achievement is to improve performance, to help managers to manage better in the future. In a marketing-focused organisation objectives are not written as a means of discipline. Reinforcement is positive and people are motivated by achievement, not fear of failure.

Without written objectives it is unlikely that optimum performance will be achieved. It follows, therefore, that the setting of objectives is a key management skill. One that *must* be mastered.

Effective managers automatically and routinely think in terms of quantified objectives, and the best ones are expressed in SMART terms.

The acronym stands for:

S – Specific

M – Measurable

A – Achievable

R – Relevant

T – Timed.

An objective, to be SMART, must be quantified and capable of evaluation against a control.

Objectives can, of course, be concerned with quality – where it is very difficult to quantify. There is almost always, however, a way to convert a quality judgement into a quantifiable objective. Semantic differential scaling, for example, allows attitude, opinion and behaviour to be quantified, as we shall see in Unit 8.

It is also necessary to distinguish between objectives which deal with effectiveness and those concerned with efficiency:

- Effective – getting the right result.
- Efficient – doing the right things.
- Effective and efficient – doing the right things to get the right result.

ACTIVITY 7

Rewrite the following 'objectives' into SMART terms. (If you find this too difficult, read through the first example below.)

a) We need to respond effectively to customer complaints.

b) Service Engineers must respond urgently to calls from Category A clients.

c) Patients must be comfortable.

d) Orders must be despatched as soon as possible.

Hints:

1 It is often easier to begin by writing out what you want to achieve at some length before editing it down into a SMART objective.

2 When you find the word 'and' in an objective it shows that you have two objectives which must be split so that each can be subjected to control.

---

a) We need to respond effectively to customer complaints.

This may first be written out as:

Our customers complain because they are unhappy. It may not be our fault; there may not be anything actually wrong with the product, but the customer thinks there is. We need to deal with both real and perceived complaints – there is no difference in the customer's mind. But there is an absolute need to pick up and deal with those we shall call 'urgent', because they appear to indicate a serious problem – perhaps of a life-threatening nature. 'Routine' complaints are those where we have seen it before, know the solution, and have an effective and efficient procedure in place. We need customers to tell us when they are unhappy. If they don't tell us, they will tell their neighbours. Far better that they tell their neighbours how concerned, helpful and friendly we are – how we take matters seriously and deal with them in a friendly fashion.

We can then produce objectives to cover the handling of customer complaints. In part they will read:

- An acknowledgement will be posted to each complainant on the day their complaint is received.
- Within two hours of receipt all complaints will be sorted into Urgent and Routine.
- Urgent complaints will be:
  - given total priority over any other business.
  - personally dealt with by the Senior Manager responsible for area that is the source of the complaint.
  - in the Senior Manager's hands within three hours of being received.
  - categorised for action on the day they are received.
  - continuously monitored to ensure the optimum solution is secured.
- Routine complaints will be...etc.

b)   Service Engineers must respond urgently to calls from Category A clients

Here we are concerned to give our best clients excellent service. But what does 'urgently' mean? It should be interpreted as it is defined in the *Concise Oxford Dictionary:* pressing, calling for immediate action. But do we really want a Service Engineer dropping a job in progress and travelling perhaps 100 miles simply because a client calls? 'Respond' means: make answer, show sensitiveness to, correspond. It does not mean visit. But how many will misinterpret respond to mean visit?

We are actually saying that clients should be responded to quickly (how quickly?); but not necessarily by visiting them. It would be more sense to establish an escalating series of steps.

Perhaps we mean:

- When a Class A client calls for a Service Engineer he or she will:
  - receive a phone call from the Service Manager or his Deputy within one hour.
  - if necessary, receive a phone call from the appropriate Service Engineer within two hours.

  – if necessary, receive a visit from the designated Service Engineer
    within four hours. An alternative Service Engineer will substitute only if
    the designated Service Engineer is unable to attend through absence,
    or because he or she is already working on a Class A job.

Etc, etc.

c)   Patients must be comfortable

Normally patients are unwell – by definition – so what on earth does 'comfortable'
mean? Are we concerned solely with physical comfort? Or with mental well-being
also? Hopefully with both, since a major source of discomfort is simply being on
unfamiliar ground, and experiencing unusual smells, whilst in a state of anxiety.

Patients need a friendly environment. They need to feel secure, valued, individual.
They need to draw upon the confidence of the professional staff, to be reassured
both by tangible and intangible factors.

Helping a patient to *feel* comfortable is the issue. Feelings are internal factors that
can only be influenced – never imposed.

Thus, our objectives need to address the patient's feelings. In an attempt to
influence the medical staff's traditional attitude the NHS has now changed its
terminology. Wards are run by 'ward managers', not 'sisters', and 'patients' are
now 'clients'. Terminology changes are, on their own, useless. There has to be an
underpinning change in the behaviour of the medical staff.

It follows that to affect patients' feelings we have first to change staff attitudes.
Probably also to introduce proactive relationship training:

- Clients will always be addressed by name.
- On the day before a client is scheduled to arrive:
  – his or her file will be checked for completeness, and any omissions will
    be rectified.
- On arrival clients will be:
  – taken straight to their ward.
  – given special attention as they settle in.
  – encouraged to talk – in particular to ask questions.

Etc, etc.

d)   Orders must be despatched as soon as possible

'As soon as possible' is commonly used to denote urgency although if one analyses
what it means it could indicate any time-scale. In any case, we should be concerned
with *arrival* in good condition, not simply with *despatch*. This 'objective' can be
easily fulfilled if an urgent order, needed today, is despatched in a week (or a
month) even if it never arrives! Managers who use SMART objectives preclude this
by thinking through what exactly is needed, and providing for it to happen.

In this case our objectives may be:

- Customers will receive goods for which an official order has been placed:
  - Within three working days.
  - In perfect condition.

To facilitate this:

- Orders will be processed within three hours of receipt.

Etc, etc.

(NB The first objective, above, was originally written as:

- Customers will:
  - Receive goods for which an official order has been placed within three working days.
  - Receive goods in perfect condition.

It is necessary to draft, and then revise – writing SMART objectives is essential, but not easy. It is an acquired skill.)

Note that all of these objectives are sub-sectioned – thus allowing each element of the overall objective to be evaluated and controlled. Management will then know where they are performing well, and where there is need to improve.

3.4 Corporate marketing

Just as there is need to market products and services, so there is need to market the organisation. This was proved conclusively during the late 1970s when major companies battled for supremacy and even huge concerns found themselves the target of unwelcome bids. Many found that although their brands were known there was no appreciation – no awareness – of the organisation that owned the brands. Thus Spillers, for example, attempted to use their well-known and popular Home Pride flour brand as a support to their attempts to remain independent. The Home Pride Flour Graders (little cartoon characters) were known for their flour connection, but not recognised by the financiers who were interested in the parent organisation. Spillers, without a clear identity as an organisation, was taken over.

The message was brutal, but well learned. In the City – on the money markets – it is necessary to promote the organisation in much the same way as one promotes brands to customers and consumers. Those responsible for providing funding need to be informed and reassured in much the same way as a high street shopper needs information and reassurance. The stakes are different, but the underpinning concept remains the same.

ACTIVITY 8

Visit a public library and examine several Annual Reports. If possible, compare one or more with reports from several years ago. What does this tell you about the perceived need for effective communications at corporate level?

You may be surprised at how difficult it is to distinguish an Annual Report from a product catalogue designed for the showroom and targeted on consumers. The detailed content will vary, but the approach, style and technique will be remarkably the same.

You will also have noted that organisations have now branded themselves. Corporate management has become aware of the need to promote the organisation since it (and they) are in an exchange relationship with their stakeholders. Bankers, lawyers, shareholders – all need to be confident in the organisation, as distinct from its products or services. Thus there is a need to market the organisation in exactly the same way as one markets its products.

CORPORATE COMMUNICATIONS

The vital need for synergy naturally includes the key area of communications. It is necessary for an organisation to present a common front – to be seen to be an entity and not a disparate number of units.

One of marketing's unique features is its contact with the external environment – its role as communications conduit. Thus, when corporate management found the need to promote the organisation it would seem natural – automatic – to turn to the Marketing Director for help.

In fact many turned to Public Relations – perhaps in a guise such as Corporate Communications Consultants. Thus the importance of PR has greatly increased since the late 1970s, with many organisations relying on the PR function to set corporate communications policy. This can be a disaster for the marketing function, since communications are at the very heart of marketing. Forced to follow corporate strategy, marketing has to comply with communications policies that will be applicable to corporate issues but which may not take marketing's needs into account.

A major role for the Marketing Director, in particular, therefore, is to establish marketing as a corporate discipline in just the same way that Finance was long ago established as both a functional and corporate necessity.

CORPORATE RESEARCH

Every organisation needs to audit the environment(s) in which it operates, and for this will require a sophisticated research activity. Marketing has introduced a wide range of marketing research techniques which have been developed to provide data and information that can be relied upon.

Marketing Research

Note that the term 'marketing research' covers all the forms of research used by marketing. Thus, market research is a part of marketing research, as is promotional research, advertising research, sales research, and so on.

Many organisations have a Management Information System (MIS) in which will reside a Marketing Information System (MkIS). These systems are heavily reliant upon managed on-going research and on an effective and efficient means of dissemination. The needed information must reach the managers who require it in time for action to be taken. Anything less, and the system is degraded. Late information is worse than no information because it has been paid for!

Marketing can make major contributions to the flow of corporate information, but a fully operative MIS is a large and extremely powerful sub-function which several Directors will lay claim too. Once again, it is for the Marketing Director to ensure that his or her discipline is fully involved at corporate level.

Consider the result if marketing loses control of communications and information. Without safeguarding these two essential and key skills, marketing would be downgraded to no more than a glorified sales activity. Many would argue for this. The need to clearly identify what marketing can offer each individual team of corporate managers – and then packaging and selling the argument – is therefore key to marketing's role in any one organisation.

Note that the need is to package and sell the argument to *managers*. Not to the organisation. As we shall see in Unit 6, it is people who are targeted, since organisations have a legal presence but no decisive ability except through their managers.

3.5 Specialised training

Marketing is a specific discipline which requires a unique mixture of Attitude, Skills and Knowledge (ASK) to do well. Its basic skills can be acquired quickly, and superficial competence can lead to the belief that one is fully skilled. It is not too difficult to run a bluff if familiar with the terminology. Finally – and significantly – it is also an activity which all of us perform routinely every day.

Given that marketing is much more of an art than a science, it becomes both very difficult to define exactly what ASK factors are required, and to evaluate the level of success achieved.

We all routinely possess some basic marketing skills because we engage in exchange every day of our lives. Obviously we have commercial exchanges, and some are better at doing deals than others – but we also are concerned with our social relationships, with our appearance, with the exchange of our time for some reward we consider significant.

ACTIVITY 9

Choose any day from the last seven and take a few moments to review it. Jot down under suitable headings every event where you have been involved in an exchange. These will range from the obvious, such as exchanging money for lunch, and extend across a range such as:

● Time for improved appearance.
  – Ask why you wanted to improve your appearance?
  – What were your motivations?

● Time for status
  – As when helping a charity perhaps?

● Information
  – For immediate return or to build up or repay a debt?

● Favours
  – For mutual benefit?

● Skills and/or Experience
  – Unique to you, beneficial to others, but what was the motivation on each side ?

It is always interesting to see the surprise experienced by committed anti-marketers when they run through an exercise such as this. It tends to force people to the realisation that marketing is intrinsic to life – and that bad marketing is the result of carelessness or, occasionally, the deliberate actions of people who know exactly what they are doing.

Marketing is undoubtedly a transferable skill. Most people can improve their marketing abilities. Thus many managers are adding a certain level of marketing understanding to their basic qualification(s). Unfortunately, many then consider themselves to be fully qualified marketers.

Many professionals suffer from the fact that their skills appear simple to onlookers. Especially to those who do not try to do the job themselves. The Chartered Institute of Marketing is actively working to improve the image of marketing as a profession – of marketing as a valuable management discipline. It does seem odd that the one function charged with promoting image should have made such a bad job of defining and promoting its own role!

Marketing training is about securing the basic understanding, and then developing skills in depth within one or more of the sub-functions. Marketing, as we shall see in this course, is applicable everywhere, but it needs to be adapted to circumstances. The consumer marketer is similar, yet different, from the retail marketer. Both are very different from the industrial marketer working on big-budget projects. The social marketer is different again, and those working in education and the health services have yet another set of attitudes, knowledge and skills.

Underpinning all, however, is the key concept of exchange for mutual benefit. Where this exists, so must the need for marketing.

ACTIVITY 10

Select a quality newspaper that runs specialised job advertising on specific days. Over a period of one week select job adverts for a range of professions: finance, human resource management, production, secretarial and marketing. Analyse the key requirements that appear regularly for each profession. How many are consistent across the range? Which are specific to each profession? What does this tell you about the blend of ASK factors required to succeed in each profession?

You should have found many general management qualities, which transcend all professions – including secretarial. You will also have found, implicitly if not explicitly, that certain character requirements (in the area we term 'attitude') are required to be successful in different areas. Perhaps you have also identified areas in which you would like to work – perhaps even found a possible job?

Summary

Marketing management has a valuable contribution to make at both corporate and functional levels. Whether or not professional marketers operate at corporate level their discipline is needed and will be applied by management. Objectives must be established in SMART terms to facilitate effective management. Specialised training is needed, both in the professional marketing skills and – importantly – in the skills of management.

SECTION 4

Functional marketing

Introduction

This section introduces several concepts essential to the function of marketing – the 'tools' of the marketer. They are only dealt with briefly here and will all be covered in much greater depth later in the module. The main purpose of this introductory visit to each tool is to familiarise you with terminology and help you to understand how all the tools interrelate. It will also give you an overview of the marketing function so that you can begin to appreciate the importance of relating each concept to both the external and internal needs of an organisation.

This aim of this section is to help you to:

- begin to understand the importance of the concept of the 'marketing mix'
- appreciate the complex process involved in selection and purchase of an item
- recognise the correlation between the 7Ps and the 7Cs
- understand the term 'marketing research'.

4.1 Marketing's mixes

A cook works from a basic range of ingredients and, with additions, uses them to produce different things:

- flour, milk, eggs and salt make pancakes and Yorkshire puddings.
- add sugar and savoury pancakes and puddings are possible.
- add butter and Victoria sponges and Madeira cakes can be made.
- add cocoa, or coffee, or fruit to create flavoured pancakes, puddings, sponges and cakes.

The ingredients matter, but they are only one part of the process. Also in the equation are the utensils, the method and the type of cooking. It really matters to a cook if the mixing bowl is porcelain, Pyrex or stainless steel; how the mixture is to be cooked, and on what form of stove. Techniques vary with need, every kitchen has its own peculiarities and every cook their own preferences and short cuts.

A marketer works from a basic range of ingredients, adding specialist utensils, skills and techniques as necessary. The generic term for this is 'marketing mix', and the basic marketing mix is considered to have either four or seven constituents.

4Ps or 7Ps

The original marketing mix is known as the 4Ps. In the early 1980s, in order to recognise the importance of the marketing of services, a further three Ps were added to give a mix of 7Ps.

In fact, the 7Ps can be used for products and/or services; it provides a far more useful set of tools than the 4Ps alone.

The original 4Ps are:

- Product
- Price
- Place (distribution)
- Promotion.

The additional 3Ps are:

- Physical Evidence
- Participants
- Process.

The whole of the 7Ps are often referred to as the 'Extended Marketing Mix'.

The subject of the marketing mix will be dealt with in more detail in Unit 5: The Marketing Mix. For the moment, it would probably be helpful to define what is meant by each of the above terms.

PRODUCT

A product can be thought of as having three attributes. It is tangible, has a function and also a symbolic value.

- **Tangibility** – physical presence – is what distinguishes a product from a service.

- **Functionality** is the purpose to which the product is put. A house brick, for example, has tangibility – but it is its function that adds value. A brick can be part of a house, a door stop, a weapon. It can provide a stepping stone in a puddle, prop up a caravan, add ballast to a boat. It can be smashed to pieces to provide material for the foundations of a new building.

- **Symbolism** is brought to the product by the purchaser. This is intangible, and will vary from person to person. A wristwatch, for example, has physical presence (lots of bits and pieces put together in a case), it has a function (to show the time) but above all it has a symbolic value. People buy for other than functional purposes *whatever they may say in answer to a direct question.*

ACTIVITY 11

See if you can identify any product which is bought purely for its functional purpose.

If you have thought of one, think about it a bit harder, because it is unlikely that it is really bought for its own sake.

To take one example:

A Rolex watch can be bought for any number of reasons additional to the basic function of telling the time sufficiently accurately for everyday purposes:

- Pilots need precise timing and so buy a chronometer.
- Status-conscious people need symbols of their taste and so buy goods that are held in esteem.
- Would-be achievers need recognition and so buy goods known to be expensive.
- Fashion-conscious people buy watches as jewellery.
- Those needing to impress and/or reward buy gifts of high status and/or high cost to meet the perceived needs of both the recipient and themselves.
- Financially focused people need to buy goods that will appreciate in value faster than inflation.
- Even a Rolex watch collector needs the pleasure/recognition of the collection rather than the physical presence of the watches themselves.

See Resource Item 1.2: Diamonds are Forever, for an explanation of how the deliberate addition of status transformed the world's diamond markets – and how different values were identified as necessary for different products and different markets. Value as perceived by customers is thus seen to be paramount and should drive product design.

A service is similar to a product, except that it does not have a physical presence. On the whole, neither the customer nor the consumer distinguish between a service or a product. They seek whatever is necessary to fulfil a particular need. It is the marketer for whom the difference between a product and a service has a significance, because of the different approaches that need to be taken to each.

Package

This term has two meanings:

- the physical pack in which a product is supplied
- the 'package of benefits' that are offered to the consumer.

Note how the diamond marketers in Resource Item 1.2 drew upon different elements to create overall 'packages', of value to their consumers. Usage is normally made clear by context. If it is not, the term will be taken to mean the 'package of benefits'.

Product life cycle

The concept of the product life cycle (PLC) is valuable in providing an overall understanding that products have a period of conception, fast growth, maturity and decline. It is a useful shorthand term which marketers use to broadly describe the type of marketing mix that is likely to be most appropriate.

It is difficult, if not impossible, to enter a market (such as for detergents) which is itself in the maturity phase of its life cycle and has several well-established products also in their mature phase. Better to identify a market opportunity which is in its growth phase or, far better, to identify a way of opening a new market (as did the innovators who designed the radial tyre).

This is something that will be looked at in much more detail in Unit 5, Section 3.

PRICE

What the marketer may regard as 'price', the customer and consumer think of as 'cost'. This is, of course, the difference between receiving and making payment. But price/cost are the least important issues in this part of the marketing mix.

Consumers buy **value,** and price/cost is only one element of value.

ACTIVITY 12

Consider several recent purchases that you have made. Select one that is routine – a grocery product, perhaps. Another that is low-value but bought rarely – a toothbrush, possibly. A further one that is expensive, but basic to your needs – a washing machine would be ideal. Finally, choose something that you regard as a luxury, even a frivolity.

For each, identify your needs. What drove you to make the purchase? What issues did you take into account in making your choice. How important was cost in the value equation ?

You will have found that you took many considerations into account. The colour and shape of the toothbrush was probably more important than the price. Did your need for healthy teeth sway your choice ? If so, how did you make your decision – on the manufacturer's promotional packaging, or on unbiased advice from, say, a dentist.

If you simply re-bought, as with a jar of salad cream, what is it about your regular choice that makes you simply rebuy, rather than assessing the competition? Is it of value to you not to waste time choosing a basic product that is 'good enough'? Would you approach the task differently if your partner had complained, or if you were planning a special meal for people you wanted to impress?

The value part of the more expensive purchase has to do with cost-in-use, longevity, guarantee and after-sales support – perhaps with free delivery and installation. Maybe you had to pay more for delivery because you couldn't take it cash and carry? If so, was it worth it in value terms? Did it free you up to do something else or provide skills you do not have ?

Your luxury purchase will have tapped into a different part of your purchase behaviour. Was it something you had saved for, wanted desperately enough to sacrifice something else to achieve? If so, why? Was it a spontaneous purchase? Do you make that kind of buy very often? What benefits do you get from your actions?

Understanding why people behave as they do is the key to the packaging of both products and services.

Remember that marketing is an exchange of value. In each of your purchases you have exchanged something you value in return for something at least of equal worth *in your perception*. Your friend, neighbour, parent, child will have their own value sets that may or may not coincide with yours. There are no rights and wrongs, but we have to recognise – across the whole marketing mix – that people are different and that we have to package the same product differently to meet the different value requirements of a range of potential consumers.

Such issues as discounts, credit terms and special offers are pricing tools used in support of value packages. What the customer (who resells) conceives of as value differs markedly from the consumer's perception. Both have to be taken into account.

In just the same way, marketers have to package their plans to secure acceptance by their peers across the organisation. Never forget that marketing is an exchange relationship between people who want to market something for at least an equivalent value and others who have needs and the ability to pay in a 'currency' valued by the marketer.

PLACE

This P is a contrived way to distinguish distribution. Goods and services have to reach the consumer and so **channels of distribution** exist. Manufacturers and producers have a range of options from which to select, and their choice will be based on a range of factors.

The intention is to provide convenience: to take the product or service as near as possible to the consumer, to make it easy for both the customer(s) and the consumer.

Channels of distribution are in constant flux as new methods of distribution are invented and/or become socially acceptable. Traditional insurance brokers, for example, believe that consumers welcome a high-street presence. Direct Line is busily proving this is now wrong, since it is a highly successful, fast-growing and extremely profitable operation that offers insurance and financial services by telephone.

A middleman can only survive in a channel whilst 'adding value'. This has traditionally been by 'breaking bulk': manufacturers deliver in van loads to wholesalers who then supply in mixed van loads to retailers. The advent of the supermarket, and then the hypermarket enabled the major retailers to cost-effectively replace the wholesaler by absorbing the function into their internal channels of distribution. This has had a disastrous effect on the smaller retailers, who cannot buy in bulk, and the whole pattern of grocery distribution has changed beyond all recognition within a single decade.

PROMOTION

This area is at the very heart of marketing. It is the one undisputed core skill. The major tools making up the promotional mix are all to do with effective communication. Each has a specific role, and each sub-divides into a range of specialist tools and techniques.

The four major tools divide into non-personal, which work at a distance, and personal. Non-personal tools are:

Public Relations

This involves stimulating demand for a product or service by securing significant news coverage in published media. PR is also concerned with prevention of the publication of harmful news, and with damage limitation should a damaging report be published.

PR, as has been said in Section 3, is beginning to take a major role at corporate level, where the target audiences are relatively few and can be tightly defined.

Advertising

The placing of messages (for a fee) in the media by an identified person or organisation.

The *Concise Oxford Dictionary* defines advertising's role as 'to disseminate, to inform' – and that is exactly what it does. We shall see in Unit 6, Communication in Marketing, that there is a steady progression from a consumer being unaware of a need, through:

- Awareness – which must be created in the customer/consumer
- Attitude – which needs to be identified, modified, maintained
- Action – which is demonstrated by trial of a product followed by repeat purchases.

Advertising in all its forms has a major role to play in making people aware of a product and service, and in the development and maintenance of a favourable attitude.

Sales promotion

This includes anything that provides an impetus at point-of-sale. The need for point-of-sale impact was identified in the 1960s, as the trend to self-service removed the personal contact between the purchaser and the retailer. Rather than relying on the personal sales skills of a shop assistant the product had to make independent impact.

Sales promotion techniques have been honed in the fiercely competitive grocery market, but are now in use throughout the whole spectrum of marketing.

The intention is that the PR and Advertising tools should create an inclination to purchase, or repurchase, so that sales promotion can influence the decision at point of sale. With many retail customers making their purchase decision at the point of sale, and with brand loyalty beginning to show signs of weakening, mastery of sales promotion is becoming ever more important to the marketer.

It is important to note that the overall purpose of marketing communications is not to *sell* a product or service. Its purpose is to influence target customers in their decisions about which products and services to buy.

You may feel that this is a very fine distinction – are there not salespeople who pressure their contacts? Of course there are. But evidence clearly shows that long-term success comes only from repeat business, and that repeat sales are not generated by high-pressure and/or unethical means. The distinction between 'encouraging purchase' and 'selling' is important to an understanding of the subtlety needed to be an effective marketing communicator.

Sales force

This is the only personal communications activity. Members of the sales force have direct contact with customers, and sometimes with consumers. An effective sales force is essential to every organisation, and it usually accounts for a comparatively large proportion of the promotional budget.

Effective and efficient sales people not only secure above-average business, they can also secure information about the market and, in particular, about competitive activity. Such events as the launch of a new competing product and/or a revised price list from a competitor can be reported back in hours if the sales force is motivated to do so. Or the marketer can wait for the trade press to report developments!

PHYSICAL EVIDENCE

Environmental factors have some degree of influence on any relationship. This will vary from the obvious – I'm not buying there, the cabinets are dirty – through to the subliminal – I can't put my finger on it, but I don't feel comfortable.

Customers always look for confirmation – for factors which support and confirm the appropriateness of what they are considering buying. When a purchase has been made they look for confirmation that they have made a wise decision.

The potential purchaser is seeking tangible clues to build confidence; the wise marketer takes care to provide them. Issues which have an impact in this area include:

- furnishings
- colour
- layout
- noise level
- preparedness
- personal confidence on the part of the sales staff.

COGNITIVE DISSONANCE

This term, borrowed from psychology, describes the state which purchasers can find themselves in immediately after purchase. It is important to recognise that buyer behaviour is equally important after purchase as before, and to make provision to manage it.

The classic example comes from the motor trade, where a new car purchaser tends to be intensely aware of car advertising *after* purchase, and notices exactly how many other new cars he sees of both the model he selected and those he rejected. He is particularly aware of any that display any form of problem, one actually broken down can cause anxiety.

The buyer is – of course – seeking reassurance that the decision was wise. Expensive items, such as a motor car, are purchased rarely, if at all, the decision process is therefore not routine, and the price is likely to be a major element in the budget.

Marketers should, therefore, take positive steps to maximise the positive and supportive elements of the process and to protect the purchaser from any potentially negative elements.

PARTICIPANTS

This area includes anything to do with personnel that may have an impact on the transaction being made. Unless sales people are well trained, knowledgeable, and – above all – have the right attitude, a sale is unlikely to proceed if there are alternatives available.

Consideration is the key. People look for considerate treatment. We all tend to regard our own needs as paramount, and look for others to understand and provide for them.

The following areas of concern come under this P:

- personnel quality
- training
- discretion
- commitment
- appearance
- interpersonal behaviour
- degree of involvement/interest
- customer contact skills
- product knowledge
- level of authority
- concern for the customer/consumer's long-term benefit.

PROCESS

Every purchase requires some formality. This can be complex, difficult to follow, time consuming – as when required to queue at a bank counter to secure authority to draw cash and then queue again at a different window to have the cash paid over. Or it can be easy – as when you put a plastic card into an automatic teller machine and draw cash without any personal involvement.

Something of the reputation that banks have acquired through their processes is indicated by research that shows that the majority of customers prefer to wait in the rain outside their branch to use a cash dispenser, rather than go inside where there are unoccupied tellers!

It is necessary to co-ordinate activities in such a way as to show concern for the customer. Thus, marketing must be involved with such issues as:

- policies – to facilitate not prevent
- procedures
- employee discretion
- customer involvement
- customer assistance
- merchandising.

ACTIVITY 13

Marketing is, as we know, concerned with customer and consumer satisfaction. Yet the 7Ps are essentially centred on the organisation – they describe various components of its function. Today's marketers are moving away from the internally focused 7Ps and replacing them with '7Cs', which relate more directly to the consumer or customer.

Take ten minutes to work out customer-oriented concepts beginning with C to match those of the 7Ps. (These are all concepts that have been touched on in the above discussion of the 7Ps.)

Your Cs may not tally exactly with those suggested here, but hopefully you were along the right lines. You should have matched Cs to the Ps something like this:

Product	=	Customer Value
Price	=	Cost
Place	=	Convenience
Promotion	=	Communication
Physical Evidence	=	Confirmation
Participants	=	Consideration
Process	=	Co-ordination and Concern

You will note that we have actually suggested 8Cs !

The marketing mix provides a range of useful tools, but these are of little use unless they are held together in some way – by strategic planning. They also need to be based on some working knowledge of the market to which they will be applied. A helpful image in this context is that of the toolbox, in which the base consists of marketing research, and the whole thing is supported by the handle of planning:

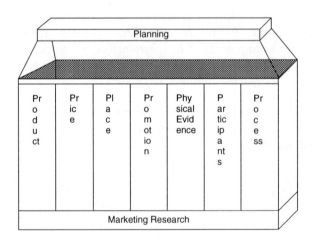

Figure 5: The marketing toolbox

4.2 Planning

Much of this unit has been concerned with the need for marketing to adopt a management role that extends beyond the function to influence corporate thinking. Corporate plans drive the organisation, and each function within it, and functional management needs to be proactive if it is not to be forced into a reactive state.

Planning is required at all levels of management and in this sense management extends to the most junior members of the organisation. Tactical issues that should be planned include: each individual sales call, each telephone conversation, each letter. Time should be managed – which requires planning. Relationships should be planned. In short, everything the members of an organisation do can be planned, and most of it should be.

This is *not* to say that planning is dictatorial. Far from it. Planning can and should be developmental. The intention is to improve, not to discipline. An example of planning in use at a tactical level is as follows:

TELESALES

Telesales have now developed to the point where contact calls can be made automatically by computer. The computer schedules the calls so that a sales agent is free when a respondent answers. When a call is put through to the sales agent, details of the respondent appear on screen automatically. The computer also provides suggestions for the most appropriate approach, given what is known about the particular respondent and others of a similar type. Thus the technology automatically provides the information the agent needs without imposing an automated solution.

Results of the call are entered by the sales agent into the real-time data base which automatically updates so that the next time a caller of the same type is contacted there will be more information about their likely tastes, requirements and values.

Planning – completed as always by Control – monitors activity to maximise value from each sales agent, suggests a line of approach, updates the data base, and monitors results against objectives. Individuals can evaluate their achievement against objective, and learn how different approaches either improve or reduce their chance of success. Given that the feedback is positive, the benefits are considerable. Individuals become more effective. Clients have appropriate information to help them decide, the organisation has a more motivated team, higher sales and improved profits.

4.3 Marketing research

Every aspect of research of use to marketing is contained within the term 'marketing research'.

- Quantitative research deals with numerical data.
- Qualitative research is concerned with measuring attitude and behaviour.

Both of these are covered in Unit 7, Section 3.

Data contains information, and information is essential to effective management and marketing planning, but it has to be processed in order that the needed information can be extracted.

Broadly speaking, data comes in two forms:

- Secondary data is that which has been collected for another purpose.
- Primary data is collected specifically for a given purpose.

Primary data automatically and immediately becomes secondary when used for anything other than the purpose for which it was originally collected.

- Secondary data should always be considered *first*. It is readily available, comparatively cheap to obtain, and often contains everything one needs to know.
- Primary data is only commissioned to fill information gaps left after secondary sources have been exhausted.
- The terms 'desk research' and 'secondary research' are synonymous and describe a secondary data search.
- 'Primary research' is also known as 'field research'.

This subject will be dealt with in much greater detail in Unit 7: Market Research.

Summary

The marketing function has its own set of 'tools', which sub-divide into specialities. Selecting the most appropriate tools, and blending them into a series of mixes enables the marketer to effectively and efficiently manage the interface with customers and consumers, potential, new and established.

Marketing is an exchange relationship between people, and it does not matter whether the people are internal or external to the organisation. Marketers, thus, should take equally as much care with the internal marketing of their plans and services, as with the external marketing of the organisation's offerings.

UNIT REVIEW ACTIVITY

Resource Item 1.3 is a report from the *Times* which deals with a 'new marketing approach to politics'. Read it carefully, and:

1 Describe in a hundred or so words how it relates to the understanding of marketing that you have secured from this unit.

2 Select an area you know well (such as a sports club) and determine the results you imagine a similar approach would obtain.

3 Outline the actions that ought to be taken following your analysis in (2).

Unit summary

Marketing is at heart an exchange process between people. In a marketing-focused organisation the marketing concept will permeate throughout and marketers should be active in both corporate and functional management.

Marketers are managers within their organisations and this prime need must not be neglected in favour of a focus on purely functional marketing issues. Managers lead people to the achievement of results and marketers should be trained in both management and marketing skills.

Organisational focus is provided by a mission and by policies which allow corporate objectives to be set to guide the functional strategies and tactics. As responsibility is delegated, so each manager's policies are established by the tactics of his or her superior. Thus, it is important to clarify the level of objective, eg marketing strategic objective, sales tactical objective, and so on. Objectives should be established in writing and should be SMART, with each tied to a specific control.

Marketers interact with people, who 'buy' in response to need. The needs of members of target audiences must be identified so that they can be provided for. It is far easier to identify and satisfy need than to create a need to match a product offering. The marketing mix of the 7Ps/7Cs, plus planning and research, are used to achieve marketing's objectives.

Glossary

You may find it helpful to refer to this brief glossary of terms when reading the rest of this module.

Consumer A person who uses up the value of a product or service. NB: Customer and consumer are sometimes wrongly used as interchangeable terms. The term 'final consumer' is unnecessary if customer and consumer are used correctly.

Customer Person or organisation that buys a product or a service, either for use by a consumer or for re-sale. Note: A customer can also be a consumer.

Management Information System (MIS) A formal method of making available to management the accurate and timely information necessary to facilitate the decision-making process and enable the organisation's planning, control and operational functions to be carried out effectively. (Stoner & Freeman)

Marketing Information System (MkIS) Consists of people, equipment and procedures to gather, sort, analyse, evaluate and distribute needed, timely, and accurate information to marketing decision makers. (Kotler)

Package 1 The physical protection that protects a product all the way to consumption. 2 Promotional 'packaging' of user benefits/'solutions package' sought by customer. Except when otherwise stated, 'package' is used in the second meaning.

Price Money or other consideration for which a thing is bought or sold.

Product A product has physical presence, function and symbolic value. (See Package.)

Service Any activity of benefit that one party can offer to another that is essentially intangible and does not result in the ownership of anything. Its production may or may not be tied to a physical product. (Kotler) A service has function and symbolic value, as does a product.

Value The intangible package of benefits that the decision-making unit believe attaches to the product.

References

Adair, J (1987) *Not Bosses But Leaders,* Talbot Adair

Adair, J (1988) *Developing Leaders,* Talbot Adair

Drucker, P (1967) *The Effective Executive,* Heinemann

Hatton, A & Worsam, M (1995) *Effective Management for Marketing*, Butterworth-Heinemann

Stoner, J A F & Freeman, R E (1992) *Management,* Prentice-Hall, 5th edn

Answer to Unit Review Activity

1   The report shows that people have deeply felt attitudes. These are hard for a researcher to access since many are held at an unconscious level, and even the most articulate people have difficulty in expressing attitudes and beliefs. Thus, indirect techniques have been developed to achieve the desired information. In this example the similes used appear to clearly indicate the attitudes held.

The example shows how skilled researchers approach the problem of extracting and interpreting attitudes, and that these attitudes are likely to affect actions. It further shows that long-term attitudes are hard to shift (Duracell rabbit getting slower and slower) and change is hard to make from a deep-seated position (voting Labour would be like taking medicine).

It follows that attitudes need to be identified, converted if necessary, and then consolidated. Changing people's attitudes takes considerable financial resources, and clarity of purpose, determination and time are needed.

2. Your choice will have either shown positive and supportive imagery – which need to be monitored and reinforced continuously; or negative images which require positive actions, both tangible and intangible, if they are to be corrected.

3. Your actions should make use of all the 7Ps because there will be need for some physical activity – either of maintenance or change – and of intangible activity – in personnel attitudes and communications.

The whole will come together in a marketing plan which should fit within the organisation's policies, be expressed in SMART objectives that cover both strategies and tactics. You may even have found a need to recommend policy changes since, without them, marketing activity will be hamstrung.

Don't worry if you found the third part of this question too difficult. There will be other opportunities to draw up marketing plans later in the module.

UNIT 2

APPROACHES TO ENVIRONMENTAL MONITORING IN MARKETING

Introduction

The environment in which firms and organisations operate has become increasingly diverse and is predicted to increase in complexity. Factors such as environmental groups, government organisations, international shareholders and cross-border operations and customers, as well as the increasing effects of supranational organisations, must all be considered by an organisation formulating its direction and strategies.

Customers in all markets are becoming more sophisticated and make greater demands on the quality of products and services provided.

In addition to this, the distance between suppliers of goods or services and their actual customers has increased, both geographically and organisationally, with many firms operating from central headquarters, directing the actions of subsidiaries.

The attempt to offer a consistent quality of products and services through standardisation of procedures and processes (such as the British Standard BS5750) also means that a clear understanding of all factors affecting the marketing environment is essential before decisions on objectives and strategies are taken. Changes at a later date may be difficult and costly to implement.

The greater the variety of market factors a company has to consider, the greater the level of risk facing an organisation. Products may fail, or consumers may be dissatisfied with the way a product is manufactured or even transported (as was the case early in 1995 when Animal Rights protesters caused a transport company to abandon the transport of live animals). Legal changes may force entire product groups out of existence, as has happened with products containing asbestos and CFCs. Each unknown aspect adds to the potential risk a company faces and can lead to losses in profit or market share, added costs or increased management complexity. In the worst case it can lead to companies going out of business.

Organisations have at their disposal a range of techniques and processes that assist them not only in reducing uncertainty and risk, but also in obtaining information on developments in their markets which enables the development of new products and services. All involve a thorough understanding of the marketing environment a company faces and therefore require extensive research.

Tools are employed to assess the quantitative and qualitative changes occurring in the environment and to analyse the impact of these changes on the actions of all 'players' involved. The impact of these players' actions on corporate activity are, in turn, assessed. Only through continuous scanning of the environment are organisations able to continue to satisfy all stakeholders involved in their markets.

The first part of the unit - Sections 1, 2 and 3 - is concerned with the internal environment of organisations. This includes their legal status, their objectives and the way organisations choose to organise themselves.

In Sections 4 & 5 the factors in an organisation's micro-environment are introduced. These include competitors, various publics faced by companies and the legal and regulatory environment. The notion of stakeholders and corporate responsibility to these, as well as their effect on marketing strategies will also be explored.

The third aspect of an organisation's environment, the macro-environment, is dealt with in Section 6. This includes the economic, political, socio-cultural and technological environment.

Review Activity 8 will consider some of the aspects a firm may face in its pursuit of international markets.

(To complete Review Activities 7 and 8, at the end of Section 6, you will be required to do some library research.)

Objectives

By the end of this unit you should be able to:

- identify ways in which the legal foundation on which a company is based affects the way it functions
- distinguish between the concepts of mission, objectives, strategies and plans
- analyse a company's strengths, weaknesses, opportunities and threats
- identify different organisational structures
- identify stakeholders in an organisation and assess their influence on it
- identify forces in the competitive environment
- identify strategies to enhance an organisation's position in the competitive environment
- assess the effects which changes in the macro-environment might have on a specific organisation.

SECTION 1

The Internal Environment of Firms

Introduction

This section is primarily concerned with internal factors affecting a firm or organisation. Marketing has been defined as 'the management process which identifies, anticipates and supplies customer requirement efficiently and profitably' (Chartered Institute of Marketing). Organisations need to develop systems that facilitate the process of providing customers with appropriate products or services. Equally, to ensure efficiency and profitability, firms have to identify clearly their own goals and the forces impinging on or obstructing these goals, and to develop aims and procedures that are achievable.

The focus of this section is on the management structures that facilitate the process of supplying customers with goods and services.

The aim of this section is to help you to:

- appreciate the complexity of the internal environment of organisations
- understand the importance of organisational goals and how these affect corporate objectives
- appreciate the effects of a company's internal environment on the development of marketing strategies.

1.1 The purpose of organisations

Organisations exist to provide a whole range of products or services for consumer or business markets – for profit or not for profit. Whatever the actual function of the company, it will usually have a purpose particular to it. In order to stay in business or to continue providing the service, organisations strive to maximise a set of objectives which may be unique to them. To achieve these objectives, they aim to structure their organisation in such a way that this maximisation is possible.

ACTIVITY 1

Consider an organisation in the public sector, such as a hospital, and another one in the manufacturing sector, producing either consumer or industrial goods. Write down a list of what you believe to be their main aim or purpose of their existence.

Under the heading of public organisation you may have listed the effective provision of the service, the minimisation of costs, the maximisation of the number of clients patients treated, an increase in satisfaction with the service. Although you may have listed similar points for the manufacturing company, reasons for its existence may also include profit maximisation, maximisation of market share, minimisation of loss, minimisation of customer complaints, maximisation of sales revenue, etc.

As can be seen, organisations can exist for a number of reasons and may be motivated by different aims.

These aims are affected by a number of factors and we will look at these in turn. The structure of the business, that is its legal entity, is one aspect; its mission, or the direction in which it ultimately wishes to go, together with clearly defined objectives, are another; finally, the size and number of functions in each organisation and the channels of communication and integration that exist within the organisation affect whether it can manage the process of supplying customer needs efficiently and profitably.

1.2 The business as legal entity

Organisations need a framework in which to operate if they are to achieve their objectives. The size of business and the complexity of products or services offered by an organisation, are some of the factors that affect the legal framework a firm adopts. The following are some of the legal frameworks used by firms.

SOLE TRADER

This type of business is owned by one person, who provides all the initial capital to form and operate the business. It is the most common type of business found in Britain and the easiest to start. However, the figures below indicate that it is also very vulnerable to failure.

	Stock	Registration %	Deregistrations %	Net change %
1980	1288	158 (12.3)	142 (11.0)	16 (1.2)
1981	1304	152 (11.7)	120 (9.2)	32 (2.4)
1982	1336	166 (12.4)	145 (10.9)	21 (1.5)
1983	1357	180 (13.3)	145 (10.7)	35 (2.6)
1984	1392	182 (9.2)	152 (7.7)	30 (2.2)
1985	1422	182 (12.8)	163 (11.5)	19 (1.3)
1986	1441	191 (13.3)	164 (11.4)	27 (1.9)
1987	1468	209 (14.2)	167 (13.4)	42 (2.9)
1988	1510	235 (15.6)	170 (11.3)	65 (4.3)
1989	1575	265 (16.8)	178 (11.3)	87 (5.5)

Note: Figure in brackets is % of stock at start of period
Source: *Business Briefing*, 20 July 1990

Table 1: Business Stock, registrations and deregistrations in the UK 1980-1989 (000s)

The main advantages of this type of enterprise are:

● It is easy to set up and often requires very little start-up capital.

● The owner/entrepreneur has full control over all business decisions.

● Profits are not shared.

● Owners are often near to their customers and are therefore able to respond to niche markets or special requirements of customers.

● Because these businesses often have a low turnover, they are exempt from VAT registration.

● Accounts need not be published, ensuring maximum amount of privacy.

ACTIVITY 2

List the possible pitfalls you might encounter as a sole trader?

Disadvantages of this type of business include:

● The fact that the owner's assets are at risk should the business fail.

● Lack of expertise in a variety of business functions often leads to inefficiency or the high cost of buying-in specialist services.

- Shortage of capital may restrict the potential for exploiting market opportunities.

- Raising capital may be difficult and restricted to the amount of private assets owned by the sole trader.

- Income is directly related to the number of hours worked by the sole trader. This makes continuity of income difficult during times of illness and holidays.

PARTNERSHIP

Some of the difficulties faced by a sole trader may be overcome by forming a partnership. These are regulated under the Partnership Act and involve at least two, but usually no more than twenty, individuals. (Some professions are allowed to have more than 20 partners, such as accountants, solicitors and members of the Stock Exchange.)

Partnerships involve written agreements regarding the amount of investment and profit share. Where no such deed exists, profits are shared equally.

All partners are equally responsible for any debts incurred by the business. This also applies to sleeping partners, that is, those who invest only in the business without taking any active part in its operation. Although it is possible to form a limited partnership, at least one member of this is required to have unlimited liability. For this reason, limited partnerships are rare.

ACTIVITY 3

Look back at the advantages and disadvantages of sole traders. List the advantages a partnership has over sole traders.

You may have identified the sharing of management responsibilities, losses and risks as one of the advantages of partnerships. The ability to raise more capital when the need or opportunity arises may also be among the advantages you listed. In addition to this there is also greater continuity should one of the partners be absent, the ability to specialise and the spread of risk.

Among the disadvantages you may have included the possibility of conflict, as well as the limit of twenty partners for this type of organisation. The costs of any disagreement may also feature in your list.

REGISTERED COMPANIES

Registered companies are legal entities in their own right and are registered as limited companies. This means that the firm, rather than the owners, is responsible for any debts incurred and that the company can be sued and can sue. Both private and public companies are often referred to as joint stock companies because the investment of the shareholders forms a joint stock of assets which forms is the basis on which the company generates further income and assets. This is then divided among the shareholders.

Registered companies must provide audited accounts as well as a directors', or annual, report. Both private and public companies are required to have at least two shareholders. The internal structure of the company must be outlined in the Articles of Association, and the Memorandum of Association must clearly define the external responsibilities and liabilities of the organisation.

Private limited company

This type of company must carry the letters 'Ltd' after its name. Shares of private limited companies cannot be publicly advertised for sale and may only be traded within a particular group of people, such as friends, family etc. A director and a secretary are required by law.

Public Company

Where a company wishes to become a Public Company, it must file a prospectus (or a statement *in lieu* of one) and a statutory declaration before it is granted a trading certificate. It may include the letters PLC in its name. Its shares are available for public sale. Share owners are responsible for any debts the company incurs to an amount which equals the investment capital. For this reason, public companies may also carry the suffix Ltd. Public companies can be quoted, that is, listed on the stock exchange, or unquoted. Capital raising is helped when the shares are listed on the Stock Exchange. Investment in shares entitles shareholders to a proportion of profits, as well as a vote in Annual General Meetings, which often determine the general direction the business is aiming for in the short- to medium-term future.

ACTIVITY 4

List the advantages and disadvantages of the public company in terms of their ability to react swiftly to market changes

One of the advantages of public companies is their capacity for raising investment. As a consequence, such organisations are more easily able to provide funds for innovation. Their size often enables them to achieve economies of scale both in production and purchasing, reducing costs and increasing competitiveness. However, the formation of a public company involves considerable expense. Its size also means that the organisation may become detached from its owners and customers, and become obsessed by red tape. Annual accounts must be available for public inspection, thereby reducing the confidentiality of the firm.

Where more than 50% of a public company is owned by another organisation, this company is termed a **holding company**.

In addition to the structures outlined above, organisations may also engage in particular relationships which affect their operations. Two of these are co-operatives and franchising.

CO-OPERATIVES

Co-operatives are a distinctive form of business organisation which falls outside the normal scope of free enterprise; indeed the original co-operative movement was set up to supersede the prevailing commercial and industrial order. Co-operatives are registered under the 1965 Industrial and Provident Societies Act and are usually limited companies. This means that individual members may lose their investment in the society's shares but are not otherwise liable.

The main principle of co-operative societies is that the members themselves are their chief customers. As owners, these people do not receive a dividend on their capital, but fixed interest on their capital investment in shares. The remainder of the profit available for distribution is returned to these owners in their capacity as customers as a (variable) dividend on purchases. In contrast to a company dividend, dividends from a co-operative are not subject to an income tax deduction, as they are regarded as a deferred rebate – a method of charging lower prices to customers.

Membership to co-operative societies is permanently open. Although there is a minimum requirement of seven members (but no maximum number) these may join and leave at any time. Societies may repay the shares of leaving members, although some co-operatives insist on members holding a certain proportion of shares which are transferable only. A purchaser must therefore be found by the owner of the shares. As a result, the capital of Co-operatives has no fixed limit and is constantly fluctuating as shares are subscribed for and withdrawn. The ruling that no members is allowed to own in excess of £1,000 means that membership tends to be large.

In place of a board of directors, co-operatives are controlled by a committee of managers elected by their members. These are elected at the annual meeting, at which accounts are also presented. Elections are held on a one-member, one-vote basis, rather than in proportion to number of shares owned.

ACTIVITY 5

Read the article 'Home shopping set to mushroom' (*The Guardian* 24/6/95) in the Resource Section (Item 2.1) and list some of the difficulties which co-operatives may face in the light of the predicted changes.

The predicted changes will affect different co-operative societies differently. Those large enough, and with sufficient members to offer a wide range of products may be able to invest in the technology required to take part in the anticipated home shopping boom. Inefficient, often small, outlets may be closed, with resulting reduction in overheads, which may increase profitability. Indeed, the fact that profits are returned to members as a fixed interest on their investment in shares may be regarded as a unique marketing tool against other competitors.

Smaller, specialist co-operatives could suffer loss of custom as buyers order goods from their armchair rather than venture into shopping centres. However, the rationale underlying the co-operative movement increases the probability of alliances with like-minded organisations, resulting in reduced overheads for a number of firms, with a chance that all will benefit from the change in shopping patterns.

FRANCHISE

This is one of the fastest growing sectors in many economies and is particularly popular in the retail sector. Franchising allows a company to use the name, products or techniques developed by a franchiser against payment of a fee. This fee may be a combination of up-front payment plus a share in the profits. Any losses are the responsibility of the franchisee. Franchising offers a relatively cost-effective way of owning a ready-made business. Marketing services, such as advertising, product development, consumer research and supply of equipment are provided by the franchiser. The range of products and services in the franchising sector is growing rapidly and includes film processing (Prontaprint), shoe repairs (Mister Minit), printing and car valeting. Increasing use of franchising is also made in the provision of business services.

ACTIVITY 6

1 List a number of franchise operations known to you.

2 Taking one franchise operation as an example, describe the features that all the outlets have in common?

3 What do you believe are the main drawbacks for a customer of a franchise operation?

The most famous of the franchise operations is, perhaps The Body Shop. Others include Sox Shop and the Tie Rack. The most common features shared by franchise operations are shop fittings, standard prices, similar or uniform standards of customer care. The location of the outlets may also be very similar: busy retail parks, shopping centres, or railway stations.

The disadvantages of franchise operations from the point of view of the customer (and therefore ultimately of the franchisee) include lack of product adaptation, lack of response to special requirements, and non-negotiable prices even for business customers.

PUBLIC AND VOLUNTARY SERVICES

The forms of organisations dealt with so far have all been concerned with the private sector. Many services and products 'consumed' are, however, provided by organisations in the public sector, such as national or local government or quasi-government agencies (Quangos). Of increasing importance are the voluntary sector and charities, which in 1994 was estimated to contribute 4% to Britain's Gross National Product, or £16 billion to the economy.

Public services

Into this sector fall services such as education, fire and police services, tax collection, health care and many more. In recent years many of the previously public services have been privatised or regulated, affecting their operations in vital areas such as pricing, share holding, the ability to promote their services as well as the required level of customer service that needs to be offered. Many of the former public utilities fall into this category, and 'watchdogs' such as Oftel (British

Telecom) or Ofgas (British Gas) regulate price increases, act as ombudsmen and ensure that fair trading standards are observed. Consumer Charters have been widely publicised regulating issues such as public transport and patient care in hospitals. Organisations within this sector have been encouraged to develop relationships with private suppliers and customers and as a result have developed the range of marketing activities.

ACTIVITY 7

Recall your dealings with at least two public service providers, such as the library, hospital or local government office.

1 Describe the evidence of any marketing activities you have observed.

2 How did this differ from the marketing activities evident by organisations in the private sector?

3 What, in your opinion, are the reasons for the difference between the public and private sectors?

Your answer to the first question may include items such as timetables, information leaflets, customer service or help desks and sponsorship events which enhance the service and attract 'customers'. Your public library may provide exhibition space to advertise local services, such as mother and toddler groups attached to health clinics.

Differences between the public and private sector may include lack of professionalism (hand-written notices), different channels and methods of promotion, or the absence of promotion in the public sector and a lack of perception of the need for making the public aware of the existence of the service. In the case of the public service, the 'customer' is often assumed either to have prior knowledge of the service or actively to seek out the service provider.

Your answer to the third question may include lack of competition, customers' prior knowledge, lack of substitutes, homogeneity of customer needs, lack of funds or marketing expertise.

VOLUNTARY SERVICES AND CHARITIES

As with the public sector, organisations in the voluntary and charity sector have become increasingly concerned with the need to market themselves. Organisations as diverse as community action groups providing childcare or education for women trying to return to work, charities supporting the need of the homeless or disabled groups and environmental organisations have all raised their profile in an attempt to raise awareness and attract funds from the public and private sector.

REVIEW ACTIVITY 1

In this section it was stated that the legal entity of organisations may have an influence over how the management function of supplying market needs is organised.

Look back over the different forms of businesses and summarise what you believe to be the essential differences between each legal entity. Then try to answer the following questions:

1 How might the ability to raise capital affect the organisation's ability to respond to new product opportunities in the market?

2 How does the fact that some companies are responsible to shareholders affect their planning cycle? Do you believe that sole traders think in the longer term than, say, public companies or co-operative societies? Give reasons for your answers.

3 Why do you think some companies have attempted to buy back their shares?

(A possible answer to this activity can be found at the end of the unit.)

Summary

We have examined the legal structure in which organisations operate. The advantages and disadvantages of each one of these will be reflected in the goals and objectives pursued by these different organisations, which is the subject of the next section.

SECTION 2

Corporate Missions and Objectives

Introduction

As stated in the first section, organisations exist for a purpose. The reason for an organisation's existence is defined in its mission, which is a statement of the general direction an organisation intends to pursue in the medium to long term (usually within the next five to ten years). It also defines an organisation's general commitment to the market areas and sectors it intends to serve.

The aim of this section is to help you to:

- appreciate the importance of an organisation's mission statement and its role in shaping a firm's long term objectives

- distinguish between the concepts of mission, objectives, strategies and tactics

- appreciate how different goals and objectives shape the actions and functions of a firm.

2.1 Corporate mission

A mission statement could be called the 'grand plan' or 'vision' of where a firm wishes to be in the long term. It should contain the essence of what the organisation is all about, and how it differentiates itself from other, similar, firms. For instance, it could be that an organisation believes that it has the ability to become market leader in its field of expertise, or that it wishes to produce a product or service of exceptional quality for a small range of clients or customers. Whatever the vision, employees, intermediaries and (often) customers must be convinced that the organisation is realistic in its overall direction, and that the final goal of its mission is achievable.

ACTIVITY 8

Below are a number of mission statements from a range of organisations. Read these first and then attempt to write a mission statement for your own university, college or the company you work for.

CADBURY SCHWEPPES

Cadbury Schweppes is a major global company in beverages and confectionery whose quality brands and products are enjoyed in over 170 countries around the world. Our task is to build on our traditions of quality and value to provide brands, products, financial results and management performance that meet the interests of our shareholders, consumers, employees, customers, suppliers and the communities in which we operate.

BABCOCK

Babcock International Group plc is a broadly based international engineering business supplying specialised products and services to its customers worldwide.

The common aim of its five operating divisions is to provide the highest possible quality of service combined with technical excellence of design and product.

The group's primary objective is to maximise profit opportunities and earnings through organic growth, appropriate acquisitions and the effective, pro-active management of existing resources in the interests of shareholders, customers and employees.

AMERSHAM

Amersham is a leading speciality biochemical, healthcare and quality assurance company which provides reliable, innovative products and services to customers in the life science, medical and industrial communities around the world.

Amersham is committed to enhancing the quality of human life in striving to provide customer benefits from both its radioactive and non-radioactive technologies:

in Life Science
assays for the detection and measurement of the key components of living cells and improved understanding of biological processes and disease state

in Healthcare
in vivo diagnosis of human psychological disorders
cancer diagnosis and treatment

in Industry
industrial sterilisation
non-destructive testing and detection
instrument calibration.

DHL WORLDWIDE EXPRESS
Worldwide Mission Statement

DHL will become the acknowledged global leader in the express delivery of documents and packages. Leadership will be achieved by establishing the industry standards of excellence for quality of service and by maintaining the lowest cost position relative to our service commitment in all markets of the world.

Achievement of the mission requires:

- Absolute dedication to understanding and fulfilling our customers' needs with the appropriate mix of service, reliability, products and price for each customer.

- An environment that rewards achievement, enthusiasm, and team spirit and which offers each person in DHL superior opportunities for personal development and growth.

- A state of the art worldwide information network for customer billing, tracking, tracing and management information/communications.

- Allocation of resources consistent with the recognition that we are one worldwide business.

- A professional organisation able to maintain local initiative and local decision making while working together within a centrally managed network.

The evolution of our business into new services, markets, or products will be completely driven by our single-minded commitment to anticipating and meeting the changing needs of our customers.

If you wrote a mission statement for a company, you probably included statements about the company's overall aim, and how it intends to achieve this. The focus of the mission statement is likely to be the customers and the benefits that can be offered them. The words 'maximise profit' are likely to have occurred as well.

If you wrote a mission statement for a college or university you may have included the following aspects: providing challenging education to a range of students, developing students from a variety of backgrounds with the skills for life-long learning. Similarly, the university or college may consider the development of international recognition as a main priority, may wish to focus on furthering its research excellence, or focus on providing an excellent teaching environment.

Each one of these broad goals will help to prioritise and guide the allocation of staff and financial resources, as well as assisting with the formulation of objectives and procedures when developing new courses or modules. For instance, where the focus is on encouraging access to study, the university would be involved in negotiations with local colleges of Higher Education to ensure that their ACCESS courses provide students with the relevant qualifications needed to pursue degree level studies. Similarly, where a university focuses strongly on attracting mature, part-time students, appropriate timetable arrangements must be considered at every course level. The provision of a crèche and nursery facilities will also have to be considered.

The importance of organisations developing a coherent direction cannot be stressed sufficiently. Before any organisation can do this, however, it is necessary for it to take careful stock of its current situation. There are a number of tools, or models, available which an organisation may use to help it find out where it is now. These will be looked at later on in this section. First, we need to identify likely objectives organisations may wish to pursue.

2.2 Corporate objectives

Just as individuals have different objectives which they try to achieve, so do business organisations. Personal objectives shape the way we plan to spend our resources, our time, and whom we wish to associate with. They influence where, how and what we purchase, our desire for education and training and a multitude of other aspects in our lives. Personal or business objectives are subject to a number of constraints which affect choices of action.

Corporate objectives, often called business goals, identify the aims a firm wishes to achieve in the medium term. As we saw in Unit 1, Section 3.3., SMART objectives state measurable and achievable positions a company wishes to reach by a particular point in time, often within the next five years or so. They relate to the environment an organisation is operating in and may depend on that environment being stable. As a company's internal environment is dynamic, objectives have to be reviewed regularly to ensure the organisation's arrival.

ACTIVITY 9

1 Write down what you believe to be the objectives of the following organisations?

a) car manufacturer

b) blood transfusion service

c) insurance broker

You may have noted profit among the objectives of the car manufacturer and perhaps also the insurance broker. However, this is obviously not the prime concern of the blood transfusion service, which may have objectives such as obtaining a certain number of blood donors per year (objective 1) in order to save supply a predetermined number of hospitals with blood (objective 2).

Objectives must be achievable and quantifiable. Size and structure of an organisation are therefore important constraints when firms set their objectives. For instance, it may be unusual for a small company operating in a large market to try and maximise market share. It would be equally difficult for a small, 'cottage hospital' to maximise the health education of the region.

The objectives outlined above are by no means the only ones organisations pursue. Companies may aim for growth and quality leadership; they may wish to be at the leading edge of technology and be perceived as innovators. In addition to this they might be involved in making it difficult for other organisations to enter the market (raising entry barriers). Whatever the ultimate objective of firms, without clear goals it is impossible to measure successes and failures and improve business performance.

2.3 Corporate policies, strategies and tactics

In order to achieve their overall mission, companies need to develop policies and strategies which will, if implemented successfully, ensure arrival at the desired end point. When a company aims for profit maximisation, it may decide to do so through price competition or through product adaptation; the company may equally decide to manage its product portfolio in such a way that products are abandoned at a particular point in their life cycle when profitability is low. The actual strategy chosen depends on the circumstances and individual company, but often involves the use of either price, product, promotion or distribution strategies.

Business Plans, or Marketing Plans are a series of connected schemes – which aim to utilise a suitable mixture of price, promotion, product or distribution strategies to ensure that the organisation achieves its objectives. For instance, if a firm decides on a **policy** of making promotion its main **strategic** 'weapon', it will estimate the best time to launch its promotional campaign, establish the budget available, goals to be reached in terms of increased sales or awareness, for instance, and how to measure its effectiveness. These steps constitute **tactics,** which will need to be carefully **controlled** – evaluated against objectives.

2.4 Identifying corporate capability

The objectives of any organisations must be achievable. It is therefore vital that companies are aware of their own capabilities and areas of weakness in order to set realistic goals that meet demands, opportunities and threats of a dynamic external environment. It is only when the organisation's capabilities are assessed that strategies and plans can be developed and implemented.

ACTIVITY 10

Read the following case study and write down the firm's strengths and weaknesses.

STOLLWERCK AG

Hans Imhoff, aged 67, knows more about chocolate than anyone else. He has been eating 'at least one bar a day' for the last thirty years. No wonder he weighs in at over 100 kilos (16 stone).

Imhoff, however, who owns 97% of the shares of Kollner Stollwerck AG, the chocolate empire (turnover in 1989: DM 709 million; 1100 employees), knows precious little about marketing. He has always been a mass-goods man. Even the purchase of such venerable brands as Stollwerck (1971), Waldbaur (1976) and Sprengel (1979) did not change a thing. Imhoff made his name as a cost-killer, never launching innovations, but always 'me-too' products.

Yet for the last few years, the 'Chocolate Napoleon', as he is known in Cologne, has been attempting to reform. Spectacular losses of market share to major Suchard brand Milka, which has been attacking Sprengel in its stamping grounds in the northern German states of Saxony, Schleswig Holstein, Hamburg, Northrhine Westphalia and Berlin, and a critical McKinsey report forced him to act.

The management consultants ascertained considerable defects in the Company's marketing and product policy. They concluded that Stollwerck AG had too many products which were scarcely differentiated from each other, contributed little to sales, had low profit margins and increased fixed costs.

Imhoff took action and appointed Franz Kraus, aged 32, as Director of Marketing 1988; Kraus was formerly Lila Pause brand manager with Jacobs Suchard.

Kraus's first step was to do his own survey, which showed that market share was modest. Stollwerck's products were not very attractive to retailers. There were hardly any synergies with other products, such as Sprengel chocolate creams. Profitability was low and products were little known. Consumer attitudes were indifferent and repurchase rate/brand loyalty was low. Competition throughout Germany was tough.

Imhoff's aim was to establish Sprengel, a traditional but faded brand, permanently in the up-market segment, and to double its national market share (1989: 4.2%) over the next five years, thus bringing Stollwerck AG into a leading position in the cholocate market throughout Germany.

Kraus was promised a budget of DM 24 million per annum for the period 1989-1994 to sort out Stollwerck's problems.

Kraus and his team decided on a new corporate design concept, changing everything from company letter-heading, sales booths and company lorries, in an attempt to guarantee what they called 'total brand display'.

Sprengel, Sollwerck's showpiece range, is now displayed in new packaging in bright red in order to contrast with Milka's lilac blocks. It also boasts a new slogan: 'Sprengel – light and sensual'.

It is aimed at well-heeled people over thirty years of age who aspire to a certain standard and style. Posters and television commercials make it clear which is meant here: ageing yuppies – a growing market.

To address this target group, the marketing team reduced the Sprengel range from over 100 to 40 items and created, together with the research and development team, two new products: Dacapo (fine chocolate sticks) and Tiamo (chocolate creams), thus complementing the tired old chocolate cream mixtures called India and Marie Theresia. The launch was supported by advertising at over 7000 billboard locations and in national monthly magazines such as *Stern, Brigitte* and *Fur Sie*.

Kraus's solution appears to have been successful. Imhoff described his company's performance in 1992 as 'outstanding', with a 20% increase in turnover to DM 1.2 billion. Stollwerck is now acknowledged to be one of Germany's leading chocolate producers, and, with significant profits, plans to diversify into biscuits through a Hungarian acquisition and to expand chocolate production at a site in Budapest.

Imhoff is bullish about the future of the company, investing DM 75 million in capital and product development. Kraus, however, issued a recent warning that inroads into the Eastern European market, whilst strategically important for the long-term growth of the company, should not be relied on. He argued that competition from other European chocolate manufacturers should be warded off by entry into other EC markets, utilising the new capacity created in the Hungarian site to supply much of this new market.

The strengths you have identified may include expertise in the market, the appointment of an experienced marketing manager, and successful repositioning of some of its products. If you have included the increasing number of 'ageing yuppies' under the 'strengths', reflect on whether this is a result of action undertaken by the organisation. **Environmental factors that are outside the direct control of an organisation are termed 'opportunities'.** Firms may have the strength – such as financial resources, know-how, personnel or contacts – to exploit and develop these opportunities into strengths. Equally, however, many companies face the same opportunities but do not have the strengths to exploit them.

'Weaknesses' could include the business philosophy of 'pile them high and sell them cheap', the interference of the proprietor, the weak positioning of the product, leading to lack of loyal customers, etc.

As with strengths, weaknesses are internal to an organisation. Check again whether the weaknesses you have identified are really under the firm's control to change. For instance, could the company change them by investing in training of personnel, increasing its production capacity, lowering the price, increasing the level of promotion, or by improving distribution? **Where a factor cannot be redressed by the resources or marketing tools available to an organisation, it is a 'threat', which the company must defend itself against through creative strategies.**

ACTIVITY 11

Now go over the case study again and note down any opportunities or threats which the company faces.

The process of identifying strengths, weaknesses, opportunities and threats is often referred to as a SWOT analysis. It forms the basis on which companies build their strategies and plans. Such an analysis enables organisations to assess the resources required in terms of personnel, finance, capacity and marketing costs and establishes the likelihood of achieving their objectives.

REVIEW ACTIVITY 2

Ingvar Kampman, the founder of the IKEA furniture group, formulated his mission (called the IKEA testament!) in the early 1970s and, as the article from the *Financial Times* in your Resource File (Item 2.2) shows, this has led the company through very volatile times. Please read the article below and carry out the following tasks:

1 Write down what you believe to be the mission of this firm.

2 Given that a company has a number of options, that is, it can use pricing, promotion, distribution and/ or product strategies to achieve its objectives, what were the main choices made by IKEA?

An answer is given at the end of this unit.

REVIEW ACTIVITY 3

Select a company known to you and carry out a SWOT analysis. Can you suggest ways in which the company can overcome its weaknesses and make more of its opportunities?

Summary

In this section we have identified the difference between corporate missions, objectives, strategies and tactics and marketing plans. We have established the importance of clear goals for organisations and the need to establish clearly the current capabilities of a firm in order for it to decide on its future direction. This can be summed up as follows:

MISSION   What is the purpose of the organisation?

OBJECTIVES   Where would we like to be?

STRATEGIES   How do we get there?

TACTICS   What do we need to do in order to ensure arrival?

MARKETING PLAN   The document that links these together.

In the next section we will examine the internal management structure of organisations and their effect on corporate activity.

Section 3

Organisational Structures

Introduction

We have seen in the first section that organisations can be of different sizes, comprise different people and legal status. Section 2 examined the need for direction via missions, objectives and tactics. In this section we will look at how organisations can provide an internal framework to support the firm in its drive to succeed and how the framework shapes the actions of organisations.

The aim of this section is to help you to:

- understand a range of different organisational structures and their advantages and disadvantages.

3.1 Changing orientations

The functions of even the smallest firm require a framework in which to operate. Even sole traders, where one person carries out a variety of functions, need to plan which proportion of their business is devoted to manufacturing, selling, administration, product development, research etc. Although sole traders are usually more flexible in the allocation of their time to tasks than personnel in large organisations, without an organisational structure, chaos will reign.

With an increase in the size and complexity of an organisation, the need for division of labour becomes more apparent, as does a greater degree of formality. Lines of authority and responsibility need to be established in order to co-ordinate, implement and manage the various tasks.

The need for an integrated marketing function is not recognised in all organisations. At the beginning of this century, when demand for goods often exceeded their supply and when firms were preoccupied with streamlining and maximising their production facility and capacity, there was thought to be little or no need for either internal or external marketing activities. As long as organisations could produce the service or product in question, they could usually find a market for their goods. For this reason, resources and management focus were very concentrated on the production department and on product development.

The growing affluence of consumers, increased competition and an evening out of supply and demand after World War II necessitated a shift in focus. Greater use was made of promotion in order to increase sales and market share, thus reducing unit costs and staying competitive through an economy of scale. Consumer demand remained fairly homogeneous and was influenced by price factors. The expression:

'Pile it high and sell it cheap' is typical for this period and reflects the sales orientation of firms prevalent until the 1970s. Resources were focused, and management concentrated on, the sales function and price and promotion strategies.

Development in consumer sophistication, greater disposable income, the need for organisations to differentiate their products to stand out from the crowd and target these products at a specific market segment led to the refinement of marketing tasks and skills in many organisations. The recognition that firms that serve specific customers or groups of customers better than competitors are more successful led to division of labour within the marketing function and departments. Resource allocation and management focus began to shift from pricing and selling to the management of a range of interrelated tasks.

Marketing departments were often added as an afterthought, however, and often only provided marketing services, rather than contributing to the customer focus of organisations. Although these organisations have incorporated the marketing philosophy to some extent, there is often conflict between different departments over allocation of resources, management time and responsibility for decisions.

The notion of market-led and consumer-focused organisations is relatively new and a result of not only intense competition in the late 1980s, but also the influence of the manufacturing and marketing techniques introduced by increasingly multinational, often Japanese, operations. These adopt the premise that a carefully researched market leads to appropriate product development subject to corporate objectives; that knowledge of customer behaviour, needs and aspirations results in appropriate positioning strategies and satisfied, loyal customers. This philosophy of 'getting things right first time' permeates the whole organisation and not only enhances customer perception and satisfaction but also reduces cost to the organisation. Allocating resources to research, and directing staff training at maintaining quality procedures are the result of this management focus.

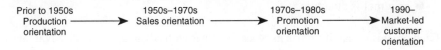

Figure 1: The development and focus of organisations

ACTIVITY 13

1 Name three companies that each demonstrate, in your view, one of the orientations given in Figure 1. Give your reasons.

2 If your companies includes one which is product or sales orientated, suggest a number of changes that may improve your level of satisfaction in dealing with this organisation.

Your chosen organisations might include a service such as a dry cleaning company that has kept you waiting some time for your items to be found. Perhaps they were not ready, making a further journey necessary? Or you might have tried to get through to a department in an organisation on the telephone and were treated discourteously by the receptionist, put through to the wrong department, found that the person in charge is not available and there was no-one else who can help. Product manuals may have been found less than useful after getting the goods home, causing frustration and delay in installation. A company may have attracted you to their outlet with money-off offers, only for you to discover that the delivery or installation of the product requires additional expense.

All these are examples of firms organised on the basis of out-of-date principles which have failed to recognise that customer orientation not only increases customer satisfaction, but in the long run also reduces cost. Firms that have adopted a customer-focused outlook usually find that it is cheaper to get things right first time, compared with the cost of rectifying mistakes at a later date.

3.2 The structure of organisations

The structure of organisations and the place of the marketing function are often an expression of the overall focus described above. They may also be symptomatic of the external environment the firm operates in. A shift in management concern therefore often requires restructuring of parts of, or the whole, organisation.

Companies may organise their operations in a number of ways:

- by function
- by market need – either customer or region
- by product
- as a matrix structure

Each organisational form has its place, together with advantages and disadvantages. It is part of the management task to evaluate alternatives and to achieve a structure that optimises the organisation's chances of fulfilling its mission and objectives.

ORGANISATION BY FUNCTION

Many small or developing organisations adopt the approach shown in Figure 2. Each function is led by a manager who is responsible for forecasting, obtaining feedback from the market and co-ordinating that particular function. She or he ultimately reports to a board of directors which decides on the direction of the company.

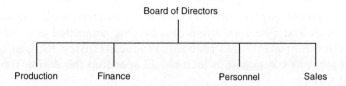

Figure 2: Organisation by function

ACTIVITY 12

Write down what you believe to be the advantages and disadvantages of the type of organisational structure shown in Figure 2.

Small or medium-sized companies often find that this is the most efficient structure for them, as the limited number of personnel often involves one person holding more than one position anyway. It allows for division of labour according to specialism and creates clear lines of communication and control.

The main disadvantages of this structure, particularly for large organisations, can be lack of communication between departments, leading to duplication in management tasks and consequent increases in costs. Feedback on changes in the market may not be passed on to production management and may lead to delays in product development or adaptation, resulting in lost opportunities to gain competitive advantage. Conversely, the production department may become concerned with efficiency of production rather than availability of a range of products at any one point in time.

EXAMPLE

A well-known manufacturer of components for the construction industry which adopted the structure outlined above, faced increasing competition from manufacturers both at home and abroad. At the same time, demand for an increasing range of products, such as differently coloured roof tiles, bricks, and accessories, increased. The main raw material used was clay and the production processes involved mixing compounds, moulding the mixture to the required shapes and sizes and kiln drying. The company focused its attention on producing with greater efficiency. New kilns, which required less energy, were installed, production runs became automated and switching time between products was reduced. Product research focused on the development of compounds which would speed up the drying time and reduced wastage.

Although the objectives of the production department were achieved, the company found itself having to store large quantities of products, thus increasing the cost of stockholding. In addition to this, it also discovered that its flexibility to respond to customer requirements was reduced. Customised orders, which would have attracted premium prices, were often rejected. Indeed, the large stockholding led to a reduction in the number of products stocked and product variety available. In addition to this, the company found that its production schedule led at times to delay in delivery of essential accessories which, due to their lower demand, were only produced intermittently, causing customers to buy not only the accessories from competitors, but also the main products, as this was perceived to be more convenient and less costly in terms of management time.

Although production efficiency was maximised, the company experienced falling profits and was eventually taken over by one of its competitors.

ORGANISATION BY MARKET NEED – CUSTOMER OR REGION

Where an organisation offers one product or service to different markets, it may break down its marketing function to serve the specific needs of that segment. For instance, a producer of instant coffee may distribute its product through multiple retailers, to wholesalers, to hotel chains who buy centrally, or to franchise operators of vending machines who use the coffee as part of their service and have specialised packaging requirements.

Each segment may be approached by employing different aspects of the marketing mix tools available to the producer, such as specialised packaging in sachets for hotels, or creating different on-pack promotions for one of the large multiple retailers. Each firm may have different objectives, strategies and plans and may therefore be best served by specialist personnel. Similarly, when an organisation is large and its markets regionally dispersed, markets may be best served by regional personnel.

One important feature of firms that are organised according to market need is the separation of the sales and marketing function. They operate on the premise that sales is one of the tools used to promote goods and services (the others being public relations, publicity, promotion and advertising), rather than believing that sales *is* marketing, as had been traditional view until the 1970s.

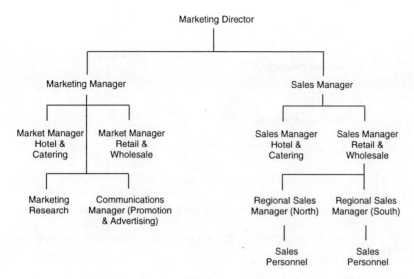

Figure 3: Organisational structure by market need

ACTIVITY 15

Write down what you think might be the advantages and disadvantages of the type of organisational structure shown in Figure 3.

The advantages of this type of structure are the ability to respond to changes in either regional or customer markets and the degree of specialism that companies can draw on. However, competition for resources and conflict between sales forces may ensue where, for instance, the company is dealing with a customer with buying centres in two or three different regions. Research has also indicated that this kind of structure leads to a preoccupation with financial performance rather than with market focus.

ORGANISATION BY PRODUCT OR BRAND

Organisations that own a large portfolio of diverse products may structure their business by brand or product. Pedigree Petfoods is an example of this type of organisation. Brand or product managers are responsible for all aspects affecting their brand, including decisions about product modification and brand extensions, promotion strategies and plans, monitoring of sales performance and corrective action affecting all marketing mix variables.

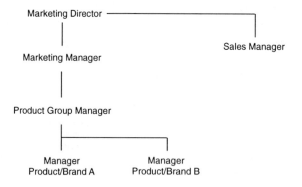

Figure 4: Organisational structure by product/brand

ACTIVITY 16

Write down what you believe to be the advantages and disadvantages of the type of organisational structure shown in Figure 4.

The advantages of this structure include a clear focus on all aspects of a product or brand and responsiveness to market changes. In-depth market knowledge is acquired by product managers and group product managers are able to balance resources according to performance and market requirements.

This structure often leads to inefficiencies and inter-brand rivalry for resources, however. In addition to this, brand managers are often relatively inexperienced and may lack the expertise required to make complex decisions. It may also lead to a lengthy chain of command and responsibility which may result in lack of communication, duplication of tasks and inefficiencies.

MATRIX ORGANISATION

Where organisations find that greater co-operation between functions, divisions and products are necessary, they may adopt a matrix structure. In this, a programme manager draws on the expertise of different departments or functions to achieve given objectives. Members of a programme team report both to their functional and programme head. This allows for speedy flow of information, the use of specialism as required, and the greater devolvement in decision-making processes.

The increased involvement of different functions can also lead to speedier acceptance and implementation of new ideas. It is also claimed, however, that organisation by matrix structure can slow down development processes when strong rivalry between departments exists. The costs of developing programmes may increase as a consequence.

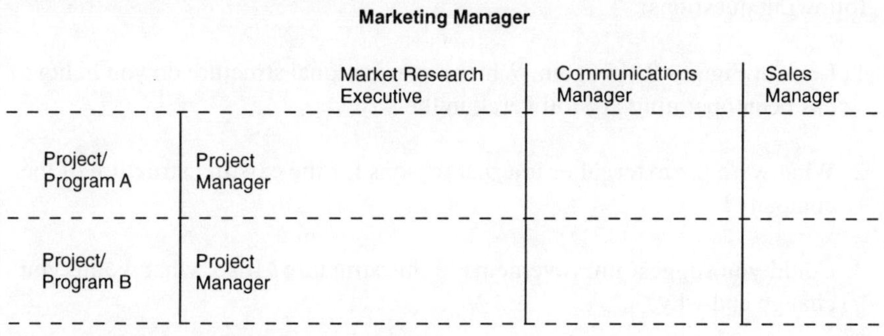

Marketing Manager

		Market Research Executive	Communications Manager	Sales Manager
Project/ Program A	Project Manager			
Project/ Program B	Project Manager			

Figure 5: Organisation by matrix

ACTIVITY 17

Consider the structure of an organisation you are familiar with. This may be your own college or university, or a company you have worked for.

1 Draw a diagram of the organisational structure.

2 Write down what you believe to be the main advantages and drawbacks obvious to you.

3 What changes would you suggest to the organisation to improve efficiency and customer satisfaction?

REVIEW ACTIVITY 4

Please read the Stollwerck case study in Section 2 again, and answer the following questions:

1 Look at Figures 2 – 5 again. Which organisational structure do you believe has been operating at Stollwerck in the past?

2 What were the external or internal reasons for the existing structure of the company?

3 Could you suggest improvements to this structure? If so, what would you change and why?

(A possible answer to this activity is given at the end of the unit.)

Summary

This section has explored the importance of an organisational framework to assist companies achieve their missions and objectives. The relationship between this framework and objectives and marketing plans or programmes has also been examined. Different management philosophies have been encountered and their effect on a company's focus and structure has been discussed.

The next two sections will look at the micro-environment of organisations and their impact on the functions and successes of organisations.

SECTION 4

The Micro-Environment of Organisations

Introduction

The second half of this unit is concerned with the micro-environment in which organisations operate.

Section 4 explores the various publics that companies in all sectors of an economy must consider when planning and executing their objectives and programmes. Examples of the relative importance of different stakeholders, the growth of the power of stakeholders and the need for monitoring changes in stakeholder concerns and expectations are examined. The impact on corporate strategy will also be discussed.

The second section is concerned with the competitive environment of organisations. This includes suppliers, competitors and intermediaries such as financial or marketing services used by a firm. Strategic options available to organisations in their pursuit of competitive advantage are introduced and their impact on the effectiveness of organisations analysed.

Regulatory pressure, which in many textbooks is dealt with separately, is exerted on firms from a variety of sources. These include stakeholders and factors in the competitive environment. For this reason there is no discrete section on the regulatory environment, but it is dealt with where appropriate. It will be expanded upon in the third section of this unit when we look at the legal environment and how legislation regulating products, competitive activity, trading conditions and consumer protection affect corporate activity.

The aim of this section is to help you to:

- appreciate the importance of publics in the formulation of corporate objectives, strategies and plans
- understand the wider social responsibility organisations face
- estimate the likely impact publics may have on corporate actions
- evaluate a number of options available to organisations in dealing with their publics.

4.1 The organisation and its publics

Marketing has been described as the process that facilitates satisfactory exchanges between two or more parties. Whereas traditionally these parties were considered to consist of sellers and customers, companies in the last ten years have had to satisfy an increasing number of parties, called 'publics', not directly associated with the exchange process. The concern of these publics is often not the exchange process, but the effect organisations have on the well-being of the wider society in attempting to facilitate this exchange.

ACTIVITY 18

Read the Resource Items 2.3 and 2.4, 'Calf protesters win legal battle' (*Guardian* 23/2/95) and 'Asda blocked on cut-price books' (*Financial Times* 9/2/95) and briefly sum up the wider issues at stake. List the 'publics' who are affected by these issues.

In the first article, the issues involved are animal welfare – that of the animals being shipped to the Continent – and public safety – that of the residents and protesters, one of whom was crushed by a lorry. The publics affected include not only the farmers and hauliers involved in the transaction, but the people living near the airport, the protesters trying to stop the transportation, and the owners of the Coventry airport.

In the second article, the issue is the complex one of whether a 'free market' should be allowed to operate in the sale of books, or whether a fixed price, established by the publisher, should be obligatory. The supermarket, Asda, and the purchasers of the books, were involved in the transaction, but the 'publics' involved include the publishers of the books, and other booksellers, who are being undercut by Asda.

Publics may comprise pressure groups, regulatory bodies including industry watchdogs, residents' associations or the media. They may be local, national or, as is the case with some environmental groups, international. Their influence on corporate strategies and marketing plans affect the ability of organisations to achieve objectives and may therefore be perceived as a threat to which companies are forced to react. However, as later examples will show, the emergence of pressure groups has also provided new market and product opportunities and may help to create competitive advantages.

4.2 The notion of stakeholders

Stakeholders, as Figure 6 below shows, surround the activities of a firm. They affect its action in various ways, and the organisation in turn depends on many of its stakeholders to carry out its functions. An organisation therefore needs to research the interests of its publics and communicate effectively with them to provide an environment in which it can meet its desired goals.

Figure 6: The organisation and its publics

Public stakeholders may consist of a variety of groups, all with different focus, resources and expertise. The table below summarises the main groups.

It is important to note that single-issue causes, which start off as the focus of a local group, may develop wider implications nationally or internationally. Many recent examples have shown that single issues can escalate and become a national and international issue when solved supra-nationally. The article at the beginning of this section on live animal transport is an example of how a single cause issue spread to become a local issue, with residents supporting the small group of protesters. It escalated, partly because of its wide media coverage, to develop into a national, then international, issue when the European Parliament became involved. Organisations must therefore carefully research the objectives of their publics and develop responses which minimise the effect on their scarce resources.

Cause	Example	Focus	Resources	Complexity
Single	Conditions of employment	Individual	Often very limited	Low
Local issues	Planning issues	Specific	Limited	Medium
Multiple	Heritage		Limited	Medium
Economic	CBI	Specific benefits to members	Often extensive	High
Social	Health & Safety	Benefit to society	Often extensive	High
National/ International	Environmental groups	Operations & standards	Extensive	Very High

Table 2: Classification of stakeholder groups by cause

ACTIVITY 17

1 Try and identify a specific pressure group in your area for each of the following categories: consumer group, local residents, environmental pressure group, regulatory stakeholders, trade union. (Your local telephone directory may be able to help)

2 Try to classify them according to the table above. Are they single, multiple, social or economic? What is the main focus of their cause(s)? Do they command extensive resources, including expertise?

Obviously the answers you give are going to depend on where you live, but the following are general comments about the way in which these 'publics' exert pressure on organisations.

CONSUMER GROUPS

Consumer groups have had an extensive influence on the safety of products, on trading conditions, on the use of marketing mix tools, the availability of credit, data protection etc. National groups affiliated internationally have had extensive lobbying powers with politicians and trade associations that has led to legislative changes.

Consumer groups have also used various media to publicise their concern. TV programmes like 'Watchdog' and 'That's Life' and publications such as Which have advanced concerns by individual consumers and consumer groups and alerted the public to dangerous products and questionable business practices.

LOCAL RESIDENTS

Local residents often fall into the single cause/low resources category of publics. They may be concerned about plans to build a motorway in the vicinity, or group together to fight for compensation, as has happened with people who own property near the Channel Tunnel rail link. By combining their resources, these groups can have a powerful influence on the actions of a firm.

Unlike multiple-cause or social-cause groups, however, once the issue is resolved these groups are usually dissolved.

Organisations must therefore consider carefully all the parties affected by their actions and plans in order to reduce the likelihood of future conflicts.

ENVIRONMENTAL PRESSURE GROUPS

Environmental pressure groups need to be distinguished from political parties which focus on environmental concerns. Unlike other groups encountered, however, the line is sometimes unclear.

Membership of environmental groups may be local, such as the Groundwork Trusts which involve local people in environmental projects, or national and international, such as Greenpeace. They may grow beyond their initially local concerns into national or international issues.

An example of a project that started as a local concern, but which grew to national level was the campaign to prevent the destruction of Fox's Wood. The case was ultimately resolved when the Court of the European Union confirmed that the area was of special scientific interest and could therefore not be developed. Another case in point is the concern over the destruction of the ozone layer, which led to manufacturers replacing CFCs with other propellant gases and resulted in an international timetable for the reduction of products containing CFCs. This has affected the product strategy of many firms, some of whom immediately sought competitive advantage by publicising the fact that their products were environment friendly.

REGULATORY STAKEHOLDERS

Pressure from regulatory stakeholders comes in a number of forms: self-regulatory, through trade associations and professional bodies, through regulatory institutions such as the Monopolies and Mergers Commission, and, as a result of commercial interest. Although regulations often become enshrined in laws at a later date, companies are not obliged to adhere to many of the self-regulations applied by a range of organisations.

Many industries combine their interests to safeguard standards from rogue competitors and draw up codes of practice which are the result of consultation and negotiation. The British Press Association, when threatened with tighter privacy laws as a result of public protest against infringement of privacy, drew up its own ethical code to prevent legal restriction. It communicated the issues widely through its own media and sought support from the wider public for its improved standards to counteract action by private individual or groups.

Similarly, the Advertising Standards Authority intervenes when it believes that one of its members contravenes its self-regulated codes of practice. As a result of over 800 complaints against the new-born baby poster advertisement by Benetton, and a large number of protests against a recent Levi TV campaign, both companies were forced by the ASA to withdraw their advertisements.

Other professional bodies, such as CORGI, the confederation of registered gas appliance installations, add credibility to their members' skills by determining standards of operation.

The Monopolies and Mergers Commission affects organisations if it believes that the power of a firm or industry is reducing consumer choice and leading to monopolistic practices.

EMPLOYEES AND TRADE UNIONS

Organisations require employees, who are often recruited from the local community. Their skill level may enable firms to increase their effectiveness and save training cost. For instance, when Nissan and Toyota decided to manufacture cars in the UK, one of the factors in favour of the chosen sites was the fact that they could draw on a large pool of skilled workers who had been made redundant from other engineering firms.

The power of representation of workers is another factor that is considered by some organisations before setting up in an unfamiliar area. Union agreements are often negotiated at length with the local workforce to safeguard production and improve effectiveness of communication.

As well as monitoring the external environment to avoid potential conflict, organisations must consider how they are perceived by their own employees; they must communicate effectively with their employees to ensure that changes affecting the organisation, the employees and trade unions are clearly understood. Failure to monitor the opinions of employees and to communicate can lead to misunderstandings and misconceptions. The result is often a reduction in quality, work-to-rule or even strikes.

ACTIVITY 20

Read the article 'Fresh Ferment for the Brewers' in the Resource Section (Item 2.5), and answer the following questions:

1 What were the main effects of the 1992 enquiry by the Monopolies and Mergers Commission?

2 How did brewers attempt to counter the effects of the orders issued by the Office of Fair Trading?

Your answers to the first question might include some of the following: The desire by the MMC to increase competition has forced brewing firms to examine their current aims and practices and to revise these in the light of the new ruling. This involves the firms in added cost. Brewers attempted to counter the effects of the ruling by changing their strategic focus (closing down brewing operations and concentrating on retailing). The companies also invited smaller brewers, who offer unusual products, to run special promotions in their licensed premises and used the guest beers to attract customers. This resulted in an increase in consumer choice.

4.3 Responding to stakeholder pressure

Companies have limited resources to respond to the pressures of their publics and must evaluate the immediacy and potency of pressures.

One way in which organisations may evaluate the different demands made on their resources is by use of matrices. Important factors such as the size or membership of the pressure group, the legitimacy of the claim, the immediacy of the threat, potential risks to their operation faced by firms in case of non-response, the probability of litigation, the probability of competitive action and the likelihood of adverse publicity are evaluated for each of the pressures an organisation faces.

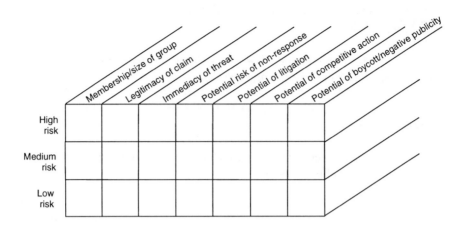

Figure 7: Evaluation matrix of competing stakeholders

By attributing high, medium and low risk to each of the identified factors (which may differ between firms), those pressures which pose the greatest threats can be identified and resources allocated accordingly.

An organisation must also evaluate its ability to counter the threats posed by its publics.

ACTIVITY 21

Assume a local council has issued a Notice of Planning Application for a new industrial estate to be built close to a residential area. It receives a number of objections from a range of publics. These include a local residents' association, environmental groups and local competitors.

List below the actions available to the council and to the organisation wishing to build the industrial estate?

Your answer may include a number of the following actions:

Consultations with publics

The council could invite comments and alternative suggestions that would reduce the environmental impact. It could impose regulations on the builders to reduce noise pollution and provide access which minimises danger and inconvenience to local residents.

Opposition

The council could choose to oppose the publics and enforce the plans. This could involve it in litigation, adverse publicity and cost.

Public relations

The organisation involved could use the public relations element of its marketing mix and attempt to ensure public support from other publics, such as unemployed residents and the building industry. Indeed, at the end of the 1980s, public relations was the fastest growing element of the promotions mix in many firms and sectors of industry. This approach was taken by British Nuclear Fuels, who attempted to reduce public fear of its industry. It built a visitors' centre at one of its power stations, provided extensive press coverage and now offers guided tours of the facilities to visitors.

Sponsorship or competition

The organisation could involve the pressure group in the planning process by sponsoring facilities or offering competitions for the best design.

Do nothing

The organisation can ignore the concern of its publics when it believes the concern to be a temporary fad or it is confident that objections will subside.

Whatever action an organisation chooses, it must be certain that it has evaluated the options carefully. One method of calculating and evaluating threat and action is through scenario analysis. Here, organisations research comparable previous cases, either from their own experience or that of other firms, and estimate the likely cost as well as a probability value for each likely outcome. The firm also estimates the cost each alternative would incur and the probability of its occurrence. Cost can include that caused by inconvenience, the need to counter adverse publicity, boycotts etc.

By multiplying the cost of each option by the likely probability of its failure and success, the organisation may be able to assess the likely cost of each option. For instance, a firm may compare two options, one with a relatively low cost but a high probability of failure (say 60%), whereas a second option may be twice as expensive but has a failure rate of only 5%. In the short term, the first option appears more attractive, particularly if the resources of the firm are very limited. Organisations considering long-term risk would, however, be more likely to opt for the second solution.

Companies can also evaluate options by plotting on a pair of axes (see Figure 8) the probability of success (high or low) and the cost of each option and choose those with the lowest likely cost and the highest probability of success. Needless to say, careful research of the probability is vital before either method is used to evaluate the likely responses of stakeholders.

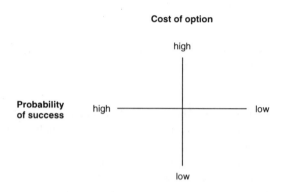

Figure 8: Evaluation axes

ETHICAL INVESTORS

Ethical investors comprise an important group of people whom organisations often cannot afford to ignore. Many investors select carefully the type of business they wish to invest in. So-called 'ethical funds' are a growing source of finance in the British economy. They guarantee to the investor that their money is not used to finance certain predetermined activities: animal testing and exploitation of less-developed communities for instance.

The term 'ethics' is extremely difficult to define and may change over time. However, companies increasingly find themselves scrutinised with regard to their business practices; the production technology and raw materials used may be objected to, as may be the methods employed by the suppliers of production inputs; remuneration of some of its staff may raise public concern; management processes and sources of funding may be subject to scrutiny.

Word-of-mouth is often regarded as one of the most persuasive channels of communication and, if negative, can do long lasting damage, as shown in the Resource Item 2.6: 'Ethics men at odds over Body Shop', (*Guardian*, 27/8/94)

Examining all aspects of corporate activity is therefore important for firms not only to attract the funds for future investment, but also to ensure that its shareholders do not engage in a rush of selling, thus affecting the value of the company.

REVIEW ACTIVITY 5

The BBC as a broadcasting organisation is involved in TV and radio broadcasting in the UK and worldwide through its World Service and sale of programmes. As a public-service organisation it is accountable to, and scrutinised by, different publics and organisations.

1 Look back over the previous section and try to identify both the main stakeholders of the BBC and how they are able to affect the activities of the organisation. Enter these into the table below.

2 Now assess whether the influence exerted by each stakeholder group on the BBC is high, medium or low, and identify those groups or individuals that have the greatest effect on the organisation.

You could use the blank matrix below:

	Stakeholder Group
Influence	
High	
Medium	
Low	

3 Go over Section 4.2 Responding to stakeholder pressure, and suggest how the BBC should respond to the pressures and scrutiny exerted by its publics. Enter this in the blank table below in order of priority.

(A possible answer is given at the end of the unit.)

Stakeholder	Suggested Response

Summary

This section has examined the growing importance of publics in deciding corporate objectives and strategies. A number of different publics has been introduced and you have attempted to evaluate the relative importance of different interest groups according to their cause, their likely resources and impact on organisations.

Various strategies which firms can employ to communicate with their publics have been examined, and methods of predicting the likely effect of these strategies have been introduced.

SECTION 5

The Competitive Environment

Introduction

The previous section examined the publics that organisations face in their micro-environment. This section looks at the actors or parties that make up the competitive environment. The nature of competition and its likely effects on marketing strategies of firms will be examined. We will also address methods and models that assist firms in analysing the competitive environment and, finally, examine options available to companies to address some of the threats and opportunities they face.

The aim of this section is to help you to:

- understand how important it is for firms to take into account the competitive environment when formulating objectives and developing marketing strategies

- identify some of the important forces in the competitive environment of a number of organisations

- appreciate the usefulness of some models to evaluate a firm's competitive position.

5.1 The competitive environment

Organisations face competition both for their resource input and their final output, whether that is a service or a product. Companies must take into account the nature of the competition when assessing their current position and future direction, and the options they have available in achieving objectives. The competition may respond to any action a firm takes through their pricing, promotion, distribution or product strategies, as well as internal management structures.

ACTIVITY 22

Consider the competition faced by

a) a carpet manufacturer

b) a water authority.

List the players in the competitive environment that may affect the actions of these firms.

You may have identified other carpet manufacturers, manufacturers of rugs, or others producing substitute products, such as alternative wooden, vinyl floor covering, or ceramic tiles. You may also have considered producers abroad who distribute to the same sales outlets as your own.

The list of competitive players for the water authority may have been difficult. You may have identified producers of bottled water as competitors, but apart from that you may well have drawn a blank.

ACTIVITY 23

Spend a few minutes thinking about, and listing, the reasons, why there are no competitors, or very few, to the water companies?

One of the factors you may have identified is the product. There are very few substitutes available for the main use of water in industry or consumer usage. The way the product is produced and distributed may also be a consideration. Carpets are 'mobile' products, which require relatively little by way of infrastructure and investment to transport to their final consumers. The same goes for most of the substitutes available. Water, however, requires extensive investment in wells/extraction, filtering and transportation equipment, as well as the internal infrastructure to deal with its supply, breakdown etc.

Another factor is that the supply of water is regulated because of likely effects on health and safety and the fact that it was, until fairly recently, a public utility owned by the nation and managed on its behalf.

A firm which faces many competitors, as in the above example, as well as a large range of substitutes, operates under conditions of **imperfect competition**. Buyers select goods on the basis of different prices, quality of material, and many other personal preferences. Most firms operate in an environment like this and must therefore carefully monitor competitive action as well as their own goals and resources in order to ensure survival and growth.

Although rare, organisations may operate in environments that could be described as **perfect competition**. Members of the recently abolished milk marketing board, or farmers, benefited from the lack of competition through predetermined prices of a virtually homogeneous product, with differentiation occurring at the later production stage. Entry barriers to milk production are relatively low, as are the exit barriers, should the producer decide to change from milk production to that of another produce. Prices paid by the buyer, the milk marketing board, were identical, regardless of the different grades of milk (related to fat and vitamin content). This meant that the milk producers did not need to differentiate their products or develop communication, promotion or distribution strategies to develop a competitive advantage. The abolition of the milk marketing board and the end of 'guaranteed prices' has resulted in farmers trying to undercut each others' prices and to promote the quality of their milk to ensure the sale of this perishable product.

ACTIVITY 24

Consider the situation of the milk producers. In the light of rising competition, which may have an effect on prices, what do you suggest they do to safeguard their income?

Whereas under perfect competition there are many organisations producing virtually identical products at similar prices, **monopoly power** is said to exist where one company produces an undifferentiated good or service for which it faces no competition. Entry barriers to the industry are often very high, as are exit barriers. The privatisation of public utilities in the UK led to a number of private monopolies, which are carefully regulated to ensure that the control they exert over price and distribution is not abused. OFWAT (Water Regulators) and OFTEL (Telecommunications Regulator) are examples.

When a market has a small number of powerful suppliers who offer very similar products or undifferentiated products such as petrol, they are said to operate under **oligopolistic** market conditions. The high investment required in equipment, and also the problem of gaining access to the necessary infrastructure and skills, all form barriers to entry. Although still relatively high, these barriers are, however, lower than those under monopoly conditions, enabling more companies to enter the market.

Although the structure of the market is important in that it affects the threat of new entrants, there are, according to Porter, other factors which must be considered and analysed before firms can develop achievable objectives and strategies. Porter (1980) identified five crucial forces impinging on the competitive environment of organisations. These are illustrated in Figure 9.

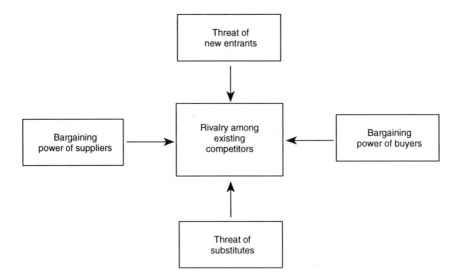

Figure 9: Porter's Five-Forces Model (Porter, 1980)

The components of the model are dealt with below:

SUPPLIER POWER

Suppliers may be classified as 'direct' or 'indirect'. Direct suppliers provide inputs required for the production process, such as raw material, components or machinery to produce the goods. Indirect suppliers, or auxiliary firms, provide a range of services needed by an organisation to facilitate the operation of a firm, for instance banks, insurance firms and consultants. Both not only affect a firm's ability to produce goods and services, but also affect the actual product and the final price.

Where suppliers are able to exert pressure on buyers because their products or services have few substitutes, require long-term contracts, or because there are only a few suppliers, buying organisations may find that these suppliers heavily influence both the product and its final price. For instance, if a supplier changes the specification of a product, say by using different materials, the buying organisation may have to accept these changes and, in turn, modify its own products. This involves cost and time. Similarly, where suppliers can dictate prices, the cost of production inputs rises. Both would result in either lower profit margins or higher prices, thus making the organisation less competitive.

ACTIVITY 25

Supplier power can affect both organisations and individuals. Where the supplier power in consumer markets is great, consumer choice is, usually, reduced.

1   Try to identify suppliers used by you, who exert an influence on your choice of product and your buying behaviour.

2   Analyse the factors that give the suppliers the upper hand.

You may have noted distribution as one factor. The concentration in the retail sector has reduced the choice of outlets. Whereas previously, communities may have been able to purchase most products locally, many consumers now have to travel considerable distances to obtain goods and services. Pressure to buy a supplier's ancillary products, such as services or replacement parts (dust bags for vacuum cleaners, for example), or the requirement to use only authorised service engineers for the guarantee to be valid, are also signs of supplier power. In this way suppliers can control the distribution and the price.

Payment terms may be another factor, both in consumer and organisational markets. Where supplier power is high, cash with order may be required rather than offering credit, thus raising the cost of the product. Pressure to engage in reciprocal deals may also be exerted on industrial buyers, who may be required to offer some of their output to the original supplier. Undue exploitation of supplier power may, however, lead to accusations of unfair trading practices and may be investigated by the Office of Fair Trading.

BUYER POWER

In consumer markets, which consist of millions of individual buyers making frequent purchases, buyer power tends to be low. However, some multiple retailers, recognising the importance of buyers who increasingly buy in bulk or less frequently, have implemented customer feedback systems which invite buyers to state their preference for products or annoyance about the absence of products.

In industrial or business sectors of industry, buyer power may be considerable, and may put pressure on suppliers, who have little choice whether or not to accept the conditions of buyers. Increasingly, distribution arrangements are being changed from infrequent bulk deliveries, which need to be stored by the buying firm, to Just-in-Time (JIT) delivery, which ensures supply just before the buying organisation requires the goods. This affects the producer's production schedule, the cost of stockholding by the supplier, and often increases the cost of distribution.

On-line ordering systems used by many retailers and manufacturers also involve firms in the additional cost of installing and servicing the new technology. Customers may also demand additional services from manufacturers, such as special promotions and product training. Many Japanese firms require suppliers to undergo an extensive quality audit as a condition of supply. This involves the buying team inspecting the premises and production processes of the suppliers at pre-determined intervals. Failure to satisfy the buying organisation may lead to the withdrawal of custom or conditions imposed on the supplier.

THREAT OF SUBSTITUTE PRODUCTS OR SERVICES

In a speech in January 1995, Sir Ralph Robbins, Chairman of Rolls-Royce speculated that '90% of products sold at the end of the decade have not yet been invented'. Changes in consumer demand, not only nationally but internationally, and the speed with which products reach the end of their life cycle, necessitate constant vigilance against new competing products and services. Organisations that operate in an environment that has many competing substitutes find themselves more vulnerable to a whole range of macro-environmental factors. These will be covered in depth in the next section.

It is, therefore, important for firms to distinguish between different substitute options and to learn more about the decision processes buyers undergo.

A jeans manufacturer, for example, would analyse the market accordingly, distinguishing between:

direct substitutes, which are products of almost identical nature, but positioned differently in the mind of the consumer (such as Levi and Wrangler jeans)

close substitutes, which are those products that fulfil a similar function (such as cord jeans purchased in place of denim jeans)

similar substitutes, which could be any item of clothing purchased

indirect substitutes, which are all the other products that vie for the disposable income of a customer. These are the most difficult to predict. For instance, if you have had an unexpected amount of money given to you to 'treat yourself' you may be tempted to spend it on a holiday, an item of furniture or even reduce outstanding bills.

Firms must constantly monitor consumer behaviour to estimate likely substitution behaviour of customers and develop strategies that make their product the first choice.

Switching behaviour can be identified in a number of ways. One is through observation, where customers in retail environments are either filmed by a hidden camera, or observed by a trained member of staff. Time taken to evaluate options, say of different brands of soup, is noted and analysed. This may be followed up by face-to-face interviews to ascertain reasons for the customers' apparent indecision.

Focus-group interviews, where customers are invited to discuss their reasons for particular purchases with the help of a trained interviewer, also help to identify some of the factors that influence final customer choice. If carried out at regular intervals, organisations can develop a chart, showing the changes in customer perception in response to product modifications and competitive action, such as new product launches or promotional pricing.

THREAT OF NEW ENTRANTS

Even where barriers to entry into a market are significant, there are few, if any, markets which do not attract new entrants. Those markets which appear to offer a good return on investment – the potential of a high market share with low investment cost – are obvious examples.

ACTIVITY 26

List a number of other reasons why firms may wish to enter a market which, at first glance, does not appear to offer very good returns on investment?

You may have considered the take-over of another firm, either a supplier or a distributor in order to gain greater control. This is called **vertical integration,** and enables firms to ensure consistent quality and quantity of supplies and/or distribution. It also enables organisations to get closer to their markets and to benefit directly from any feedback about the product or service they supply. Sony, for instance, have recently opened a number of retail outlets in a market which is extremely competitive and therefore at first sight not very attractive. Peters and Waterman, in their book *In Search of Excellence* (1987) found that organisations that remain in close contact with their market usually perform better than those which are remote from their customers.

5.2 The role of distribution intermediaries

Many organisations, unless they control the entire process from production to final distribution, are reliant on the services of one or more distribution intermediaries. These may include wholesalers, retailers, distributors and agents.

Distribution intermediaries provide the vital link between an organisation and its customers. They share stock-holding and promotion costs and provide ancillary services to enhance a product or service. With the exception of agents, members of the distribution chain are simultaneously customers and for this reason the relationship between producers of goods and services and their supply chain is of particular importance.

In their search for competitive advantage, firms increasingly move away from their concept of 'selling' to their customers, whether they are industrial or private customers, and try to develop relationships. This new focus on long-term satisfaction and customer loyalty necessitates a different approach to distribution channels. Manufacturers and intermediaries in manufacturing, services and consumer markets, increasingly work together to develop processes that maximise the satisfaction of all parties involved.

5.3 Monitoring the competitive environment

As can be seen, organisations have many factors to consider in their competitive environment. Continuous scanning of competitive action is therefore vital, as is the assessment of their own position in relation to that of their competitors.

Product development engaged in by competitors may render a firm's offering obsolete, competitive pricing strategy can have a devastating effect on revenue and recovery of investment, and promotional tactics can result in customers selecting competing substitutes.

Information about competitors may come from a variety of sources, including the salesforce, media, industry reports, members of the distribution chain and customer feedback. To manage this wealth of information, organisations must develop effective marketing information systems and processes of passing on the information to the relevant internal departments. Effective communication channels in the internal marketing environment are therefore essential. Factors such as new product development by competitors needs to be passed on to the Research and Development (R&D) department, who may well be able to incorporate the innovations into the design of their own products or services; information about delivery and packaging systems and processes may enable the despatch department to exceed the techniques employed by rival firms; changes in pricing strategies must be communicated to the relevant sales department so that the organisation's own tactics can be adapted if it is considered necessary and/or desirable. Peters and Waterman (1987) conclude that 'excellent companies do better competitor analysis'.

Firms can adopt a number of methods to evaluate their competitive position. One measure of success is market share. A declining market share may indicate growing competitive pressure, either through new entrants, new products or new developments in the market place. (The external environment will be dealt with in the next section.) It may also be indicative of the end of a product life cycle.

One method of evaluating competitive position is the portfolio analysis developed by the Boston Consulting Group (1970). The BCG Matrix (Figure 10) is a grid composed of market share and market growth axes. Each resulting quadrant (for example, high market share/low market growth) both indicates market position and points to certain product strategies.

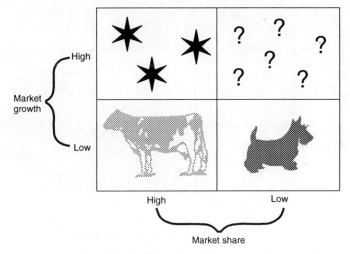

Figure 10: Boston Consulting Group (BCG) Matrix

The quadrants have been characterised as follows:

High market share/high market growth is indicated by means of a **star**. Such products generate large amounts of income, but also require much investment to deter other companies from entering the market. An example is the Nintendo Game Boy when it was launched.

High market share/low market growth are indicated by **'cash cows'**. Cadbury's Dairy Milk is one of these products.

Low market share/high market growth is indicated by **question marks,** as such products or services require much investment and face an uncertain future. They may develop into a dog (see below) or a star.

Low market share/low market growth are represented by dogs. The products in this quadrant are usually at the end of their life cycle. The company may wish to hold on to them because it has a secure and large market share, or it may liquidate these.

Most firms find that both their own and their competitors' product portfolio contains products in all four quadrants. Their aim, however, is to maximise the number of stars and cash cows and minimise the number of dogs in their own portfolio, whilst reducing the number of stars and increasing the number of dogs in the portfolio of their competitors through appropriate marketing mix strategies.

An extension of the BCG Matrix is the McKinsey/General Electric approach to analysing an organisation's competitive position which uses the two axes: market attractiveness and business position. (See Figure 11.)

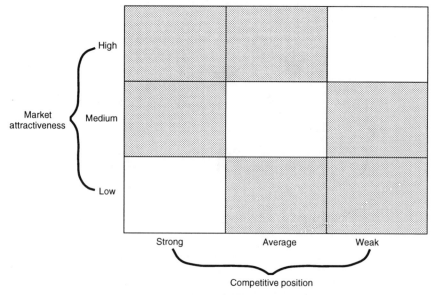

Figure 11: McKinsey/GE Business Screen

Companies, or, as may be the case, independent parts of a firm called Strategic Business Units (SBUs), are best placed when their products are situated in the upper-left sphere of the matrix, with positions of products or strategic business units in the lower-right sphere, requiring either particular attention or divestment.

Unlike the BCG matrix, this model does not point to appropriate strategies companies might adopt in response to their market position, but indicates changes in position over time. It also enables comparison between an organisation and its competitors and thus may be used as a foundation on which to formulate strategies.

BUSINESS GIFTS – CASE STUDY

Business Gifts Ltd are wholesale suppliers of a wide range of gifts and novelty items to firms and organisations, who give these to suitable clients or customers as gifts. These are often inscribed with the name or logo of the donor and range from inexpensive pens and diaries to desk utensils and expensive items, such as briefcases and personal organisers. Larger or more costly items are often personalised with the name of the recipient.

In addition to gifts, the company also supplies large quantities of so-called 'freebies' for use at exhibitions or large-scale promotions. These include key fobs, soft toys, and stationery items.

Although the company has many competitors in the UK providing a similar range of goods, Business Gifts Ltd has been in the market for longer than most, having branched out from its original business of supplying office stationery.

All items featured in the company's catalogue are bought in from a wide range of manufacturers, some of which also offer an inscribing service. Where this is not offered, Business Gifts Ltd subcontracts this out to a local company.

Timing is crucial for the company, as a missed deadline may result not only in dissatisfied customers, but also in the company being sued for non-compliance with agreed delivery conditions. In addition to this, Business Gifts Ltd may be left with a quantity of unsellable items.

Time delays are often caused when large quantities of goods are inscribed by the manufacturer. To overcome this problem, Business Gifts Ltd keep small amounts of the most popular items in stock for rush orders, which are then inscribed by its local sub-contractor.

The company currently uses no distribution intermediaries. Orders to the mainly local customers are usually dispatched using company-owned vehicles. Where customers are situated at considerable distance, a commercial haulier is employed to deliver the goods.

REVIEW OF COMPANY RESULTS

When the board of directors reviewed the 1993 results of the company, they noted that while the market share had remained virtually unchanged at 19% of the market, their profits had declined by approximately 6%. Further investigation showed the following:

Sales of small, inexpensive items had increased from 28% of turnover to 34%. However, this was achieved through the supply of one unusually large order to a large multinational organisation.

Turnover from the supply of stationery products had decreased from 48% to 42%)

Sales of larger, more costly items had remained almost static in spite of a costly promotion aimed at large corporate clients in the middle part of the year.

Competition had become more intense in the fight for a decreasing corporate gift market, with the result that prices had been maintained, even though suppliers had increased their prices, thus squeezing the profit margin of the firm.

An added worry for Business Gifts Ltd for the future was the recently announced takeover of the local inscriber by a competitor, who had decided to integrate this operation into its business.

Business Gifts Ltd realise that it needs to address the difficulties it faces. A similar erosion of its profits in the following year would leave the company in an extremely vulnerable condition and might result in closure of the business.

REVIEW ACTIVITY 6

Please read the Case Study above and answer the following questions.

1 You describe the competitive environment in which this company operates.

2 Using Porter's Five-Force Model, assess the competitive environment of this firm.

(A possible answer is given at the end of the unit.)

Summary

Organisations must scan the competitive environment to ascertain their position, identify competitors' weaknesses and identify niche opportunities which serve customers better. They need to develop appropriate answers or strategies to respond to changes by using one or a number of the marketing tools – that is, pricing, promotion, product, or distribution to counter competitive action.

In addition to this, firms may engage in extensive personnel training to ensure that a customer's experience of the firm – from switchboard operator to the installation and after-sales service of a product – conforms to the quality expected.

Unit summary

This unit has looked at environmental factors that can have an impact on an organisation. It started with the environment created within the organisation itself – its management structure, legal status and corporate objectives – and considered how these might affect the functioning of the organisation. The second half of the unit looked outwards to the people (the stakeholders) and the other organisations (competitors) who were likely to have an effect on the way the organisation functioned. Finally, it looked at the macro-environment: the socio-cultural, political, economic and technological factors that come into play.

References

Henderson, B (1970) 'The Product Portfolio', *Perspectives,* no 66, Boston Consulting Group

Peters, T J and Waterman, R H (1987) *In Search of Excellence*, Harper & Row

Porter, M E (1980) 'Industry Structure and Competitive Strategy: Keys to Profitability', *Financial Analysts' Journal,* July–August , p33

Eurostats (1992), European Union

Plummer, J T (1974) 'The Concept and Application of Life Style Segmentation', *Journal of Marketing,* January 1974, pp33–37

Further Reading

SECTION 1
Kotler, P & Armstrong G (1991) *Principles of Marketing,* Prentice-Hall International, 5th edn, Chapter 1

SECTION 2
Kotler & Armstrong (1991) Chapter 2

SECTIONS 3, 4, 5 AND 6
Kotler & Armstrong (1991) Chapter 3

Answers to Review Activities

Review Activity 1

Your answer to the first question might include the following:

SOLE TRADER AND PARTNERSHIP

Funds for product development are likely to be limited, with its main source being private capital, banking finance or venture capital. The last named is an investment by individuals who use the services of venture capital companies to find worthwhile projects to support.

Legal agreements between small companies and investors vary, but there is usually a share in profit. The investors tend to carry most of the risk. Careful vetting of new products or services by venture capitalists is the norm, to protect the level of risk to investors. Bank loans, which attract interest payments, can be relatively difficult for small companies to obtain, as income projections from a new product or service may be difficult to make. As a result, sole traders often fail to respond to new opportunities.

LIMITED COMPANIES

These may raise funds from their existing shareholders, either in the form of new share issues or debentures. New shares are often allocated on a proportionate basis, with individual shareholders trading shares between them. Debentures are loans to an organisation from each shareholder, which the organisation undertakes to repay. These firms do have a number of options not available to sole traders and partnerships, thus extending the scope of raising finance. This may lead to a greater ability to exploit new market or product opportunities.

PUBLIC COMPANIES

The value of quoted companies and the attractiveness of any share offer to raise new capital depends in part on the firm's past performance and its future prospects. In addition to this, because many shares are owned by overseas investors, the value also depends on wider macro-environmental factors, such as the interest rate and the exchange rate. As a result, forecasting returns on new share issues is difficult. However, public companies do find it easier to raise investment capital through the variety of sources available to sole traders, partnerships and limited companies.

It is important to remember that raising finance is only one aspect of responding to changing market needs. Opportunities may arise for product variations or differentiation which a sole trader may be able to assess and respond to much more quickly than a limited company with many interested parties. A partnership, although able to raise finance more easily than a sole trader, may be encumbered with conflicting views on how to respond to the opportunities presenting themselves.

The second question may have produced a mixture of responses.

SOLE TRADERS AND PARTNERSHIPS

Although it was pointed out above that these forms of firm may have difficulties in raising finance, the existence of the decision makers does not depend on the vote of shareholders. The horizons of these firms may therefore reach beyond the current financial year and the next shareholders' meeting. However, because the income generated provides the business with its livelihood, short-term thinking may prevail.

LIMITED AND PUBLIC COMPANIES

The financial structure of these companies tends to encourage short-term thinking in the UK. Studies undertaken in other European countries and in Japan indicate that raising funds through issue of new shares rather than personal investment by the owners encourages short termism. In countries where the *majority* of shares in firms are family owned (BMW in Germany, for example and Mitsubishi in Japan), long termism is considerably more common. Similarly, where national governments have a large stake in companies, as is the case in many French industries, this, too, affects the time horizon, with medium-to-long-term planning cycles prevailing.

CO-OPERATIVES

The structure of co-operatives has changed significantly in the last 15 years, with smaller co-operatives joining forces in order to remain competitive. Large superstores have replaced many of the small convenience store and regional societies, such as the Greater Manchester Co-operative Wholesale Society, have been formed. The capital investment has necessitated a longer planning cycle, with merchandise often determined 6 months prior to their introduction to all stores. This has put greater pressure on supplying society members to alter their planning cycle in turn.

Organisations in the public sector may be affected by the electoral cycle, with longer-term horizons shortly after a general election, which tend to shorten towards the next electoral round.

FRANCHISES

Many franchise operations, as well as large organisations with a significant share holding by one of its chief investors, have found that loss of control over the planning cycle and, often, over the quality of management and products have adversely affected their overall competitiveness. The Body Shop, for instance, found that many of its overseas outlets suffered from poor standards of retail outlets. Management and training of staff was also difficult. By purchasing back some of the shares, tighter control over product development and quality has been possible. The need for firms to obtain quality standards to be considered credible also encouraged a move towards greater centralisation.

Review Activity 2

The belief that furniture of simple, Swedish design would attract customers throughout the world, as well as the conviction that the management process employed by IKEA was its major strength, led the company to expand into new markets using the same techniques and products. However, rapid growth and external factors such as the worldwide recession, had an impact on the original management philosophy of providing 'quality furniture at prices the majority of people can afford'.

The resulting losses forced IKEA to re-examine its operations and led to a slow-down in expansion, involvement in market research and product adaptation, particularly for the US market and the new venture into China. In spite of these changes, the company intends to adhere to its basic principles because, according to Ikea's chief executive, their 'identity is extremely important'.

Review Activity 4

1   Prior to the appointment of Franz Kraus the company was structured along functional lines. Marketing was considered a function of sales (rather than the other way round).

2   This was partly due to the beliefs of the major shareholder Hans Imhoff and his views on, or lack of, market development (internal factor). While rival companies were not involved in aggressive marketing programmes, and consumers were less discerning in their chocolate eating, this structure was successful for the company. Changes in consumer tastes and income, mergers and acquisition in the chocolate industry with Nestle taking over Rowntrees, for example, resulted in a need to reorganise (external factors).

3   The company may consider organising along product/ brand lines. The strategic aims of each product or brand would be determined in line with corporate goals, with brand managers responsible for the management and implementation of marketing programmes.

Review Activity 5

Likely publics the BBC needs to consider include the Broadcasting Standards Authority, consumer groups, ethnic groups, employees and their unions and the funding authorities, including sponsors of programmes. Political parties and individuals may also object to the broadcast of certain programmes. This was the case in early 1995, when a court decision prevented the screening of an interview with the British Prime Minister prior to local elections in Scotland, after complaints received from opposition parties. Similarly, the broadcast of a reconstruction of a murder case was strongly objected to by the family of the victim, which resulted in adverse publicity about practices employed by broadcasters.

The effect of stakeholders can vary. They may influence finance, programme content, timing of programmes, employment practices and the ability to film at certain locations. Often the pressures of stakeholders conflict with each other. For instance, the filming of many popular sporting events requires payment to the event organisers before a license to film is issued. While the broadcasting of popular events may be demanded by one group (the viewers), other groups, such as those regulating the finances, may not make the required amount of money available to obtain filming rights.

If you have identified the Broadcasting Standards Authority as one of the stakeholders, you might have assigned a fairly high influence value to this. It sets guidelines about the suitability of programmes for different age categories and time of screening. Employees and individuals may have been assigned to the categories of medium and low influence respectively, whilst local groups or residents may have relatively little influence, although, as was pointed out earlier, companies must be aware that single cause/individual issues can escalate.

Where you have identified a group that exerts considerable influence on the BBC, communication is vital. Consultation with the BSA is important. Research may be necessary when the filming of a programme involves considerable inconvenience to a locality. Local involvement, in which residents are asked to play very minor parts, is one option, as may be negotiation with local councils about environmental improvements after filming has ceased. Advertising, although not allowed commercially, is also an available option to create goodwill amongst viewers. This is often done at the beginning of a 'new season'.

Lobbying of some groups is an alternative when the organisation anticipates objections from another. For instance, when the financial regulators were considering the price for the broadcast of the Wimbledon Tennis Tournament too high, public concern was raised among viewers, who protested over the potential loss of the 'British tradition' of broadcasting the matches to everyone, rather than limiting it to satellite viewers only.

Review Activity 6

1   The company operates in an imperfect market, where buyers select goods and services on the basis of many different criteria. Price, quality and fashion may be among these.

2   Your answer to the second question may include some of the following points:

- The company faces a wide range of competitors for the corporate gift expenditure. Direct competitors are those who offer similar products to

Business Gifts Ltd. These are relatively easy to identify. More difficult to establish are substitute products and competitors, for instance organisers of corporate hospitality-sporting weekends, conferences and other social events.

● The power of buyers in this market may be considerable. This may increase even further if the company is forced to rely on few orders placed by large organisations, who may dictate terms and conditions.

● Supplier power is relatively weak, as there appear to be many suppliers of very similar goods.

● Due to the relatively low amount of stock-holding required by an organisation such as Business Gifts Ltd, the threat of entrants is potentially large. However, the fact that this market is contracting may make it less attractive to new entrants.

● From the evaluation of the competitive environment it appears that in all but one area, that of threat of new entrants, the firm appears extremely vulnerable.

Review Activity 7

You may have discovered the following changes:

The population's age structure has changed, showing an increase in the number of 'under fives', but a decrease in the number of 'under 16s' and 'under 18s'. With the exception of the 70-74 year olds, all age groups above 60 have increased.

The distribution of gender has not changed markedly, with the exception of the older age groups, where in some age categories the increase in the number of females is proportionately higher than that of males.

For pension providers this means that they may find themselves with fewer, younger customers, but also with having to pay pensions for a longer period of time. Both will have an effect on pension premiums. Similarly, the changing market may necessitate a range of new products or services and different messages to create awareness of, or interest in, the market for these new products.

A pharmaceutical company may find that its demand for products has altered, with products for age-related diseases in greater demand, whereas the demand for products related to children, vaccines for instance, may have decreased in the UK.

UNIT 3

THE CHARACTERISTICS OF INDUSTRIAL, CONSUMER AND SERVICE MARKETS

Introduction

Markets in the late 20th century are changing – and rapidly so. The increased concentration of industries, the need to become and remain competitive, greater availability and use of technology are some factors that have affected the buying behaviour of firms both in the manufacturing and service sectors. Better-educated consumers, who benefit from wider choice of goods and services, easier access to a range of suppliers, technological advances which facilitate purchasing and changing social structures also have an impact on the buying process of this market.

Markets are also becoming less distinguishable. Whereas the supply of goods and services were clearly separable between different markets, customers of industrial, service and consumer markets are now found to cross boundaries. American-style warehouse clubs, where both private customers and small retailers may purchase in bulk either for consumption or retail, and wholesale office stationery suppliers dealing with both private consumers and small businesses, are two examples.

Communication between suppliers of goods and services and their customers is also undergoing change. The number of media channels available, the regulatory forces monitoring some of these channels, customer expectations and the complexity of managing communication processes pose challenges for marketers today.

In the increasingly competitive environment firms find themselves in, knowledge of characteristics, buying processes and the needs and wants of each market they serve is vital; niche market opportunities may remain undiscovered, resources may be wasted, corporate goals may not be reached and the risk of business failure increases. Above all, a company will only be able to maximise its competitive advantage when information about the needs of each market and its own ability to supply this need can be analysed and a suitable match found.

This module will introduce you to the concepts of, and differences between, consumer, business and service markets served by firms. It examines the essential characteristics and differences in their structure, their needs and their buying behaviour. The implications of these differences for organisations marketing their products and services to these buying groups will also be discussed.

ACTIVITY 1

Before progressing with this module, try to recall and write down a definition you have read of marketing. This need not be a sentence. You could just list a number of key tasks of a marketer:

If you identified key words only, these should include:

Identification of customer needs, evaluation of the external environment, analysis of market opportunities, developing a suitable offer, communicating with the market, developing suitable channels of distribution, managing the relationship with customers, developing feedback systems from the market.

This unit will give you an opportunity to consider the different needs of the three markets under consideration, their buying behaviour, changes that have occurred in each of the market and, finally, strategies that organisations develop to accommodate both the different needs and recent changes.

Objectives

By the end of this module, you will be able to:

- show an understanding of recent developments in industrial, consumer and service markets.

- appreciate the essential characteristics that differentiate the needs of customers in consumer, industrial and service markets

- be familiar with the different behaviour exhibited by customers in consumer, industrial and service markets

- appreciate the implications of different needs and behaviour on the planning, execution and control of marketing strategies and tactics aimed at consumer, industrial and service markets.

SECTION 1

Business Marketing

Introduction

Before we venture into this section we need to define very carefully what is meant by the term 'business marketing'. 'Business marketing' and 'industrial marketing' are often used interchangeably, although strictly speaking, industrial marketing is defined as the anticipation and identification of the needs of manufacturing firms, and the satisfaction of these needs at a profit; business marketing (or 'business-to-business marketing') recognises the different needs of organisations and pays attention to the growing importance of *organisational* customers, who require goods *and* services. The term 'industrial marketing' and 'business' marketing will be used interchangeably in this section.

Most of the consumer marketing activities may be fairly familiar to you. Daily you are confronted with organisations communicating the benefits of their products to you via advertising and public relations or, simply making their presence felt through sponsorship. You are familiar with your responses to direct mail, price offers and newly developed products, and have considered perhaps with some guilt the impulse purchase of confectionery or an item of clothing.

Each product we purchase has, at one time or another, been part of many different marketing strategies, most of which are hidden from the consumer.

ACTIVITY 2

Consider an item you have recently purchased. This could be clothes, food or an item of furniture. Examine the item and try to list the components which make up the product. How many different manufacturers were, in your estimate, involved in producing the item?

If the item is a garment, you may have listed some of the following:

- farmers to produce the cotton or wool, or firms to produce the synthetic fibre
- textile companies to produce the fabric, which may purchase patterns from a design company
- thread, supplied by a further organisation
- fashion designers, delivery firms, wholesalers or agents will be required to facilitate production and distribution.

Each of these firms also requires a whole range of equipment, machinery or further material such as paper, telephone services.... the list is endless. The process by which each of these components is 'marketed' to the next organisation down the chain is that of business-to-business marketing.

Industrial or business marketing can therefore be considered as dealing with the bulk of the iceberg, whereas consumer marketing addresses the final tip of the same iceberg. This is not to say that either is more or less important. What is important is that the needs, motivation and processes of each target market are recognised clearly so that a suitable offer can be made or developed by the supplying organisation.

In the first part of this module we will focus on the nature of business marketing. The needs and motivation of business markets, purchasing behaviour displayed by organisations and the different purchasing methods employed will be examined. Having identified some of the idiosyncrasies of industrial markets, we will identify some of the techniques employed to identify target markets and position products to satisfy industrial buyers. The concept of 'relationship marketing' and its significance will be explored and its effect on the marketing mix variables outlined.

The aim of this section is to help you to:

- understand the importance of business marketing
- distinguish between the different needs of buyers in various sectors of business markets
- evaluate the relative importance of marketing mix variables in the formulation of strategies aimed at different business sectors
- understand the importance of relationship marketing and its effect on the formulation of strategies and tactics.

1.1 Needs and motivation of business markets

Customers in both consumer and industrial markets purchase products to satisfy a perceived need. But whereas consumers may satisfy their perceived needs through a variety of unrelated products, often in a fairly irrational manner, buyers in industrial or business-to-business markets acquire goods and services as a result of clearly defined needs and to solve specific problems. Most importantly, they purchase these to *safeguard value-added operations*.

Goods fulfil a variety of functions in the value-adding process and we need to distinguish between:

- those purchased as direct inputs into a production process, for instance tyres or door panels in the manufacture of a car

- those that facilitate production, such as grease to ensure the smooth operation of machinery and computer disks to store accounting information on

- consumer products, such as paper and cleaning fluids or coffee, which are used by staff to enable the operation of a firm.

Establishing the exact need for the product is vital to formulate the appropriate product, pricing, promotion and distribution strategies. An example will illustrate this point.

EXAMPLE

Coffee is a commodity that is purchased by different organisations. For companies such as Nestlé it is a vital ingredient in the manufacture of a consumer product. Coffee beans are purchased in bulk quantities on the commodity market and processed to produce the final product. There are no substitutes for this input. A retail outlet, such as the franchise operation Costa's Coffee House, is supplied with coffee for resale to the final consumer. There may be a number of suppliers who offer coffee from different countries of origin, already roasted and packaged in sacks, with smaller quantities ground and packaged on the retail premises according to customer requirement.

In contrast to this, a café will purchase coffee as part of a range of beverages. It may be required as filter coffee prepackaged in cup- or jug-size quantities, or as instant form packaged in sachets or large containers. In each of these instances coffee is a product which is sold to generate revenue. Large quantities may also be purchased by organisations who supply their workforce with free or subsidised drinks.

Recognising the function which coffee fulfils in an organisation as well as the way it is used by each customer enables the coffee producer to target customers with an appropriate product. The price, distribution and communication channels chosen will further reflect these different needs and usages.

ACTIVITY 3

Fill in the matrix below, identifing companies or industries that use the products listed in the left-hand column:

a) as inputs into a production process

b) to facilitate production

c) to assist in the operation of the business.

| Product | Company or Industry | | |
	a)	b)	c)
Water			
Oil			
Paper			
Tyres			

In the case of water your answers may have included: a) soft drinks, b) water used in cooling towers of electricity generators, and c) water used, say, for cleaning premises such as a café. Oil could be used: a) for the production of synthetic materials such as carrier bags, b) to enable machines to run smoothly in the production process or c) in the form of petrol, allowing sales personnel to reach customers. Paper could be used: a) as an input in the publishing sector, b) as patterns to enable garment manufacturers to produce prototypes and c) in offices, where it is used in a variety of applications. Tyres are used: a) as components in the car industry. (Indeed, used tyres are now the basis of a flexible material used to cover children's play areas to reduce injury.) Tyres are also used as: b) necessary components for heavy-duty conveyor belts and c) as a vital part for many delivery services.

1.2 The buying behaviour of business purchasers

We have already mentioned that business buyers purchase goods for a range of applications with the purpose of maximising at least one of their corporate objectives. Profitability may be such an objective but is not always the only one.

The processes involved in business buying are usually more complex than those in consumer buying. They not only depend on the demand of the product, but also on the type of firm and its organisational structure. For instance, private firms, government departments and institutional buyers exhibit very different purchasing behaviour and processes. Similarly, one customer, or company, may have different purchasing locations with differing needs for very similar products.

Unlike consumer purchasing, buyers in organisations are specialists and have considerable technical expertise. Buying decisions are often the result of discussion by committees, task groups or buying groups.

The time span involved between identifying a need for a product and service and its purchase point are usually much longer than in consumer buying. Impulse purchases are virtually non-existent.

Legal and contractual agreements are the norm in business marketing. Each transaction is regulated by conditions of sale, payment terms, delivery clauses etc. This is usually not the case in consumer marketing.

BUYING TASKS

New buy

Industrial buyers may be faced with different purchasing situations, similar to consumers. Where a new need is recognised by a primary area within the firm, this will have to be evaluated carefully by a range of interested parties. Users may be consulted to identify a range of solutions. 'Gatekeepers', which can be unions or health and safety personnel may be involved in this process. The implications of a purchase for different departments – such as the need for related training of personnel, the cost of change-over, the cost of redundancies, as well as the effect on customers – may need to be considered.

This 'new-buy' situation involves all stages in the organisational buying process, shown in Figure 1 below, and can take many months to complete.

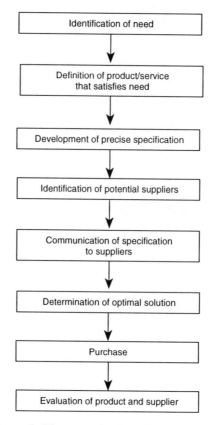

Figure 1: The organisational buying process

Re-buy

Not all purchasing occasions involve all steps in the buying process. Where there is a list of approved suppliers and the product is one that is frequently purchased, we speak of a 'straight re-buy', which involves fewer people and may even involve on-line ordering, with prices and conditions only renegotiated periodically.

Modified re-buy

A third situation that may face a buyer is the modified re-buy, when a new product may have come on to the market which is believed to fulfil the function of another product better, cheaper or with greater performance consistency. Faced with this purchase situation, industrial buyers must involve a range of people to examine the new product, to test its performance and establish whether this product has beneficial effects on the operation of the business or the manufacture of the product or service produced by the organisation. The buyer must also evaluate the cost of this new input and evaluate its effect on the final price of the product and on the profitability of the company. In addition to this, a new production or service input may be evaluated in relation to how well this assists the company in developing its own unique selling proposition.

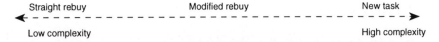

Figure 2: Degrees of complexity of purchasing situations

Organisations marketing their products to other businesses must be fully conversant with the processes of the purchasing firm. To be effective, they must understand the motives in primary areas, that is, the areas where the products are *actually* used, through regular contact with the customer. This presence with current or potential customers enables firms to recognise needs, understand the negotiation and consultation processes within the purchasing firm and to develop a suitable offer.

Targeting business customers, however, can be very difficult. In the most extreme case, every buyer may have its specific needs and usage for the product or service, its own buying motives, characteristics and purchase behaviour. As a result, product positioning and branding is complex and above-the-line advertising, which facilitate positioning in the consumer marketing, is often not engaged in.

Targeting is further affected by the structure of the purchasing organisation, which may be centralised or decentralised. When there are many small markets in the firm, purchasing is said to be decentralised. This usually means each buyer has less power, and for the marketer this may mean sales enquiries are easier to convert into sales because each contract may consist of small orders. Where purchasing is centralised, the power of the buyer or buying group is usually much greater. These purchases often involve greater quantities and, although buying centres are easier to contact, sales enquiries are more difficult to convert into sales. Price is often of greater concern to centralised buyers than to decentralised purchasers, because of the quantities involved.

Relationships between buyers and sellers are often long term and critical to the ultimate success of the marketing effort. These relationships can be very unequal at times, when small companies are reliant on large, powerful organisations for the supply of their inputs. In addition to this, some firms may also have reciprocal arrangements, when one partner in the relationship, usually the more powerful one, demands a return from the smaller, less powerful organisation. This can be in the form of goods or services.

ACTIVITY 4

Please read the case study below and try to identify:

a) products that you believe require extensive decision making and the purchase of which is likely to involve all steps in the organisational buying process

b) products, the purchase of which involves limited decision making and therefore follows only some of the steps outline in Figure 1

c) products that you believe are purchased routinely and therefore fall into the 'straight re-buy' category.

DIXEM PLC

Dixem plc is a company that produces plastic items for a variety of uses. These include watering cans, household items such as buckets, rubbish bins, lunch boxes for schoolchildren aged between four and ten years old, drinks bottles purchased by individual private customers, and many more.

In addition to products that are used by private customers, the company also manufactures plastic containers for a variety of industrial uses. Dairies and soft drinks producers require containers for their products, local governments and/ or private refuse collection companies provide Dixem's wheely-bins to each household, and many manufacturing companies purchase Dixem baskets for storage of small components.

The manufacture of plastic products requires many different components and items of machinery. Plastic molecules are either melted and then moulded or pressed, for later 'extrusion' by customers. This process involves gases to blow up compact forms into the final product (similar to blowing up a balloon). Extruded products are used by all soft drinks manufacturers, as this saves them storage cost. Instead of storing large quantities of bottles, a machine extrudes the compact components immediately prior to entering the conveyor belt for filling.

Plastic molecules are available in various densities for different purposes. Milk containers, such as those used by dairies and sold to retailers, require a different density from containers used for motor oil. Dyes are required to produce coloured plastic items, and moulds are needed to produce different shapes, thicknesses and sizes. To ensure the smooth running of machinery, the company has entered into a service contract with the foreign manufacturer of the machines it uses, which provides one service engineer on a permanent basis. They also provide any spare parts, and lubricants.

Apart from products required in the manufacture, the company also uses products that help in the running of its business. Fork-lift trucks are needed in the warehousing and despatch operation; lorries deliver to the widely dispersed customers; computer equipment stores manufacturing and sales data used by various business functions such as marketing, finance and production. Office furniture, carpeting and electrical items are purchased infrequently, but consumable products such as stationery, toner for printers and developer units for photocopiers are bought on a regular basis from a wholesale office supplier.

Dixems employ the services of a number of marketing agencies. These are usually appointed on a project-by-project basis, according to their field of expertise. For new product launches, for example, a highly creative marketing agency is required, whereas catalogues and leaflets tend to be produced by a printer who also offers graphic design and layout facilities. For the design of their trade advertisements, agencies with knowledge of specific target markets are often used.

Buying decisions on capital items and production inputs are taken by the managers of the relevant departments in consultation with other staff and with advice from the purchasing and finance department. Where services have to be bought in, the relevant managers, in consultation with staff, usually appoint the service provider for a fixed term or on a project-by-project basis, renewal of contract being determined by the quality of service provided. Smaller items, or those purchased frequently, are often either routinely re-ordered or purchased on an ad-hoc basis.

Of the many purchases necessary for Dixem, you may have broken the complexity of the purchasing decision down as follows:

Extensive Decision Making	Limited Decision Making	Straight Re-buy
Machinery	Printing services	Service engineer
Marketing Services Agency	Office furniture	Stationery
Moulds	Components	Plastic compound
Warehousing equipment	Advertising agency	Office consumables
Computing equipment	Dye	

1.3 Effects of external factors on business marketing

As in the consumer market, businesses are subject to a number of external factors. These may act more powerfully on firms than they do on private consumers. Webster and Wind (1972), in their article 'A General Model of Organisational Buying Behaviour' identified the following factors:

Environmental factors: Socio-cultural, technological, political economic, legal and physical

Organisational factors: Goals, objectives, corporate structure

Buying-centre factors: Resources, roles, authority

Individual factors: Status, politics, ethics

ACTIVITY 5

Read the two articles: 'Fleet sales drive car recovery' (Resource Item 3.1) and 'Lucas wins £1bn deal to supply VW' (Resource Item 3.2), that appeared in *The Guardian* (7/3/1995).

Note down some of the factors that you believe have contributed to the increase in fleet car sales and the new contract between VW and Lucas.

In the case of Lucas, you may have identified public concern over fuel economy and exhaust emission as a socio-cultural or technological factor. However, it is also important to remember that, given the competitive nature of the car industry (which is also apparent in the second article), VW is hoping to gain a competitive edge over its competitors by incorporating this new component in its vehicles. If the company is successful, it may be able to obtain its wider goals and objectives (**organisational factors**). **Political and legal factors** may also have influenced VW's decision to purchase Lucas components, rather than those offered by, say a US or Japanese organisation. Since both the UK and Germany are members of the European Union they do not face tariffs, customs procedures and import tax. This would have been the case if a supplier outside the EU had been chosen by VW.

The second article indicates an unexpected rise in fleet cars, which companies purchase for their employees. This may indicate a change in the economic cycle from the prolonged recession that the UK experienced in 1990-95. This is also confirmed by the fact that truck sales have increased by 25.8% in the first two months of 1995 (**economic factors**). However, the article also shows a growing trend among UK firms to purchase imported cars. The increase in foreign competition, combined with the fact that private consumers are still reluctant to purchase new cars, may increase the need for UK car manufacturers to source better, cheaper or different car components to maintain market share through competitive pricing. Organisational and buying centre factors may well be affected by this. Single-source suppliers may be favoured by firms to reduce costs, and the buying process may become more centralised as a result of this.

ENVIRONMENTAL FACTORS

The **social and cultural environment** in which firms operate has an increasingly important effect on buyer behaviour. In an attempt to reduce distribution and stockholding cost and to facilitate joint product development, many firms prefer to do business with a supplier in their vicinity.

The increase in the number of **customs or economic unions,** such as ASEA (South East Asia) and NAFTA (North American Free Trade Association), and the widening of the membership to the European Union, have affected the choice of country of origin.

Technological changes have had a significant impact on purchase behaviour. Information on suppliers and products is stored more easily; the widespread use of media such as fax machines, video-conferencing and on-line systems have improved the speed and efficiency of communication. But while this has improved the efficiency of the buying organisation it has not significantly altered the effort of firms competing for business. Indeed, the cost of new technology is often considerable and may lead to strategic alliances or joint ventures between supplying and buying organisations. Whereas the long-term benefits of joint ventures for both supplying and purchasing organisations are obvious, firms not included in the strategic alliance will find it increasingly difficult to obtain business from the purchasing organisation.

Both the technological and physical environments are influenced by **political and legal/regulatory factors.**

ACTIVITY 6

Consider a production process, such as the manufacture of paper. What effects
have political and legal/regulatory factors had on this industry?

The composition of raw material has been affected, with pressure from
environmentalists and, increasingly, governments, for firms to recycle paper.
Ingredients such as some bleaching agents are no longer permitted. A paper
manufacturer may require investment in better filtering equipment or incur
transportation and disposal costs of waste material. Health regulations may affect
the chemicals used and buyers may have to draw up new product specifications and
face modified or new buying situations. This will provide new opportunities for
suppliers who anticipate the needs of the company better than their competitors.

ORGANISATIONAL FACTORS

Organisational factors include the **goals and objectives** of organisations, as well
as the buying organisation's knowledge about the processes engaged in by the
supplying company. In-house design expertise also affects the buying process.
For instance, if a company designs its own components and subcontracts the
manufacture to a supplier, relationships and contracts may be relatively short. If an
organisation expects suppliers to add value to the in-house blueprint through
advanced manufacturing or processing techniques, or by adapting standard
products, longer term relationships ensue. The success of many Japanese companies
is ascribed to the long-term relationships they establish with their supply chains.

THE BUYING-CENTRE STRUCTURE

The buying-centre structure also affects the relationship with suppliers. In
decentralised organisations that operate autonomously, there may be a number of
smaller centres with different, and often competing, needs. They purchase smaller
quantities than centralised organisations and there is probably more variety. It is
important to note the increasing centralisation of multi-national organisations,
who may produce a standard design but require local manufacture. For instance,
McDonalds, the fast food chain, requires local manufacturers to reproduce the
standards it has developed in everything from counter fittings to the size of chips
and burgers, although some ingredients, such as spices, may vary with the country.

The relative roles people play in different organisations also affects buying
behaviour. In privately owned, smaller organisations the proprietor may want to
make the final decision about suppliers. Similarly, in companies that are structured

by department or strategic business units (SBUs), with their own budget responsibility, there may be different buyers, according to the need of the unit or department.

INDIVIDUAL FACTORS

Individual factors, although not as predominant as in consumer purchasing, must not be ignored. Many a business deal was not concluded because the buyer and salesperson simply did not get on. In the increasingly international environment in which firms operate, this becomes ever more important. Buyers bring their own personality, ambitions and experiences to the negotiation table. Business buyers also try to reduce risk both to themselves and the organisation. As a result they often choose a well-known company's product in preference to a superior product from an unknown supplier. Internal politics may also play a part that cannot be ignored by the selling organisation.

1.4 Marketing strategies in business marketing

Whether marketing to private consumers or businesses, organisations have a range of strategies at their disposal that enable them to offer a suitable product to a previously defined target market. It is the combination of a tangible or intangible product, its price, the way it is promoted and the distribution channels a firm selects that positions the product in the customer's mind and leads them to purchase it. We will look at each of these four strategies in turn and examine how strategic options differ between private consumer and organisational customers.

THE PRODUCT IN BUSINESS MARKETS

We have already established that the range of products and services in business markets is vast. New products are introduced at a faster rate than ever before, shortening the product lifecycle and the time in which organisations need to reach the break-even point – that is, when the firm's revenue exceeds the costs incurred in developing and manufacturing the product or service.

There is also a greater trend for organisations producing consumer goods to offer standardised products, thus reducing the range of components required in stockholding for manufacture and repair. This can be seen in hi-tech industries such as the computer industry, where a standard or benchmark is established, such as Microsoft or Intel processors, which are adopted by most computer manufacturers. In the increasingly competitive business environment it is therefore vital that firms attempt to develop products that fulfil the need of business customers better than those of the competition.

The development of products is also increasingly affected by events in international environments. Newly emerging countries and economies pose a threat to successful products in developed markets. As the article referred to in the next activity shows, they are also often able not only to develop and manufacture products more cheaply, but also to leap-frog technology and omit expensive research and development costs that were incurred by the original manufacturer.

ACTIVITY 7

Please read the article 'Beating the west to the medicine cabinet' from the *Financial Times* (21/3/1995) (Resource Item 3.3) and write down what you believe to be the effect of competition from newly emerging countries on the product development process of drugs in developed economies.

Your answer may have referred to all the stages in the development process of a new product. These are:

1 Idea generation
Companies may have to pay more attention to disposable income of future customers and ideas generated by clients or customers as well as the international business environment. For instance, if some foreign governments spend only $1 per head of population on drugs per annum, it may be advantageous to concentrate on ideas for basic health products or on reducing costs of manufacture.

2 Idea screening
Firms may need to enlist other organisations in this process, such as future users, international health organisations (for instance the World Health Organisation) or members of their distribution chain, which can include foreign government administrators. Increasingly, joint project development teams are set up, containing members of the buying organisation and manufacturers. Ideas also need to be screened as to their likely success in international markets and vis-à-vis foreign competition in their home markets.

3 Business analysis
An organisation needs to assess how well the proposed product is likely to do in the marketplace. Research may need to be carried out with regard to the likely demand and sales, the profitability of the new product or service, as well as the effort the company may have to invest in getting the product accepted by its markets. A further consideration is the effect this product will have on the overall product portfolio of the firm. For instance, producing cheaper medication may reduce the demand for higher priced goods, thus eroding the profitability of that product.

4 Concept development
Only those products that have successfully passed the previous stages will be developed into a prototype. This process enables firms to consider the difficulties

and full implications of, for example, changing machinery, using different inputs requiring different kinds of staff expertise for the production of the new product.

5 Product testing

When a new product is tangible, this is often tested in-house and by potential users. Market research may be carried out to ascertain the opinions of buyers. In the case of drugs, the packaging and quantity contained in each pack may be crucial as they affect the shelf life of the product. Product testing will also take considerable time with this particular product as trials must show that the drug does not have any side effects before a licence to produce can be obtained.

The testing of business services, however, is often not possible. Only an evaluation of the service's success over time may show whether the development process has been successful.

6 Commercialisation

Only after successfully passing all previous stages in the development process can organisations market the new product fully.

PRICING IN BUSINESS MARKETS

Pricing is another strategy available to marketers. The price of a product or service reflects the value that both customers and producers attach to the exchange. In consumer markets, if the price is perceived as too high by the customer, then the demand for this good or service usually falls. Similarly, where a good or service is considered to be competitively priced, demand usually increases. (See Figure 3.)

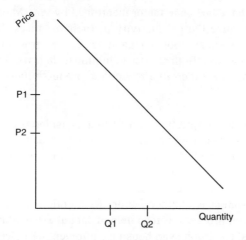

Figure 3: The normal demand curve for a consumer product.

Whilst price is of relatively high importance to private consumers, the relationship between the two is not as simple in business markets. It could be that organisational customers believe that an initial price rise is the first indicator of further price increases. As a result, demand may actually increase with rising prices. This was the case when microchips used in the manufacture of computers increased in price.

The response of business markets to a fall in price is not necessarily to purchase more of a product. It depends on factors, such as:

- the ability of the customer to store raw materials and products
- the relative importance of the product in relation to the final price of the product
- customer expectations.

ACTIVITY 8

List a number of other factors that may determine whether a business will increase its demand in response to the falling price of a product.

Cost of storage may have been one factor mentioned by you. Manufacturers and retailers need to maximise the productivity of their premises. Retailers often calculate this as sales per square foot and manufacturers as gross margin or output per production line or process. Both also try to minimise their fixed cost. Providing additional storage space may therefore reduce the productivity of their revenue-generating space.

The **price** of the product in question is a further consideration. If the product represents a major investment, organisations will be unlikely to be tempted to purchase additional items by a decrease in price, as this would tie up valuable resources and affect the cash flow of a firm.

The **nature** of the product is another factor. As mentioned above, businesses purchase a large range of products. Is it an item of capital expenditure, such as new machinery, computers, electronic warehousing equipment, or indeed an input into the production process that is perishable?

Another factor is the ability of the purchasing organisation to **increase the demand** for its own output. For instance, if a manufacturer of computers offers their products at a reduced price, will a distributor, in turn, be able to stimulate customer demand sufficiently to ensure a fast turn-round of these goods? The firm may risk being left with last year's outdated stock. This would also apply for manufacturers of fabrics and garments, the fashion for which changes colour.

When an organisation uses the just-in-time principle of supply, by which inputs are delivered on a continuous, contractually agreed basis to avoid stockholding, a decrease in price may have no effect on the purchasing organisation. Greater quantities cannot be purchased because of lack of warehousing facilities. However, the purchaser may try to alter the long-term contract to include the new, lower price, or may extend the current contract for a further period of time to benefit from this price decrease. This would make future planning of the pricing strategy of the purchasing organisation easier.

Even when organisations are able to hold stock, a decrease in price may not provoke a response. Buyers may believe that this is only the first of a series of price reductions and may only purchase greater quantities at the point at which the price is, again, increased. Figure 4 shows that when customers expect further decreases in prices, demand may not initially alter. It will change at the point at which companies see the first signs of price rises, resulting in a shift of the demand curve.

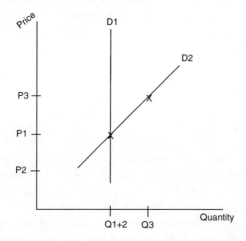

Figure 4: A decreasing price (D1) may not have any effect on demand until the point at which the price starts to rise (D2).

If the reduced-price product makes a relatively unimportant contribution to product being manufactured by an organisation, the purchasing organisations may, again, not respond to price reductions. The overall effect on the price of the finished product may not warrant reorganising the warehouse to accommodate extra stock. In addition, where the product being purchased is covered by a one-year guarantee, storing this for six months would mean only half the value of the guarantee being utilised. Of course, if the product in question is perishable, then no increase in demand will occur. Similarly, in cases where the demand for this product depends on the demand for other goods, such as tyres in the manufacture of cars, price changes of tyres will only have an effect if the demand for finished cars also rises. Such joint, or derived, demand often results in two manufacturers (that of cars and tyres) engaging in joint promotion or pricing strategies to attract new customers.

Business markets are, like consumer markets, susceptible to cross-elasticity of demand. This means that a decrease in price for one good may increase the demand for this good, but may in turn reduce the demand for another good also offered by the same manufacturer. For instance, where a paper supplier reduces the price of one type of paper, the purchasing organisation may switch from a higher priced product to this new lower priced product, thus affecting the profitability of the supplying organisation.

As with price decreases, business organisations may respond differently to price rises. Whereas in consumer markets a price rise often causes a decrease in demand for this good, business organisations may, in fact, increase their demand in anticipation of further price rises that would affect the final cost of their own products. This is called 'reverse elasticity of demand' but, again, depends on the relative importance of the actual good or service in question.

PROMOTION TO BUSINESS MARKETS

Identifying the function that a product or service fulfils is imperative to the development of appropriate products. It is also vital when positioning the product in the minds of purchasers and to create a message that attracts the attention of the business buyer. This is not unlike the process of marketing to private consumers.

Organisations consider a range of audiences when formulating their communication strategy. These include shareholders, various publics, members of the distribution chain as well as the business customer or the ultimate private consumer. Messages must therefore be suitable for each of these and not conflict with each other. Lucas, the motor component suppliers, in its recent drive to capture the replacement part market for motor components, evaluated its entire communication strategy and developed suitable plans to achieve their aims. Components supplied to manufacturers are now branded under the Lucas name, consistent with those offered through wholesalers for the car repair sector and the retail sector. The company believes that customers, whether trade or private, are more likely to choose parts from the range of the original supplier, since this reduces evaluation and increases peace of mind at having selected the correct part. At the same time, Lucas has paid attention to display of their products in wholesale and retail outlets and promoted more conveniently located distribution centres to all their customers, including manufacturers (Beavis, 1995).

ACTIVITY 9

Identify all the media for conveying promotional messages that you observe in consumer markets and write them down. Then consider whether these may be appropriate for business marketing. If you decide they are not appropriate, try to give a reason for this.

Fairly high on your list of media may be **television advertising**. It is probably the most visible form of promotion, partly because it engages both sight and hearing, and often emotional involvement as well. Although you may have decided that this is not appropriate for business promotions, think again. Some organisations dealing with both private and business customers sponsor programmes. Diamond producers, who sell their product to jewellers, have engaged in a pull strategy to increase demand for diamond jewellery, and increasingly you may find advertisements for office equipment. However, for the vast majority of industrial or business products, this medium is not suitable.

Apart from personal selling, the largest part of most promotion budgets is spent on **press advertising** and **directories**. Trade publications are available for every conceivable industry. These include paid-for magazines, trade association newsletters, trade directories, and many more. It allows organisations to target very specific markets and even user groups, such as the 'IBM System User Group' and to provide information, via press releases, about new products or updated features. User groups or interest groups may also be addressed to support a pull strategy and to encourage new needs in the primary use areas.

Exhibitions may not feature in your list above. However, because of their specialist nature, they, too, allow organisations to reach their desired target markets. Indeed for many firms wishing to enter international markets they are often used as a market-entry strategy, as well as a promotional tool. Exhibitions are also used as a Public Relations vehicle, for the company as a whole, rather than for specific products. Innovative products exhibited at exhibitions may also gain media attention and free coverage in the trade press.

Direct mail is extensively used both in consumer and business marketing. Although the Data Protection Act curbs the sale of some trade lists, companies may compile their own data bases of customers, target companies and individuals from a range of trade directories or contacts. It has the drawback of receiving a low response rate unless the product is truly innovative but is a low-cost promotional tool, which has the added advantage that it can be personalised. Direct mail is usually accompanied by **brochures** and/or **price lists,** which update existing and potential customers on an organisation's latest products or range.

Free samples may have been one of the promotional tools you wrote down. Particularly where a product is new, industrial producers may offer free trial samples to their existing or potential customers. In addition to this, companies involved in the sale of large equipment may select one of their customers to act as a so-called 'beta-site' – a trial site to test the equipment and to reap endorsement from the user for later promotions.

Other methods mentioned by you may have been **product** or **price promotion.** These, too are employed in business marketing. Product promotions may be offered in the form of, for example, 'free toner for three months with every photocopier sold or leased'. Similarly, many organisations offer price promotions, if these are considered to increase the sales volume. As mentioned above, in the section on pricing, price promotions may not always have the desired effect, however.

Hospitality and **gifts** are common in business marketing but need to be treated with great care. Companies must establish the very fine line at which gifts move into the category of bribes. Where organisations deal with international customers, ethical and cultural norms must be considered with even greater care.

Personal selling may have been identified as one of your promotional tools. This consumes by far the largest part of any company's marketing or sales budget. With many organisations changing their strategic focus from straightforward selling to being more market-led, the training of sales staff in a range of aspects has become more important. Technical training of a company's own products and an understanding of customers' applications and needs leads increasingly to the concept of 'relationship marketing', where the aim is to maximise the benefit for both organisations through suitable product or service solutions. Joint product development may ensue, as the following brief example shows.

EXAMPLE

British Airways, in the mid 1980s, developed its automatic booking system, which allowed travel agents to check availability of flights and make bookings while the customer was still on the premises. BA intended to sell or lease the complete booking facilities to travel agents, thus gaining revenue from its information system. At the time, other major airlines were developing similar systems with the same intentions.

The system required a label printer that could print serial tickets, was able to print very closely to both the top and bottom margin and had a tear-off facility. Printers had to be of the impact variety and had to be capable of printing through seven copies, with the last still being clearly legible. Many printers in those days either could not cope with seven copies, had no tear-off facility or had to lose a ticket between each printed ticket, thus wasting expensive stationery.

BA approached a number of British companies with its specification. One of these, a distributor of computer peripherals with considerable experience of converting standard peripheral for specialist applications, redesigned a printer it imported from the US to meet all of BA's requirements. The company then approached its supplier Datasouth in the States and offered the re-engineered product, under a royalty agreement, back to the original manufacturer who were able to incorporate the new features and offer a 'new' product to all its customers.

DISTRIBUTION IN INDUSTRIAL MARKETS

Distribution outlets, in both industrial and consumer markets, help manufacturers to ensure an adequate supply of the products they need. They provide convenient opportunities to purchase. Members of the distribution members, also called 'channel members', assist in providing regular levels of goods, such as spare parts and finished items. In addition to this, they may offer maintenance and repair services and provide feedback about the market place.

The customer base of most organisations is considerably smaller than those found in consumer markets. Indeed, they may have only a handful of customers, as is the case in the defence industry. In addition to this, customers are often concentrated in particular areas. The need for microchips, for example, is greatest in the Reading area (often called the British Silicon Valley).

Where the customer base is small and concentrated, distribution is often direct from manufacturer to customer. Direct distribution is also becoming more widespread in cases where the customer is a multiple retailer or a large manufacturer. These firms operate automatic re-ordering systems via computer links to the manufacturer, which is activated once stock levels reach a certain point. The practice of just-in-time delivery, which helps to reduce the cost of stockholding by customers, also leads to direct deliveries from manufacturer to customer. In many cases the cost of long-term JIT delivery contracts makes it necessary for the manufacturer to set up warehousing facilities close to the customer's premises to ensure regular supplies.

Even when intermediaries are used, channels of distribution are often much shorter, with agents or distributors appointed on a regional basis.

ACTIVITY 10

From your previous reading and your own experience, identify and list possible distribution channels in an industrial market. What are their main functions? What are the drawbacks and advantages?

You may have identified any of the following:

Wholesalers or wholesale distributors

These purchase from manufacturers for resale to other business markets and are used extensively for many products. Most trade sectors rely on distribution via this channel, for instance electrical wholesalers and timber merchants. Smaller retailers, such as convenience stores, also purchase through this channel. The advantages of using wholesalers includes sharing of promotion cost. Since wholesalers purchase the goods from manufacturers, they help to maintain a constant supply of goods to the markets they serve. However, wholesalers add a significant margin on to the manufacturer's price, thus often reducing the competitiveness of the products.

Agents

Unlike distributors, agents do not take title to goods – that is, they do not actually buy and stock the goods for further distribution. Both in product and service marketing, they develop links between the producer and the business customer, for which they are paid commission only. This means that, whilst they use their knowledge of the market, they do not facilitate distribution flow through stockholding. In addition to this, agents often act for a number of competing firms, selling on the product or service that maximises their own objectives (often income). In spite of this drawback, agents are, however, widely used in business marketing.

Own sales office or sales force

Most organisations employ sales personnel, either based at head office or in sales outlets, who negotiate with potential customers. As mentioned above, the quality of sales personnel in assessing the requirements of customers is becoming increasingly important, with many business customers expecting solutions to problems from supplying firms rather than products. The training of salespeople is therefore gaining in importance.

The choice of channel option depends on a number of factors.

Firms may wish to keep regular contact with their customers; in particular when the product is of a technical nature and has a relatively short product life, feedback may be required to remain at the leading edge of developments in the market. When companies engage in relationship marketing with their final customers, they are unlikely to involve intermediaries.

The level of service, both prior to delivery and post delivery, as well as installation requirements may influence whether, and how many, channel members a firm may wish to appoint. When the customer base is widespread, the organisation relatively small and a high level of service and technical assistance is needed, organisations are likely to appoint servicing intermediaries.

The cost of operation plays a major role in deciding the number and type of intermediaries. When the cost of maintaining relationships with customers is high compared with that of appointing channel members, then the latter option may be chosen, provided all other factors have been taken into account and lead to the same conclusion. Companies may well opt to deal directly with customers when a high level of control over the relationship is required, even if this does mean an increase in cost.

Products that constitute a minor cost element in the final production process, such as small items of hardware, paper and lubricants, but which are purchased in large quantities, may require more selling activities than, say items of capital expenditure. When this is the case, intermediaries are frequently appointed.

The table below summarises some of the aspects organisations may consider when selecting and evaluating channel members and options.

	Number of Final Customers	Contact required by final customer	Contact required by intermediary	Control required
High	Multiple sets or intermediaries	Stocking/service intermediary	Stocking/service intermediary	Own channel
Medium	One set of intermediaries	Stocking intermediary	Stocking intermediary	Mixed channel
Low	Direct channel	Selling intermediary	Selling intermediary	Independent channel

Table 1: Evaluating Channel Options

1.5 Future trends in business marketing

A number of issues are currently changing the nature and processes of business- to-business marketing and are anticipated to grow in importance. Increasingly, firms are forming strategic alliances and joint ventures to overcome the pressures that rapid product change and intense competition places on their resources. These alliances may be between complementary firms, such as a manufacturer and a distribution firm, or between competing organisations. Convergence of consumer tastes in international markets and the rate of mergers and acquisitions in the global market place are creating new opportunities, but also increase the level and intensity of competitive pressure on firms. Technological changes affecting customers have an increasing impact on suppliers, as does the increasing power of many buying organisations. Green issues will continue to affect firms, requiring changes in products and production processes.

The changing environment requires organisations to scan their market carefully in order to anticipate developments in the marketplace. Ignoring new threats and opportunities will eventually lead to business failure.

REVIEW ACTIVITY 1

Produce a report for a purchasing manager listing the reasons why it may not be a good idea always to buy from the cheapest supplier.

(A possible answer to this activity is given at the end of the unit.)

Summary

In this section we have examined some of the aspects governing marketing processes in business marketing. Needs and motivation of business markets, as well as the buying process and buying behaviour have been dealt with. Factors determining pricing, product, distribution and communication strategies have been identified and a range of strategies proposed that facilitate the marketing process in this environment.

SECTION 2

Consumer Marketing

Introduction

This section is concerned with consumer behaviour and the considerations marketers have to bear in mind when developing strategies. Strictly speaking, consumers are defined as all the people involved in making the decision whether or not to purchase a product or service for use or consumption. This includes organisational consumers. However, when we speak of consumer behaviour, we usually mean the behaviour of individuals who make purchasing decisions for private or household use or consumption. These consumers buy a large range of fast-moving consumer goods (FMCGs), durable goods and services, which are not part of a value chain, and the purchase is (most of the time) not for the purpose of generating profit.

Consumer markets are, generally speaking, considerably more dispersed than organisational markets. In addition to this, buying behaviour, both prior to and after the actual purchase, tends to be less rational than that of organisational buyers. Needs are more individual to the consumers and, since they are coloured by a range of internal and external stimuli, they are more difficult to predict. Consumer purchasing decisions are often referred to as a 'black box', which is difficult to access but gives vital clues as to the factors that determine purchases.

Organisations need to ascertain what happens inside this black box. Even in business-to-business marketing, the ultimate consumer or customer must be borne in mind. If companies fail to remember this, inappropriate products may be produced which, though technically sound and extremely well designed to fulfil their function, may be unattractive to the consumer. Similarly, organisations must compare their abilities and objectives with those of consumers to establish whether they are able to serve the market with appropriate products profitably.

Figure 5 indicates the process that marketers try to identify when researching consumer markets and developing suitable offers.

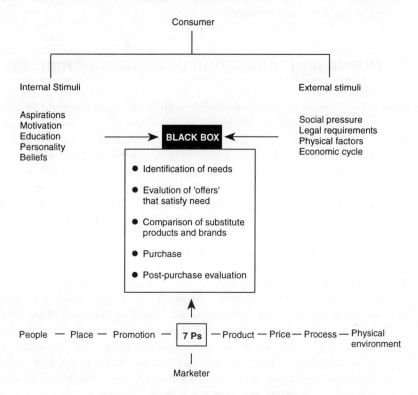

Figure 5: The consumer's 'black box'

Organisations selling in consumer markets must not only try to identify what goes on in each customer's black box, but estimate whether there is a sufficient number of potential purchasers that will be satisfied with their offer. Marketers must also identify whether they are able to position their product or service in the mind of their purchasers in such a way that buyers will prefer their offer in significant enough numbers to warrant the effort of production, distribution etc.

Organisations therefore have to identify market needs, segment the myriad of needs into groups of potential purchasers who are likely and able to purchase the offer, and to position the product or service as an attractive alternative to competing offers in the minds of these target segments. In addition to this, research into value perceptions and preferred purchase locations of the chosen group enables firms to make products and services available at appropriate locations and prices.

The aim of this section is to help you to:

- gain an understanding of the difference between needs and wants and how this translates into buying processes

- become familiar with the consumer purchasing process and appreciate the importance of marketing research to ascertain the players and processes involved in this

- be able to recommend alternative segmentation and targeting strategies on the basis of given information.

2.1 Needs and motivation of consumer markets

Goods and services in the consumer market fulfil a variety of functions in addition to the core function they are designed for. Consider the purchase of food, for instance. If the customer's need is that of satisfying hunger, then there are numerous options available. Take a fresh look at your local supermarket and appreciate the vast range of products that are designed to fulfil that need. If the need is for food *now,* then customers are again faced with a multitude of options from fast-food outlets to restaurants, cafés to pubs serving snacks. What the marketer wants to know is how people make choices, and what the likely choices are that customer groups or segments will make, under what conditions. They also need to know what price customers are willing to pay for the use they derive from the purchase.

NEEDS, WANTS AND MOTIVATION

It is important to distinguish clearly between the needs and wants of customers. Needs are perceived levels of deprivation. According to Maslow (1943), this can be of food and drink, but also of higher needs such as esteem or friendship. Wants can be defined as the product that we believe will satisfy the need. For instance, we may wish to improve our home to gain satisfaction, approval (or hygiene). The choice of products, – wallpaper *vs* paint, curtains *vs* blinds, carpets *vs* floor tiles etc – are the result of internal and external stimuli. Similarly, the motivation to purchase, as well as the purchase location, may be the result of stimuli. A special offer, peer pressure, health reports etc may all act as triggers.

Maslow grouped people's needs into a hierarchical order, arguing that, as human beings satisfy one level of needs, they become preoccupied with another level to strive for. Figure 6 summarises this hierarchy:

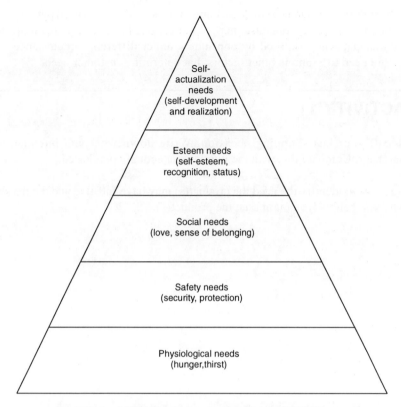

Figure 6: Maslow's hierarchy of needs (1943)

Physiological needs refer to the basic human requirements for survival, such as food, drink and oxygen. Maslow argued that only when we have satisfied these elementary needs does the next level of needs arise: the need to protect these.

Safety needs are those for security, stability and predictability in people's lives. Often this need is satisfied through services, such as insurance, guarantees, even membership of a neighbourhood watch scheme.

Belonging and love are seen to drive people to join clubs and associations where they experience affiliation with others and affection.

Esteem, the penultimate need, expresses itself in the search for status, recognition and achievement. Many products and services – such as perfumes, motors vehicles and high-tech products – 'promise' this as a reward. Only after successful satisfaction of these needs, so Maslow argues, will people seek to achieve their self-fulfilment and their potential. This is often expressed in concern for external issues such as volunteer work.

Although useful for an initial understanding of needs, Maslow's need pyramid often does not help in predicting customer responses. Neither does it explain different behaviour patterns exhibited by consumers under different circumstances. We therefore need to examine other factors that determine customer need.

ACTIVITY 11

Recall your last shopping occasion. Write down what you intended to purchase. Compare this with the item(s) you actually purchased.

Next, try to identify the need the product(s) may have fulfilled and the reason why you believe you purchased the product(s).

You may have identified a whole range of reasons why you purchased the products. Many of these may, on the surface, have very little to do with needs.

You may have written down 'fancied the product', 'persuaded by friend'. Perhaps the usual product was not available, or you wanted to impress someone else... All are valid reasons for purchases. What becomes apparent from your list, though, is that consumers often purchase irrationally, and regardless of needs. This is quite different from organisational purchasing.

One school of thought, that of Motivation Research, attempts to uncover the hidden meaning of these often irrational-seeming decisions. Based on Freudian ideas, they make the assumption that product choice and use is often based on unacceptable motives, which are channelled into acceptable outlets. Studies carried out by Dichter in the 1950s found that product choices were frequently associated with latent or underlying motives of which the purchaser was unaware. Dichter conducted lengthy in-depth interviews on over 200 products, combining general questions with those on product usage and perception. Whilst his findings have been subject to criticism, in particular that it may be used to manipulate consumers, they are nevertheless used by marketers in the positioning of products. Table 2 shows some of the major motives identified by Dichter, as well as associated products (Dichter, 1964).

Motive	Associated Products
Security	Ice cream (feel like a loved child again), hospital care, home baking, neatly folded washing
Individuality	Gourmet food, foreign cars, perfume, fountain pens
Reward	Alcohol, ice cream, confectionery
Status	Scotch, carpets, designer clothes (these indicate a high stress/ high powered job)
Femininity	Cakes, silk, tea, dolls, household ornaments (they are decorative and have a significant tactile component)
Masculinity/Virility	Coffee, red meat, heavy shoes, shaving with a razor, power tools
Moral purity/Cleanliness	Cotton fabrics, harsh household detergents (make housewives feel moral after use), bathing, oatmeal
Mastery over environment	Household appliances, sporting goods, boats

Table 2: Consumption motives identified by Dichter

Learning, conditioning and memory are also believed to influence both our motivation to buy and the way we purchase.

Classical Conditioning Theory (Dichter, 1964) argues that marketers are able to elicit desired responses when one stimulus which causes a response, say thirst leading to drinking, is paired with another, say the drinking of a cola soft drink. Over time, so they argue, the second stimulus, for instance the recognition of a brand of soft drink, leads consumers to experience the first stimulus. In other words, we feel thirsty when we see a particular brand of cola. The two become synonymous.

According to classical condition theories, successfully marketing a product would require the building of strong brands which are heavily promoted so that wherever an original stimulus is present, the satisfaction of this is achieved with the same product. The verbal cues, too are important to enhance the probability of product loyalty. 'Don't leave home without it', one credit card company urges us. Another assures us that our 'flexible friend' is always available when we are in difficulties. Being able to repeat the purchase and to rely on the availability of the product or service is, according to this theory, vital. When the stimulus – response pattern is interrupted, customers will need to switch products and, when this happens frequently, are not able to associate products with needs and wants.

Whereas classical conditioning theorists (McSweeney and Bierley, 1984) see brand purchasing as an automatic response, cognitive learning theories see buying behaviour as heavily influenced by mental processes, which may be conscious or unconscious. Hoch and Deighton (1989), for example, argue that the association of products with desirable outcomes reinforces the wish to own such a good or use the service. Lack of purchase may lead to 'punishment'. For instance, many household detergent manufacturers use this principle. The image portrayed is that clean washing is rewarded with esteem and love (Maslow's hierarchy of need appears relevant here, too); not using the product results in socially unacceptable, dirty clothes. The use of widely accepted role models to endorse the product message, as well as easy-to-remember 'jingles' reinforce the process of associating the product with a desired outcome.

ACTIVITY 12

Look at the following advertising slogans. Note down what you perceive to be the desired outcome for customers using each of these products? What is the punishment element?

The best a man can get
(Shaving foam)

It makes them come home to you
(A stock cube)

Your flexible friend
(Credit card)

The desired outcome for using the shaving foam is being attractive to 'the best' of the opposite sex, being admired and loved. Absence of the 'close shave', therefore could be construed as leading to loneliness. The same message is often portrayed in advertisements for the female equivalent, the perfume.

The credit card's reward is certainty and reliability (the qualities one expects from a friend) and freedom to go anywhere, do anything (flexibility). Not owning a credit card restricts freedom and can lead to embarrassment. The stock cube slogan conveys promises to keep the family together, to stop its members straying from the nest.

Attitudes, too, shape our buying behaviour. These may be the result of cultural influences or of past experiences and are considered by many marketers to give vital clues about buying intentions. Attitudinal research attempts to correlate particular viewpoints of customers with past purchase behaviour in order to predict future buying patterns. One technique employed is the use of questionnaires that ask interviewees to respond to a number of statements on an agreement/ disagreement scale. You may have encountered such questionnaires inside the packaging of products you have purchased. Inclusion with products allows marketers to form an attitude profile of the purchasers. An attitude survey carried out by the European Commission, for example, established that even in low-income households, which are traditionally perceived as satisfiers of lower needs, purchasers were prepared to spend an additional 5% on products if they were environment friendly. A similar study carried out by the UN found that in less developed countries, which tend to have lower literacy and education levels, this pre-occupation with environmental factors was less predominant. Attitudes to risk taking, and therefore the degree to which consumers may try new products, are established using a variety of research methods. The findings influence whether a product becomes a 'New Improved' product with a familiar brand name, or the beginning of a new brand.

Attitudes, unlike needs, do change with varying degrees of speed. For instance, in the late 1970s many multiple retailers brought out 'no-frills' brands. Tesco packaged a number of essential goods such as toilet paper, baked beans and other household items, and called it the 'Yellow Brand'. Consumers, however, were not drawn to these products as this basic brand was perceived to be inferior. This situation is quite reversed in the 1990s, when the brands of many multiple retailers are seen to offer similar quality at lower prices, or in the case of the Marks and Spencer brand St Michael, superior quality at competitive prices.

The **level of involvement,** or the importance of the need or want in comparison with other, competing, goals plays a further part in the motivation for purchases. When an item is perceived as essential, or satisfying more than one need, this product may be purchased in preference to another. A car, for instance, can satisfy the need for transport, but also save time when public transport is unavailable or inconvenient. In addition to this, it may also act as a status symbol. For someone, who enjoys tinkering with cars it may even become a leisure pursuit.

The **level of utility** derived from the purchase may also explain how consumers evaluate various purchase options. Some goods cease to provide utility or benefit, once a certain level of consumption has been reached and consumers may then switch to other priorities. For instance, when a household does not have a television, the first set purchased may provide a high level of benefit. A second set may be used in another room but may offer a slightly different kind of benefit: that of which channel to watch. Further additions may decrease the level further, until the purchaser derives zero utility from further purchases.

Although it is difficult to ascertain the exact need or want that products or services fulfil, marketers nevertheless need to carry out careful research to find groups of benefits sought by a number of consumers. The results may be analysed and displayed on a scatter diagram for different customer profiles, such as is shown in Figure 7.

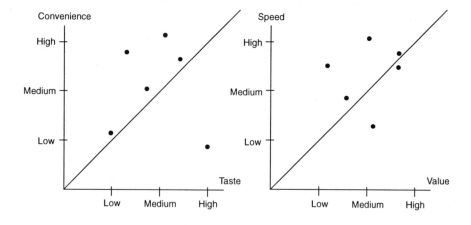

Figure 7: Scatter diagrams of utility derived from the purchase of convenience food.

The diagrams show that consumers consider convenience more important than the taste of the product, and are prepared to pay a premium for the ability to produce a meal speedily. Many more variables would need to be considered to arrive at a conclusion about the purchase motives for this type of product before a picture emerges of what will provide maximum satisfaction to purchasers.

2.2 External factors influencing consumer buying behaviour

SOCIAL FACTORS

External factors affect all of us in our daily lives and, as a result, influence what, how and where we purchase, as well as quantities bought. They can be grouped into primary factors, which are culture, social class, family and reference groups, and secondary factors, which comprise the wider environment we live in.

Cultural influences

Culture has been defined as a set of shared values that guide human behaviour. Examples of cultural influences are language, which shapes the way we communicate with each other, and social structures and hierarchies that determine our 'place' in society and how we address each other. For instance, in England it is becoming common to use first names even with people who are older/superior in status. This is not acceptable in cultures such as the French or German, which even have different words for 'you'. How we live and spend our time is also shaped by cultural forces. In societies, for instance, that place a lot of emphasis on possessions we tend to find people living spacially further apart than in those where this is less important. Products such as garden fences and services such as block paving are therefore needed less.

Cultural factors shape not only the products we buy, but also how we purchase. Multi-pack products require a certain degree of storage facilities, ownership of fridges and freezers, the disposable income to make bulk purchases and motorised transport to be able to get the purchases home. When these factors are absent, consumers may well purchase one fruit yogurt, rather than a pack of eight or more.

Cultural changes tend to happen slowly over time and may only be identifiable when comparing different eras. However, each culture also consists of sub-groups that affect the way we behave. We will look at these next.

Subculture and reference groups

Almost every member of a larger society or culture also belongs to a subculture, which defines more subtle behavioural norms. Religious groups, shared interests such as membership of a golf club, or common beliefs all shape our choice of products and the way we purchase. Think, for instance, of the contrasts in punk and Yuppy culture in the 1980s, which dictated a range of product choices, such as hairstyle, clothing, jewellery, etc.

ACTIVITY 13

Write down factors that would influence your purchasing behaviour if you went for a meal with the following:

a) family

b) friends

c) colleagues

d) recent acquaintances

You may have identified choice of venue as one factor. For instance, you would probably not go and visit a McDonalds with colleagues. The degree of formality may also be different, which may be reflected in your choice of meal and drink. The amount spent and how you pay may also differ. For example you would probably pay separately if you went out with recent acquaintances rather than sharing a kitty, which could be the case with colleagues or friends.

ACTIVITY 14

Read the article 'Cast-offs are back in fashion' from the *Observer* (6/6/93)
(Resource Item 3.4) and consider the target market for these clothes. Try to
describe the buyers you believe are most interested in purchasing these clothes.

Social class

Like internal and cultural factors, social class affects our choice of products. In
addition to this, however, it also influences to a large extent our ability to purchase.
Often called socio-economic group, the social class we belong to is made up of a
mixture between income level, education and occupation. An example may
illustrate this.

Consider a street in your village or town that consists of mixed housing. You
could envisage two families that consist of, perhaps, two adults and two children
with similar age profile. Both families do their main shopping on a weekly basis in
the same supermarket. Grouping these two families by geography, gender and age
profile may lead us to the assumption that they have very similar needs, values and
attitudes. On closer examination, however, we discover that one family has a joint
income of £15,000 and the other a joint salary in excess of £70,000. We can now
assume that their spending patterns and the amount spent is rather different.

Different categories of social classes exist and care must be taken when comparing
data from different countries. In Britain we tend to use a seven-category system to
define membership of social class, as is shown below (Chisnall, 1976, pp114-5).
However, five-category and even three-category models, that break down class into
blue collar/ grey collar/ white collar or upper, middle, lower class also exist.

Class	Indicator
Upper Class	A
Upper Middle Class	B
Lower Middle Class	C1
Upper Working Class	C2
Working Class	D
Others	E

Identifying the social class or socio-economic group to which individuals and
households belong is crucial when developing products and services that are not
only attractive, but also affordable. In addition to this, it is often the upper classes

that adopt products first, with their use 'cascading' down as products become more widely available and usually cheaper in price.

A further difference between social classes, and usually connected with the different levels of education achieved by different classes, is the choice of newspapers or magazines read or television channels watched. For instance, *Home and Garden*, a British publication, is aimed at the upper/ upper-middle-class female reader, whereas magazines such as *My Weekly* is targeted at the working-class female reader. Among magazines with primarily male readership, *Private Eye* is aimed at the upper- and lower-middle-class male.

ACTIVITY 15

Imagine that you are the owner of two specialist retail outlets, selling a variety of household items, including ornaments and soft furnishing. One store caters for the upper middle class (B) and the other for the working class (D). How would the difference in social class affect:

a) product lines and style of goods

b) advertising and media selection to your target groups

c) prices and usual payment method.

Product lines in the outlet catering for the B socio-economic group may be 'wider' – there may be more co-ordinating products on offer such as matching curtains, pillows, rugs etc. Or they may be deeper – offering slightly different variants of the same products. For instance, if the outlet sells glasses, you may find red wine, white wine, sherry, champagne, whisky and many more glasses of the same design. The quality of the goods may also vary from that of the outlet aimed at socio-economic group D. Products may carry a famous brand name in the former shop, but be unbranded in the second.

The **advertising** message may differ, using different language and images and buying motives. Similarly, the quality of any print material used will reflect the difference in product quality offered. When mass media, such as magazines or newspapers, are used, the outlet catering for group B may use a local magazine rather than a local newspaper, which is often delivered free of charge to households.

Price levels will differ in line with the different product quality. Price promotion in the outlet targeting the group D may be more widespread. Payment methods, too, may vary, reflecting the different purchase amounts. The outlet aimed at group D may find more cash payments, whereas that targeting group B may find more payments made by credit cards or debit cards.

In addition to social class, many environmental factors discussed in Unit 2, influence choice and timing of purchases. One further factor, termed 'environmental dynamism' also influences the perceived needs of consumers. External pressures, and the materialist culture within a society, affect the goals that individuals set themselves and may lead to a shift in hierarchy levels. For instance, when an economy is in recession, individuals, although in secure employment, may change their spending patterns as a result of media coverage and heightened awareness of possible insecurity. Changing social norms, aspirations and expectations, too, influence purchasing patterns. This can be observed in many societies, where spending on home entertainment, for example, is often great in social groups that are deprived at lower level needs on Maslow's hierarchy, but are very susceptible to peer pressure in their choice of products.

2.3 The consumer buying process

Unlike professional buyers in organisational markets, private consumers take a less formalised approach to their purchases. They tend to purchase a wider range of goods in smaller quantities and, as a result, exert very little power over the supplying organisation. However, having said that, there are an increasing number of consumer or interest groups trying to influence the range of products stocked by retailers.

ACTIVITY 16

Think back to a recent purchase of an expensive item, such as a bicycle, car or hi-fi equipment and describe the process you went through from the moment you considered the purchase until the point at which you took the product home.

You may have decided to purchase the article for a number of reasons. For instance, someone may have suggested this as 'a good idea', or you may have decided to replace a previous item. Someone, perhaps you yourself, may have been the

initiator of the buying process. At this point you may only have felt a desire to own a new product.

The next step may well have been a conscious or unconscious **search for information**. Perhaps you browsed through catalogues or brochures, suddenly took time to read the advertisements in the press or visited retailers to collect information. At this point you may have sought the opinion of others, an **influencer**, to help you gather further evidence about the right purchase. Having collected information, you may have sat down, in the case of a car purchase perhaps with the local paper, and highlighted or **evaluated alternatives**.

If you were the buyer, you may also have been the **decision maker** about the final purchase. However, it may well be possible that the item was a gift, with you acting as an influencer, but someone else making the buying decision and/or the purchase. Similarly, when the item was a present bought by you, you may have made the purchase decision, but were not the final **user** of the product.

Most people also experience **cognitive dissonance** after purchasing major items of expenditure. Also termed 'post-purchase anxiety', we wonder whether we have made the correct decision. One way of reducing this anxiety is to look for confirmation that the choice was a correct one: we ask friends to approve of our purchase, notice the number of other, identical, cars on the road or, in the case of a house purchase, continue to look at estate agents windows to assure ourselves that we paid a fair price for the property.

Marketers need to establish both the stages that people pass through in their buying patterns, as well as the people who are usually involved in the buying process, and develop a presence with the person or people who play the dominant role at each stage.

ACTIVITY 17

Write down possible actions that marketers can take to ensure customer awareness at the different stages in the buying process:

1 Need recognition

2 Information search

3 Evaluation of alternatives

4 Purchase decision

5 Cognitive dissonance

You may have identified some of the following tactics for staying with the customer at all stages of the buying process:

Public relations
This is relevant at all stages to ensure consumer awareness of manufacturers and brands.

Brochures and catalogues
The presence of these assist customers, particularly at the information search stage. Distribution through retail outlets, as loose inserts in other publications or sent directly to households at key purchasing times are some available options.

Sales assistance or helplines
These can add personal reassurance during the evaluation, purchase and post purchase stages. Needless to say that the level of training is vital to convey a positive impression about the product or service.

Price incentive
This can be in the form of credit facilities or price reductions and is a tool often employed at the purchasing stage.

Warranties, guarantees and no-quibble money refund
Such promises often reduce indecision at the point of purchase, but also reduce post-purchase anxiety. Trials, such as extended test drives, also reassure customers.

One other important aspect is the choice and intensity of distribution. When customers cannot find their chosen good in the expected outlet, they may well switch to their second choice.

The involvement of consumers in arriving at a decision is not dissimilar to that of organisational buyers. Buying a completely new item will involve all stages in the purchasing process; the modified rebuy, when the consumer finds that the usual brand is not available and chooses a similar, less familiar product will probably involve stages 3 onwards, and the straight rebuy involves simply stage 4.

In the consumer market, however, there is also a fair amount of impulse buying, although this is heavily influenced by cultural and economic factors. Marketers should take this into consideration when developing particularly promotions other than advertising in mass media (called below-the-line promotions). British consumers top the list of impulse purchases in European comparisons!

REVIEW ACTIVITY 2

Please read the article 'Supermarkets get ready for a new generation of YABS' (Resource Item 3.5), which outlines changes in consumer buying behaviour. Identify at least three different categories of shoppers and suggest a range of product, price or promotion strategies that would attract each of the different groups into the store.

(A possible answer is given at the end of the unit.)

Summary

We have identified that product choice is subject to a number of personal and environmental factors that act on consumers when selecting product options. Theories that try to explain the motivation of consumers and their needs have been examined. It has become apparent that marketers must evaluate carefully the appropriate product, pricing and distribution strategies for different consumer groups and offer those that not only meet the organisation's, but also the consumer's requirements.

SECTION 3

Service Marketing

Introduction

The service industry has been gaining importance in all countries since World War II and indeed employs the largest number of people in industrial and post-industrial societies. In the UK, the number of people employed in the service sector rose by almost 35% between 1972 and 1990. Whereas in 1972 approximately 50% of all employment was in the service sector, in 1990 68% of all employees were found in the service industries. (Source: *Social Trends,* 22, 1992).

The range of services offered by organisations has also increased. New technology has necessitated the creation of new or changed occupations and firms to support products or enhance existing services. For example, the advent of the video recorder created new opportunities for video hire outlets and maintenance services for recorders, while increased ownership of home computers has created a new market for computer games and service facilities.

With growing affluence and experience of a range of services, customer expectations have changed. Foreign holidays, for instance, are now widely taken by many households. This has had the effect of increasing the number and size of airports, and requiring the provision of hotel facilities and ancillary services provided at airports. The use of leisure facilities such as fitness studios has experienced significant growth, as have the number of retail outlets selling a large range of fitness-related products.

Deregulation and privatisation of many public utilities, such as water, energy generation and distribution and air transport, within the UK, continental Europe and the US, has intensified the competition in some service industries. Diversification of a number of organisations from manufacturing to service industries has also impacted on the level of competition. In non-service industries, firms increasingly try to gain competitive advantage through customer services or by adding service products to their products. For instance, in the car industry, many manufacturers now offer a range of financing options or even their own credit cards.

In the light of industry growth, changing consumer demand and increased competition from domestic and foreign companies, the marketing of services has become increasingly important. This section is concerned with the additional complexities companies face when marketing an often intangible product.

The aim of this section is to help you to:

- understand the added complexity involved in the marketing of services
- be able to assess some of the issues and stages involved in the development of service facilities
- have an understanding of the importance of the service encounter
- appreciate the importance of quality in the production process of services.

3.1 The nature and role of services

Every day, we experience a whole range of services. The radio programme that wakes us up, the roads taking us to work, meals provided in the canteen and electricity we take for granted throughout the day are all examples of services most of us consume. Indeed, services are absolutely vital for the operation of any household or economy and their importance is growing. Even when we purchase manufactured goods, most of these will have been made available to us with the assistance of a range of services.

Services are provided by private and voluntary organisations, national and local government and their agencies. They may be provided by for-profit or not-for-profit organisations (when the providers are charities or government agencies). Services may be a core product, or part of the augmented product of another manufactured good. Their nature is often intangible, such as health services or life insurance products that provide quality of life or peace of mind. All these factors make a definition of services and their product difficult. How do we, for instance, define the service provided by air-quality monitoring services. The product may be cleaner air, or accurate information about the level of sulphur; convictions of offenders may be another output.

In her interactive model of an economy, Dorothy I Riddle (1986) attempts to classify services under a number of headings, as follows:

Business – such as accountancy, consultancy, finance

Public – such as tax collection, legal services

Infrastructure – such as broadcasting, planning, transport

Trade – such as retailing, haulage

Personal and Social – such as leisure and health services

Services in each of these classifications supply both the manufacturing and the extractive sectors (mining of raw materials) of an economy with the foundation needed to supply private and business consumers with goods, as well as providing service products directly to customers.

One of the difficulties with this classification is the development of 'boundary crossing', which many firms have engaged in order to gain customers or competitive advantage. For instance, traditional business services, such as printing services, may offer printed stationery to private customers; pension plans, which were once confined mainly to the business sector, are now widely available to private individuals. Recognising that many service products also require an element of physical products, Shostack (1982) developed a 'scale of elemental dominance' of a range of goods and services. This illustrates the proportion of services to manufacturing input of a range of 'service products' (Figure 8).

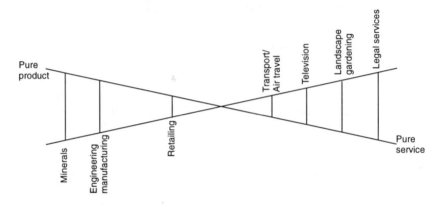

Figure 8: A scale of elemental dominance (Shostack, 1982)

ACTIVITY 18

Identify and list below a number of services you use on a regular basis. Then examine Figure 8 above and try to position the services you use on the elemental dominance scale, giving reasons for your choice of position.

You may have positioned services such as postal services, newspaper publishing and financial services somewhere between television and air travel, whereas your position for hairdressing may be between the theatre and nursing.

Reasons you may have given could include the degree to which the service is tangible or intangible, or whether the largest cost involved in producing this service is in the material used to provide the product or the people providing the service. Other reasons may be the degree to which the customer's presence is essential in the production process or the number of supplementary services required to provide each one of these.

3.2 The service product

When talking about the service process and the production of a service, the word 'servuction' is often used. The major differences between a service and a product are as follows:

- Most services, in order to be produced, require the presence of customers.

- Whereas most tangible products may be sampled, inspected or returned, services are primarily experienced and consumed at the time of production.

- Standardisation of the service product is often difficult, particularly when service personnel interact with customers.

- Service products are often time-perishable: an unsold theatre seat cannot be 'stored' for the next performance, for example.

All these factors need to be taken into account by organisations developing service products.

Services can be grouped according to the degree of customer presence. We can distinguish between those services provided to objects and those affecting people. We can further sub-divide each of these two categories into tangible and intangible actions to produce four product categories:

Service for objects		Service for people	
Tangible (car maintenance)	Intangible (banking and insurance)	Tangible (hairdressing/café)	Intangible (education/theatre)

Car maintenance requires minimal customer presence and is carried out on a physical object. Its results can be seen (new exhaust) and the service action experienced (better performance). Banking and insurance services, on the other hand do not require the presence of the customer and are intangible. (The transfer of funds cannot be seen and the benefit of life insurance is only experienced by the beneficiaries.) Tangible services requiring the presence of people include hairdressing, restaurants and fitness studios, whilst health screening, theatre visits and education are examples of intangible services requiring people, whose exact effect cannot be seen or measured.

Distinguishing these four categories of service can assist us in assessing the complexity of the servuction process and thus in the development of the service product. It also offers vital clues about the relevant importance of distribution, promotional messages and pricing strategies. Figure 9 presents the four product categories on a scale of increasing complexity.

Directed at tangible objects	Directed at intangible objects	Directed at people's bodies	Directed at people's minds or feelings
Low complexity			High complexity

Figure 9: Degree of service complexity

Where a service is intangible, and affects objects, customers often require much written information, guarantees and, in the case of banking and finance, the assurance of an ombudsman, should customers be unhappy with the service. Although these services require distribution outlets (eg banks), the main part of the distribution system is usually invisible. Pricing of such services is called professional pricing, with customers expecting a particular price (or price range) for the type of service rendered.

Where a service requires the presence of customers throughout the servuction process, for instance in a café, the final price is determined by the amount of service received, the physical environment which the owner provides, added services etc.

The complexity of services grows with greater customer involvement. If we compare the service provided by a vending machine with that of a restaurant this becomes apparent:

The **vending machine** will not require interaction with customers. The quality of the product remains the same with each purchase. Customisation of the final product is not possible. In case of breakdown or complaints, there is no, or little, interaction between customers and service provider.

A **restaurant** will be expected to provide other service facilities which affect the perceived value of meals purchased (cloakrooms, for example). Training of staff varies, depending on the nature of the restaurant (self-service or table service). Products may be customised to suit individual customers.

ACTIVITY 19

Consider at least three services that you have recently used and work out where they are positioned on the 'degree of complexity' scale.

You may have included the following services under the heading **low complexity**:

repairs to your car, dry cleaning services, plumbing or electrical repairs in your home. Because you are – usually – not involved and leave a specialist to get on with the job, your only involvement is at the beginning of the service and when payment is required.

Services involving **high complexity** may include a visit to a nightclub. Your presence, as well as the reason for your visit – probably to have a good time – makes careful planning of the location necessary. Access, parking, the right music for different visiting groups (eg over-25's night), security, cleanliness of the venue, as well as special promotions, may all be part of your expectations. The price you are willing to pay will almost certainly depend on the number of facilities provided by the nightclub.

SERVICE PRODUCT DIFFERENTIATION

The intangible nature of many products necessitates attention to those aspects of a product that positions the service in a customer's mind. This could be branding, with companies often developing strong family brands and differentiating their offers according to their target market. The black horse symbol used by Lloyds Bank is an example of family branding. When Lloyds Bank acquired a range of estate agents in the late 1980s, it found that strong brand recognition assisted it in developing a quality image.

In consumer markets, organisations also add a range of tangible products to increase awareness and brand recognition. Hotel chains, for instance, offer a range of gifts with the hotel name inscribed. When the film Jurassic Park was launched in 1993, a vast range of merchandise featuring dinosaurs was manufactured under license and introduced to coincide with the opening night of the film. Leisure parks offer their own T-shirts and sports bags and even the blood transfusion service in the UK gives away free car stickers and other items such as calendars to donors. Harrods and Liberty also offer durable shopping bags that cause the customer to recall the service experienced long after the service encounter.

3.3 The service delivery system

Because of the nature of services, their delivery takes on different dimensions to that of consumer or industrial goods. Customer presence necessitates service facilities, which in turn need to be designed to maximise efficiency for the customers and the organisation, create a pleasant ambience and, because of the time-perishable nature of services, avoids excess demand and queuing. Services that require one-to-one contact with service personnel require well-trained staff who are empowered to make decisions regarding their area of responsibility to provide a positive impression of the service encounter and maintain quality and customer loyalty.

In the late 1980s, post offices in the UK were the main service point for the payment of many social security benefits. Insufficient staff at key times, as well as inefficient processes often lead to long queues and a negative customer perception of the service offered. As a result, many customers requested automatic transfer to their bank accounts, when this became an option. Post offices not only lost the income generated per transaction, but since many sub-post offices were also general stores, they forfeited income from additional sales.

When designing delivery systems, organisations often attempt to break down each step required to achieve service delivery through a process called 'blueprinting'. Used for many years in the manufacturing industries, it aims to give a pictorial representation of the service process. Blueprinting aims to identify high and low contact points between service staff and customers, potential bottlenecks or waiting time that could cause customer dissatisfaction and points in the servuction process when the firm may be reliant on other services. New delivery processes may be designed, such as the automatic despatch of chequebooks once the customer has used the nth cheque, or, when waiting cannot be prevented, the addition of facilities that improve the customer's perception of the company. These facilities can themselves be other services that generate revenue. Airports provide a whole range of income-generating facilities to reduce the perceived waiting time. Blueprinting also enables managers to identify those areas that require staff trained in customer service and to develop appropriate training schemes.

Another approach to the design of service facilities is flowcharting. This aims to maximise throughput of customers, minimise inefficiencies such as waiting time and so improve customer satisfaction. Each process necessary for delivering the service is examined and timed and a solution that optimises the organisation's resources while maximising customer satisfaction is sought. The example below shows how altering the design of the delivery system may reduce waiting time and increase efficiency of staff.

EXAMPLE

A self-service petrol station with one pay kiosk experiences the following pattern:

1   Customer drives up to kiosk (approximately 10 seconds)

2   Payment by customers (an average of 45 seconds)

3   Customer puts away his/her wallet/purse and drives off (approximately 15 seconds)

This system requires every customer to wait for at least 70 seconds. The operator is idle for 25 seconds between every transaction.

By installing a second lane, the following pattern now emerges:

Customer 1 enters lane 1(10 seconds)
Customer 1 is served (45 seconds)
Customer 1 departs (15 seconds)
Customer 3 enters lane 1 (10 seconds)
While customer 1 departs customer 2 is served in lane 2 (45 seconds)
Customer 2 departs (15 seconds)
Customer 4 enters lane 2 (10 seconds)
While customer 2 departs, customer 3 is served in lane 1 (45 seconds)

Using the one-lane system, at peak times, it takes 225 seconds to serve three customers. The two lane system reduces the total time taken to 145 seconds. Operator idle time in the one-lane system was 60 seconds and has been reduced to 10 seconds. Customer 2 now has to wait a maximum of 45 seconds, assuming that (s)he arrives at the same time as customer 1. Customer 3 has to wait for 30 seconds and customer 4 and subsequent customers have to wait 20 seconds.

ACTIVITY 20

Reflect on the operation of a canteen or a fast food outlet known to you. Demand for meals probably fluctuates, reaching a peak between noon and 2.00 pm.

Draw a flow diagram, showing the processes involved in providing meals to customers, from entering the premises to sitting down with the purchased meal. What potential bottlenecks exist in this process? How could they be avoided?

Bottlenecks identified may be waiting to be served. This may be due to lack of staff or insufficient service areas. Food may have to be fetched from the kitchen or coffee machines refilled. Slow or inexperienced staff may cause a hold-up at the cash desk, or there may be lack of small change. An insufficient number of seats or tables not cleared may cause further delay.

Part-time staff may be employed to carry out a range of functions at peak time. It may also be possible to alter the flow of traffic, separating different types of food, thus creating more than one queue. Similarly, some operations may be automated, such as drink dispensing, while utensils and condiments may be situated outside the main serving area, encouraging faster throughput. Pre-packaged food items and self-service counters of individual products may also help to disperse the traffic flow. Staff training may be required to ensure that staff anticipate the effect of any shortages on customers, and procedures to monitor efficiency will need to be developed.

Organisations may take different approaches to the design of their service facility. One of these is the **production line approach**, which tries to reduce the amount of decision making by service personnel through implementation of standard procedures. Many fast food restaurants are examples of this. Customers are encouraged to take part in some of the processes like carrying their food to the table and clearing away rubbish. This approach aims to remove discretion exercised by staff with set procedures and operates on clearly defined divisions of labour. When this approach is taken, customers need to be educated about what they can not expect.

Another method is that of increased **customer participation**. Multiple retailers and self-service petrol stations and vending operators employ this principle. The customer is responsible for almost the entire service process. Because staff cost is minimised and economies of scale are high, service organisations can place strong emphasis on the service environment and training of those staff essential in the encounter, such as cashiers, help-desk staff and telephone operators. Other advantages of this approach are the ability to manage demand more easily, as is the case with bank cash dispensers and automatic ticket sales at stations.

ACTIVITY 21

Look at your answer to the previous exercise. Did you suggest a system that relies primarily on customer participation or on the production line approach? If you suggested service at the tables, list ways in which this would affect the price of your meal and the speed of service.

Organisations are increasingly trying to reduce the human element in non-essential parts of the service delivery system with automation. One of the benefits of this is that quality can be more easily controlled this way, as it eliminates decisions otherwise made by serving staff.

3.4 Service quality

Perception of service quality depends not only on the actual service product, but on many other factors. The consistency of the service, the level of training that staff receive and their ability to make decisions when customers have special requirements, the physical environment in which the service outlet is placed, as well as the service class which, for instance, a hotel is placed in, all affect customers expectations and therefore their perceived level of quality.

ACTIVITY 22

Read the letter of complaint in the Resource File (Item 3.6), and the reply from the firm (Item 3.7) and answer the following questions:

a) What do you believe were the expectations of the customer prior to the visit?

b) What were the specific quality issues complained about by the customer?

c) How well do you believe the proprietor responded to the complaint?

d) Suggest a number of ways in which the owner could redress the negative impression gained by the customer.

The quality expectations of the customer were high prior to the visit. The restaurant had obviously positioned itself as a premium priced, up-market establishment, leading to expectations of quality surroundings, service and products, with the customer anticipating to pay a premium price for this.

The main quality issue was the poor service. Indeed the customer praised the meal itself and had no complaints about the ambience and surroundings.

The owner blames a number of factors 'beyond her control' for the bad quality of service: lack of staff in the area, staff sickness and a high rate of custom that night. As it is part of the service package offered by the proprietor to hire experienced staff, her abnegation of responsibility is highly unsatisfactory for the customer.

Training of staff is obviously one aspect the owner or manager must address. The difficulty of finding new staff could be overcome by national, rather than local recruitment advertising, which would require the organisation to look at the incentives and remuneration offered to staff. Careful analysis of the service process may also identify gaps or inefficiencies that may be redressed. An offer of compensation (preferably in the form of another meal so that the quality impression can be altered) rather than reimbursement, would seem to be appropriate. Finally, careful management of the supply and demand, through promotion and price discrimination and/or incentives may also be an option to the proprietor. We will examine these in turn.

3.5 Managing supply and demand

We have already identified that services are time-perishable in nature: an unsold airline or concert ticket cannot be stored. Similarly, the capacity of most service firms is finite. Multi-storey car parks can only accommodate so many vehicles; the transport industry must observe safety regulations on maximum passenger numbers when selling tickets; and a marketing consultancy can only deal with a certain number of clients before it must employ more consultants and/or move to larger premises. Because of the demand fluctuations of many services, the demand for these must be carefully forecast and managed. Flexible systems, such as more cash desks than are usually required and a register of part-time staff who can be called on at short notice, are two ways of managing rising demand. When demand at peak times is unavoidable, firms may use a number of tactics to increase customer satisfaction levels while queuing.

Animating the waiting situation, by providing televisions in hospital waiting lounges or revolving advertising holdings, for example, often reduces the perceived length of time spent in a queue. Similarly, involving service customers in the process by asking them to complete necessary stages in the service process may also reduce annoyance. Informing customers in advance about the likely time it will take to be served allows customers to choose how to spend the waiting time or whether to return. Theme parks often use time indicators, when visitors are told to expect a certain waiting time at different queue points, as do telephone answering systems, that tell customers that they are in a queuing system.

When demand is cyclical, or intense at certain times of day or year, pricing and promoting strategies and incentives may be used to smooth excess demand.

Pricing

The intangible nature of services, that is the fact that customers can usually not see in advance what they are buying, requires careful research into customer expectations before pricing new and existing services. Many services are divided into price categories, with prices rising according to ancillary services offered. For instance, a leisure centre may charge an entry fee plus a price for the use of swimming pool, solarium and fitness room. If this is a public leisure facility, customers will expect the price to be considerably below those of a private leisure and sports centre. The latter may, in fact, charge an annual membership fee according to the quality rating it has gained. Hotels have star categories, and a guest staying in a two-star hotel will have very different price and quality expectations from one staying in a five-star hotel.

In professions, such as consultancy or accountancy and legal services, 'customary pricing' is often used, when the fee is usually a minimum price plus expenditure incurred.

ACTIVITY 23

1 Contact your local railway station and find out the price of a second and first class return ticket from your home to London (or your capital city if you do not live in the United Kingdom) at the following times: 7.00 am and 10.00 am, Mondays and Saturdays.

2 How do you explain the difference in price?

Many public transport operators employ price discrimination – charging different prices for the same service at different times. The price difference is intended to reduce the demand at peak times during the week (7.00 am) and increase the demand for seats at other times. This assists planners in sending the correct number of carriages around the country, reduces customer frustration with inadequate services if they cannot find a seat, enables smoother operation of buffet services and staff rota planning and avoids excessive queues at the ticket kiosk. The overall effect is increased customer satisfaction and reduced cost in dealing with customer complaints.

Many of the factors mentioned in the discussion of business-to-business marketing in Section 2 of this unit apply to the purchase or use of business services. Demand for services in business markets are subject to the same decision processes that would affect the purchase of a physical product. Price changes, too, may not affect the demand at all. For instance, whereas a private customer may decide quite spontaneously to take a short break in a foreign city as a result of low-cost flights, organisations are unlikely to plan their business trips around the availability of special offers. Although airlines realise that they may be unable to affect the level of demand, they offer services to business customers to increase loyalty. This could be conference facilities at airports, access to fax machines and computer systems, or greater in-flight comfort. In addition to this, they also attempt to influence the choice of airline by offering bonuses (for instance air miles) to users.

Price incentives are frequently offered when demand for a service is seasonal. We will discuss this in the section below.

PROMOTION

There is little difference in the promotion of services and products to private users and consumers. All kinds of media are employed for most services on offer. Until recently a number of legal restrictions applied to professional services such as legal firms, dentists and doctors surgeries and this has affected their use of promotion even after deregulation, with few service providers making use of all media. In addition to this, many small service organisations are local and therefore tend to favour either small ads in local papers or direct mail, sometimes distributed as a loose-leaf insert in local media.

Because of the cyclical nature of many services, incentives are often employed. These may be in the form of price reductions, such as offering a reduced fee for boiler maintenance in the summer, added-value premiums, such as two travelling for the price of one, or other rewards promised. Joint promotions with tangible products are also frequent such as repair services or extended warranties, which are, in essence, insurance services.

3.6 Voluntary services and public services

The range and number of voluntary services, or not-for-profit organisations, has been increasing in the last 15 years. Unlike conventional services, they are involved both in marketing their services to gain suppliers (of funds, expertise, supplies) and to their target groups. Whereas the service product of some organisations is easily defined, such as that of consumer protection groups or shelter groups for the homeless, others are extremely difficult to define.

Public services are similar to voluntary service providers inasmuch as they tend to operate as not-for-profit organisations. They exist to maximise their respective objectives, such as improved health care, an effective legal system, efficient fire service etc. Employees in these services, unlike the voluntary sector, are always paid and are required to fulfil the quality standards and procedures laid down by the service provider.

One essential difference is the fact that the public services do not rely on donations, but on government (central, regional or local) funds. They are therefore required to meet the funding and cost requirement laid down.

Both voluntary and public services have begun to embrace the marketing concept in recent years and as a result have changed their service products, their delivery systems and ancillary service provision, as well as their PR strategies and budget allocations.

REVIEW ACTIVITY 3

Imagine you have been given the brief to organise a Live Aid concert to obtain funds for a worthy cause and note down answers to the following questions:

a) What is the nature of your service and what ancillary services might you have to supply in order to produce it?

b) Who are your customer?

c) How would you deliver your service?

d) What areas of promotion are open to you?

e) How will you price your service?

(A possible answer is given at the end of the unit.)

Summary

In this section we have examined the nature of services and the difficulties in defining a service product, partly because of its intangible nature. The importance of the servuction process, which requires the customer to be present as well as the importance of this for the design of the service product and the delivery system have been encountered. This section has also highlighted some of the pricing and promotion issues that apply to the marketing of services and has suggested strategies that facilitate greater effectiveness in the marketing of services.

UNIT REVIEW ACTIVITY

Bettasoap is a manufacturer of skin cleansers that are used in a variety of markets, such as industrial firms that require large quantities of the cleansing product for their workforce, the hotel and catering industry, which uses the products both for its employees and, in miniature pack form, for use by its visitors. As a fast-moving consumer good liquid soap in pump-action bottles is sold under the Bettasoap brand name to retailers.

The basic ingredients used in the production of the skin cleanser are water, lanolin and perfume, as well as a number of preservatives to ensure that the product stays fresh. By varying the amount of each ingredient, the product receives its consistency, which can range from cleansing fluid to soap bars, and its scent.

The company is already equipped with the necessary filling and packaging machines but finds that relatively short production runs, which involve down-time of machines during the change-over from one product to another, increases its costs significantly.

Excess production capacity has now caused the company to re-examine its target markets and you have been asked, in the role of marketing assistant, to provide information on the following:

a)   likely new target markets

b)   an outline of the different needs that the product serves in these new target markets and the effect of these needs on the product portfolio

c)   factors that the company should consider when pricing, promoting and distributing its products

d)   any other issues that you feel Bettasoap should consider when marketing its range of cleansing products.

(A possible answer to this activity is given at the end of the unit.)

Unit summary

This unit has introduced you to some of the differences marketers encounter when offering products and services to business and private consumers. It has explored difference in buying behaviour between these two purchasing groups and examined their effect on product, pricing, distribution and promotion strategies.

The nature and complexity of services, and the importance of understanding customer involvement to ensure a satisfactory servuction process, were examined in the final section.

References

Beavis, S (1995) 'Lucas wins £1bn deal to supply VW', *The Guardian*, 7 March

Chisnall, P M (1976) *Marketing: a behavioural analysis,* McGraw-Hill

Dichter, E (1964) *Handbook of Consumer Motivation,* New York, McGraw-Hill

Hoch, S J & Deighton J (1989) 'Managing What Consumers Learn from Experience', *Journal of Marketing,* vol 53, April, pp1–20.

Maslow, A H (1943) 'A Theory of Human Motivation', *Psychological Review,* vol. 50

McSweeney, F K & Bierley, C (1984) 'Recent Developments in Classical Conditioning', *Journal of Consumer Research,* vol 11, pp619–31

Riddle, D I (1986) *Service-Led Growth,* Praeger, New York

Shostack, L G (1982) 'How to Design a Service', *European Journal of Marketing,* vol 16(i), pp49-64

Social Trends (1992), no.22

Webster, Jr, F E & Wind, Y J (1972) 'A General Model for Understanding Organisational Buying Behaviour' *Journal of Marketing,* April, vol 36, pp12–19

Further Reading

SECTION 1
Dibb S, Simkin L, Pride W and Ferrell O (1994) *Marketing Concepts and Strategies,* Houghton Mifflin, 2nd edn, Chapter 5

SECTION 2
Dibb *et al* (1994) Chapter 4

SECTION 3
Dibb *et al* (1994) Chapter 24

Answers to Review Activities

Review Activity 1

Your report should at least include an introduction, your main findings and a conclusion and recommendations. If you are unfamiliar with report writing, please seek advice.

There are many benefits of seeking out the lowest cost supplier: the buying department will stay in touch with current price and product trends; a supplier who was previously considered unsuitable may have changed their production methods or materials required in the production of the relevant product, thus reducing the cost of production and the final selling price; lower cost alternatives enable the buying company to keep its own costs down and, if necessary, pass these savings on to their customers.

Drawbacks of buying goods on the basis of a low-price are also numerous: a lower price may be the result of inferior materials employed in the manufacturing process, or of inexperienced staff. Changing suppliers for the sake of price may result in the company changing production methods and product specifications. Where a product has a particular quality standard, such as BS5750 or ISO9000, the adherence to these standards may be in danger. Similarly, if the company's own customers expect a particular component or material, and have had their own standards approved, a change of component or raw material may jeopardise the quality of the customer's products.

Most Japanese car manufacturers, for example, when buying raw material or components for their cars, insist on visiting, not only their suppliers, but also the suppliers of suppliers, to ensure satisfactory products and production techniques.

Review Activity 2

Some of the shopper types and potential strategies to attract these are outlined below:

HARRIED HURRIER
This type of shopper requires services from the supermarket that go beyond those usually accompanying the purchase of goods. A crèche for small children, parking spaces that are wide enough to cope with pushchairs and/or wide trolleys, as well as sweet-free zones and possibly 'family' check-out counters, may all prove popular. Packing services, too, would assist this type of shopper to complete the shopping trip quickly.

Magazines aimed at women may be a suitable medium for advertising this enhanced service, as may be the radio or national TV, with the time of broadcasting coinciding with popular viewing times for this type of shopper.

YOUNG AT HEART

This customer group may be attracted by special events or themed-product weeks, at which they can taste or experience unfamiliar products or brands. Supermarkets could schedule these events at off-peak times. Coffee shops offering a suitable menu which facilitates trials of dishes for sale in the supermarket could also be considered. These facilities could be promoted together with other incentives (such as over-50s discounts at certain times or days) in the local press.

YOUNG AFFLUENT AND BUSY

The supermarkets may consider offering snack meals or convenience food in a section that is separate from the main shopping area, allowing these shoppers to make their purchases quickly. Premium prices could be charged for this service, which may be promoted on national television. (Most multiple retailers do advertise on this medium.) Time-limited parking slots near to the 'quick-food' section may also make the shopping trip less stressful for this type of customer.

The detailed behaviour and motives of all these customer groups would need to be researched carefully to ascertain the most important motivating factors that would attract them to the store.

Review Activity 3

You may have struggled with these questions partly because in order to deliver the central service, the raising and distribution of money through the vehicle of a Live Aid concert, you may have to consider a whole range of other services. Just staging the concert would require the services of a venue, performers, security, catering, media channels to broadcast the concert and many more. In addition to the service product – the concert – there may be other physical products to consider: CDs or tapes of the concert and memorabilia such as T-shirts.

Customers are also two-fold. On the one hand everyone visiting or viewing the concert or donating toward the cause could be considered a customer, but the recipients of the funds, too, are customers or clients. The question as to the position of the ancillary service providers may also be raised. Are they suppliers? If they give their services free of charge in return for a mention at the end of the program, are they then not also customers using your concert as a vehicle for promotion?

The concert event will be the delivery process, but if it is broadcast, then TV channels will be used for delivering the product, free of charge, to home viewers. Delivery of merchandise items may be through retailers, perhaps jointly with other charities that own retail outlets, or by direct mail. A third delivery issue is the transfer of funds or donations. This may require the services of financial institutions. Finally, the aid products will need to be delivered to the recipients of the cause, providing a further delivery issue.

All conventional channels of promotion may be used by the organisers, funds or donation of air-time or advertising space permitting. But promotion may also be in the shape of street collections (which then makes it difficult to distinguish the promotion from the actual product!), sponsorship and other public relations support for the cause.

Pricing the service may be at different levels. The concert tickets and merchandise need to be priced in such a way that they reflect the one-off experience and utility gained by the spectators, but no price can be fixed for donations. Neither can a price be charged to home viewers who therefore can experience the service free of charge.

Unit Review Activity

Likely new markets that the company may wish to approach are government organisations, as well as organisations such as the health service, which may require additives to the product, such as sterilising fluid. The product could also be offered to multiple retailers for branding under their names. Provided the Bettasoap brand continues to be sold by the multiples, this would ensure considerable shelf space for the company. Targeting large hotel chains that provide customers with conveniently sized soap products would also be a viable option for the company.

The buying behaviour of corporate buyers will have to be researched carefully. When the product is offered free to the customer (in wash rooms for instance) the cost and convenience of supply may be extremely important. However, when the product is offered as part of the corporate image, such as hotels, packaging and the quality of scent and ingredients used may be essential. When it is offered as a fast moving consumer product, issues such as reliability of supplies, potential selling price and profit margins are some of the major factors to be considered. Research may need to be conducted among consumers purchasing the current, Bettasoap, brand to find out their reasons for purchasing this brand and their likely switching behaviour, should the company offer the same product under the brand name of a multiple retailer.

The advantage of producing the product for other organisations would be a reduction in promotional cost. This would enable the company to reduce the price sufficiently to offer it at the often significantly lower price required by multiple retailers and other customers who may use the product to facilitate the operation of their business.

Relationship marketing and the possibility of entering into a strategic alliance with manufacturer of dispensers are relevant. It may be possible to share the marketing cost of gaining access to new markets, distribution costs and promotion, as well as offering customers a superior product and service.

UNIT 4

MARKET SEGMENTATION

Introduction

It was Henry Ford who was described as both the world's best and the world's worst marketer. The design development and launch of the black Ford Model T was classic marketing. Henry Ford identified a need for an automobile that, whilst a luxury, should be affordable. The development of mass-production techniques to produce the car was a planned strategy to enable the Model T to be marketed at an affordable price for the mass market. Ford became the dominant car producer in a matter of years, in an apparently unassailable market position.

Whilst Henry Ford's entrepreneurial vision should be applauded, his subsequent product strategy misfired! Consumers could own a Ford T as long as they wanted it in black in the only available model. Whilst undoubtedly a quality car, the Model T did not meet all the needs of the market. Chevrolet recognised this opportunity and developed a product range that offered the consumer choice and the opportunity to upgrade the model. The identification of unmet market needs enabled Chevrolet to penetrate into and subsequently dominate the American automobile market. Chevrolet succeeded where Ford failed by analysing and segmenting its market and developing products that more closely met individual consumer needs.

The case history of the Model T offers us the opportunity to understand the importance of meeting consumer needs. More importantly, it introduces you to some of the marketing terminology that will be introduced in this unit.

ACTIVITY 1

Write down what you think the following words mean:

● market

● needs

● mass production

● product range

● strategy

● market segment

● targeting.

How close are your answers to the following short definitions?

Market	– The set of actual or potential buyers of a product/service.
Needs	– The complex physical and psychological requirements of an individual.
Mass production	– The organisation of resources to enable large-scale production of standardised products that benefit from economies of scale and therefore lower unit costs.
Product range	– The supply of product items within a specific category that offers the customer a choice of specifications.
Marketing strategy	– The analysis, planning, implementation and control of marketing actions.
Market segmentation	– The subdivision of a total market into groups of people with similar needs.
Targeting	– The evaluation and selection of specific customer groups within market segments. A specific 'marketing mix' will be developed for each segment targeted.

We will return to the car market later on and apply the above terminology throughout this unit.

The process of market segmentation, targeting and position, is outlined opposite in Figure 1. Stages I and II of the process involve gathering and analysing market data to identify possible market segments. From this data a range of possible market segments is identified which then requires further detailed analysis and planning. These market segments are evaluated to determine which are worth targeting in terms of commercial viability, and potential growth. The selected segments will represent the target market that the organisation wishes to reach, and the marketer moves on to Stage III. The product's position in the market is determined and appropriate marketing strategies developed and implemented.

Each of the three main stages and the steps within them will be described and discussed in the course of this unit.

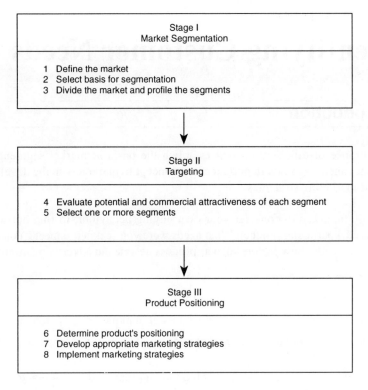

Figure 1 The three-stage model of market segmentation, targeting and positioning

Objectives

By the end of this unit you should be able to:

- identify the benefits to the marketer of segmenting the market
- identify the consumer demand category represented by a specific market
- select the most appropriate method of market segmentation in a specific case
- analyse the market segmentation strategy adopted by a specific organisation
- draft a market segmentation plan for a specific product
- identify market segments in an industrial context
- assess the attractiveness to the marketer of a specific market segment
- identify the targeting strategy being used by a specific marketer
- identify ways in which products have been differentiated and positioned in the minds of target customers.

SECTION 1

Identifying Customer Needs

Introduction

The purpose of this section is to establish the basis of market segmentation – customer needs – and its importance as a concept to marketers in the development of their marketing strategies.

You will be asked to consider your own buying behaviour, to find out why you purchased a particular product. What needs were you seeking to meet? You are also asked to consider how factors such as product design and advertising might appeal to you.

The aim of this section is to help you to:

- appreciate the importance of the concept of market segmentation
- begin to understand how market segmentation works in terms of your own specific needs
- identify the different demand categories represented by the markets for specific products.

1.1 Why is market segmentation necessary?

The very essence of the marketing concept itself leads us to the need to segment markets. All definitions of marketing have at their core the identification and meeting of customer needs – which in itself is the key factor that lies at the heart of market segmentation.

Whilst it is possible to manufacture products or provide services to meet individual needs this, for most organisations, is currently not profitable or possible. Such customisation is available but generally only for premium-priced, specialist products and services. Equally, the notion that a market does not need to be segmented and that one standardised product will suffice for all, is within a short time-span doomed to failure.

ACTIVITY 2

Can you identify any products for which people have an identical need?

Do the following examples fit the bill?
        Toilet paper
        Water
        Education

At first glance, customers' needs for these products might appear similar. When looked at in more detail, however, the range of needs these products might satisfy is actually quite wide. All markets can be broken down into identifiable groups of **primary** and **secondary** needs. Some markets are more homogeneous than others, but even in these markets a range of needs can be identified that offer opportunities for market segmentation. For any market, consider the multitude of brands that are now available. Each brand is targeted at a specific market segment. The following analysis of the toilet paper market is based on the advertising and packaging of each brand.

Product	Primary needs	Secondary needs	Brands
Toilet paper	Cleanliness	Emotional	Andrex
		Value-for-money	Dixcel
		Environmental	Nouvelle
		Comfort	Kleenex

All toilet paper brands satisfy the primary need of cleanliness. Manufacturers therefore need to identify underlying needs that can be targeted.

Even water comes in many different forms and fulfils a range of needs:

Tap water	Primary needs	Secondary needs
	Refreshment	Health
	Cleanliness	Low cost

Bottled water	Primary needs	Secondary needs
(still/carbonated)	Health-giving properties	Social status
	Fear of tap water	
	Drink/refreshment	

While tap water and bottled water satisfy the same primary need of refreshment, many other underlying needs can be identified. For instance, a primary need for bottled water is purity of water. Bottled water is positioned to meet this need. However, brands of bottled water can also meet needs for social esteem and belonging. Manufacturers will target market segments at the secondary need level in order to differentiate their product from the competition.

Education, is also a fragmented market. Although the majority of children go to state schools (within which there is a hierarchy of desirability), the parents of a significant number elect to pay for their children's education and make their purchasing decision on the basis of a whole range of needs – some central to the concept of education, others not.

Education	Primary needs	Secondary needs
(state, private,	Knowledge	Self-esteem
public school,	Job prospects	Professional status
Montessori,	Security	Social ranking
Steiner etc)	Location	

Different individuals have varying interests, tastes, aspirations, and characteristics and it is unlikely that one single product will satisfy all needs. This provides the rationale for market segmentation. Individuals with similar specific needs are likely to exhibit similar purchasing behaviour or motives that can be targeted. It is through the process of identifying different consumer needs and grouping these together that market segments are identified. From this information, marketers can develop specific products and services that closely match consumers' needs. Increasingly, marketers in both consumer and industrial markets are recognising the need to segment the markets in which they are operating. Marketers can then decide which segments to target.

ACTIVITY 3

When you next visit a supermarket, note down the different brands of bottled water. Look at their packaging and price. Consider who the brand is targeting. Is it you? If not, why not? What brand do you purchase and why?

By analysing your own buying behaviour you can often work out what particular need of yours the product is meeting. Why do other products not appeal to you in the same way?

Products are designed to appeal to different sets of needs. The advertising that communicates the brand to you is designed to appeal to those needs. You form part of a market segment that is being specifically targeted. The product will be positioned in that market to appeal to you. Remember that the process of market segmentation targeting and positioning begins with the identification of people/organisations with similar needs.

Two major benefits accrue from the process of segmenting markets.

1   Customer needs can be met more effectively.

2   New market opportunities can be identified.

We will look in more detail at the benefits of market segmentation later. It is appropriate at this stage to look at the stages involved in developing the market segmentation process.

1.2 The process of market segmentation

The following are definitions of market segmentation.

> Market segmentation is the subdividing of a market into distinct and increasingly homogeneous subgroups of customers, where any subgroup can conceivably be selected as a target to be met with a distinct marketing mix. The danger of thinking in terms of a single mass homogeneous market has been recognised. Market segmentation, as an approach, emerged from the recognition of this danger.
>
> (Cannon, 1980, p82)

> Market segmentation is the subdividing of a market into distinct subsets of customers, where any subset may conceivably be selected as a target market to be reached with a distinct marketing mix.
>
> (Kotler, 1995, p286)

DEFINING THE MARKET
The total market for a product or service consists of all the people and/or organisations who desire or potentially desire it, have the resources to buy and are willing and able to buy. It is necessary, therefore, to determine the nature of the market in terms of its size and pattern of demand.

The potential automobile market can be defined as the potential number of people who are 17+ years old, have the disposable income to afford the purchase of a new car and are able to drive.

Analysis of a market will reveal a range of possible patterns of needs (see Figure 2). These have been termed 'alternative demand categories'. The analysis of these demand categories will determine the extent to which a market can be segmented. **Homogeneous demand** suggests that all consumers in a market have similar needs and wants. The danger in accepting this outcome is that more detailed market analysis may identify previously unseen clusters (segments). **Diffused demand** suggests the need for customisation. This trend can increasingly be seen in markets today and new technology is making it possible for traditional mass-marketed products to be customised. **Clustered demand** recognises that market segments exist which represent groups of consumers with similar needs. As will be seen in this unit, these clusters can be identified from a wide range of possible market-segmentation criteria.

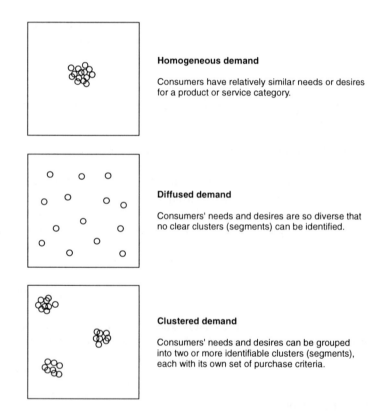

Homogeneous demand

Consumers have relatively similar needs or desires for a product or service category.

Diffused demand

Consumers' needs and desires are so diverse that no clear clusters (segments) can be identified.

Clustered demand

Consumers' needs and desires can be grouped into two or more identifiable clusters (segments), each with its own set of purchase criteria.

Figure 2: Alternative consumer demand categories (Evans & Berman, 1992)

ACTIVITY 4

Using your knowledge of the following markets, and with reference to Figure 2 above, identify the most appropriate demand category for the following.

1 The car market ....

2 Cosmetics market ....

3 Overnight delivery market ....

The car market is relatively clustered, with a range of market segments identifiable, each with its own purchasing criteria, ie safety, comfort, family, sporty etc.

The cosmetics market is fairly diffuse, particularly in the case of lipsticks and nail polish. No clear market segments are identifiable. Manufacturers supply hundreds of colours and shades of lipstick and nail polish to ensure that customers' varying needs can be met.

The overnight delivery market is relatively homogeneous. Most customers require speed, reliability and reasonable prices.

From this analysis of demand category, possible bases for market segmentation can be developed.

SELECTING THE BASES FOR SEGMENTATION

Various methods of consumer and industrial market segmentation are outlined in Sections 2 and 3 of this unit. These fall into broad categories: demographic, socio-economic, psychographic/behavioural and geodemographic.

Identification of market segments may be based on detailed market research, or on basic analysis of customer data held within an organisation. Many organisations hold customer records detailing information such as age and gender. In the early 1980s Harrods analysed the information it held on its credit card holders. Prior to this analysis it believed its core target market was from higher socio-economic groups (A/Bs). In fact, it found that over 70% of its customers were middle class (C1/C2) or tourists visiting the store. Their main reason for shopping at Harrods was to fulfil aspirational needs.

It is possible to overlay various market segmentation techniques and thus define the target market extremely narrowly. There is danger in over segmenting, however, in that you may end up with too small a market to support your product!

DIVIDING THE MARKET AND PROFILING THE SEGMENTS

The process of dividing the market into identifiable market segments is carried out from any research data that has been gathered. Initially, demographic and socio-economic variables might be used and then psychographic, behavioural and geodemographic variables overlaid. This can be reversed, depending upon the nature of the market being investigated.

The information obtained will give details as to the nature of the market segment. This is called the segment profile. This will result in groups of people with similar characteristics being aggregated and separated from those with different characteristics.

The next section will be devoted to looking in detail at the various bases for segmenting consumer and industrial markets. This will show how markets are divided and market segment profiles developed.

REVIEW ACTIVITY 1

Consider the market needs of school leavers who are thinking of going to university to study a business degree.

1 What do you consider is the appropriate demand category in this market?

2 On what basis have you made this decision?

(A possible answer to this activity is given at the end of the unit.)

Summary

This section has looked at the importance of using customer needs as a starting point when defining a target market. It has introduced the three steps involved in market segmentation and laid the foundations for the more detailed description of segmentation techniques in the next section.

SECTION 2

Consumer Market Segmentation

Introduction

Market segmentation techniques are becoming increasingly sophisticated. This has led to a more detailed understanding of consumer buying behaviour and the improved targeting of messages and products/services.

This section describes the main techniques of consumer market segmentation. The principle behind each technique is outlined and activities enable you to explore them in further detail. The advantages and disadvantages of each technique will be explained in order to demonstrate how and when specific techniques might be used.

Two sectors will be outlined:

● consumer market segmentation

● industrial market segmentation.

Within these two sectors a range of techniques is used.

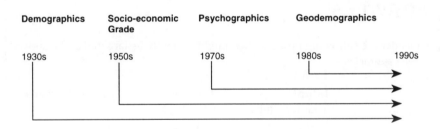

Figure 3: Evolution of consumer market segmentation

Figure 3 shows the evolution of the broad techniques of market segmentation now used by marketers. All of these techniques are currently used, as illustrated by the arrows. Within each technique a range of market segmentation criteria is applied.

This section aims to help you to:

● understand the basis of the main segmentation techniques

● assess the advantages and limitations of each technique

● apply segmentation techniques to a specific market.

2.1 Demographics

The term demographics refers to the analysis of population profiles. Populations are traditionally broken down by age and gender. Further demographic segmentation is possible by looking at marital status and ethnicity. Demographic data makes a significant contribution to the marketing analysis conducted by organisations. The information is easily attainable and it provides a useful basis upon which further market segmentation variables can be added. Bingo clubs and discos often target specific age groups, for example, and will offer entertainment designed to appeal to these groups.

Government statistics provide information on the UK population broken down demographically. It is also relatively easy to obtain. When conducting surveys age, gender and ethnicity are among the simplest categories to identify.

Segmenting markets demographically appeals intuitively to the marketer. Consider the following segments:

- infants
- teenagers
- senior citizens.

Each of these represents distinct market segments comprised of consumers with broadly similar sets of needs. We would not expect the needs of teenagers to be the same as those of senior citizens.

ACTIVITY 5

Consider the following products that might typically be targeted at the above three categories

	Infant	**Teenagers**	**Senior Citizens**
Holidays	Toddler Clubs	Club 18-30	Saga
Toys	Postman Pat	Nintendo	–
Computers	Junior Alphabet	Apple/PC	–
Magazines	Comics	*Just 17*	*Young at Heart*
Food	Baby Foods	Beefburgers	Health Foods

1 Do you think that segmenting markets by age is a satisfactory means of closely targeting audiences?

2 What disadvantages are there in this method?

3 Does the same criticism apply to ethnicity?

To reinforce this point consider the question: 'Do all people over 65 years of age desire to buy Des O'Connor records'? It is obviously unlikely that *all* people over 65 years of age would want to do so, but on the assumption that the records he produces are appropriate to this age group, we can assume that *a proportion* of those over 65 years old may enjoy Des O'Connor and purchase his records.

The problem with using broad demographic criteria is that it ignores fundamental differences within each age bracket. All people over 65 years of age do not have the same needs, attitudes, characteristics and motives. Whilst it is true to say that such music appeals mostly to this age group, other factors will be influencing the decision to purchase, not just age.

LIFE STAGES

Demographics can be made more effective if further criteria are applied, such as the stage of life that a person has reached and the circumstances in which they live.

Some life stages are outlined below. They are based on people's household and marital status. At each stage it can be reasonably assumed that different motives and attitudes will be exhibited because of the environment that a person is living in.

Bachelor/Single Woman

Young/Single
Living with parents/away from home

Not married – 25/45
Not married – 45+

Newly marrieds – young, no children

Full nest 1 – Youngest child < 5
Full nest 2 – Youngest child > 5

Full nest 3 – Older couples – dependent children

Empty nest 1 – Older couple – working, no children at home

Empty nest 2 – Older couple – retired, no children at home

Solitary survivor 1 – working
Solitary survivor 2 – not working

Divorced – 21/35
Divorced – 35+

Further categories can be added to this list. The life stages are selected by establishing market segmentation criteria that are appropriate to the product being offered. For instance, older singles and married couples with no children could be included as additional categories, if it was thought relevant. If a particular life stage represents an identifiable group of similar needs then it represents a potential market segment.

ACTIVITY 6

1 Spend a few minutes thinking of a four or five examples of products (product ranges, or services) that are likely to appeal to a single life stage exclusively.

2 Think of a four or five examples of products (product ranges, or services) that will appeal to a range of life stages.

3 What do you consider are the benefits of 'life stages' as a method of market segmentation, compared with demographic criteria such as age, gender or ethnicity?

It is likely that the following products and services will appeal to specific life stages:

Club 18/30 holidays	Young single
Singles clubs	Not married 25/45+
Saga holidays	Empty nest 2
Camping holidays	Full nest
Baby/children's clothing	Full nest 1

The following products, however, have a slightly wider, appeal:

Discos/Bingo clubs	Young single/Divorced
	Empty nest 1, solitary survivor
DIY	All
Computers	Full nest 2 & 3
Computer games	Full nest 2 & 3
Eating out	Young single/not married/full nest 3
	Empty nests
Life assurance	Newly married/Full nest 3/Empty nest 1

The key benefits that can be identified for life stages as a market segmentation technique are that it relates purchase behaviour to current circumstance, and that it does not assume that age brackets determine behaviour. It recognises changes over time due to family circumstances, and has some empirical research support. It is used, by Granada television amongst others, in audience research profiles.

Life stages does offer a slightly more sophisticated approach to demographic market segmentation than standard demographic data. The major criticism is that in assuming that all people within each life stage have the same or similar needs, this technique still represents a broad-brush approach to the breaking down of markets into distinct groups of needs.

2.2 Socio-economic grade

The social class of a person is likely to influence buying behaviour. While it is difficult to define social class because of the number of factors involved (income, education, status etc), nevertheless it is one of the most commonly used methods of segmenting consumer markets. The National Readership Survey (NRS) scale, based upon the occupation of the main wage-earner of the household, uses the following classification.

Grade	Social Classification	Occupation
A	Upper Middle Class	Higher managerial, professional or administrative jobs
B	Middle Class	Middle managerial, professional or administrative jobs
C1	Lower middle class	Supervisory or clerical jobs. Junior management
C2	Skilled working class	Skilled manual workers
D	Working class	Unskilled and semi-skilled manual workers
E	Subsistence level	Pensioners, unemployed, casual or low grade workers

ACTIVITY 7

1 List three different products or services that you believe can be effectively segmented by socio-economic grade, and indicate the grade that you feel is most appropriate to each of them.

2 What do you consider are the major disadvantages of this classification?

An enormous number of products can be classified in this way, but perhaps the most obvious are the following:

Newspapers/magazines	*Sun/Mirror* C2/D/E
	Daily Telegraph B/C1
	The Times A/B
Cars	Ford Fiesta C2/D1
	BMW B1/C1
	Mercedes A/B
Fashion Clothes	Multiple chain stores C2/D/E
	(Top Shop, Tammies, Primark)
	Design Boutiques B/C1
	Gautier/Dior A

There are several major disadvantages to this method, however. It divides the population into six large groups and therefore lacks precision. It is often difficult to identify significant differences in behaviour between adjacent classifications. The classification is based only on the occupation of the head of the household and does not, therefore, reflect the income of the whole family. Discretionary disposable income is not consistent within each category. It does not reflect the lifestyles/aspirations of individuals.

The socio-economic grade developed by NRS is extensively used, particularly in the field of advertising. Target Group Index, a market research organisation that supplies data to the advertising industry, classifies individuals by socio-economic grade and age and links this to heavy and light usage of a product. It is felt that, despite the limitations outlined above, socio-economic grade does provide marketers with sufficient information to discriminate between different market segments. For products that are suited to mass markets, such grading is probably applicable, even if relatively unsophisticated. The major advantage is in the data's availability and simplicity of use. In the 1980s and early 1990s, however, there has been a growing trend of dissatisfaction by users of this data. This has been caused by a need for more focused and targeted marketing, an increasing fragmentation of market needs, and the availability of new technology that can manage more complex data.

	Heavy Users				Light Users			
	A	B	C	D	A	B	C	D
		%	%			%	%	
	'000	down	across	index	'000	down	across	index
ALL WOMEN	2462	100.0	10.7	100	3790	100.0	16.4	100
15–19	439	17.8	19.7	185	449	11.9	20.2	123
20–24	522	21.2	24.8	233	492	13.0	23.4	142
25–34	447	18.1	11.9	111	782	20.6	20.8	126
35–44	313	12.7	8.5	80	524	13.8	14.3	87
45–54	224	9.1	7.4	69	285	7.5	9.4	57
55–64	245	10.0	7.8	73	319	8.4	10.1	61
65+	272	11.1	5.3	50	939	24.8	18.4	112
AB	315	12.8	8.0	75	742	19.6	18.8	114
C1	553	22.5	10.3	96	919	24.3	17.1	104
C2	707	28.7	12.2	115	955	25.2	16.5	100
D	525	21.3	13.0	121	545	14.4	13.4	82
E	361	14.7	9.2	87	628	16.6	16.1	98
H/D Income £20,000 or more	126	5.1	9.9	93	239	6.3	18.8	114
£15,000 – £19,999	189	7.7	11.6	108	336	8.9	20.5	125
£11,000 – £14,999	239	9.7	9.8	92	467	12.3	19.3	117
£9,000 – £10,999	239	9.7	12.3	115	311	8.2	16.0	97
£7,000 – £8,999	184	7.5	9.9	93	274	7.2	14.7	89
£5,000 – £6,999	204	8.3	10.1	94	340	9.0	16.7	102
£4,999 or less	614	24.9	10.3	96	950	25.1	15.9	97
Not stated	666	27.1	11.3	106	873	23.0	14.8	90

Figure 4: TGI data

A further development of the life-stages socio-economic grade model is SAGACITY, developed by Research Services Ltd (Wilson *et al,* 1994, p204). This model combines life stages with income and social class, as shown in Figure 5 below.

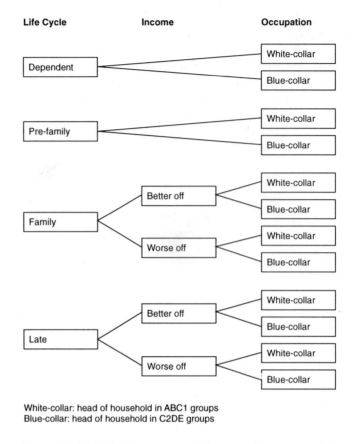

White-collar: head of household in ABC1 groups
Blue-collar: head of household in C2DE groups

Figure 5: SAGACITY (Wilson, Gilligan and Pearson, 1994)

This segmentation method recognises that social class and income will influence individual behaviour. The major problem with this technique is the progressive and continued blurring of the boundaries that differentiate blue-collar from white-collar workers. This blurring is caused by changing economic and social circumstances and individual aspirations. The assumption that income is a relevant influence on purchase behaviour can also be questioned. Other factors, such as lifestyle and situation will have an impact on, and influence, buying behaviour more than income. It is possible that high-income families may have high debt burdens and therefore less disposable income than a person earning a moderate income.

ACTIVITY 8

1 Summarise the major forms of demographic segmentation techniques in the space provided below and list the advantages and disadvantages of each.

2 Compare your answers with the descriptions of the techniques outlined so far in this section. How did you do?

2.3 Psychographics

As can be seen from the above, the traditional forms of market segmentation all have their limitations. The data, whilst of some use, lack the precision and depth required to gain a detailed understanding of market needs. In response to this, more sophisticated methods of market segmentation have been developed. Psychographics attempts to classify individuals by their personality, attitudes and lifestyle.

To obtain psychographic data it is necessary to conduct detailed research into the behaviour of the consumer. The research is often conducted with individuals or in focus groups and an attempt is made to classify individuals on the basis of statements they make about themselves or on how they perceive a product.

Guinness used psychographic data to understand better the Guinness drinker. They asked respondents to draw pictures of how they perceived Guinness. From these diagrams the company was able to analyse what it was that consumers looked for in the drink. Consumers saw the brand as rich and warm, dark on the outside but refreshing on the inside. The advertising that developed from this research led to Rutger Hauer being used to personify a pint of Guinness.

Guinness drinkers emerged from this study as individualists who also liked to be part of a crowd. From this psychographic survey an advertising campaign was developed using a character dressed in black and white to personify the Guinness drinker. This was targeted at a new market of young drinker, but designed not to alienate the traditional older Guinness drinker.

SEGMENTATION ACCORDING TO LIFESTYLE

The major growth in psychographics has come from market segmentation according to lifestyle.

> The concept of lifestyle refers to the distinctive characteristic ways of living adopted by certain communities. It relates to the general attitudes and behaviour towards the allocation of time, money and effort in pursuit of objectives considered desirable by particular types of individuals. (Chisnall 1985).

Examples of lifestyle market segmentation are given below. The technique recognises that consumer behaviour is determined by the way we live our lives. It arises from a complex relationship between our aspirations, current situation, perception of self, income and attitudes. Marketers cluster individuals into groups of people with similar lifestyles. They then identify the most effective media to reach them.

The lifestyle categories used are derived from market research. Most commonly they will derive from an analysis of attitude statements.

'I agree with equality'
'I am proud to be a man/woman'
'I enjoy gardening'
'I prefer being at work than home'
'I enjoy fast foods'
etc

Levi Strauss considered extending its brand into casual clothes and suits. Extensive market research was carried out and four lifestyle categories were identified as

- Classic Independent
- Mainstream Traditionalist
- Price Shopper
- Trendy Casual.

Each segment represented a significant share of the men's clothing market. Levi identified from its research that the 'classic independent' segment represented a potential market opportunity. No competitor directly targeted this market segment. The research identified some clearly defined needs. Individuals had a strong liking for wool clothes, enjoyed shopping on their own and were willing to pay that little bit more if it meant they got a tailored suit. However, individuals in this segment strongly indicated that they would not buy a suit if it had the Levi brand name. Levi's subsequent marketing strategy unfortunately ignored this last factor and the launch of the new product was unsuccessful.

Lifestyle represents a powerful indicator of how we behave and what we buy. It relies, however, on fairly complex data-gathering techniques. Lifestyle data is now heavily used by advertising agencies and major FMCG manufacturers and retailers.

Two lifestyle analyses are shown in figures 6 and 7. These were based on empirical attitude research. The two agencies that constructed them used the lifestyle data to advise their clients on how best to design and position existing and new products at target segments made up of people with similar lifestyle characteristics.

Can you see yourself or someone you know in one of these lifestyle categories?

No? Never mind. There are hundreds more classifications that exist that classify people by lifestyle. There is no escape from being categorised!

Man	Woman
Avant Guardians. Concerned with change and well-being of others rather than possessions. Well educated, prone to self-righteousness.	**Avant Guardians.** 'Liberal left' opinions, trendy attitudes. But out-going, active, sociable.
Pontificators. Strongly held, traditional opinions. Very British, and concerned about keeping others on the right path.	**Lady Righteous.** Traditional, 'right-minded' opinions. Happy, complacent, with strong family orientation.
Chameleons. Want to be contemporary to win approval. Act like barometers of social change, but copiers not leaders.	**Hopeful Seekers.** Need to be liked, want to do 'right'. Like new things, want to be trendy.
Self-admirers. At the young end of the spectrum. Intolerant of others and strongly motivated by success and concerned about self-image.	**Lively Ladies.** Younger than above, sensual, materialistic, ambitious and competitive.
Self-exploiters. The 'doers' and the 'self-starters', competitive but always under pressure and often pessimistic. Possessions are important.	**New Unromantics.** Generally young and single, adopting a hard-headed and unsentimental approach to life. Independent, self-centred.
Token Triers. Always willing to try new things to 'improve their luck', but apparently on a permanent try-and-fail cycle. Includes an above average proportion of unemployed.	**Lack-a-daisy.** Unassertive and easy going. Try to cope but often fail. Not very interested in the new.
Sleepwalkers. Contented under-achievers. Do not care about most things, and actively opt out. Traditional macho views.	**Blinkered.** Negative, do not want to be disturbed. Uninterested in conventional success – in fact, few interests except TV and radio.
Passive Endurers. Often economically and socially disenfranchised. Expect little of life, and give little.	**Down-trodden.** This group is shy, introverted, but put-upon. Would like to do better. Often unhappy and pressurised in personal relationships.

Figure 6: Lifestlye analysis developed by McCann-Erikson

Self-explorers. Motivated by self-expression and self-realisation. Less materialistic than other groups, and showing high tolerance levels.	**Conspicuous Consumers.** They are materialistic and pushy, motivated by acquisition, competition, and getting ahead. Pro-authority, law and order.
Social Resistors. The caring group, concerned with fairness and social values, but often appearing intolerant and moralistic.	**Belongers.** What they seek is a quiet undisturbed family life. They are conservative, conventional rule followers.
Experimentalists. Highly individualistic, motivated by fast-moving enjoyment. They are materialistic, pro-technology but anti traditional authority.	**Aimless.** Comprises two groups: (a) the young unemployed, who are often anti-authority, and (b) the old, whose motivation is day-to-day existence.

Figure 7: Lifestyle analysis developed by Taylor Nelson

ACTIVITY 9

1 Try and identify yourself in one or both of the lifestyle analyses. (If you can't, devise a category into which you would fit, but remember that to be of use to the marketer it has to be broad enough to encompass a group of people, and not just you as an individual.)

2 Consider how the characteristics given under 'your' category might affect your purchasing behaviour. Give an example of a recent purchase you have made that reflects your lifestyle.

If you find this activity quite difficult, don't worry. Lifestyle classifications involve fairly sophisticated research methods and your difficulties simply reflect this.

Consider the following examples. Young and Rubicam, a large London advertising agency, developed four lifestyle categories based upon extensive market research. Specific advertising campaigns were targeted at these lifestyle categories.

Mainstreamers	Buy British. Conservative. Shop at Debenhams and Marks & Spencers. Buy mainstream branded products.
Advert	Legal and General – bright umbrella adverts, symbolising friendliness, reliability and security.
Achievers	Buy status symbols. Motivated by money. Enjoy showing off their possessions. Like the good things in life.
Advert	Gold Credit Card
Succeeders	Like to be in control. Prefer not to advertise their wealth. Tend to be at the top of their profession. Motivated by security and comfort.
Advert	British Airways' 'Club Class'
Reformers	The most educated of the groups. Environmentally aware. Heavily involved in local community. Are not motivated by wealth or possessions. Tendency to buy own label products.
Advert	*Guardian* newspaper – A picture seen from one angle leaves one impression. From another angle it leaves a different impression. It is not until you get the whole picture that you see events for what they really are.

Lifestyle market segmentation offers a detailed view of buyers because it encompasses numerous characteristics related to their activities, interests and opinions. It goes beyond personality and enables marketers to understand some of the underlying motives that determine behaviour.

ACTIVITY 10

Read the following extract about the Target Group Index. Identify the types of information contained in it that would be useful to a marketer. Geoff Wicken, marketing director of BMRB International, explains how his TGI classification breaks the 'Grey', 'Third Age' or 'Gold' market down into five lifestyle groups – each with their own distinct patterns of media consumption.

TGI BREAKS DOWN THE MARKET

BMRB is about to launch a more detailed TGI Gold study into the key product and media consumption in this age group, due for publication by August of this year. In the meantime, here is a TGI view on our elders and betters. This may allow specialist titles such as *Sage, Yours* and *Choice* to be surveyed.

The **Thrifty Traditionals** are 17% of the age group. They are not well off, budget for every last penny, have trouble saving, prefer paying by cash, and are most likely to read down-market tabloids, listen to local radio, and be heavy TV viewers.

Outgoing Fun-lovers make up a further 20%. They are magazine orientated, reading titles such as *BBC Holidays, Country Homes* and *High Life,* and enjoy newspapers like *Today,* the *Star,* the *Mail on Sunday.* They love travelling, entertaining people at home, and eating out. They are above-average viewers of TV, as are most people in the age group, but look forward to an increasing number of TV channels.

Astute Cosmopolitans account for 18%. These are the ones with most money, and far more likely to read the *FT, Guardian, Independent* and other broadsheets. Magazines such as *Golf Monthly, Country Living* and *Moneywise* get a look in here. Astute Cosmopolitans find it easy to save and invest, and like spending money on foreign holidays, foreign food and restaurants. They are the only section of the grey market who are light TV viewers.

Apathetic Spenders are nearly 22% of the group. They are similar to Thrifty Traditionals, but more likely to take on debt through credit cards, do not enjoy planning foreign holidays or entertaining at home. *The Sun, News of the World* and the *Mirror* are favoured newspapers here.

> **Temperate Xenophobes** are the final 21%. They most definitely do not like travelling abroad or eating foreign food, are heavy TV users, love the *Radio Times* and *Reader's Digest,* the *Mail* and *Express,* and, curiously, given their unease with foreign travel, *National Geographic.*
>
> *(Marketing,* 19 January 1994, p30)

A range of useful information is contained in this extract on the following topics:

- income
- payment preferences
- reading habits/viewing habits
- hobbies
- products consumption
- home life
- attitudes
- interests
- thriftiness.

Such information can be extremely valuable to a marketer, in helping to determine the appropriate positioning of a product in the market and in developing an appropriate market strategy. In identifying the media that these individuals listen to, read or watch, the information allowing the marketers to target the consumers effectively.

This technique does have its limitations, however.

ACTIVITY 11

Write down four possible limitations of lifestyle segmentation.

Data is hard to collect, as it relies upon extensive and accurate research methods. And the more detailed the research, the more segments you are likely to uncover. The problem then arises of estimating the size of the segments (the size of the target market). This is particularly difficult to measure. Lifestyle segmentation uses more qualitative data compared with, say, demographic techniques, which are more quantifiable.

Added to this, the relationship between a lifestyle segment and purchasing behaviour is not always clear. Nor is it always possible to identify a method of reaching a particular segment if no particular media or store dominates their lives. Finally, respondents may not always tell the truth in their response to attitude/behaviour surveys, for a number of complex psychological reasons.

It is the job of market researchers to overcome these problems and they are always in the process of determining new and more sophisticated techniques.

2.4 Benefits sought

This technique for segmenting consumer markets considers the *motive* for a purchase. It groups consumers according to the specific benefits they seek from a product. (The concept of 'benefit' is discussed more fully in Unit 5, Section 2.1.)

Even when two consumers are buying exactly the same product, the expected benefits may vary. Purchasers of Miller Lite beer may seek the lightness of the drink, or the brand image that goes with the drink. It may simply be bottle size or shape that determines their decision to purchase. Through research it is possible to determine a range of benefits being sought by consumers. Marketing decisions can be made to ensure that the product/service meets these needs. Travel Lodge Hotels were launched in the United Kingdom and targeted at the travelling sales executive whose requirements were for comfortable and competitive 'no frills' hotel accommodation. No breakfast facilities or bar are provided. These represent high overhead costs in the running of a hotel. The Travel Lodges are located out of town and next to fast-food outlets. Such a hotel would probably not appeal to a family going on a weekend break, who would require leisure facilities and food to be provided.

'Benefit segmentation' is therefore based on **behavioural processes,** involving thought and action, as opposed to age and socio-economic class, which are defined according to individual characteristics. It closely identifies the customers needs and represents a powerful method of understanding and influencing behaviour. It is now a commonly used method of segmenting markets.

ACTIVITY 12

Consider the primary benefits which the following cars are designed to offer the customer:

- Volvo (all makes)
- Renault Clio
- 4 x 4 Range Rover
- Suzuki Jeep
- Ford Escort XR3I

You may consider that the main benefit offered by the Volvo is safety. Certainly, this is emphasised in much of their advertising. The Renault Clio appeals to people who want a small car to use in town but care about their image. The Range Rover is targeted at two groups of people: those who live in the country and frequently drive 'off-road', and those who live in towns and like other people to think that they frequently drive 'off-road'! It therefore combines the benefit of four-wheel drive with image enhancement. The Suzuki Jeep is targeted at those who like motoring to be fun, and the Ford Escort offers the benefit of good performance.

2.5 Geodemographics

The final consumer market segmentation technique to be described in this unit is geodemographics. This system is based on the proposition that the neighbourhood area in which you live will be reflected in your professional status, income, life stage and behaviour. The neighbourhood types are initially identified using national census data. This data is overlaid with a range of other data, including such items as credit references.

ACORN (A Classification of Residential Neighbourhoods) and MOSAIC are examples of geodemographic systems. In the case of ACORN, some 40 variables, derived from the ten-yearly census, have been analysed and the emerging clusters of households has led to the creation of 39 neighbourhood types. The neighbourhood types are then combined with postcodes to enable marketers to target specific households with mailshots.

It is claimed that these classifications, based on neighbourhood types, are more discriminating than traditional demographics primarily because they are founded on a national census, and not on a sample of the population. When geodemographic data is combined with internal company records and other market research data, such as TGI and lifestyle classification, a fairly powerful tool of market analysis and segmentation is possible.

Neighbourhood types are given names to signify the type of social group they represent. Table 1 below lists 12 generalised descriptions of different types of housing, derived from the more detailed ACORN classifications.

ACORN groups	1981	
	Population	%
A Agricultural areas	1,811,485	3.4
B Modern family housing, higher incomes	8,667,137	16.2
C Older housing of intermediate status	9,420,477	17.6
D Older terraced housing	2,320,846	4.3
E Better-off council estates	6,976,570	13.0
F Less well-off council estates	5,032,657	9.4
G Poorest council estates	4,048,658	7.6
H Multi-racial areas	2,086,026	3.3
I High-status non-family areas	2,248,207	4.2
J Affluent suburban housing	8,514,878	15.9
K Better-off retirement areas	2,041,338	3.8
U Unclassified	388,632	0.7

(*Wilson* et al, 1994, p203).

Table 1: Broad-based ACORN classifications

Many retailers use geodemographics to assist them when deciding to locate a new store. Many companies use existing customer information held on their database to create a profile of their typical customer(s) and then compare this profile to those held by a supplier of geodemographic data in order to find out in which areas their customers are likely to predominate. New possibilities can be identified and targeted with mailings.

ACTIVITY 13

1 Consider your nearest town. Select four contrasting areas and classify them according to the broad classifications given in Table 1 above.

2 Is there a fairly strong similarity between the types of people that live in these neighbourhood areas in terms of age, income, social class, families?

3 Do you think there is a close correlation between the type of housing and the purchase behaviour of the people living in it?

4 Look at the direct mail you receive. Why has this mailing been sent to you? Have your neighbours received the same mailing. Is the product or service being offered relevant to your needs?

Your answer will obviously depend on where you live. The classifications are, however, developed from very rigorous statistical analysis and you should be able to identify neighbourhood types and similarities between the people living in these areas.

Households can be even more precisely defined if additional variables are added, such as age and financial status. Thus geodemographic profiling provides accurate data and a good correlation between type of house and the purchase behaviour of people living in it.

Mailing that arrives through your door may have been targeted at you using geodemographic data. It has been shown that responses to mailings increase on average from 2% to 10% of those mailed using these systems. Irrelevant mail is wasted money for companies. It is expected that improvements in this area will continue as database systems become more sophisticated. The growth in use of geodemographic data has been substantial and can be closely linked to the development of the information technology that is required to use this data. It has been shown to improve the effectiveness of direct mailing and retailers have benefited from the use of such data to identify opportunities for store locations. The system is not expected to achieve a 100% response. The key question is, was the mailing relevant to you?

A number of companies, as well as CACI, offer geodemographic data.

PINPOINT – Pinpoint identifies neighbourhoods. It uses information from a range of sources and overlays this with the Ordnance Survey.

FINPIN   –   Financial Pinpoint combines financial data with census and other data.

While in principle this method of market segmentation offers a tighter classification than earlier examples, a range of limitations has to be considered.

ACTIVITY 14

Briefly describe any limitations you can think of with this system of classification.

The census is only carried out every ten years and the degree of accuracy of the data is therefore likely to diminish over time, as people move house and the character of neighbourhoods changes.

The assumption that households in similar neighbourhood areas will exhibit similar purchase behaviour does not always apply. 'Mixed' neighbourhoods exist, particularly in areas of large, older housing, some of which may have been converted to multi-occupation while the rest is occupied by a single household.

The most powerful data a company holds about its customers is that held on its own internal records. It is possible, with good geodemographics, to profile an existing customer database to identify the key neighbourhood types that purchase a particular product or service. This information can then be compared with UK maps of neighbourhood types and potential new customers targeted who have similar profiles to the existing customer base.

The problem with this technique is that the information may not be as accurate and useful as it appears at face value. Grattans used geodemographic data to identify potential purchasers of a £1000 grandfather clock. They profiled and identified potential customers but only sold a few clocks after the first direct mail shot. They then analysed further the profile of those customers who had purchased, remailed to the new profile and sold all the stock.

It is clear, then, that used intelligently, geodemographic market segmentation offers a sophisticated tool for analysis and targeting. The data, if managed carefully, offers the marketer a relatively accurate profile of target markets.

The techniques of lifestyle analysis and geodemographics can now be combined, using up-to-date information technology. This allows the marketer to develop a more sophisticated understanding of the consumer and enables increased opportunities for more closely targeted marketing.

REVIEW ACTIVITY 2

Read the brief item below about the Lego Company's marketing segmentation, and answer the following question:

1 What do you think was the aim of the Lego company in segmenting the market in this way?

2 What do you think might be the benefits sought by the parents purchasing Lego?

3 Looking back at the ACORN classification, which categories of housing might the Lego company select for a direct mail shot?

(A possible answer is given at the end of the unit.)

LEGO

The Lego building brick is one of the most successful children's toys ever developed. It has achieved its long-term success through a process of protecting its trademark, but more significantly by ensuring that it meets the needs of its markets through the development of new product ranges, and by communicating its core benefits to its target markets.

Lego was established in 1930 and entered the UK market in 1950. Its core product was the small building brick and it was aimed at children aged 4 to 10 years old. It became the market leader in the toy construction sector. New competitive threats emerged, either directly from other toy brick manufacturers or from manufacturers of more advanced construction toys, such as Meccano. Lego began to lose market share. In response to these threats, Lego segmented its markets.

Age	Development of Duplo for younger children. Development of mechanical Lego for older children.
Sex	Construction kits for boys. Fantasy land kits for girls.
Interest groups	Themed kits (ie farms, trains, houses etc)

REVIEW ACTIVITY 3

Spend about 15 minutes segmenting the market for wine in the UK.

Consider   Consumer-related variables
                   Product-related variables
                   Industry/market related variables

(A possible answer is given at the end of the unit.)

Summary

This section has covered in detail the various methods of market segmentation used in consumer markets. While the principles behind the use of market segmentation have essentially remained the same, the methods of segmenting markets have become increasingly sophisticated. Traditional methods are still extensively used in marketing because of their ease of use and the availability of data, but the introduction of more sophisticated behavioural techniques and geodemographic systems has enabled marketers to develop an increased understanding of consumer buying behaviour. These modern techniques require sophisticated research and analysis of data and that requires the most up-to-date technology.

SECTION 3

Industrial Market Segmentation

Introduction

This section will consider the segmentation of industrial markets – the marketing of goods by organisations for sale to other organisations. The goods concerned might be part of the machinery and equipment used in manufacturing, or could be the raw materials that are turned into goods to be sold on to the end user.

The aim of this section is to help you to:

- appreciate the range of criteria that can be used in the segmentation of industrial markets

- assess the appropriateness of different criteria in specific instances

- understand some of the models that are used for the segmentation of industrial markets.

3.1 The differences between consumer and industrial markets

The principles behind the segmentation of industrial markets are similar to those behind the segmentation of consumer markets. Many of the same variables can be used and the reasons for market segmentation are similar. Several important differences do exist, however, which require industrial market segmentation to be considered as a separate area of study.

The most obvious difference is that the population we are describing is now made up of organisations and not individuals. The criteria for industrial market segments therefore tend to relate to such things as the size of an organisation, or the volume of its sales. Within organisations, the buying decision-making process is often more formalised than that of an individual consumer, and it is often possible to identify potential segments *within* a buying process, even down to the level of the individual within the buying organisation.

Industrial market segmentation has evolved more slowly than consumer market segmentation. This section will introduce the different criteria for industrial market segmentation and show how such methods can be applied by industrial marketers.

The section will demonstrate that while the nature of the buying process may differ between industrial markets, and while techniques for segmenting these markets is less well developed than that for consumer markets, it is still extremely important to segment and understand these markets.

3.2 Segmentation criteria

A range of criteria on which the segmentation of industrial markets can be based is outlined below and described in detail during the course of this section:

DEMOGRAPHICS

Industry
On which industries that use this product should we concentrate?

Company
On what size of company should we concentrate?

Location
In which geographical areas should we concentrate our efforts?

OPERATING VARIABLES

Technology
Which customers' technologies are of the greatest interest to us?

User status
On which types of user (heavy, medium, light, non-user) should we concentrate?

Customer capabilities and user status
Should we concentrate on customers with a broad or a narrow range of needs and on those which are heavy or light users of our product?

PURCHASING APPROACHES

Buying criteria
Should we concentrate on customers seeking quality, service or price?

Buying policies
Should we concentrate on companies that prefer leasing, systems purchases, or sealed bids?

Current relationships
Should we concentrate on existing or new customers?

SITUATIONAL FACTORS

Urgency
Should we concentrate on customers with sudden delivery needs?

Applications
Should we concentrate on general or specific applications of our product?

Size of order
Should we concentrate on the few companies that place large orders, or the majority of companies that place small orders?

PERSONAL CHARACTERISTICS

Loyalty
Should we concentrate on customers who exhibit high or low levels of loyalty?

Attitudes to risk
Should we concentrate on risk-taking or risk-avoiding customers?

(Adapted from Bonoma and Shapiro (1984))

The above list includes the major variables that can be used for segmenting industrial markets. You will notice that the criteria used are less sophisticated than those applied to the segmentation of consumer markets. Nevertheless, the importance of market segmentation to organisations selling in business-to-business markets should not be undervalued.

DEMOGRAPHICS

Industry type

ACTIVITY 15

Briefly outline how you would segment industries by type.

The criteria for segmenting markets by industry types can be broad or narrow. It is possible to classify industrial markets under manufacturing or service, public or private or by the type of activity they are mainly involved in (such as glass manufacturer, electronics or catering). It is possible, however, to classify organisations within each activity in further detail, so that the type of manufacture or service is specified. For instance, a glass manufacturer could be classified under 'windows', 'bottles', or 'glasses'.

It may be that a manufacturer is only involved in one part of a process. There will be a classification under shoemakers, but a further classification under leather manufacturer for shoes. This level of detailed information is available through the Standard Industrial Classification codes, published by the government (see figure 8). It is possible to identify key industry types by region to assist in the targeting of marketing effort.

7. Selling
   054 Sales supervisors
   055 Salesmen, sales, shop assistants, shelf fillers, petrol pump, forecourt attendants
   056 Roundsmen, van salesmen
   057 Sales representatives and agents

8. Security and protective service
   058 NCOs and other ranks UK armed forces
   059 NCOs and other ranks foreign and commonwealth armed forces
   060 Supervisors (police sergeants, fire fighting and related)
   061 Policemen, firemen, prison officers
   062 Other security and protective service workers

9. Catering, cleaning, hairdressing and other personal services
   063 Catering, supervisors
   064 Chefs, cooks
   065 Waiters and bar staff
   066 Counter hands, assistants, kitchen porters, hands
   067 Supervisors – housekeeping and related
   068 Domestic staff and school helpers
   069 Travel stewards and attendants, hospital and hotel porters
   070 Ambulancemen, hospital orderlies
   071 Supervisors, foremen – caretaking, cleaning and related
   072 Caretakers, road sweepers and other cleaners
   073 Hairdressing supervisors
   074 Hairdressers, barbers
   075 All others in catering, cleaning and other personal services

10. Farming, fishing and related
   076 Foremen – Farming, fishing, horticulture, forestry
   077 Farm workers
   078 Horticultural workers, gardeners, groundsmen
   079 Agricultural machinery drivers, operators
   080 Forestry workers
   081 Supervisors, mates – fishing
   082 Fishermen
   083 All other in farming and related

11. Materials processing: making and repairing (excluding metal and electrical)
   084 Foremen – tannery and leather (including leather substitutes) working
   085 Tannery and leather (including leather substitutes, workers
   086 Foremen – textile processing
   087 Textile workers
   088 Foremen – chemical processing
   089 Chemical, gas and petroleum process plant operators
   090 Foremen – food and drink processing
   091 Bakers, flour confectioners
   092 Butchers
   093 Foremen – paper and board making and paper products
   094 Paper, board and paper product makers, bookbinders
   095 Foremen – glass, ceramics, rubber, plastics etc.
   096 Glass and ceramics furnacemen and workers
   097 Rubber and plastics workers
   098 All other in processing materials (other than metal)
   099 Foremen – printing
   100 Printing workers, screen and block printers
   101 Foremen – textiles materials working
   102 Tailors, dressmakers and other clothing workers
   103 Coach trimmers, upholsters, mattress makers
   104 Foremen – woodworking
   105 Woodworkers, pattern makers
   106 Sawyers, veneer cutters, woodworking machinists
   107 All other in making and repairing (excluding metal and electrical)

Figure 8: Extract from SIC codes

Size of company

ACTIVITY 16

1 What criteria might you use to classify companies by size

2 As a marketing manager, to what use might you put such information?

The size of a firm can be determined by turnover, number of employees or capital employed. The segmentation of a market by company size is useful for determining supply and pricing policies and also the amount and type of marketing effort that should be expended in trying to reach these organisations. In several industries, such as the electrical cable industry, wholesalers are classified by size and appropriate discount structures determined prior to any business actually being conducted.

Location
Many industry types are concentrated in specific regions. It is therefore possible to concentrate marketing efforts on these regions. It is also possible to break a customer base down by distance travelled or location of sales offices.

OPERATING VARIABLES

Technology
It is possible to segment the market according to the level of technological development organisations have reached on the assumption that needs will vary according to the knowledge, expertise and systems that are in place. Market opportunities can be identified and products/services developed according to this criteria.

Customer capabilities and user status
This technique focuses on the range of needs organisations have that require servicing. It may be decided, for example, that no organisation will be approached unless it offers opportunities for cross-selling of products. A finance company offering facilities to lease products (a form of hire purchase) may only target those business that are identified as potentially needing a factoring (credit control) services. Similarly, it might be decided to target only those companies that use a certain quantity of the product annually.

PURCHASING APPROACHES

Buying criteria

Organisations can be segmented by the criteria upon which they place most emphasis in their purchase decisions.

ACTIVITY 17

Give examples of criteria on which a company might base its decision to purchase a product.

For some organisations quality and service may be key criteria. Other organisations may simply require a product that offers only basic functions at a low price. Quality and service may not be key criteria.

Buying policies

The way in which a firm purchases its products/services can lead to useful segmentation criteria. Types of negotiation (ie aggressive, open etc), a centralised/decentralised buying process, and whether the firm prefers certain types of buying arrangements can all influence marketing decisions.

Current relationships

The level and type of relationships that exist between organisations can be used to segment markets. Where close long-term relationships exist, strategies will differ from those where a more casual relationship exists. Multiple retailers vary in their need for close relationships with brand manufacturers. Traditional 'push/pull' marketing strategies will be adopted at multiples that do not want close relationships. These organisations will require heavy promotional support for a particular brand, and trade incentives to stock the brand. This transaction-focused approach is the opposite of a more open partnership in which the retailer and manufacturer work together to build a complete brand category as opposed to individual manufacturer brands.

SITUATIONAL FACTORS

Urgency

Is there a market opportunity in targeting organisations with urgent delivery needs? Most courier services deliver urgent mail/parcels. (Note that those companies operating flexible manufacturing systems and requiring regular and prompt delivery will, over time, develop their own distribution systems.)

Size of order

Pricing and distribution strategies will be influenced by this classification, as will the level of service and sales-force commitment.

Applications

The industrial market can be segmented by the level of sophistication required in applications. Certain companies require specific products because of their need for superior performance or finish.

PERSONAL CHARACTERISTICS

Loyalty

If degrees of loyalty can be established, then markets can be segmented according to this criteria. It may be decided to focus on those customers that exhibit loyal behaviour and reward them accordingly.

Attitudes to risk

Risk-aversive companies will require different products and communications from those companies that are established as risk takers. Pricing and credit facilities may also be influenced.

ACTIVITY 18

Read the following case study, and list the three most significant ways in which this market could be segmented:

MARKET ANALYSIS

A manufacturer of foam products has decided to conduct an analysis of the foam market. The uses for foam are many and varied. The company felt that it would require a means to classify different groups of customers by different needs.

Foam converting is neither a technically sophisticated nor capital-intensive industry. There is, however, a wide range of different industries using foam either for packaging or in the manufacture of a product. Within this diversity of uses there is a range of technical requirements, some dictated by law and others simply by the quality standards required by individual firms.

The size of firms within these sectors also varies significantly, from large multinational companies with sophisticated buying requirements and processes, to the small sole trader with fairly limited and unsophisticated requirements. Many small firms are using sophisticated technology to develop new markets, and their requirements, while not high in terms of volume, offer the opportunity for higher prices.

A recent trend noticed by the company is that customers in technology-led industries are now requiring their suppliers to develop closer relationships with their suppliers. This is in contrast to many of the traditional users of foam products, who appear intent on driving the price down at every possible opportunity.

The professionalism of buyers has also steadily increased, particularly in larger companies with buying departments. The information and service requirements are now being specified very strictly in these companies, with a system of bonuses or financial penalties on completion of the contract. While this is an important market, it can increase the risk of doing business with such companies.

For this activity you should have been able to identify the full range of market segmentation discussed in this section. This shows the diversity of possibilities within most industries for using market segmentation techniques. The activity specifically asks you to make a value judgement about the most important ways of segmenting industrial markets. Your answer should consider such factors as size of organisation, size of order, frequency of purchase, uniqueness of requirements. While it is appropriate to use broad-based market segmentation techniques, particular for low-value, frequently purchased products, it is more likely in industrial markets than consumers markets that there will be a need for customisation and individual relationships. Specific industrial market segmentation techniques are therefore of equal validity, depending on the nature of the market and purchase.

3.3 Models of industrial market segmentation

Recognition of the need for more effective segmentation techniques in industrial markets has led academics to investigate and develop models based upon a step-by-step hierarchical approach. An example of this approach is shown in Figure 9 below.

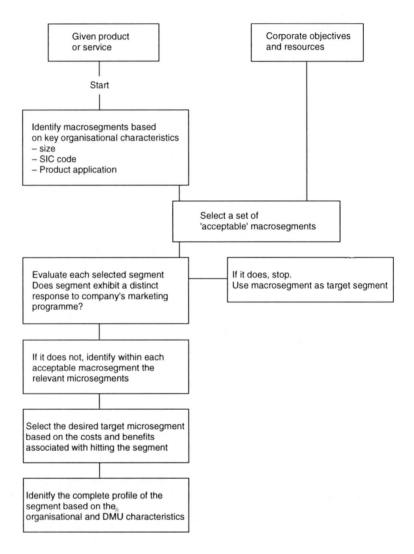

Figure 9: An Approach to Segmenting Industrial Markets
(Adapted from Wind and Cardozo, 1974)

This model attempts to develop a sequential approach to segmenting industrial markets. It firstly differentiates between macro and micro variables. It emphasises the need to research the potential market segments at this level to see if these represent a suitable basis for segmenting the market. If it is found that no competitive advantage is gained from targeting these segments, then further segmentation is necessary. The micro segments are based on specific characteristics of an organisation – such as purchasing style or management culture – that may identify new opportunities for targeting.

This model can be criticised for its fairly broad and simplistic approach to segmenting industrial markets. Some of the conclusions initially drawn from it appear fairly banal. The model does, however, show a sequential approach, using broad and then narrow segmentation criteria, and suggests the importance of organisational characteristics in the industrial market segmentation process.

The Shapiro and Bonoma model (Figure 10) does not adopt a sequential approach to the market segmentation process. It identifies broad and narrow market segmentation criteria, but suggests that to effectively segment an industrial market these criteria need to be layered. Essentially, the model suggests a multidimensional approach to market segmentation where broad criteria (demographics) are combined with each further level. Essentially, a nest is formed of market segmentation possibilities which can then be assessed in terms of market potential. With the advent of information technology such multi-attribute criteria can produce fairly sophisticated and closely defined market segments.

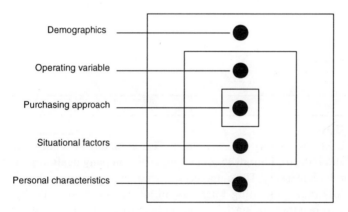

Figure 10: A 'nested' approach to industrial market segmentation
(Shapiro and Bonoma, 1984)

This model uses standard industrial market segmentation criteria, but by combining each layer, the 'nests' offer a more precise identification of market segments. The model uses a multi-segmentation approach, using broad data initially and then overlaying more complex data to develop these into more precise and targeted segments. The model indicates how industrial market segmentation criteria can be applied in practice.

REVIEW ACTIVITY 4

You have been asked to do a presentation to your board of directors. You are required to outline the arguments as to why market segmentation is important in an industrial business to business context. Write down five key arguments that you would present.

(A possible answer to this activity is given at the end of the unit.)

REVIEW ACTIVITY 5

Imagine that you are the office assistant in the following case study. List the ways in which the market could be segmented.

(A possible answer to this activity is given at the end of the unit.)

CASE STUDY

In 1992 the Blinds Factory was launched. This company specialised in both consumer and industrial blinds manufacture. The company dealt directly with end users in both markets. The company enjoyed reasonable growth in its first two years of trading, gaining business on an *ad hoc* basis, and by 1994 employed two members of staff: a fitter and an office assistant with a recent marketing qualification.

Very quickly it was identified that the company needed to develop a more cohesive and planned strategy to ensure continued growth and better use of the limited resources. Initial analysis identified that 80% of the Blinds Factory business in 1994 was coming from 20% of its accounts and these were all in the commercial sector. More importantly, the contribution to profit was considerably more than much of the work being obtained from the consumer market. It was decided to explore how the commercial market could be effectively segmented to assist the development of a marketing strategy.

The office assistant was given the task of initially identifying possible ways in which the commercial market could be segmented.

Summary

Industrial market segmentation has not developed to the level of sophistication of consumer market segmentation for several reasons. Consumer marketing, particularly in the field of fast-moving consumer goods (FMCGs) has, for several years, used extensive research data and sophisticated market segmentation techniques to identify market segments. In recent years there have been further developments, particularly in the use of information technology, that have enabled more detailed market segmentation to occur. Industrial marketing has only in recent years adopted more sophisticated methods of market segmentation. The need to accurately identify market segments has meant that manufacturers have adopted many of the techniques of marketing traditionally used in FMCGs.

This section has shown that industrial markets are not homogeneous, that they consist of a range of complex needs from broad-based demographic to behavioural. It is as imperative to segment industrial markets as it is to segment consumer markets. While the techniques of industrial segmentation remain relatively unsophisticated, compared with those of consumer market segmentation, it is now recognised that behavioural and organisational criteria can be applied to industrial markets and provide a useful means of identifying unmet needs.

Competitive market forces are increasing the pressure in both consumer and industrial markets to use more effective market segmentation techniques. This section has outlined various techniques that can be used in combination to create more detailed market segmentation criteria, enabling industrial marketers to develop better-targeted and more-effective marketing strategies. The future is likely to see rapid developments in this area.

Summary of unit so far

This unit has now covered stage one of the market segmentation process, including:

- defining the market
- selecting the basis for segmentation
- dividing the market and profiling the segments.

When defining the markets it was shown that they can vary in terms of shape and size, and also in terms of the needs that might exist. Some markets consist of consumer groups with relatively similar needs for a product or service, (homogeneous demand). Other markets demonstrate a diverse range of needs (diffused demand). Thirdly, a market may consist of clusters of needs each with its own identifiable purchase behaviour, (clustered demand). From an analysis of these needs it is possible to select basis for segmenting the market.

A range of consumer and industrial market segmentation techniques was identified. In both cases, market segmentation techniques have become more sophisticated as marketers try to identify more closely potential consumers or buyers. Five broad categories of consumer and industrial market segmentation were identified. While consumer market segmentation techniques are more sophisticated, industrial market segmentation is just as important and relevant. The principles are the same for both areas.

After selecting the basis for segmenting the market, the process of segmenting the market can begin and a profile of each segment developed. It is possible to overlay various market segmentation techniques to more closely define your market, but taken too far this can result in identifying market segments that are too small.

The activities you have carried out in this section required you to segment various markets, identify the benefits of market segmentation and the advantages and limitations associated with various market segmentation techniques.

SECTION 4

Targeting

Introduction

Having worked through Stage I of the three-stage model you are now able to segment your potential market. Stage II of the three-stage model involves evaluating the potential of each of the segments and making a decision on which to target. (See Figure 11: The Three-Stage Model.) The process of targeting essentially enables the marketer to focus activity more accurately at those market segments that offer the most potential. The attributes of the market segment will influence the nature of any planned market activity.

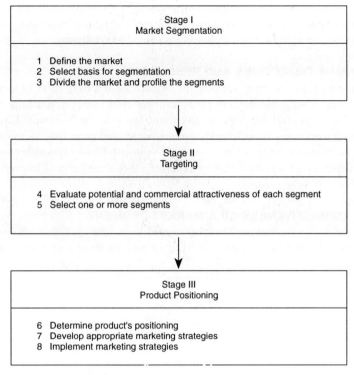

Figure 11: The Three-Stage Model

The aim of this section is to help you to:

● establish criteria by which market segments can be assessed

● identify the most suitable segment to target in a specific instance

● identify different techniques of targeting.

4.1 Evaluating segments

Philip Kotler (1988) identifies three criteria that help identify those segments that offer the most potential.

1 SEGMENT SIZE AND GROWTH

The market segment must be of a size that enables the organisation to exploit it profitably. The most appropriate segment size is in direct relation to the size of the organisation and its manufacturing/service capability. A large manufacturing company will probably require market segments that offer large sales volumes, whereas smaller organisations can profitably exploit smaller, narrower segments.

The market segment's expected growth rate is also an important consideration. A rate of growth that can be matched by the organisation's capability is the ideal outcome. The faster the growth rate, the more likely that competitors will be attracted to the segment. A fast-growing segment is also more difficult to service. On the other hand, a slower growth rate will affect company performance, as it may give rise to spare capacity, price pressure and loss of efficiency.

2 COMPANY OBJECTIVES AND RESOURCES

The segments selected must support the organisation's long-term objectives. A segment may offer considerable potential, but if it is not consistent with the organisation's overall strategic focus then this may be harmful. Equally as important, the company must have the competencies and capability to establish and maintain its competitive position in a market segment. Unless it is able to maintain a competitive advantage by offering superior value then its position will not be sustainable.

3 THE ATTRACTIVENESS OF A MARKET SEGMENT

Michael Porter's Five-Forces Model (referred to in Unit 2, Section 5.1) (Porter, 1980) is useful when assessing the level of attractiveness of a market segment.

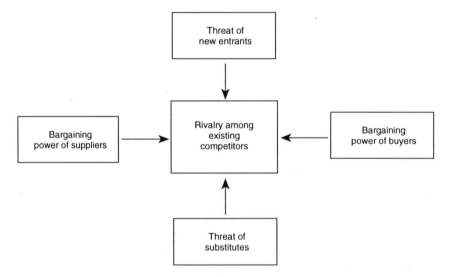

Figure 12: Michael Porter's Five-Forces Model

Competitive rivalry

The level of competitive rivalry will have an impact on the performance of the company. The lower the competitive rivalry, the more attractive the segment.

Threat of new entrants

A market segment for which entry and exit is easy is less attractive because of the increased threat of competition. Barriers to entry are high when heavy investment in technology, equipment, expert knowledge etc, is required.

Threat of substitutes

Where a product or service is easily substituted by competing products prices and profits will be driven down, making the segment less attractive to the producer.

Level of buyer power

Where the level of buyer power is high, the negotiating strength and manoeuvrability of the supplier will be reduced. The UK food retail market is a good example of the effect that buyer power can have on a supplier's products and profitability.

Level of supplier power

The negotiating strength of a supplier will be enhanced where the level of concentration of suppliers is high. The brewery market until recently was dominated by a few major breweries. New government legislation forced them to open up the market to smaller breweries.

ACTIVITY 18

You are a marketing director at Ford in charge of a new product: a battery-powered Ford Escort with a top speed of 65 miles per hour and maximum travel distance of 200 miles before recharging is necessary.

The market segment you are considering targeting is the 'environmentally friendly ABC1 consumer'. Analyse the attractiveness of this segment, using Porter's Five-Forces Model.

It may be necessary to make some assumptions, but the market attractiveness would appear to be relatively high. The market segment identified (ABC1 consumers interested in environmentally friendly products) is fairly large and is growing. The level of **competitive activity** in this segment is low. Other manufacturers have shied away from developing such a car. The **threat of new entrants** is low, as the technology required to develop a car with such a specification is to your knowledge currently not developed. The possibility of a **competitive substitute** product being developed is low as this is new technology.

The level of **buyer power** is low, and once suspicion of the new technology is overcome and accepted, both for car distributors and the final consumer there may be a willingness to pay a premium for the benefits the product offers. The level of **supplier power** is more difficult to ascertain. The assumption could be that the availability of raw materials to manufacture the battery-powered car could be obtained from anywhere in the world, therefore supplier power is low. If specialist technology is required, however, then fewer suppliers may be available and supplier power would therefore be high.

The major concern would be the time period it would take for competitors to develop a competitive product and enter the market.

This process of evaluation can be further developed by evaluating the market segments in terms of the following criteria (Zikmund & d'Amico, 1995, p182). Segments must be capable of identification. They must be able to be profiled in terms of distinctive needs that set them apart from the rest of the market. These criteria, which must be met if a market segmentation strategy is to be successful, are illustrated in the following case study.

SONY WALKMAN

The Sony Walkman was targeted at the 16- to 25-year-old single male or female who enjoyed music and a busy social lifestyle. Such a person was fashion conscious and not constrained by traditional values. They were likely to be active and avid listeners of music and watchers of trend-setting television programmes.

Characteristics such as lifestyle may be intangible and require careful research (see Section 3), but the basic characteristics alone offer a broadly identifiable market segment that can be refined by further analysis.

Responsive

Members of the identified segment must be likely to respond to your message. Evidence for this can be found by market research, testing promotional material or by test-marketing a product. Focus group sessions are frequently conducted by marketers with a small number of consumers taken from the target market.

Focus group sessions were carried out among members of the target audience to test their reaction to the Sony Walkman concept. Trial products were left with these individuals for a period of time and then further research carried out to test for behavioural reactions.

Adequate

The market segment must offer an adequate market potential. There must be sufficient numbers of people in the segment to justify the expenditure in reaching them. Market potential can be defined as the number of people potentially willing or able to purchase a product.

Demographic data alone would have indicated a large potential market for the Sony Walkman. This criteria alone would not, however, have indicated the true market potential of this product. Only a percentage of this age group would be likely to purchase it. Further market segmentation using lifestyle data was necessary before a more accurate idea of market potential was formulated.

Accessible

Marketers must be able to reach the market segment. One of the key characteristics of markets in the 1990s is their fragmentation into smaller and smaller market segments. A proliferation of new media (magazines, satellite TV, independent radio etc) means that audiences are now harder to reach. Careful media planning is essential and therefore a good knowledge of the audience's media habits and social interests is essential.

The Sony Walkman target audience was reached through selected radio, magazine and TV programmes. Media audience research data was used to determine the most appropriate media in which to place advertisements.

Stable

Because it is likely that to penetrate and establish a product in a market will require fairly substantial investment, the segment must show that its size, shape and composition are not going to change radically, at least in the short term. Ideally, the segment will show signs of growth as well as being stable.

Example – The Sony Walkman required that the target market would not perceive the product as a fashion item. It also had to ensure that the age group's interest in music was not just a passing fad and that the market was sustainable over the longer term.

It is likely that Sony would have investigated various market segments and assessed them against these criteria. A decision could then be made as to which, if any, of the segments offered the most potential.

The Sony Walkman was successfully launched on to the UK market and represents one of the most successful new product launches of the last two decades. The application of market segmentation and targeting lay at the heart of this product's success.

ACTIVITY 19

For a product and market of your own choice, evaluate the attractiveness of the market segment you feel is being targeted. Use the five criteria outlined above and support your conclusion with evidence about the nature of the market segment.

When carrying out this exercise, simply apply the above criteria in a similar manner to the Sony Walkman example. The product you choose can be successful or unsuccessful. Either way, use the criteria to identify the importance of market segmentation in determining such an outcome.

4.2 Selecting target markets

Each market segment that is identified has to be evaluated in order to identify which is most attractive and offers the best potential. It also has to be determined whether an attractive segment fits in with the organisation's overall goals. The choice of market segments that you will target is partly determined by the available resources and capabilities of an organisation. An organisation can concentrate on one segment or pursue many segments. Evaluating market segments identifies those market segments worth entering. The next stage is to select those market segments you *wish* to enter.

It is only after selection of the market segment(s) that the organisation can design marketing strategies that are appropriate to the needs of the target audience.

ACTIVITY 20

Consider the marketing strategies of the following car manufacturers: Ford, Toyota, Skoda, Mercedes, Morgan.

Note down whether they are targeting low-volume or high-volume segments (or both), with low-value or high-value products.

One possible answer is the following:

Ford – High-volume segments, both consumer and fleet car customers.

Toyota – High-volume and low-volume segments across the product range.

Skoda – High-volume market segments. Focused on low value.

Mercedes – Low-volume, high-value segments. Recently looked at higher-volume segments with the launch of a smaller Mercedes.

Morgan – Narrow, low-volume market segments. Targeted at car enthusiasts.

Each of the market segments will consist of consumers with identifiable and similar characteristics and needs. The understanding the marketer has of the market segments enables him or her to develop specific strategies targeted at each segment, as opposed to developing a single strategy aimed at all market segments. There are four strategies a company can choose when targeting market segments.

UNDIFFERENTIATED TARGETING

This strategy (see Figure 13) is rarely used by organisations that have researched their markets. If it were found that there was little diversity among market segments then a single targeting strategy for all market segments might apply. Markets where this may be applicable are, for example, the supply of hacksaw blades, or brass or silver polish, but in general such an undifferentiated strategy would result in the needs of many market segments not being satisfied.

Figure 13: Undifferentiated marketing strategy

CONCENTRATED TARGETING STRATEGY

This strategy (see Figure 14) identifies one market segment and develops a single marketing mix that focuses on this segment. This concentration allows the firm to specialise and avoids its resources being spread too thinly. The danger is that the market segment reaches its decline stage and the organisation then faces financial difficulties. Examples of companies using concentrated strategies are the Morgan car company, exclusive perfumes suppliers, and holiday companies such as SAGA.

Figure 14: Concentrated marketing strategy

DIFFERENTIATED TARGETING

This strategy (see Figure 15) identifies more than one market segment that can be exploited. For each segment identified, the organisation develops an appropriate marketing mix. This strategy – which is the most commonly adopted – reduces the risks associated with reliance on one market segment. It is used to increase sales and market share through the identification of new market opportunities and new product development.

The disadvantages of this strategy are the increased costs incurred in having to develop a separate market mix for each segment and the need for separate production processes. The danger is that the organisation cannot defend all its markets from competitors because its resources are spread too thinly.

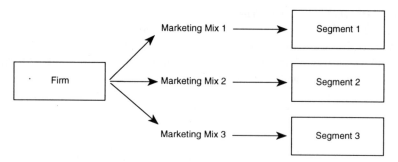

Figure 15: Multisegment (Differentiated) strategy

CUSTOMISED TARGETING

This strategy (see Figure 16) is traditionally used for exclusive goods. Saville Row tailors and solicitors are among those who adopt such a customised strategy. The advent of new technology and in particular the database has, however, enabled more organisations to explore the potential for customised marketing. Many direct marketing companies are now able to communicate directly with individuals, sending the appropriate message at the appropriate time. (An example would be toy catalogues being sent to parents a few weeks before their child's birthday.) Each customer is dealt with in a unique way.

Industrial markets commonly customise products to meet the individual requirements of their customers. New technology is making the customisation option an interesting dimension to explore and many companies are developing future strategies along these lines.

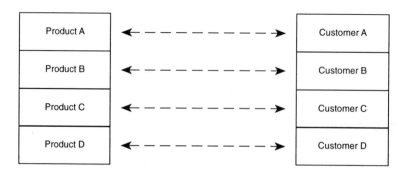

Figure 16: Customised segment strategy

ACTIVITY 21

Identify which targeting strategy is being adopted for the following products and services.

Johnson's Baby Powder
Häagen Dazs Ice Cream
Readers Digest
RAC/AA
Next Clothing
Travel Lodge Hotels
British Airway
The National Lottery

Johnson's Baby Powder is traditionally a concentrated strategy, focusing on the parents of young children, but it now targets adults as users of the product as well.

Häagen Dazs Ice Cream adopts an undifferentiated strategy. The message is singular and simple: indulge yourself. It is targeted at a broad market segment of people across age and socio-economic classes who are silently protesting against health food and healthy living.

Readers Digest also adopts an undifferentiated strategy. Who doesn't receive a mail shot from Readers Digest? The RAC and AA, on the other hand, adopt a differentiated strategy. A range of services is available and is targeted at different user groups.

Next Clothing adopts a differentiated strategy in terms of men's and women's clothing, in-store and Next Directory, but concentrates on the age bracket 18/35 and on those with fashionable lifestyles.

Travel Lodge Hotels concentrates on the commercial traveller who simply requires a low-cost room for the night.

British Airways adopts a differentiated strategy. A range of air-travel packages are available for different market segments.

The National Lottery adopts a completely undifferentiated strategy, making the point that the finger of fortune could alight on absolutely anyone!

4.3 Relationship between market segment and company objectives

Company objectives include the mission statement, corporate objectives and marketing objectives. The mission statement sets out the values and overall purpose of the company and will determine the nature of the corporate objectives and marketing objectives. The overall setting of objectives will therefore determine the types of products and markets the company operates in and its overall positioning in these markets. The selection and targeting of market segments is a critical part of the strategy-development process and will be a major determining factor in the achievement of the company's objectives.

REVIEW ACTIVITY 6

Consider the following list of dental hygiene products and, selecting a segmentation technique from those given in Section 2, identify which segment you believe each product is targeted at.

- Orange-flavoured infant toothpaste
- Herb-based 'natural' toothpaste
- Denture-cleansing tablets
- Mint-flavoured dental floss
- Listerine mouth wash.

(A possible answer is given at the end of the unit.)

REVIEW ACTIVITY 7

An average news-stand has over one hundred magazines on its shelves.

1 Suggest six ways the magazine market has been segmented?

2 Browse through three magazines. Identify which segment the magazine is targeted at and see if you can find an advertisement in the magazine precisely tailored to that targeted segment.

(A possible answer is given at the end of the unit.)

Summary

The accurate measurement and evaluation of market segments is a critical phase in the process of segmentation and targeting. The success or failure of future marketing campaigns is dependent on identifying those market segments that are profitable and accessible. They should be large enough to generate the required sales volumes and offer future growth potential. The appropriate market segment size and growth are related to the size of an organisation, the nature of the product and the profit margins that can be secured.

The segments selected must support a company's long-term objectives and strategic focus. Also the company must have the capability to exploit the targeted segments. Unless the company has the capability to sustain its competitiveness over a period of time then it may be better not to exploit the opportunity. This will require both internal organisation analysis and external market and analysis.

On completion of this evaluation, appropriate targeting strategies can be developed. Four strategies have been described: undifferentiated, concentrated, multi-segment or customised.

These strategies will be selected on the basis of the nature of the market, competitive activity and the flexibility of manufacturing systems. In particular, technological developments have enabled organisations increasingly to customise products to individual needs.

SECTION 5
Product Positioning

Introduction

This section introduces you to the final stage of the three-stage model – product positioning (see Figure 17). The concept of positioning is critical to a product's success in the market place. The section defines the purpose and meaning of positioning and show how products can be positioned against competing products on selected criteria. Positioning maps are shown to demonstrate this process. The section then looks at how products can be repositioned if their traditional markets go into decline.

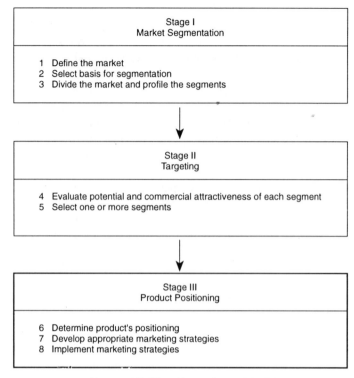

Figure 17: The Three-Stage Model

The aim of this section is to help you to:

● understand the concept of positioning

● identify a product's position in the market place.

5.1 What is positioning?

Consumers are overloaded with information about products and services. They cannot re-evaluate products every time they make a buying decision. To simplify the decision-making process, they organise products into categories – they position products, services and companies in their minds. *A product's position is the complex set of perceptions, impressions, and feelings that it induces in consumers, compared with competing products.*

Positioning involves designing your product or service so that it occupies a distinct and valued place in your target consumers' minds. To position a product or service, your organisation must select the differences it wishes to appeal most strongly to its target audience and communicate these differences clearly.

The concept of positioning therefore has a strong influence on both the development of the product and on the way its attributes are communicated to its target market. Positioning is communicated through product design, performance and marketing communications – all of which have to present a consistent approach.

DIFFERENTIATION

In order to create a unique position in the consumer's mind, it is important to differentiate your product from its competitors, both in terms of its design and in the communications you make about it to your target market.

EXAMPLE 1

Nike charges over £80.00 for its Air Jordans. They have identified a target group and designed a basketball shoe that is differentiated from all other basketball shoes on the market. The design of this shoe offers benefits that add value to that product. The targeted consumer is willing to pay a price premium for these perceived benefits. Nike has successfully communicated the brand's values using high-profile media and celebrity endorsement to ensure that the product is clearly positioned in the consumers' mind.

EXAMPLE 2

The Toyota Lexus is targeted at professionals in their early forties with annual incomes of £80,000+ who are ready for their first luxury car. The car is designed to offer luxury at an affordable price. Toyota has ensured that the targeted customer receives a service compatible with the car's marque, using exclusive showrooms and high-quality support services. Leading-edge technology was used in the manufacturing process.

The Toyota Lexus was positioned as a exclusive family saloon car, offering superior comfort and style. Performance was not a key factor when determining the car's position in the market. These values were communicated using appropriate up-market media.

ACTIVITY 22

Identify the target audiences for the following products. How have these products been differentiated? How have these products been positioned in the minds of the targeted consumer?

Bold washing powder
Levi jeans
Häagen Dazs ice cream
Benetton

Bold washing powder is targeted at the C2, D, E family household who required a washing powder that emphasised clean more than 'green'. The product was positioned as bold, brash and capable of cleaning the worst stains. This positioning was communicated through advertisement in the style of family home videos.

Levi jeans are targeted at the 18- to 30-year-old fashion-conscious age group who are motivated by good looks and image. They require a quality symbol on their clothes. A pair of Levi jeans retails at £40.00+. They are positioned as a high-quality fashion accessory, despite their apparent ruggedness. These values are communicated through TV advertising.

Häagen Dazs ice cream is targeted at the 25- to 45-year-old age group. On its launch it broke all the rules by encouraging people to indulge themselves when most organisations and media were communicating more healthy values. The product was communicated as an indulgence and at a premium price compared with other ice creams.

Benetton has repositioned itself. Its traditional positioning was based upon its unique designs of hand-crafted jumpers. Is message was the 'United Colours of Benetton', which gave it a globally acceptable image. Recently, however, Benetton's positioning has changed. The product is the same, but a more controversial approach has been adopted, focusing on social issues. Its aim (which has to some extent backfired) is to position Benetton as a socially aware and concerned company.

5.2 Determining a product's position

Within one market segment it is possible that several products will be in competition. It is likely that these products have different images, specifications or design. These unique properties are communicated to consumers in such a way as to position the product in the consumers' mind. For instance, the *Sun* and *Daily Mirror* newspaper are both targeting C2/D/E consumers. However, the *Sun* has positioned itself as less serious and politically right-wing, whereas the *Mirror* is more serious and politically left-wing.

To identify the position of a product in a market, it is necessary to conduct fairly in-depth research to understand the parameters that are most important to the customer and how they perceive different products. Management intuition is often not appropriate. Research can explore attitudes, desires, perceptions and motives. It can identify what factors are most important to the consumer when making a decision to purchase. This information can be analysed and the product's positioning determined against specified parameters. These parameters may be as simple as price and product variables, or can involve quite complex psychographic variables.

The important aspect to remember with regard to this research is that the parameters and variables are arrived at by reference to consumer perceptions. This information can then be shown on a product positioning map, which visually depicts consumer perceptions of brand attributes. Two examples of a market position map are shown below.

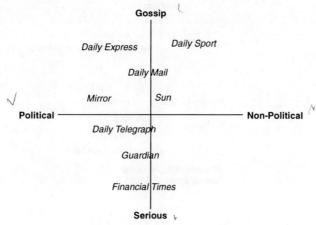

Figure 18: Market-position map for newspapers

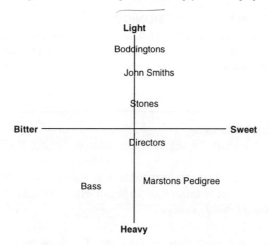

Figure 19: Market-position map for beer

ACTIVITY 23

Draw a market-position map based on your own perception of the market for savoury snacks.

To a certain extent the answer to this activity depends on your own personal perception. Here is one possible version.

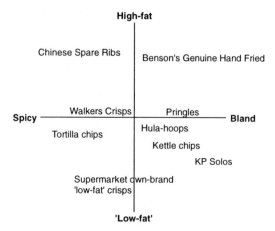

Figure 20: Market-position map for savoury snacks

PRODUCT POSITIONING/REPOSITIONING

In Unit 1, Section 4.1, you were introduced to the concept of the product life cycle. The cases outlined below demonstrate how two products that appeared to be in the maturity/decline phase of their potential life cycles were successfully repositioned.

EXAMPLE – LUCOZADE

Lucozade was successfully launched as a brand in the 1930s. It was positioned as a drink that would restore the energy and health of people who had suffered illness. The product's essential attribute was its glucose. The product's position was clearly communicated through effective advertising and a distinctive packaging/bottle design.

In the 1980s Lucozade sales went into decline. The decision was made after careful analysis of the market to reposition Lucozade from a medicinal product to a sports product. New market segments were identified and targeted away from children/mothers to teenagers/young adults. The product's 'isotonic' properties of restoring body fluids was successfully communicated using a famous sports star (Daley Thompson). The essential attribute of the product (its glucose) was consistent with the brand's new positioning. The product launch was extremely successful and Lucozade sales grew rapidly.

EXAMPLE – MENU MASTER

Menu Master was launched into the UK Market in the 1970s. This range of pre-cooked foods targeted traditional families who enjoyed wholesome food. It maintained market leadership in a growing convenience food market until the 1980s, when its sales went into decline. Analysis revealed that Menu Master's traditional market segments were becoming smaller. Psychographic market segmentation techniques were used to analyse the market. A competitive product had recently been successfully launched targeted at health-orientated individuals. This product was branded 'Lean Cuisine'.

Menu Master was repositioned into this health-food segment with no change in branding or product ingredients, however. Despite extensive promotional support, the product repositioning was unsuccessful because the brand's attributes were not consistent with the product's new position.

A new brand was developed, Healthy Options. The product was essentially the same as the traditional Menu Master, but with effective branding and communication, Healthy Options was successfully launched. Menu Master was repositioned back to its original market segment where it is still selling today.

ACTIVITY 24

Outline the key lessons that can be learned about product repositioning from the examples given above.

New market segments offer opportunities for products that are approaching the end of their traditional life cycles. If a product is to be successfully repositioned, its attributes values must be visible and consistent with its new positioning. To be successful, the product's attributes must be clearly communicated and carefully targeted. If traditional brand values cannot be broken down, then it is unlikely that a repositioning strategy will be successful.

REVIEW ACTIVITY 8

Responses to the in-depth questionnaire on perfumes, shown in Resource Item 4.1, give details of consumers' perceptions of six perfume brands. These people have sampled a range of perfumes and answered a pre-prepared set of questions.

1 From this information select the two *key* attributes for perfume, and label the axes of the perception map accordingly.

2 Develop a product positioning map that shows how each product is positioned in the minds of the consumer.

Summary

Positioning is a critical phase in the market segmentation process. Positioning involves identifying key product attributes or emotions that are then communicated to the targeted customer. This communication 'positions' a product in the mind of the consumer relative to other products. A product's position is the complex set of perceptions, impressions and feelings that consumers hold for the product.

Positioning offers marketers the opportunity to compete more effectively for the mind of the consumer. It is critical that the brand's style, design performance and communications consistently reinforce this positioning. Positioning maps can be developed usually against two criteria to show how competitive products are positioned in the market. The appropriate positioning of a brand is fundamental to that brand's success.

Some brands are repositioned, as their traditional market positions become less attractive. The examples of Lucozade and Menu Master show the importance of the product's core attributes and values being recognised and accepted by the consumer. Positioning is not simply about communicating values. The product has to have the attributes to support the desired position.

Unit summary

This unit has outlined the market segmentation process from the initial analysis of the market through to segmenting the market, selecting viable market segments and determining a product's position within that market segment.

This process lies at the heart of the overall philosophy of marketing. Success stories abound of companies who have successfully adopted and implemented market segmentation into their planning process. Equally, stories of failures are all to frequent as companies poorly define their markets, treat all customers in that market the same, do not evaluate market segments rigorously or finally, fail to position the product appropriately or communicate this position effectively.

The lessons you have learned from this unit are relevant to marketing in industry, commerce or the public sector. Market segmentation techniques are becoming increasingly sophisticated, but the important principles that underline this process will always remain essential for the development of effective market strategies.

The following activities review the unit as a whole.

UNIT REVIEW ACTIVITY 1

In order to rescue the Close Shave brand you have been called in by the Managing Director of B & G Shoprite Ltd (see case study below). Write a short report to the MD advising him of:

1   The importance of market segmentation, targeting and positioning for a branded product aimed at the consumer.

2   How B & G Shoprite Ltd might consider segmenting the market for A Close Shave.

3   Some possible parameters by which A Close Shave might be positioned.

(A possible answer to this activity is given at the end of the unit.)

SEGMENTATION IN ACTION

B & G Shoprite Ltd is a national manufacturer of a range of cosmetics and over-the-counter drugs. It has developed a good reputation in the industry for supplying own-label cosmetic products and generic drugs direct to chemists and convenience stores. This reputation has been achieved through close attention to quality, excellent service and competitive pricing.

The company is unknown outside the industry. It has never launched any product of its own into the consumer market. As a company, it works very closely with its retail customers and will develop products to their specification.

Recently, the company has considered diversifying into men's shaving products. The product would be bought at similar outlets to its existing products and could be developed within the company's existing research and development department.

The shaving product that the company has developed is a men's shaving cream that is applied on the face, left for 5 minutes and then washed off. This process will not require any use of a razor. Initial research has shown that the product might appeal to people who are in the age band 18-30 years old, but no further detailed research has been carried out. The shaving product is revolutionary in that no such product is currently available on the men's shaving market. Extensive tests have been carried out and no risk of harm is entailed in its use, except for those men with sensitive skin.

The company decides to develop this product as its own brand. The brand name chosen is 'A Close Shave'. The product is supplied in tubes or containers. It is priced at approximately double the price of existing shaving foams on the market, but no replacement razors will ever be required. It has been initially distributed through existing channels and not supermarkets because of their likely price requirements. The launch of the product took place in the South East of England and used prime-time television slots. The adverts emphasised that the product was 'manly enough for men'.

Despite rave reviews the product launch was a flop. The company only reached 30% of its targeted sales in the first 3 months.

After consultation with its advertising agency, the company decided to commission more extensive research with 250 consumers in the targeted age group. The responses can be summarised by the few quotes given below.

'The shaving foam I use is manly enough for me. I had to laugh at that advert. It wasn't me at all.'

'I can't imagine any of my mates being seen putting a cream on their face. I like the idea but no I wouldn't buy the product.'

'I might use it but only if I was convinced it was not harmful to my face.'

'It's a bit expensive. I wouldn't pay that much for a shave.'

'I like my dry shave and nothing will shift me from that.'

References

Berman, B & Evans, J (1992) *Marketing,* Macmillan, 5th edn

Bonoma T & Shapiro B (1984) 'How to Segment Industrial Markets', *Harvard Business Review,* May–June, pp104–10

Chisnall, P (1985) *Consumer Behaviour,* McGraw Hill 2nd edn

Cannon, T (1980) *Basic Marketing – Principles & Practise,* Holt, Rinehart & Wilson

Kotler, P (1995), *Marketing Management Analysis Planning and Control,* Prentice-Hall, 8th edn

Kotler, P (1988) *Marketing Management: Analysis & Decision,* Prentice-Hall, 6th edn

Porter, M E (1980) 'Industry Structure and Competitive Strategy: Keys to Profitability', *Financial Analysts' Journal,* July–August, p33

Wilson, R M S, Gilligan, C & Pearson, D (1994): *Strategic Marketing Management,* Butterworth-Heinemann

Wind Y and Cardozo Y (1974), 'Industrial Market Segmentation', *Industrial Marketing Management,* March, p156

Zikmund, G W & d'Amico, M (1995) *Effective Marketing – Creating and Keeping Customers,* West Publishing

Further Reading

Evans, M & Baker, M (1994) 'Market Segmentation', *The Marketing Book,* Butterworth-Heinemann, pps303–332

Mercer, D (1993) *Marketing,* Blackwell, pp243–282

McDonald, M & Dunbar, I (1995) *Market Segmentation,* Macmillan

Bearden, Ingham & La Forge (1995) *Marketing Principles & Perspectives,* Irwin, pp178–205

Zikmund & d'Amico (1994), pp178–205

Answer to Review Activities

Review Activity 1

The market needs of school leavers for higher education business degrees are many and varied. The most appropriate demand category would be clustered. Student needs will vary according to personal issues, income, status, interests, ability etc, but each category is unlikely to be unique to one student. However, in the future it may be possible for a student to determine his or her own programme of learning and location. Information technology creates increasing opportunities for such 'customisation' in education. If this is developed, it is likely that the demand category would become diffused.

Review Activity 2

The basis for this process of market segmentation was the need to develop an increased understanding of the market and to break it down into more identifiable and targeted groups. Lego developed new product ranges to meet the needs of these markets and communicated the appropriate themes through carefully targeted media. The aim of Lego was to supply its product range to all possible market segments, thus reducing the threat of competitive entry. This is an ongoing process and Lego is continually developing and updating its product ranges to ensure its products are relevant to today's children,

The benefits sought by parents (the main purchasers of Lego) fall into two categories: the benefits they seek for their children (which include the development of motor-coordination skills and imagination) and the benefits they seek for themselves (peace and quiet while their children play!).

The ACORN groups that Lego is most likely to select for a direct mailing are: B (modern family housing, higher incomes), E (better-off council estates), J (affluent suburban housing).

Review Activity 3

1   Consumer-related variables

Geographic   UK Regions
                  Urban
                  Suburban
                  Rural

Demographic	**Groups**	
	Young/old age groups	
	Male/female	

Usage	Occasion	
	Usual –	with food
		without food
		with mixer
	Light	
	Medium	
	Heavy	
	Connoisseur/Novice	

Income	Disposable income

2   Product-related variables

Red/White/Rose
Dry/Medium/Sweet
Low/Average/High alcohol
French/German/New World/East Europe etc.
Bottle size
Method of dispensing/merchandise display:

Bottle
Carafe
Draught
Cabinet
By the glass
By the case

3   Industry-related variables

Managed 'on trade'
Pubs, restaurants, hotels, leisure centres

'Off trade'	
supermarkets –	major
	minor

off licence –	tied
	free

wholesalers

Review Activity 4

Market segmentation is important in an industrial business-to-business context for the following reasons. Industrial markets are becoming increasingly competitive and it is essential that more effective and targeted markets activity are developed. The identification of businesses with similar needs that form identifiable segments enables marketers to exploit market opportunities more effectively. If a new segment can be identified, it is likely that the organisation can establish itself as market leader in that area. Market segmentation enables the company to explore new opportunities, monitor competitors, develop appropriate strategies and therefore compete more effectively.

Review Activity 5

The commercial market could be segmented by:

- Sector (retail/manufacturing/service)
- Region (counties/city zones)
- SIC code (contractors/interior designers/surveyors, draughtsmen)
- Benefit sought (functional/corporate/specialist applications)
- Buying criteria (quality v price)
- Situational factors (development areas/renovations of buildings).

Review Activity 6

Orange-flavoured infant toothpaste: Segmentation according to age, targeted at toddlers and young children.

Herb-based 'natural' toothpaste: Segmentation according to psychographics – targeted at environmentally aware, health-conscious consumers.

Denture-cleansing tablets: Segmentation according to age, and possibly socio-economic grade, since dental problems are more prevalent amongst people with low-incomes (and consequent poor diets) – targeted at over-60s, possibly C2DE socio-economic groups.

Mint-flavoured dental floss: segmentation according to age and psychographics – possibly targeted at young adults (who might need to be encouraged to floss their teeth) and health-conscious.

Listerine mouth wash: segmentation according to age – targeted at young adults (advertisements featuring the curry-eating dragon with bad breath trying to seduce the captive maiden).

Review Activity 7

The newspaper/magazines market can be segmented in a number of ways, amongst them the following:

- Age – children, teenagers, adults, senior citizens
- Sex – men's and women's
- Socio-economic grade, A/Bs, C1/C2s, D/Es
- Lifestyle – modern, traditional, humorous/satirical, careerists, reformers
- Hobbies/interests – sports, cars, computers etc

There are obviously any number of answers to the second half of this activity, but a couple of examples would be:

Private Eye: segmentation according to lifestyle – targeted at anti-authoritarians, non-conformists. The advertisements it carries include a high proportion for products intended to amuse or entertain.

Country Life: segmentation according to age, socio-economic grade and lifestyle – targeted at people over 30, in the A/B socio-economic grade, conformist in approach. The advertisements it carries are generally for items at the top end of the price bracket, including those for expensive fabrics and furnishing, and for antiques and jewellery auctions.

Review Activity 8

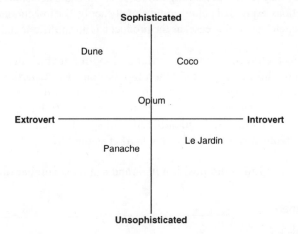

Unit Review Activity 1

As suggested, the new product, 'A Close Shave', does not have mass-market appeal. Men's self-perceptions matter and the product was not seen as being manly by certain segments of the market. The research findings do suggest, however, that the product does appeal to certain individuals. Market segmentation is therefore critical to the launch of this product to ensure that it is targeted at the right people and that the marketing budget is not wasted on a 'shotgun approach'.

The identification of appropriate segments will give B & G Shoprite Ltd a clearer idea of the market size and potential for this new brand. Appropriate communication and distribution strategies can also be developed that target the market segments. As the sales for this brand develop, the company can explore new market segments and attempt to increase the market with new strategies and messages. It may be that the brand's positioning will be varied as it moves along the product life cycle to reflect opportunities in new market segments. Finally, the new product once established in the market will be able to defend its market position more effectively if it closely meets the needs of a carefully defined market segment. If the company attempts to establish mass-market appeal, then its ability to defend the brand's position will be weakened.

It is possible that over time such broad market appeal will become possible as the concept of shaving without razors becomes more broadly acceptable. It is likely, however, that a product range will have then been developed that appeals to each specific segment within this mass market.

B & G Shoprite Ltd can segment the market along a range of criteria. The research findings suggest that age is a criteria but is too broad. Within the 18-30 age group, a range of attitudes and personal needs exists. While the female market does not consume the product, they may represent a strong influence on purchase decisions and therefore many of the options expressed below could equally apply. Socio-economic criteria do not appear to be relevant in this case, as the product has no specific social class appeal.

Psychographic techniques, in particular behaviour techniques, offer good segmentation possibilities and should therefore be considered, particularly in view of the strong attitudes expressed about the brand. It is further possible that the market could be segmented by lifestyle groups (ie young trendies, self-admirers, experimentalists etc). Finally, the identification of specific 'benefits sought' offers the company possibilities to identify new market segments.

3   B & G Shoprite Ltd could position its brand against a number of criteria. For instance:

- modern man
- individualist
- smoothness of shave
- ease of use
- a gift for men
- unique experience.

UNIT 5

THE

MARKETING MIX

Introduction

The purpose of this unit is to develop understanding of the marketing mix, which was introduced in Unit 1. The marketing mix is comprised of the tools available to a marketer in order to optimise the return from the exchange of value with customers and consumers. It does not relate simply to the elements of a product or service – rather it identifies all the variables over which a marketer has control.

This unit will examine in depth the different components of the marketing mix and will discuss the way in which these components are controlled and adjusted to make a product or service more competitive.

The unit will then proceed with an analysis of each of the key variables of the mix. A product is defined and analysed in terms of a series of levels. Products, including goods and services, are classified for ease in understanding. Every product has a life cycle, and this is evaluated in terms of its importance to marketing managers. The way in which the market adopts a new product is evaluated.

Pricing strategies and tactics are considered in Section 3, including the many factors that affect the price placed on a product or service. The way in which products are made available to customers is by distribution and this is introduced as an important part of customer service. An overview of this important concept is studied in terms of the level of customer service offered, alongside the different methods of distribution.

Promotion, which covers the communication between an organisation and its target audiences, is put into context ahead of Unit 6: Communications, which is devoted to this important area. The physical surroundings in which a service is delivered or a product sold are also considered, along with the people involved in the process of ensuring customer and consumer satisfaction. These must all be brought together to provide a seamless and positive support to every transaction.

Objectives

This unit deals with the components of the marketing mix and looks at ways in which they can be managed to optimise return on investment.

By the end of this unit you will be able to:

- identify the components of the marketing mix in the marketing of a product or service
- identify ways in which the variables of the mix can be used to the mutual benefit of the organisation and its clients
- select the appropriate marketing strategy for a product
- identify the benefits provided to the consumer by a product

- identify the characteristics of a service and use these to assess the benefits provided by a service

- use the product life cycle concept as a guide to marketing understanding

- select the appropriate marketing mix strategy for a product offering at different stages of its life cycle

- identify pricing strategies used to make products and services more attractive.

SECTION 1

The Marketing Mix

Introduction

The marketing mix, a concept central to modern marketing, has been defined by Kotler & Armstrong (1989, p45) as 'the set of controllable marketing variables that the firm blends to produce the response it wants in the target market'.

The aim of this section is to help you to:

- identify the components of the marketing mix

- identify the variables within each component

- appreciate the ways in which the variables of the mix can be adjusted in order to achieve a specific strategy or tactic

- appreciate how the targeting strategy affects the marketing mix.

1.1 What is the marketing mix?

The marketing mix has traditionally been considered to consist of four components, known as the '4Ps'. This classification was first introduced by McCarthy in the 1960s and has remained in popular use since then. A further 3Ps have been added to create the Extended Marketing Mix, as greater understanding of the importance of both services and service has developed.

ACTIVITY 1

Check on your memory from Unit 1. Write down as fully as you can, your understanding of the significance of each of the 7Ps in the purchase of a new car.

Product

Price

Place

Promotion

Physical evidence

People

Process

Your answer may have been along the following lines:

PRODUCT

When you buy a new car it is not simply the physical product that you purchase. We saw in Unit 1 how the underlying need for a product is to do with its function, but how the symbolism of a product or service – the status it affords the consumer – is an important part of every purchase. The buyer receives far more than transportation when taking delivery of the new car.

PRICE

This is the amount of money the customer is asked to pay for a product or service. The price of a car is set at a specific level but is often open to negotiation between the retailer and the customer. The final agreed price is a reflection of the customer's perceived value of the car and the competitive atmosphere in the market.

PLACE

This is the method by which a product or service is made available to the customer, more accurately referred to as 'distribution'. A car is distributed through retail dealers and agents as well as at auctions and through second-hand car dealers. The image of the retail outlet, and its proximity to the customer, are major factors affecting the buying decision.

PROMOTION

This is the way an organisation communicates the values inherent in its product or service to its target customers. It is necessary first to achieve awareness of need, then build a positive attitude to purchase, move on to secure the sale and finally to ensure that there is on-going satisfaction.

It is clear that each of the above components of the marketing mix has many variations and that skilful marketing 'blends all of the marketing mix elements into a co-ordinated programme designed to achieve the company's marketing objectives'. (Shapiro, 1985).

PHYSICAL EVIDENCE

This covers all aspects of the physical environment in which the service occurs. How the environment is designed, decorated and maintained influences consumer perception of the service. This refers to everything noticed by the potential and actual customers that will either increase or reduce the likelihood of purchase. All aspects are important: from the obvious – cleanliness of the premises – to the subliminal – a faint smell of dog in a second-hand car.

PARTICIPANTS

This can be summed up, for now, in the classic phrase used about President Nixon: 'Would you buy a used car from a man like that?' The people involved in every transaction – even those 'behind the scenes' – have a major role to play, and can be a major force in the customer's decision processes.

PROCESS

This refers to the actual documentation involved in the purchase, the stages of negotiation, the simplicity or complexity of making it happen. Obviously all legalities have to be complied with, but in as simple and fast a way as possible.

In a wider definition, it also involves every stage of service development and delivery described by Mudie & Cottam (1993, p6) as 'converting inputs to outputs'. It includes an organisation's policies and procedures, the way in which the service activities combine and flow, the training of employees and how flexible they can be when working with the customer.

The addition of the 3Ps to the original four has arisen because of two factors:

The first is a move towards the more active marketing of **services**. This has come about because marketers have come to understand that from the viewpoint of the consumer there is no difference between a product and a service. They are buying a **bundle of benefits**. They want to be able to do something that is currently difficult or impossible. They don't mind what the supplier calls the solution. Thinking 'product or service' is useful to a supplier, but is of no significance to the consumer.

The second is a realisation that every product sold has a degree of service associated with it. Try to think of any purchase you have made of a physical product which did not involve some degree of service. Even routine purchases in a supermarket carry a return-and-exchange-if-not-liked guarantee.

CONTROL OF THE MARKETING MIX

The composition of the marketing mix is controlled by management, and depends upon:

- the resources available
- the developmental stage of the product or service
- the managers' knowledge of the market and predictions as to its behaviour.

Resources are the ultimate control upon what is possible. It may be necessary to support a new product offer with a national television campaign, for instance, but if some £5m is not available this route is closed and, perhaps, the intended launch cannot go forward. A frozen product requires a specialised and costly distribution network. If this cannot be afforded, and/or the networks are not available (owned by the competition, perhaps) then the project will founder.

There is always competition for resources and a marketer has to be able to make a compelling cost-benefit argument over the medium- and long-term if a project is to be given an approval.

Product offerings pass through developmental stages, as we shall see a little later, and the mix must be amended to suit the needs of each stage.

Knowledge about how a market is likely to change and develop allows marketing decision-makers to change the marketing mix in a timely way, to make the most of their customers' changing needs and wants. For example, additional options or features can be introduced, the packaging can be developed, or new credit terms or price allowances can be used. The aim is to make the best possible decisions about the marketing mix in order to gain maximum customer satisfaction, at a profit, more effectively than the competition.

The management and control of the mix is *internal* to an organisation, but the way the mix performs in the market is *external*. The marketing mix must be the best possible combination of variables which the organisation can create. This, of course, will vary according to the target market segment and what is known about the customers within that segment. When making decisions about the composition of the mix the significance of data in a customer profile becomes paramount. The way in which the variables of the mix are developed and changed must at all times reflect the fact that it is going to be challenged by the competition in the market.

The market is in a constant state of flux, and anticipating change is a major concern of strategic management. Having tactical plans to handle the change efficiently is at the heart of quality in marketing management.

1.2 The variables of the marketing mix

It is timely now to explore in more detail the 7Ps of the marketing mix. Each of these components of 'the mix' can be varied in order to enhance or reduce the quality and image of a product or service. An important part of strategic management is that all aspects of the mix must blend together in a uniform identity so that the mix is communicating a coherent message to its target customer group. If the different variables within the mix are in conflict, then the message will be confusing for potential customers, who will tend to look elsewhere for alternative products.

The marketing mix is planned essentially to influence the level of customer response. Some examples of variables within the 7Ps are as follows:

Product	Place (Distribution)	Participants
Quality	Location	Personnel
Service line	Accessibility	Training
Capabilities	Distribution channels	Discretion
Goods	Distribution coverage	Commitment
Clues		Incentives
Personnel	**Promotion**	Appearance
Environment	Advertising	Interpersonal behaviour
Delivery	Sales promotion	Attitudes
Brand name	Personnel	Other customers
Warranty	Personal selling	Behaviour
Facilitating	Public relations	Degree of involvement
Tangible	Physical environment	Customer/customer contact
Price	Facilitating goods	
Physical	Process of service	**Process**
Process of service	Tangible clues	Policies
	Delivery	Procedures
Price		Employee discretion
Level	**Physical evidence**	Customer involvement
Discounts & allowances	Environment	Flow of activities
Payment terms	Furnishings	
Customers' perception of	Colour	
Value	Layout	
Quality/price	Noise level	
Interaction	Goods	
Differentiation	Tangible clues	

These variables are altered to create a variety of mixes to achieve given strategic and tactical objectives, such as: to defend the market share or to stimulate further sales. Some product or service are, for example, sold in a number of different versions.

ACTIVITY 2

Give an example of a product or service that is sold in different versions, depending on the specific needs of the consumer.

An example would be shampoos, which were originally offered as single products to facilitate the washing of hair. To secure competitive advantage, however, manufacturers began to introduce different versions targeted at the differing needs of consumers. Thus, those with dry, greasy, or 'fly away' hair found they could buy different versions of their favourite brand (and those of the competitors).

More recently, the competition in this market has intensified through the development of shampoo and conditioner being sold as a single item. The 'Wash & Go' range, which initiated this development, exemplifies excellence in promotion since it encapsulates the shampoo's benefits in a catchy and accurate description that doubles as the brand name.

(Note that the initial pressure for change came from consumer demand, fuelled by competitive pressure. Left to themselves suppliers would prefer to sell the simplest products in plain labelled packs in a market where they hold a total monopoly. Unfortunately, this apparent utopia does not stand up under examination since where such monopolies have been broken the almost universal results has been increased demand and sales as a result of competition.)

Even within a tightly defined market, such as that for shampoo, there is need to modify the marketing mix to meet the needs of the members of each target market. The promotion for a branded baby shampoo, for example, differs from that for the same brand offered to young women, and again differs from that targeted on older women. In this market the variation is marginal, but in other branded markets the differences are quite marked. Consider the difference in marketing a car radio to the automobile trade and to retail customers and consumers. Or the differences needed in selling the identical soup mix in sachets for home use and in 5kg tins for the catering trade.

EXTERNAL INFLUENCES

It is preferable, but not always possible, that the influence of all the external variables likely to have an impact on the marketing mix should be anticipated. In addition there should be an allowance or contingency for unanticipated variables. For example, an organisation must know how it would respond if a competitor introduced a price discount.

There are many external variables, in addition to competitor behaviour, that marketing decision-makers must allow for when selecting the combination of variables for the mix. These have been covered in Unit 2: Approaches to Environmental Monitoring in Marketing. Section 5 looked at the competitive environment, and Section 6 at the socio-cultural, political and legal, economic and technological environment.

Taking all these factors together, and adding in the issue of education and training, they can be referred to as the STEEPLE factors:

S   Social/Cultural

T   Technological/Product innovation

E1 Economic/Market competition

E2 Education/Training/Employment

P   Political

L   Legal

E3 Environmental protection.

(Worsam and Wright, 1995, p77)

ACTIVITY 3

The variables below are outside the control of a commercial organisation. Give an illustration for each one, and suggest how they can have a negative influence on the performance of the mix. (You can use examples from a range of contexts.)

● environmental protection

● government policy

● economic change

● social/cultural change

Examples of possible answers are as follows:

Environmental protection refers to the way attitudes and values change in society. In the Western world, especially in the UK and USA, attitudes towards the killing of animals for their pelts has changed over the past ten years, with public opinion so strongly against such practices that the retail fur trade has been badly affected and many businesses forced to close down.

Government policy can also influence developments in the mix. Concern was expressed over the high number of people killed in household fires. Evidence showed that soft furnishings on chairs and settees burned particularly rapidly, and gave off poisonous fumes. The government passed legislation requiring material used for soft furnishings to be flameproofed.

The extra process involved in the manufacture of the product caused cost increases which led to a price rise for the consumer. Good promotion strategy has been important to make consumers aware of the reasons for the price increase and the benefit, in terms of increased safety, that the change has brought to them.

Economic changes can seriously affect export markets. Firms for whom Iraq was a major export market, for example, were hard hit by the advent of the Gulf War and the subsequent trade embargo. Conversely, the 'freeing up' of some former Soviet Union countries and China for international trade has created opportunities.

The UK is undergoing major social and cultural changes as a result of the immigration policies of the 1950s and 1960s. The children and grandchildren of immigrants are demanding their rights to be treated equally as British citizens. There are major marketing opportunities to meet the needs of individuals from markedly different cultural backgrounds, with widely varying social customs.

1.3 Strategy and tactics

There has already been discussion of the terms 'strategy' and 'tactic' in Unit 1 of this module, but it is worth revising the subject here, and relating it specifically to the marketing mix. Both strategy and tactics are frequently used words. It is easy for them to become intertwined and for their meanings to have blurred boundaries. In this module the term is used as follows:

A **strategy** is a *plan of action* by which an organisation intends to achieve a goal over a set time-scale. Strategy should be viewed on a long-term basis. Marketing managers spend much of their time planning and implementing marketing strategy. A marketing strategy :

- identifies the target customer group whose needs and wants the company can satisfy at a profit
- sets objectives to achieve specific levels of performance
- identifies how the marketing mix or mixes is to be planned to achieve the objectives.

Tactics are short term and are directed by strategy. They have been described as manoeuvres in the field of battle (Fifield, 1992, p239). An effective strategy should change very little after planning, but tactics are likely to change fairly frequently. Their role is to respond to changes in the market and in competitor behaviour. Tactics are the tools by which strategic policies are interpreted and implemented. For example, discounting the price of a product for a short period is a well-used tactic to strengthen market share.

ACTIVITY 4

Give an example of a strategy that could be adopted by the following manufacturers/service providers, and the tactics they could employ to implement that strategy:

● sweet manufacturer
● chiropodist.

(Use the 7Ps as a frame for your answer.)

A sweet manufacturer might, for example, decide on a strategy to increase the market share of one of its chocolate bars by 2% within 3 months. Its tactics might include: enlarging the size of the chocolate bar (product), whilst maintaining the price; advertising the product on television; offering retailers a stocking bonus to encourage them to stock the product and to give it a favourable position in their shop (place and promotion). The manufacturers employees must be alerted to the tactics so that they can encourage retailers to take part and to benefit. The physical evidence will, as always, need to be supportive – sales people must, for example, have the necessary promotional material and briefing, in time to be effective.

A chiropodist in private practice might decided on a strategy to increase the size and scope of the business by a specified amount in a specified time. The tactics that might be employed include: leafleting the local area (promotion); offering home visits at no extra charge (physical environment/process); moving the practice location to make it more accessible (place); taking on an assistant/trainee (people).

1.4 Market selection strategies

As we saw in Unit 4, knowledge and understanding of the market and the selection of appropriate target segments is the starting point for the marketing of any product or service. It is only once this has been established that resources can be allocated to the various parts of the mix. Even if an organisation has only one product or service to offer, the decision will still need to be taken on

● how many target segments to aim at

● how many different marketing mixes to employ.

An organisation might choose to adopt a mass marketing strategy: offering one product or service, using only one marketing mix, but trying to attract as many segments as possible.

Marketing managers may wish, however, to divide the market into smaller and more distinct segments, adopting a strategy of selective marketing. In this case, the tactics used must produce a range of marketing mixes, designed to satisfy the needs of each of the segments targeted.

If a strategy of niche or concentrated marketing is being adopted, a marketing mix needs to be devised to meet the needs of the targeted segment.

ACTIVITY 5

Consider each of the products listed below. Write down whether a Single Marketing Mix has been devised for it, or a range of Marketing Mixes. If the latter, give two examples of the markets these mixes are targeted at.

● Bic biro

● Mars bar

● Reebok trainers

● Student textbooks

● Nissan car range

● Scuba-diving equipment

● Domestic lawn mowers

Both Bic biros and Mars bars are mass-marketed, and a single marketing mix has been devised for them, the aim being to appeal to as wide a range of consumers as possible. Both are widely available through many different retailers, and are sold in large volumes at relatively modest prices.

Scuba diving equipment and student textbooks are niche marketed and sold through specialist retailers or dealers. A single marketing mix will have been devised, appealing to the group of specialists requiring the product.

Domestic lawn mowers, Reebok trainers and Nissan cars are sold by using selective marketing strategies, targeting identified segments with variations on the basic product. A different marketing mix will, for example, be used by the manufacturers of Reebok to attract the young adolescent seeking a fashion item, from that which is used to attract serious athletes.

REVIEW ACTIVITY 1

Select an item which you have chosen, bought and paid for yourself over the last few months, and preferably something which is central to your lifestyle, such as a musical instrument, a piece of sports equipment, a CD player, a ticket for a special event, or a holiday.

1 Now describe each element of the marketing mix associated with it, in a comprehensive way, using the variables of the mix mentioned earlier.

2 Make comparisons in your analysis with alternative products which you examined and subsequently rejected for your preferred choice.

3 Show how the mix for your product could be modified to give a better offer to you as the consumer, and to improve the performance of the product for the producer.

(A possible answer to this activity is given at the end of the unit.)

Summary

In this section we have defined the marketing mix as seven different components or variables, which a company can manage in order to gain competitive advantage. The seven components have been briefly outlined in terms of what they comprise. It has been pointed out that the success of a product or service is also subject to external influences which, although difficult to control, should, as far as possible be allowed for when planning.

We have defined the term strategy as determining the direction of an organisation or department, and the term tactic as aiding the implementation of the strategy. We have also begun to identify reasons for selecting specific marketing strategies.

SECTION 2

Products and Services

Introduction

Products and services are arguably the most significant part of the marketing mix because this is what delivers the customer benefits. It is important that the product does not disappoint the customer. *The word 'product' in the title of this session is intended to encompass anything that is given to a customer in exchange for money. It thus covers everything from a haircut or theatre ticket to a car parking space (services), and tangible goods, such as a compact disc, a jar of coffee or a house.*

The aim of this section is to help you to:

- use analytical models to identify the intrinsic properties of a product or service
- classify products into different types
- analyse the characteristics of a service in terms of the consumer's perception of it.

2.1 What is a product?

Several different models have been devised to explain the properties of a product. The following two are the most useful.

FAB ANALYSIS

One way of looking at a product or service is to describe it in terms of the features it displays, the benefits it offers to the consumer, and the advantages it offers to the manufacturer.

Features

A product or service can be described in terms of a number of **features.** The features of a product will usually relate to its physical attributes. Thus, an electric kettle can be described in terms of its capacity, shape, colour and ability to switch off automatically. The features of a service such as a cut and blow dry would be the washing of the hair, including the shampoo and conditioner used, the cutting and blowing dry of the hair and any hair spray or hair mousse applied.

A list of features describes a product or service at its most basic level. It is quite likely that such a list would apply equally well to a competing offer.

Benefits

The most influential aspect of a product or service in terms of how well it sells is the **benefits** it offers the consumer – the characteristics which make it more attractive than its competitors.

Benefits can be hard to identify since they are often subjective. What attracts one purchaser, puts off another. To return to the example of the kettle, a particular model might include a decorative floral motif on its casing. This would be considered by some purchasers to be a desirable feature (a benefit to them since it will enhance their kitchen), while others might consider it to be overly elaborate and prefer a more utilitarian look. In the case of the haircut, a particular salon might specialise in loud rock music which will attract some customers but repel others. Benefits also include such things as the performance of a product or service, brand identity, and price. (Both low and high prices can be attractive to different customers: some people are keen to save money (even at risk of low quality); others equate high price with high quality and are happy to pay 'over the odds' because it gives them peace of mind.)

Indeed, not all the benefits associated with a product are necessarily founded in that product. Lancaster and Massingham (1993, p.79) believe that 'products should be distinguished not only by their actual utilities, but also by the perceptions that consumers have of them'. Sometimes these 'perceived benefits' will actually exist, but in other cases they are generated in a collective or individual imagination. Products which become fashion objects are a case in point. The perceived benefits of a specific brand of trainer relate not only to its physical properties but, for a teenager, to its 'acceptability' amongst a peer group. Such 'image' benefits can be created by manufacturers, by the use of clever promotion, but they sometimes take even the producers by surprise. There are examples of certain toys that suddenly become incredibly desirable because of the success of a related television programme, and of the manufacturers being completely unable to keep up with demand. The perceived benefits of these toys (in the eyes of children) exceed even the imaginations of their adult creators!

Advantages

There is a third component in this analysis: advantages. These are even harder to define but they relate to the features of a product or service that offer a competitive advantage to the producer or service provider. Frequently they will coincide with the benefits, as perceived by the consumer (since these are likely to give a competitive advantage), but they also include aspects of a product or service that make it cheaper to produce or provide than those of its competitors, or perhaps easier to distribute.

A dry-cleaning firm might, for example, purchase a new machine that processes the cleaning slightly more quickly than the old . Although the time saved isn't enough to make much difference to the consumer (the firm already offers a two-hour service), it means that the firm can take on more cleaning while maintaining the same number of staff, and thus increase its profitability.

ACTIVITY 6

Use the FAB analysis as a tool to help you understand the degree you are currently working on, your reasons for choosing it and the university's reasons for offering it.

1 Describe the degree, and the organisation providing it, in terms of its features – the basic components of the degree and the elements of the service provided by the university.

2 Pick out from the list of features those which attracted you and describe the benefits that you consider you will gain from them. Add any benefits which you value and which are not tied directly to a feature.

3 Consider the degree from the point of the view of the university. What might be the advantages to them of offering this particular degree, in this format?

Your answer will obviously depend on which organisation you are enrolled with and what type of degree you are working on (part-time, full-time etc). The list of **features** might include the syllabus, its structure and content, and the location and characteristics of the university. Amongst its **benefits** you might indicate the vocational nature of the degree, that it enables you to continue in employment or that it enhances your job prospects, the fact that you can easily reach the university by public transport and the facilities offered by the university in terms of the way in which they affect your lifestyle. The **advantages** to the university might include the increased number of students they are able to take on by offering part-time degrees.

THREE LEVELS OF BENEFITS

Another analytical model looks at a product purely in terms of the benefits it offers. It classifies these on three main levels, as illustrated in Figure 1.

At the first level is the **core benefit** (goods and services): the reason for the product's existence. This describes the product at its most basic level (in an electric kettle this would be to boil water), but is not the most significant level in terms of aiding the sale of the product. Core benefits are usually taken as routine by buyers. We *expect* an electric kettle to boil water.

The second level is the **real product,** a physical item or service (the 'features' in the previously discussed model, such as the kettle's shape, capacity etc.), plus additional benefits (such as the kettle's ability to switch off when it boils, and its display gauge which tells you how much water is in it).

The third level is the **enhanced product,** which has had a series of additional benefits added to the first two levels to improve its competitive nature. (These might include, in the case of the kettle, an extended guarantee, or a pair of free mugs with each purchase.) It is this final added range of benefits that reveals an organisation's understanding of the life style and want-satisfying needs of its target customer group.

What is being created is a **bundle of benefits** targeted at a specific customer segment. It is a way of saying to customers that the organisation cares about its ability to satisfy their needs through its products. It is this bundle of benefits that is promoted and purchased.

So, for a Parker fountain pen, the product analysis would be:

Core Benefit   Writing implement for communication

Real Product   A physical fountain pen

Enhanced Product   Brand identity, (Parker), guarantee period, repair and
                                maintenance service, matching biro and pencil
                                available through brand extension

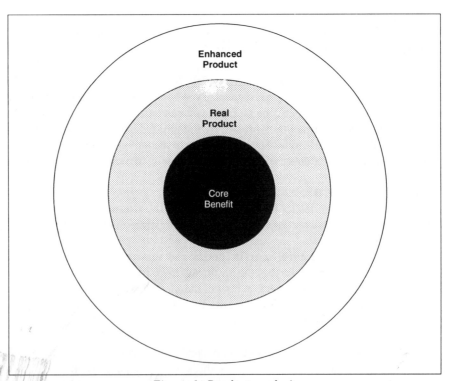

Figure 1: Product analysis

ACTIVITY 7

Apply the three-level model, as given above, to the product and service provided by a fish and chip shop.

List its core benefits, a description of the real product, and the benefits provided by the enhanced product.

(Note: You will need to take into consideration all the 7Ps, since many of the benefits and advantages are concerned with such things as the physical evidence and the people serving.)

The end product is fish and chips and its **core benefit** is a ready-prepared food.

The **real product** is a service which makes available a product: fish and chips. The additional benefit is that it is both tasty and filling (one hopes). The product cannot exist without the service process, the people who make it and the physical environment in which this occurs. Indeed, an integral part of the experience of buying fish and chips is enjoying the sight and smell of it being cooked – or being repelled by the smell of stale oil or the dirtiness of the staff's clothing!

The **enhanced product** is an extension of the benefits described above. This includes the optional extras (such as mushy peas, sauces etc), which can be bought or are provided free with the product. It also includes the packaging of the food, both the protective wrapping paper and the disposable container to store and carry the food away in. These must be effective and keep the food in good condition.

The staff involved have a significant role to play in the service process. Their manner and behaviour, and the way in which they take the order and deal with the customer are all important parts of the service encounter and help create an enhanced product. The style and cleanliness of uniforms are further illustrations.

The physical environment influences consumer perceptions of the outcome of the process. The size and layout of the waiting space, the length of the waiting period and a TV to watch are all benefits which enhance the service for the customer.

2.2 Types of products

Economists have classified products into a number of groupings. This is of value when studying the overall market behaviour in context of a national economy, but the concept is of limited value to a practical marketer, who must work from identified consumer need.

The main headings are:

CONSUMER PRODUCTS

They are bought by the person who will use them. This classification further sub-divides, as follows.

Convenience goods

Convenience (or non-durable) goods are those we buy regularly and need constantly to replace, such as food, household cleaning materials, etc. Generally these are of relatively low value and – important to a marketer – are seen as low-risk purchases.

Shopping goods

Shopping goods are bought and used relatively infrequently. They are expected to be durable. Because of their relatively higher price and their longer life expectancy they are seen as higher risk purchases and more care is taken in their selection. (The term derives from the phrase 'shopping around'.)

Marketers need to be aware that the decision process for shopping goods is likely to be longer and more complex than for convenience goods, and the marketing mix must provide the needed depth of information and reassurance in the form of guarantees, instructions, etc.

Speciality goods

Kotler & Armstrong (1989, p245) define speciality goods as having 'unique characteristics or brand identification for which a significant group of customers is willing to make a special purchase effort'. The price of such a product is usually high and the number of target customers is usually small. Purchasers of these products usually seek a great deal of information about them. A Rolls Royce is an example of a speciality good.

ACTIVITY 8

An umbrella is a difficult product to classify. Try and give examples of types of umbrella which would fit under the categories of convenience good, shopping good and speciality good, and indicate where each might be purchased.

Many cheap umbrellas are bought on impulse during a rainstorm; these can be classified as convenience goods. A golfing umbrella with a brand identity, might, on the other hand, be classified as a shopping good. It has to be sought out in a specialist shop, and is likely to be relatively expensive. It could, on the other hand, be classified as a speciality good, as could a fashion umbrella with an exclusive design for use at a wedding or when visiting Ascot.

INDUSTRIAL PRODUCTS

This term refers to goods that are mainly bought to be used in the manufacture of other goods. They can be subdivided as follows:

Capital Goods

This term covers plant and equipment, which tends to be purchased for use over many years (buildings, printing presses). They involve a large financial investment and are usually purchased after an extensive and thorough decision-making process involving many people and considerable time.

Consumables and accessories

'Consumables' refers to all those goods that are used in the working day and which need to be frequently replaced. They include such things as lubricants, and goods for maintenance and repair of machinery. 'Accessories' refers to relatively low-price capital goods, such as portable office equipment. These tend to be purchased as routine re-buys once they have been carefully selected. Once established, a supplier is hard to dislodge.

Materials and component parts
These are bought because they are required in the manufacturing process. A manufacturer of agricultural machinery would buy steel as a raw material, with the engine parts classified as components. It is important for a manufacturer to try to become involved at the design stage. A component which has been 'designed in' has secure sales through the life of the product.

2.3 Characteristics of services

We have seen earlier that there is a service element to all transactions. In many cases it is taken for granted, not noticed by the buyer – but if this is so it is a tribute to the seller. One of the worst things a salesman can hear is the comment 'Thanks, you are a good salesman'. A truly good salesman sells without the customer being aware that he or she is being helped to buy.

Conversely, almost all services involve a product. Shostack's Scale of Elemental Dominance (Figure 2) shows how product/service balance varies across a range of offerings.

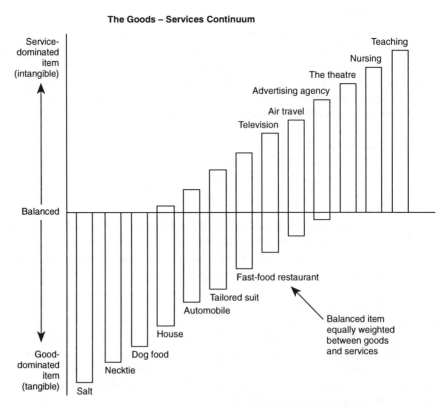

Figure 2: Shostack's Scale of Elemental Dominance (Shostack, 1982)

While recognising that there is no such thing as a product-less service, some services are less tangible than others. It is useful, therefore, to have a model with which to analyse those services at the 'intangible' end of the continuum. Unlike the model of a product, with its three levels of benefits, services can more easily be analysed in terms of a core benefit or service and a range of secondary services, or products that enable the benefit to be gained (as shown in Figure 3).

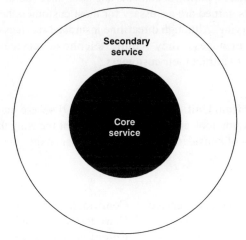

Figure 3: Service analysis

ACTIVITY 9

Consider the service offered by a hotel and an insurance firm. In the two inner circles below write down what you believe to be the core benefits of each? Note down in the outer circle all the secondary benefits that are essential for the customer to gain the core benefit.

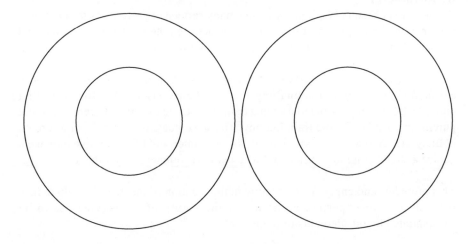

You may have identified 'bedroom' as the core benefit of the hotel group. It is inconceivable, however, that this is offered without a range of added services. These may include a restaurant, cleaning services, receptionist, parking facilities, entertainment or leisure facilities, room service and more.

The core benefit sought from an insurance company may be security or peace of mind. However, advisers, policy documents and assurances about the length of the contract and benefits gained are necessary for most customers before committing themselves to the service. Although direct-line insurance services often remove the need for premises or access, they require telephone services, together with freephone numbers, to attract their customers.

THE 7CS

You may remember from Unit 1, Section 4, how the 7Ps were matched by 7Cs (or 8, depending on how you look at). The 7Cs are a way of focusing the marketing mix on to the consumer – of considering how the consumers experiences the product or service.

To recap, the 7Cs are:

Customer value (product or service)	Confirmation (physical evidence)
Cost (price)	Consideration (people)
Convenience (place)	Co-ordination and Concern (process)
Communication (promotion)	

In the activities that follow, you will be find it helpful to analyse the service that is being offered in these terms.

Services are by their nature intangible. They tend to be produced and consumed at the same time and they also tend to be perishable. There can be difficulty defining ownership and it is difficult (impossible!) to provide heterogeneity. Let us take these issues one at a time, in context of the 7Cs.

INTANGIBILITY

Rushton and Carson (1985) investigated many service organisations to see if they had any clear perceptions of the differences between the marketing of goods and services. Many of the respondents emphasised the intangible nature of the service.

Of course, a service may have an end-product (such as a hair-cut or a tooth extraction), but it is not something that can be experienced before it is first purchased. It is not possible to try out a train service and examine its benefits before purchasing a ticket for the train journey. The same goes for a haircut, or a foreign holiday. (Of course, once experienced, the consumer will be better able to make a choice as to whether to return – and whether to recommend it to others.)

This provides challenges for marketing in the creation of the mix. To help reduce the risk of poor experiences the intangible nature of the service has to be substantiated by the elements of the mix.

ACTIVITY 10

Imagine that you have moved to a foreign country where you speak and read the language and need a dental check-up. You are not in pain and so the problem is not urgent.

How will you approach the problem? Remember to use the 7Cs framework – you are a consumer, not a supplier.

Your approach may have been something like this:

Customer value (Product/service) and Cost (price)

It is important that my teeth are well cared for. I need to be sure of a good dental surgeon because I want to build a long-term relationship for me and my family.

What does dental treatment cost here? Am I covered by insurance? How do I find out? Does any dental surgery help out I wonder? If I go to the Town Hall they will either know, or point me in the right direction? And can I ask them to recommend a dentist (and to suggest who to avoid)?

Convenience (Place)

How many dentists are there in my village? Can they all be accessed easily? My wife is handicapped, will she be able to get into the surgery when she needs attention? Are they open in the evenings and at weekends? What about emergency cover?

Communication (Promotion)

Can dentists advertise? Are they in the Yellow Pages. Do any stand out for the imagination/creativity of their approach? When I pass their door does the surgery look clean and inviting? Does it look welcoming, or forbidding? Has the brass name plate been cleaned today?

Confirmation (Physical Evidence)

Who do I know who can give me reliable advice? What can I deduce by actually going in to each surgery just to get information?

Consideration (Participants) and Co-ordination and Concern (Process)

How am I welcomed by the receptionist? Is my newness and uncertainty noted and responded to. If I meet the dentist (or even see him through an open door) am I impressed by his appearance. Are my questions answered – anticipated even? Is it assumed that I will be a supplicant expected to do what I am told, or will I be treated as a valued client?

In short, which dentist has put his or her marketing mix together with concern for my needs? That's the one I'm going to try for my check-up. If that goes well I'll consider signing up with him or her, at least as far as my first actual treatment.

INSEPARABILITY

The production and consumption of services is inseparable in that they both happen at the same time. When having dental treatment you are part of the service process. You are involved in the production process, which only exists through you.

The personality and skill of the person providing the service is obviously an intrinsic part of the service, which cannot be separated from it, but, perhaps to a lesser extent, the personality of the consumer plays a part. Both bring different motives, values and expectations into the situation. The service provider has got to get the service right the first and every time, so there is no room for mistakes.

PERISHABILITY

A service cannot be stored. Once the train has left the station the seat has gone; it's impossible to put it on the shelf and bring it out the next day. If the train leaves with empty seats that means loss of revenue, so strategies and tactics must be devised to maximise consumption and profit. Differential pricing according to the time of day the train departs is a widely used tactic to regulate demand. A lower priced ticket, or two for the price of one, will encourage other consumers to travel at different times during the day. Careful pricing and promotion activity can also stimulate consumers to travel who would not normally use the service. Decisions about service provision can considerably aid efficiency and profitability.

OWNERSHIP

In the main there is no tangible or legal ownership of a service. The consumer is paying for a process, an experience, the use of a facility, or a combination of these, as in a package deal.

HETEROGENEITY

Services vary because human beings are involved in both the production and consumption. It is possible to visit the same bank twice and not receive the same service, due to the 'people factor'. The quality of the service may vary according to when, how and who provides it. One restaurant waiter may give a fast, courteous and efficient service, whilst another in the same restaurant may be slow and inefficient. Marketing managers need to devise ways for customers always to feel that the quality of service is sound.

ACTIVITY 11

Think of a service that you have used frequently, and spend a few minutes describing it in terms of the above characteristics.

You might note the **intangibility** of a bus service on a route you use often. There never is a bus there when you need one! Then two come along together, or one comes and won't stop because it's full. Most frustrating! You have no control over this lack of **co-ordination,** are forced to be patient – probably in the rain.

You have to fumble for change to pay as you enter, and the person in front pays with a £20 note that the driver won't accept. The fare has gone up, again, and the whole operation is beginning to look unsatisfactory. The whole process is degrading and **inseparable** since the bus won't move until payment has been made and all are aboard. Part of the service is the physical environment, which you translate into **confirmation** that there is little **consideration** or **concern** and the overall **communication** encourages you to take the car next time – at least you own that.

Mind you, on most days the bus does come on time, the driver is very pleasant and the service operates functionally. Compared to the hassle of trying to park, and the risk of theft whilst the car is left all day, it really is better (marginally perhaps) to use the bus!

REVIEW ACTIVITY 2

You have identified the need for a boarding cattery to look after pet cats whilst their owners are away on holiday. Each cat will stay for anything from 2 to 14 days and your daily cost per cat, assuming 80% occupancy, will be 65p. You can accommodate up to 20 cats.

1 Identify the FAB factors that apply to your offering.

2 Use the 7Cs framework to establish the customer needs that you will address with your marketing mix.

(A possible answer to this activity can be found at the end of the unit.)

Summary

This section has described the different ways in which a product or service can be analysed, in terms of what it offers to the customer and consumer. It has also introduced terms that can be used to classify consumer and industrial products.

Services have different characteristics from products but has been shown that there is little difference in the actual marketing of a product or a service. The key is to approach the problem from the perspectives of the 7Cs.

SECTION 3

Product Mix

Introduction

This section looks at the product in greater detail, and in particular at the range of products a single organisation may offer. It is important for an organisation to maintain a balance between the products it offers, in terms of, for example, the stage in its life cycle each product has reached.

The aim of this section is to help you to:

- understand the concept of a product mix
- appreciate the usefulness and limitations of the concept of the product life cycle
- analyse how the marketing mix changes during a product's life cycle
- understand the concept of the diffusion of innovation.

3.1 What is a product mix?

A product mix is the set of all product lines and items that a particular seller offers for sale to buyers. For example, British Aerospace's product mix includes civil aircraft, military aircraft, guided weapons and satellites. Within each of these categories, there may be several different types of product, such as the range of passenger jets made by the company.

Marketing strategists have to decide:

- when new products and product lines are needed
- which existing products need a facelift
- which products should be dropped.

They make these decisions in the context of changing consumer and market behaviour and developing technology. Reasons for changes include:

- technological obsolescence in the face of new inventions
- style obsolescence
- changing production costs
- need to fill gaps in the product line
- changes in consumer habits
- activities of competitors.

ACTIVITY 12

Take each of the reasons for change listed above and name a product that has changed for that reason.

There are many illustrations which can be given to answer this question. A personal computer is an example of a product that has changed for technological reasons, with more powerful models coming on to the market every few months. Clothes are the best example of products that are affected by style changes, with the fashion industry dedicated to the task of stimulating consumer demand.

Production costs might increase, or they may conceivably decrease. Typically, when a product requires a lot of hand-finishing, production costs are likely to increase, with the result that they may well be phased out (unless a specialist niche market can be found for them). When production can be increasingly automated the production costs may well decrease. When products drop in price as a result (such as is happening in the home computer market) there may come a point when it is cheaper to purchase a new product, rather than have an older model repaired.

The need to fill gaps in the product line is closely linked to the activities of competitors. A sweet manufacturer might, for example, bring out a new snack, to match that of a competitor, rather than risk losing overall market dominance.

Changes in consumer habits and expectations obviously affect the products and services being offered, and vice versa. The technological development of the VCR created the opportunity for people to spend their leisure time watching videos in the comfort of their own home (as opposed to going to the cinema or the pub). The ownership of some many video recorders has resulted in 24-hour television, enabling programmes to be videoed for later viewing.

3.2 Product life cycle and strategies

Every product passes through a series of stages, which can be compared with the natural life cycle. An idealised PLC curve is shown in Figure 4. You will see that the stages are:

- Development – from conception of the basic idea, through research, concept testing, business analysis to market test and then to the...

- Launch – placing the product offering on to the market in a chosen segment with strategic and tactical objectives in place and the resources in support to maximise the probability of success.

- Growth – as the offering is successful it attains market share until the growth curve slackens and the decision is taken to move to a strategy of...

- Maturity – the product offering can stand alone and contribute profits to support the organisation and further new product development. It is from this stage that the product starts to move into profit; up until now expenditure on development will have been offset against profits.

- Decline – eventually the offering will come to the end of its useful life and it is no longer valid to support it.

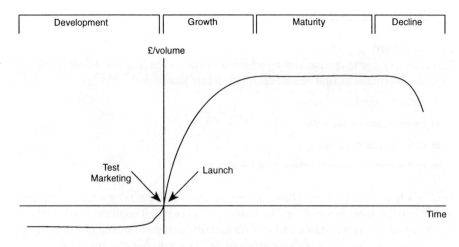

Figure 4: The product life cycle

The shape of the life cycle varies from one product to another, but it is hoped that the product will have a fairly lengthy life cycle, and be profitable for many years. Short life cycles are high-risk strategies and may only cover the research and development costs, failing to meet the organisation's criteria for profitability. Wilson, Gilligan & Pearson (1993, p273) argue that 'the product life cycle is one of the best-known but least understood concepts in marketing'. This may be because it is difficult to be precise about the shape of the life-cycle curve and the precise position of the products on the curve at any particular moment in time. Others, such as Dhalla and Yuspeh, believe that the concept of the product life cycle is flawed and impossible to use operationally.

While the PLC is a useful introductory concept, it is actually difficult to use, since it does not allow for the input of hard data, nor does it show what the market is doing in terms of the actions competitors are taking. It also only shows one product offering in isolation. These deficiencies caused the Boston Consulting Group to devise a quantified way to study the PLC. The Boston Matrices have already been introduced in Unit 2, Section 5. They allow the marketer to quantify and predict and are suitable for computer modelling, and so allow 'what-if?' scenario planning. They also allow a range of product offerings – known as a portfolio – to be shown together on the one matrix.

What, then, is the value of the PLC? The PLC is an ideal way of illustrating certain basic concepts to those coming new to marketing. The life cycle simile is easy to relate to, and the concept is superficially easy to grasp and to use. It provides a useful shorthand for speedy, but generalised, descriptions of a product offering's place on the curve.

It is useful to expand on each of the PLC stages. We shall use the retail market as the basis for our examples.

STAGES IN THE LIFE CYCLE

Development

This is the pre-launch phase, during which the idea for the product is conceived and gestated. Its role is to find and develop a product which will:

- satisfy a consumer need
- be profitable over time
- fit the product range
- fit the organisation's image and resources.

This is a heavy investment phase, as the product concept is generated, created, tested and developed up to the point at which it is launched on to the market. It can also be quite a lengthy period and it is financially supported by the profitability of other products, already in the maturity and decline stages in the life cycle.

Launch

This is the stage when the product is launched onto the market and is a period when the growth in sales is fairly slow as it takes time for the market to respond. It is not likely that the product will be profitable at this stage as the heavy investment in the R&D phase needs to be recovered. Promotional activities, and possibly the development of new distribution channels, may also prove costly.

Some products linger at this phase, which can prove costly if the competition is keen and able to follow quickly into the market with a copied product or a product with enhanced benefits. The product which is launched is the best that can be produced at the time but developments will quickly occur. Also in this phase, the 'gremlins' in the manufacturing process tend to surface and need to be resolved efficiently.

Growth

This is hopefully a period of rapid sales growth as new consumer groups buy the product. If the product takes off, there is likely to be more competition, with new entrants into the market. At this stage the product may be subject to modifications, with more benefits added to increase its appeal. It may also require new routes to the market. New market segments will be targeted, as part of the strategy and promotion activity, and advertising, in particular, may be used to encourage purchase. Price reductions may be used tactically to encourage purchase, and profitability will rise as volume and unit production costs start to decline.

Much of the profit will, at this stage, be ploughed back as market share is crucial to long-term profits.

Maturity

Most of the products we see on the shelves are in this stage and they tend to remain there much longer than the first and second stages after launch. This tends to be the period of greatest competition and many offensive strategic opportunities arise. There is more emphasis on tactical tools, such as sales promotion, and there are likely to be price reductions, as cost-benefits allow. Some competitors will leave the market, whilst others will perhaps modify their product and relaunch it before it goes into decline.

It is important to know the stages of the product life cycle because each one gives opportunities to manage the marketing mix differently. In this way the product will become more competitive and be better able to satisfy consumer need.

Decline
This marks a decline in sales of the product, usually for a whole variety of reasons including changing fashions. A product in the decline phase can still be profitable, however, because there is little or no further investment needed and costs are now as low as they will ever be. Products in decline can be 'milked' until no longer cost-effective.

The market performance of products in this stage of their life cycle needs to be carefully monitored. Some organisations leave the market or reduce the number of segments they serve. An effective strategy is to suspend all advertising and promotion activity, reduce the number of outlets and rely on consumer pull and brand loyalty to keep the sales and profitability going. One tactic is to raise the price at this stage. Although it will accelerate the decline of a product, the profit will be high on those sales made.

3.3 Price/promotion strategies for a new product

There are several ways of maximising profits from a new product, and different strategies will be adopted, depending on the nature of the product and the target market.

SLOW-SKIMMING
This strategy is used in situations involving:

- a high-price product
- low promotional activity.

It applies to luxury products where the market segment is small, its members are already aware of the product and are willing to pay a high price. The threat from competition must be little or none, with good barriers to entry. This is a high-profit strategy, since the price of the product is high and promotion is limited. The strategy is not to maximise sales, but to skim a lot of profit from those sales that are made.

RAPID SKIMMING
This involves a high promotional spend. Typically this strategy is adopted when only a limited production capacity is available (perhaps to test the product's acceptability before heavy investment). Then a high price has the dual effect of limiting demand and establishing the product as highly desirable and – probably –

of high status. The first calculator wristwatch was sold in Harrods for £1,000. Five years later they were on the high street at £9.99.

The strategy rests on the assumption that once the market becomes aware of the product and what it represents then consumers will be both willing and able to pay the high price. The heavy promotion is designed to convince the market of the value of the product. In time, as the top of the market is skimmed, prices will be reduced to allow those less willing or able to pay the original price to buy the product.

SLOW-PENETRATION
This strategy is used in situations involving:

- a low price product
- low promotional activity.

The low price should encourage a warm market response and if the promotional costs are low then profitability levels should be very acceptable. This is a useful strategy if the market is large, already aware of the product and includes some competitor activity. Significantly, the market is also likely to be price sensitive; that is, if the price were to be raised marginally they would turn elsewhere.

Unfortunately, it tends not to be very successful, since volume markets normally require a high-spend/high-volume approach – especially if competitors already have products in place.

RAPID-PENETRATION
There are times when the potential of the competition may be quite strong and it is wise for the organisation to adopt a rapid penetration strategy. This should help them to gain a large, if not the largest, share of the market. Its feature is:

- a low-price product
- heavy promotion.

On the surface, this looks as if the high costs of the latter will erase any profits. For this strategy to be successful the market needs to be large and the turnover high. Economies of scale feature, with low unit production costs falling as productivity rises, and with the benefits that arise from accumulated experience. The market is also likely to be price sensitive, and fluctuations in price will quickly affect consumer demand.

ACTIVITY 13

Describe the marketing strategy you would select (giving your reasons) for each of these products:

- pocket-size colour TV

- a new Japanese small car

- a new brand of toothpaste with refillable dispensing facility

- a new Kellogg's breakfast cereal for children.

Pocket-size colour TV: slow-skimming strategy followed by rapid penetration

The slow-skimming strategy is designed to pick up the status market, followed rapidly by a rapid penetration strategy to secure a share of the market and block off the competition. There will be a new stream of product enhancements coming rapidly behind, and the product life cycle will be short because of rapid technological developments.

Japanese Small Car: rapid-penetration

The small car market is a large one and a key part of the tactic will be to gain as large a share of the market as possible and to hold onto it. Heavy promotion activity will therefore be used, with many offers and incentives to the consumer to purchase. The price will probably be in line with the rest of the market. Some of the incentives to purchase will be financial, such as 0% finance, to encourage purchase without resorting to an official lower price which will pull down the overall market price as competitors react.

New brand of toothpaste: rapid-skimming

This new and unknown brand of toothpaste offers an innovative benefit to the consumer. It ought to be attractive to a market concerned with controlling waste and other environmental factors. Since this is a very topical issue the product is likely to face competition, and marketing managers will want to get established quickly. The price will be higher than the average toothpaste because of the additional benefit offered. There will be heavy promotion to convince the market to accept the product.

New Kellogg's breakfast cereal for children: slow-penetration

The breakfast cereal market is large and most of the top ten brands are produced by Kellogg's. This means that the new product will have an established brand identity. There is some competition, however, and the strategy of low price will be attractive, since cereal is an essential product in a price-sensitive market. The consumer must easily perceive the additional benefits to make the purchase worthwhile.

3.4 Diffusion of innovation

The theory of the diffusion of innovation is part of classical marketing theory and has been well researched by Roger (1962, p162). The theory assumes, according to Lancaster and Massingham (1993), that there are four elements to a new product launch and these are :

- the innovation (the product)
- the communication of this innovation among individuals
- the social system
- time.

The theory is concerned with how consumers react to new products and how long it takes for a product to be adopted by a given society. 'Adopted' in this sense means bought by target customer groups. Obviously, this has implications for the product life cycle. Some consumers respond quite quickly to new products and like to try them. Others wait until friends have bought them and some adopt the product much later. This leads to a classification of customers into 'adopter categories', as shown in Figure 5. The adoption process – the time taken for target customers to buy – is shown in this example as an approximate normal distribution curve.

When the innovation is introduced on to the market only a few people buy. The innovators (2.5%) are consumers who are willing to try new ideas. These are followed by the early adopters (13.5%), who are careful in adopting new ideas. The next group are the early majority (34%), followed by the late majority (34%), who like to wait until most others have tried the product. The final group are the laggards (16%), who are very traditional and only buy when the product is well established.

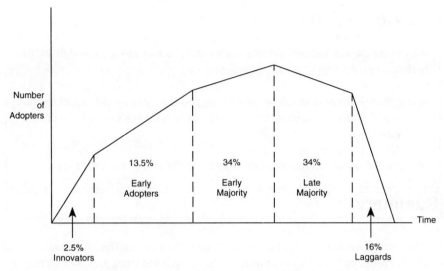

Figure 5: Roger's Adoption Theory or The Diffusion of Innovation

Note that the shape of the curve will vary with the product or service being offered. This example is a typical curve shown to illustrate the concept.

Each of these groups has different values which marketing managers need to know about through research. Each group will require a different approach for each aspect of the mix. Diffusion theory is important for managing totally new products, since there will be no previous sales history to give information about who buys, how, where and when. Identifying the characteristics of each group enables marketing efforts to be targeted at them, particularly the innovators and early adopters, as these are the two groups likely to buy early. Innovators are likely to be relatively young, better educated than the other groups and also have a better income. They are likely to be more willing to take risks and to rely on their own judgements and values rather than allowing their attitudes to be influenced by others. The influence of others is more likely to affect the later adopters.

Note that the 100% represented by the curve refers to all those who eventually buy the product or service under consideration. It does *not* refer to the 100% that comprise the entire market segment (the population).

There are many aspects of the product and its characteristics that affect the rate of adoption and the product life cycle. If the product is perceived to be better quality than existing products, it is more likely to be quickly adopted. The extent to which the product matches the values and lifestyle of customer groups also affects its rate of adoption. If the product is complex, and needs use in order to understand how it works, this will slow down the level of market penetration.

REVIEW ACTIVITY 3

Why does the marketing mix change as the product moves through its life cycle?

Apply the information in this section to suggest how you would expect the mix to change for an innovative home exercise kit as it moves through the product life cycle.

(A possible answer to this activity is given at the end of the unit.)

Summary

In this section we have looked at some of the influences on the range and type of products produced by a manufacturer. We have assessed strategies for entering the market with a new product and described the product life cycle and its reaction to market behaviour.

SECTION 4

Pricing

Introduction

The price of a product is its value expressed in monetary terms. It is a quantitative measure of the worth of a product and is usually related to the price of competing products. The more one knows about the way the market behaves the more reliably one can fix the price. Pricing decisions are among the most difficult that marketing managers are required to make. They often have to be made quickly and without testing, but almost invariably have a direct effect upon profit (Wilson *et al*, 1993, p325).

This section aims to help you to:

- identify some of the pricing tactics used by manufacturers and retailers
- appreciate some of the factors affecting price.

4.1 Price setting

Pricing is an extremely useful tactical tool – aggressive or defensive – to use against competitors. The way in which price is manipulated as a variable in the marketing mix will depend upon its role in an organisation's objectives. Without doubt, a financial objective will be a key objective and this will influence the type of pricing strategies used.

ACTIVITY 14

When fixing a price for a new product, what should one know about the market and its customers?

It is necessary to know the size of the market, both in terms of its value (in sterling) and the total volume of trade (the number of units sold). An organisation will usually have internal data to show what customers have paid in the past (historical sales data) for other similar products. The price of competitors' products should also be taken into account. Other information needed includes the type of outlets in which the product is sold and the frequency of customer purchases. Finally, it is important to know if the market is static or growing, and, if the former, whether or not it can be stimulated to grow. Channels of distribution, their needs, availability and cost, all impact on price decisions.

The level at which the price of a product is set has to be a careful balance between the cost of production and the price that wholesalers, retailers and consumers are prepared to pay. Costs set the floor, and the market and demand sets the ceiling (Kotler & Armstrong, 1989, p310). When establishing the price of a specific product, the anticipated sales volume must be measured against several price levels to monitor the expected effect on the target share of the market.

Threats are likely to come from:

- directly similar products
- substitute products on the market
- unrelated products which draw upon the same consumer finance.

Some products are **price elastic.** This means that if the price is lowered the demand for the product will increase. Others are **inelastic** and manipulating the price, up or down, will not affect consumption.

The price expected by wholesalers, retailers and consumers will strongly influence the manufacturer. For some customers, a low price is an important benefit, but for others such a price is unattractive. They become suspicious about the product's quality. Some like the status associated with a high price; they feel it enhances their image.

PSYCHOLOGICAL PRICING

Psychological pricing involves the manipulation of numbers and is well used in the car market. To many people £7,995 is a substantially different price from £8,000, even though in reality such a modest difference is almost irrelevant. Equally, £200 per month for a year, may appear more attractive than £2400 (or even £2000!).

Other tactics under this heading include:

Trade and cash discounts

Trade discounts are offered by manufacturers to wholesalers, in order that the latter can make a profit on the sale. A discount may also be offered if a bill is paid within a specified time period. If the size of a purchase is large, then a quantity discount may be offered. Seasonal discounts may be offered to stimulate out-of-season buying. Solid fuel is, for example, often discounted in the summer months.

Loss-leader pricing

This tactic is well used by supermarkets. The price is reduced to cost, or close to cost, and the product well promoted. Normally the product is something frequently purchased and is used to encourage consumers into the store so that they may buy other products.

Same-as-competition pricing

If a product is priced at the same level as the competition then there must be additional or alternative benefits to encourage consumers to purchase. Adding more, and increasing the bundle in a way which will save the consumer from having to make an extra purchase, can be perceived as an enormous benefit. Putting radios in new cars as part of the standard price, for example, used to be seen as a tremendous benefit by many consumers. Now a radio-cassette and all-round stereo is coming to be expected. In real terms it is not all that costly to the car manufacturer to add some benefits that have a major effect on the consumer, particularly considering the order size and discounts available to them. This is a well-used strategy.

4.2 Factors affecting price

COSTS

Since the price a product is sold must cover production, distribution and sales costs, it is obviously desirable to reduce these to the minimum. This does not mean that the product's price will drop accordingly, however. An organisation with low production costs has the flexibility to decide whether to price its products as low as possible, or to keep its prices in line with those of competing products. The first strategy may mean that the organisation captures a larger share of the market (with lower profit margins), whereas the second strategy may mean that it has to split the market with competitors (but with higher profit margins).

A product has two costs: **fixed** and **variable.** The **fixed** costs include things like the rent and rates of a factory, and interest rates on any loans. **Variable** costs fluctuate according to productivity levels. Each unit of production has set costs, but the total unit costs vary according to levels of production. The total cost of production are the sum of fixed and variable costs. Each unit produced shares some of the fixed costs, so the more units produced, the smaller the share of the fixed costs each has to carry. The unit costs are important when setting the price at which a product will sell. 'In the short run, variable costs may have more influence on a product's price, because the company loses money on each item if variable costs are not covered' (Kotler and Armstrong, 1989, p307) .

PRICE-VALUE RELATIONSHIP

An important term is the price-value relationship, which refers to a consumers' perception of the value of a product. If consumers believe that Product A is better quality and has more benefits than Product B they will be willing to pay more for it. Here, branding plays an important role as a strategic tool, and the investment in time and promotional activity to develop a brand identity has been shown to reap substantial rewards.

Another aspect of the price-value relationship is **added value.** The value of a pound of potatoes may be 20p, but this can be considerably increased by adding a few (inexpensive) additional ingredients and making up a recipe dish such as Potato Dauphinoise – potatoes and onion layered with cream. If this is then given a name typical of French cuisine, the price can be increased to whatever customers are willing to pay. This is the difference between price value/perception and cost/value reality.

ACTIVITY 15

Explain how consumer perception of price might be used by a marketer in the exchange process.

The key to understanding pricing is to understand value. Value is a package of benefits that includes price, but often, more importantly, such issues as: availability, branding, ease of installation, guarantee, expected life, free delivery. Customers expect to pay a certain price level – determined by 'benchmarks' which, interestingly, tend to vary by culture. Thus, a female dog can be sterilised in the UK for about £50 on a 'day patient' basis. In France an overnight stay is needed and the cost is FF2,000 (some £240).

It can easily be seen that to set a price which differs widely from customer expectation is to invite a bad response. The actual cost is of no importance to the average buyer and should only be used by the marketer to ensure that an acceptable profit will be made at the intended price.

This is *not* to say that 'what the market will bear' is the correct, or even the best, way to establish prices. Ethical considerations must be taken into account, along with the need to remain a friend of one's customers over the long-term.

Pricing policy, therefore, should set out to offer value for money with 'value' determined by the purchaser. Alongside this goes the need to compete and to secure profits over the long term

IMAGE PRICING

Often people need to express the importance of a relationship, or to mark a special occasion, and certain product offerings have become associated with these. They are priced accordingly. Although it is generally known that the astringent effect of after-shave can be obtained from simple chemicals available over the counter in a retail chemists, after-shave products sold as 'fragrances' are priced at anything from £3 to £100.

Patisseries in France are highly priced, as are flowers, because they are used as gifts to mark the importance of a relationship or to say 'thank you'. Grandchildren are often bought huge ice creams because the grandfather (always the man!) wants to show how much they are valued. Interestingly, as an overall rule of thumb, women differ widely from men in their perception of price, and their use of money. They are just as likely to want to pay a price set deliberately high as men, it is their perception of what items to pay for that alters.

Hard-nosed businessmen also need to pay image prices. One consultant has just gone on record as saying that as her daily fee increased from £400, to £600, to £750, to £1,000, so the demand for her services increased. Same woman, same skills, same dedication. But now charging what a segment of her market wants to pay.

ACTIVITY 16

Describe the circumstances in which an image price might be discounted.

The whole point of image pricing is that price is unimportant to the purchaser. The purchase motivations are to do with love, reward, appreciation. A gift bought at a discount destroys the image of generosity that underpins the purchase decision.

The only time when discounts appear to be used for image-priced goods is when stocks of a replaced model, or a slow-selling product are reduced in price to clear them – but this is a price reduction not a discount. **[The difference is not clear to me and needs to be explained.]** Note how upset air-line passengers become when they realise they have paid full price for a seat and next to them they have a traveller who paid some 60% less. What does that do for the perception of the airline and its integrity? What does that do to the overall price levels in the airline industry? The airlines are seen to be greedy in over-charging when (apparently) they could charge less – and passengers learn to shop around to obtain special offers rather than pay the full price.

COMPETITION

The **competition** has a strong effect on price and 'the price setter must gauge the effect of price on the behaviour of current and potential competition. At some high price level new entrants are tempted into the market and customers are tempted to switch'. (O'Shaughnessy, 1992, p337). If there is limited competition, or even a single supplier, then the latter can demand a high price. Competition is healthy since it encourages greater fairness in pricing. In terms of tactical pricing, an organisation must always consider how the competition will react to a price change since price wars can prove to be costly. Collecting data on the competitors' prices (and costs if possible) for every alternative product makes for efficiency and this should occur both in the developmental stage and at each stage through the life cycle. This data and information, along with a fairly flexible organisation, will enable optimal prices to be fixed and maintained.

PRICE WARS

A price war occurs when one competitor reduces the price of a product or service and another follows. Then the first reduces further and is again followed. One pair of filling stations in Belgium in 1992 met and beat the other's price until both were selling for five cents a litre. Queues of motorists blocked the city for hundreds of metres and the police were needed to control the traffic jams and to deal with angry motorists who had to wait as the storage tanks were emptied and new supplies came forward.

This dramatic example is not typical, but a prolonged price war can only benefit the customer since, while prices go down, costs remain much the same. Thus the overall level of profit across the industry is reduced as prices stabilise at their new lower level.

Dominant suppliers may use price as an aggressive weapon to force smaller competitors into line – or to block entry to a market. But then the price war is of limited duration, with a clear tactical objective. It is, in fact, more of a battle than a war.

To achieve a promotional impact, limited periods of price reductions are widely used – especially in the retail sales of petrol. Note how the filling stations near you run lower prices for a limited time, but always return to the base level set for their type of filling station. (Main brands are always higher than second brands, but both discount from their established level.)

REVIEW ACTIVITY 4

INTERNATIONAL AIRLINES

International Airlines, based at Manchester, offers a range of discounted fares, including a return fare of £99 for a flight to Bruges as part of their off-season, winter programme. A special fare for a week-end visit to London is being introduced at £70, in line with the daily fare during the week for passengers travelling between 11.00 am – 3.30 pm. There will also be special offers for a week-end visit to Rome at £130 throughout November and February only, and also Amsterdam for £95 through the same period. Special four-day breaks are being introduced between Manchester and New York, and also Boston to encourage consumers to combine shopping and sightseeing during late October, November and early December and these prices are to be set at an all inclusive and low level of £245. including hotel accommodation but no meals. Normal transatlantic fares will rise by 4% in line with inflation from early December through to early January. The special prices will not apply over the Christmas period for European destinations. These special offers apply to Economy Class only and are not available for Business Class or First Class Seats.

1   Give three reasons why International Airlines vary their prices?

2   Are airline prices elastic or inelastic?

3   Why is a fare of £99 attractive to both airline and customer?

4   Name one other organisation which raises and lowers its price:
    ● at different times of the day
    ● at different times of the year

5   Why are these special offers only available for Economy Class seats?

6   Why are prices described as being raised 'in line with inflation?'

7   Can the price for special offers ever be too low for the customer?

8   Identify any other factors that influence the prices charged for airline travel.

(A possible answer to this activity can be found at the end of the unit.)

Summary

In this section we have explained the meaning of the term 'price' in marketing and looked at some of the pricing strategies and tactics that can be used in the management of the marketing mix. We have also considered some of the factors that affect the level at which the price of a product is set.

SECTION 5

Distribution

Introduction

Distribution is a more informative term for 'Place'. (It just doesn't happen to begin with 'p'!) The task of distribution is to make product and services easily available to customers. Christopher (1991, p378) has written widely on this aspect of the mix and states that 'we have come to recognise that a crucial source of competitive advantage can be achieved through superior market place service.' People and offerings have to be brought together in the market place. Either the offering must be delivered to the consumer, or the consumer must be encouraged to come to the offering.

The costs of distribution must include everything which physically assists in the movement of offerings from point of manufacture (even services are made) to the consumer. Getting as far as the customer is not enough – the offering has to be *used* if it is to be repurchased.

If the product or service is new, and new routes to the market have to be found, then the costs will be very high. It is considerably cheaper to route a new product through existing channels to the consumer. No matter the number of benefits being offered, nor the quality, if the distribution strategy is weak it will invalidate all other aspects of the mix. And if a product is promoted and the consumer then can't find it, a lot of damage will be done to a brand or organisation's image. Sales will, of course, be lost.

The aim of this section is to help you to:

- identify the different distribution channels used to get a product or service to the customer or consumer
- recognise the objectives of effective distribution channels
- identify the costs involved in the different channels.

5.1 Distribution channels

Channels are the routes down which products or services travel on their journey to the consumer. Intermediaries such as wholesalers and retailers exist to facilitate this journey and remain in business as long as they are cost-effective within the channel. The UK's grocery wholesalers, for example, were forced into liquidation as the big supermarket chains found they could distribute far more cost-effectively, and the smaller retailers were, at the same time, forced out of business.

Major decisions involve the choice of market and how it is to be reached. A market is likely to have well-established channels of distribution and organisations need to develop good relationships along these routes. Such channels are a defence against competition. New entrants to the market may be forced to look for what Chisnall (1989, p164) defines as 'non-traditional channels of distribution'.

Direct-line insurance has revolutionised the motor insurance market by opening new direct-marketing channels which leap-frog the traditional high street insurance brokers. By siting their telesales operation in an area of cheap labour, cutting out much routine and time wasting process, and by developing an expert database they have been able to build on-going business relationships. We shall return to direct-line insurance in Section 7.

Some suppliers sell directly to the consumer but most do not, although there is a clear shift occurring towards direct marketing. It is noted by Lancaster & Massingham (1993, p230) that 'today's business transactions are often characterised by a diverse range of complex and interacting activities which are required in order to facilitate the process of exchange'.

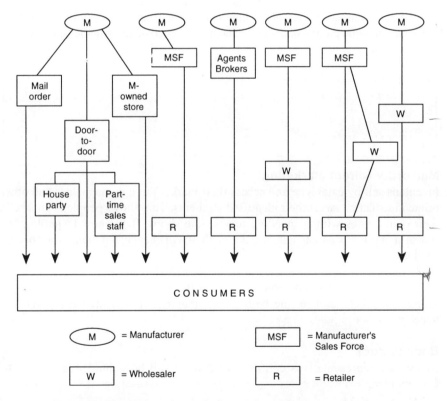

Figure 6: Marketing channel alternatives (Consumer Products)

The main routes open to a manufacturer are shown in Figure 6. The choice of channel depends on the requirements of the product or service, the market need and the availability of channels, but can be either:

- direct or
- indirect.

Direct channels include mail order (the old term for what is now beginning to be known as direct marketing), the manufacturer's own stores, or door-to-door, using parties and their own part- and full-time sales staff).

Indirect channels involve agents and brokers, wholesalers and retailers. These last two exist to break bulk. A large shipment can be dropped off to a wholesaler who can then use economies of scale to mix a range of goods from several suppliers to make cost-effective deliveries to retailers. Retailers facilitate the individual purchase of single cans and packages.

ACTIVITY 17

Give an example for each of the channels of distribution shown in Figure 6. Explain in what circumstances the channel is effective and whether it is likely to change.

Mail order (direct marketing)

Freemans sell by catalogue and access their market through magazines and other printed media that target their identified segments. This allows people to choose in their own homes without needing to visit the shops. If the new technology of 'home shopping' is adopted, their order method will change, but their basic concept need not.

This whole channel is mushrooming, with the advent of ever tighter ways to segment markets, and in line with the ever more sophisticated computer and telecoms technology.

Door-to-door

Betterware representatives call door-to-door to sell household items direct to householders.

These are routine items which can be demonstrated but, more importantly, are often not replaced as often as they need to be as they wear down gradually. They are also not seen as important enough to buy in the high street and people tend to postpone purchase. No reason why this activity should not continue.

House party

Ann Summers sell lingerie and marital aids through parties organised for a group of friends by a local housewife located by an Ann Summers part-time sales person. Potentially embarrassing products can be dealt with in the company of friends and in private. It is hard to try lingerie on in a retail store. Sometimes it is not allowed. Women find sex shops forbidding, and so access to marital aids in private is of great benefit to many.

Agents

Car manufacturers, sell through retailers who are accredited Ford Agents. The need is not only for sales – it is for a complete package to last the lifetime of each car, and beyond. It is hard to see how cars can ever be sold in any other way.

Manufacturer's sales force

Manufacturers sell through their own sales forces when the value of the purchase is sufficiently high to require negotiation. Thus Boeing sells direct to airlines (who retail airline seats and cargo). Philips sells consumer goods through electrical wholesalers, as well as direct to big chains such as Comet. They also sell their X-ray equipment direct to hospitals and medical centres (but using a dedicated sales force in each case). Whilst big ticket sales continue (as they must) there will be need for sales forces.

Marks & Spencer acts as a wholesaler for their own stores and manufacturers supply direct to them. Initially, a relationship had to be established, often by the manufacturer approaching M & S, but once agreement is reached the control passes to the wholesaler. We have achieved a degree of 'vertical integration'. The tendency towards integration – horizontally as well – is likely to continue as the cost-benefits of integrated channels becomes ever more apparent.

PHYSICAL DISTRIBUTION

This is part of the channel function and involves the transport of products via the various intermediaries to the customer.

Shipping physical products about is time consuming and adds cost. But it also adds value when done well. Customers and consumers expect product offerings to be available where and when needed – and by 'available' they mean in good condition.

Channel management is a specialised skill and the discipline of physical-distribution management is now established in its own right. Marketers are well advised to take expert advice on the management of this crucial area, just as one would when establishing a pricing policy or developing a new product.

5.2 Distribution objectives

Distribution must be seen as a total system that takes responsibility for the product's safe and secure arrival at the point of use at the time when it is needed. This can be explained by a well-used conundrum:

- When is a refrigerator not a refrigerator?
- When it is in York and wanted in Torquay.

Distribution adds cost, and so reduces profit, unless it adds sufficient value to make up for all (or some) of the costs. It has a strong gearing effect on the cost to profit ratio and good physical distribution management can result in substantial savings, which increase the profit margin markedly.

When planning distribution strategy and tactics, the output, the interface with the consumer, is the starting point . The key decision for marketing managers is what level of customer service the organisation is seeking as part of its marketing mix? This decision is paramount because the level of service, whether tied to goods or services, is a tool to gain competitive advantage and therefore needs to be planned and implemented well for good market performance.

ACTIVITY 18

What factors would you think were important to fast-food organisation in terms of customer service?

A fast-food operation, such as Burger King, is concerned to offer a total package of customer service. This must permeate everything that the organisation is, does, is seen to be. How it behaves, the importance it puts on each and every facet of how it operates, how it actually is.

No matter how hard an organisation may *pretend* to offer customer service, its real self will be exposed and the sham of the pretence will do more damage than if it had taken an obviously hard-nosed product-centred take it or leave it attitude.

Therefore Burger King must set its customer service intentions at corporate level. Unless they are encapsulated in the Mission and Corporate Objectives they cannot be expressed in Marketing Strategies and Tactics.

Issues of importance to Burger King, who operate through franchisees rather than through company-owned outlets, must include factors such as:

● developing and reinforcing the customer service ethos in each franchisee

● SMART objectives for every aspect of the offering

● precise specifications for each item offered across the counter

● thorough training and re-training of all staff

● monitoring (through 'mystery shoppers') the quality of the totality of the service provision at each outlet

● providing a full, effective and efficient back-up service to ensure all equipment is to specification, that food items are pre-portioned where possible, that support goods such as napkins, straws and cartons are to hand when needed.

Fast food operations such as Burger King have detailed manuals that cover every aspect of the needed operation in minute detail. They know exactly what their customers have come to expect and plan not only its provision, but also monitor its perceived value. They are so organised that a new outlet can be up and running from a bare site within 48 hours.

The key issues of importance within distribution are:

Order and delivery time

Customers want the goods they have ordered supplied as quickly as possible and long order periods or unreliable delivery times will encourage consumers to purchase from the competition. Reducing the expected waiting period is a bonus and could result positive word-of-mouth communication about the organisation. Distribution managers have to consider what is an acceptable length of time for an order to be completed and to monitor how often this target is achieved.

Ability to meet emergency needs and orders

An organisation which responds promptly to its customer's needs in a crisis will create a grateful customer who is likely to remain loyal.

It is fashionable to refer to the customer as 'king' and with this as background the handling of complaints can be a daunting task. Beware the trap of making a judgement about whether or not complaints are 'justified'. From the consumer's point of view all complaints are justified. Internally there is need to sort into the routine, which are easy to handle, and the urgent where special attention is needed – urgently.

Even a king cannot have everything he may want, but a courtier will try very hard to meet his wishes. In just the same way, an organisation should try to meet the wishes of its customers and consumers. The original instant tea needed hot but not boiling water. It failed in the UK back in the 1960s because the British insist that tea be made with boiling water – and then didn't like the product. Today's instant teas are designed to be made with boiling water, and some even have milk powder added for extra convenience.

Complaints should be monitored very carefully since they provide valuable information to assist the marketer improve the product offering.

Availability of parts, repairs and installations

Customers seek reassurance that if they are spending a large amount of money on, say, an automatic washing machine it will be easy to install or that the organisation will install it for them. Also that a parts supply and repair service will be readily available. The charge for installation is best incorporated into the purchase price as part of the benefits offered by the product, since additional charges at the point of purchase tend to irritate consumers. It is a useful sales tactic to mention the free, or easy, installation when the customer is at the point of making a decision.

Inventory level

Inventory is stock which an organisation will sell to a customer. It is a valuable asset which has cost a lot to produce. Having stock available when it is required is part of sound strategy, but having too much stock is inefficient strategy. Getting the balance right so that inventory is always ready when needed is a skill gained from experience and is achieved by monitoring the movement of stock to prevent stock piles or stock out.

5.3 Costs of distribution

An efficient distribution system clearly has a cost attached to it, and this is the input side of the equation. If distribution proves too costly, profit margins will be reduced.

ACTIVITY 19

List the areas in which costs are incurred by manufacturers and distributors for the service they provide to their customers.

TRANSPORT

This is part of physical distribution and is concerned with getting the product to the market. It does not necessarily follow that the cheapest transport is the best transport. There are instances when high transport costs must be borne. For example, a regular overseas customer may be willing to purchase a piece of complex machinery providing that it is delivered within a few days. It is wiser for the manufacturer to send the machinery by air, rather than the longer journey by sea, even though the cost is higher. The organisation will then have given a quality service and met the needs of a regular customer. It may, of course, be possible to charge the additional cost to the customer.

STORAGE AND WAREHOUSING

Storage and warehousing involves a large investment, which may be borne by the manufacturing organisation if it owns the distribution network. Alternatively, the manufacturing organisation may sell the product on to the business in the next stage of the demand chain on the route to the market. In either case, the costs have to be borne since they will be incurred.

INVENTORY LEVEL

There must be a balance between supplying every need from stock, and holding every order until stocks come forward from a central depot. A major strategic decision is concerned with the levels of stockholding that are needed to meet the corporate customer service objectives.

Stocks are an investment which have to be financed and so minimum stock holding is attractive to the finance director. On the other hand, the sales team would like everything to be ex-stock. A point between the two extremes must be established, set as an objective and monitored for effect.

CENTRALISED ACCOUNTING AND MANAGEMENT

The need for businesses to be increasingly efficient in their day-to-day running is emphasised by the move in recent years towards centralising financial functions. Prior to this, the duplication of accounts just added to management costs.

Overall, the picture of **total distribution costs** is:

Total distribution costs = Transport costs + Warehouse fixed costs + Warehouse-variable costs (inventory) + Potential profit loss on sales by delayed orders

PART 1

Describe briefly the difference between **physical distribution management** and the **channels of distribution** used by the manufacturer of, for example an own-brand cereal.

PART 2

What channels of distribution would you consider for:

● a new drip-dry summer skirt

● a lightweight pair of binoculars

● a car valeting service based on a laser cleaning technique?

(A possible answer to this activity can be found at the end of the unit.)

Summary

In this section we have identified the two components of distribution – the physical movement of goods and channels of distribution – and considered the appropriateness of different channels for a variety of products. We have also considered the need to balance the level of customer service with its cost, while at the same time meeting the main objectives of distribution.

SECTION 6
Promotion

Introduction

Promotion is the only variable in the marketing mix under the direct control of the marketer. Responsibility for all the other elements are shared with other managers. Wilson, Gilligan and Pearson (1993, p345) refer to promotion as 'the major forms of marketing communications, namely advertising, personal selling, sales promotion and public relations, which we can call the promotional mix'. Writers such as Kotler and Armstrong (1989, p415) use the term 'marketing communications mix', rather than 'promotional mix', since promotion is actually part of an organisation's communication strategy.

This difference in terminology has been tackled by the UK's Chartered Institute of Marketing. 'Marketing communications' is taken by them to include all issues of communication that concern marketing, and this includes internal marketing and corporate communications policy. The 'promotional mix' is seen as the major tools available to marketers when communicating *with* (never to) their target audiences. We shall come to communication issues in Unit 6.

As we saw in Unit 1, the four promotional tools can be classified into those that use impersonal media – public relations (PR), advertising, sales promotion – and the only one to use personal media: personal selling (often referred to as the sales force). Each of the four major tools sub-divides into a myriad of specialist activities but, fortunately, there is only need to delve into minute detail when beginning to specialise. For the purposes of this course it is sufficient to have a grasp of the major principles and to understand why and how each tool is used.

The aim of the section is to help you to:

- appreciate the differences between the four promotional tools
- identify the most appropriate tool for the job in specific circumstances
- begin to assess the advantages of and disadvantages of each tool
- identify ways in which each tool can be made most effective.

6.1 The promotional tools

Promotion exists to assist people in an organisation in making contact with the people who are going to buy and use the products and services they are offering. (It is worth noting that communication is between *people;* organisations do not have souls – it is the people within them that one is concerned with.)

Promotion is concerned with helping people's behaviour to change. At any one time we are all established in our ways, and many see no need to make changes. Marketers, of course, believe that they have identified needs and that they have a product or service to satisfy those needs. Therefore they have to influence people – to encourage them to change their behaviour so that it now incorporates the new product offering.

ACTIVITY 20

Identify three ways in which the behaviour of your parents has changed from when they were in their mid-20s. Consider why this might be? What forces were at work?

You may have come up with any one of dozens of examples, because people act so differently now compared with even 10 years ago, let alone from how they behaved 15 or even 20 years back.

Women's behaviour and role in society and in the home has changed beyond all recognition. Many say this is because of the birth control pill, but there are more complex factors at play. This change was, however, undoubtedly greatly facilitated by some research chemist's determination to find a reliable method of birth control, by finance being made available (in expectation of a high return on investment) and by marketing's effective communication.

Self-entertainment has declined with the advent of television and, now, of computers and computer games. There is no reason why people should not play card games, or monopoly, nor why they shouldn't entertain at home as the Victorians did. But most do not. Is the technology a cause or effect? How important was/is the persuasive role of marketing? Remember that marketers are working hard to sell self-entertainment packages. Cards are still in the shops, board games are popular at Christmas. But overall there has been a massive change in behaviour.

People's shopping habits have changed. They no longer go to the local shop, daily or weekly, but to the superstore, weekly or monthly. This was not an immediate move. It has taken over 40 years from the first self-service shop to the present situation. How much is the change due to consumer demand and how much to the marketer's skill?

Marketers are concerned with people and their behaviour. They are interested in what people want, why they want it, and how to show them that a solution is available. They are also, of course, concerned to reinforce positive behaviour and to keep customers loyal for as long as possible.

We shall see in Unit 6 that there are three states through which marketers need to move members of their target audiences.

First, individuals have to become Aware of the product offering. . .
    then a favourable Attitude must be secured before. . .
        a desired Action can occur.

Each promotional tool has a unique role to play in achieving the overall strategic objectives.

6.2 Public relations

PR is the non-personal stimulation of demand for a product offering or business unit by planting commercially significant news about it in a published medium, or obtaining favourable publicity about it on radio, television or stage without payment. Philip Kotler describes it as 'A variety of programs designed to improve, maintain, or protect a company or product image.' (Kotler, 1991, p567)

The essence of PR is its role as an influencer. Space is not purchased and so what is printed is in the hands of the journalist and the editor. Obviously, if the PR specialist provides material in a suitable form it is more likely to be used, but there is no guarantee that it *will* be used or, if it is, that it will be used in full or in context.

A major benefit is derived from this anonymity, however. Because the copy appears under a journalist's by-line the reader attributes it to the journalist and to the publication. Typically, one is more influenced by the opinion of the motoring correspondent of the *Sunday Times* than one would be by the motor manufacturer's advertising. We believe that the journalist is unbiased – as he or she should be.

They can be unbiased, but can still be influenced. If you received detailed copy, with supporting photographs and interesting statistics, would you not be tempted to use it? Especially if it was written in your style? The clincher, of course, is if you – as a journalist – can believe the claims that are being made. Hence, it is vital to encourage the journalists to try the product or service, in the expectation that they will be favourably impressed.

Immediately before the launch of Eurostar, the channel tunnel express between London and Paris, in 1995, all travel and holiday journalists were invited to take a pre-launch trip. The resulting copy should have run ahead of the launch and praised the service. Instead, the publicity was awful, because the day was a disaster. It started with the train being over an hour late – not even at the platform ahead of time! – and went downhill from there. The journalists had a field day and tore the service and its management to shreds. It even made the financial pages and share values fell, while initial bookings were 'disappointing'.

Publicity or PR? It is easy to remember the difference. Publicity happens. PR encourages it to happen. Publicity following PR is usually favourable, but publicity will also follow an event which an organisation would prefer not be made public. Then the PR role is one of damage limitation.

PR AND DAMAGE LIMITATION

The PR specialist really comes into his or her own when working in areas where a catastrophe may be reasonably expected. Public service transport operators, for example, should face up to the fact that accidents will occur, and that they will be reported. Unless there is a contingency plan in place the company can be destroyed – as in the case of Townsend Thorensen, when the *Herald of Free Enterprise* sank – or enhance its public reputation and standing – as in the case of British Midland after one of its planes crashed into the M1 at Kegworth.

PR, as has been explained in Unit 1, is beginning to take a major role at corporate level, where it operates with the organisation itself as its subject.

The major roles for PR are then:

- in the generation of interest
- the building of positive attitude
- the reinforcement of positive offering
- damage limitation.

Although media space is free, a substantial budget is needed because there can be major costs in putting across the information you wish to convey. The Ford Capri was, for example, launched in the island of Capri and journalists were flown in from around the world for a two-day visit and the chance to drive all models of the car. Personal cars were then available for them to road test at length. All the costs of this event were charged to the PR budget, but the media coverage, measured in terms of space alone, would have cost many times the PR budget, if it had been purchased for advertising. And it would not have achieved the same impact.

6.3 Advertising

'Any paid form of non-personal presentation and promotion of ideas, goods or services by an identified sponsor.'
(Kotler, 1991, p567 quoting from American Marketing Associations 1960)

Advertising exists to inform. It is understood to be sponsored by the organisation responsible for the product offering being advertised (this has by law to be made clear) and so it is treated as biased communication. People, thus, expect it to show only the best side of the story and it has long ago been established by the courts that a certain amount of 'puff' is allowed. One therefore sees adverts that quite clearly overstate the case, usually in a humorous way, so that it is clear that one is not expected to take the claims totally seriously.

Before individuals can consider a purchase they have to *know* that a need exists. They have to identify this need for themselves, and until then will take only a passing interest, at best, in any advertising. Research shows that we may be exposed to as many as 5,000 adverts every day (when one counts the logos printed on shirts, jeans pockets, etc) and that we cannot possibly take notice of them all. So we devise our own screening process to filter out those we don't immediately perceive as being of interest. A major advertiser's task is to penetrate these protective filters.

As always, SMART objectives are needed but, in common with PR, those for advertising will deal with qualitative issues. Behaviour change is sought, and such change cannot be measured quantitatively. You will therefore deduce that advertising does not seek to *sell*. Its role is to inform, and to help effect behaviour change by building a positive attitude and encouraging prospective customers to move to a state where they believe that a solution is available to them.

Note that in direct marketing 'advertisements' do seek some form of response, but in these cases the message contains not simply advertising, but also sales promotional messages.

TARGETING OF ADVERTISEMENTS

All promotion is targeted at individuals, usually falling within identified segments of the market. Advertisements should therefore be judged from the perspective of the individuals for whom they are intended. The skilled job of designing a message in terms of the interest of the target audience should not be destroyed by marketers and senior managers who judge the proposals from the perspective of 'would I respond to it?' (Unless, of course, they are representative of the target audience.)

The major roles for advertising are to generate awareness and interest, to provide information, to stimulate a desire for further information and/or action, to reassure after purchase. The reassurance role is very important, especially for big-ticket sales where the decision has been a major one. Many individuals become very nervous after they have agreed to buy and will consciously revisit the advertising to reassure themselves.

Advertising therefore has to address several audiences: those who are coming new to the area; those who are partly convinced that they should be interested; those who are actively seeking to buy; those who have bought and are about to use; regular users; those who have ceased to use. Campaigns have to be co-ordinated around these very different needs, with the awareness that every advert will be seen by people in each of these action states. It is not a job for amateurs.

(Note that direct marketing is a channel of distribution that uses the tools of promotion. It is not a form of promotion any more than retail or wholesale is a promotional type.)

ACTIVITY 21

Monitor the daily press for a few days in a search for an article that carries a report on some new development. Then note the subsequent advertising.

Identify how many of the points made in the PR piece are featured in the ads. Which points are they? Why were they selected? Were they carried in copy or visually, or both? What imagery was used, and was it suitable for the subject?

This is an activity that will occupy you for a few days, but it is worth the effort. Probably you will remember how the legislation on the advertising of feminine hygiene products changed to allow products to be featured on television – but were you aware of the long campaign waged by their manufacturers using PR and lobby strategies to influence the legislators and pressure groups?

Are you also aware of the outcry at the banality of the imagery used when the first ads ran, and how the marketers have amended their style and approach in line with market demand?

There are many examples, not as dramatic as this perhaps, that are worth looking for.

6.4 Sales promotion

Sales promotions can be defined as 'short-term incentives to encourage purchase or sale of a product or service'.((Kotler, 1991, p567)

As was explained in Unit 1, Section 4, the necessity for sales promotion arose as the trend towards self-service removed the personal contact between the purchaser and the retailer. Instead of being able to rely on a person to discuss needs and to recommend products, the suppliers suddenly found that the product had to sell itself from the retail shelf.

'Sales promotion' describes a variety of techniques, all designed to achieve a sale – now. It is the role of sales promotion to convert the *intention* to purchase action into the *act* of purchasing. It does this by adding an incentive that will appeal to the target customers.

The offered advantage should be time-limited to convey urgency and stimulate action. It should also be designed to achieve one or more specified sales objectives. In every form of sales promotion there is need for well-conceived promotional material, to be available at the point of sale.

ACTIVITY 22

List five different sales promotion techniques that might be used to encourage people to buy a new product.

List five different sales promotion techniques that might encourage people to remain loyal to a product.

As you probably worked out, different sales promotion techniques are likely to achieve different results. Here are some of the possibilities:

GENERATING FIRST PURCHASES

- Samples can be distributed door-to-door and supported by offers redeemable in-store.
- Samples can be banded on to sister products that already sell to the target market.
- An introductory price discount can be offered.
- Coupons can be mailed out, attached to products, provided on the shelf or handed out in store.
- Prizes can be offered to all, if small, or by competition or free draw if larger.
- A free gift can be given with every product bought.
- Free trials remove the risk from purchase, as does no-questions-asked exchange.

STIMULATING LOYALTY

- Cash refund or rebate can be offered in return for a specified number of purchases.
- A premium offer can be made at low price in return for purchases.
- Patronage awards in the form of trading stamps and/or vouchers reward loyalty.
- Prizes can be used in a variety of ways.

- Second purchases of a complementary product can be encouraged through offers in the first product. For example, a toaster can go a discount voucher for a blender purchase.

- Tie-in promotions associate similar products, sometimes from different companies. Shut out competition.

- Two-for-the-price-of-one prevents repurchase (and hence temptation to purchase competing product) for double the normal time – and may generate higher usage.

- 20% extra is the equivalent of a discount and makes the product appear better value for money than the competition.

- Special refill packs that fit only the original attractive and useful packaging may well represent a cheaper alternative to the competition.

The list of opportunities for and methods of sales promotion is limited only by the marketer's imagination and budget. It is such an important part of promotion today that in many markets more is spent on sales promotion than on advertising. Heinz have become the first major company to abandon all but the minimum of advertising in favour of direct marketing tactics with heavy investment in sales promotion.

TRADE PROMOTIONS

Trade promotions are a form of sales promotion used to stimulate action from traders who, of course, have to 'buy' the proposition if the product is to find its way into their stores. These tend to be more directly associated with the cost, but are not exclusively cost centred. 'Thirteen for the price of twelve' (a baker's dozen) is a long-established trade promotion, but today 'advertising allowances' and 'stocking bonuses' are far more likely. In the less obvious area are such as: sale or return deals; free demonstrators in store and incentive schemes for the dealer's staff.

Sales promotional techniques are now used in virtually all markets, even really big budget selling has found ways to utilise the concept of adding inducement at point of sale.

6.5 Personal selling

Personal selling can be defined as 'oral presentation in a conversation with one or more prospective purchasers for the purpose of making sales'. (Kotler, 1991, pp 567, quoting from American Marketing Association, 1960)

A sales interview is often described by sales trainers as a 'conversation with an objective'. This objective may not be to make sales on this occasion. In much of selling there are major hurdles to overcome before a sale can be made, and each of these must be seen as an objective to secure before one can move on. Gaining information is always an important sales tactic.

Two of the most important selling skills are asking questions and listening, as this scenario will show:

The scene is a high-street electrical retailer. Enter a middle-aged man and woman. They look around for a moment and go over to the fridges. A sales person joins them.

SP: A good range, isn't it?

Woman: Yes

SP: We have over 16 in stock at the moment, and they are all covered by our 3 year extended guarantee.

Woman: Really?

SP: The four cubic foot models are best for smaller kitchens – we have these (waves arm) which all have 4 star freezer compartments except the Philips which has a 5 star. (Pause) Doors can be left- or right-hung and we can supply in a range of colours if you don't mind waiting a couple of days (Pause) Finance isn't a problem, you'll be glad to hear sir – your wife won't bankrupt you in our store! – we have a 12-month zero interest option on units over £100.

Woman: We're just looking.

SP: Let me give you some brochures and my card. Do come back when you have decided.

On their way out the couple are met by another sales person:

ASP: Did you get what you were looking for?

Woman: No.

ASP: Oh dear. What was it you wanted?

Woman: We came in to see about a replacement for our fridge, but you seem only to have fridge freezers in stock.

ASP: Oh we also have plenty of larder fridges without the freezing compartment. We carry the biggest range on the high street – they are with the other fridges – but you can't tell the difference from the outside. Tell me why do you need a new fridge?

Woman: Well we don't really, but I am a professional photographer and need to store my film. We thought we could put a new bigger fridge into our kitchen and then I could use the nearly-new smaller one for my film.

ASP: Fine. Now just how much space do you have where the fridge is to go?

The conversation continues, with the sales person asking open questions and listening to the answers. By not assuming and by asking questions he has already ascertained that they are not married, that the woman is to buy, that she wants a larger fridge but is not really certain of the need. As the conversation proceeds extra information will come out and the subsequent fridge demonstration can be focused on the two that best suit the needs that have been expressed. At no time will the seller monopolise the conversation, nor pressure the couple. In a high percentage of cases a sale will follow, quite often then and there for comparatively low-budget items, especially if the zero finance offer is time limited.

SUBSIDIARY OBJECTIVES

The need to set subsidiary objectives can best be illustrated in the context of business-to-business marketing, but the principles apply across all selling.

In business-to-business marketing, the purchase will be made by a team of people who comprise a buying unit. This can be shown to comprise:

- Gatekeepers – who control access to the others. Secretaries, receptionists, junior staff have gatekeeping power. An objective is to get past them.

- Users – those who actually use the product offering. Often junior staff they may have no voice in the purchase decision, but never assume that this is the case. On occasion, their voice can be very strong. Always set an objective to confirm the users' status and influence.

- Influencers – those who have an influence, for one of many potential reasons, on the decision. Unless these are identified, and their needs provided for, a sale may be impossible to achieve.

- Approvers – those who have to approve the buying decision. They may be on site, or they can be in a different continent, but without their approval the sale cannot be confirmed.

- Deciders – these have the power of decision, subject to approval. It is frustrating to work hard to secure a 'decision' only to find that the true power did not lie with the person you were dealing with.

- Buyers – the obvious people to negotiate with, but a professional buyer works to obtain the best terms that meet a specification prepared by somebody else. He is a professional negotiator, not a decision maker.

These roles are present to some degree or other in every purchase decision. The wise sales person works hard to identify (research) the position before attempting to put a sales proposition together.

The importance of this approach is emphasised by Roy Hill and Terry Hillier (1982, p43), who show that there are four levels of decisions behind each business purchase.

- Precipitating decisions form the basis for product decisions.
- Product decisions form the basis for supplier decisions.
- Supplier decisions form the basis for commitment decisions.
- Commitment decisions allow the contract to be signed.

It should now be obvious why a simple objective like 'Sell five Boeing 737s to National Airlines by June 199X' is naïve. That is the strategic objective, but the subsidiary sales objectives have to take the overall task and break it down into manageable pieces.

SALES FORCE

The sales team are likely to be the only people in the marketing department who work in isolation, and they must be selected for their special abilities to operate away from base, to motivate themselves, and to be able and willing to take decisions (within clear policies).

ACTIVITY 23

The job of the sales person can be broken down into several different tasks. See if you can think of at least three of the components of the job.

Typical sales tasks include:

- Prospecting – searching for new opportunities.

- Selling – structuring and managing the sales conversations is a skill that must be learned and continually practised.

- Servicing – customers need constant support and advice. The sales person is the direct conduit to the organisation.

- Research – sales people can provide an immense amount of research information if they are motivated to do so.

- Allocating – scarce resources must be allocated. This includes everything from the sales person's time to product offerings that are in limited supply.

Sales people need skilled management to ensure that they are recruited and selected with integrity, that they receive initial and on-going training, and that they are motivated and rewarded in line with achievement. In particular, they should be required to set tactical objectives for their areas and for every call on each customer. Success should be evaluated against these objectives, rather than on overall sales performance. This will follow automatically if the tactical objectives are defined correctly and achieved.

REVIEW ACTIVITY 6

Identify and describe how the Ministry of Defence uses the promotional mix to attract recruits to the armed services.

(A possible answer to this activity is given at the end of the unit.)

Summary

This section has considered the four tools of promotion – PR, advertising, sales promotion and personal selling – in general terms, looking at the circumstances in which they might be used, and the advantages and disadvantages of each.

SECTION 7

Physical Evidence, Participants and Process

Introduction

The last 3Ps are better taken within one section, since there is a considerable overlap between them, with issues from one area having a major impact on the others. People are, for example, part of the physical evidence as background, and also responsible for the processes. Required processes have an impact on the type of personnel needed, and on the environment.

A clerical person working in a building society has much the same attitude, skills and knowledge as another working in the accounts department of a manufacturer

– but the one will be in uniform, behind a security screen and handle cash and numeric figures in direct contact with the public. The other will have a looser dress code, be in an open-plan office, handle figures only and have indirect contact with customers.

The aim of this section is to help you to:

- recognise the interrelationship between physical evidence, personnel and process
- apply the concepts in context.

7.1 Physical evidence, personnel and process

It is easier to understand the interrelationships in context.

THE MOTOR INSURANCE MARKET

Motor insurance is provided by underwriters, who provide the capital to support an insurance policy. Brokers exist to sell insurance on behalf of underwriters. They act as middlemen between those who want to be insured and those providing the insurance. Typically, a broker will earn 15 per cent commission on revenue. This is his income from which all costs and profits have to come.

Some brokers have concentrated upon niche markets. (Endsleigh's relationship with the National Students' Union, for example, gives it privileged access.) Others trade from the high street. A broker needs first to secure the business from individuals and then to invite renewal each year. It can take three or more years before the profit on any client covers the 'acquisition cost' of that client.

Some insurance companies (underwriters) have always traded through their own sales forces, effectively keeping their brokerage service in-house. The disadvantage to the consumer of this type of service is their inability to select the most competitive quote from a range of underwriters.

A recent, and very worrying, development for the brokers is the invention of Direct Writing by Direct Line Insurance. There are now some ten direct writers. Direct writers underwrite their own insurance but deal direct through 0800 and 0500 (free) telephone lines. They have no high street presence – seen as a major strength by many brokers – but run powerful advertising campaigns in the media.

It has come as a major shock to the traditional broker to find that many of today's buyers of motor insurance are prepared to effectively become their own brokers and shop around for the best quotation. Direct Writers have introduced a dynamic to the industry and are exploiting the power of database marketing to great effect.

Motor insurance – the traditional process

Proposal - Would-be insurers complete a proposal in which they detail the facts about their vehicles, their insurance history, driving record, health, age, sex and so on. This information is the basis for an insurance quotation.

Quotation – Brokers use their skills to select what they consider to be the most suitable quote from the range available. In practice this often means that they check out the two or three underwriters they most commonly use. In exceptional cases they will investigate the market to locate an underwriter willing to provide cover.

Acceptance – Would-be insurers accept the most suitable quotation and pay in advance. The broker issues a 'cover note', which provides temporary evidence that the vehicle is insured. In due course the insurance policy and a certificate of insurance is raised by the underwriter and sent, via the broker, to the client.

Renewal – A short time before the policy is due for renewal the broker will receive pre-prepared details of the renewal offer from the underwriter. He may add an alternative quotation before sending the renewal offer to the insured. Traditionally, the majority of insured have simply written a cheque, put it in the post and in due course received a cover note and then a new certificate of insurance.

Claims – When an accident occurs the insured contacts the broker with the details. The broker passes the information to the underwriter and follows whatever procedure is in place to settle the claim. Sometimes this is all handled by the underwriter; alternatively, it is dealt with by the broker working to the underwriter's instructions.

It is in the claims process that many insured become dissatisfied, since it is only then that the effectiveness of their insurance is tested. Ensuring that the insured is well looked after at claims time can be a major marketing benefit.

Motor insurance – the direct writers process
Direct Writers use real-time databases. This means that their information bank is constantly increasing in size, and becoming more refined.

Proposals, quotations and acceptance – Because they have direct personal contact by phone with their potential customers direct writers can change the questions they ask in the light of the information they know they need. (By contrast, the high street broker tends to use a standard proposal form acceptable to a range of underwriters.)

If their quotation is accepted they accept payment by credit card over the phone and issue a cover note which is subject to a written proposal confirming what has been stated on the telephone. Quotations that are not immediately accepted are sent out in the post and then followed-up by telephone in a few days' time.

All documents are raised automatically and typically reach the insured within two working days.

Renewals – Invitations to renew are raised, personalised to individual clients and sent out automatically. They are followed up by telephone.

Any enquiries received during a year, including those from people who asked for quotations but did not take them up, are included in the 'renewal' cycle, since it is the insured's renewal that is at issue. He or she must be taking out new insurance and the direct writer's know, courtesy of their database, exactly when.

Claims – Claims are handled by a database system using a nationwide chain of accredited repairers.

Brokers – the future

A traditional broker has tended to accept any customer so long as an underwriter can be found to provide cover. Direct writers have, from the first, been very selective in their choice of customer. By 'cherry picking' only those with the lowest risk they were able to offer very competitive rates, and begin the development of their databases. As they gained in experience they widened their criteria for selection and added further clients. The result is that direct writers are managing their risk, in real time, whereas other underwriters are assessing risk on historical evidence.

An additional problem for the traditional underwriter is that their customer base is skewing towards those with the highest likelihood of making claims. Claims must be processed and costs met out of the overall 15 per cent commission. Therefore, claims reduce the profit margin available to a broker. With the number of claims rising and the number of low-risk clients falling, there is an insupportable pressure being placed on brokers' profits.

The European Union opened its internal borders on 1 July 1995, to allow free trade in insurance. This will enable UK insurers to sell into the other countries of the EU, but has also allowed competition from other countries within the EU.

It seems that traditional brokers cannot expect to survive unless they make changes to the way in which they do business.

ACTIVITY 24

Using the 3Ps – physical evidence, participants and process – identify and contrast the differences between a traditional broker and a direct writer.

PHYSICAL EVIDENCE

Environment/furnishings/colour

The broker must cater for customers actually entering the premises and meeting face to face with the staff. The direct writer needs only to provide for reasonable staff working conditions. It is even possible that some staff will be home workers, linked into the database by modem and telephone line.

Layout/noise level

Privacy must be assured by the broker, where several customers may be discussing their private business alongside others. The ambient noise level, including that from the street, must be controlled so that a businesslike atmosphere is created.

Facilitating/goods

The staff must be easily able to facilitate the process. Today this will most often mean a computer linked to a database, but a small broker may not be able to go on-line to underwriters and so not be able to give a hard and immediate quote. A direct writer has a real-time database on screen and can initiate the insurance on the spot.

Tangible clues

A broker can establish clues to support its credibility. They have the three-dimensional physical office in which to work, and often a shop front as wel'. A direct writer has to establish credibility through promotion, and directly in the relationship between sales person and client.

PARTICIPANTS

Personnel

Recruitment and selection of suitable personnel will most likely be more difficult for high- street locations, where there is it may be difficult to obtain staff with the needed levels of customer-contact skills and numeracy. A direct writer can establish itself anywhere and so can select areas where staff are more likely to be available. Given a reasonable personnel policy, a direct writer is more likely to retain staff for longer than a broker.

Training

This is especially crucial for the direct writer since everything hangs on short telephone contacts. Initial training with regular monitoring of calls in progress will be needed to achieve and maintain the needed level of professionalism. The broker will have the ability to personally supervise his or her staff, visually as well as aurally, and will be more able to move in to assist if needed.

Discretion/commitment

These attributes are needed by both, but the direct writer is more reliant on self-motivated and self-disciplined staff.

Incentives
Can be the same for each type of business.

Appearance/interpersonal behaviour/attitudes
Appearance has been covered under environment. Interpersonal behaviour internally is more likely to be an issue in a broker's office, where a team can be developed, than in a direct writer's, where individuals work at computer stations.

Other customers/customer/customer contact
The broker's customers will meet, briefly, in the office. They, especially, must not become frustrated in the broker's office since this attitude will quickly be noted by others. Direct writer's customers will only meet each other if one has a claim and is telling others about the level of service. It is important that on these few occasions the customers report a good impression of the service.

PROCESS

Policies
Organisational policies must take all the issues, plus those in the other 4Ps, into account.

Procedures
Insurance quotations and the issue of policies is necessarily a complex business - but it need not be complicated, as the direct writers have shown. Staff must be aware of the need to help customers complete the needed documentation, and not expect them to be able to do it for themselves, unaided. They, after all, see it only rarely.

Merchandising
There are opportunities for the display of various product alternatives in the broker's office. There is far less opportunity for the direct writers.

Employee discretion
Vital in both cases.

Customer involvement, direction and flow of activities
Customers must be highly involved, since accurate and truthful answers are needed to personal questions. Clear direction is needed to steer the customers through the process with the minimum difficulty and at the maximum speed.

Summary

It can easily be seen that the original 4Ps do not address all the issues of concern to a marketer. We must always provide for the supporting issues covered by the whole of the 7Ps. These additional 3Ps overlap to a considerable extent and they must, therefore, be addressed together.

UNIT REVIEW ACTIVITY

As a traditional insurance broker, consider what actions you could take to counter the threats from the direct writers. Itemise your recommendations, using the framework of the 7Ps.

(A possible answer to this activity is given at the end of the unit.)

Unit summary

In this unit we have seen that the full 7Ps are needed if a marketer is to effectively manage the marketing mix. We have also seen that, although the 7Ps framework remains useful, it is better to work from the perspective of the customer and consumer and translate each P into a C.

Those managers who do not shift to a 7Cs approach, even if they continue to use the Ps framework for convenience, cannot call themselves marketers. Nor will their organisations be as successful as their potential would indicate.

None of the 7Ps stands alone. The whole of the marketing mix interrelates and decisions taken in any one area have repercussions across the other six.

Of the 7Ps, only Promotion is totally within the marketer's control. Each of the other six Ps exists within another function of the organisation, and marketing communication skills are needed to negotiate the needed actions so that the objectives within a marketing plan can be achieved.

References

Adcock, D, Bradfield, R, Halborg, A and Ross, C (1993) *Marketing Principles and Practice,* Pitman Publishing, 1993

American Marketing Association (1960) *Marketing Definitions: A Glossary of Marketing Terms*

Chisnall, P (1989) *Strategic Industrial Marketing,* Prentice-Hall, 2nd edn

Christopher, M (1991) 'Distribution & Customer Service', *The Marketing Book* (M J Baker ed) Butterworth-Heinemann, 2nd edn

Dhalla, N K & Yuspeh, S 'Forget The Product Life Cycle Concept', *Harvard Business Review,* vol 54, no1, pp102-112

Fifield, P (1992) *Marketing Strategy,* Butterworth-Heinemann

Haley, R I (1968) Benefit Segmentation : a decision-oriented research tool, *Journal of Marketing,* vol 32, no 3, pp 30-35

Hill, R and Hillier, T (1982) *Organisational Buying Behaviour,* Macmillan

Kotler, P & Armstrong, G (1989) *Principles of Marketing,* Prentice-Hall International, 4th edn

Kotler, P (1991) *Marketing Management: Analysis, planning, implementation and control,* Prentice-Hall, 7th edn

Lancaster, G & Massingham, L (1993) *Essentials of Marketing,* McGraw-Hill, 2nd edn

Levitt, T (1983) *Differentiation of Anything: The Marketing Imagination,* Collier Macmillan, London, pp 72-93

McMurry, R N (1961) The Mystique of Super-Salesmanship, *Harvard Business Review,* vol 39, no 2, pp113-122*

Moncrief, W C (1986) Selling Activity and Sales Position Taxonomies for Industrial Sales Forces, *Journal of Marketing Research,* vol 23, August, pp261-70*

Mudie, P & Cottam, A (1993) *The Management & Marketing of Services,* Butterworth-Heinemann

Oliver, G (1993) *Marketing Today,* Prentice-Hall International, 3rd edition

O'Shaughnessy, J (1992) *Competitive Marketing,* Routledge, 2nd edition

Roger, E M (1962) *Diffusion of Innovation,* Free Press, NY

Rushton, A M & Carson, D J The Marketing of Services: Managing the Intangibles, *European Journal of Marketing ,* vol 19 (3) pp 19-40

Shapiro, B P (1985) 'Rejuvenating the Marketing Mix', *Harvard Business Review,* vol 63, no5, pp28-34

Shostack, L G (1982) 'How to Design a Service', *European Journal of Marketing,* vol 16(i), pp49-64

Teboul, J (1988) 'De-Industrialise Service For Quality', *Management of Service Operations: Proceedings of the Operations Management Association Annual International Conference,* (ed R Johnson) IFS Publications/Springer-Verlag, Bedford, UK, pp131-138

Wilson, R M S, Gilligan, C & Pearson, D (1993): *Strategic Marketing Management,* Butterworth-Heinemann

Winkler, J (1991) 'Pricing', *The Marketing Book* (ed M J Baker), 2nd edn*

Worsam, M & Wright, D B (1995) *Marketing in Management,* Pitman

*cited in Further Reading only

Further Reading

The following articles and sections of books are recommended as further reading The full publication details of all books and articles listed are given under References

SECTION 1: MARKETING MIX
Adcock *et al* (1993) pp140-53

Lancaster & Massingham (1993) pp307-18

SECTION 2: PRODUCTS
Lancaster & Massingham (1993) pp170-211

Mudie & Cottam (1993) pp3-21

SECTION 3: PRODUCT MIX
Baker, ed (1991) pp284-09

Lancaster & Massingham (1993) pp190-7

Oliver (1993) pp176-82

O'Shaughnessy (1992) pp177-88

SECTION 4: PRICING
Kotler & Armstrong (1989) pp303-21 and pp326-40

Oliver (1990) pp344-60

O'Shaughnessy (1992) pp329-66

Winkler, J (1991) 'Pricing', *The Marketing Book* (ed M J Baker), 2nd edn, pp297-316

SECTION 5: DISTRIBUTION
Adcock *et al* (1993) pp214-32

Oliver (1993) pp312-42

Answers to Review Activities

Review Activity 1

To answer this question you will need to discuss each of the 7Ps of the marketing mix for your product. The brand identity and the image of the *product* are important variables, along with aspects of the style and design which influenced your decision to buy. Which factors were you most attracted to and why? Comment on the packaging and labelling of the product. Do these link with the quality and the price? What do you understand by the term 'quality'? Does the product have a guarantee or any safety features? Is there an after sales service facility?

How did you pay for the product and were alternative methods of payment offered? Did you pay the list price or negotiate a discount. Were there any price incentives?

Where did you go to buy the product? Was there a good choice of locations which stocked the product and were there alternative products to choose from? Was the product delivered to you? Were there other ways you could have bought the product such as a mail order facility?

How did you know about the product? Were specific sales techniques or sales promotion used to help you make your decision to buy? What advertisements, brochures or leaflets have you read about the product both before and after you bought the product.

What physical evidence did you actively look for? Which did you find? Were you encouraged or forced to proceed by other factors (such as a compelling price offer)? What affect did the salespeople have on you? Did they know their product? Were they interested in you and your needs? Were they helpful and enthusiastic? Was the process made as easy as possible? If necessary, were you helped to complete any forms, such as an application for credit?

Overall were you pleased with the transaction, and will you return to the retailer when next you need something that is on sale there? If so, why? If not, why not?

Modification to the marketing mix would include making the product more widely available so that it is sold through more types of outlets. The product could have more features, and a change in design or style, to make it more attractive to the consumer and more competitive for the producer. Promotional material which provides more information may influence the consumer. Changes in the design and additional features may affect the price which should be acceptable to both customer and supplier.

Review Activity 2

Depending on your conception of the offering your answer should be something like this:

Features:

- large, weatherproof garden shed
- spacious and secure living quarters for each cat
- cat toys and interesting items to play with
- diet: top-quality cat food and/or specific diet for each cat, as owners want
- low daily price.

Benefits:

- individual treatment for each cat
- cats can be given their own brand of food, so more likely to eat well, despite unfamiliar surroundings
- looked after by dedicated cat lover
- 'home from home' comfort
- secure and safe.

Advantages:

- is not a full-time occupation
- payment will be in advance
- much payment will be by cash
- high profit potential as price can be set at market expectation
- drop-off and pick-up can be at set hours or by appointment.

From the customer's viewpoint the offering will be seen:

Customer value

My cat will be safe, secure and well looked after. I can go away on holiday with a clear conscience.

Cost

As a part of my overall holiday budget I think up to £2.00 a day is value, especially as I can make appointments to drop off and pick up.

Convenience

The cattery is close to where I live. Well, close enough not to be a problem.

Communication

I saw the ad at my local vet's, and the local Cat Protection League said it was a well-run place.

Confirmation
When I visited I was reassured that the cats in residence were happy and well looked after. And my friend's cat was there for a fortnight and came home sleek and content.

Consideration
The lady I spoke to was so helpful. She even said I can ring from abroad if I am in any way concerned. She has three cats of her own and is obviously a cat lover and a nice person. Her house is so clean and both it and the cattery smell so fresh.

Co-ordination and Concern
It's so simple to make a booking, and the whole package is reassuring. I have never left Tabitha before, but I feel pretty sure that she will be as happy here as anywhere.

Review Activity 3

The marketing mix must change as the product life cycle unfolds since strategic objectives change and tactical opportunities occur. It should be obvious that what is right for a new product that is rapidly climbing the growth curve and building market share is inappropriate for a developed and ageing product at the end of the maturity curve and assaulted by products from a new technology.

Obviously, effort is needed to maintain the product in its mature (and profitable) phase – but not at the expense of high promotional spending that could be better used to bring forward successors to the product.

A HOME EXERCISE KIT
The following is a possible scenario for the life cycle of an innovate home exercise kit:

Introduction
At the introduction stage the innovative product is quite basic but the best that can be produced at this point. There has been extensive research and development previous to the launch. Production and marketing costs are high. The competition is limited and unfocused, sales are low and the price strategy is low, and costs per customer are high. Distribution is selective through a few outlets. It is important to make consumers aware of the product, and this will involve all aspects of the promotional mix. Promotion is extensive and targeted to encourage consumers to try the product.

Growth stage
At this stage sales increase rapidly, and costs per customer drop. The price level is set so as to maximise penetration of the market and profits start to increase. These are ploughed back. The product is also improved by modification, such as streamlining the features of the exercise kit and adding more benefits. The service levels for the product rise. The competition increases, and there are some imitation

products on the market. There is likely to be a battle for market share. Distribution of the product becomes intensive and many new outlets open up. The spending on promotion continues to increase awareness, build a positive attitude towards the product and encourage mass-market consumption.

Maturity

At this stage sales are high and will peak, and profits are high too. The model is a price leader and meets and beats the competition. More modifications to the product occur and there is a specific attempt to differentiate the product to make it more competitive. The distribution of the product continues to be intensive with good discounts to encourage the trade to stock the product. The promotion tools are mainly advertising and in-store promotion.

Decline

At this stage sales are falling, profits begin to decline and some competitors start to leave the market. The price is low. The product strategy is to phase out the exercise kit if it is a weak brand. If the brand identity is strong, then marketing expenditure is reduced so that the brand can be 'milked' for profits. Distribution levels are reduced to a selective level and the less profitable outlets are discontinued. The product is promoted only at a level to attract the loyal customer.

Review Activity 4

INTERNATIONAL AIRLINES

1   International Airlines varies its prices to encourage consumers to travel outside peak or popular times. Their aircraft are incurring costs if they fly empty and so carrying passengers at lower fares generates 'marginal' income. They also broaden their customer base and show that they care about their customers by offering them chance of relatively cheap travel.

2   Airline prices are elastic – if the price goes down the demand will go up.

3   The price of £99 attracts the customer because it is perceived as substantially less than £100. It is attractive to the airline because they know that it is as near to £100 as makes no difference!

4   Examples of other organisations varying their prices at different times of the day and year include British Rail, cinemas, and double-glazing companies who offer special discounts in early summer.

5   Airline profits rest on selling Business and First Class seats at full price. These are never discounted because there is no need; the business traveller has to travel and needs to travel in comfort. But there is a limit to the number of passengers who can, and will, pay that price. Thus, price differentiation is an attractive way of encouraging a wide range of consumers to purchase. The majority of tickets sold are economy tickets. British Airways, in the autumn of

1994, introduced their new Club Class with a great fanfare of publicity. Special seating was designed so that existing seats could easily be changed from economy standard to Club. The dividing curtains in cabins was put onto sliders so that the availability of Club seats could quickly be changed to meet demand. Thus, a popular route, such as London-Montpellier can have seven rows of Club seats on weekdays and perhaps only two rows at weekends, when the demand for tickets is mainly from tourists.

6   Price changes 'in line with inflation' mean that prices can go down as well as up. This policy is adopted to show that a fair price is being charged and that it will not be amended simply to increase profits.

7   Total revenue should never drop below total costs, but a proportion of revenue can be above marginal cost and still make a contribution to fixed costs. Selling below cost is a deliberate act to achieve specified objectives and should be funded from the promotional budget or in some other way that does not disguise the true situation.

8   A further factor that influences the prices charged for airline travel, is the need to be competitive. Airlines watch each other's prices very carefully and usually move quickly to match a competitor's 'special offer'. Another factor influencing the price is the desire by the airlines to get money 'up front'. The earlier a ticket is bought before the date of the flight the more likely it is that the price will be fairly low, particularly for long-distance flights. This is to encourage those who know they are going to travel on a particular date to buy a ticket. The money generates interest for the airline during the waiting period. As the flight date gets closer, ticket prices tend to rise as the proportion of seats allocated to the cheaper bands is exhausted. On the day of the flight itself, and especially as the flight is about to close, it is often possible, however, to secure a really low fare since at this stage any income for the airline is virtually all profit.

Review Activity 5

PART 1

Physical distribution management is concerned with the storage, handling and movement of goods. Channels of distribution are the routes down which products travel.

An own-brand cereal is shipped direct from the manufacturer to either a store chain's central warehouse or – possibly – direct to individual stores. If a central point is designated it will be because the store chain's management has determined that it is more cost-effective for them to distribute (as quasi-wholesalers) rather than to pay the additional price the manufacturer would charge for store delivery.

PART 2

Hopefully you have determined that you need much more information before you can really deal with this part of the activity. If not then you are still not yet thinking management, nor marketing!

How are the products to be positioned? Are they low value, high volume, or exclusive, high status, high priced? How large is each organisation, and does it manufacture or is it a distributor? Are there similar products already established in channels which could simply be used by the new items? It is crucial that you understand all these issues before you attempt to make recommendations.

For example, the skirt could be throw-away and sold at beach resorts, or it could be sold under an exclusive label. The binoculars could be plastic and suitable for a free offer (send in three packet tops and receive a pair of binoculars free), or they could be state of the art and priced at £1,500. It would make a difference! The car valeting could be portable – we'll come to you; open opportunities for franchise operations, or be sold directly to garages, etc.

Without hard information we cannot decide! And when we can't decide, we should not decide. Rather, we should identify what else we need to know and then set out to get the information.

Review Activity 6

The MoD uses **PR** to generate interest and pride by providing active encouragement and budget to allow military bands to play at events around the world. Sports players are allowed time to represent their country. The Navy sponsor the top 100 sea scout troops in the country. Demonstration teams perfect their skills and demonstrate them to an appreciative public. Who has not been thrilled by the Red Arrows and marvelled at their professionalism? How many youngsters have not been stirred to at least consider a military career?

Advertising is used – mostly in press and TV but supported by posters – to inform potential recruits about what individual services have to offer, and to provide the addresses of recruiting offices, etc.

Sales promotion is used when young people are sponsored through university as a factor in their recruitment. Some units offer 'experience' periods that allow would-be recruits to try the service out for a time.

Personal selling occurs in the recruitment centres.

Unit Review Activity

OVERALL

The brokers are in trouble. Their previous market strength has now become a liability since they have no experience of proactive marketing and little opportunity to change locations.

Given that they want to stay in the insurance business, they need to identify the Critical Success Factors before considering what actions to take. They may see the factors as:

Claim handling   Clients see this as of major importance. It affects renewals. It is cheaper to keep than to recruit clients.

System efficiency   Especially access, closely followed by speed of response. (The phone should be answered on the second ring, for example and written response should be within 24 hours.)

System effectiveness   To confirm that the right things are being done with those with whom we are currently in contact.

Product mix   Is it sufficient. Does it have flexibility, variety and opportunities to add value?

Follow-ups   Of those who expressed interest. At renewal time.

Promotion   Positioning, segmentation, targeting.

Marketing research   Promotional effectiveness.
Client satisfaction.

Control systems   Based on SMART objectives.

Corporate issues   STEEPLE factors, mission, corporate objectives.

Internal systems   Co-ordination and simplification, e.g. standardise on computers and network.

Database   Establish client database.

Using the marketing mix headings we can then determine what needs to be done:

Product

In this section it is necessary to cover each of the opportunities that have been identified, and to show how they relate to Customer Value. Remember that today's customers value and respond to brands and the broker currently has no brand identity.

Price

Remember to show that cost is the issue. That the price paid is only one element of the customer's costs. Time, energy and effort have to be committed by customers and they want to minimise their expenditure of each. In particular, in this market, is the opportunity to sell the cost benefit of the broker's insurance when (if) there is need to claim. A difficult conceptual sale but an essential one.

Place

With place equating to convenience, it seems that the broker has little choice but to get into real-time data management very quickly, and then to use it pro-actively to secure and retain business.

Obviously the existing client base needs segmenting so that packages can be tailored, but new business must be secured as well. This will, of course, depend to a great extent on the strategic direction, but a beginning can and must be made. Dedicated phone lines, for instance, can route clients more quickly than a traditional switchboard.

Promotion

The major communication aspects can only be devised when segmentation issues are determined. In the immediate and short-term, however, there is need to determine what the broker means by promotion and marketing and to apportion spend in line with intended achievement. Thus, communication objectives are needed immediately and, in particular for this market, there is need to track enquiries and determine the true costs of acquisition and retention. (See Unit 6)

Physical evidence

Confirmation that clients and potential clients are making the right decisions is needed throughout. We need to set standards so that issues such as performance standards and staff training can be put into place.

Participants

Consideration of the individual needs of clients must be provided for in the database and in training staff to be proactive. The benefits of a total package need to be identified and converted into user benefits so that the training can be effective.

Process

Co-ordination and Concern are linked, in that the processes are identified and provided for. At a minimum these will be:

- taking out insurance
- renewing insurance
- making a claim.

Processes should be seamless, yet tailored to individual need. Concern must be expressed by, for example, following up on claims to ensure that the client is fully satisfied. This probably means improving the use of computers, and cutting back on staff numbers.

Research

In addition, we shall need management and/or marketing information. Obviously there is urgent need to get a segmentation system up and running, but to achieve this we need hard information.

UNIT 6

COMMUNICATION IN MARKETING

Introduction

The marketing departments of today have developed from a more narrowly focused function, that initially included only advertising and sales, to include public relations and sales promotion. Just as finance is concerned with money in all its forms, so marketing has communication as its prime focus. We have seen in Unit 1 how marketing acts as a communications conduit between the organisation and its markets. The management of these communication processes is a key marketing skill that requires detailed understanding of the behavioural processes that underpin 'communication'. Section 1 of this unit will look at various models that have been devised to explain the communications process. Section 2 looks at how to select the most appropriate promotional tool and Section 3 at the use of advertising agencies. Section 4 deals with the management of marketing communications.

Communication is a two-way process. To be a successful communicator it is necessary not only to deliver a message, but to ensure that the message is heard, understood, accepted and acted upon. Evidence is therefore needed that the communication has been effective, and monitoring feedback is a process that continues until a desired end result is achieved. This may be relatively short-term or continuous.

When a family sells its house they are concerned to select an estate agent; advertise it; welcome prospective buyers when they visit; communicate with lawyers, buyers, agents, removal firms and service providers. But when they move out, the process stops. The communications task is complete. When marketing a product such as Persil (which has been a market leader for 90 years), however, there is the need to maintain a relationship with existing users, secure new users from rival brands, ensure that young people growing up become first new users and then loyal users, develop the brand image to keep pace with current market expectations, legal requirements and product developments, and be proactive in meeting competitive actions.

'Marketing communications' and 'promotion' are often used synonymously but they are, in fact, different. The one describes all communications emanating from marketing. The other describes the communications processes intended to 'promote' one or more courses of action. The distinction is to some degree artificial, since the underlying purpose of most (if not all) communication is to persuade, but as we saw in Unit 5, 'promotion' is aimed at sectors external to an organisation and is under the sole control of the marketing department.

Effective communication relies upon effective and efficient management – upon establishing strategies and tactics that are managed within a budget. Section 4 will be looking at the setting of promotion objectives and the management of communications. A communications budget is especially hard to manage, since communication is intangible, but the days are long past since Lord Leverhulme was forced to say that he knew half of his advertising was wasted – he wished he knew which half!

Objectives

By the end of this unit you should be able to:

- determine the factors that make up effective communication
- select and correctly use communication tools appropriate to a given purpose
- set and monitor communication objectives
- select, brief and manage promotional agencies.

Activity 7 (Section 2) requires student to use a public library. It is to be conducted over the course of several months.

SECTION 1

Communication

Introduction

This section examines the mechanism by which marketers communicate their message, and explains the need for a thorough understanding of the behavioural processes that underpin communication, including buyer behaviour. It examines the practical use of communications theory and distinguishes the need for separate areas of communications expertise.

The aim of this section is to help you to:

- understand the mechanism of communication by breaking the process down into its component parts
- appreciate the importance of communication in the context of marketing
- recognise the stages of the higher level response set
- identify the most appropriate promotional tool for each stage
- design a promotional campaign.

1.1 The communication process

It is commonly assumed that communications is a one-way process – as can be validated by simple observation. In everyday life many 'conversations' are in fact dual one-way flows, with each person waiting for the other to draw breath before he or she can get in with what he or she wants to say. Good listeners are hard to find; the human animal needs to express rather than suppress – except that one can never be sure that some information is not being held back, or modified for some reason that seems important to the 'communicator'.

The child's game of Chinese Whispers – in which a message is whispered by one person to another, around in a circle – is a simple way to prove how difficult it is for people to receive and transmit a message accurately. A well-known example starts as 'Send reinforcements I am going to advance' but may be received as 'Send 34 pence I am going to a dance.'

You will also notice, through simple observation, how many people transmit orders as a one-way process, without checking that they have been understood – still less that they have been accepted and will be complied with.

Effective communication only exists when a message is received, understood, accepted and correctly acted upon.

1.2 Communication models

The starting point for communication is:

Figure 1: Model 1

This shows the basic one-way process of a sender transmitting and a receiver (hopefully) receiving.

Validation is introduced in the more complex model, with a feedback loop:

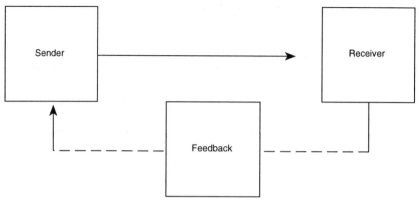

Figure 2: Model 2

Note that one of the most useless questions is: 'Do you understand?' This always produces the answer 'Yes'. It is essential to develop techniques to ensure there has been true understanding of exactly what was transmitted.

The communications process is considerably more complex than indicated in these simple models. Model 2 provides the basic framework, but we have to identify the key factors that combine to make up the full process. Only when these are in place can we consider the subsidiary issues that are within each main factor.

ACTIVITY 1

Spend 20 minutes carefully examining some examples of communication from your immediate environment. What are the key factors that make up effective communication? What does the effective communicator have to take into account when planning to communicate?

Hint: You are looking for language and images that are comprehensible to the receiver and used correctly by the sender.

The key factors can be summarised as: Receiver, Message, Channel and Feedback.

Receiver

The intended receiver(s) must be identified and their capabilities determined. It is essential to direct the message to the right person/people – in a form that allows them to access it psychologically as well as physically.

Message

What is to be transmitted must be clear, unambiguous, acceptable to the intended receiver; the selected language and syntax must be appropriate to the receiver. This is not simply a choice of a major languages: dialects and localised terminology must be taken into account, as must intellectual capability.

Jargon is an acceptable language – but only to those who understand it. The Morse code is a language, and so is a message translated into a commercial code created by merchants to abbreviate phrases into short form to reduce the length of messages and economise on transmission time. In communications jargon a message is said to be **encoded** when an appropriate language has been selected. Receivers must be able to **decode** it accurately.

Messages must also be psychologically acceptable; cultural background plays an important part in communications. What is acceptable in one culture may be taboo, even illegal, in another.

The form of message should suit the receiver. Americans, for example, respond better to a request than to a direct order – but a correctly phrased request has the power of an order.

Channel

Messages must be able to reach the Receiver(s) physically, in time for action. The channel must therefore be selected for its accessibility to the receiver, and for the speed with which it communicates. A Sunday newspaper, for example, has a colour supplement that goes to press two months before it is available to the public. The paper it is supplied with goes to press at 3.00 a.m on the Sunday morning. Both reach the same target audience, but one carries information that is far more immediate than the other.

Feedback

Unless the sender is monitoring the response from the receiver there can be no way to judge the effectiveness of the transmission. Feedback often indicates the attitude of the receiver towards the sender. Messages originating from a sender who is liked and/or trusted have more power than those from a sender who is disliked and/or distrusted.

Feedback should evaluate not only whether a message is being acted upon, but also why? Why it is, or why it isn't, or why only partly. Unless we know why, we cannot improve our communication skills and therefore our effectiveness. Lord Leverhulme would today be delighted with the amount of detailed feedback on advertising effectiveness that comes from research to determine why and how communication works.

A developed model of the communications process is:

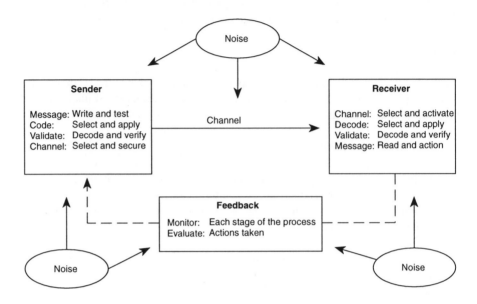

Figure 3: Model 3

Note that this model shows that messages have to be transmitted through 'noise'.

Noise

The term noise is used to describe all those factors that have the potential to disrupt a communication. It includes everything from a 'dirty' telephone line to anything distracting a receiver so that full attention is not given to the message. Noise also extends to such issues as examination nerves which cause a candidate to write about segmentation benefits (the benefits of segmentation) when the question calls for an answer about the value of benefit segmentation (which is a particular form of segmentation).

Marketers are concerned, more than most, with communication that is intended to have a persuasive effect. Over time it has proved necessary to understand something of human behaviour, since communications that synchronise with preferences are more likely to be received favourably than those which do not.

1.3 Behaviour

An understanding of individual and group behaviour is essential to an effective marketer. For an in-depth coverage of the topic, see the Further Reading list at the end of this unit. The following represents a brief survey of current thinking.

SOURCES OF BEHAVIOUR

Our behaviour stems from three main sources.

- Simple reflexes take care of our routine needs. We breath without conscious effort, our breathing being constantly ordered and controlled by our unconscious mind. These simple reflexes are, however, conditioned over time to take environmental factors, such as heat, cold, rain, storm, etc into account.

- We have simple habits that introduce routine into our everyday lives. Once a habitual pattern begins we are likely to follow it through to conclusion without thought. We can also be triggered into a habitual response by an appropriate stimulus. It is sometimes scary to find ourselves 20 miles down the road, without being able to remember covering the distance.

- Voluntary behaviour is superimposed upon habitual behaviour and is subject to conscious decisions. It depends on our frame of reference, and is derived from basic drives – either directly or indirectly. As a child, much of our behaviour is drive-directed, but by the time we reach adulthood little if any of our behaviour is directly drive-instigated. Instead, the drives have been built into systems which enable them to operate more effectively within our environment.

LEARNING

Edward de Bono, famous for the concept of 'lateral thinking', asks an interesting question: 'What is the purpose of thinking?'. He answers: 'To stop thinking.'

His contention is that people routinise as much as possible so that time is freed to do more interesting things. Once an acceptable result has been achieved, people tend to take the same route when presented with the same stimuli. Only when faced with a new, or rare, experience will the average person devote thought to how to achieve the needed result.

ACTIVITY 2

1 Make a list of everything you have purchased in the last week.

2 Against each item note how routine the purchase was, how much time and effort you devoted to it.

3 How much original research was needed, and to what extent did you call for, and then rely on, advice from outside sources ?

You may find it informative to repeat the exercise, using a close friend as the subject.

You will have found that the majority of your shopping is completely routine and requires no research or advice at all. You have learned which supermarket is best to use, where items are to be found within it (except when they move things around!) and many of your purchases will be straight re-buys to replace products you are familiar and happy with. It may be, however, that you found that one of the products you regularly buy was out of stock and you had to select a new brand. Did you find it difficult to make the choice?

Perhaps you will have found marked differences in your friend's purchase behaviour. If so, was it to do with age, sex, experience – or a combination of factors? Perhaps he or she uses different stores – because they are best in his or her experience. Are you right, or is your friend?

Now we are referring to target marketing, of course, which we covered in Unit 4. It is, you will understand, impossible to target without detailed understanding of human and especially purchase behaviour.

Learning is a natural process, which every living organism engages in to some degree. Formal learning is often resisted because it is forced, but learning itself is as natural and necessary as breathing. Without learning we should never be able to cross the road in safety, for example, since we need to learn road safety rules, and to be able to judge the speed and predict the likely behaviour of approaching vehicles.

A brief explanation of learning theory is necessary because it underpins much of the work done in understanding communications and especially advertising.

Conditioned responses

These can be developed in humans, just as they can in animals. Pavlov showed that dogs could be conditioned to salivate at the sound of a bell. In the early days of advertising much effort was put into a straight **stimulus-response** approach. Unfortunately, the process of human learning, and response, is far too complex to support a simple S-R approach and we now know that there is no direct relationship between advertising spend and sales results. We cannot say that X spent in advertising will bring Y results.

Operant conditioning

This works in reverse to Pavlov's approach. He elicited a response from a stimulus. In operant conditioning one's results stimulate and then reinforce the learning. Thorndike carried out the original work in this area by putting cats into boxes from which they could escape and get food by pressing levers. Each cat stumbled on the solution by accident, but it was found that subsequently the cats could escape from the boxes in a shorter and shorter time until they came out as fast as they were put in.

This response, because it is always rewarded, becomes a conditioned response. A consumer who always finds the instant coffee she likes in every jar of a certain brand will become conditioned to purchase that brand. A major problem for the marketer then becomes how to encourage the first and then the repeat purchases *and usage* needed to establish the conditioning.

Response patterns

These apply to complex situations. In a maze, for example, there will be certain points where decisions must be made. Initially we are confused, but as we gain experience of the maze we gradually identify certain features of each decision point and remember which way to turn. In time, the whole maze becomes familiar and no longer presents us with any difficulty. It does, however, retain its level of difficulty for those trying it for the first time. We may decide to help them, but they may be unwilling to accept our aid.

Customers and consumers who have learned how things operate may actively resist change, even if it can be proved logically that the change is beneficial. Think how many typists still cling to electric, even manual, typewriters, rather than move to a computer!

Pattern helps the learning process because we are able to group what needs to be learned and remember the groups rather than the individual items. Thus, 20 items are hard to remember, but four groups of five are really quite easy. Try it and see.

ACTIVITY 3

Spend a minute memorising the 20 items in the box below. Turn the book over and write down as many as you can. Then check back.

---

button	armchair	airship		razor blade
camera		poodle		can of petrol
	pencil		modem	
bench	mermaid			beer mat
			match	
rose bush				
	trailer	loaf		
duck				street lamp
	flag		sun	

You probably found it hard to remember more than half of the words.

ACTIVITY 4

Now try to remember 20 more items. After one minute turn the book over and write down as many as you can. Then check back.

straw	bucket	bus	footballer
bottle	spade	fountain	canyon
glass		statue	alligator
	towel		
ice cube		bell	hot dog
	boat		
lemon		clock	policeman
	harpoon		

Without doubt you found the second activity far easier because the words have been grouped, and in such a way that it was quite easy to make connections between them. (You probably found the last column the hardest because there is no apparent connection between the words.)

If the first 20 words had been grouped it would have been far easier to remember – and the memory would last far longer. Consider the effect of adding a narrative:

1 While sitting in an ARMCHAIR (not a BENCH) with the POODLE on my lap I sharpened a PENCIL with the RAZOR BLADE.

2 Never put a MATCH to a CAN OF PETROL unless you want to fly like an AIRSHIP towards the SUN which is brighter than a STREET LAMP.

3 A MERMAID was chasing a DUCK who wanted to get to a LOAF that had fallen from a TRAILER and had FLAGged its presence by a splash.

4 The digital CAMERA is great. It has an easy BUTTON release and can zoom to photo from BEER MATs, to ROSE BUSHes. It even has a MODEM built in.

Marketers, like teachers, can aid their communication if they take the time and trouble to present their material in a user-friendly form.

PERCEPTION

This refers to the making of meaning out of stimulus patterns. We are uncomfortable with random events and automatically and unconsciously attempt to 'make sense of them' – to put them into a frame of reference which we understand and are comfortable with. What will you do with these random letters?

X	X	X	X	X
X	X	X		X
X	X	X	X	X
X	X	X	X	X

And with these:

X	X	X	X	X
O	O	O	O	O
X	X	X	X	X
O	O	O	O	O

In the first example many will have not have noticed the missing X in the second line and 'completed' the pattern by believing they have seen 20 Xs.

In the second the Os and Xs are seen as rows – until you turn the book round by 90°, when they become columns. In either case they have been grouped by you – where no grouping may have been intended – because you have learned through life to turn data into patterns that make sense to you. If you have learned how to see the 3D images in the Magic Eye books you have added a further form of perception that enables you to decode messages that many others find incomprehensible.

If we were not capable of immediately reacting to stimuli we should spend our entire life struggling to interpret the mass of data which assaults our sensory system every moment. It is estimated that we receive some 50 million signals per second! Even our highly developed brains cannot process that amount of data and so we each put a series of discriminators and filters into place to limit the number of signals that reach our brain. In the process we, of course, censor out much data that could potentially be of value.

All communicators are trying to penetrate a series of discriminators and filters, which will vary from person to person. Ideally, each individual should be approached with a unique message, but since this is clearly impossible, the aim is to target groups of individuals with similar backgrounds, experiences and needs.

Selective perception

This refers to the tendency to take notice only of the evidence that supports a previously held position or attitude. Thus, parents of criminal youngsters captured on video commonly claim that their son 'wouldn't do anything like that'. One mother, presented with video evidence of her son's hooliganism, resorted to the explanation, 'Well perhaps his body was there, but his mind wasn't.' This example shows how entrenched a belief can be. Even unequivocal evidence that is of direct and personal concern can be filtered out, and the effort to do so probably strengthens the belief even further as a self-defence mechanism. It is important to understand that perception can be, and is, selective because marketing communications have to be at the right 'level', and couched in an appropriate tone if they are even to be read or watched.

Flip through a magazine and see how many adverts catch your attention. Then check back to see why those did – and why the others didn't. You will be on your way to identifying some of the discriminators and filters that you have personally established.

ATTITUDES

Relatively enduring attitudes are a major influence on behaviour. Usually deeply entrenched, attitudes are established through experience and predispose a person's viewpoint and actions.

Attitudes influence the lives of everyone; they affect the ways in which individuals judge and react towards other people, objects and events. Much of life is governed by attitudes – which are essentially emotional rather than logical. It follows that an appeal couched in emotive terms – whether or not supported by logic – is likely to have far more effect than a logical case, however powerful. Put simply: we do what we *want* to do rather than what we *should* do, sometimes rather than what we *need* to do.

Attitudes are not permanent, but become very strongly established over time and with reinforcement. Every time someone routinely rebuys the same instant coffee and receives positive feedback – it's good, the family like it – that person's attitude to the product is reinforced. So, also, is their attitude to the brand. If they buy Tesco coffee, and like it, they will be more inclined to buy other Tesco products. In time they will actively search out Tesco branded products and may become a strong advocate of them.

Attitudes linger even when reinforcement ceases. Even when there is negative reinforcement – a jar of coffee is unsatisfactory – the first response is likely to be 'that's most unusual, not like Tesco at all'. Providing that the supplier deals with the matter effectively it will be written off (but not forgotten). If the supplier handles it badly it will weaken the attitude and set back customer loyalty. It may even destroy loyalty altogether – and for all Tesco-branded products and their store group as well! The effective and efficient management of customer complaints is therefore a vital part of marketing.

Attitudes are not permanent, but they can be deep seated. Thus, whilst change is possible it is likely to take considerable time and expense. The first requirement is to identify the attitude state, then determine what you want it to be. The gap between the two determines the magnitude of the task, and helps establish the time and resources budget that will be needed. Clear objectives are required, usually staged so that attitude shift can be monitored.

There is *always* need to take attitude into account. Every communication, internal and external, should be constructed on the basis of an understanding of the attitudes which prevail in the targeted receivers.

1.4 Awareness – Attitude – Action

There are three key stages that underpin effective communication:

AWARENESS

Unless our intended receiver is aware of the communication, *and* of its importance to him or her, it will either be ignored, or, if noticed, disregarded. It is necessary to identify needs, and attitudes so that the whole of the communication package can be designed to achieve awareness.

There is usually a complex double task at this stage because the receiver has to become aware of a need before he or she will take notice of the communication, and yet the communication must help him or her to *identify* the need.

A major task of marketing is to create awareness within the target audience. Only from awareness can the next stage develop.

ATTITUDE

Once the receiver is aware of the need, and has opened some filters to communication, the task is to influence attitude. The need is to create a favourable attitude to the subject of the communication.

ACTION

Only when a favourable attitude has been created can action be sought. The desired action may be a trial, a first purchase or a repurchase. The purpose of the communication is to recover a lapsed user. On occasion it may be to induce the buyer actually to *use* the product. (A surprising number buy a new product, but do not get around to actually using it.)

The desired action is a full commitment to regular and on-going usage of a product, wholehearted and committed acceptance of a principle, and routine use of a new system in place of one that has been discontinued. Marketing profits come from repeat purchases. Almost anything can be sold, once. The skill comes in achieving repeat sales, in creating an on-going circle of Buy – Use – Like – Rebuy.

HIGHER-LEVEL RESPONSE SET

The 'higher level response set' is also known as the 'continuum of behaviour', or the 'marketing continuum'. It has been developed by a number of academics to explain the communication process necessary to move a purchaser from a state of unawareness to commitment as a regular and repeat buyer.

The detailed stages vary with the product, the market, and the target audience. To be precise, each marketer should develop his or her own HLRS. In practice, however, the three stages of Awareness, Attitude and Action serve across all markets.

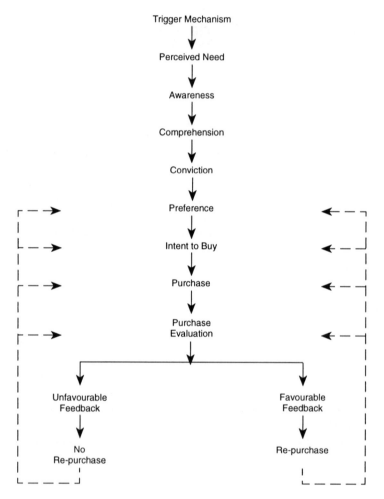

Figure 4: The higher-level response set for a fast-moving consumer good

A HLRS for a fast-moving consumer good shows that 11 stages are needed in the full process. First there has to be a **'trigger'** that will be noticed and cause a need to be perceived. Typical triggers are an almost-empty jar, a special offer in a shop.

Once a need has been **perceived** the individual will be **aware** of the necessity for information, and will begin an active search for a means to satisfy the perceived need.

The next stage is **comprehension** of the actual nature of the need, and of the potential ways to satisfy it.

Then comes a **conviction** that the need can be satisfied, and should be dealt with now. Once this stage is reached, the individual is committed to a desire to buy (or take whatever other action is appropriate).

The **preference** stage is one of choice between alternatives. At this point all those who offer a solution to the identified need have an opportunity to complete the transaction – whoever it was who initiated the process.

Intention to buy is an active decision, often made away from the point of sale. In any event, the individual approaches the market place having made a decision to purchase.

The **purchase** will be made if the product is available and the process is user-friendly. If not, there may be confusion; certainly there will be disappointment. An alternative may be taken, the purchase may be postponed or in some cases the impetus will diminish and the purchase process will be set back and may never be restarted.

All purchases are **evaluated** and there are two possible outcomes. Both affect attitude as the one leads to **repurchase** and the other to a **disinclination to rebuy.**

When this process is fully understood it can be seen that a single communication tool is unlikely to be able to achieve all that is necessary. Also that the most appropriate tool should be used at each stage.

Note that the whole process can be almost instantaneous – as when one sees a mobile ice cream van, feels hot, buys an ice cream, consumes it, and decides if it was value for money. It can also be extended over years, as when an airline requires new aircraft to come on stream in a decade, but has to start the process of ordering them now.

ACTIVITY 5

The Promotional Mix, you will remember from Unit 5, is composed of four tools: public relations, advertising, sales promotion, sales force. Identify which of the tools is best suited to each of the stages represented in Figure 4.

(Remember that we have to deal with at least five target audiences: those who are unaware, others who are moving down the continuum, purchasers, regular users, lapsed users.)

Public relations exist to influence through non-paid-for media space. Thus it can help throughout the stages of the HLRS, but is especially powerful in the earlier stages, when attitudes are formed (or influenced) and *trigger mechanisms* need to be found and tripped.

Advertising works alongside, and picks up from, PR. Because it is known to be paid for by the advertiser it is assumed (correctly) to be biased and so its messages are less trusted than those of PR, which carries the imprint of the journalist and media that carried the message. Advertising is especially powerful in provoking *awareness, comprehension, conviction* and *preference*. It also has a major role to play in reinforcing the purchase decision. As an on-going activity it has an on-going effect on attitude in particular.

Sales promotion deals with the all-important point-of-sale, where the decision is made to *purchase*. SP tools exist to add a last-moment incentive to buy – *now*. Some are targeted at securing a trial of the product offering, others at encouraging repeat purchase, still others at achieving sales volume. Sales promotion came into existence to replace the sales assistants in retail, but has now extended into almost all markets as a sales support tool.

The sheer volume of low-priced goods in the retail market means that the **sales force** concentrates its activities on obtaining orders from retailers, on securing space for their product. The higher-level response set for the purchasing departments of retailers is, however, much the same as that for the individual consumer/customer. The **sales force** is best targeted at increasing *comprehension,* and encouraging *conviction, preference, intent to buy* and the *purchase* itself. When seeking to obtain orders worth a considerable sum, however, then they can be cost-effectively used across a wide range of stages, becoming involved in triggering awareness of a perceived need.

PHYSICAL PACKAGING

Although not part of the promotional mix, the physical packaging has a major role to play. As a media it carries promotional messages, as a silent salesman it helps to achieve attention on the shelf. A well-designed user-friendly package will reinforce attitude and add aesthetic value in the place of use.

ACTIVITY 6

A new tramway is to be built to link Bromley in Kent with Croydon in Surrey. This will swing around south London and open a cross-town route free from traffic congestion. You are the communications advisor to the project. Your task at this early stage is to list:

1 Who is most likely to use the route

2 What they are likely to seek from it

3 The disadvantages they may perceive

4 The product features that are required

5 The product features that are desirable if affordable

6 The central core appeal that may be most suitable.

1 Likely users include:
   ● children travelling to and from school
   ● shoppers
   ● a relatively few commuters
   ● retired people shopping and visiting friends
   ● individuals and couples at weekends for shopping and entertainment
   ● teenagers – unemployed and/or out of school.

2 This mix of clients is likely to look for:
   ● safety
   ● reliability
   ● punctuality
   ● accessibility
   ● spaces for bikes, wheelchairs, prams, etc
   ● plenty of stopping points
   ● price
   ● car parking.

3   The disadvantages they may perceive include:
- danger from muggers, sneak thieves, etc
- low frequency of service
- fares too high
- difficult access and egress.

4   Product features required must include:
- security – a patrolling security officer?
- reliability
- punctuality
- ease of access and egress
- space for equipment and luggage.

5   Desirable features include:
- low price
- car parks
- more, rather than fewer, stopping points.

6   A suitable central core appeal would be 'Travel easily and safely'. On to this can be added appeals of interest to specific target groups.

REVIEW ACTIVITY 1

BROMLEY–CROYDON TRAMWAY

Now that you have clarified the planning issues you can go ahead and produce an outline promotional plan for the launch of the tramway. Take the main headings of public relations, advertising, sales promotion and selling, and indicate what you intend to do, when, and in what media. (You don't need to go into too much detail; just indicate which medium you intend to use, and give a rough idea of the message you intend to put across.)

You will need a name for the service.

(A possible answer to this activity is given at the end of the unit.)

Summary

It is crucially important to plan communication so that it will be received and acted upon. To achieve this it must pass through the protective systems of discriminators and filters which we all have put into place so that we are not overwhelmed with stimuli from the environment. An understanding of human behaviour is essential if cost effective communication is to be achieved.

To attain the desired outcome it is necessary to take receivers through stages that can be summarised as Awareness, Attitude and Action.

Specific promotional tools exist for use at each of the stages, but to achieve maximum effect they should be integrated to ensure that there is a clarity of purpose and a consistency of message.

SECTION 2

Promotional Tools

Introduction

This section will examine the way that promotional tools are used. It will relate the promotional process to the processes of physical distribution and examine the range of media that is available. The identification of target audiences and publics will be a key consideration, as will the need to select a blend of mixes that are appropriate to the target market and the task.

The aim of the section is to help you to:

- understand the art of promotion by an analysis and comparison of real-life campaigns
- develop the skill of writing a good product-positioning statement.

2.1 Promotional process

The system of distribution requires that manufactured goods pass down a channel to reach the end user. The purpose of the middlemen in the channel is to 'break bulk' – buy in bulk and redistribute in smaller quantities – and they survive as long as their contribution helps make the channel more cost-effective.

In support of this system the sales operation used to be one of **pushing** goods down the channel. The manufacturer's sales people would sell to the wholesaler, the wholesaler's sales team would sell to the retailer and the retailer would sell to individual customers. The same principle applied in all markets.

It was only when the last link in the chain was removed in favour of self-service retailing outlets (supermarkets) that marketers and their agents were forced to devise an alternative sales contact at the vital point of sale. It became necessary to directly address the consumers – to induce a desire to purchase at point of use which would affect behaviour at point of sale. In effect, to 'pull' the consumers in.

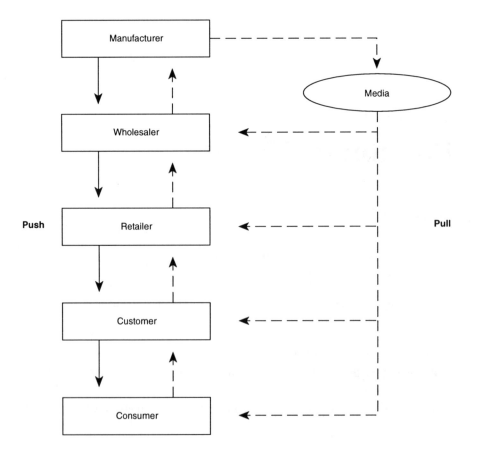

Source: Marketing Operations, Worsam (1995)

Figure 5: The push and pull models of promotion/distribution

The 'pull' approach requires the consumer to generate demand and so a range of media is needed so that all the target audiences can be addressed in the most effective way. A 'positioning statement' (see Section 2.4 below) underpins effective campaigns so that messages are congruent and synergy is maximised.

Sales responsibility has now shifted from the retailer to the supplier, with the main responsibility of the retail sales force now being to ensure that stocks are available in store and – crucially – on the shelves in sufficient quantity. The big retail groups hold the reins and enforce their stocking policies on the suppliers, and it is now quite normal to find only the brand leader and the store's own brand on sale. The power over the channel has shifted to the retailers, who demand a fully integrated promotional campaign as a condition for their making space available. (This changing relationship will be examined in greater depth in Unit 9.)

POINT OF SALE

The importance of promotion at point of sale is almost impossible to calculate. Research commissioned by NDI Visual Merchandising and Display indicates that sales increased 5.84 times when advertising was supplemented by point-of-sale activity. Other research shows that only around 20% of shoppers go into the store knowing which product and brand they intend to buy. Of these, 20% substitute alternatives whilst in store. Around 40% go in knowing the product, but not the brand they intend to buy, and some 40% make purchases of products they had no prior intention to purchase.
(NDI promotional leaflet, 3 January 1995)

ACHIEVING A POSITIVE RETURN

It is relatively easy to secure a short-term advantage using heavy promotion. Alan Scaping, when Nescafé marketing manager, said 'I can take 2% market share off Maxwell House any time I want. Trouble is they will take it right back the next month.'

The true value of effective promotion comes from the long-term benefits. If you merely encourage people to buy two months' supply this month, but then nothing next, as in Figure 6, you have given away profit for no gain (unless the need to stock up customers, perhaps ahead of a competitive new product launch, has been your objective). Figure 7 shows a result that is very much more to be desired.

2.2 Media

Marketers use the term 'media' to describe anything that can carry a promotional message. As you would expect, marketers mix media to achieve their communication objectives.

Major media types are classified as 'broadcast', 'press', 'outdoor', etc, and each sub-divides into units that are ever more specifically targeted, such as:

> Broadcast: television and radio
> > Television: terrestrial, satellite and cable
> > > Terrestrial: BBC1, BBC2, ITV, Channel 4

(Each channel then sub-divides into segments based on the programme carried and time of day.)

The audience for the commercial slot in ITV's News at Ten is highly valued, for example, because it mainly consists of ABC1 business people, who cannot easily see an earlier news broadcast. In 1994 there was pressure from the programme makers to shift News at Ten to an earlier time so that major films could be shown without an interval for the news. This proposal was successfully opposed by the schedulers because of the comparatively lower income that the new ad slots would command.

Each media targets a unique audience. Advertising inside taxi cabs is a different media to that carried outside; InterCity lines have different audiences to the Gatwick Express, which in turn differ markedly from a commuter service from the Thames valley.

It will be seen that media buying and scheduling is a highly specialised skill which can literally make or break a campaign. It is an area into which only highly skilled professionals should venture!

The majority of media now have determined their profile in terms of the major segmentation tools such as ACORN and MOSAIC (see Unit 4). Thus, it is possible to match target audiences specified by a marketer with appropriate media. Such is the proliferation of media that virtually any target audience that can be identified can be reached by one or more targeted media.

Media usage should be complementary. A typical campaign will use:

- press and TV news, current affairs and specialist interest sections to create awareness
- advertising on TV, radio and in the national press to develop awareness, build attitude and carry SP coupons and/or facilitate direct response
- PR and advertising in the trade press to target the middlemen ahead of the main campaign
- specialist press – magazines, etc. – to target readers with a high potential level of interest in the product
- local press to carry the main message, supplemented with local buying point information and/or SP coupons, etc.
- door-to-door distribution to carry samples and/or SP coupons
- retailer promotions to feature the product/offer

- in-store merchandising, which will require specialised display material
- sales promotion schemes to motivate purchase
- on-pack coupons to motivate repeat purchase.

WHICH MEDIA TO CHOOSE?

In order to select the most appropriate media a promotions manager will have to ask the following questions:

- What is the background and circumstances of my need?
- What is the media objective (information/entertainment)?
- Whom do I want to reach – described in terms of target audience profile?
- Where are my target audiences – geographically wide-spread or tightly clustered?
- Are there creative requirements to:
    - demonstrate the product?
    - use sound and/or colour?
    - create a specific mood?
    - build an association?
    - carry a detailed message?
    - elicit an immediate response?
- Is the message appropriate to the media?

There is a vast range and depth of media available, and it is used in a wide variety of ways. The best way of fully understanding the scope of this aspect of promotions, is to undertake a study of a specific promotional campaign. The next activity (which may take you several months to complete) will lead you through this process.

ACTIVITY 7

1 Select two promotional campaigns that are just breaking in an area in which you have an interest (perhaps connected with a hobby of yours).

2 Visit a public library and search the media available to see which are carrying an advertisement for the products or services. Check for variations between advertisements and cross-relate those you find to the profile of the media concerned and the profile of the campaign (so far as you can deduce what it is).

3 Widen your search to include the most likely specialised media – e.g. women's glossy magazines.

4 Widen it further to include TV and radio.

---

5 Extend it to outdoor media – in fact, extend your search as far as your imagination, perception and time allow.

6 Back-track through selected media (especially trade press) to pick up the pre-launch promotion. Relate what was promised to what you are finding.

7 Carry your search forward into stores, spending some time observing purchase behaviour.

8 Finally, relate the on-going campaign over several months to what happened in the launch. Is the same theme continued, amended or abandoned?

9 In all of this you should be asking questions. What was the purpose of the campaign, and of each element within it? In your judgement did it appear to succeed? Why? Why not? How could it have been improved? What might you have done differently?

MEDIA INFLUENCE

The above examples relate to retailing because that is an area in which we all have direct experience. The range of media available allows marketers to select those most appropriate to their needs. Table 1 (overleaf) summarises the main characteristics of each medium and allows a comparison to be made between them.

Different media are used when targeting personnel in British industry. Table 2 (overleaf) shows the result of a survey in which managers were asked to name the two media most likely to influence them. The figures indicate the percentage of each category of manager asked who named that particular source (i.e. 66% of Board members rate Sales Engineers as one of the two most important sources of information).

| | TV | Radio | Cinema | PRESS | | | Posters | Direct mail |
				Daily, evening and Sunday	Regional	Magazines		
A U D I E N C E								
Audience size	Some wastage large and national (some international)	No national coverage	Small, no national coverage	Large and mostly national	Small, no national networks	Mostly national (and international)	National coverage is difficult	Large national and international
Audience type	Few 15-24 year olds	Many housewives, commuters	many 15-24 year olds	Socio-economic	Geographic segments	Lifestyle segments	Commuters, car drivers etc	Any target available
Audience state of mind	Relaxed and passive TV couch potato = visual wall paper	Background/audio wallpaper?	Captive audience-willing suspension of disbelief	Deliberately read		Relaxed and involved with magazine		
M E S S A G E								
Extra advantages	Adds credibility to product or company	Trans-portable medium	High impact and captive audience					
Variable/senses	Sight, sound, colour, movement time constraint	Sound and time constraint	Big impact enhanced sight and sound	Mostly black and white some colour	Black and white	4-colour	4-colour big impact	4-colour and 3-D possibility
Serial ad sequence	Viewed seriously – no competition from other ads or editorial but zoo	Seriously, less zapping	Seriously and no zapping	Must compete with the other ads and editorial on same page			Add clutter	
Transitory	Highly transitory since you cannot refer back to ad once shown (unless taped)			Can keep clippings or refer back if desired			Can refer back walk back or drive past	Can refer back/keep coupon
Demon-stration	Ideal for usage and impulse purchases	Difficult	Yes	Benefits or results can be shown but not product usage demonstration			Only short image benefit	Yes
Detail/technical	Viewer cannot absorb detail	No urgency and topicality	No	Yes	Yes	Yes	No	Yes
Urgency/topicality rub-off	No	Unique-immediacy, urgency and topicality	No	Yes	No	Magazine image splits onto ad	Cult image?	

| | TV | Radio | Cinema | PRESS | | | Posters | Direct mail |
				Daily, evening and Sunday	Regional	Magazines		
C O S T S								
Cost of production	High	Low	High	Low-med	Low	Low-med	Med	Low
Minimum cost of space	High	Low	Low	Med	Low	Low-med	Low-med	High but can experiment in small quantities
Average cost per thousand	Low less than £2	Very low less than £1		Low-med £8	Med £30	Med £12-£70		High £500
E A S E O F M E D I A B U Y I N G								
Flexible	Inflexible and pre-emptible	Flexibility		Flexible			Inflexible	Flexible
Lead times	Long	Short	Long	Short			Long	Short
Clearance	Script(1-week) finished film (1-week) ITVA	Same day clearance ITVA	One week clearance cinema and assoc.	Code of advertising practice (clearance is not compulsory)				
Audience research*	BARB and TGI	RAJAR	CAVIAR	NRS	JICREG	NRS and ABC	OSCAR	
High frequency facility	Hourly and daily	Hourly and daily	No	yes	Weekly	Weekly/ monthly		
National coverage	Experts job but network exists and international cable/ satellite	No national network		Yes	No national network		Difficult	

Table 1: Summary of media characteristics

	A	B	C	D	E	F	G	H	I	J
Catalogues	39	36	45	64	34	64	52	32	44	76
Direct mail	12	9	14	6	31	21	23	14	5	27
Sales Engineers' visits	66	61	60	67	78	64	64	60	73	40
Trade press ads	14	32	28	22	21	15	12	23	24	24
Exhibitions	15	17	11	11	47	15	9	19	14	12
Manufacturer demos	50	41	35	26	37	21	37	38	45	22
Other	6	4		6			5	5	35	

Key:

A	–	Board members and general management	F	–	Research
B	–	Operational management	G	–	Buying
C	–	Production engineers	H	–	Finance
D	–	Design and Development engineers	I	–	Sales
E	–	Maintenance engineers	J	–	Others

Table 2: Sources of information

MEDIA COSTS

Each medium has a 'rate card', which indicates the cost of advertising in it. This can be calculated in costs per column or part of a page, for example, or per 30-second commercial slot. The rate card also carries all the technical details of the medium so that material can be submitted in appropriate form for reproduction. Rate cards also carry contact details, copy dates and target audience information in terms of audited figures, where available. (Segmentation profiles are becoming quite common.) All media owners allow a range of discounts and price variations, however, and these are not published.

When investigating costs it is important to know what one wishes to buy. The cost of space does not indicate how many people, of what quality, will see it. It certainly does not include how many will read an advert carried within it. It is necessary, therefore, to buy in terms of the 'cover' or 'reach' of the ad, the 'frequency' with which the ad needs to be run and the number who have the 'opportunity to see' it (OTS).

- 'Cover' or 'reach' refers to the percentage of the target population who have 1 OTS. If the News at Ten reaches 10 million viewers, 70% of whom are ABC1 male, then an ad in the mid slot will reach 7 million ABC1 males.

- 'Frequency' is determined by the number of OTS (or impacts) that are required. A frequency of 60 can be built up by having the same ad run four times an evening over three five-day weeks, or by running it twice a week for 30 weeks.

- OTS relates cover to frequency. 7 million x 60 equals 420 million OTS during the campaign.

Appropriate measures are used by different media – it is at this stage only necessary to know that advertising should be selected not on the basis of the price, but on what is expected in terms of target audience impacts.

2.3 Target audiences

Advertisers have traditionally used 'target audience', whereas in public relations the term is 'target public'. Both mean exactly the same.

A target audience is an identified and specified group of individuals who share sufficient common attributes to justify a tailored communication. It is easier to explain through an example.

ACTIVITY 8

You have been commissioned by the Chief Executive of Acme Computers plc to advise her on a corporate communications need. Acme is planning a rights issue to finance expansion but is concerned that a strong rumour to the effect that redundancies are planned will affect the issue.

There is no truth in the rumour – in fact Acme plans to increase the workforce by about 10%. At the same time it intends to renegotiate working practices with the two unions involved.

Because Acme is a high-profile UK operation on the cutting edge of technology there is considerable interest in its activities across a very wide range of target audiences.

Your task is to produce a draft list of the target audiences as a basis for establishing the communications plan with the CE and the Marketing Director.

Hints:
1 You may be surprised just how extensive a range of contacts has to be made.
2 'Mind mapping' is an excellent technique to use in this kind of situation. (See Buzan (1993, chapters 6 – 9)

The mind map in Figure 8 is a possible preliminary draft which will serve as a basis for further work. Each section and sub-section will need to be broken down into detailed segments, each of which should then be carefully profiled.

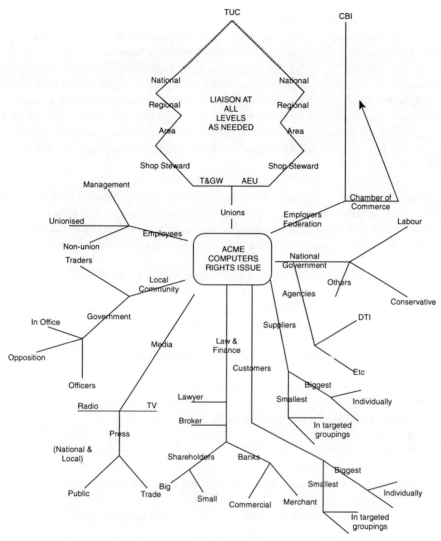

Figure 8: Acme Computers plc: Target Audiences

2.4 Positioning

Product positioning has already been discussed in Unit 4: Market Segmentation, where it was established that a product's position 'is the complex set of perceptions, impressions and feelings that it induces in its consumers.' The position you require your product to adopt (the messages you are trying to ensure it sends) is the focus of marketing communications. In order to ensure that everybody is working towards the same end, a positioning statement is required. This is a succinct statement of the exact position that the product takes (or will take) in the minds of individuals within the target market.

Very great care, and considerable time, is taken to ensure that the statement is as accurate and detailed as possible. Once established, it will serve to focus all subsequent marketing effort; the creative management time devoted to it will, therefore, hopefully be repaid in substantial long-term benefit.

Products can be repositioned – and very often are. Qualcast repositioned itself when faced with a strong challenge from Flymo. KitKat repositioned itself as a snack as well as a chocolate bar and immediately qualified for the snacks and biscuits section of a supermarket as well as the confectionery counters. As seen in Unit 4, Lucozade has repositioned from 'healthy' for invalids to 'energy-giving' for sports people.

It may be necessary to change a product, in order to achieve the desired position in the market. Usually, however, the change that matters is almost cosmetic in nature. Name, pack and label changes are not true *product* changes, yet singly or in combination such changes will be perceived by the prospective customer.

Anything can be positioned. Remember that in marketing communications one is working with a package made up of a bundle of concepts. There is no difference in principle between the positioning of a product or a service, an industrial or a consumer good, a charity or a political candidate.

HOW TO WRITE A GOOD POSITIONING STATEMENT

1   Identify the market position you want to occupy.

2   Itemise (research) what the brand will do for consumers:
    ● uniquely
    ● identically?

3   Determine why the customers and consumers should believe your claims.

4   Enlist the help of some top-quality people to help draft the statement.

5   Aim for brevity – with completeness. This is one reason why a statement takes a long time to write.

6   Include the competitive issues. Try to include the words 'only' and 'unique'.

7   Emotional values are very powerful. Build them in – but only if they can genuinely be sustained.

8   Solicit the assistance of technical and production people where possible.

9   Aim to secure total commitment at all levels in the organisation; the best statements come after very hard discussion.

10 Publish the statement internally when you are reasonably sure that you have it right, but you should not be committed to it at this stage since there will be comments you will want to consider.

11 Publish the final version as declared policy, and ensure that its receipt and importance is acknowledged by all.

12 Use the statement at the beginning of promotional review meetings as a focus for the discussion. Some marketers keep framed versions in their offices as constant reminders.

13 Update the statement as necessary – but be as careful in the re-drafting as you were with the original statement. Don't rush. Time must be invested. A positioning statement is a key policy document.

REVIEW ACTIVITY 2

Begin the process of writing a positioning statement for yourself. You can only *begin* the process within this activity because you will need to devote time and energy to its perfection, and you will require the assistance of others whom you know (and trust) as your drafting develops. You will find the exercise of major benefit, however, in terms of short-term marketing study but, much more importantly, when creating your CV ahead of applying for work.

Summary

There is need to ensure that effective communication reaches target customers and consumers. The push method of disseminating product and communication has been superseded by the pull strategy, which generates demand. Virtually every conceivable target segment has media that will reach it, when media is defined, correctly, as anything that can carry a promotional message.

Different media often need to be used within a single campaign in order to ensure that each target audience receives a message. To ensure synergy there must be a central positioning to underpin the communications strategy.

SECTION 3

Agencies

Introduction

This section examines the use of agencies in promotion and research. It explains why agencies are needed, the different types available, and the different functions they fulfil. It is intended to give you an insight into the process of selecting and recruiting an agency and of managing the relationship. It will also give guidance on how to brief a creative and a research agency.

The aim of the section is to help you to:

- devise a checklist of areas for consideration when selecting an agency
- draw up a procedure for selecting an agency
- analyse the way in which responsibility is divided (or shared) between agency and client
- identify information on a promotions campaign that is essential for a proper assessment of the effectiveness of that campaign.

3.1 Different types of agency

A wide variety of agencies is available to provide specialised communication services. As the key principles of selection, briefing and management apply across all types of agency we can generalise to some extent.

(The term 'agency' is used in a casual, everyday sense, but is actually incorrect because advertising agencies long ago ceased to be 'agents' of the media, dependent upon media commission for their income. Sales promotion 'agencies' are spin-offs from advertising, but in PR and marketing research the correct term is 'consultancy'. We shall, however, follow tradition and for convenience use the traditional collective term 'agency' within this section.)

WHY USE AN AGENCY?

Agencies should be used only because they have specialised skills that you need and which it is not cost-effective to provide in-house. They survive only as long as they add value in the area to which they contribute.

Agency staff are highly opinionated people – which is their major strength – but their sheer competence can lead a client to accept what they say, and to follow their direction. Always remember that the client is in charge. He or she controls the budget and has to live with the results of any action!

Within advertising there are three types of agency:

Full-service agencies

These offer a complete package, including planning and research, creative services, media planning and buying and production. Some full-service agencies have departments which specialise in forecasting, market intelligence and business planning. They will have an excellent range of contacts through subsidiary companies and associates to provide international cover, and support needs such as SP, training and sales support materials.

Hot shops

Also known as 'creative shops', these specialise in creative work. Saatchi and Saatchi started as a hot shop.

A la carte

This is a term used to describe a client who manages the whole process 'in house' but selects from a range of agencies, each with specialist skills, to provide support. This is also known as 'using specialist services'.

Generally speaking, there will be a specialist agency to handle every aspect of the promotional business. Agencies or consultancies specialise in such areas as media planning and buying, new product development, public relations, product naming, sales promotion, sponsorship, direct response, posters, etc.

There are three ways to manage promotion: via an agency, through specialist services or in-house. The advantages and disadvantages of each are:

	Agency	Specialist Service	Keep in-house
Advantages	All-round skills. All-round experience. Objective, outsider's view of your business. You benefit from mistakes made by others. They do the whole job for you. Continuity of contact. Specialist skills are available that you couldn't afford on the full-time staff.	You pick and choose the experts for each part of your job. You can fill gaps without having the expense of a full agency. May be cheaper. May be faster.	Everything in your own control. Full understanding of the problems. Confidentiality assured. Learn as you go with no embarrassment. May be faster. Probably cheaper.
Disadvantages	Lack of specialist knowledge of your business (usually). Cannot devote all their time to you. May do a poor job for a small client. May not put their first team on to your account. May give your work low priority unless you are a major client. Probably expensive – but you should receive high quality work.	Need careful control and co-ordination: this needs experience from you. Requires extra careful briefing – every time. Difficult to get extra services in a hurry. The best people are always busy – you may have to wait or accept second stringers. Can be very cost-effective, <u>if well managed by you.</u>	Easy to make mistakes – no one there to cross-check. Limited view – no outside, impartial critique. No input of experience gained with a range of clients and industries. Lack of specialised skill in some areas of need. Lack of specialised know how. Lack of 'hot contacts'.

Table 3: Advantages and disadvantages of the three ways to handle promotion.

ACTIVITY 9

A checklist can help considerably when making your decision as to whether an agency is needed. Itemise the areas you think need to be considered and the questions you might ask yourself about them.

There is obviously no definitive list, but an example would be:

Knowledge
Do I know about advertising/SP/PR, etc.? If so, I have the option to do it myself.

The task
Is it simple or complex? Can I actually do it?

Resources
Can I afford to hire an agency? Could an agency do it on my budget because of their contacts and experience?

Confidence
Do I need a second opinion? Is one available in-house?

Workload
Have I the time to do the task? How long will it take? Is there a mass of detail? Can I actually fit it in?

Staff
Do I have staff who can do it for me? If so, are they experienced?

Back-up
Is there a corporate department I can call on? If so, are they any good? How much priority will I get?

ADVERTISING AGENCY PERSONNEL
The key personnel and functions are:

Account Executives
These liaise between client and agency and should be a senior member of the client's marketing team.

Planners
These are skilled managers of research, who ensure that it is commissioned and carried out effectively. They provide an objective voice, and must not be confused with 'business planners', who operate in a similar way to marketing consultants.

Creatives
These are the people who visualise the ideas and concepts that make the promotion work. They translate these into copy and visuals and so often work in pairs, a copy writer and an artist.

Media planners and buyers
They have an intimate knowledge of the media – its availability and price. They plan the space needed to achieve the objectives of Reach, OTS and Frequency, and they buy the space. Media planning and scheduling are different activities from buying and so the two activities are often separated.

Production staff

These are concerned with actually making the advertisement. Some of the very large agencies can do almost everything in-house, but all sub-contract as needed.

Account management teams

They will be formed to handle a specific client. Whilst some staff will be members of more than one team, the tactical core will usually be dedicated to a single client. A typical account management team may comprise: account director, account executive, planner, creative director, copy-writer, artist, art director, TV producer, media director, media buyer. It will be an active team, with tight focus on the briefings and feedbacks from the account executive.

CONSULTANCIES

Specialist consultancies exist to help with every aspect of promotional planning, execution and control. Consultants can take much of the load from a hard-pressed marketing director, especially in regard to one-off assignments. They are highly skilled people who can be hired without the need for commitment to a full-time post. They can also serve as 'whipping boy' or scapegoat in the event of need.

Trust is vital when using any consultant. Full disclosure appropriate to the level of operations is vital if a consultant is to work effectively. The client may find this emotionally problematic, but when looked at logically it is obvious that consultants do not survive without being able to maintain security – often far better than their clients because it becomes routine with them. Survival as a consultant depends not only on competence – which must be above average – but also on speed of assimilation, the ability quickly to come to grips with new situations and to compartmentalise each client.

3.2 Selecting an agency or consultancy

Choosing the right agency or consultancy is a complex matter because so many subjective judgements are required. When contracting for the supply of raw materials the major part of the negotiation has to do with physical matters, such as quality, quantity and availability. There is a degree of concern over integrity, and personal chemistry must never be overlooked, but the central issue must be the product.

People are the central issue when choosing an agency: people, and the quality of their work. Thus the subjectivity quotient is extremely high.

Roderick White (1980, p34) refers to selection as 'a marriage business'. David Ogilvy (1983, p66) uses the same analogy: 'Make sure the chemistry between you works. Happy marriages fructify, unhappy ones don't.' Ogilvy also puts the professionalism needed into perspective 'Don't insist that an agency negotiates its terms of business with your Purchasing Department. Would you do this with lawyers and accountants?' (1983, p67)

ACTIVITY 10

You are the Marketing Director of a regional chain of second-hand car sales agents. You have not been satisfied with the quality of your promotion and want to take your £2,000,000 account to another agency. Itemise the steps you will take to maximise your probability of success. (Hint: Agency recruitment is very similar to personnel recruitment.)

As with personnel recruitment and selection the key stages and details are:

● Define your requirements. List the key elements that must and must not be present, such as: Agency size: small enough to allow you to be an important client, large enough to have gained experience; current clients: none who compete with you.

● Audit the market. In advertising this means searching the media that targets your markets for advertising that impresses, then tracking examples back to the originating agency. From your long list exclude all those that are obviously impossible (such as those already working for a competitor).

● Attract applications. The market is such that you will be overwhelmed with solicitations as soon as word gets out that you are seeking to make a change.

● Develop a short-list. You need a check list of key characteristics – track record, experience in your market, creativity, technical expertise, integrity. The agency is to join your team and so include the inter-personal aspects that you would look for in a Personal Assistant.

● Know what to expect. Brief each of the short-list identically. (This will be looked at in more detail in a moment.) Offer a fair fee for the work they must do in preparing their pitches. Include details of your key policies so the basic ground rules are clear. (We shall come to briefing a little later.)

● Decide how to analyse the applicants and how to select a winner. Set up a panel of three or four key people from your organisation to receive the pitches. Provide each person with a copy of your checklist against which to write detailed comments immediately each pitch concludes and before you allow any discussion. Hold back all but minimum discussion until all pitches are complete – this may mean up to a week in total. Convene a meeting of your panel and analyse each pitch, and each agency. Take a decision to either appoint one, or none.

If you decide that none of the short-list is suitable, then do *not* make an appointment. Client/agency relationships must be close and based on mutual trust for them to succeed. They are also intended to be long-term and so it is vital to be certain from the start. Negotiate and sign the contract before you announce the appointment. Be courteous and kind in your notifications of rejection.

MANAGING THE RELATIONSHIP

Relationships are dynamic. They need to be managed carefully. The best relationships work on the basis of a joint interest in results and clarity in areas of responsibility.

ACTIVITY 11

List the main areas of knowledge and responsibility under the headings 'client', 'agency' and 'joint'.

Under **client** you might well have included the management of the product or service, and knowledge about the market. The **agency,** on the other hand, will know a lot about customer behaviour, communication, evaluation and more than you may think about the market. While the client has the final word, it is would be foolish for them to argue about technical issues to do with promotion with an agency, and equally foolish of an agency to offer advice about the manufacturing of the client's product.

Overall strategy is open to discussion, of course, but not areas of high technical competence. You can remember this by considering the relationship you have with your doctor. Discuss with him or her what ailment he or she is about to treat, but be very careful about querying his or her prescription.

Client management of an agency relationship depends for its success on agreed, specific and achievable objectives, regular review, praise when deserved, shared responsibility where appropriate, clear definition of individual areas of responsibility.

3.3 Briefing an agency

When briefing competing agencies, provide only the essential information necessary for them to put together their pitch. A creative agency will be much more likely to have need of detailed information than a research agency. Creative agencies must be trusted with strategic-level information because they must work from the same facts as the client team if they are to be truly effective. Research agencies exist to obtain specific information to aid in a particular decision. They are *not* part of the decision process and so only need briefing on the exact information required. They may not even need to know why it is required. Although you are likely to repeatedly use the same agency there is never any requirement to brief them other than on a need-to-know basis. (Briefing of research agencies is covered separately.)

MARKETING COMMUNICATION BRIEFS

Based on the need-to-know principle, these specifically brief an agency or a consultancy on the need to achieve certain limited objectives within the overall Marketing Communications Plan (see Section 4). There is no set format, but a brief must be written in report style.

Key points to remember:

- Briefings may be oral, but must always be supported in writing.
- The agency should repeat back the brief to show full understanding.
- Improvements should be encouraged.
- Take time to plan, brief thoroughly and carefully, listen for suggestions and critique. Go firm only when both you and the agency are happy.

Each brief will be unique to its purpose, but there are key points that must be covered in every brief. They are:

Situation

Where you are now. The agency will need a full background of your position in the market, your strengths and weaknesses, policies that must be taken into account, competitive activity, etc. This can be given first in outline and then fleshed out later in the brief.

Objectives

Provide the marketing communications objectives and, if appropriate, the supporting marketing objectives.

Strategy

You will need to describe, in broad terms, how you intend achieving the objectives.

Tactics

These are likely to be formed in consultation with the appointed agency, but you may wish to outline your initial ideas at this stage.

Budget

State the budget, if known. If the agency is required to recommend a budget, this requirement must be explicit.

Product technical specification(s) and customer satisfactions

Give details of the product (or service), how it works, what it does –the product benefits. The team will probably need to have samples of the product, to try it for themselves. They should be encouraged to think of additional product benefits.

Organisation profile

This is especially important when inviting agencies to pitch for an account. An agency should not have to waste resources locating facts that you can give them easily.

Market analysis

Information on the market must be provided. Raw data is of little value, it is for the client, who knows the market, to provide useful information.

Pricing and/or pricing policy

This must be provided as it is a vital component of marketing tactics.

Distribution

The agency must know when, where and by whom the package will be sold.

Criteria for evaluation of campaign effectiveness

Good marketing communications objectives establish the control criteria. Methodology for measurement should be asked for – it is for the agency to provide it.

A time-scale should be given for submission of the proposals, and for the decision to be made. The people who will be involved in assessing the pitch should be listed, and a name given in case further information is needed.

You will have an opportunity to draft a creative brief in the Unit Review Activity

RESEARCH AGENCY BRIEFING

Research involves two areas of concern: the information needed and methodology. The information needed is determined by the client. The brief must concentrate on the need, never on the research technique. The methodology is recommended by the research agency as a response to the brief.

The research effort is managed by the researcher once a proposal has been accepted. Note that it is not for researchers to recommend a course of management action. They do not have full knowledge of the situation and any such recommendations may be inaccurate, simply because the briefing was deliberately restricted. If you want management recommendations you should brief a consultant and let him or her brief a research agency as necessary.

Key points to remember:

● Give a sufficient briefing into the background of the problem (see below).

● Objective discussion is required – do not allow pre-conceived ideas to intervene.

● Adequate information is the need – specify the degree of confidence that will be sufficient.

● Indicate if a security problem exists.

● Brief thoroughly – take time.

● Specify that the formal research proposal includes:

   – the research to be undertaken

   – methods of enquiry

   – sample design

   – data to be collected

   – time estimate

   – cost estimate

   – security controls (ie checks on the effectiveness of the interviewers).

Only give authority to proceed after the proposal has been checked against the brief.

Research briefs relate to specific need. The major headings which must always be included are:

Security
The implications for security must be explicit. The degree of security needed for a market test of a new product varies considerably from that needed when post-testing an ad campaign.

Objectives
The exact purpose(s) of the research must be specified. This means that the manager must state what questions need to be answered – what information is required. The client does not specify a research methodology.

Background
This should be provided only in sufficient detail to place the objectives in context.

Budget
The agency will probably need only an indicative figure, although a maximum may be set. Include your requirement that methodology, etc., be specified.

Time-scale
You need to specify a date:

   ● for receipt of proposal

   ● for agreement to proposal

   ● for stage reports and for the final report.

Personnel
Who requires the information, and the person co-ordinating the research.

ACTIVITY 12

As the newly appointed Marketing Officer to a private college you have access to a wealth of secondary information covering such areas as the number of students recruited, their ethnic background, place of residence, fees paid, attendance and examination results achieved.

You have no reliable information on the response to your efforts to promote the college, nor on why students choose your college. You are also concerned at an apparently high drop-out rate. This is explained by your colleagues as 'typical' and the result of poor motivation on the part of the students.

You have decided to allocate a small amount of your budget to research. Itemise the key information that you need and classify it as 'essential', 'desirable', 'nice to know'. Indicate how this information might be secured.

Essential information will include:

● Response to each promotional vehicle. Sub-classified by timing of appearance. Each ad to carry a code which enquirers must quote when making contact.

● What features of the promotion attracted response.

● Discovering a link to the perceived needs of the respondents.

● How each potential customer's enquiry progressed.

● Monitoring drop out at each stage, from initial response, through interviews, formal application to join, fees payment, visa application – and so on.

● Student reaction to the college, sub-classified into areas such as: rooms, refectory, library, administration, support, teaching, assessed work, etc. Secure this through interviews with all who leave (face-to-face if possible. If not, by phone and/or post).

Desirable information if the budget allows includes:

● Attitude studies to ascertain expectation before, during and after courses.

● Market studies to determine detailed information about how the market segments.

Nice-to-know information:

● This should automatically be discarded because no research budget can ever extend to secure merely nice-to-know material. The addition of even a single question will considerably increase survey costs, depending on how much the data is cross-referenced and cross-tabulated.

REVIEW ACTIVITY 3

You are the marketing product manager for a range of fragrances targeted on the C2D young female market. You are very happy with your agency and with the approach they are taking. Results are excellent, budgets are being hit, all is looking good.

Your managing director, who is an accountant, bumps into you in the corridor. 'Not too pleased with our advertising. It is so noisy and is projecting a most unsuitable image. Come and see me this afternoon at 4 o'clock.'

What are you going to say at the meeting.

(A possible answer to this activity is given at the end of the unit.)

Summary

Agencies provide added specialist strength in a cost-effective manner. Relationships should be managed for the long-term, and careful selection is necessary. It is often necessary for an agency to be a part of the client marketing team, for without total access at strategic level they cannot give of their best.

Client confidentiality comes automatically to both agencies and consultants. They are, in fact, often far more secure than their clients!

A creative agency requires a more comprehensive briefing than a research consultant because of the different roles. Creatives are concerned with an on-going situation which must be managed in the light of events. A researcher exists to secure specified information and does not need to know why it is wanted. Briefings should always be confirmed in writing, even if they are initially delivered orally.

SECTION 4

Managing Communications

Introduction

This section examines the way that the communication process is managed, including the monitoring of promotional objectives. It also covers the different techniques used in promotional research and the control of a research budget. The purpose and contents of a marketing communications plan is discussed, and guidance will be given on how to draw up a marketing communications brief.

The aim of this section is to help you to:

- appreciate the problems involved in setting and evaluating promotional objectives
- devise an approach to evaluating the effectiveness of advertising
- appreciate the difficulty of obtaining objective data on consumer awareness and attitude
- assess different approaches to budget setting
- prepare a briefing document for an advertisement agency.

4.1 Monitoring promotion

The desire to believe in a simplistic approach whereby promotional expenditure is in a direct relationship to sales encourages the manager to use factual measures of success:

- How much business is generated for each unit of spend in advertising?
- How much from the overall spend on advertising and sales?
- How many orders are secured from how many sales calls?
- How many repeat orders are secured?

The problem with this approach is that whilst the end result will be counted in numbers – eventually in terms of profit or loss – the individual achievements needed to ensure overall success are often non-numeric.

We know the aim is for potential purchasers to move from being unaware of a product to repeated purchase of it, and that the major stages are awareness, attitude and action. Once this is understood it becomes obvious that awareness and attitude objectives can only be non-numeric, since they measure behaviour. Even the 'action' stage requires some non-numeric evaluation, since a purchase may be prevented by circumstances such as an out-of-stock position.

Promotional objectives can easily be written:

Product A, Target Market 1.

By 31 July, to generate:

- awareness   50%
- attitude   35%
- repeat usage   22%
- new users   2%

They are easy to write – but fiendishly difficult to evaluate!

ACTIVITY 13

Consider the above objectives. What evaluation problems do they present to the tactical marketer?

What, exactly, is meant by 'awareness'. What response will indicate that a person is sufficiently aware of the product? Simple recognition of the label, or of the branding overall? Guinness found that when they tested round labels on their bottles the product disappeared from the perception of their regular buyers, who were looking for oval labels and couldn't find Guinness without that perceptual cue.

'Attitude' is extremely difficult to define, let alone to measure. But unless there is a clear definition *in writing,* a researcher cannot measure attitude. It is not sufficient to say 'Well, we all know what we mean.'

Purchase intention is a form of attitude. It is easy to build desire – many have an intention to buy a house in the country, to run two or three cars, to send their kids to good schools and on to university. But is this a dream or a serious intention to purchase? In the early days of the pop stars there were stories of long-haired youths being thrown out of up-market car showrooms even though they could buy anything they wanted on their platinum credit cards. If the intention is thwarted how will this be known?

Sales achievement should be easy to measure – but how does one know who has made the purchases? It could easily be that the sales were made to another segment altogether. This was the case with the Yorkie bar. Targeted on youngsters it was bought in quantity by young women. It is believed that they were responding to the unintentional sexual appeal of the lorry driver used in the ad to attract the kids. Some rapid rethinking at Rowntrees changed the promotional tactics to concentrate on the driver and abandon the planned tug boat captain who was to follow!

New users are difficult to identify, especially if they are one-time purchasers. If the volume of sales increases, it could be for one or a combination of several reasons.

Setting promotional objectives

Promotional objectives must be set in terms of desired behaviour; effective action can only be taken when this has been done. This is because without objectives we cannot know what we are trying to achieve. How many customers do we want to take what action? Are we looking for purchases, repeat purchases, responses to an offer? If we don't know what we need to achieve, it is unlikely that we shall succeed?

It is then necessary to measure the number of prospective customers at each stage of the continuum, and to decide how many must be helped to move further down, and how many must be held in the positive action repurchase loop. When desired behaviour has been established and quantified, it is possible to consider which tools are appropriate, and how much budget to allow. We shall come to promotional budgeting a little later.

Linking objective to mechanics

There is a well-established link between certain types of objective and the promotion most likely to achieve them. Each marketer, of course, needs to build a detailed understanding of what works best in his or her market – here an experienced agency can be of the greatest value, especially as it is able to cross-fertilise ideas and techniques across markets.

Table 4, devised by Julian Cummins (1990), ranks the effectiveness of specific marketing tools (described as 'mechanics') against various common objectives.

Objectives	Mechanics	Immediate free offers	Delayed free offers	Immediate price offers	Delayed price offers	Finance offers	Competitions	Games and draws	Charitable offers	Self-liquidators	Profit-making promotions
Increasing volume		9	7	9	7	5	1	3	5	2	1
Increasing trial		9	7	9	2	9	2	7	7	2	1
Increasing repeat purchase		2	9	2	9	5	3	2	7	3	3
Increasing loyalty		1	9	0	7	3	3	1	7	3	3
Widening usage		9	5	5	2	3	1	5	5	1	1
Creating interest		3	3	3	2	2	5	9	8	8	8
Creating awareness		3	3	3	1	1	5	9	8	8	8
Deflecting attention from price		9	7	0	7	7	3	5	5	2	2
Gaining intermediary support		9	5	9	5	9	3	7	5	1	1
Gaining display		9	5	9	5	9	3	7	5	1	1

Each square is filled with a rating from 0 (not well matched) to 10 (very well matched). Use it as a ready reckoner for linking your objective to the mechanics available.

(Source: Cummins, J 1990)

Table 4: Linking the objectives to the mechanics.

EVALUATION

It is apparent that some advertising works better than others. Why this should be is not always self-evident.

ACTIVITY 14

A list of headings is given below relating to an advertising campaign. Fill in some questions that you feel would need answering if a proper assessment were to be made of that campaign.

Media selection
Content
Market
Competitors
Environment

Media selection

Was the spend wisely split between the media? Which media generated the higher response rate? Why?.

Content

How did the advertisement content affect sales?

Market

What did the customers and consumers actually need and want? Did the advertisement address the correct issues?

Competitors

What were the competitors offering? What advertising were they doing and where? What special offers were they making?

Environment

What external factors, such as unemployment, inflation, social changes, natural disasters, etc, need to be taken into account when evaluating the campaign?

OBJECTIVE RESEARCH

The first information to gather is factual – such data as advertising spend, media circulation, coupon redemption, sales calls made, orders taken, etc. Care must be taken to understand exactly what the figures relate to. Circulation, for example, is not the same as readership. Circulation measures the average number of copies sold, readership the number and kind of people who read the publication. Sales calls can be simply a two-minute head-round-the-door-nothing-needed-today-thank-you, or a twenty-minute detailed sales conversation that achieves one or more pre-determined sales objectives.

Primary research must be targeted at a specific information need. Promotion research is required either to predict how a new launch or campaign will be accepted, or how well a campaign met its objectives. It is therefore mostly concentrated on obtaining subjective, rather than objective, data.

Careful, realistic, slightly cynical management is required in marketing, since although a representative sample of 2,000 adults will provide sophisticated breakdowns of actions, perceptions and attitudes it may be that only 4% purchase your product. If so, you will only get a sample of 80, which may not be satisfactory.

There is no point spending money on research which brings back unsatisfactory results. It is essential to ensure that the predicted results will provide what is needed, and then to confirm that the survey delivered what was expected.

SUBJECTIVE DATA

To discover levels of awareness and attitude it is necessary to probe in depth – hence the invention of Depth Research (also known as Motivation Research). Depth researchers are concerned to identify the subjective rationale that underpins buying behaviour. In Unit 1, you will remember, we drew upon a report of the work of depth researchers in the *Times,* who considered differences perceived in the political parties.

Depth research is now a routinely used tool of the specialist researcher, but its finding are non-numeric and from a background of social, not natural science. (In other words, experiments are not necessarily repeatable, as they have to be in 'true' science.)

Subjective research reports usually contain data in numeric form – but they are not 'true' numbers in the sense that they can be manipulated mathematically. Nor can they be directly compared. The problem is that whilst people can quantify their feelings, preferences, etc. on a scale of 7 = Excellent – 1 = Poor we have no common agreement on a base. Without a base zero and a fixed unit of measurement between each scaler point we cannot know how respondents perceive the range. It may be very difficult to split levels 1 and 2, and perhaps 3 and 4 are close, but clearly better than a 2 ranking. 5 and 6 may be much the same, with 7 only awarded for exceptional excellence. We can't know, because we can't get into the respondents' minds and the numbers are not *scaler.*

Because responses are numeric but not scaler we cannot say that a grading of 7 means anything other than 'best' in the opinion of the respondent. We certainly cannot compare a 7 for one product from one survey with a 7 for another product from a different survey. Non-scaler results can be used for comparison, but only when comparing results using the same research instrument administered to matched samples of respondents. Thus, a trend can be determined, but not a comparison across products and/or markets.

Non-scaler numeric techniques are widely used because they make it possible to evaluate a general opinion by using techniques such as semantic differential scaling.

Providing the results are used with knowledge and care they can be extremely valuable.

ACTIVITY 15

To prove to yourself that people's behaviour is more important than any other aspect of marketing communications consider why:

1 Reported circulation (from face-to-face or telephone surveys, for example) for the quality press exceeds the print run by 1,000%, and popular papers printing in millions reportedly sell very few.

2 When asked for an opinion on the Metallic Metal Act (which did not exist) the respondents answered:

- A good thing if dealt with by government   –   21%

- A good thing if at local government level   –   59%

- OK for foreigners, but not here   –   16%

- It is of no value   –   4%.

Obviously, status is important to individuals, and the press is clearly positioned as media that reflects status. Newspaper-buying habits are felt to reflect something of an individual's behaviour and so securing answers even to apparently simple questions becomes difficult because individuals want to impress the researcher. (A more accurate picture of newspaper purchasing habits is obtained from an analysis of household rubbish, and waste sent for recycling.)

The readiness to give an opinion, regardless of knowledge, allows researchers to secure answers to what they want to know. The answers to the Metallic Metal Act question show much about attitude to government, even though the question was superficially invalid.

Issues that impinge on behaviour tend to be complex and have to be approached indirectly. One way to discover preferences for different brands of biscuits, for example, is to set up a discussion about anything that will interest the group. Then serve tea and a range of biscuits. Observe the quantities in which the biscuits are consumed and ignore the discussion findings – and *don't* tell the group what has been done!

As part of an ongoing activity while you are working on this course, monitor behaviour around you. Note how many people say things such as 'Oh, I've only got a X – I know you have a Y.' What does that tell you about X, Y, and the person? What would it mean to you if you were marketing X, or Y?

In the same way, monitor the way people select items in a store, how many buy a quality paper but do not read it, where people choose to shop. (Is a Harrods shopping bag really worth the higher prices?) Note how people choose to keep some shops' bags (e.g. Harrods again) and to spurn others. Also ask yourself why a sports brand on a T-shirt allows about £20 extra to be charged (and paid) for it? And why a sportsman's endorsement can add some £40 to the value. The function doesn't change, but the symbolic value obviously does.

Always check what it would mean to you if you were working in that market.

4.2 Promotional research techniques

We shall concentrate upon advertising research because the basic principles spill over into other promotional areas and this area is key to the approach to the others. The following techniques are all used:

Copy testing
Respondents are asked to look through a collection of alternative advertisements and are then questioned as to what they can remember. The aim is to hone the copy for optimum effectiveness.

Content research
This is concerned with the ability of an ad to achieve impact and to project the desired message to the target audience. People not in the target group are of no interest and so an ad must be judged only from the perspective of its target audience. The purpose is to confirm that the copy platform, the general theme and presentation of the advert, achieves the desired results.

Pre-and post-testing
The one is ahead of publication to confirm that the ad will work as intended. The other monitors the actual results.

Post-tests may be 'same day' or 'day after'. The major techniques are of recall and recognition. Tests may be oral and/or pictorial. In 'unaided recall' (spontaneous) respondents are asked if they have seen a particular advert, and if so what they remember about it. In 'aided recognition' (prompted), also called 'aided recall', respondents are shown stills from a series of adverts and asked how much of each of the advertising messages, brands, etc. they can remember.

Split-run testing allows two different ads to run in alternate copies of the same publication. Post-testing can then determine which was the most effective.

Tracking study

The purpose of this is to monitor change over time. A tracking study is a piece of continuous research that allows trends to be identified and tracked. Persil is reputed to have kept a tracking study running for nearly 90 years.

Focus groups

Discussion groups are formed around experienced researchers so that a proposal for an ad, a new product, a below-the-line scheme, can be addressed by typical members of the target audience. They can be very powerful, but must be in the hands of highly experienced researchers. It is very easy to misuse a focus group through bad briefing, bad selection and/or bad management. It is often necessary for the group members to remain in ignorance of the purpose of the research, at least until well into the discussion, and a researcher that allows a bias to show, or cues the group too soon can destroy the value of the exercise.

Market tests

Testing through market tests and pilot studies take the product and/or promotion into a limited area to check how it stands up within the market place. Their value is limited because a test cannot replicate a full launch, and there is danger that competitors will pick up the test and be prepared to counter the full launch.

ABOVE AND BELOW THE LINE

Traditionally, advertising agencies were paid by the media owners (rather than the organisations placing the ad), and were considered as agents of the media, not of the advertisers. The commission was standardised at 15% of the charge made by the media for the space (known as the 'billing'). Competition led to agencies offering added value in terms of design, copy writing, research, etc.

When it became necessary to carry the 'advertising' message through to point of sale as a replacement for the sales assistants, a new technique was needed and sales promotion was born.

A problem immediately became obvious. How should the agencies be paid without media to offer a commission? The solution was to charge a fee for sales promotion work. In marketing jargon the term 'above the line' refers to the use of media on which a commission has traditionally been paid, 'Below the line' refers to media for which a fee is charged.

There is a tendency for advertising agencies to move to a fee structure in place of commission. This does not affect the use of the terms, however, which are used as shorthand to indicate the type of promotion being used.

The term 'through the line' simply means that a campaign contains both above- and below-the-line media and techniques.

PROMOTIONAL BUDGETING

It is quite difficult to set a promotions budget because one is dealing with qualitative rather than quantitative issues. There are many examples of high-budget campaigns failing, and as many of low-budget campaigns succeeding beyond wildest expectations. The difference is in the *quality* of the spend, not in the *quantity* of money invested.

The problem becomes one of attempting to judge how members of designated target audiences will respond to any proposed campaign. As always when one is forecasting, it is impossible to take environmental changes into account. What appears from all the research and pre-testing to be a winning campaign may therefore be negated by events prior to or coincident with the campaign actually running.

The cost of a campaign, or of a particular media, cannot be directly relevant. 'Expensive' and 'cheap' are value-laden terms. It may seem expensive to use £1m in one media against £100,000 in another. But what response is pulled? If the one brings in business worth £5m and the other only £50,000 which, then, seems the best value? If one produces 10,000 responses and the other only 400 where is the money best spent?

This is a trick question because 10,000 responses from a £1m spend works out at £100 per response. 'Only' 4,000 from £100,000 come out as £25 each. Further complexity is added by the value and volume of the potential sales. If it is a big-ticket operation, such as a world-wide time-share scheme, a lot of responses at £100 each may be acceptable. But what of the quality of the response? The 4,000 responses are more welcome if there is an 80% chance of conversion, compared with only 10% of the 10,000.

The marketer must establish clearly, unambiguously and in writing what his or her objectives are. Only then can a budget be established, and an evaluation plan put into place.

Budweiser in the US ran what has become a famous experiment in an attempt to understand the budgetary process. They ran field trials using seven levels of advertising budget across six marketing areas. Stringent controls were put in place to evaluate every aspect of the campaigns. In comparison to what they had done previously their levels of advertising budget were:

-100%   (i.e. no advertising)
- 50%
  0%   (i.e. the same as last year)
+ 50%
+100%   (i.e. double the previous year)
+ 150%
+ 200%   (i.e. treble the previous year)

Results showed that the same sales level was maintained when advertising was withdrawn! The -50% budget produced a sales increase! Budweiser unfortunately did not publish their detailed results and so we do not know what the long-term effects were (or would have been). Nor do we know how, or if, the quality of the advertising was changed. We can only guess at what competitors were doing at the time Budweiser withdrew its advertising – but the inference is obvious. It is not the amount spent, but the quality of execution that really counts.

It is crucial to evaluate the quality of the execution ahead of budget approval. The problem is how to judge quality, since most promotion is not directed at the segments to which marketers and promotions experts belong. When you evaluate promotion remember that you judge it through your own filters and discriminators. Even if you happen to belong to one of the target segments, it is still difficult to evaluate the effect of the advertising because you will have a very strong attitude which is supportive of your product, and you cannot avoid being biased.

Attempts to pre-test can be frustrated by the fact that respondents are put into an unnatural situation. A typical comment is 'Because I was asked to help I tried very hard to follow the commercial. I didn't like to say I didn't understand.'

4.3 The budgeting process

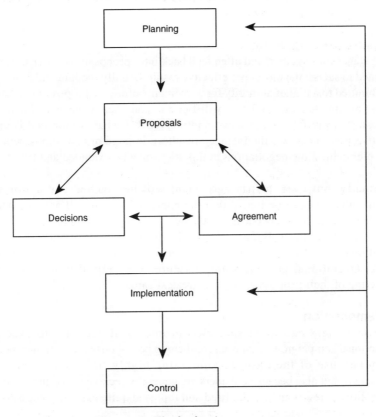

Figure 9: The budgeting process

Planning

Careful and thorough planning is needed if the budgeting process is to have meaning and value. It is crucial to:

- Identify and quantify the target markets
- Identify and quantify the target audiences within the target markets
- Determine the appeals that will have the most power within the defined audiences
- Use the detailed records, and the experience of specialists, to prepare scenarios which allow the results of various budget levels and funding splits across the promotional and media mixes to be worked through.

Proposals

Before authorising any creative work one needs to receive or prepare considered proposals for overall budget level and for the splits across the promotional mix, media and target audiences. Clear objectives are essential. Remember that marketers are concerned to move individuals within audiences through awareness, attitude and into action – then to hold them in the action phase for as long as possible.

Objectives, therefore, should be detailed and deal with each identified target audience within each target market.

Decisions and agreement

These stages run together, and often feed back into 'proposals' in a dynamic process designed to secure the most cost-effective result. Usually recommendations have to be submitted to a higher authority for agreement before the proposals can be firmed up into action plans. It can be very difficult to convince managers who are one or more steps away from the product and market that what is proposed is the most effective way to achieve the intended result(s). In large organisations, with multi-level hierarchies, the negotiations at this stage may be extended and frustrating.

Eventually, however, a firm agreement will be reached and action can be implemented. It is to be hoped that the approved action will achieve what was intended, but on too many occasions the negotiation process results in compromise and, often, in reduced budget. If stated objectives are not achieved, it is the operational marketer and/or the promotional agency who have to shoulder the blame. Operational marketers are therefore best advised to plan the internal marketing of their proposals with the greatest care.

Implementation

Most marketers call upon specialist promotional agencies to execute the promotional campaign. It is unusual for there to be in-house promotional specialists, partly because of the cost of maintaining highly trained and experienced technicians, but also because outsiders are generally reckoned to bring a refreshing, non-political view – and can be fired and replaced quite easily if necessary.

It is for the marketer to establish the objectives, secure the budget and select the teams to secure the results. He or she sets and manages the strategy which the tactical promotional specialists will implement. This is achieved through an overall Marketing Communications Plan (see 4.4 below), and in detailed Marketing Communications (Promotional) Briefs (already covered in 3.3).

Control

No plan should ever be implemented without the needed control measures being identified and in place. How else can the degree of success be evaluated? How else can the whole process be improved?

ESTABLISHING THE BUDGET

There are essentially four methods of setting a promotional budget.

1   Percentage of Sales – the forecast sales revenue determines the amount to be spent on promotion.

2   All you can afford – the budget is set at the maximum possible.

3   Competitive parity – matching what competitors are spending.

4   Objective and task – setting the budget to achieve specified tasks.

ACTIVITY 15

Consider each of the above methods of setting a promotional budget. Make detailed critical notes about each method and determine which you think is the most effective. Explain your conclusion.

Percentage of sales

This can only be a crude method since it relies on past precedent. We know that advertising and sales are not directly related and, in any case, sales should surely result from promotion and not dictate the amount to be spent?

Under this system the successful products will have more spent on them than those which are newly introduced and others that are struggling to attain or hold market share. If funds are reallocated across products from a main budget derived from overall sales it is hard to see what objective basis for the allocation can be used.

All you can afford

This can be a formula to waste money. If all you can afford is not sufficient to reach the objectives then it is money thrown away. The good manager budgets sufficient funds to do the job. Too high a spend is wasteful, too low is ineffective, and therefore also a waste.

Competitive parity

This allows the competition to set your budget! Do they have the same promotional strategy? Do they have the same costings, the same short-, medium- and long-term objectives?

There can be a case to ensure a presence in the same media as the competition, but this refers to only one part of the promotional spend. The Nestlé marketing manager, for example, ran advertising in the trade press not because it was judged to be cost-effective but in response to calls from the sales force. They were concerned that competitors were advertising, and that Nestlé did not have a presence. The cost of trade-press advertising was judged a cost-effective way to restore and maintain the morale of the sales force.

Objective and task

This is the most difficult to introduce, but is by far the most valuable. It depends on clear objectives, specific planning and detailed controls in order for the effectiveness of the spend to be measured. Promotional objectives in SMART terms (see Unit 1) should underpin all promotion, but for 'objective and task' are essential.

The introduction of the objective and task method of setting a promotional budget requires:

- initial data as a foundation for budget experimentation
- control systems that are used effectively
- investment in promotional research.

4.4 Marketing communications plan

Communications requires as detailed planning as any other aspect of marketing. The marketing communications plan is an internal document that sets out the entire plan for a product, product range, department, division, organisation. It will be highly confidential since it contains strategies to achieve and maintain the desired market presence.

There is no universally recognised format for a marketing communications plan, but it should be presented as a report. It should clearly communicate intention and brief all those who will have a part in the communications processes.

A typical marketing communications plan will have nine sections to show in outline how the promotional mix will be used to achieve a specified strategies. From this overall plan, individual briefing documents will be produced so that each strategy has the needed tactical planning to underpin it. The nine sections are:

1   Objectives

2   Target audience(s)

3   Copy platform*

4   Media

5   Creative platform*

6   Timing

7   Budget

8   Schedule

9   Evaluation.

*   The positioning statement provides the themes that copywriters and creative people, such as designers, use as guidelines.

The order in which the sections appear, and their length, will vary with need – there can be no hard-and-fast rule. But all sections must be covered if a plan is to be of value. Remember, however, that the full plan is a confidential and internal document. Sometimes it is restricted only to senior management, with other management (and agencies) having only sufficient access to allow them to function effectively.

ACTIVITY 16

You sell your product range to the building trade through builder's merchants who tend to be independently owned, rather than in large chains such as one finds in retail. You have carefully segmented the market and identified customer and consumer needs. You have been running a very effective promotional campaign which is based on:

● Your sales force making regular contact with the bigger buyers on a monthly call schedule, and with the smaller ones each quarter. They also call on building contractors to ensure that they are receiving a service that is up to standard.

● Trade press advertising. Black and white, half-pages.

● Sales promotions to tie in with each season and to encourage stockholding ahead of demand.

Results are on budget, everybody in head office marketing is pleased.

Your sales manager reports that his team is unhappy because major competitors are running full-colour advertising, and taking big stands at national and local exhibitions. They feel, he says, that the competition will run away with the market.

You believe this to be nonsense, since the product range has many advantages over the competition, and your sales team is in far more regular contact at customer *and* consumer level.

What can you do? What will you do? Why?

You can:

- Ignore the comments and go on with the proven policy.
- Follow the competition into colour and exhibitions.
- Select a response that meets the sales team's needs at minimal extra spend.

You do:

- Recognise that the sales force's morale is more crucial than the marginal cost of a small increase in the promotional spend.
- Find ways to spend as little as possible to achieve the objectives that the sales force seems to want.
- Justify the cost against sales force morale, and *not* against the original promotional objectives. This may mean moving to colour advertisements in the trade press. It may mean taking exhibition space at selected high-profile exhibitions. It should not mean both – and it should not match what the competition is doing.
- You will also ensure that the sales force knows what is being done. 'Pulls' of the advertising must be sent out, photos of the exhibition stands should be taken and circulated at sales meetings.

Why?

- Because you have established the sales force as a major promotional tool and you need it to be sharp.
- Because it will lose its edge if it feels handicapped by competitive action to which you are not responding.
- Individuals will be flattered that you have taken notice, and also have taken action.

Overall the cost will be small, against a very high probability of falling sales if it is not incurred.

Summary

Communications must be managed every bit as thoroughly and precisely as any other part of management. A major difficulty comes from the necessarily subjective nature of response, which is conditioned by people's behaviour. This is compounded by the need to plan communications for a future time, when the prevailing attitudes and perceptions of target audiences are likely to have changed from their present state.

Management's problems are made even more complex by the difficulty of securing an unbiased response to communications research, and to test marketing. The nature of marketing management as more akin to an art than a science is clearly demonstrated in the communications area.

UNIT REVIEW ACTIVITY

This is a major activity to which you should devote at least two hours.

Acme Sail Training's Strategic Plan is given as Resource Item 6.1. As Jason McCall, the director with management consultancy experience, you are required to prepare a briefing document as a basis for advertising agencies to pitch for your account.

You are not prepared to specify a budget, but require that each agency costs their proposals and indicates how they recommend that promotional results be evaluated.

Note that you will need to 'flesh out' the case, making what reasonable assumptions enable you to complete the activity. Assume that you have detailed research into the market which you will attach as an appendix.

There is no 'correct' answer to this assignment. Much will depend on your personal interpretation of the case. Your answer should, however, be close to the specimen brief that is given at the end of the unit.

Unit summary

Section 1 demonstrated how communication is a two-way process and that for effective communication, four factors have to be taken into account: receiver, message, channel and feedback. Messages are received through a set of filters and discriminators which each individual automatically puts into place to manage the surfeit of sensory signals that reach us every second. In order to be effective in their work, marketers need to study and understand the behaviour of individuals, and the ways in which they perceive and filter out messages.

It has been demonstrated that purchasing is based on learned behaviour and that learning is reinforced by a retention of rewarding experiences. Individuals progress from unawareness of a product, through the three stages of Awareness of the product, Attitude towards it, and Action. Marketing's promotional role is to help the progression from unawareness to regular usage.

The higher-level response set (HLRS) shows how each major stage can be sub-divided into smaller steps, each of which has to be achieved in turn.

Section 2 discussed the promotional mix: public relations, advertising, sales promotion and sales force. Each tool has a specific role to play, but all components should interrelate. Physical packaging has a dual role: as protection for the product and as a medium for the product message.

It is important to determine who you are trying to communicate with. Target audiences, composed of individuals who share the same attributes, must be identified. The communication process needs to encourage demand in consumers and customers so that product is 'pulled' down the channel of distribution.

The importance of the point of sale cannot be over-emphasised. Different media (by which we mean anything that can carry a promotional message) impact differently on a range of apparently similar individuals.

A product or service is mentally positioned in the minds of individuals who make up target audiences. A positioning statement is required as a strategic focus from which all communications are derived.

Section 3 concentrated on agencies and consultancies – which can provide a valuable service, based on highly professional standards and cost-effectiveness, and which should be used when they add value to management's efforts. Agency recruitment, selection and management is a crucially important activity. Briefings must be thorough and confirmed in writing. Promotional objectives must underpin all communication.

Section 4 considered the different aspects of managing communications, including the difficulty of obtaining reliable data on the effectiveness of communications. It stressed how promotional budgets should be set in line with the specified objectives, and described a marketing communications plan as an *internal strategic* management document. A marketing communications brief was described as an *external* document that establishes exactly what has to be achieved in one or more strategic and/or tactical areas.

References

Buzan, T (1993) *Use Your Head* , BBC Publications [Section 2]

Cummins, J (1990) Table – Linking the objective to the mechanics: how they match up, in P R Smith (1992) *Marketing Communications: An integrated approach,* Kogan Page

Ogilvy, D (1983) *Ogilvy on Advertising,* Pan

White, R (1980) *Advertising: What it is and how to do it,* McGraw-Hill

Worsam, M (1995) *Marketing Operations,* Butterworth–Heinemann

Further Reading

Chisnall, P M (1975) *Marketing, a Behavioural Analysis,* McGraw-Hill

Foxall, G R (1980) *Consumer Behaviour,* Kogan Page

Hill, R W & Hillyer, T J (1982) *Organisational Buying Behaviour,* Macmillan

Smith, P R (1993) *Marketing Communications,* Kogan Page

Adcock, C J (1970) *Fundamentals of Psychology,* Pelican

Answers to Review Activities

Review Activity 1

SPEEDLINK

The new tramway linking Bromley and Croydon will enable people to *travel easily and safely,* at convenient times. Prices will compare favourably with the bus services, but the journey time will be halved, with no traffic delays.

Public relations

The PR campaign is already running and has secured initial permission and focused the response of the local community. It will step up a gear in the months and weeks ahead of opening.

It will be especially concerned with creating awareness of Speedlink's positive benefits, but contingency plans to deal with the inevitable setbacks must be prepared in detail. We must expect the media to pick up on any problems, and security and safety are bound to be major concerns.

We should budget to take journalists and prominent local people to visit the tramways that are up and running in Newcastle and Amsterdam, so that they can sample the service and talk to actual users about any concerns.

The PR activity should not be stood down until at least six months after Speedlink is operating, although we should be able to gradually wind it down as confidence in the service grows.

Advertising

The major thrust will be in local media, by which we mean London south of the Thames and Kent, Surrey and East Sussex down to the coast. Ads in close proximity to the line will stress the daily convenience factor – school journeys, commuters, shoppers, etc. Those further away will join with Bromley and Croydon's Local Authorities and major shopping centres to encourage day visits to the shops, theatres, cinemas and restaurants. 'Why go to the West End when you can Speedlink?'

Sales promotion

A whole range of special fares will be offered, firstly to encourage travel, and secondly to encourage travel within specified time bands. The 1000th, 5000th and 10,000th passenger will be especially feted.

Selling

Ticket machines will be state of the art, and tickets will also be available wherever bus tickets are currently sold (newsagents, etc). Daily, weekly, monthly and annual tickets will be available. Annual tickets will also be available on monthly direct debit terms.

Bulk concessionary sales to major concerns in the area will be handled by a sales team of two outside representatives and three sales office staff.

Review Activity 2

Your positioning statement should encapsulate the key issues that sum up the essential you – the issues that make up your overall image – what you offer to the outside world. Your behaviour will change, depending on context (at work, with friends, with parents, at home), but not the underpinning values that direct your approach to life. You may (probably will) find issues about youself that need work if you are to present an image with which you are satisfied. Equally, there will be areas of strength that you will be able to capitalise on.

Review Activity 3

You could agree with the MD and change the advertising. Alternatively, you could explain just why it had been planned the way that it is, and support your position with clear evidence that sales and profit budgets are being met, and that the target customers and consumers are happy.

You will need to be prepared to cope with unreasoning criticism, however, because without a marketing background your MD will be using inappropriate criteria as the frame of reference. The point is not whether the MD likes it, but whether the target market is responding well.

If what you are doing is having a detrimental effect on corporate image, then the overriding need of corporate communications policy may force you to change – but you should have structured your brief to the agency within corporate communication guidelines.

The bottom line – unfortunately – is that the MD outranks you, and you cannot *prove* that a change of advertising will have a detrimental effect – only that it would cost a lot of money. So, in reality, whatever the theory, you are likely to have to make changes. (And then, unfortunately, be held to account if there is a fall-off in sales.)

Unit Review Activity

ACME SAIL TRAINING BRIEFING DOCUMENT

1 Situation
Acme Sail Training has been set up with a prime focus which we summarise as 'Enjoy learning to lead'. A secondary focus is 'Qualify while you Holiday'. We shall operate on the South Coast of France, which is particularly attractive to the British.

2 Objectives
2.1 To generate a revenue of £ 200,000 in the first year and £500,000 in year two.

2.2 To generate an awareness in our major markets of:
- 20% awareness amongst Human Resource Directors of UK companies with over 10,000 employees.
- 10% awareness amongst UK amateur powerboat owners and drivers, water-ski and scuba enthusiasts.

2.3 To secure bookings from:

Year one
- 5 major companies, to train a minimum of 10 managers each.
- 400 persons for a two-week package.

Year two
- 20 major companies, to train a total of 400 managers.
- 700 persons on two-week packages.
- 500 persons on action-centred weekend packages.

3 Strategy

3.1 Management:

Our broad intention is to build on existing client contacts by using personal contacts such as letters and direct visits. This will be supplemented by carefully targeted direct mail. We shall possibly also use targeted trade press.

3.2 Holidays:

Targeted promotion to powerboat and sailing club secretaries supplemented with advertising in the RYA magazine and selected boating monthlies. Possibly linked promotions with makers and agents of top of the range craft.

4 Tactics

Detailed tactics will be established in collaboration with the appointed agency once strategies have been finalised.

5 Budget

Our maximum promotional spend must not exceed £150,000 in year one.

6 Product

6.1 Our clients will benefit from our guarantee that as an EU Recognised Training Establishment we shall maintain the highest standards of instruction and use only modern and well maintained equipment.

6.2 Safety measures will be above the standards laid down by all interested bodies.

6.3 Clients will leave, subject to having qualified, with diplomas and certificates that will have true value in the employment market.

6.4 Holidaymakers will benefit from our exclusive beaches and from individual attention from highly qualified staff.

6.5 All will enjoy the high standard of the accommodation and – in particular – of the cuisine and fine wines.

6.6 Our unique benefits are:
- the south of France
- highly qualified staff

- full travel service from UK and return
- guaranteed to be able to get on the water (UK weather often prevents)
- instruction in English, by British qualified staff
- quality of fellow guests.

7 Organisation

7.1 We are a small organisation in terms of full-time staff, but our main need for staff will come in a very limited period. There are many highly qualified and eager young men and women coming down from university who are anxious to earn good money during their holidays. We shall recruit from the best qualified of these.

7.2 Our four directors have each earned a high reputation in their field, and we work together as a 'seamless team'.

7.3 In the summer we shall have six full-time British staff in France to manage the facility and lead the activities. These will be supplemented with part-time staff to handle the individual instruction, maintain the equipment and administer the centre. The kitchen and all domestic arrangements will be staffed by French people, but led by an on-site British Director.

8 Market analysis

Our marketing research has been thorough and we believe that clear market opportunities have been identified.

9 Pricing

9.1 For the management market we shall work to parity with the leading competitors – but with the proviso that our prices will include travel to the facility.

9.2 For the secondary market we aim to be well above the package rate for the same area. At £350 per week, inclusive, and a targeted two-week course we aim to segment by price. We shall not allow a discount for a non-sailor companion. Payment will be by substantial deposit with booking, with the balance to fall due two weeks before departure.

10 Distribution

We intend to market direct. Our target customers are well defined and media is already targeted upon them. Specialist magazines exist, dedicated clubs provide access and direct mail is available through national institutions to whom we are affiliated.

11 Evaluation

We shall measure effectiveness through response and then conversion. We shall welcome specific input upon this point.

12 Time-scale

We confirm that your pitch should be made at our offices at 10.00 am on the 10th of next month.

13 Personnel

We shall positively welcome your creative input, ahead of your pitch, if this will help to clarify points or improve the brief. For this, or any other matter, simply contact me, rather than any other Director, at our Redhill office.

Signed
Jason McCall

UNIT 7

MARKET RESEARCH

Introduction

The purpose of this unit is to introduce you to the principles and methods of market research. The data and information which arise from market research activities influence many decisions in the marketing department of an organisation. It is thus an important part of marketing.

The term 'market research' is used in this unit to mean a specialist activity involving the collection of data and information through questionnaires, observation and other techniques. It is part of the marketing function and its importance has grown alongside the growth in importance of the marketing concept.

The initial stage of any market research project is to assess the quality and relevance of available secondary data – data which already exists and which may provide some answers for the researcher. Useful sources of published data – both internal and external – are recommended in Section 2. The next stage of research is the collection of primary data – that collected specifically to find answers to the problem under scrutiny. Sections 3 and 4 consider different types of primary data – quantitative and qualitative – and simple research design.

The final section of the unit covers the design of questionnaires. A questionnaire is a valuable form of measurement, and a control document, but it cannot be prepared until the researcher has identified the exact information that is to be collected. Attention is given to the style and layout of a questionnaire, the type of questions used and the sequence in which they are presented to the respondent. You will be given an opportunity to analyse questionnaires, and to plan a market research project.

Objectives

By the end of the unit you should be able to:

- identify the information that can be obtained by market research
- identify what information about the market can be obtained from internal sources
- identify appropriate sources of external data
- define the difference between data and information
- select the appropriate form of question to elicit specific information
- design a simple piece of market research
- select the appropriate mode of research to obtain specific information
- evaluate the effectiveness of a questionnaire
- design a simple questionnaire.

SECTION 1

The Role of Market Research

Introduction

This section introduces you to the concept of market research, and draws a distinction between it and marketing research. It goes on to demonstrate how market research lies at the heart of the marketing concept, providing evidence, as it does, about the customer. Market research has an important part to play in the development of new products.

The aim of this section is to help you to:

- understand what is meant by the term 'market research'
- appreciate the importance of the information gained as an aid to decision making, particularly in the initial stages of product planning
- identify some of the limitations of market research.

1.1 What is market research?

The Market Research Society defines market research as 'the means used by those who provide goods and services to keep themselves in touch with the needs and wants of those who buy and use these goods and services.' This definition applies to market, social and economic research, but it fails to specify what the process involves.

Many marketing writers confuse the term 'market research' with the term 'marketing research', and sometimes these two terms are used interchangeably. There are significant differences between them, however, as will be seen in the following quotations. A comprehensive definition of marketing research emerged among key writers of marketing theory in the 1980s, and this is now widely accepted. It defines **marketing research** as:

> the function that brings the consumer, customer and public to the market through information – information used to identify and define marketing objectives and problems; generate, refine and evaluate marketing actions, monitor marketing performance; and improve understanding of the marketing process. (American Marketing Association, 1987)

This clearly shows that marketing research is wide ranging in its concerns. The term **market research** is, according to Adcock *et al* (1993, p101):

> used to define the specialist activities involved in collecting information directly through the use of questionnaires and other associated techniques...it is useful to

consider market research as a specialist activity which is within the scope of the marketing research function [and is] concerned with collecting primary information.

Market research is the 'intelligence tool' of management in any type of organisation that is managed by business principles, and which wants to be efficient in the market it serves. It includes opinion polls, such as those used to monitor the public's attitude towards the government's handling of its national responsibilities, or those that measure the voting intentions of the public in the period leading up to a general election.

In addition to the Market Research Society, mentioned earlier, there is also the Industrial Market Research Society; these two bodies represent the interests of professionals involved in market research. Since their inception earlier this century, they have both been actively involved in raising the status of market research, and of aiding the development of rigorous techniques for use in planning and carrying out polls and market research projects.

ACTIVITY 1

Write down three key adjectives that describe the most important features of good market research.

There are a number of adjectives that would fit the bill here, but they should convey the importance of market research being systematic, objective and accurate.

Market research is defined by the European Society for Opinion and Marketing Research (ESOMAR) as:

> The systematic collection and objective recording, classification, analysis and presentation of data concerning the behaviour, needs, attitudes, opinions and motivations of individuals and organisations within the context of their economic, social, political and everyday activities.

The term 'systematic' means that the market research project or opinion poll must be planned and organised in an efficient way, and that the type of research design to be used must be established before the research begins. The type of data to be collected must be stated, along with the method of analysis for that data. Objectivity in the method of recording will mean that the research activity will be 'unbiased and unemotional in performing its responsibilities'. (Kinnear and Taylor, 1987, p18).

The ESOMAR definition also refers to the presentation of the data. Raw data is transformed into useful information by analysis, and should be presented in a written research report to management. It is in this form that it is most useful as an aid to managerial decision-making, and the style and presentation of the written report is as important as the research activities that have preceded it. Boyd and Westfall (1956, p195) emphasise that 'no matter what the proficiency with which all previous steps have been dispatched, the (market research) project will be no more successful than the research report'.

MARKET RESEARCH AS AN AID TO DECISION-MAKING

All marketing managers need information for 'planning and control purposes' and, in particular, information is 'needed regarding the controllable and uncontrollable variables in the marketing system'. (Kinnear & Taylor, 1987, p13) Market research managers must have a regular supply of information about the marketing system, and this information must be co-ordinated and distributed in a way that enhances the planning and control activities of the organisation. This enables marketing managers to be more effective in their work of allocating resources in the marketing function, of defining and developing marketing objectives and carrying out a performance audit.

It is critical for the well-being and future of the organisation that decision-makers make the most effective decisions every time. Market research information helps to reduce uncertainty. Some marketing managers seem to require only a small amount of market research information, the reason being that:

> certainty costs a lot of time and money, and . . . most businesses are able to tolerate a great deal of uncertainty in market research results, because they understand the environment in which they work and have a platform of certainty based on their sales to existing customers which they can use to evaluate results of field surveys.

> (Clifton *et al*, 1992, p58)

Decisions are often taken in a routine way. As Simon (1960, p1) points out: 'the vast majority of decisions made by [marketing] managers are programmed and involve recurring situations which have been dealt with previously.'

Some decisions are, however, not routine and involve an evaluation of alternative courses. For example, if the early demand for a new car has been much greater than expected, then the marketing manager will want to make a decision which capitalises on this market opportunity. There will be more than one course of action to choose from, and market research information is essential to evaluate the alternative decisions. It should help to reduce the uncertainty within any chosen course of action.

Sometimes a major marketing decision has to be taken extremely quickly, in response, say, to the behaviour of a competitor, as the following example demonstrates.

CHOCOLATE WARS

The launch of Cadbury's Wispa Bar created a competitive threat to Rowntree Mackintosh's Aero Bar. The Wispa Bar was a small oblong bar of textured chocolate which was informally packaged. Aero Bar, at that time, was also a bar of textured chocolate but the outcome of the texturing process produced something slightly different from the Wispa Bar. It was also quite different in shape, since it was designed as a finger bar like the highly successful Kit-Kat, which was also part of Rowntree Mackintosh's range.

The decision the marketing management of Rowntree Mackintosh had to take was how to respond to protect their market share against this new entrant into the market. They chose to copy the competition – the 'me-too' approach – and immediately changed the shape of the Aero bar to one almost the same as Wispa Bar. They had to be confident in making this decision that the new shape would still be pleasing to their current customers, and attract more frequent purchases, that it would prevent customers from trying the new Cadbury brand, and that it would help to attract new customers. To this extent they had to have a clear image of their customer groups and their lifestyles, habits, values and attitudes so that they could be confident about the quality of their commercial judgement.

This kind of information comes from good-quality market research data, which has proved over time to be reliable, and valid, and which is collected on a regular basis. It provides the company with a clear picture of their customers and their buying behaviour, and on the basis of this it is possible to predict how they will respond to change.

This is an illustration of decision-making which has to be taken quickly. Markets, like society, are dynamic and in a constant state of flux. There is no guarantee that a product that has performed well for a company will continue to do so. Being able to predict how and when the needs of the market will change is critical in successful marketing, and an area where quality in market research data and information is essential.

1.2 Market research as part of the marketing function

It is important to set market research activity within the context of the marketing of an organisation.

As has already been stated, market research is an activity within the marketing research function. Both have grown in importance alongside the development of the marketing concept. Business orientation moved earlier this century from an emphasis on products to an emphasis on selling, and then on to a marketing orientation, as managers became increasingly aware of the need to be more efficient in a highly competitive environment. The massive growth in communications and information technology has made the world markets into a 'global village', so the need to attain a sustainable competitive advantage and to be increasingly responsive to rapidly changing market conditions has become more urgent. A supply of high-quality market research data to aid decision-making is essential, although this cannot be a substitute for experience, commercial insight and judgement skills.

The marketing concept, as described in Unit 1, uses the customer as its starting point when making plans. The concept of marketing 'is founded on the belief that profitable sales and satisfactory returns on investment can only be achieved by identifying, anticipating and satisfying customer needs and desires'. (Barwell, 1965, p3) It is obvious that in order to do this it is necessary to ask customers questions.

The marketing concept is put into practice though the management of the marketing mix. It is through the marketing function that an organisation identifies:
    the current and future needs and wants of specifically defined target markets. This information is then acted on by the whole organisation in bringing into existence the products and/or services necessary to satisfy customer requirements. It is the marketing function that forms the interface with the firm's existing and potential customers. (Lancaster & Massingham, 1993, p5)

1.3 The scope of market research

Arpi (1970, p15) said that 'realistic market planning implies knowledge of the present and future state of the market, in so far as the future can be predicted'. Knowledge of the kind required comes from research involving both primary and secondary data.

An organisation's research department may just serve the needs and wants of the organisation, or it may submit a competitive tender for research projects from other businesses. Research projects that are carried out within the organisation are known as in-house activity. Alternatively, an organisation can commission the services of a market research agency and other organisations, such as a university. The market research industry is a large, multi-million-pound market made up of businesses of all sizes, many of whom specialise in certain areas of consumer or industrial markets, and in specific approaches to market research. Clifton *et al* (1992, p197) identify four reasons why a research agency may need to be used. These are if:

- the company lacks adequate personnel resources
- there is a need for anonymity in approaching a market
- disagreements within the company on the potential of a market make an independent assessment desirable
- speed in getting information is critical.

As was shown in Unit 2, a business exists not only within its 'micro-environment' of customers and competitors, suppliers and distributors. In addition, there are the factors of the macro-environment impacting upon it, such as legislation, social, political and economic changes, and as well as technological developments. All of these influence the nature of problems with which the organisation has to cope and thus the products it plans to develop for its customers and markets.

PRODUCT DEVELOPMENT

All aspects of product development, from idea generation to concept testing and development, through production, to launch and the post-launch period, require research strategies. Even at the stage of 'idea generation' market research can provide information on the perception of the product by those in the trade, of its acceptability and whether it fits with the company's image. It can also help to establish the consumers' perception of the product's benefits and whether or not they are likely to purchase it. If this stage is not accurately and efficiently researched, then every decision that follows may be erroneous and lead to serious financial losses for the company.

ACTIVITY 2

List three aspects of a product and its potential market that might need to be researched before a decision was taken to go into production.

Market research techniques may be used to gauge reaction to:

- the design, form and functional characteristics of the product in the range
- the relationship between quality in the product and its price
- the brand name, positioning strategy and the way in which the core brand proposition is written and described.

The steps involved in providing back-up research for the initial stages of product development are:

Identifying the target market

This involves identifying the customer groups that are to be served and establishing their characteristics:

- what reasons do they have for purchasing the product or service?
- what is their current pattern of purchasing behaviour: from whom do they buy, and why?
- what sort of benefits do they seek from the products they purchase?

- what are their attitudes and opinions, and how are consumer tastes, and thus needs and wants, changing?

Information is sought about changes in fashion trends and lifestyle trends which will influence consumer purchase patterns.

Analysing the market

The size of the market and its potential for growth will also be researched, with such questions being asked as:

- Can the market be stimulated so that more sales can be made? This involves identifying potential changes in the characteristics of the market that may create conditions in which the market can grow, or respond to stimulation to grow. Changes may be demographic, social or geographic.

- What is the effectiveness of current activities in the market, and are these activities suitable for transferral to new markets?

- Are there niches which leading competitors are failing to satisfy? It is unlikely that such niches will not have been noticed, but the competitors may have decided that it is not in their commercial interests to satisfy the needs of the niche. This will create an opportunity for a small business to exploit.

- What influences the demand for products and what has influenced demand in the past?

Methods of distributing the product

This involves establishing:

- available locations and opportunities for distributing the product

- current methods of distributing products, and possible alternative methods.

Suitable sales and promotion methods

This involves assessing:

- which methods of selling and promoting a product appeal to target customers

- the coverage and frequency of a media (who will see it and what they will see)

- the types of media that should be used, depending on their audiences.

ACTIVITY 3

Identify some of the information that a marketing manager would find beneficial when making decisions about the price of a new product.

A marketing manager would need information about the price of competing products, but also about how price-sensitive the market is. A survey could be constructed to gauge demand at different price levels, leading to an estimation of the optimum price.

1.4 The limitations of market research

Market research should not be thought of as the answer to every marketing manager's problems. It does not provide all the answers, and it does not make decisions. Market research, while a useful tool when used properly, has its limitations.

ACTIVITY 4

List what you consider to be the limitations of even the best market research.

One of the major weaknesses of market research is that it is a **time-consuming** activity and in commercial life it is an old but true cliché that 'time costs money'. Invariably, management wants market research data 'yesterday' and is impatient for research results. It is for this reason that many large companies are willing to pay high fees to research agencies for data to be collected speedily and efficiently.

Market research data reports on **current and past behaviour,** and from the moment the research activity ceases the data becomes historical. The data is measuring human behaviour, and human behaviour patterns are continually developing and changing so the data is quickly out of date. Data can be used, along with other factors, to predict future patterns of behaviour, but it should not be relied on alone.

Market research data is **never complete;** there is always some further information that managers would like to know in order to make their decision. It can, however, give a clear picture of several key issues, depending upon the nature of the project.

The data can be **interpreted** in a variety of **different ways** and there can easily be quite significant intellectual differences between those who carry out the research, and those who use the information that arises from it. It is important, then, for the key findings to be presented in a succinct and easily understandable format, and with a fuller account of the findings also included in the report. Managers want to be able to absorb the many points from a research project quickly and easily, and not feel overwhelmed by research technology and technical jargon. They want information that they can use in a practical way.

As mentioned above, market research is a tool to be used when making a decision; it does not make the decision for you. Lehmann (1989, p14) stresses this when he points out that 'market research does not make decisions . . . research takes data about a confusing/uncertain market and rearranges them into a different form which hopefully makes the market more understandable and consequently good decisions easier'. He then adds: 'market research does not guarantee success. The real value of research can be seen over a long period where increasing the percentage of good decisions should be manifested in improved bottom-line performances and on the occasional revelation that arises from research.'

Other limitations of market research occur during the research design and in the implementation of the design. Sometimes the analysis of the marketing problem may be inadequate, which may lead to the wrong data being collected. Then there are problems in carrying out the research project, such as surveying the wrong target population or too few of the target population. Similarly, faults in the design of a questionnaire can generate poor-quality data. Also, respondents may give answers to impress the interviewer.

REVIEW ACTIVITY 1

Imagine you are the manager of a car dealership, selling both new and second-hand cars for Rover and Nissan, which is being established in a small town with a population of approximately 50,000 people.

What type of market research data and information would help you to compete more effectively? What questions might you need answers to?

(The answer to this activity is to be found at the end of the unit.)

Summary

This section has explored the nature of market research as a specialist activity within marketing research. It has set market research within the context of an organisation and shown how and why it has grown in importance. Market research has been shown to be intrinsic to the development of new products or services, but its limitations mean that it should be treated carefully and used with circumspection.

SECTION 2

Sources of Secondary Data

Introduction

'Secondary data consists of information that already exists somewhere, having been collected for another purpose'. (Kotler & Armstrong, 1989, p97). There are two sources of this data:

● **Internal sources.** This is data that is available within the company, although as Chisnall (1992, p40) points out 'many companies do not make full enough use of the information that is routinely collected'.

- **External sources.** This is data that has been published for commercial reasons. A key source of secondary data is the library service and most good libraries have a wide range of sources. Some government data is available free; secondary data from private sources can be very expensive.

This section will look at the internal sources of data available to a researcher working for a well-managed and well-resourced organisation. It will give some guidance as to where to look for external secondary data and the range of publications available.

The following section will look at the collection of **primary data:** that which is gained first-hand from customers.

There is an absolute mass of secondary data available to the researcher and it is important to select sources carefully and use them prudently. Otherwise, the task can be overwhelming. Without doubt, there is much material available, giving information on markets and the companies who operate within those markets. A well-managed organisation will identify and record those sources of secondary data that are most appropriate for its efficiency.

When planning a research project which may go on to include the collection of primary data, it is important to know what data is already available, since this will guide the structure and format of any fieldwork. It can also influence the choice of the data collection methods used. It is even possible that secondary data sources can provide the complete answer to the problem under scrutiny, thus saving both time and money. The least it will do is limit the scope of the fieldwork in a useful way.

The aim of this section is to help you to:

- identify the most appropriate sources of secondary data (internal and external).

2.1 Internal sources

Internal sources of data are those which are found *within* an organisation. Most organisations have masses of data which, if well organised, can be very useful. It is important that a system is devised so that:

- important data and information are recorded efficiently
- all those who should know about the system are aware of it and use it
- data and information are distributed internally to all those who need to receive it at a time when it is needed.

There are many different kinds of data within an organisation and quite often this type of data is a much under-used resource. Data that is not useful must be discarded on a regular basis to stop it cluttering the system.

Data can be captured in a formal way, such as by monitoring trends in sales, or informally through personal conversations. No source of data should be overlooked, but its usefulness to the company must be discerned.

ACTIVITY 5

What sort of data would you expect an organisation to have on the markets it serves?

It is important to have data on the size of the market, and the market share held by the organisation. Good details about customers is critical so that this profile can be used to attract similar others. How the organisation sells its products, where and by what method, and if any salespeople are used essential areas from which data should be collected.

The type of data that is particularly useful for marketing decision-making consists of the following:

- sales figures, past and present, broken down by product, product range or brand
- sales figures broken down by market segment to observe trends in the market
- analysis of sales figures by different type of sales outlets to monitor different performance levels, and the analysis of order size to monitor the volume and value of sales
- the relationship between sales figures and the cost of sales force expenditure, and promotional activities, including packaging
- information about competitors, their products and the segments they serve. The data should be so comprehensive that it should be possible to predict how they will respond to changes in your company strategy.
- articles from the trade or business press that are relevant to both the company and its products and markets.

Information technology is widely used in storing and retrieving market data, since large amounts of information about sales and customers can be processed very quickly. This is an important growth area, particularly for mail order and direct mail businesses who need to be able to access information speedily.

It may also be possible to refer to primary research which has been commissioned in the past by an organisation. If nothing else, it will give good background information and a picture of the situation as it pertained at the time the research was commissioned. It can then be used as a measurement of change, and may well give useful information that can guide steps in the research process.

Many organisations employ sales personnel, who have direct access to the customer, and who are sources of both formal and informal information. Sales people work in a variety of situations, in business-to-business markets, in offices taking orders over the telephone, in over-the-counter sales or by visiting customers at their premises. They have access to much information about customers, and their needs, and to what is happening in the market overall. It is important that they have a routine for systematically reporting back. Frequently, much valuable information can be gleaned from an informal conversation, carried out in a relaxed way with a customer. Attendance at conferences, exhibitions and meetings also gives opportunities to observe competitors in action.

The customer service or complaints section in an organisation is also important, and many ideas for product modifications have arisen here.

ACTIVITY 6

What type of data and information do you think could be obtained from a customer complaint?

Extremely useful data and information can be obtained from a customer complaint, and this is often the starting point for modifications and additional benefits which are added to the product. A constant and repeated request for a specific type, style, design or colour in a product, for example, might eventually lead to a worthwhile research project, to more fully assess market demand. Some customers love to comment on the strengths and weaknesses of products, and if they receive a suitable response to their comment, it makes them feel valued.

Customer complaints will reveal customers' perceptions of the product or service. This may not be the same as the organisation's perception of its product or service. Where there is a disparity, the organisation may well need to reposition the product correctly in the eyes of the consumer. Comments may relate to the way the product is packaged and presented, and the usefulness of any labels. Equally, the instructions for use given by the manufacturer may not be easy for the consumer to follow, and may affect the way the product is used by the consumer. Overall, customer complaints will show if the product does what it is supposed to do.

REVIEW ACTIVITY 2

A manufacturer of domestic lawn mowers in the UK wishes to expand its market. It already has the largest share of the UK market, and is selling well in France. It wishes to expand into other European Countries, such as Spain and Germany, and you have been asked to advise its Board of Directors on the research necessary to assess these new markets.

What information will the company need, and how should they obtain it? Use the information in this section for guidance.

A proposed answer to this Review Activity is at the end of the Unit.

Summary

This section has defined desk research and secondary data and identified the key sources of such data. It has noted the useful forms of internally available data that can aid decision-making and listed the types and sources of published data normally available in libraries and through inter-library loans.

SECTION 3

Collecting Primary Data

Introduction

Once the desk research is complete, and all possible sources of secondary data have been referred to, the researcher will have a much clearer idea of:

● the up-to-date and relevant data already available

● what data still needs to be collected to find a solution to the problem under scrutiny.

The next stage is to:

- identify data that it is absolutely essential to gather
- differentiate the above from data which it would be good to know but which is of lesser importance and is peripheral to requirements.

All data that is to be collected in the research must be directly relevant to finding an answer to the problem. This data, which is generated specifically by and for the project and is collected by the use of fieldwork, is **primary data.** To achieve the data and information the research team needs to answer certain questions:

- What is it necessary to know?
- Who will have the information that is sought?
- What is the best method (quick and efficient) to use to collect this data?

It is important to streamline the answers to these questions to avoid collecting a mass of irrelevant data by inappropriate or inefficient methods.

There are two different types of data, both of which are important and yield different insights. They are:

- quantitative data
- qualitative data.

It is usually appropriate, particularly in a large research project, to collect both types of data, as the information gained from either sort on its own is normally insufficient.

The aim of this section is to help you to:

- understand the difference between quantitative and qualitative data
- identify when it is appropriate to gather each kind of data
- weigh up the costs and benefits of each type of data
- begin to appreciate the problems and importance of achieving an accurate sample.

3.1 Quantitative data

As the term implies, this is data that is expressed in numbers. Quantitative data is quite easy to collect, and a large amount of reliable and valid data can be collected, largely by questionnaire or observation, in quite a short period of time, in a fairly formal approach. This data arises from what is termed 'closed questions' because the respondent is restricted in the choice of answer he or she can give.

ACTIVITY 7

Try to define the difference between data and information.

Data is expressed quantitatively, in numerical terms. It is translated into information by analysis.

TYPES OF QUESTIONS ASKED

Sometimes the respondent may be asked to:

Choose one answer from a selection of alternatives, such as:
Where do you prefer to do your shopping?
(a) Town Centre ☐
(b) Out-of-town shopping complex ☐
(c) Both ☐

Select one or more answers from a selection of alternatives, such as:
Place a tick against the word(s) that come closest to your image of Stoke-on-Trent?
(a) Historical ☐
(b) Industrial ☐
(c) Pleasant ☐
(d) No image ☐
(e) Dirty ☐
(f) Clean ☐
(g) Has character ☐
(h) Developing city ☐

Rank a series of alternative answers in a specific order of priority, such as:
Rank in order of importance the following benefits in a new washing machine:
(a) Good brand identity ☐
(b) Installation and free services for two years ☐
(c) Automatic wash and dry programme ☐
(d) Fits the available space in the kitchen/laundry room ☐
(e) Has a wide variety of programmes ☐

Choose the answer YES or NO in response to the set questions, such as:
Do you live in this town?   YES☐   NO ☐

In all of the above illustrations the respondent answers by placing a tick in the box. Other variations in questionnaire style will be considered in Section 5; they all restrict the type of response and collect quantitative data.

This type of data is a systematic record of response or measurement. A quantitative approach is also taken in the selection of those members of the population to question as part of the survey.

ACTIVITY 8

Which of the above types of question would you use in a survey to find out if there was:

● a perceived need for a new swimming pool in the centre of town and if so, where?

● satisfaction with the service at a hospital out-patients?

The answer to whether or not consumers perceive a need for a swimming pool can be quickly discovered by a set question with a restricted choice of answer: that is, answer Yes or No. To discover the preferred location for the swimming pool, a question listing the alternative locations could be set, and consumers asked to choose one answer from the selection of alternatives.

A question to discover the level of satisfaction with the service at a hospital out-patients, would need to identify the components of the service. Respondents could be asked to rank these in order of their importance for a satisfactory service to occur, and then express their satisfaction with the service they have experienced by means of a score out of 10.

SAMPLE SELECTION

In an ideal situation all members of the population with the characteristics or qualities being measured would be questioned. For example, a tobacco manufacturer planning a new blend of pipe tobacco would ask all people who smoke a pipe about their smoking habits. This would mean that the target population would be:

● too large to manage

● too difficult to locate

● too time-consuming for the parameters of the project

- far too expensive to achieve.

It is therefore necessary to select a only sample of the target population, but it is important that this smaller, selected group possesses all the characteristics of the target population, so that the results are as close as possible to those that would be gained by asking every single person. It is essential, therefore, first to define precisely the characteristics of the population under consideration, so that the researcher can draw up a sampling frame – a list of the characteristics/social/marital status of the people to be researched. Lancaster & Massingham (1993, pp291-2) suggest five criteria that can be used to evaluate the suitability of a sampling frame. These are:

- **adequacy** – it should cover all of the population to be surveyed for this specific research purpose.

- **completeness** – it can be difficult to assess the completeness of a sampling frame, but the sample will be biased if the population to be surveyed is not complete.

- **accuracy** – it is impossible for a sampling frame to be up-to-date and it may contain people or houses that no longer exist. This occurs when using the Register of Electors as a sampling frame, because people move house.

- **lack of duplication** – a business may be entered more than once on a list, say in telephone directories. The bias created by this duplication can be allowed for in subsequent statistical analysis.

- **convenience** – sampling list can be obtained from commercial sources, although the price will be linked to the nature of the list and how easy it is to compile. The sampling techniques used in market research are well tried and tested and make it possible to research only a small sample (5-10%) of the total group available in a meaningful way. Providing that the sample techniques are appropriate used and the data collection method is properly prepared, then the results should be both reliable and valid.

Most importantly, the sample must be of sufficient size to be subject to accepted for statistical analysis and interpretation. Analysts and statisticians can gauge the sample size from a mathematical expression, given a specific margin of error and confidence level.

In the final stages of the project, during the report writing, quantitative methods of expressing and displaying findings are widely used, as in the following example:

> 42% of male pupils in the age range 11-13 years were found to eat school meals, whereas only 18% of the females within this age group partook of the school meals service.

Similarly, pie charts and bar graphs can be used to give support to the results through visual presentation.

3.2 Qualitative data

Qualitative data comes from group discussions or in-depth interviews and its findings are based on content rather than numeric analysis. Crimp (1990, p10) says that 'qualitative work . . . is widely used when markets are being explored, products and services developed and unexpected findings from quantitative surveys probed'. Qualitative data is said to be much more subjective than its counterpart. While **quantitative** data may reveal consumer patterns of behaviour and purchasing trends, it does not show *why* consumers behave in a particular way. **Qualitative** data can give meaning to their behaviour and provides an opportunity for consumers to explain and provide insights into patterns and trends, inasmuch as they are prepared to be truthful.

When obtaining qualitative data, questions can be open-ended and can lead to a free-ranging and in-depth discussion on a specific point that provides a variety of rich data. An example would be to ask respondents: 'What further facilities would you like to see in the leisure centre and why?' There will be no numbers or digits in this data and it is not suitable for statistical interpretation. Instead, analysis can be done by hand, rather than by computer, and the statements made can be grouped into generalised categories.

The number of respondents is obviously going to affect the way the data is dealt with. Ideally, the research will, in the main, be carried out in small group discussions or focus groups that last up to two hours. But one or two qualitative questions are commonly included in a large survey, perhaps towards the end of the questionnaire, when the respondent is well-primed. An open-ended question placed at the end of the survey can be structured to seek a response that confirms or denies the truthfulness of the responses obtained in an earlier quantitative question placed on the same document. Alternatively, it provides the respondent with an opportunity for free expression, and as such can produce a variety of rich and meaningful statements.

Discussion groups are the main method of collecting this data and these tend to be small, which means both lower costs and a shorter time-scale for qualitative projects than for quantitative ones. Sometimes a qualitative approach is used to develop and test a hypothesis or hypotheses; the results can then be used as the basis of a quantitative survey.

3.3 Quantitative or qualitative?

When trying to evaluate quantitative and qualitative methods of data collection Birks (1991, pp183-4) suggests that the researcher should 'examine the characteristics that information should possess if it is to be of practical value to the decision maker'. He then uses R A Peterson's framework for evaluation and says that information must be:

- **accurate** – a *valid* representation of the phenomena under investigation, that has come from a *reliable* or consistent measurement, and that is *sensitive* to differences. Combining these three criteria refers to the degree to which information reflects 'reality'.

- **current** – the information should reflect events in the relevant time period, past and present.

- **sufficient** – the data should present as complete and clear 'picture' as possible of the phenomena under study.

- **available** – relevant information should be easily accessible when a decision is imminent.

- **relevant** – the information given should 'makes sense' to the decision-maker, who should be able to use it to build upon their foundation of existing knowledge.

It is almost impossible to fulfil the above criteria in data collection, but they provide a useful framework on which to base decisions about what type of data to obtain.

REVIEW ACTIVITY 3

Read the Nissan Customer Care Survey (Resource Item 7.1).

How many qualitative questions are there?

What sort of data is collected in questions 1–13 and why?

(A proposed answer is given at the end of the unit.)

Summary

This section has defined the term 'primary data' as part of the research process, and discussed the different types of primary data, quantitative and qualitative. Illustrations of different styles of questions have been given, and methods for selecting a sample have been discussed.

SECTION 4

Simple Research Designs

Introduction

Designing the research process is about creating a framework within which to work. It is the structure for the research activity and ensures that all aspects of the research process are planned and co-ordinated. This principle applies to all research designs, whatever the nature of the problem. It is the same for consumer and industrial markets, and also the not-for-profit sector, including charities and educational establishments.

The aim of this section is to help you to:

● understand the different types of research design and the uses to which they can be put.

4.1 Types of research design

Market research seeks a solution to a problem that has been identified by the client, and agreed upon by both client and research team. It is active research and will be used to aid decision-making, as discussed in Section 1.

There are three main types of research design:

EXPLORATORY

Exploratory research is investigatory and the researcher is helping to determine the true nature of a problem. 'Its main purpose . . . is to uncover the salient variables that are at play in the situation of interest'. (Webb, 1992, p21). It is a preliminary to all research and helps to shape and direct the real research design. Exploratory research is particularly valuable when the problem is unfamiliar to the research team and the organisation. If an organisation is interested in expanding into new and unknown markets, for example, exploratory research would be used.

The research approach taken is usually fairly informal and creative and the direction may change according to the discoveries that are made; it is used because not enough information is known to create a specific research plan. The issues that need to be probed further will be highlighted until the direction of the research and what the research can expect to achieve becomes clearer. Intuition, hunches, 'educated guesses', and judgement all play a part in exploratory research. All the normal data collection methods are used in its approach, until it becomes clear how to proceed, or even whether this exploratory phase has produced enough information for decision-making.

CAUSAL

Causal designs seek to discover the relationship between the cause and the effect of events in the market place. Causal research might be used, for example, to determine whether a massive increase in the sales of a high-quality branded product has been caused by increasing the promotion budget and having an extensive advertising campaign – or whether there is another variable within the marketing mix that may have influenced consumers to behave differently. Will there be a mass swing to the use of the Channel Tunnel by domestic consumers because of price, speed and availability, or because recent disasters with Roll On-Roll Off ferries make consumers fearful of travelling by sea? It is easy to 'guess' the cause-and-effect outcome but it is unwise to do this for specific market situations, nor to predict future patterns of purchase behaviour on the basis of guesswork.

DESCRIPTIVE

Descriptive research is probably the most well used and covers issues such as customer profiles, or consumer perceptions of the product/organisation amongst other things. As exploratory research finds 'something of interest and points the camera, descriptive research takes the photograph.' (Webb, 1992, p21) For example, a university that has recently changed its identity from a polytechnic may be keen to know how the community perceives its image – what members of the public think and know about the role of the university, at that moment in time. A descriptive approach would provide the answer.

ACTIVITY 9

Identify (giving your reasons) the type of research design you would recommend:

● to discover the acceptability of a new brand of low-calorie jam

● to set the price level for a children's computer game

● to consider the possibility of developing a new market in the Far East.

A **descriptive** research design would be suitable to find the acceptability of a new brand of low-calorie jam. It would measure consumer perceptions of the brand identity, and other products in the brand range. It would measure understanding of the term 'low-calorie', at a time when this is a topical concept.

A **descriptive** research design would be suitable also for setting the price for a children's computer game. It would be measured against consumers' perceptions of the value of the game and also that of any similar competing products that are already on the market. The image of the manufacturer who has made, and is marketing, the computer game would also be measured. The price of the game must fit with the quality and image of the company and with its other products in the market.

An **exploratory** research design would be suitable to consider the possibility of developing a new market in the Far East. This would discover any barriers to entry, competitor activities, selling procedures and buying behaviour, and details about the potential of the market on a long-term basis.

4.2 Designing a research project

Perhaps, at this point, it is right to identify the stages involved in planning and defining a research project. Each stage must be carefully carried out, since failure to do this will invalidate the subsequent steps of the project. If insufficient thought is put into the first stage – that of identifying problem – the data and information that is collected may well turn out to be irrelevant to the real problem.

The stages of a market research exercise are identified below in Figure 1. For success, the plan of the research project must be known to all who contribute to the research, and a time-scale should be identified. This means that every member of the team knows the planning constraints within which they are working and the point by which each stage must be completed.

PLANNING AND DESIGNING MARKET RESEARCH

Briefing
Meet the client to define the problem

↓

Research Proposal
Write the objectives and plan the research in a written research proposal

↓

Desk Research
Check the internal and external sources of secondary data

↓

Data Collection Methods
Prepare and test the documents for collecting data, eg questionnaires

↓

Fieldwork
Collect the data. Code the questionnaires and analyse

↓

Report and Presentation
Write a business report with an executive summary.
Formally present the findings and recommendations to the client.

Figure 1: Stages in a market research exercise

REVIEW ACTIVITY 4

The president of the Students' Union at your university is concerned about the membership figures of the union, which have not risen in line with the massive increase in student numbers over the last two years. Many of the new students have not joined the union. She has asked you to carry out a market research project to show why membership remains static.

Using the headings given in Figure 1 for guidance, discuss how you would plan this project.

List the objectives of your research and how you will achieve them. What main question areas would you include in your questionnaire? How many students would you interview and how would you identify them?

(A proposed answer is given at the end of the unit.)

Summary

This section has stressed that successful research arises from a good research design. It has described the three main types of research design in marketing theory and identified the stages involved in planning and designing a market research project.

Section 5

Questionnaire Design

Introduction

A questionnaire is a standardised form of measurement and is a control document. It ensures that every respondent is asked the same questions, with the same opportunities for response, in the same order. It is designed when the researchers have identified exactly the information to be collected and it is 'the vehicle whereby the research objectives are translated into specific questions'. (Lancaster & Massingham, 1993a, p292)

Questionnaires are a well-used form of measurement in market research and produce a mass of reliable and valid data quite quickly. For greater accuracy and better research credibility it is always better to use an additional form of measurement that will verify the results. Since most market research is based on human behaviour and human response patterns, another useful form of measurement is by observation. It would be good to see this data collection method more widely used, since it reveals much data about what consumers do, especially if they are being observed without their prior knowledge. Kotler & Armstrong (1989, p104) believe that 'questionnaires too often leave out questions that should be answered and include questions that cannot be answered, or will not be answered, or need not be answered'. Unless a question contributes to achieving the research objectives it should not be included.

Data from questionnaires is mainly quantitative, although a little qualitative data is often gathered. These data are then coded and subjected to analysis, usually on an appropriate computer package.

This section aims to help you to:

- assess the appropriateness of different ways of collecting data and information
- select the most appropriate form of question for a specific purpose
- order and phrase questions within a questionnaire.

5.1 Who are the respondents?

It is important to know who the respondents are likely to be (in terms of their relationship with the organisation commissioning the survey), since this is likely to influence the style and format of the questionnaire. There are three main groups who might be questioned:

Consumers
Any male or female who is an actual or potential user of the organisation's actual or potential goods and services. That covers most of us! It is important to question consumers balanced by gender, using an unbiased sample method. The wording of the questionnaire should be in plain English, with simple questions and phrases. Questions should be phrased in such a way that the least able respondent can cope with them.

Industry
All manufacturers of goods and services need to use market research data to monitor performance of their goods and services in the market. This applies to

products for business-to-business selling, or those sold to the end customer in the high street. Industry also generates valuable data about the market in which it functions in terms of its structure and operations and by competitors. Questionnaires for this group may include technical terminology because respondents are likely to include technical experts, and questions must be pitched at an appropriate level.

Trade
This largely refers to the distribution or retail trade, but also includes wholesalers and other intermediaries in the channel of distribution. Their market data includes knowledge of which brands or products are consumed and in what volume.

5.2 Information gathering

Information is gathered for questionnaires by *four* separate methods. Those are:

Mailed survey
A mailed survey is one that is posted 'cold' to a respondent.

ACTIVITY 10

List the advantages and disadvantages of this kind of survey.

The advantages of a mailed survey are as follows:

- It is fairly low cost.
- A large sample can be used.
- It is completed in the respondent's own time, and no pressure is applied.

The disadvantages are that:

- There is a low response rate. People usually need to be offered an incentive (a voucher or free gift).
- Although the survey can be addressed to somebody by name, there is no guarantee that they are the person who actually completes the questions. (This affects the accuracy of the sampling.)

Personal interview

Webb (1992, p76) describes this as 'one of the most popular data collection methods'. A personal interview is by appointment and its features are as follows:

- It is an in-depth interview up to two hours
- It gives a good opportunity for quality discussion on critical issues
- The interviewer must be skilled in probing and recording
- A tape recorder may be used, although this can distort behaviour
- The respondent may have been told to speak to the researcher by a superior, rather than by choice
- It is expensive in time and money.

Street or doorstep interview

Another form of personal interview, this is usually short, perhaps no more than a few minutes. Its features are as follows:

- It is a quick way of gathering a large amount of data.
- Interviewers only need a modest training.
- It is important to choose the right time of day to 'catch' the respondents.
- It is sometimes hard to get potential respondents to agree to take part.
- It is sometimes hard to find respondents that fit into certain age brackets or sample groups, necessary to maintain an accurate sample.

Telephone interview

This is increasingly used and its features are as follows:

- The interviewer can get direct to the potential respondent.
- It is expensive on time and money but it costs less per completed interview, compared with the personal interview, which can incur travel costs, and additional time costs.
- Only a few questions can be asked.
- Some potential respondents are eliminated because not everyone has a telephone, and not all of those who are have an entry in the telephone directory (precisely so that they won't get this sort of call at inconvenient moments!)
- Some consumers think it is intrusive and refuse to answer because they may feel the interviewer is trying to sell something.

ACTIVITY 11

How would you gather the following information:

● feedback from customers at the end of the warranty period for a new car

● information on why people in a small community subscribe to the local paper

● an industry view of changes in legislation affecting a major manufacturing process?

A mailed survey would be an effective way to obtain feedback from customers at the end of the warranty period for a new car. This should be sent to all customers. This would collect mainly quantitative data, but some qualitative responses should be allowed for. A telephone interview using two or three short questions to respondents would be appropriate to obtain information about why people subscribe to a local paper. It would be satisfactory to survey a sample of the population, using housing and geographic variables. A personal interview, using unstructured questions, would be suitable to monitor an industry view of legislative changes. This is likely to be with senior personnel, by appointment, and last for up to two hours to allow a wide-ranging discussion. In this way, all the major issues will be covered.

5.3 Planning a questionnaire

The secret of success in questionnaire design is summed up by Clifton *et al* (1992, p76) who states that 'the only way to learn about questionnaires is to devise one, test it and find out how it is understood'.

When writing a questionnaire, questions must be carefully prepared and should move from introductory general questions on to specific questions, rather like a funnelling process to focus the respondent's thoughts. In general, questions should be:

● easy to understand and should only ask one point at a time

● relevant to the problem

● avoid leading questions

● avoid technical terms, except in industrial questionnaires

● unbiased

● carefully selected

● fairly brief

● easily coded for subsequent analysis.

TYPES OF QUESTIONNAIRE

Structured
This, the most common method, contains formal questions in a set sequence, and almost all responses are controlled. It can be completed fairly quickly by the respondent.

Semi-structured
As above, but with some open-ended questions.

Unstructured
A few classification questions will be used to start with, and then suggested topics for discussion in a personal interview.

ACTIVITY 12

Which type of questionnaire would you use for a street interview and why?

The most suitable type of questionnaire for a street interview would be a structured one, because it is easy and convenient to complete and responses are controlled. Respondents may not be willing to give much time in the street and they will be of a wide variety of ages, abilities, and occupations.

5.4 Writing a questionnaire

STYLE AND LAYOUT
It is important that the questionnaire is professional in its presentation and appeals to the respondent. The initial part must make clear the:

- status and identity of the organisation
- the purpose of the questionnaire.

Experience has shown that 'a badly presented, messily printed questionnaire is just as likely to cause non-response or measurement error as badly constructed questions.' (Webb, 1992, p107)

The diagram in Figure 2 illustrates how to plan the introductory section of a questionnaire. (Crimp (1990, p90) advises that 'if the questionnaire is mailed the introductory remarks are more likely to be the subject of a covering letter'.) This is followed, in Figure 3, by a sample layout.

Name of Organisation		Questionnaire Number
Introductory remarks – no personal names		
Question Numbers	Questions and Response Boxes	Coding column

Figure 2: Diagram of introductory section of a questionnaire

SAMPLE LAYOUT FOR A STREET OF DOORSTEP INTERVIEW		
ABC Research Agency Nether Poppleton Shopping Survey		Questionnaire Number ☐ ☐ ☐ ☐ 1 2 3 4
Introduction		
Will you please help with some research into shopping by answering a few questions: It will only take a little time and all answers are confidential.		
Thank you.		
1	Do you live in this town? (a) Yes ☐ (b) No ☐	☐ 5
2	Sex? (a) Male ☐ (b) Female ☐	☐ 6

Figure 3: Sample layout

CLASSIFICATION QUESTIONS

These are the important personal details about the respondent that need to be collected for sampling purposes. Some favour placing these in the middle or at the end of the questionnaire because they can be seen as 'sensitive' questions.

This data covers:

age, sex, occupation,	)	
marital status	)	Consumer questionnaire
income group	)	
respondent's status	)	
company sales/turnover	)	Industry or trade questionnaire
number employed	)	

QUESTION SEQUENCE

Avoid bias, or questions that may influence later answers. For example, do not state in the introduction that the survey is for 'The Potteries Shopping Centre', if a later question asks 'Which shopping centres do you visit?'

The early questions should generate awareness about the research and 'warm up' the respondent using closed questions, as in the following examples:

Do you shop separately for food, and clothing?
(i) Yes   ☐   (ii) No   ☐

How do you travel when you go shopping for clothes?
(i) Car   ☐   (iii)   Train   ☐
(ii) Bus   ☐   (iv)   Other   ☐

How far would you be prepared to travel when shopping for clothing?
(i) Up to 10 miles
(ii) 11 – 20 miles
(iii) 21 – 30 miles etc.

This should be followed by questions that give the respondent a choice in his or her response but deal with specific issues to discover attitudes. For example:

Are any of the following facilities important to you in a shopping complex?

	Very Important	Not Important	Important
(i) Chain Stores	☐	☐	☐
(ii) Exclusive shops	☐	☐	☐
(iii) Food shops	☐	☐	☐
(iv) Catering facilities	☐	☐	☐
(v) Toilets	☐	☐	☐
(vi) Banking facilities	☐	☐	☐
(vii) Crèche	☐	☐	☐
(viii) Car park	☐	☐	☐
(ix) Information desk	☐	☐	☐

Have you ever visited any of these shopping centres? (Tick one or more)
    (i) Chester Grosvenor Centre ☐
    (ii) Nottingham Victoria Centre ☐
    (iii)Potteries Shopping Centre ☐
    (iv)Manchester Arndale Centre ☐
    (v) Wolverhampton Centre ☐
    (vi)Shrewsbury, Charles Darwin & Pride Hill ☐

Open-end questions should identify the reasons for the responses in the above two questions. For example:

Which of the shopping centres listed is your favourite and why?

ACTIVITY 13

Give reasons why these words should not be used when setting questions:

● normal   ● various

● expensive   ● sensible

● ordinary   ● believable

These words can have different quantitative or qualitative meanings to different groups of people. What is 'normal' for one person may be quite abnormal for another: equally, what is 'expensive' to one person may be quite 'a fair price' to another person. They are relative and subjective and so have limited meaning to a researcher seeking data that is of good quality, objective, and can be easily coded for analysis.

5.5 Rating scales

A rating scale enables the researcher to convert a qualitative response, the attitude statement, into quantitative data.

Sometimes a market researcher needs to know the intensity of a reaction to a particular issue. The normal approach is to ask questions about past and current buying behaviour and about future purchase intentions. The latter results can be unreliable because sometimes what consumers *say* they will do, compared with what they *actually* do, can be very different. If we ask questions about consumer attitudes to products or issues, and combine the findings from this with their buyer-behaviour profile (past and current purchases) this proves to be a more likely prediction of future behaviour.

Crimp (1990, p90) defines an attitude 'as a learned pre-disposition to respond in a consistently favourable or unfavourable manner with respect to a given object'. Crimp continues that:

> attitudes are the product of experience (what has happened to the respondent), awareness (what has been noticed and learnt), and volition (what is wanted or willed). Attitudes are recorded to help explain behaviour so that informal assumptions may be made about future behaviour.

This type of information enables marketing managers to predict fairly well the future behaviour of markets.

A cigarette manufacturer might need to identify consumer attitudes to cigarette smoking among 20-30 year olds, for example, because it is interested in launching a new brand of cigarettes targeted at that age group. The first stage would involve exploratory research to discover all the ideas that the population to be surveyed has about cigarette smoking, and how the age group expresses its ideas about smoking. By talking to young people in discussion groups, a series of statements or an 'attitude battery' is gathered. Much skill is needed to decide the order in which the ideas are introduced to the young people, and the total number of attitude statements associated with each topic.

These attitude statements, taken from the discussion groups, are then measured against respondents' reactions. To find out the relative strength or weakness with which an attitude is held, **rating scales** are devised. There are two commonly used types:

LIKERT SCALES

Using this method, respondents are asked to show their level of agreement/disagreement with a particular statement by using a five-point scale that ranges from 'strongly agree' to 'strongly disagree'. The statement can be:

- written on the questionnaire (mailed survey)
- written on a card to show the respondent (personal interview)
- read out by an interviewer with the response scale shown on a separate card (personal interview).

Weights are used for each position on the scale and the responses are then analysed.

Weighting	5	4	3	2	1
	Strongly Agree	Slightly Agree	Neither Agree nor Disagree	Slightly Disagree	Strongly Disagree

If the range of attitude statements includes negative and positive statements, 'strongly agree' for a negative statement should be weighted 1 and not 5.

The statements are chosen to represent the total body of ideas held by the population being surveyed. The sample's total response to individual statements can be compared with its response to the total battery of statements.

OSGOOD'S SEMANTIC DIFFERENTIAL SCALE

Marketing managers may want to measure how consumers perceive the products they present to them, particularly in comparison to offers made by the competition. This can be done by using a semantic differential scale. This is a well-used scale for measuring attitudes towards, say, a brand image, against the competition's brand image. The scale has seven points and is double-ended. Respondents are asked to position their attitude about a product on the scale. This enables the researcher to evaluate both the direction and intensity of the respondents' attitude 'towards the product.' (Webb, 1992, p168) At either end of the scale are a series of opposite adjectives, statements or phrases that are bi-polar, such as:

heavy ————————————————————— light
good ——————————————————- bad

or:

sweet ——————————————— not sweet
heavy ————————————————— not heavy

Baker (1991, p152) states that 'one of the key aspects in devising a semantic differential scale is the selection of pairs of adjectives (or statements, or phrases) that are appropriate to the concept or object to be rated, are of interest to the researcher, and are meaningful to the intended respondents'. Exploratory research is used initially to identify the relevant attributes. When the researcher is preparing the scale, the positive and negative adjectives should be placed randomly so that the respondent does not develop a set response.

An illustration of a semantic differential scale is given in Figure 4.

Indicate on the scale below which adjective best describe this unit of study on Market Research:

Good	☐	☐	☐	☐	☐	☐	☐	Bad
Non-rigorous	☐	☐	☐	☐	☐	☐	☐	Rigorous
Analytical	☐	☐	☐	☐	☐	☐	☐	Descriptive
Interesting	☐	☐	☐	☐	☐	☐	☐	Boring
Challenging	☐	☐	☐	☐	☐	☐	☐	Routine
False	☐	☐	☐	☐	☐	☐	☐	True
Negative	☐	☐	☐	☐	☐	☐	☐	Positive

Figure 4: A semantic differential scale

5.6 Piloting a questionnaire

Once the questionnaire has been prepared, the next stage is to test, or pilot, it to check for weaknesses and inefficiencies. It should be tested on a selection of the target population and in the light of the results modifications should be made. By this means the data eventually collected will be as accurate and reliable as possible.

REVIEW ACTIVITY 5

Look again at the Nissan Customer Care Survey (Resource Item 7.1). Study this and discuss how each of the questions, or groups of questions, will help Nissan improve its Customer Care Service.

(A proposed answer to activity is given at the end of the unit.)

REVIEW ACTIVITY 6

Design a questionnaire to discover why the membership of the Students' Union is static, despite the massive increase in student numbers over the last two years. Use the contents of this unit and the Nissan Customer Care Survey (Resource Item 7.1) for guidance.

Also use the material you have prepared for Review Activity 4 on planning a market research exercise.

Summary

This section has introduced questionnaires and identified the different groups of respondents who may complete a questionnaire. It has evaluated several key methods of gathering information for questionnaires and identified the different types of questionnaire in popular use. You have been given guidance on writing a reliable and efficient questionnaire, and the varieties of question styles and the reasons for choosing them have been discussed.

UNIT REVIEW ACTIVITY

Read the following case study and answer the questions listed below

– a press release for a community newspaper that is having a special feature on local businesses

1 What might a market research project find out about a new pack design for a plant feed?

2 Explain why question setting is a job for a specialist.

3 Interviewers are trained for three months. Draw up a set of rules that interviewers should always use.

4 Why is it important that interviewers should be defined as 'classless'?

5 Looking at the press release, what personal qualities do you feel an interviewer for market research should have?

RJF RESEARCH AGENCY

Assessing the suitability of a new design for the packaging of a plant food is a typical market research project. It is important to know if the new packaging will enhance the image of the product, or damage it. How do we, at the R J F Research Agency, carry out market research and find out what people think about the different products?

We are a fairly small, London-based business, carrying out research for Bison's Fertilisers – a major manufacturer of garden food products and small gardening tools. Most of our work is for this one organisation, although Bison's has its own market research department and therefore does some of its research in-house. There are fifteen of us in the team, including a manager, question-setting specialists and analysts, and research interviewers. Question setting is a skilled task, and we can't leave anything to chance. If the questions are not worded correctly, the answers will also be incorrect.

Our interviewers are mainly women over 35 years of age, who have undergone three months' training. It is not an easy job, and requires maturity and tolerance as well as having a 'classless image' to deal with such a wide range of people. We like to take a 10% sample whenever possible, using a wide range and cross section of jobs, ages and social groups, so we need a particular type of personality to cope with this. Our interviewers have to have a very positive attitude, since it is hard work and may involve talking to over 100 people in a single day to get to the right number and type of respondents.

There's a lot of travelling and paperwork too, but most of the interviewers seem to enjoy it. A lot of our research is done within a radius of 60 miles of Central London, but our interviewers also go as far afield as York and Southampton. The interviewing stage of a research project normally takes a week and a half, with over 300 people interviewed, although many more may have been spoken to in order to find the correct balance of respondents.

When the survey is finished, the results are fed into the computer in our office for analysis. This takes a few days. They are then sent to Bison's for them to use as they choose. We do up to 50 tests per year and work on everything from package and pack design, to finding out how easy a proposed new garden tool is to use.

Most of our interviews are either held in the home, at work or in the street. Finding and getting access to the people can be difficult, particularly when looking for a non-working 25-35 year old woman without children! We sometimes have to find working males and females, further broken down by age and job type. There's no doubt this job gives a wide outlook on life and we see some interesting domestic situations! However, we do have to be careful about some of the areas we go into for interviews. We always do the job properly, according to Market Research Society guidelines.

Unit summary

This unit has introduced you to the main techniques of market research. It has considered its role within the marketing function, its scope and its limitations. You have been reminded that the place to start with any market research is with already existing (secondary) data, both that which is internal to your organisation, and external, published information.

When, and if, you come to the point of needing to commission or organise the collection of primary data, it has been emphasised that careful planning is essential to the success of any survey. The subject of questionnaire planning has been touched on, and the problems of identifying a suitable sample of the population were discussed.

The kinds of questions, and the types of responses they elicit, were also discussed, and you have been given an opportunity to design your own questionnaire, and to consider how the data might best be collected.

References

Adcock, D, Bradfield, B, Halborg, A & Ross, C (1993) *Marketing Principles & Practice,* Pitman Publishing

American Marketing Association (1987): *Report of the Definitions Committee*

Arpi, B (1970) *Planning and Control Through Marketing Research,* Hutchinson

Baker, M J (1991) *Research for Marketing,* Macmillan

Barwell, C (1965) 'The Marketing Concept', *The Marketing of Industrial Products,* Hutchinson

Birks, D F (1991) 'Market Research', *The Marketing Book,* ed M J Baker, Butterworth-Heinemann, 2nd edn

Boyd, H & Westfall, R (1956) *Marketing Research Text and Cases,* Homewood, Illinois, Richard D Irwin

Chisnall, P (1992) *Marketing Research,* McGraw-Hill, 4th edn

Clifton, P, Nguyen, H & Nutt, S (1992) *Marketing Research: Using Forcasting in Business,* Butterworth Heineman

Crimp, M (1990) *The Marketing Research Process,* Prentice-Hall, 3rd edn

Kinnear, T C & Taylor, J R (1987) *Marketing Research: An Applied Approach,* McGraw-Hill International, 3rd edn

Kent, R (1993) *Marketing Research in Action,* Routledge*

Kotler, P & Armstrong, G (1989) *Principles of Marketing,* Prentice Hall International, 4th edn

Lancaster, G & Massingham, L (1993) *Essentials of Marketing,* McGraw-Hill, 2nd edn

Lancaster, G & Massingham, L (1993a) *Marketing Management,* McGraw-Hill

Lehmann, D R (1989) *Market Research and Analysis,* Irwin, 3rd edn

Oliver, G (1990) *Marketing Today,* Prentice Hall International, 3rd edn*

Simon, H A (1960) *The New Science of Management Decision,* New York, Harper & Row

Webb, J R (1992) *Understanding and Designing Marketing Research,* Academic Press

* cited in Further Reading only

Further Reading

The following articles and sections of books are recommended as further reading. The full publication details of all books and articles listed are given under References.

SECTION 1
Adcock *et al* (1993) pp121–139

Birks (1991) pp169–174

Clifton *et al* (1992) pp19–38

SECTION 2
Chisnall (1992) pp40–46

Crimp (1990) pp18–23

Webb (1992) pp40–43

SECTION 3
Chisnall (1992) pp32–40

SECTION 4
Kent (1993) pp312–326

Kinnear & Taylor (1987) pp123–152

Oliver (1990) pp112–116

SECTION 5
Chisnall (1992) pp109–135

Baker (1991) pp132–156

Crimp (1990) pp79–104

Answers to Review Activities

Review Activity 1

As the manager of a car dealership you would need to have data and information on a variety of issues about Rover and Nissan products, and information about the performance of the manufacturer in the UK car market.

Information about the market and its size and any influences working upon it is also essential. This would include details of all major competitors and their products and the way consumers respond to these products, and why they buy them. The data and information should show you the features and benefits of each new Rover and Nissan model.

Details of the competitor's equivalent product in the two ranges should be available to you. What do their products offer to the customer which is different from your offer to them?

You also need to know what type of customer buys which type of car and how the benefits of the different modules are promoted to them. For example, a large hatchback is frequently bought by someone running a small business – such as a photographer, or antiques dealer – who may need to carry equipment as part of his or her work. When you know which type of customer buys which type of car then, as a manager, you can begin to satisfy, more easily, potential customers within your small town community, and treat them accordingly.

A car is an expensive purchase and your information should show you the different methods available to a customer for paying for the product. Most importantly, you need to know which type of customer is likely to choose which type of payment method. This is important to help salesmen negotiate deals that are acceptable both to the customer and the dealership.

It is necessary to know about the competition in the area in terms of who they are, where they are located and whether their location gives them a competitive advantage. It is important to know their reputation in the community and how they promote their image to the small town.

Review Activity 2

It is necessary to use both internal and external sources of information to answer the question thoroughly.

The management of the company should analyse its sales records for both the UK and French market, looking in particular at the similarities and differences between these two markets in terms of models sold. Sales patterns will vary from one country to another because of cultural and lifestyle variables. The desk research should highlight these differences and offer explanations for them.

A consumer in the UK market will buy a lawn mower using a set of criteria to aid decision-making that will be different from the criteria used by a consumer of similar status, in Spain. Internal sources of data will show which models of the product have been purchased, at what price and through what type of outlet. It will also show details of the salespeople and any sales and promotion strategy.

The external, or library sources of information will reveal valuable information about the countries into which the manufacturer wishes to expand. Demographic trends should be identified, such as the age structure of the population and whether it is static, rising or in decline. The number of households and types of housing is important. Details of the market, in terms of value and volume, and the number of competitors in the market by share and size will also be needed. Where products are sold, which models and at what price must be known. The promotion methods used for each country should be evaluated, alongside the amount spent on promotion by the main competitors over the last five years.

Review Activity 3

There are six questions in the survey that collect qualitative data. (These are easily spotted because they provide a box for the respondent to write in.) They are all, however, with the exception of question 37, asking for data which can be used both qualitatively and/or quantitatively.

Questions 1-13 provide information and data that will probably prove useful in a quantitative summary.

Many respondents feel insecure about answering questions for a survey because they may feel they have to provide a particular answer which could result in their response being highlighted as a right or wrong answer, and they want to get it right. Those questions that require a simple unambiguous response allow respondents to feel more confident.

Review Activity 4

BRIEFING

A discussion will take place with the President of the Students' Union, who has commissioned the report. This will give an opportunity to identify trends in membership figures over the last few years, and assess ways in which the Union tries to maintain and increase membership. It is important to note how this is done, and when, what procedures are used and who is involved. Any changes in procedures need to be highlighted, as do any other factors that might impinge upon the problem. The President may have details of membership trends across other societies.

RESEARCH PROPOSAL

This is a formal working document, showing what will be included in the research, when it will be carried out and by whom, over what time-scale and at what cost. Within the proposal you should identify the major areas in which you expect the research to produce results.

Objectives of the research

The objectives of this research are to:

- identify the benefits of membership of the Students' Union
- identify how these benefits are promoted to the target customer group
- explore reasons why some students join the Union

- examine alternative reasons why some students do not join the Students' Union
- discover what ways can be used to bridge this difference
- analyse what students want from the membership of university organisations.

The objectives will be achieved by using a postal questionnaire sent to students through the internal mail. Current members of the student union will be used to encourage other students to complete and return the questionnaire. This data collection method will be supplemented by holding four discussion groups, each made up of eight students, who will be drawn from different years and courses across the university.

DESK RESEARCH
The extent of the desk research will depend upon how far the researcher is allowed access to the required information by the university authorities.

The following figures should be analysed:

- number of registered students by age range, course, full or part-time, undergraduate or postgraduate.
- union membership figures for the last five years.
- membership figures of all clubs and societies in the university, if that information is available.

DATA COLLECTION

By questionnaire
Classification questions: age and course

Whether they are members of the students' union

What they know about the union and its benefits

Clubs and societies they belong to at university and pre-university

What they want from membership of any university society

What they want from the students' union

Costs of membership

Discussion groups
The question areas will be similar to those for the questionnaire but they will be unstructured. The students' response to the initial questions will be used to generate further questions and probe issues as well as possible. The intention is to have a full and wide-ranging discussion to draw out all of the issues of relevance.

FIELDWORK

5–10% sample of students on different courses across the university and in different Schools/Faculties. To include undergraduate and postgraduate students, and members and non-members of the students' union.

Computer analysis and interpretation will be used for the questionnaires and the results of the discussion groups will be analysed by mental/hand analysis.

REPORT AND PRESENTATION

The key headings for the business report will include details of organisations to which students belong; a classification of students who belong to the Students' Union; the benefits that students seek from their membership; and reasons why students do not belong to the union, with recommendations for change.

Review Activity 5

THE DEALER WHO SERVICES YOUR VEHICLE (QUESTIONS 1–3)

The information will show if customers are having their car serviced at the dealership where the car was purchased, or elsewhere. It also shows the reasons why the visit was made and the frequency of those visits. If a new car is frequently being returned to the dealer for attention, then this implies some fault of which Nissan should be aware.

BOOKING THE APPOINTMENT (QUESTIONS 4–6)

This covers the method by which the appointment is made and the manner in which the initial contact was handled. The dealer representative is at the interface with customers and should be trained to provide high-quality service at all times. The service given must be right the first time it is given, and at all times.

OUR SERVICE RECEPTION (QUESTION 7)

This seeks consumer perceptions of the physical environment in which service is given. The layout and style of the service area is all part of the service offered to the customers and should be in line with its quality image.

OUR SERVICE RECEPTIONIST (QUESTIONS 8–11)

These questions are specifically about the behaviour, manner and presentation of one member of staff in the service area. They will identify any weaknesses in the staff training programme on customer service, or transgressions of the rules.

ALTERNATIVE TRANSPORT (QUESTIONS 12–14)

Sometimes it is difficult to leave a car for servicing at a garage when the owner needs it to travel to work. These questions highlight this problem and whether alternative transport was required and provided. This area of service may be very important to customers.

OVERALL SATISFACTION (QUESTION 15)

A general question allowing customers to express a level of satisfaction/dissatisfaction on a graduated basis.

VEHICLE COLLECTION (QUESTIONS 16–22)

These are comprehensive questions covering the type of work carried out on the vehicle, the way this was explained to customers, and the manner in which customers were treated and handled during the collection time. It gives customers a chance to say if work was carried out for which they had to pay but about which they had not been informed, and if all the requested tasks had been satisfactorily handled. Overall, it is a thorough section for data collection.

OUR CHARGES (QUESTION 23)

Customers can show if they are satisfied with the explanation of what they are paying for.

OUR WARRANTY (QUESTIONS 24–26)

The warranty should be of value to customers if things go wrong, although one would not expect this with a new vehicle. Customer confidence will be severely dented if the warranty is not comprehensive and if they have to pay for repairs that were not anticipated.

FOLLOW UP (QUESTIONS 27–29)

This shows if the dealer's personnel followed up the service to reassure the customer, build confidence and generate goodwill for future purchases.

PARTS AND ACCESSORIES (QUESTIONS 30–31)

It is an important part of customer service that parts and supplies are available when required. These questions show the efficiency of the dealer in this area. A delay in obtaining a part will cause irritation to the customer and perhaps affect future purchases.

OVERALL SATISFACTION WITH THE SERVICE DEPARTMENT (QUESTIONS 32–34)

These questions provide a general impression of the customers' overall satisfaction and provide an opportunity for customer comment. It is important that customers want to recommend to others the quality of service they have experienced.

YOUR SATISFACTION WITH NISSAN (QUESTIONS 35–39)

These show customers' response to Nissan as an organisation and seek constructive criticism for improvements. It also shows if the customers are repeat purchasers.

A FEW DETAILS ABOUT YOU

These are classification questions and also seek to identify the source of finance for the car.

HOW CAN WE DO BETTER?
An open-ended question to draw a free response.

Answer to Unit Review Activity

R J F RESEARCH AGENCY

1   The researchers may be asked to discover information about the size and shape of the pack design, how easy it is to use, particularly if it has a specially designed dispenser. They might also be asked to discover whether the instructions given are clear on issues such as safety and storage, and whether it can be used for any other purpose. Researchers may be asked to ascertain whether the packaging puts across the right image, and whether it communicates the unique qualities of the product. There should also be some assessment of the price of the product and of its perceived value.

2   There is a great skill in setting and structuring questions to avoid bias and ensure the data is both reliable and valid. The position of questions and the question style is important if the data is to be relevant and useful for the project. It is critical to collect exactly the right data through the questions. A question setter will know how to 'tune in' the respondent, by moving from general to specific questions, for example. They will not use loaded or subjective questions, or those that draw upon distant memory. They will be cautious in the use of personal questions.

3   Rules for interviewers:

● Always dress appropriately for the occasion.

● Be polite and professional in conduct at all times and remember to say 'thank you' at the end of the interview.

● Carry out the work within the time-scale set, neither skipping through nor allowing others to control the timing.

● Avoid influencing the interviewee by familiarity, changing the tone of voice, facial expressions or other body language.

● Follow all instructions as set to carry out the research properly.

4   It is important that the interviewer is able to put people at ease quite quickly and create a positive reaction. Any aspect of behaviour such as dress, mannerisms, voice and speech pronunciation that identify the interviewer as belonging to a specific social class may cause a problem.

5   Interviewers should be mature, and able to handle a wide range of social groups of both sexes. Other qualities should include tolerance and stamina, a capacity to work hard until the task is complete, and a willingness to travel as part of the work. A concern for efficiency and to be able to relate well to people are also important points.

UNIT 8

THE NATURE AND ROLE OF MARKETING ANALYSIS

UNIT 8

THE NATURE AND ROLE OF MARKETING ANALYSIS

Introduction

The analysis of the market is an important part of any overall evaluation or implementation of a marketing strategy. The techniques employed by analysts can be used to assess the correct marketing mix, changing market structures, support or reject hypotheses that have been proposed and forecasting or estimating market potential, to name but a few.

You have seen, in previous units of this module some methods of data collection for analysis. This unit reinforces the differences within data, the range of data that can be encountered in marketing analysis and some of the main techniques used in the evaluation of such data.

A marketing analyst makes use of a wide selection of techniques from the quantitative methods in order to explain the market, forecast elements of the market and support management and corporate decision making.

The unit will examine techniques from the quantitative methods which find widest use in the analysis of markets, such as hypothesis testing, which can be used to examine data and statistics from samples with a view to supporting or rejecting assumptions about the market population. Regression and correlation will be examined as techniques that can be employed to assess the existence and strength of relationships within a market and also their use as a possible forecasting tool. Finally, an introduction will be made to a range of multivariate techniques, which have found widest use in marketing analysis in the analysis of data from questionnaires. It is quite common to link the multivariate methods to enrich analyses. The section covering these methods will make use of a case study to demonstrate this.

Modern approaches to analysis make wide use of questionnaires to obtain primary data and computer software to analyse data. The first section of this unit will therefore introduce different types of data and the approaches to coding data for analysis. There exists a wide range of statistical packages to analyse data; probably the most widely used package in the UK is Statistical Package for Social Sciences (SPSS), which has been used to facilitate analyses for this unit.

Objectives

After completing this unit you should be able to:

SECTION 1

- Explain the use and application of variables.
- Distinguish between the different principal types of variables.
- Explain and identify four categories of data measurement.
- Understand the procedures for coding data.
- Distinguish between the methods of summarising data using location and dispersion measures.

SECTION 2

- Calculate a standard Z score.
- Set up a confidence interval with known parameters.
- Appreciate what is meant by an hypothesis and understand the difference between a null hypothesis and an alternative hypothesis.
- Undertake an hypothesis test and appreciate the importance of significance in hypothesis testing.
- Undertake a chi-square test on two-dimensional data (hypothesis on non-parametric data).

SECTION 3

- Understand the nature of bivariate data and straight-line relationships.
- Measure the strength of linear relationships between variables using coefficients of correlation and determination.
- Determine a least squares regression equation and line.
- Estimate and forecast future data values using technique of interpolation and extrapolation.
- Be familiar with one approach to the analysis of a time series set of data.

SECTION 4

- Explain the concept of multivariate analysis in marketing.
- Describe the application and use of a range of multivariate methods as individual techniques.
- Describe the application and use of a range of multivariate techniques linked in an analysis.
- Interpret printouts from a statistical package (SPSS).

SECTION 1
Data Type and Preparation

Introduction

This section will examine the differences in data and types of data with which an analyst can be presented. The majority of organisations that undertake marketing research and analysis functions process data by initially editing and then coding response or numerical observations into categories. This is usually undertaken on spreadsheets such as Lotus or Microsoft Excel. In this section you will see that data may then be subject to a variety of tabulation, graphical and statistical summarisation procedures which can be the basis of analysis. These procedures can be undertaken on the spreadsheets themselves, or on specialised statistical packages, such as Statistical Package for Social Sciences (SPSS).

This aim of this section is to help you to:

- distinguish between the principal types of variables
- explain and identify four categories of measurement
- apply coding and summarisation techniques
- calculate measures of dispersion.

1.1 Data types

Most of the analysis undertaken for marketing purposes is on data from surveys or observations, and the techniques used are usually statistical. The actual techniques used depend on the type of data obtained.

Data can be generated either by a process of counting or of measurement. Whatever the method, the result will be a collection of numbers, which will normally vary in values (rather than all being identical). This characteristic is referred to as a **variable**. Examples of variables can be seen in data relating, for example, to:

- ages of people
- amounts of produce purchased in different retailers
- the number of children per family.

The observations themselves – the **values** of the variable – consist of two principal types:

Discrete variables, which consist of integer (whole number) values only. These are normally obtained by counting, such as when determining the number of cars produced on a production line.

Continuous variables, the values of which are usually recorded as decimal numbers with a number of digits after the decimal point being determined by the accuracy or precision of the measuring apparatus. An example of this is the weight of assembly components.

ACTIVITY 1

Which of the following are discrete or continuous variables:

(i)   The speed of a car during a journey

(ii) The daily value of stock market transactions

(iii) Pub prices of lager in different parts of the country (in pounds)

(iv) Supermarket prices of one litre of diet lemonade in different parts of a city
      (in pence)

The measurement of the speed of a car over a period of time will result in a **continuous** variable, because the speed will include measurements of a fraction of a mile per hour. The same is the case for the price of lager measured in pounds – the prices will include up to two decimal points (pence). The prices quoted in the stock market, and the price of diet lemonade, both given in terms of pence, can, however, be considered as **discrete** variables, since no fractions of a pence will be given.

1.2 Categories of measurement

In addition to classifying data consisting of continuous or discrete variables, a further classified can be made according to the level of measurement. There are four categories of measurement:

- nominal (or categoric) variables
- ordinal variables
- interval level variables
- ratio scale variables.

The taxonomy of these classifications is represented as follows:

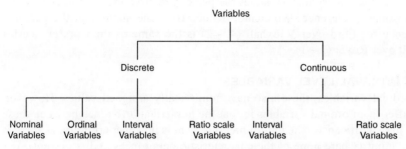

Figure 1: Taxonomy of classification of variables

1.2.1 NOMINAL VARIABLES

A nominal variable consists of data which is non-numeric in nature. In test marketing a new product, for example, marketing researchers are often interested to establish whether consumer reaction to the product is associated in any way with the social class of the consumer. The product designers and the market researchers may think that the colour of the product is an important factor in designing an effective advertising campaign. With this in mind, they are likely to test market the product in a range of colours with a sample of consumers from a wide range of social and economic backgrounds. Results of such a survey may appear as follows:

CONSUMER PREFERENCE

		Red	Blue	Green	Black
	A/B	10	42	25	57
SOCIAL	C	24	20	36	16
CLASS	D	48	20	34	7

Here we could use a numeric code for the different social classes and the colours, for example 1 for A/B and 4 for red. Such a code would facilitate recording and computer processing of this data, but the values of 1 and 4 are simply labels, even though they are numeric.

1.2.2 ORDINAL VARIABLES

These are variables that can be arranged in a meaningful *order* but whose *numeric* values represent rank only. For example, if someone prefers Ford cars to Renault cars and Renault cars to Vauxhall cars, then they can list these in rank order. They are not giving any measurement of by *how much* they prefer one car over the other.

Suppose a person's ranking for four manufacturers of cars is as follows:

4   Ford
3   Renault
2   Vauxhall
1   Rover

where a rank of 4 is most preferred and 1 is least preferred. The rank values assigned to these says nothing about the persons relative preference, only about their absolute preference. We cannot deduce from the above that the person's preference for Ford over Vauxhall (4 – 2) is the same as their preference for Renault over Rover (3 – 1).

1.2.3 INTERVAL LEVEL VARIABLES

Like ordinal variables, these also have numerically assigned values. However, they differ from ordinal variables in that the numerical difference between these values has significance. The unit of measurement is however arbitrary, as there is no zero point (where none of the characteristic being measured is present). For example, a survey question may be ask a person's concerning opinions on driving a car thus:

State your opinion on the safety of the car by ticking the box that most closely accords with your views:

Strongly agree			Neutral	Strongly disagree		
-3	-2	-1	0	1	2	3

Not comfortable to drive:

While the data collected from a response to this question can be used to rank preferences, if used in a comparative way, it can be described as *interval*, because the respondent is being asked to quantify their opinion.

1.2.4 RATIO SCALE VARIABLES

The ratio scale has both an absolute zero point and equal intervals of measurement. Marketing research data that qualifies as ratio scale data would include such measures as age, income, price and market share. These items have a very definite zero point at which none of the characteristic is present and, a value twice as high as another does indeed represent twice as much. (So, for example 60% of a market share is twice as much as a 20% market share, and someone who is 30 years old has been alive for twice as long as someone of 15 years old.).

Whilst the ratio scale is nearest to our accepted number system and is therefore considered as the most frequently used measurement, most marketing research data will be nominal, ordinal or interval form.

It is also worth noting that **discrete variables and data** can be given in any of the four levels of measurement, but **continuous variables and data** can be given in terms of interval or ratio scale only.

ACTIVITY 2

In each of the following cases, state whether the variable is nominal, ordinal, interval or ratio scale.

(i)   The incomes of bank managers

(ii)   The preferred colour for a product in a consumer test

(iii)   Social class

(iv)   The strength of feeling for political policies

(v)   Results of awards for best product design

(vi)   the number of visits to a shop per week by a customer

The income of bank managers and the number of visits made to a shop per week are both examples of ratio scale data: the value represents an actual amount or event. The preferred colour of a product and a person's social class expressed numerically are, however, nominal, since the value used to record them do not relate in any absolute sense to what is being recorded. The feelings of the respondent for different political policies will probably be expressed in terms of interval level variables, and the results of a design award will be ordinal.

1.3 Data manipulation

The processes involved after categorisation of data involve preparing it for analysis. For statistical analysis of data, computer packages are usually employed. Convention dictates that data is subject to a set of processes prior to analysis. These include:

● editing

● coding

● analysis (on a spreadsheet or statistical package).

1.3.1 Editing

This involves examination of the raw data to ensure accuracy, that the data set is complete and, if not, appropriate omissions or additions are made to the data to ensure a full set. The steps involved would be:

- **Screening** of responses for consistency, legibility, completeness and any other adverse factors that may have occurred. This may involve re-visiting the source of the data.

- **Categorising** answers which may be difficult to code, such as opinions and comments, and also responses that are non standard. (For example, a respondent may have been asked to score an opinion between 1 and 5, but have provided a score of 6. This would have to be correctly categorised or addressed.)

- **Editing** the data. This can occur in the field, at the point of data collection, where ambiguity may arise, and involves completing or interpreting comments or observation. Alternatively, the process can be undertaken centrally by a single editor or team, to provide consistency.

1.3.2 Coding

This involves assigning responses to categories. Each set of responses or observations needs to be identified with a number associated with the category. Coding can proceed in two ways:

Precoding

This is appropriate where questions or observations are such that only a limited set of responses is available. In this case the analyst can predetermine the numbers that can be assigned to different responses or observations. Aside from the conventional data gathering on spreadsheets, data may be found in a report, submitted initially within a word-processed document or non-compatible file format. Ultimately, any data must be converted to numbers for analysis.

As an example of how coding can occur for a structured questionnaire, consider the coded data for 10 respondents to a questionnaire with 32 **descriptors** (the questions within a questionnaire that have coded responses to them, subjected to a numerical analysis):

data list free
/1 id rating1 to rating32.
begin data

```
01 2 2 1 4 2 5 3 2 4 5 2 4 3 1 2 5 3 2 1 4 2 3 2 4 2 5 2 4 4 1 2 3
02 3 1 4 2 5 3 2 4 5 2 4 3 1 2 5 3 2 1 4 6 3 2 4 2 5 2 4 4 1 2 3 4
03 4 3 2 4 5 2 4 3 1 2 5 3 2 1 4 3 3 2 4 2 5 3 2 1 4 6 3 2 4 2 5 2
04 1 1 4 2 5 3 2 4 5 2 4 3 1 2 5 3 2 1 4 2 2 4 5 2 4 3 1 2 5 3 2 1
05 5 5 4 1 4 2 5 3 2 4 5 2 4 3 1 2 5 3 2 1 4 3 2 4 5 2 4 3 1 2 5 3
06 3 5 2 4 3 1 1 4 2 5 3 2 4 5 2 4 3 1 2 5 3 2 1 4 5 3 2 4 1 5 4 5
07 2 1 4 2 5 3 2 4 5 2 4 3 1 2 5 3 2 1 4 4 3 2 4 2 4 5 2 4 5 1 3 3
08 4 4 1 4 2 5 3 2 4 5 2 4 3 1 2 5 4 1 4 2 5 3 2 4 5 2 4 3 1 2 5 4
09 2 4 1 3 4 4 1 4 2 5 3 2 4 5 2 4 3 1 2 5 5 2 3 1 4 3 2 3 1 5 4 2
10 1 5 2 3 4 2 4 5 3 4 1 4 2 5 3 2 4 5 2 4 3 1 2 5 3 1 4 2 5 5 5 5
```

Figure 2: Example of coding

The coded data in the example contains a number identifying respondents in the first column. Each row then contains numbered responses for 32 descriptors, each separated by a space. It is common to avoid use of zero, if possible, and blanks (for example for a nil response). Use of a number code for such an eventuality is usual practice, because most software packages do not recognise a zero as a valid response. Additionally, the inclusion of a zero in any subsequent statistical calculations can present misleading and confusing results.

Postcoding

This is appropriate for questions of an open-ended type, for example those that are unstructured. Here, responses are assigned to categories after data has been collected. The process requires that an editor categorises any open-ended responses into an assigned set of categories as numbered responses. This may necessitate use of several coders, depending on the size of a survey or questionnaire.

1.4 Summarisation of data

After coding, data can be summarised for presentational purposes which may also contribute to an analysis.

1.4.1 TABULATION

Simple tabulation of data may allow us to examine data one variable at a time, but in marketing analysis it is usually the relationships between variables that is of interest. In this event, two-way cross tabulation (in two dimensions) is preferred. Here, one variable can be compared with another, or more than two variables can be examined in a cross tabulation. It can allow marketing analysts to identify statistically significant data, as you will see later in this unit.

1.4.2 GRAPHICAL SUMMARISATION

Graphical summarisation can be a useful tool with which to explain data. At one level it is simply presentational, rather than analytical, and this will not be examined in this unit. However, the extent to which graphical displays, produced by statistical software, contribute to analysis, will be covered in Section 4 of this unit.

1.4.3 MEASURES OF LOCATION

Statistical summarisation can be undertaken on marketing data in an attempt to provide a value that best represents the central point of the data or variable. This is generally known as an average. There are several averages available for use, the three most common being the **mode, median** and **mean**.

The **mode** is the value that occurs most frequently in a data set. Consider a variable age. Ten observations of age were made as follows:

$$25 \quad 23 \quad 24 \quad 23 \quad 25 \quad 26 \quad 28 \quad 25 \quad 29 \quad 25$$

The most commonly occurring value is 25 (occurring four times). The value is determined by inspecting data and counting the number of occurrences of each value. The mode, when determined, is usually nominal scale data.

The **median** is the value of the middle item in the data set when the data have been arranged in ascending or descending order. For example the age data could be listed in ascending order as:

$$23 \quad 23 \quad 24 \quad 25 \quad 25 \quad 25 \quad 25 \quad 26 \quad 28 \quad 29$$

In this example there is no single middle item, in this event the mean of the two middle items – 25 and 25 – is taken to represent the median (in this case 25). As a measure of central tendency the median is usually more representative than the mode. The median is usually treated as ordinal scale data, due to its selection being based on its position in an ascending array.

The **mean** is the most commonly used measure of location for a set of data and is known generally as the average. In statistical terms it is the sum of the data or variable divided by the number of data points. The variable or data, X, is summed, denoted by the instruction ΣX (sum X), where the symbol sigma (Σ) instructs summation. This sum is then divided by the number of data points (n). The mean has the symbol , it is correctly known as the arithmetic mean and is calculated as follows:

$$= \frac{\Sigma X}{n}$$

If we consider the age data, the mean age would be:

$$= \frac{23+23+24+25+25+25+25+26+28+29}{10}$$

$$= 25.3$$

The key weakness of the mean as a location measure to represent centrality is its susceptibility to distortion by extreme values. For example, if one of the ages (25) was observed as 60 this would alter the mean age for this data to a value of 28.8 (a 14% change in the original mean age). The calculated mean is a value that can be placed on a scale for consideration, this scale being analogous to a category of measurement. The calculated mean is usually interval scale (analogous to interval level) data.

ACTIVITY 3

Consider the following set of data for the number of pints of a brand of lager consumed per week, by regular customers of a public house:

| 8 | 9 | 13 | 12 | 12 | 14 | 17 | 21 | 12 | 14 | 7 |

Find the mode, median and calculate the mean number of pints of lager consumed by the customers.

If the data is placed in ascending order as follows:

| 7 | 8 | 9 | 12 | 12 | 12 | 13 | 14 | 14 | 17 | 21 |

The mode is 12 pints (occurs three times), the median value (sixth item) is 12 pints and the arithmetic mean is 139/11 = 12.64 pints

1.4.4 MEASURES OF DISPERSION

As well as describing the location or centrality of a set of data it is also useful to determine the spread or dispersion of a set of data. There are several methods available for determining dispersion. The three most common are **the range, the standard deviation** and **variance**.

Range is defined by the extreme values of a data set. If we consider the age data given above, the smallest value is 23 and the largest value is 29. The range of the data set is from 23 to 29 years. Alternatively , the range can be expressed as 6 years.

Range as a concept has the advantage of being easy to calculate and understand. Its disadvantage is that as only the two extreme items in the data set are used for the calculation of the range, it gives no indication of the dispersion of any of the items between the extreme values. It can also be easily distorted by a single extreme value in the data set, such as the inclusion of, say, an age-value of 60 to the age data given above.

Standard deviation and **variance** are measures of dispersion which measure similar dispersive elements. The variance (s^2) is a measure of dispersion that utilises all the data values. It is based on the difference between each data value and the mean. The difference between each data value (x_i) and the mean ( ) is called a **deviation about the mean** and is written ($x_i - $).

In the computation of the variance for a sample, taken from the population, it is standard procedure to use ($n - 1$) as the divisor. When the variance, and subsequently the standard deviation, are calculated in this way, they are better estimators of the variance and standard deviation of the population from which the sample was taken. (For large samples, such as when $n \geq 30$, the use of $n - 1$ makes little difference.)

To calculate the **variance** the following formula is used:

$$s^2 = \frac{\Sigma(x_i -)^2}{(n - 1)}$$

The **standard deviation** (s) is obtained as the square root of the variance, $\sqrt{s^2}$ The variance and standard deviation for the age data can be calculated as follows:

Remember that the mean age was calculated as 25.3 years

Age (X)	$(x_i -)$	$(x_i -)^2$
23	-2.3	5.29
23	-2.3	5.29
24	-1.3	1.69
25	-0.3	0.09
25	-0.3	0.09
25	-0.3	0.09
25	-0.3	0.09
26	0.7	0.49
28	2.7	7.29
29	3.7	13.69
253		34.10
ΣX		$\Sigma(x_i -)^2$

$$\text{Variance} = s^2 = \frac{\Sigma(x_i -)^2}{(n - 1)} = \frac{34.10}{(10 - 1)} = 3.79$$

$$\text{Standard deviation} = s = \sqrt{s^2} = \sqrt{3.79} = 1.95$$

The standard deviation is an important measure because it can tell us the limits within which the majority of our data lies; a high standard deviation indicates that the data set contains widely ranging values around the mean, whereas a low one indicates that the data set contains values that do not vary widely.

The calculated variance of 3.79 in the above example is the average of the sum of the squared deviations about the mean. The mean age calculated from the data is 25.3 years and this dispersion measure (the variance) of 3.79 years is the average deviation of all the values from the calculated mean.

The calculated standard deviation of 1.95, which is the square root of the variance, is the preferred dispersion measure to use as it is in the same units as both the data and the calculated mean. It is essentially the average of the sum of the deviations about the mean. It is usually preferable to quote $s = 1.95$ years, rather than $s^2 = (1.95)^2$ years.

If we substitute an age of 60 years in place of one of 25 years, the mean would become 28.8 years and the standard deviation would now become 11.13 years. Clearly this distortion is quite large for one change in data value.

ACTIVITY 4

Consider the lager consumption data from the previous activity:

Pints consumed per week:

7   8   9   12   12   12   13   14   14   17   21

Calculate the variance and standard deviation number of pints of lager consumed per week.

The mean number of pints consumed (from previous activity) is 12.64 pints

Pints (X)	$(x_i -)$	$(x_i -)^2$
7	-5.64	31.81
8	-4.64	21.53
9	-3.64	13.25
12	-0.64	0.41
12	-0.64	0.41
12	-0.64	0.41
13	0.36	0.13
14	1.36	1.85
14	1.36	1.85
17	4.36	19.01
21	8.36	69.89
139		160.55
ΣX		$\Sigma(x_i -)^2$

$$\text{Variance} = s_2 = \frac{\Sigma(x_i - \quad)^2}{(n-1)} = \frac{160.55}{(11-1)} = 16.06$$

$$\text{Standard deviation} = s = \sqrt{s^2} = \sqrt{16.06} = 4.01$$

REVIEW ACTIVITY 1

Marketing analysts wish to profile the ages of purchasers of a newly launched Digital Audio Tape (DAT) system. They have randomly surveyed 20 people who have purchased the systems across several regions. Their ages were observed as follows:

23	24	28	36	29
28	22	24	25	31
24	22	34	31	33
26	41	44	22	27

(a) Find the mode and median for the data and calculate the mean age of purchasers

(b) Calculate the range, variance and standard deviation age for the data

(c) What type of variable is present?

(d) What is the category of measurement for this data?

(The answer to this activity is given at the end of the unit.)

Summary

In this section you have seen that an understanding of the nature of variables and categories of measurement are important considerations for a marketing analyst, prior to the summarisation and analysis of data. The analysis of data by organisations currently occurs on spreadsheets or specific statistical packages.

Understanding the nature of data is important in any such analysis, in order that you may channel and manipulate the data correctly. You have also seen the processes involved and the necessity for coding of data in order that you can best facilitate the analytical facilities within spreadsheets and statistical packages.

In this section you have also been introduced to statistical summarisation of samples of data. Later in the unit you will discover that these calculations and procedures are important contributions to the analysis of data.

SECTION 2

Hypothesis Testing

Introduction

In this section you will be introduced to hypothesis testing. At one level this process involves using calculated values (parameters), such as the mean and standard deviation of samples, to support or reject statements made about means or standard deviations of a population. At another level, you will examine how hypothesis tests can be undertaken in the absence of the parameters; this is known as a non-parametric test.

In marketing it is important to be able to calculate conditions within a population based on the results of samples from that population. The procedures involved call on statistical processes and the concept of inference. Hypothesis tests allow analysts to make inferences about the population.

In order to appreciate how inferences can be made with confidence, you must initially reinforce your knowledge of the way in which data can be distributed and the limits of confidence that can be used in supporting or rejecting statements about a population. The section will therefore enable you to revise this concept before undertaking hypothesis tests.

The aim of this section is to help you to:

- calculate a standard z score
- set up a confidence interval with known parameters and appreciate what is meant by an hypothesis
- understand the difference between a null hypothesis and an alternative hypothesis and undertake an hypothesis test
- appreciate the importance of significance in hypothesis testing
- undertake a chi-square test on two-dimensional data (hypothesis on non-parametric data).

2.1 The normal distribution and standard scores

Data often needs to be transformed into a standard score to enable meaningful conclusions to be drawn. For example, suppose an organisation undertakes a comparison of its turnover at the beginning of the decade (1990) and the middle of the decade (1995), as follows:

Year	Turnover (Ecu)
1990	900,000
1995	800,000

Clearly turnover has declined.

Two hypotheses may be formulated in an attempt to account for the decline in turnover. (An hypothesis is a supposition made as a basis for reasoning.) Statisticians usually consider an hypothesis as a statement capable of being tested. The following hypotheses could be used to explain this decline:

Hypothesis A: The market for the product has declined.
Hypothesis B: The organisation has lost some of its market share

Either or both of these could explain the decline in market share. If further information was made available about the industry, then it might be possible to decide which hypothesis was the most likely explanation. Suppose that the average turnover for all the organisations in this market is known. This mean is termed the 'population mean' and can be represented by a different symbol from that used for the sample mean. The symbol is μ (mu). We can now consider the following data:

Turnover (at constant 1990 prices) (Ecu)

	For the organisation	Average for organisations in the market
1990	900,000	760,000
1995	800,000	620,000

Two observations may be drawn from this data:

● As the average turnover for all organisations in the market has declined it may be that the market is declining.

● In both years this organisation had a higher turnover than the average of that for the market.

The data on average tends to support hypothesis A, but hypothesis B could still also be true.

Suppose the standard deviation of the turnover for organisations within the market is known. The standard deviation is termed the 'population standard deviation' and can be represented by a different symbol from that used for the sample standard deviation. The symbol is σ (sigma). We can now consider the following data:

Turnover (at constant 1990 prices) (Ecu)

	For the organisation	Average for organisations in the market	Population Standard Deviation
1990	900,000	760,000	175,000
1995	800,000	620,000	90,000

In 1990 the organisation's turnover was:

$$\frac{900,000 - 760,000}{175,000} = \text{0.8 standard deviations above organisational average}$$

In 1995 the organisation's turnover was:

$$\frac{800,000 - 620,000}{90,000} = \text{2 standard deviations above organisational average}$$

Compared with the rest of the market, the organisation performed better in 1995 than it did in 1990. Hypothesis B should therefore be rejected as an explanation for the decline in the organisation's turnover. Its market share may well have increased, and Hypothesis A is the most likely explanation.

To assess which hypothesis was correct, the statistic:

$$\frac{\text{organisation average} - \text{population average}}{\text{population standard deviation}}$$

was calculated.

This statistic is called a standard Z score and it changes the base unit of measurement for sets of data into some standard unit. It enables comparisons between sets of data using different units of measurement. If a certain **population** has a mean μ and a standard deviation σ, then for any observation x the standard Z-score is given by:

$$z = \frac{x - \mu}{\sigma}$$

(Usually, the standard Z-score is shortened to Z-score.) Such scores are crucially important to analysts for use in testing specific hypotheses.

If the observation x is greater than the population mean, the Z-score will be positive. If the observation x is less than the population mean, the Z-score will be negative.

Data can be plotted as a distribution, provided the population has a normal distribution (where the shape of the plotted data is symmetrical or bell shaped). If this is not the case we can approximate a normal distribution by obtaining a suitable number of samples of at least 30 ($n \geq 30$). Under these conditions a distribution which is plotted from at least 30 samples will always assume the shape of a normal distribution. This is the basis of the central limit theorem.

Z-scores can be used to predict the proportion within a population that is more or less than a certain value (termed x). The value of x in a distribution for which the mean and standard deviation are known, ranges between $-\alpha$ and $+\alpha$, although a glance at the diagram below shows the effective range for x is from -4 to +4

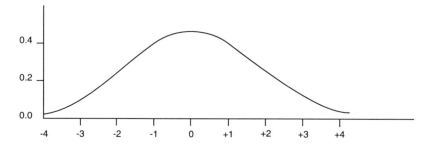

Figure 3: Normal distribution of data

In a normal distribution the mean is placed at the centre of the curve (at the zero point). The range of one standard deviation on either side of the mean represents 68.2% of the curve and therefore 68.2% of the data in a distribution. Two standard deviations on either side represents 95.5% of the data and three standard deviations, 99.7% of the data.

ACTIVITY 5

Mean and standard deviation sales figures for two products A and B have been determined as follows:

	Mean	Standard deviation
A	45,000	5,000
B	54,000	7,000

Bob, one of the sales staff, has sold 53,000 of product A, and 65,000 of product B. Standardise these scores and determine the product in which he performs better on sales?

Z-score for A = (53 – 45)/5 = 1.6
Z-score for B = (65 – 54)/7 = 1.57

Bob performed marginally better in sales of product A.

2.2 Confidence intervals

This is a statistical method which allows us to estimate the range in which a
population value will fall based on sample information with a certain degree of
confidence. You might, for example wish to find the limits containing the central
95% of sample results (95% of sample means or 95% of sample proportions).
Such limits are called the 95% confidence interval. This level (along with one other,
the 99% confidence interval) finds widest use. If the sample results are normally
distributed, then such limits can be determined quite easily. The proportion of the
normal distribution required is illustrated below:

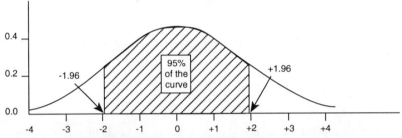

Figure 4: 95% interval on normally distributed data

The range that represents 95% of the data is -1.96 to +1.96 standard deviations on
a distribution. If you wished to estimate the value of a population statistic, such as
the mean, with 95% confidence, you should incorporate the Z-score for this limit,
of 1.96, in any calculations you undertake.

In addition, you should note that when estimating the population mean from sample
means, the population standard deviation is not known. In this event it is possible
to substitute this with the sample standard deviation. The standard deviation for this
sample mean serves, however, as a measure of error that will be encountered when
using a sample mean to estimate a population mean.

If a set (n ≥ 30) of sample means have been used to construct our distribution, this
is known as the sampling distribution of sample means and the standard deviation
of such a distribution is known as the standard error of the sample mean. The
standard error is a smaller value than the standard deviation, as it takes into account
the sample size (n). The standard error is determined as follows:

$$\text{Standard error (SE)} = \frac{s}{\sqrt{n}}$$

As n increases, the standard error decreases.

It therefore follows that if we wish to estimate the population mean, the following relationship applies (which includes the above observations):

$$\mu \pm 1.96 \quad \frac{\sigma}{\sqrt{n}}$$

This can be rearranged to give an expression for an estimate of the population mean (μ) to:

$$\mu = \quad \pm 1.96 \quad \frac{s}{\sqrt{n}}$$

where:

   is the sample mean and
   s is the sample standard deviation
   $s/\sqrt{n}$ is the standard error.

Likewise, a 95% confidence interval for the sample proportion (p) would be given by:

$$\pi \pm 1.96 \sqrt{\frac{\pi(100 - \pi)}{n}}$$

where π is the symbol for the population proportion. Again, in this equation, p can be substituted for π.

If the limits are widened, then a larger proportion of sample results would be contained within the limits: 99% of sample results would be included in a 99% confidence interval. This can also be rearranged to give an expression for an estimate of the population proportion (π), to:

$$\pi = p \pm 2.576 \sqrt{\frac{\pi(100 - \pi)}{n}}$$

where p can be substituted for π.

The 99% confidence interval would include the central 99% of the sample. The Z-score would lie between 2.57 and 2.58 (exact value 2.576) on either side of the mean.

The 99% confidence interval for the sample mean is given by:

$$\mu \pm 2.576 \quad \frac{\sigma}{\sqrt{n}}$$

2.3 Hypothesis tests

When data has been summarised, analyses can be undertaken concerning relationships between samples or populations and it is usual to reach conclusions or make decisions with regard to the significance of the results based on a set of hypotheses.

Consider the following:

> Currently, the age profile for purchasers of a particular make and model of sports car is mean age 31, with a standard deviation of 2 years. This data was collected on all purchasers since the introduction of the model. A recent survey was undertaken of purchasers of the same make and model of car on a sample of 250. The mean age of purchasers here was 36 years, with a standard deviation of 2 years.

This scenario can present us with a whole range of questions, such as:

(a) From sample evidence has the mean age changed, or not?

(b) Has the mean age increased, or not?

Clearly the mean age has changed, but has it changed significantly, bearing in mind the spread (dispersion) of data and within specified limits of accuracy?

To reach a conclusion about this data we can undertake an hypothesis test. This requires that a set of hypotheses are formulated concerning the data and tested, using the statistical values obtained.

If you consider the question posed in (a) then two hypotheses could be formulated:

> Hypothesis A: The mean age has not changed
> Hypothesis B: The mean age has changed.

Hypothesis A presents us with a particular type of hypothesis known as the **Null Hypothesis,** and is represented symbolically as H_o. A null hypothesis assumes that nothing has happened. It is always a statement made about a population parameter and not the sample statistic. In our example this would be that the mean age of 31 has not changed.

An analyst would test the null hypothesis as s/he would wish to know what to expect if it was true.

Hypothesis B presents us with an Alternative Hypothesis (alternative to the null hypothesis), and it is represented symbolically as H_1. We therefore have the following hypotheses:

H_o: The mean age has not changed (or $\mu_1 = \mu_2$)
H_1: The mean age has changed (or $\mu_1 \neq \mu_2$)

In order to test these hypotheses a level of significance needs to be selected.

2.3.1 LEVEL OF SIGNIFICANCE

Even though an analysis might lead you to reject the null hypothesis, there is a possibility that you may be in error. A rejection of a null hypothesis when it is actually true is known as a **Type I Error**. When devising a rule on which to base your selection of a null or alternative hypothesis as your decision in an analysis, you must state the level of probability of a type I error that you would find acceptable. This is analogous to a level of confidence. If the probability of a type I error is to be 5%, then you are required to state the Z-score for this limit, in any determinations you subsequently make. This value is found with reference to the normal distribution. It is the area bounded by 95% confidence, that is ± 1.96 standard deviations (a Z-score of 1.96). As both sides of the mean are considered to obtain this Z-score the test is referred to as a two-tail test.

In order to test the hypotheses, a Z-score needs to be produced from the sample information gathered and the population mean. This is obtained as follows:

$$Z\text{-score} = \frac{\text{sample mean} - \text{population mean}}{\text{standard error } (s / \sqrt{n})}$$

Therefore, if a 5% chance of a type I error is acceptable, then the decision rule would be as follows:

> If the Z-score for the sample data is larger than the Z-score for 5% significance, then reject the null hypothesis and accept the alternative hypothesis, otherwise accept the null hypothesis.

Therefore for our example:

$$Z\text{-score} = \frac{31 - 36}{2/\sqrt{250}} = -39.53$$

This value of Z known as Z_{test} (-39.53) is clearly larger than the 5% significance value for Z, known as $Z_{critical}$ (-1.96). The decision rule is: Reject H_o if $Z_{test} > Z_{critical}$. We would therefore reject the null hypothesis and accept the alternative hypothesis:

H_1: The mean age has changed (or $\mu_1 \neq \mu_2$)

We would accept this at the 5% significance level (5% chance of a type I error)

This example serves to demonstrate the use of a hypothesis test. In our example the accepted population mean age is 31 years with a standard deviation of 2 years. What we are required to test with sample information, is the possibility of these population statistics having changed, based on sample evidence. The test has shown that the mean age has changed, but there is a 5% significant chance of error in this test.

This sort of information can prove useful when selectively targeting potential customers, changing a strategy based on new evidence or justifying a move from currently targeted customer bases.

ACTIVITY 6

An insurance company has a one-star insurance premium for death of £20,000. The average income for people who take out this premium is £30,000 per annum, with a standard deviation of £3,000. A recent survey of 150 new clients showed a mean salary of £28,000 and standard deviation of £2,000. Has the population mean salary of clients for this one-star premium changed. Test at the 5% significance level.

H_0: The mean salary has not changed (or $\mu_1 = \mu_2$)
H_1: The mean salary has changed (or $\mu_1 \neq \mu_2$)

$$Z\text{-score} = \frac{30,000 - 28,000}{2000/\sqrt{150}} = 12.24$$

This value of Z known as Z_{test} (12.24) is clearly larger than the 5% significance value for Z, known as $Z_{critical}$ (1.96). The decision rule is: Reject H_o if $Z_{test} > Z_{critical}$. We would therefore reject the null hypothesis and accept the alternative hypothesis:

H_1: The mean salary has changed (or $\mu_1 \neq \mu_2$)

2.3.2 SUMMARY OF ERRORS
When applying the decision rule there is another kind of error that can be encountered: that is to accept the null hypothesis when it is in fact false. If a hypothesis is accepted when it should in fact be rejected, this is known as a Type II Error. These errors can be summarised in a table below:

		Decision is to Accept null hypothesis	Decision is to Reject null hypothesis
	True	Correct	Type I error
Hypothesis is:			
	False	Type II error	Correct

2.3.3 ONE-TAIL TESTS

To continue with the example of the average age of the purchasers of a specific make of sports car, if you consider the question posed in (b) Has the mean age increased, or not?, then two hypotheses could be formulated:

Hypothesis A: The mean age has not changed
Hypothesis B: The mean age is greater

Hypothesis A presents us with a **Null Hypothesis** and again this is represented symbolically as H_o A null hypothesis assumes that the population age is less than or equal to 31.

Hypothesis B presents us with an Alternative Hypothesis (that the population mean age is greater than 31) and it is represented symbolically as H_1. We therefore have the following hypotheses:

H_o: The mean age has is less than or equal to 31 (or $\mu \leq 31$)
H_1: The mean age is greater than 31 (or $\mu > 31$)

In order to test these hypotheses, a level of significance needs to be selected. The test is now directional and we are concerned with one side of the normal distribution curve only (that greater than the mean). If the portion of the curve of interest is shifted, as you can see on the diagram below, the Z-score for significance also changes (for 5% the Z-score is now + 1.645 or -1.645), concerned with only one-tail of the distribution.

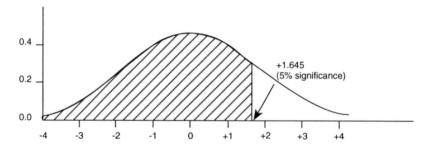

Figure 5: One-tail interval for 5% significance

The test would proceed as follows:

$$\text{Z-score} = \frac{\text{sample mean} - \text{population mean}}{\text{standard error } (s\,/\sqrt{n})}$$

Therefore, if a 5% chance of a type I error is acceptable, then the decision rule would be:

If the Z-score for the sample data is larger than the Z-score for 5% significance, then reject the null hypothesis and accept the alternative hypothesis, otherwise accept the null hypothesis.

Therefore for our example:

$$\text{Z-score} = \frac{31 - 36}{2/\sqrt{250}} = -39.53$$

This value of Z_{test} (-39.53) is clearly larger than the 5% significance level of $Z_{critical}$ (-1.645). The decision rule is: Reject H_o if $Z_{test} > Z_{critical}$. We would therefore reject the null hypothesis and accept the alternative hypothesis:

H_1: The mean age is greater than 31 (or $\mu_1 > 31$)

We would accept this at the 5% significance level (5% chance of a type I error)

The following table represents critical values for commonly used significance tests:

		Critical values	
		One-tail	Two-tail
	1%	2.33	2.576
Significance levels			
	5%	1.645	1.96

ACTIVITY 7

An engineering company has modified one of its products, a carburettor. In planning for a marketing campaign analysts need to establish if the new carburettor allows the car to travel more miles per gallon of petrol. Before modification the mean distance travelled was 25 miles. After modification, a random sample of 32 cars with the modified carburettor travelled a mean distance of 27 miles, with a standard deviation of 3 miles. Does this indicate that the carburettor increases distance travelled. Test at the 5% significance level.

H_0: The mean distance travelled is less than or equal to 25 miles (or $\mu \le 25$)
H_1: The mean distance travelled is greater than 25 miles (or $\mu > 25$)

$$\text{Z-score} = \frac{25 - 27}{3/\sqrt{32}} = -3.77$$

This value of Z_{test} (-3.77) is clearly larger than the 5% significance level of $Z_{critical}$ (-1.645). The decision rule is: Reject H_o if $Z_{test} > Z_{critical}$. We would therefore reject the null hypothesis and accept the alternative hypothesis:

> H_1: The mean distance travelled is greater than 25 miles (or $\mu > 25$) at the 5% significant level.

2.3.4 COMPARING TWO SAMPLE MEANS

This test is concerned with whether or not there is a significant difference between sample means, or if they are the result of chance variation. The test is usually undertaken on large samples. A requirement for this test is knowledge of the mean, standard deviation and sample size for each sample. The test is identical to previous tests observed, except for determination of the test Z value. This is determined as follows:

$$Z = \frac{x_1 - x_2}{\sqrt{\dfrac{s_1^2}{n_1} + \dfrac{s_2^2}{n_2}}}$$

Consider the following: Vauxhall Motors Sales team is trying to sell a fleet of a particular model of car to a prestigious company, on the basis that their model travels greater distances per gallon than an equivalent competitor Ford model (where data is available). The following data is available:

	Ford	Vauxhall
Mean distance travelled per gallon	38	42
Standard deviation	3	4
Sample size for data collection	100	64

Test the hypothesis that there is no difference between means, at the 5% level.

The test would proceed as follows:

> H_0: The mean distance travelled is not different (or $\mu_1 = \mu_2$)
> H_1: The mean distance travelled is different (or $\mu_1 \neq \mu_2$)

$$\text{Z-score} = \frac{38 - 42}{\sqrt{2.9}} = 2.35$$

This value of Z known as Z_{test} (2.35) is clearly larger than the 5% significance value for Z, known as $Z_{critical}$ (1.96). The decision rule is: Reject H_o if $Z_{test} > Z_{critical}$. We would therefore reject the null hypothesis and accept the alternative hypothesis:

> H_1: The mean distance travelled is different (or $\mu_1 \neq \mu_2$) at the 5% significance level.

It is also the case that a one-tail test could be undertaken (this would show that the distance travelled by the Vauxhall car per gallon of petrol is greater, with 5% significance).

2.4 Chi-square analysis

You have looked at several techniques that call upon descriptive statistics (mean and standard deviation) and inference for marketing. You have considered tests of confidence significance tests which you have taken sample statistics to estimate population parameters, within specified limits of statistical accuracy (the process of inference). Within the area of significance testing these are known as **parametric tests**. If the conditions of these tests cannot be satisfied (such as when you do not know that mean of a sample or population), you need to consider other test procedures. The chi-square test, denoted by the Greek letter Chi (squared) $\chi 2$, is an alternative to the parametric tests described. (The symbol $\chi 2$ has no meaning and is representational only.)

Parametric tests are used to answer specific problems concerning the parameters of a population. These tests are generally concerned with parameters such as the mean or variance of a population. Ordinarily, when testing a parameter from a population you would assume that it has a normal distribution, or that the Central Limit Theorem applies. If this is not the case, however, because data is skewed for example, the collection of large samples is usually undertaken to produce an approximately normal distribution (based on Central Limit Theory) If, for any reason this cannot be undertaken and sample sizes are small (n <30), an alternative is to use a non-parametric method of analysis, that is not based on assumptions of 'normality'.

Instead of making assumptions about distribution, as many other statistical methods do, this procedure presents us with a set of distributions which help us to measure how well theoretical data helps us 'fit' the observed data.

These distributions allow us to determine confidence intervals, and perform tests of hypothesis on the variance and standard deviation of a population that does not satisfy the requirements for a parametric test. For chi-square, as with all continuous distributions, a probability corresponds to an area under a curve. The first step in a chi-squared test is to establish appropriate hypotheses for a particular problem.

Consider the following example:

You have been asked to assess consumer preference of adults with respect to 5 varieties of pasta (labelled 1 – 5). Each is cooked in an identical manner and you invite 500 adults to taste a portion of each pasta and state which they prefer. The results are as follows:

Pasta	1	2	3	4	5
Number
preferring	170	120	80	40	90

It may be that these adults are expected not to be able to distinguish between the pasta types. This would form your null hypothesis. If you remember, the null hypothesis should infer that the population cannot distinguish as follows:

H_0 – Adults are unable to distinguish between the pasta varieties.

Using the above sample evidence you can test the validity of this. The alternative hypothesis is:

H_1 – Adults can distinguish between pasta varieties.

Note. H_0 and H_1 can alternatively be stated as

$H_0 - \pi_1 = \pi_2 = \pi_3 .... \pi n$
$H_1 - \pi_i \neq \pi_j$ for any i and j (i $\neq$ j)

where π = proportion of adults

To test the Null Hypothesis using chi-square, you require observed (O) and expected (E) frequencies. The observed frequencies are those from your sample. The expected frequencies are those which would occur (be expected) if the null hypothesis were true.

If preferences depend on chance, you would expect the preferences to be equally spread (ie all equal to 100). This expectation is probabilistic in nature. To begin the analysis the differences between observed and expected values are gauged.

Pasta variety	Observed preference	Expected preference	(O – E)
1	170	100	70
2	120	100	20
3	80	100	-20
4	40	100	-60
5	90	100	-10
	500	500	0

If you sum all the differences between observed (O) and expected (E), the resulting operator $\Sigma(O - E)$ measures the total deviation of observed from expected frequencies. As you can see, however, the value obtained for this is 0 (clearly not a reflection of deviation), resulting in a 'zero sum problem'.

Use of this data would provide a misleading representation of deviation. The sum of the deviations, when averaged, would also be zero. Therefore, to avoid this misrepresentation, statisticians have devised an alternative means of representing deviation. To avoid the zero total you must: square this difference $\Sigma(O - E)^2$. However, when this is done, notice the 'profile' for pasta 2 and 3 (specifically $(O - E)$ column).

Pasta	Observed	Expected	$(O - E)$	$(O - E)^2$
1	170	100	70	4900
2	120	100	20	400
3	80	100	-20	400
4	40	100	-60	3600
5	90	100	-10	100

A deviation of 20 on an observed value of 80 (pasta 3), is 25%, which is more important than a deviation of the same order on 120 (pasta 2), which is 16.7%. However, when the squares of the deviations are obtained, they are the same value of 400.

Due to important anomalies that can arise with observed and expected values (e.g. pasta 2 and 3) a weight is applied to the value of each squared difference: you should therefore divide each difference squared by the expected value (E) for that difference. This normalises the data. The normalised values are summed as follows:

$$\Sigma \quad \frac{(O - E)^2}{E}$$

This statistic is the sum of the normalised squared deviations and is considered to be in the same units as the original data (due to normalisation). This statistic is known as the **chi-square statistic** χ^2

Returning to your example:

Pasta	Observed	Expected	$(O - E)$	$(O - E)^2$	$(O\ E)^2/E$
1	170	100	70	4900	49
2	120	100	20	400	4
3	80	100	-20	400	4
4	40	100	-60	3600	36
5	90	100	-10	100	1
	500	500	0		94

Therefore $\chi^2 = 94$

The calculated statistic of 94 is equivalent to a test Z-score (Z_{test}) which you have seen used previously in significance testing. In this case the equivalent is χ^2_{test}. This value can be used to test a null hypothesis. This test proceeds in a similar way to a Z score (as χ^2_{test} is a standard score), but for χ^2 here are many distributions, not just the standard normal distribution. These distributions are non-normal and selection of the correct χ^2 distribution depends on two values: **degrees of freedom,** given the symbol v and critical significance, given the symbol α.

- Degrees of freedom has its basis in the statement of sample size for a distribution. Generally:

    degrees of freedom (v) = n – 1

    For your example there are five observations (n) and therefore the number of degrees of freedom (5 – 1), is 4. Thus, for the hypothesis you are free to assign expected values to four out of five varieties of pasta.

- Critical significance level is the level of significance with which you wish to test the hypotheses. It is usual to use either 5% or 1% levels of significance.

With knowledge of the above two values, a critical value of χ^2 can be obtained from statistical tables, such as Murdoch and Barnes (1991, p17). This is known as $\chi^2_{critical}$ and is equivalent in its use to $Z_{critical}$ in that the values of χ^2 test and $\chi^2_{critical}$ are compared to support or reject a null hypothesis.

Chi-square is therefore a set of distributions, each one dependent on the number of degrees of freedom.

You can now consult chi-square tables, locating 4 degrees of freedom.

2.4.1 SIGNIFICANCE VALUES
The standard normal distribution uses Z values for 5% and 1% significance, to compare with test values (Z scores) in rejecting or accepting hypotheses. In a similar way, critical values are used and are compared with chi-square test values to accept or reject hypotheses.

The critical values are obtained from chi-square tables with knowledge of the following:

- the level of significance (denoted α)
- the number of degrees of freedom (denoted v)

Convention refers to the critical value as $\chi^2_{\alpha,v}$. For example, for chi-square at 1% significance with 3 degrees of freedom, the notation would be $\chi^2_{0.01,3}$. The value can then be identified from tables.

The decision rule for the test is:

Reject H_o if $\chi^2 > \chi^2_{\alpha,v}$
Accept H_o if $\chi^2 \leq \chi^2_{\alpha,v}$

For your example the values of $\chi^2_{\alpha,v}$ are $\chi^2_{0.05,4}$ and $\chi^2_{0.01,4}$. From this information you must obtain critical values from tables.

The following is a section of chi-square distribution tables providing critical values for 1% ($\alpha = 0.01$) and 5% ($\alpha = 0.05$) levels of significance for various degrees of freedom, $(1 \leq n \leq 10)$:

a =	0.05	0.01	
v = 1	3.841	6.635	
2	5.991	9.210	
3	7.815	11.345	
4	**9.488**	**13.277**	— $\chi^2_{0.05,4}$ and $\chi^2_{0.01,4}$ highlighted
5	11.070	15.086	
6	12.592	16.812	
7	14.067	18.475	
8	15.507	20.090	
9	16.919	21.666	
10	18.307	23.209	

Critical values from tables are therefore:

9.49 at the 5% level of significance
and   13.3 at the 1% level of significance

The calculated (test) value of chi-square is 94 (far greater than both of the critical values). The decision rule is:

Reject H_o if $\chi^2_{\alpha,v} > \chi^2$

Accept H_o if $\chi^2_{\alpha,v} \leq \chi^2$

At the 5% significance level χ^2 (94) > χ^2 α, v (9.49), the decision rule is: Reject (or fail to accept) H_o.

You have seen that the null hypothesis is rejected, therefore the alternative hypothesis is accepted, that is: Adults can distinguish between pasta varieties (which is fortunate for some pasta makers, and fairly obvious from the results of the survey!)

A similar result is obtained at the 1% significance level (χ^2 (94) > χ^2 α, v (13.3)), and the same conclusion drawn, that is to accept the alternative hypothesis.

This sort of information can prove invaluable to a marketing analyst in formulating a marketing campaign or strategy.

You should now be familiar with the principles of the chi-square test. The following activity gives you an opportunity to apply the principles.

ACTIVITY 8

Bob's Food Store holds milk from three different suppliers (A, B and C). Bob has received complaints about the milk going sour after being sold to customers. Bob wishes to know whether these complaints are equally attributed to all suppliers of milk. He decides to categorise 24 randomly selected complaints to test whether complaints are equally divided amongst the three brands. The random selection results in the following number of complaints for each of the brands:

Supplier A	Supplier B	Supplier C
5	10	9

You are required to undertake the test at the 5% level of significance.

H_0 – No difference between complaints ($\pi_1 = \pi_2 = \pi_3 ..... \pi n$)
H_1 – There is a difference in complaints ($\pi_i \neq \pi_j$ for any i and any j (i ≠ j))

Supplier	Observed	Expected	(O – E)	(O – E)^2	(O – E)^2/E
A	5	8	-3	9	1.125
B	10	8	2	4	0.500
C	9	8	1	1	0.125

$$\chi^2 = 1.750$$

Degrees of freedom = n – 1 = 2

The calculated (test) value of chi-square is 1.75, which is less than the critical value (5.991). The decision rule is:

Reject H_0 if $\chi^2_{\alpha,v} > \chi^2$
Accept H_0 if $\chi^2_{\alpha,v} \leq \chi^2$

At the 5% significance level χ^2 (1.75) < $\chi^2_{\alpha,v}$ (5.991), the decision rule is: Accept H_0: There is no difference concerning suppliers.

2.4.2 TEST OF ASSOCIATION

The most common form of a chi-square test is undertaken in two dimensions, to establish if independence exists. The dimensions represent variables or specific elements of one variable of interest. For example, one dimension may represent personal characteristic variables, such as age, height, weight or specific areas of age, such as ages 18 to less than 23, 23 to less than 28, and 28 to less than 33 and so on. Additionally, use is made of contingency tables.

You may have previously observed classifications of a population into one of many categories. That situation is known as one dimensional (as each is classified by one criterion). We will extend the idea to a two dimensional situation, in which each value is a contribution from two criteria, e.g. sales and regions, sex and income level. The question to ask in these situations is: are the two criteria (or variables) associated or not? Are they dependent or independent?

Results for this type of data can be summarised in a **contingency table**. As with other chi-square tests you have so far considered, there are several factors (some differing from those examined so far) which need to be understood for this particular test. The example you will see will highlight these.

2.4.3 CONTINGENCY TABLE

For a two-dimensional analysis of data using the chi-square method, the results can be summarised in a contingency table. This consists of values based on paired or joint observations, for example how many Siesta models of car are sold in the North region (answer 106,000). This observed value arises from one dimension concerned with the model of car, and another concerned with number of sales. The observed value is placed in a cell (or position) on the table corresponding to both criteria. All outcomes for one variable are listed as row headings, and all possible events for a second variable are listed as column headings. The value entered in each cell of the table is the observed value of each joint occurrence.

It is usual to calculate probabilities using this type of table, based on observed frequencies of occurrence for the various joint events. The number of rows and columns in a contingency table can vary (is not fixed) and is important in the determination of the number of degrees of freedom. It is usual to total each column and row in order to determine **expected frequencies** for the contingency table values. Two differences that are observed for this approach are:

Degrees of freedom

For a contingency table these are determined based on a consideration of the number of rows (r) and number of columns (c). For the overall table only $(r - 1) \times (c - 1)$ values are free to vary. The table used in the following example is 4 x 4 (see below):

Expected frequencies

You will see from two-dimensional data that there are rows and columns that result in a contingency table. In the example you will examine, the row and column values are respectively totalled and used in the determination of expected values for those observed values within cells. The expected values are determined based on the multiplication rule of probability, as follows:

Let row totals for each row be denoted RT_i

Let column totals for each column be denoted CT_j

Then Expected value $Eij = \dfrac{(RT_i)(CT_j)}{OT}$

OT = Overall total of rows/columns (in the example this will be 2077).

Expected values for contingency tables are therefore probabilistic in nature.

The following example demonstrates this approach:

A large petrol company wishes to examine sales of four models of car in Britain (Siesta, Scort, Sorion, Scortina). The company sales department wishes to know if there is an association between the region (North, South, East and West) and model sold, for the purpose of refining their marketing strategy. The following sample data has been collected from the most recent financial year, for randomly selected branches of car manufacturer in each region. Use this data, with a significance level of 5%, to test a suitable set of hypotheses concerning any association between region and models sold:

Model	North	Sales (000's)\ South	East	West	
Siesta	106	196	89	94	**Contingency**
Scort	213	298	97	99	**Table**
Sorion	107	109	71	79	**For Data**
Scortina	198	210	66	45	

The hypotheses which would test for association are as follows:

H_0 – There is no association between region and models sold
H_1 – There is an association between region and models sold

Degrees of freedom = $(4 - 1)(4 - 1) = 9$

The decision rule would be: Reject H_0 if $\chi^2 > \chi^2_{0.05,9}$ (16.919)

The expected values can be tabulated along with observed values for comparison. Expected values appear bracketed below observed values.

Model	North	Sales (000's) South	East	West	Totals
Siesta	106 (145.710)	196 (189.844)	89 (75.424)	94 (75.023)	485
Scort	213 (212.406)	298 (276.741)	97 (109.948)	99 (107.905)	707
Sorion	107 (109.959)	109 (143.263)	71 (56.918)	79 (55.860)	366

Scortina	198	210	66	45	519
	(155.925)	(203.152)	(80.711)	(79.212)	
Totals	624	813	323	317	2077

Determination of chi-square proceeds as follows:

Observed	Expected	$(O - E)^2 / E$
106	145.710	10.822
196	189.844	0.200
89	75.424	2.444
94	75.023	5.392
213	212.406	0.002
298	276.741	1.633
97	109.948	1.525
99	107.905	0.735
107	109.959	0.080
109	143.263	8.195
71	56.918	3.484
79	55.860	9.585
198	155.925	11.354
210	203.152	0.231
66	80.711	2.681
45	79.212	14.776
		$\chi^2 = 73.137$

Remember the decision rule is: Reject H_o if $\chi^2 > \chi^2_{0.05,9}$ (16.919)

$\chi^2 = 73.137$ Therefore as $73.137 > 16.919$ you should reject H_o and accept H_1.

H_1 – There is an association at the 5% significance level between region and models sold.

REVIEW ACTIVITY 2

The marketing section of a Business School wishes to make a small study of age differences and course preference, based on gender, for undergraduate students. Analysts wish to know the following:

Is there a difference in age at entry between students who study a language with business (European Studies) and Information Technology with business (Informatics). Random data has been selected from a range of UK universities and from the data the following statistics have been obtained:

mean age of Informatics students at entry = 22 yrs
standard deviation age = 2 yrs
sample size (n) = 200

mean age of Informatics students at entry = 25 yrs
standard deviation age = 2 yrs
sample size (n) = 200

Formulate suitable hypotheses and test them at the 5% significance level, using sample data provided.

In addition, analysts wish to test if there is an association between type of degree chosen and gender of all business students that the Business School caters for. You are required to formulate and test hypotheses concerning any such association at the 5% significant level, using observed data that has been randomly selected. This is presented in the following table:

Degree studied	Gender	
	Female	Male
Informatics	19	35
Business	34	27
Accounting	20	29
European Studies	29	7

(An answer to this activity is given at the end of the unit.)

Summary

In this section you have seen the importance of the normal distribution and parameters such as the mean, standard deviation and sample size in undertaking estimation of population parameters, hypothesis tests and determination of the significance of such tests. Introduction to the use of statistical tables and the application of decision rules has also been made, in an attempt to highlight the importance of correct procedures in undertaking such tests.

You have also looked at a widely used non-parametric test, the chi-square test, which is a hypothesis test undertaken in the absence of commonly used parameters and does not use the normal distribution.

SECTION 3

Bivariate Analysis

Introduction

Further examinations of data analysis for marketing will be made on bivariate data (data consisting of two variables). Here you will see how to describe data consisting of paired values by examining the strength of a relationship and use of regression to describe and forecast data. An introduction will be made to the straight line equation and an evaluation and interpretation of the gradient and intercept for a straight line will be given. This approach will be extended to the analysis of data over time.

The aim of this section is to help you to:

- understand the nature of bivariate data and straight-line relationships
- measure the strength of linear relationships between variables using coefficients of correlation and determination
- determine a least squares regression equation and regression line
- estimate and forecast future data values using technique of interpolation and extrapolation
- become familiar with one approach to the analysis of a time series set of data.

3.1 Bivariate analysis

So far, this unit has shown you data in one variable. Bivariate analysis considers, strictly, two sets of data which are variables: a set of data values which can be referred to as an X variable and a set of data values which can be referred to as a Y variable. The aim is to describe the data and establish whether or not a relationship exists between the variables.

The observations for bivariate data are said to be 'paired'. Paired means that the first observation for the X variable is matched or compared with the first observation for the Y variable (second for X with second for Y etc.).

3.1.1 DESCRIBING BIVARIATE DATA
An example will serve to highlight the process:

Consider an organisation where marketing analysts consider that there may be a relationship between the variables, Advertising Expenditure (X) and Sales Revenue (Y). Examining records for the previous seven years yields the following data:

Year	Advertising (X) Ecu (million)	Sales (Y) Ecu (million)
1	1.9	240
2	2.1	260
3	2.4	278
4	2.7	288
5	3.1	301
6	3.3	322
7	3.9	339

Notice, for example, when $X = 1.9$, $Y = 240$; similarly, when $X = 3.3$, $Y = 322$

Thus, a pair of values is associated with each. The above data can be represented graphically on a **scatter diagram**, on which each pair of data is represented as one point. We can order the pairs (X followed by Y) as follows (1.9, 240), (2.1, 260) and so on. These ordered pairs provide the co-ordinates for a diagram such as that shown below:

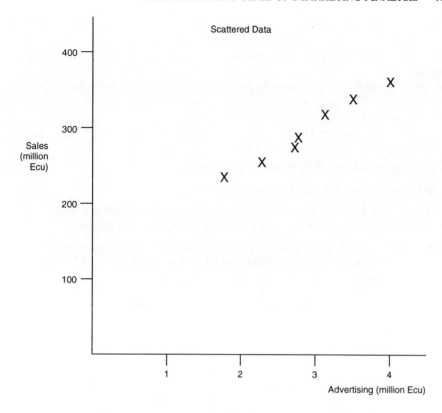

Figure 6: Scatter diagram of advertising and sales data

3.2 Correlation

Scatter diagrams give some initial insight into the relationship between two variables, but it is important to be able to measure the *strength* of the relationship. To do this you can calculate a **correlation coefficient**. The correlation coefficient (r), for a sample of bivariate data is a number we can calculate to give us a measure of the strength of a linear relationship between the two variables, X and Y.

3.2.1 DATA TYPE

In calculating a correlation coefficient it is necessary to identify the type of data you are using. If the data is cardinal (defined as data or numbers) you should calculate Pearson's coefficient of correlation (r) as follows:

$$r = \frac{n\Sigma XY - \Sigma(X)\,\Sigma(Y)}{\sqrt{([n\Sigma X^2 - \Sigma(X)^2][n\Sigma Y)^2])}}$$

This is also known as Pearson's Product Moment of correlation.

If you are examining **ordinal** data consisting of two sets of rankings, the correlation coefficient that results is known as Spearman's Rank Correlation, denoted as r_s. For such data, correlation (r) is equivalent to rank correlation (r_s) and is calculated as follows:

$$r_s = 1 - \frac{6\Sigma d^2}{n(n^2 - 1)}$$

Some properties of **r** and **r_s** should be considered.

● r is a measure that lies between -1 and +1.

● If this number is large (near to +1 or -1), the scatter pattern is almost linear and this is termed 'strong' positive or negative correlation.

● If this number is small (near to 0) X and Y variables show neither a positive relationship nor a negative relationship (ie they have little or no correlation)

The latter two representations can be seen below:

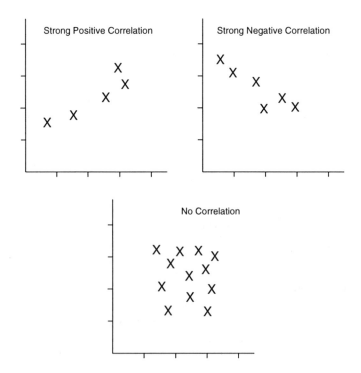

Figure 7: Extreme relationships in correlation

The data on the scatter diagram shown in Figure 6 can therefore be seen to demonstrate strong positive correlation.

The value of correlation (r) obtained can be expressed from three perspectives:

- As a measure of the strength of the relationship between X and Y
- As a percentage variation in Y, explained by a percentage variation in X
- As a measure of the goodness of fit of an idealised Least Squares line to scatter points (see later in this unit on simple regression).

The variation concept is fundamental to the relationship between variables that gives rise to the statistic which we call the 'correlation coefficient'. In examination of the above perspectives an expression can be demonstrated for Total Variation, as follows:

$$\text{TOTAL VARIATION} = \text{EXPLAINED VARIATION} + \text{UNEXPLAINED VARIATION}$$

The total variation is comprised of two types of variation: explained and unexplained variations. It is possible also to demonstrate a proportional relationship between the two variations which provides a further measure of the relationship between data. This is known as the **coefficient of determination** (r^2).

This relationship provides that:

$0 \le r^2 \le 1$

Using the contributory variations that make up Total Variation, we can determine the coefficient of determination, r^2, which is an expression of the proportion of variation in explained values to total variation. The statistic can be obtained if we simply square the calculated value of the correlation coefficient r.

You have seen, so far, reference to the correlation coefficient as a value which lies between -1 and +1. This is actually determined as follows:

$$r = \frac{\text{Explained Variation}}{\sqrt{\text{Total Variation}}}$$

In contrast to this, r^2 is expressed as a percentage, and is the percentage of explained variation in the dependent (Y) variable.

To return to the data of sales revenue and advertising for the fictitious example organisation, we are now going to examine the data with a view to establishing the possibility of strong or significant correlation with Advertising (X) and Sales Revenue (Y).

Year	X	Y
	(Ecu million)	(Ecu million)
1	1.9	240
2	2.1	260
3	2.4	278
4	2.7	288
5	3.1	301
6	3.3	322
7	3.9	339
n = 7	19.4	2028
	ΣX	ΣY

Examination of the equation used to calculate Pearson's correlation coefficient shows that you need knowledge of six quantities:

ΣX, ΣY, ΣXY, ΣX^2, ΣY^2 and n (where n = the number of paired values).

The remaining three quantities are obtained as follows:

Year	Adv.(X) (Ecu million)	Sales (Y) (Ecu million)	XY	X²	Y²
1	1.9	240	456.0	3.6	57600
2	2.1	260	546.0	4.4	67600
3	2.4	278	667.2	5.8	77284
4	2.7	288	777.6	7.3	82944
5	3.1	301	933.1	9.6	90601
6	3.3	322	1062.6	10.9	103684
7	3.9	339	1322.1	15.2	114921
n = 7	19.4	2028	5764.6	56.8	594634
	ΣX	ΣY	ΣXY	ΣXY²	ΣY²

With the required quantities in hand, the value of the correlation coefficient (r) is computed as follows:

Remember:

$$r = \frac{n\Sigma XY - \Sigma X \Sigma Y}{\sqrt{([n\Sigma X^2 - \Sigma(X)^2][n\Sigma Y^2 - \Sigma S(Y)^2])}}$$

where n = 7

Therefore:

$$r = \frac{7(5764.6) - (19.4)(2028)}{\sqrt{([7(56.78) (19.4)^2][7(594634) - (2028)^2])}}$$

and

r = 0.986

The calculated value of the correlation coefficient for the data is a positive value (r = 0.986), close to 1, indicating a high degree of association between Sales and the amount of Advertising Expenditure.

The coefficient of determination, $r^2 = 0.972$ leads to a conclusion that 97.2% of the variations in Sales Revenue can be explained by the regression equation, leaving 2.8% unexplained.

Although a 'strong' relationship is indicated with both coefficients, it does not mean a **cause and effect** relationship is established. If a scatter diagram is plotted and the appearance suggests a strong linear relationship (as with the example of Advertising and Sales), to go on to say that an increase in one causes an increase in the other is tempting, but would not necessarily be correct.

For example, in many business and economic applications we observe highly correlated variables, when each pair of observations correspond to a particular time period. An expected high correlation between average annual wages (X) and the gross national product (GNP: Y), might be expected, when measured over time. Even though wages may be a good predictor of GNP, this does not imply that an increase in wages *causes* an increase in GNP. It is much more likely that a third factor, inflation, caused both wages and GNP to increase.

Other factors must also be considered. If, for example, the product was a drug that received adverse reports of side effects, a fall in sales might result, *despite* increases in advertising.

High statistical correlation does not therefore imply causality. Other non-quantifiable factors may be an influence. Caution in establishing cause and effect is therefore advised.

3.3 Simple regression

If two variables are thought to be related, such that one variable has influence on or affects the other, then the assumption is that one is a function of the other.

That is: $Y = f(X)$

For bivariate data one is the **dependent** variable and the other is the **independent** variable.

The Y variable is known as the dependent variable, because the implication is that the value of Y depends on the value of X (independent variable). By passing an estimated straight line through points on a scatter diagram, with Y as the dependent variable, Y is regressed on X . In parallel to this physical procedure the statistical procedure of linear regression takes the dependent variable Y (which we are trying to estimate), and regresses this onto the independent variable X such that residuals are minimised. **Residuals** are the differences between the actual scattered data and a theoretical best-fit straight line.

The method of studying the relationship between two variables, with the main purpose of arriving at a method for predicting the value of the dependent variable, is known as simple regression analysis.

In simple linear regression you use only one variable X to describe the behaviour of the dependent variable Y. Simple linear regression is only suitable when the relationship between X and Y is approximately linear.

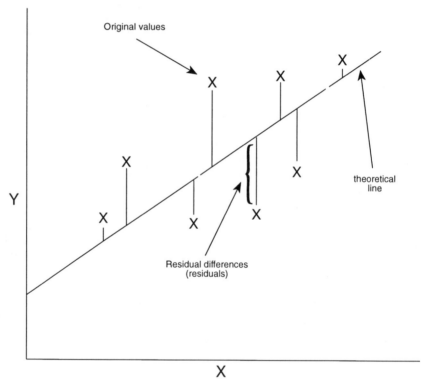

Figure 8: Scatter plot to highlight residuals

The aim of a simple-regression analysis is to find the 'best' straight-line fit for the data, in order to predict as accurately as possible the behaviour of one variable, Y, from the behaviour of another, X.

Regression analysis is based on a **statistical model**. The model can be used to explain things that are non-standard (in this case scattered data). The model allows determination of the 'best' straight line for scattered data, by calculation of the equation.

The general equation for a straight line is given by:

Y = a + bX

In regression analysis the data is usually not linear and the aim is to fit a linear relationship to 'scattered data' to minimise residuals.

As a result of this process   is determined as an estimate of Y:

= a + bX

Additionally, a and b are estimates of the **intercept** and **gradient** of a straight line

The **statistical model** approach enables us to find the values of the regression coefficients, a and b, which satisfy the **least squares criterion** of best fit. The true relationship between Y and X is:

Y = a + bX + e

where e is error, which we seek to estimate by the straight line:

= a + bX

With knowledge of Y and X data values the estimates a and b can be determined using several computational methods, the most common being use of **standard equations**

3.31 STANDARD EQUATIONS

Perhaps the most convenient methods for determining the general solution for intercept (a) and gradient (b) are as follows:

$$b = \frac{n\Sigma XY - \Sigma X\Sigma Y}{n\Sigma X^2 - (\Sigma X)^2} \quad \text{and} \quad a = \frac{\Sigma Y - b\Sigma X}{n}$$

As can be seen from the above, a value for the gradient (b) is calculated first in order to then calculate the value of the intercept (a).

Examination of the equations used show that you need knowledge of five quantities: ΣY, ΣY, ΣXY, ΣX^2 and n (where n = the number of paired values).

If you remember, for correlation analysis, a further quantity of ΣY^2 is used. If you again consider the data for sales revenue and advertising for the fictitious organisation, you will see how to calculate the values a and b with the aim of obtaining the regression equation, describing Advertising (X) and Sales Revenue (Y).

Year	Adv. (X) (Ecu Mill)	Sales (Y) (Ecu Mill)
1	1.9	240
2	2.1	260
3	2.4	278
4	2.7	288
5	3.1	301
6	3.3	322
7	3.9	339
n = 7	19.4 ΣX	2028 ΣY

In order to obtain the remaining two quantities, the following is determined:

Year	X (Ecu Mill)	Y (Ecu Mill)	XY	X^2
1	1.9	240	456.0	3.6
2	2.1	260	546.0	4.4
3	2.4	278	667.2	5.8
4	2.7	288	777.6	7.3
5	3.1	301	933.1	9.6
6	3.3	322	1062.6	10.9
7	3.9	339	1322.1	15.2
n = 7	19.4 ΣX	2028 ΣY	5764.6 ΣXY	56.8 ΣX^2

With the required quantities in hand, a and b can be determined for the regression equation:

The gradient (b) is estimated first.

$$b = \frac{7(5764.6) - (19.4)(2028)}{7(56.8) - (19.4)^2} = 47.82$$

Using the gradient estimate (b), we then calculate the intercept estimate (a), as follows:

$$a = \frac{2028 - 47.82(19.4)}{7} = 157.18$$

The regression equation representing Sales Revenue (Y) and Advertising (X) is:

$$= 157.18 + 47.82X$$

This equation can now be used to describe our data mathematically, superimpose a best-fit straight line on scattered data (see below) and (if the relationship has been established as strong or significant) make forecasts or predictions. This analysis can support planning and explain data in a marketing environment.

From the calculated regression equation above:

When Advertising X = 1 million Ecu, the estimate of Sales Revenue Y is 205 million Ecu

When Advertising X = 3 million Ecu the estimate of Sales Revenue Y is 300.64 million Ecu

These are predictions within the data limits, using the regression equation. This is known as **interpolation**. Predicting outside of the range is known as **extrapolation**. These co-ordinates help construct the graph below.

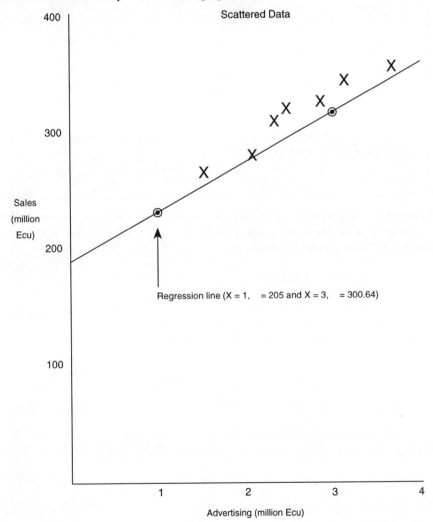

Figure 9: Scatter diagram of advertising and sales data showing regression line

This next activity gives you an opportunity to do some forecasting.

ACTIVITY 9

Marketers are particularly interested in expenditure on the proportion of monthly available net pay spent by professional people in restaurants. Data was collected for eight Advertising Executives on: monthly salary after deductions for tax and national insurance and monthly expenditure on meals in restaurants.

The dependent variable is expenditure on meals (Y).

Salary (X) £	Meal Expenditure (Y) £
2500	80
2800	95
2600	78
3400	94
3600	120
4200	160
4000	160
2700	90

Calculate the regression equation and forecast the meal expenditure for a monthly income of £4,500

Some of the values are large and you may wish to scale down your units. I have given some of the values here: $\Sigma X = 25800$, $\Sigma Y = 877$, $\Sigma XY = $ large, $\Sigma X^2 = $ large and $n = 8$. The regression equation is:

$$= -43.628 + 0.048X$$

To forecast **Y** for a monthly income value, X, of £4500 we would obtain the extrapolated estimate of meal expenditure, Y as £172.37.

REVIEW ACTIVITY 3

VDX, a national chain of record stores, has undertaken some market research to examine the relationship between populations of student halls and sales of CDs (within a three-mile radius of the halls). A set of bivariate data has been collected, as follows:

Weekly Sales of CD's and Population of Halls data:

Population of halls (X)	Sales of CDs in VDX stores (in 3-mile radius)(Y)
(00's)	(00's)
20	4
30	5
27	6
40	7
34	5
39	8
25	6

You are required to determine the correlation coefficient. Is this significant at the 5% level. In addition calculate the regression equation and forecast sales of CDs for a hall population of 3700 (37 using the above units).

(The answer to this activity is given at the end of the unit.)

Summary

The section examined the treatment and analysis of bivariate data. Two aspects were considered: correlation, which attempts to establish the strength of the relationship between cardinal or ordinal data, and regression, which attempts to obtain a best-fit straight line equation for scattered data. Regression is undertaken in order to explain data and forecast data. This concept was extended to bivariate data where one of the variables was time.

SECTION 4

Multivariate Techniques

Introduction

This section will examine a range of multivariate techniques that are currently employed in marketing analysis. These techniques find widespread application in the analysis of questionnaires and other marketing data. The techniques can be used in isolation, but provide more meaningful information when linked. The range of techniques will be highlighted in this section through use of marketing examples and printouts from analyses. A case study will introduce you to ways of linking analyses.

Multivariate techniques are those that involve more than **two** variables at the same time. They can be categorised into essentially three broad areas, depending on the nature of the variables examined and their relationship with each other. The categorisation is based on the ways in which questions are posed when designing surveys for primary data and analysing primary and secondary data. These are:

- ● *Are any of the variables dependent on one or more of the others?*
  If we are to assume that one or more of the variables may be explained and consequently predicted by at least two other independent variables then dependence is involved. Subsequent calculations yield values in the form of a linear equation for the independent variables, which are used to explain the dependent variable.

- ● *Is there more than one dependent variable?* This can also be answered by the first question. If the answer is no, then techniques such as multiple regression are suitable. If it is yes, then the technique of multiple regression, amongst others, is not suitable, and specialised areas, such as multivariate analysis of variance, would need to be employed.

- ● *What is the nature of the data?* The scale of measurement has to be considered, that is: is it nominal or ordinal scale (metric), or is it interval or ratio scale (non-metric). The independent variables should be non-metric (interval scale) data. The subsequent analyses of primary and secondary data, using multivariate techniques, has rules which govern the sequence and approach to analysis. These are best summarised in the classification diagram below.

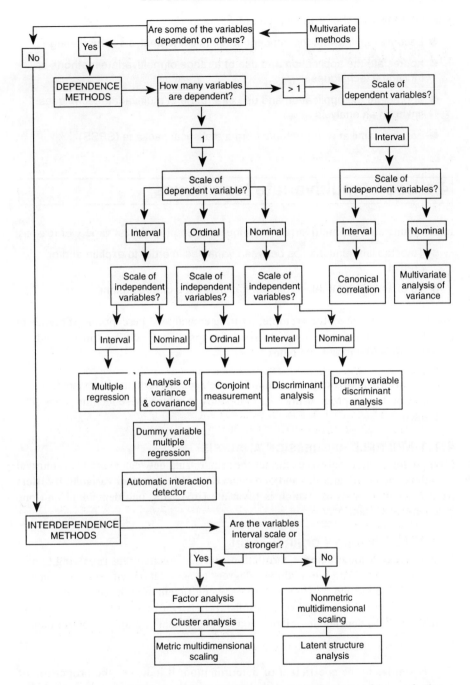

Figure 10: A classification of the multivariate techniques used in marketing research (Adapted from Kinnear and Taylor (1979), p595 and Sheth (January 1971), pp13-19)

The aim of this section is to help you to:

- become familiar with the concept of multivariate analysis in marketing

- appreciate the application and use of a range of multivariate methods as individual techniques

- appreciate the application and use of a range of multivariate techniques linked in an analysis

- become familiar with printouts from a statistical package (SPSS)

4.1 Use of multivariate techniques

In marketing analysis multivariate techniques are employed for a variety of reasons:

- To establish relationships between variables in order to explain and/or predict.

- To examine and analyse differences in groups or populations.

The latter may involve, for example, plotting consumers' perceptions of brands or other objects, on one or a series of spatial maps. (This includes those brands or objects with and without attributes.)

It may be useful at this stage to summarise the approaches that will be examined in this section, before progressing to a case study in which these techniques will be employed.

4.1.1 MULTIPLE REGRESSION ANALYSIS

Multiple regression analysis examines the relationship between at least two interval scaled independent variables and one interval scaled dependent variable. It differs from regression analysis, which is bivariate (involving one dependent and one independent variable).

4.1.2 MULTIVARIATE CORRELATION

This is an extension of simple correlation analysis, to situations involving two or more independent variables and their degrees of association with the independent variable. There are two coefficients used: the coefficient of multiple correlation, R, which indicates the strength of relationship between two or more independent variables and the dependent variable; and the coefficient of multiple determination, R^2.

This is similar to the coefficient of determination; it indicates the proportion of variance in the dependent variable that is statistically accounted for by knowledge of the two (or more) independent variables.

4.1.3 CONJOINT ANALYSIS

Conjoint analysis is a commonly used tool in market research. It enables manufacturers, for example, to find out which features of a product will have most appeal to potential customers, or conversely, which features are regarded as least important. One consequence of this is that it is possible to achieve a commercially beneficial balance: to keep costs within acceptable limits, while positioning a product favourably in the market place.

There are two methods of doing this. The 'trade-off' approach, which compares pairs of variables at a time, and the 'full-concept' approach, which provides far more detailed information, comparing all of the variables of interest together, thus enabling a fuller picture to be gained of the interactions in the dataset. SPSS uses the 'full-concept' approach, which entails producing a number of 'product profile cards' which can be rated in a variety of ways.

Analysis can be both numerical and graphical, although in the case study we will concentrate on the latter almost exclusively, as the graphs in themselves provide a very clear picture of what is happening.

4.1.4 CLUSTER ANALYSIS

This can help us to identify groups of people. The idea is quite simple, and is based on the idea of drawing a graph of particular people's scores, known as factor scores, looking at them, and noticing clusters -- that is, a lot of people with similar scores on the factors.

Computer packages allow us a variety of options in this procedure. Later in this section you will be shown how to arrange your respondents into groups with similar characteristics or attitudes.

The key piece of output from this analysis, however, is the dendogram, which helps to identify the number of groups that may be useful to us.

Items that are similar will group relatively early in the process, while distinctive groups will generally not merge until a long way through the process.

4.1.5 PERCEPTUAL MAPPING AND ATTRIBUTE-BASED APPROACHES

Perceptual mapping is concerned with describing the consumers' perceptions of objects on one or a series of spatial maps, in order that the relationship(s) between objects can be easily seen. These methods can:

- identify the number of dimensions that consumers use to distinguish objects
- determine a preferred location of an object on each of the dimensions
- provide information on the nature and characteristics of these dimensions.

These approaches require respondents or observers to evaluate a set of objects on a large number of attributes. This usually requires ranking the objects on scales such as Likert or semantic differential. The following describes three of these approaches:

Factor analysis

There may be few or many linked variables in a data set, as a result of which marketing analysts try to group responses from tests into basic clusters. This technique is known as factor analysis and can be used in conjunction with other techniques, such as cluster analysis. The analysis is usually undertaken on responses to a questionnaire. It is used to reduce the questionnaire to those questions that are really measuring different attitudes or traits of the respondent.

The starting point of the analysis is to obtain a matrix of the correlations between variables, gained from answers to questions. The analysis identifies patterns from correlations. It does not indicate variable dependence directly but offer guidance for the analyst in what patterns predominate. A hypothetical matrix can be seen in Figure 11.

	X_1	X_2	X_3	X_4
X_1	1.00	0.85	0.35	0.20
X_2		1.00	0.95	0.15
X_3			1.00	0.75
X_4				1.00

Figure 11: Hypothetical matrix of correlations between variables (Xs)

It can be seen in Figure 11 that there is a high correlation between variables X_2 (horizontal) and X_3 (vertical) of 0.95. This would indicate that they are associated with the same underlying construct or factor. You should also observe that correlations of 1 are given for variables of the same type; that is to be expected and is ignored in a subsequent analysis.

The basic concept of factor analysis is quite simple: there are certain things – such as 'love' – which are not measurable, but they do give rise to various attitudes, and these attitudes can be measured with a reasonable degree of success. These attitudes should correlate with the 'factor', or 'trait' if you prefer. Conversely, if we find that a group of attitudes correlate with each other, then they must have some common factor that links them, and all we have to do is decide what to call it.

Discriminant analysis

Discriminant analysis seeks to generate dimensions that will separate objects as much as possible. The procedure for this is analogous to factor analysis. Like multiple regression analysis, this technique has one dependent variable and a set of independent variables. Based on measurements for the independent variables, discriminant analysis can be used to classify people or objects into one of two or more groups. The technique can also be used to identify descriptive variables that best determine group membership. This occurs by examining members of known groups to determine which variables are most useful in helping us differentiate between members of each.

Correspondence analysis

Both factor and discriminant analysis require that attribute evaluations be interval data. Correspondence analysis allows the creation of visual perceptual maps, using categorical data as well as mixed data sets (nominal, ordinal, and/or interval).

4.1.6 NON-ATTRIBUTE-BASED APPROACHES

The attribute-based approaches usually require the analyst to design or develop a complete set of attributes in advance, in some circumstances producing unnecessary dimensions. Non-attribute approaches generally refer to both attribute and non-attribute approaches and are known as multidimensional scaling (MDS) techniques.

Multidimensional scaling

With this technique a respondent would be asked to rate objects in terms of similarity or preference. Attributes are not supplied in advance and respondents use their own implicit criteria to make judgements.

A summary of these approaches is represented diagrammatically below:

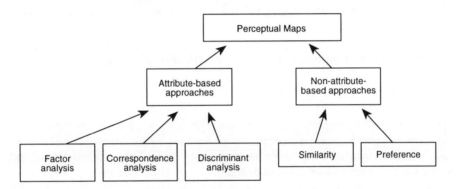

Figure 12: Approaches to generating perceptual maps
(Tull & Hawkins, 1993, p421)

4.2 Using multivariate techniques

4.2.1 MULTIPLE REGRESSION

This approach can be highlighted by comparison to simple regression:

In simple regression the bivariate analysis fits a straight line through two-dimensional space with an output and interpretation as follows:

$$= a + bX$$

Thus, with knowledge of a and b, Y could be predicted for any value of X.

For multiple regression the output and interpretation are the same, but extended as follows:

$$= a + b_1X_1 + b_2X_2 \ldots\ldots\ldots + b_iX_i$$

ACTIVITY 10

Consider the following multiple regression equation:

$$Y = 121 + 0.2\,X_1 + 5.2\,X_2$$

$$R^2 = 0.42$$

where:

= Estimate of sales, X_1 = Cost of advertising, X_2 = Demand

Describe the effects cost of advertising and demand would have on sales in this relationship.

What would be your comment on the strength of relationship?

Sales tends to increase by 0.2 units for every unit increase in cost of advertising and 5.2 units for every unit increase in demand.

42% of the variance in sales can be accounted for by the cost of advertising and demand.

The marketing applications of multiple regression are:

- forecasting
- marketing mix analysis
- monitoring effects of changes on one or more marketing variables whilst others remain fixed
- estimating for missing data.

4.2.2 CONJOINT ANALYSIS

Consider the mythical example that follows:

Several features concerning motor cars are to be evaluated. The variables that have been included ask questions about such things as engine size, brand name, colour and whether or not there is a full-service warranty included. With 7 brands, 4 colours, 4 engine sizes and 2 options for the warranty, there are a total of 7 x 4 x

4 x 2 = 224 possible combinations. Even if we wanted to produce a list of all 224 combinations, it is unlikely that people would want to sit through a market research exercise involving such a large amount of information!

Luckily, it is possible to generate what is know as an 'orthogonal array', which makes sure every option is listed at least once, and to infer from this the importance and utility of the original. This reduces the number of combinations to 32 by minimising the number of variables that have high loadings on a factor. All that is then required is for the combinations to be written up as profile cards, and for the cards to be assessed. An example card is shown below:

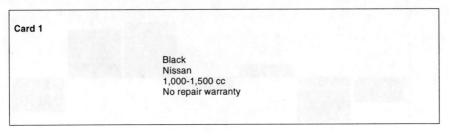

Figure 13: Profile card for conjoint analysis

There are a variety of ways of rating the cards. It is possible, for instance, to ask survey subjects to place the cards in rank order. In the example which follows, a slightly different method was used: each card was rated on a scale of 1 (strong dislike) to 5 (strong liking), and the results recorded.

Key output

From a practical point of view, the concern is frequently 'which is the most important factor to the customer?' Although there is numeric output to allow us to answer this question, the appropriate graph will provide a more immediate answer (Figure 14).

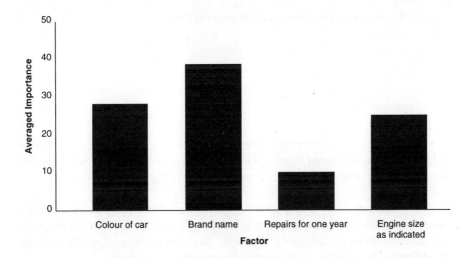

Figure 14: Importance summary from conjoint analysis

From this we can conclude that brand name is the most important attribute when buying a car, followed by colour, engine size and then warranty.

A conjoint analysis output also produces a graph for each of the factors, enabling us to examine the various options within the specified range. So, if we look at that for brand name (Figure 15) we find that Volkswagen cars would seem to be the most popular. (But please bear in mind that this is a fictional study!)

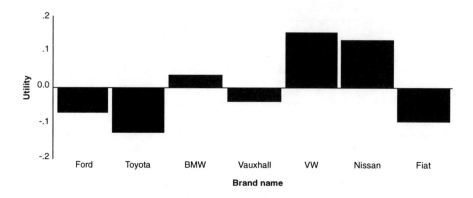

Figure 15: Utility summary for brand name

ACTIVITY 11

Use the importance and utility summaries to find:

(a)   What is the second most important factor in considering a car.

(b)   What is the second most important brand name

The second most important factor, as shown in Figure 14, is the colour of the car. The second most important brand name, as shown in Figure 15, is Nissan.

Conjoint analysis is an exceptionally useful tool, especially for the market researcher (although this technique originated in psychology!), with the one caveat that data requirements are fairly intensive: if you include a lot of factors with many levels, you will have a lot of profile cards that need rating.

4.3 Linking techniques in analysis of market research data

The following case study, based on Phoneselect Television, will help you understand the linked application of various multivariate techniques.

PHONESELECT TELEVISION

Have you ever been stopped in the street and asked some questions about your attitudes to a new product? The chances are you have. Commonly, such questionnaires take the form of Likert Scales, where you are asked to rate statements from Strongly Agree through to Agree, Neutral, Disagree to Strongly Disagree. The answers (coded in this example as 1, 2, 3, 4 and 5 respectively) are taken to be indicative of people's attitudes, either towards a product or to some social issue. Such measurement of attitude can be extremely useful in market research, as the following example demonstrates – and incidentally introduces a large variety of useful techniques along the way.

One of the advantages of cable television is that it allows a degree of interaction between viewer and programme provider. It is now commonplace to find a facility to use the telephone to select films being shown on cable TV, especially in hotels. Imagine that not so long ago, before these devices were introduced, a company developing a cable film selector carried out some marketing research, with the intention of answering the following simple question:

> What sort of people will be interested in this kind of service, and how reliably will we be able to identify them?

Such a simple question involves, statistically, quite a complicated answer – although as we shall see, the final answer will be quite straightforward, and have a certain 'intuitive' appeal.

4.3.1 THE QUESTIONNAIRE

The key components of this questionnaire are the questions, which contribute to the underlying question: 'Would you be interested in Fonafilm?'

The questionnaire consisted of a set of 21 attitudinal questions – statements is a more accurate term, perhaps – relating to entertainment. These are listed below:

ATT1   I enjoy going to the cinema
ATT2   I like a wide range of choice in the video shop
ATT4   My leisure activities are mainly pursued outside the home environment
ATT5   I would rather watch TV than go out to get a video
ATT7   The TV is always on in my household
ATT8   The choice of films on TV is limited
ATT9   I do not agree with paying the TV licence fee
ATT10   Satellite and cable is just more of the same
ATT11   I am a tele-addict
ATT12   Satellite dishes are a blot on the environment
ATT13   I often forget to return a hired video film
ATT14   I rarely have time to sit down and watch TV
ATT15   I prefer films to soaps
ATT17   There is enough choice without satellite & cable
ATT18   I get annoyed if the video I want is out on hire
ATT19   Advertisements in the middle of programmes really annoy me
ATT20   I would rather go the theatre than watch a film
ATT21   More choice from satellite & cable is needed
ATT23   Videos are an excellent form of entertainment
ATT24   I don't mind paying for extra choice
ATT25   TV is a last resort in entertainment

This set of questions was distributed to respondents and 82 responses were received. These questionnaires were coded and subject to analysis using SPSS.

Analysis of the case

Obviously, simple techniques such as cross-tabulation tables between the attitude questions and product interest could be used to try to identify those questions which may be of use in differentiating between potential customers and those not interested, but this would give us no clear idea of the psychological profile of person that made a potential customer.

The appropriate technique to use here is factor analysis, which was developed by psychologists interested in describing personality.

4.3.2 FACTOR ANALYSIS

This is not the place to go into the fine details of the procedure, but using a statistical package such as SPSS it is possible to 'explain' a large proportion of our 21 responses in terms of three factors. Not only that, we can save the factor 'scores' to a datafile and use them in further analysis.

The key part of the output from factor analysis is the **rotated factor matrix,** illustrated below (Figure 16). At first sight, this is rather daunting, but a few tweaks have already been performed to help us understand what is going on. Firstly, the loadings have been sorted to show the largest first, and secondly, small loadings have been suppressed from the printout. Loadings are analogous to correlations between factors and original questions, and allow us to find psychologically meaningful names (at least, meaningful to us – other researchers may disagree) for the factors, in order to aid our future interpretation.

Rotated Factor Matrix:

	Factor 1	Factor 2	Factor 3
ATT4	.92232		
ATT7	−.88719		
ATT1	.83365		
ATT14	.83088		
ATT9	−.80342		
ATT25	.77420		
ATT20	.74673		
ATT11	−.70688	.45963	
ATT5	−.53570	−.31653	
ATT12	.48269		
ATT19	.40777		
ATT17		−.90120	
ATT10		−.88086	
ATT21		.85903	
ATT24		.78182	.41987
ATT23		.58470	.58058
ATT8		.52039	
ATT15			
ATT18			.67289
ATT2		.52349	.57702
ATT13			.44145

Figure 16: Factor matrix

The question which has shown the highest loading, 0.92232, is Attitude 4: 'My leisure activities are mainly out of the home environment'. This loads positively onto the first factor, and since the questionnaire was coded so that a high value represents disagreement, we can see that someone with a high loading here will tend to take their entertainment in the home. Someone who agrees will actually produce a negative score here.

ACTIVITY 12

Which question (attitude) has the highest negative score?

The highest negative score is -0.90120 for Attitude 17 'There is enough choice without satellite & cable'. Attitude 7 loads negatively. This means that someone strongly agreeing will increase their factor score. The question here refers to the TV always being on.

From these two attitudes we can start to build an idea of the concept that Factor 1 represents:

- a high score, suggesting an inclination to stay in and watch the television
- a low score, suggesting an inclination to go out for entertainment.

In fact, what we have is a factor that measures what we may choose to call 'social activity'. Similar examination of the other factor loadings leads us to label Factor 2 as 'pro/anti satellite' (a high score is anti-satellite TV) and Factor 3 as 'pro/anti video' (a high score is pro-video). The next step is to rename the factors, in order that we can remember what respondents referred to.

To get an idea of the effectiveness of the factors, we can examine the data. A simple way to do this is to list some of the cases, and see how people compare. The output from the 'list cases' procedure of the package SPSS is illustrated in Figure 17. It enables us to compare two respondents: Nigel Nevamore and Susan Cinema.

Name	Social	Antisat	Provideo
Susan Cinema	−1.18243	1.28303	.80431
Nigel Nevamore	1.15523	−.50914	.20937

Figure 17: Selected list cases output

Nigel Nevamore doesn't like going out, is in favour of satellite TV, and is slightly in favour of videos – perhaps he doesn't like walking down the road to the video shop! Susan Cinema, on the other hand, likes to go out for entertainment, is fairly strongly against satellite and cable TV, but very in favour of video – maybe she likes to watch her favourite films again and again?

The next task is to try to 'pigeonhole' people, and to see if it is possible to put them into groups. To do this we use cluster analysis.

4.3.3 CLUSTER ANALYSIS

For this analysis we will concentrate on trying to find three easily identifiable groups. We can actually record people's group membership allocation in the data file, too, so you can observe this, and see how useful it becomes. The key piece of output, remember, is the dendogram, which helps us to identify the number of groups that may be useful to us. Part of the dendogram is shown in Figure 18. If you look carefully, you'll find Susan Cinema and Nigel Nevamore in different groups.

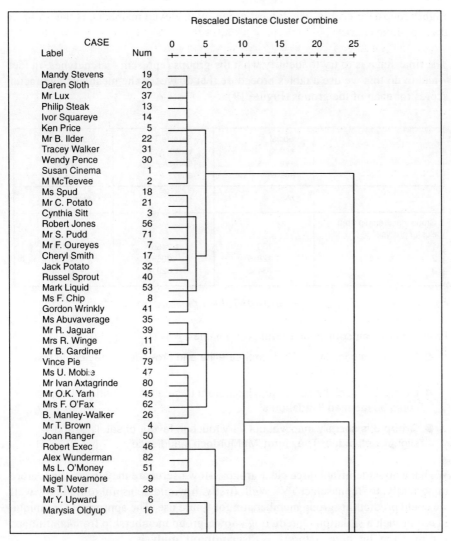

Figure 18: Part of the dendogram from cluster analysis

ACTIVITY 13

(a)   How many groups are visible in the dendrogram?

(b)   Which is the largest group visible (and with how many members)?

Eight groups are visible. The largest group, with eleven members, is the group at the top of the chart.

The final stage is to try to identify what the groups represent – archetypes, in fact – and to do this we use a tables procedure that arrives at the mean average factor scores for each of the groups (Figure 19).

	Social activity: +ve = less active	Satelite TV views: +ve score = anti	Video score: +ve = in favour
	Mean	Mean	Mean
Group membership from cluster analysis			
1	−.73319	1.24567	.22156
2	1.12845	−.00665	−.08530
3	−.73490	−1.02918	−.11644

Figure 19: Table of means

From this we can coin some useful group names:

- **Group 1** is socially inactive, anti-satellite and pro-video. They could be called 'Couch potatoes'.

- **Group 2** is socially active, and indifferent to satellite and video. They could be labelled 'Gadabouts'.

- **Group 3** is socially inactive, but very much in favour of satellite, and slightly anti-video. They form 'Mr Murdoch's audience'.

We have now identified three clear groups. How useful are they to us – and, more importantly, to Phoneselect TV? Well, firstly, it would be useful to find how well we could predict this group membership for future use. The appropriate technique to use in such a situation – predicting known-group membership from continuous variables (eg the three factors) – is **discriminant analysis**.

4.3.4 DISCRIMINANT ANALYSIS APPROACH

Phoneselect simply wishes to know how well the factors can be used to predict group membership, and would therefore examine the classification results, which cross-tabulates the 'prediction' from discriminant analysis with the known-group membership (Figure 20).

Classification results

Actual Group	No. of Cases	Predicted 1	Group 2	Membership 3
Group 1 Couch potatoes	23	23 100.0%	0 .0%	0 .0%
Group 2 Gadabouts	29	0 .0%	29 100.0%	0 .0%
Group 3 Mr. Murdoch's audien	27	0 .0%	0 .0%	27 100.0%

Percent of "grouped" cases correctly classified: 100.00%

Figure 20: Classification results from discriminant analysis

The results here are excellent: a 100% hit rate. This tells us that our three factors are very good at discriminating between the groups; that the three groups are clear and distinct. (With a large number of groups this may not be the case.)

Consolidating analyses

How much does this tell us about what we really want to know: what sort of person is interested in the product. Let's briefly review what we've done.

Firstly, we have analysed the 21 questions to find three underlying factors. We used people's scores on these factors to produce distinguishable groups of people, and finally checked on the quality of our work so far, with discriminant analysis. We are now confident that our groups can be used for further breakdown of our data, and to finally answer the original question in a useful way.

The procedure we have used here is one of the simplest available: cross-tabulation. We can also use the chi-square test for independence to see if the two variables of interest to us (group membership and interest in the product) are related.

4.3.5 CHI-SQUARED ANALYSIS

This is demonstrated in Figure 21.

BUYFONA Interested in FonaFilm
by GROUP Group membership from cluster analysis

Page 1 of 1

BUYFONA	Count	Group Couch potatoes 1	Gadabouts 2	Mr. Murdoch's audience 3	Row Total
Yes	1	11	5		16 20.3
No	2	12	24	27	63 79.7
Column Total		23 29.1	29 36.7	27 34.2	79 100.0

Chi-Square	Value	DF	Significance
Pearson	17.84649	2	.00013
Likelihood Ratio	21.11147	2	.00003

Figure 21: Final chi-square analysis of the dataset

This output tells us that interest in the product and group membership are extremely likely to be related in the market place. By examining the table, we can see that it is predominantly the couch potatoes who are interested, with nearly 50% (11 out of 23) of them expressing a desire to learn more about the product.

ACTIVITY 14

What does the chi-square analysis tell you about product and group membership? How do we know that product and group membership are likely to be related from the chi-square analysis?

This output tells us that interest in the product and group membership are extremely likely to be related in the market place. By examining the table, we can see that it is predominantly the couch potatoes who are interested, with nearly 50% (11 out of 23) of them expressing a desire to learn more about the product.

Determination of chi-square proceeds as follows:

H_0 – There is no association between product and group membership
H_1 – There is an association between product and group membership

degrees of freedom = 2 and if we find table value for 5% significance and 2 degrees of freedom this is 5.991

From the print out:　　$\chi^2 = 17.846$

Remember the decision rule is: Reject H_0 if $\chi^2 > \chi^2_{0.05,2}$ (5.991).

$\chi^2 = 17.846$. Therefore, as $17.846 > 5.991$, you should reject H_0 and accept H_1 – There is an association between product and group membership at the 5% level of significance.

The obvious next step would be to target such people with the marketing campaign – since they tend to stay in a lot and watch television, that may be the medium to use. However, that would not be all: there are other variables in the data set, and further analysis could examine the relationship in more detail, perhaps by region?

Examining groups by region

Obviously, we could use a cross-tabulation, as above, in an attempt to infer a relationship between group membership and, say, ITV region, but there are other, more advanced, techniques which help us visualise things graphically. Such techniques fall under the umbrella title of multidimensional scaling (MDS) .

4.3.6 THE MULTIDIMENSIONAL SCALING APPROACH

Multidimensional scaling is one of the techniques for data analysis which presents us with a 'distance map' requiring numerical values. When it is not necessary to represent this data using numerical values, or when only non-numerical values are available, then labels such as high/low yes/no can be used. Such data is known as categorical data. In such circumstances data can be analysed in ways that corresponds to such procedures as factor analysis. The following example uses one such method, correspondence analysis (ANACOR), and attempts to place the categories of two variables on to a 'perceptual map' to enable us to identify similar groups.

The graph below (Figure 22) shows the relationship between the groups we identified earlier and ITV region, obtained from addresses. Here we can see that the couch potatoes seem to be dominant in the Granada, TVS and Tyne-Tees regions. Perhaps our marketing programme should be concentrated in these areas?

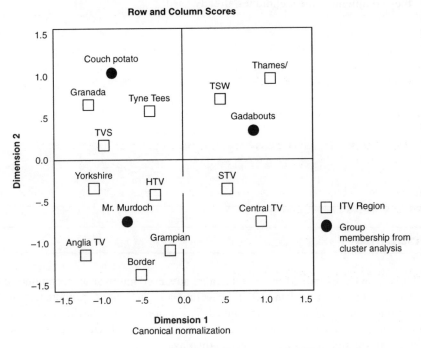

Figure 22: Perceptual map of Group with ITV region

REVIEW ACTIVITY 4

Consider that EDA is Exploratory Data Analysis. This approach uses simple arithmetic procedures to summarise data. In recent years the approach has found wide application in breaking down complex data sets to provide more effective interpretation of data sets. The procedures have been enhanced with incorporation of an EDA facility into the most commonly used statistical packages.

Write a few hundred words commenting on the analytical method and approach used for a study. Your commentary should make reference to the importance of EDA, the category of data used, and whether the overall analysis would have benefited from linking this multivariate technique with others studied in this section of the unit. If you are to recommend further techniques, include an explanation as to why you think them suitable and in what ways they complement the techniques already used.

Summary

This section has examined some of the more advanced multivariate techniques used for analysing marketing data. All of the techniques can be used individually, but are more informative and useful when linked. The majority of the calculations for these analyses require complex mathematics and therefore specialised computer packages for the production of results and visual displays.

Early in the section you saw application of multiple regression and correlation analysis and an application of conjoint analysis, all as individual approaches. A case study containing a seemingly simple question: 'What sort of person will buy my products?' involved a number of advanced statistical procedures which were linked together in order to provide a simple answer. Fortunately, the original questionnaire for the study was constructed with this process in mind, otherwise we may never have found out that selecting a cable film by phone would appeal most to couch potatoes.

Unit summary

In this unit you have looked at the types of variables and data categories which a marketing analyst may encounter. In addition to this you have examined procedures for the coding of such data prior to analysis.

An outline of the important techniques and approaches to the analysis of data was then made in sections 2, 3 and 4, where the techniques of hypothesis testing, bivariate analysis and multivariate analysis were demonstrated in terms of marketing analysis.

The concepts of statistical significance in hypothesis testing and bivariate analysis are important considerations for any analyst, as any decision-making which has to be undertaken in a marketing environment needs to be justified by sound technique, rather than judgement. You have therefore covered the essential principles of hypothesis testing and bivariate analysis to highlight these points.

In marketing analysis, primary data (usually obtained from questionnaires) is a common and valuable source of information for decision making in areas of supply and demand forecasting, consumer preference and general consumer opinion. Data sets for such analyses are usually very large, and the application of techniques can result in complex analysis.

Use of sophisticated computer software to undertake such evaluation is widely employed in marketing, and you have examined, in a case study, a range of some of the important multivariate techniques currently used by marketing analysists for which the resultant printouts were obtained using the SPSS software package.

References

Anderson, D R, Sweeney, D J, Williams T A (1990) *Statistics for Business and Economics,* West Publishing Company, 4th edn

Hughes, G, Jones, R, McClelland, R J, Purnell, K (1992) *Quantitative Methods,* Liverpool John Moores University Publishing

Kinnear, T C & Taylor, J R (1979) *Marketing Research: an applied approach,* McGraw-Hill Book Company

Kvanli, A H, Guynes, C S, Pavur, R J (1995) *Introduction to Business Statistics: a computer integrated approach,* West Publishing Company, 4th edn

Murdoch, J and Barnes J A (1991) *Statistical Tables,* Macmillan, 3rd edn

Sheth, J N (1971) 'The Multivariate Revoluation in Marketing Research', *Journal of Marketing,* vol 35, January

Simon Dunkley SPSS Training: *SPSS data bank and SPSS for windows computer package* (SPSS UK Ltd, SPSS House, 5 London Street, Chertsey, Surry, KT16 8AP)

Weiers, R M (1984) *Marketing Research,* Prentice Hall

Further Reading

SECTION 1:
Anderson, *et al* (1990) Chapters 1 & 2

Kvanli, *et al* (1995) Chapters 1, 2 & 3

Hughes, *et al* (1992) Chapters 6 & 7

Weiers, (1984) Chapter 11

SECTION 2:
Anderson, *et al* (1990) Chapters 7, 8, 9 and 17

Kvanli, *et al* (1995) Chapters 8, 9 & 12

Hughes, *et al* (1992) Chapters 11, 14, 15 & 17

Murdoch, & Barnes, (1991)

Weiers, (1984) Chapter 12

SECTION 3:
Anderson, (1990), Chapter 13

Kvanli, *et al* (1995), Chapter 13

Hughes, *et al* (1992) Chapter 18

Murdoch & Barnes (1991)

Weiers (1984) Chapter 12

SECTION 4:
Anderson, *et al* (1990), Chapter 14

Kvanli, *et al* (1995), Chapter 14

Weiers, (1984)

Answers to Review Activities

Review Activity 1

(a) There are two modes for this data (22 and 24), which both occur three times. The median is 27+28/2 = 27.5. The mean is 574/20 = 28.7 years.

(b) The minimum value is 22 and the maximum value is 44, the range is therefore (44 – 22) = 22. The variance is 39.69 and standard deviation age is

   $\sqrt{39.69}$ = 6.30 years.

(c) Age is a continuous variable.

(d) Age is a ratio scale of measurement (it has a definite zero).

Review Activity 2

For the age difference, study the hypotheses that could be used to test for difference are:

H_0 –   There is no difference between ages of students and degree chosen at entry

H_1 –   There is a difference between ages of students and degree chosen at entry

This is a two-tail test and for 5% significance the critical Z-score is 1.96.

The decision rule is: Reject H_0 if the Z-score for the sample data is larger than the Z-score for 5% significance.

The sample (test) Z-score is determined as follows:

$$Z_{test} = \frac{25 - 22}{2/\sqrt{200}} = 21.43$$

The sample Z-score is 21.43. Therefore as Z_{test} (21.43) > $Z_{critical}$ (1.96) the decision is: Reject H_0 and accept H_1

H_1 –   There is a difference between ages of students and degree chosen at entry

For the gender study:

The hypotheses which would test for association are as follows:

H_0 – There is no association between degree chosen and gender
H_1 – There is an association between degree chosen and gender

$\chi^2_{critical}$ from tables for 5% significance and $(4 - 1)(2 - 1) = 3$ degrees of freedom = 7.82

The decision rule would be: Reject H_0 if $\chi^2_{test} > \chi^2_{critical}$ (7.82)

Expected values can be tabulated (brackets) with knowledge of row and column totals, as follows:

Gender

Degree studied	Female	Male	Total
Informatics	19	35	54
	(27.54)	(26.46)	
Business	34	27	61
	(31.11)	(29.89)	
Accounting	20	29	49
	(24.99)	(24.01)	
European Studies	29	7	36
	(18.36)	(17.64)	
	102	98	200

Determination of chi-square proceeds as follows:

Observed	Expected	$(O-E)2/E$
19	27.54	2.65
34	31.11	0.27
20	24.99	1.00
29	18.36	6.17
35	26.46	2.76
27	29.89	0.28
29	24.01	1.04
7	17.64	6.42
		$\chi^2 = 20.57$

Remember, the decision rule is: Reject H_0 if $\chi^2_{test} > \chi^2_{critical}$ (7.82)

$\chi^2 = 20.57$. Therefore as $20.57 > 7.82$ you should reject H_0 and accept H_1:

H_1 –   There is an association at the 5% significance level between degree chosen and gender.

Review Activity 3

I have given the values here: $\Sigma X = 215$, $\Sigma Y = 41$, $\Sigma XY = 1304$, $\Sigma X^2 = 6931$ $\Sigma Y^2 = 251$ and $n=7$

For our example, $r = 0.750$ and $n = 7$ the table value for 5% significance is 0.666. As the value of r, $0.750 > 0.666$ (the table value). The decision rule will be reject H_0 and accept H_1 concluding that there is a significant linear association between weekly CD purchase and population of halls, at the 5% significance level.

For regression:

The regression equation is:

$$= 1.663 + 0.137X$$

To forecast for Y for a hall population value, X of 37 we would obtain the extrapolated estimate of weekly CD purchase,   as 6.73 (that is 673)

Review Activity 4

You should avoid data that is based on the ratio scale of measurement. The use of ordinal and nominal scale data analysis can fail to reveal frequency of purchase of for example brand over a time interval, which is ratio scale data.

Analyses can be partially successful in distinguishing brand choice, as this is concerned with nominal (purchase – not purchase) data, but this could not be linked with frequency of purchase (important in identifying market segments in any particular problem).

Exploratory Data Analysis enabled any anomalies to be identified, clusters for example to be assigned and misinterpretation of data avoided.

Discriminant analysis can be used as a linked or complementary analysis to perhaps cluster analysis. This may indicate how well factors could be used to predict group membership of variables. In using any approach, it presupposes that factor analysis would be undertaken first and a rotated factor matrix obtained.

EDA reinforces the importance of identifying and accounting for the categories of data used. Even if data is correctly coded, there may be obscured relationships within mixed data sets, resulting in misleading analyses.

UNIT 9

CHANGING MARKET STRUCTURES AND THE IMPLICATIONS FOR CHANNEL RELATIONSHIPS

Introduction

The aim of all organisations is to manage the marketing mix variables within the organisation to exploit to best effect the opportunities that arise in the market place. These opportunities are created through changes in the organisation's marketing environment. As we saw in Unit 3: Approaches to Environmental Monitoring in Marketing, the external environment consists of both 'macro' and 'micro' elements. Macro elements include legal, economic and political factors. Micro elements include consumers, suppliers, and wholesalers. It is likely that only for short periods of time will an organisation have a 'perfect fit' between its capabilities and strategies and its marketing environment.

The purpose of this unit is to focus primarily on the organisation's micro-environment – the market structure in which the organisation operates. The market structure will influence the strategies adopted by an organisation. In particular, the market structure has an impact on distribution channels and distribution and sales strategies. The level of competitiveness in a market and the nature of the relationships formed between organisations is often determined by structural forces operating within the market.

Changes in the macro-environment will also have an impact upon market structures and upon the behaviour of organisations operating in the market. Those organisations that develop appropriate responses to these changes will gain market penetration and leadership.

ACTIVITY 1

Write down what you consider the following words to mean:

- macro-environment
- micro-environment
- market structure
- an organisation's capabilities
- strategy
- distribution channels
- relationships.

How close are your answers to the following?

Macro-environment – The broad external factors that indirectly impact upon an organisation. These consist of social, legal, economic, political and technological factors. (SLEPT)

Micro-environment – The external factors that directly impact upon an organisation. These consist of retailers, wholesalers, manufacturers, competitors, and the customer.

Market structure – The *combination and interaction* of the micro-environmental factors. Different market structures are formed, depending on the nature and the extent to which each factor is present.

An organisation's capabilities – The resources an organisation possesses, such as finance, technology, and people. When combined together these create distinct areas of strengths and weaknesses. These strengths and weaknesses will determine the organisation's competitive capabilities in a particular market.

Strategy – The decisions made that govern the direction an organisation takes when competing in a market. For instance, should it aim to be a market leader or follower, cost leader or differentiator, market developer or product developer.

Distribution channels – The means by which a product reaches the customer, from raw material, through manufacture and either direct to the customer or through middlemen. Organisations involved at each stage are called 'channel members'.

Relationships – The channel members within a distribution channel will transact business within some form of relationship. This relationship may be close or distant, based upon trust and partnership or upon conflict.

This unit will introduce you to the changing nature of market structures and its implications for channel relationships.

Objectives

By the end of this unit you should be able to:

- Outline the factors that combine together to create market structures
- Identify the key forces of change that are impacting upon market structures
- Identify the different types of channel relationships that exist within different market structures
- Relate changes occurring in market structure to the changing nature of relationships within distribution channels

SECTION 1

Types of Market Structure

Introduction

This section looks at the factors in the micro-environment that, when combined, form the market structure in which an organisation operates. The market structure consists of suppliers, competitors and buyers etc. The performance and behaviour of firms will be influenced by the nature of the market structure and the relationships that are formed in it. The competitive dynamics that exist in any market are introduced and explored using a case study. This demonstrates the forces at work within any market and shows how any market structure can be analysed. The key factor that influences this behaviour is the economic relationship of supply and demand. This economic relationship can be analysed by looking at the number of buyers and sellers that exist in a market.

The aim of this section is to help you to:

- become familiar with four key market structures that affect the market relationship between supplier and buyer
- appreciate the extent to which power is a key factor in the relationship between supplier and buy.

1.1 Marketing environment and market structure

As described in the introduction to this unit, organisations operate in what is termed a 'marketing environment'. This environment can be considered in terms of macro and micro factors.

The macro factors consist of the following:

S ocial
L egal
E conomic
P olitical
T echnological

These are often termed the SLEPT, or PEST (Political, Economic, Social and Technological) factors, and they also include an element of demographics.

The micro factors are made up of the following elements:

Competitors
Suppliers
Distributors
Customers.

Figure 1 represents the situation graphically, showing the micro-environment encircled by the macro-environment.

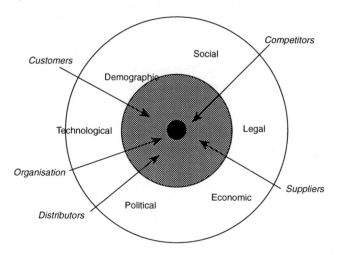

Figure 1: An organisation's marketing environment.

As stated earlier, it is the combination and extent to which each of the factors in the micro-environment are present that form the market structure. The market structure will exert considerable influence upon an organisation in its ability to market its product. The extent to which this influence affects the organisation depends on such factors as the number and size of organisations that operate in that market, the relationships that exist between each organisation and the relative power that is held between them. The ability of an organisation to distribute its product often depends upon its ability to gain control or develop strong relationships with other members in the market.

Channels of distribution are therefore an integral element of the market structure, which, in turn, impact upon the organisation's marketing strategies and its relationship with consumers and the trade. It may also determine the relative attractiveness of the market in terms of its stability, competitiveness and profitability.

Traditionally, brand manufacturers have focused their marketing activity on the consumer. On average 75% of marketing spend would be directed at the consumer market in the form of advertising. The remaining 25% would be targeted at the trade, in the form of trade promotions and incentives to encourage them to stock and sell the brand.

These brand-building strategies proved very successful in the 1960s and into the 1980s. In recent years, however, a major change in market structure and market dynamics has occurred. The consumer has become wiser and less willing to accept brands that do not provide value. The power of retailers has grown at the expense of manufacturers and wholesaler power. Retailer brands have become established in their own right.

Two examples will serve to illustrate this point:

HEINZ

In May 1994 Heinz announced that it was to abandon its famed 'Beanz Meanz Heinz' commercials in favour of a huge direct-marketing campaign. Television advertising for all its individual branded products was to end. 50% of Heinz' total marketing spend would be used for promoting the corporate brand name; the balance would be used for 'below the line' activities, including trade promotions, sales promotions and direct marketing. Heinz' justification for this move was that it was a strategic response to the increasing threat posed by own-label products sold increasingly by supermarket chains, coupled with increasing ineffectiveness of television advertising to reach large audiences as a result of changing social/leisure trends and advances in communication technology, which has fragmented television audiences in the UK and made the television medium less effective.
(Information based on article in *Sunday Times*, 8 May, 1994)

NESTLÉ

In 1992 Nestlé chose the United Kingdom as a test market for a new Buitoni pasta brand. The strategy adopted by the company to launch and manage the brand represented a radical departure from its traditional brand-building strategies for fast-moving consumer goods, which had focused on intensive advertising campaigns through mass media. The Buitoni brand was launched in 1993, using direct-response advertising to build a database of potential or actual users of the brand. Consumers who responded to the advertisements were sent recipe sheets, money-off vouchers, new-product information etc. Respondents were also offered the opportunity of joining the 'Buitoni club'. By the end of 1993 the club had 75,000 members, and by the end of 1994 projected a membership of 200,000.

The new strategy was developed in response to six factors:

- the increasing difficulties Nestlé was experiencing in directly reaching the consumer as a result of increasing retailer power

- the balance of power with regard to information, which increasingly lay in the retailers' favour, particularly as a result of the new retail electronic point-of-sale scanning systems (EPOS)

- the increasing strength of the retailers' 'own label' brands

- the increasing need, on the part of consumers, for a more personal relationship with producers

- the declining cost-effectiveness of traditional mass media

- the advances in new technology and alternative distribution channels, and the need to be first in the market to exploit these opportunities.
(*Marketing*, 9/11/92)

Market behaviour can therefore be analysed by identifying the dynamics operating in a market and assessing the impact of these forces on the relationships that are formed between distribution channel members. These relationships and strategies are outlined in detail in Section 4.

Figure 2 shows the competitive dynamics that exist within any market structure.

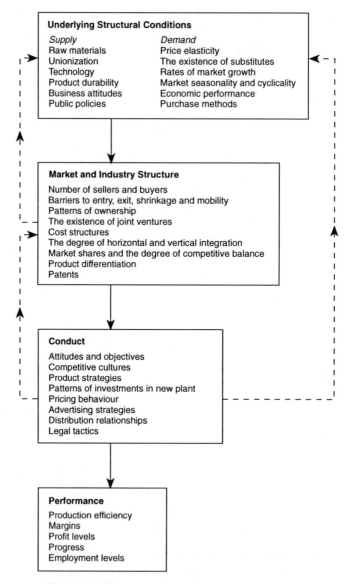

Figure 2: The competitive dynamics of an industry
(Wilson, Gilligan & Pearson, 1993)

The example below applies the above model in an assessment of the competitive dynamics of the newspaper market.

NEWSPAPER WHOLESALE MARKET – W H SMITH

UNDERLYING STRUCTURAL CONDITIONS

Supply side – The availability of paper (raw material) for newspapers is not a cause for concern except for environmentalists. However, national and regional newspaper owners are considering, in the longer term, new forms of media technology that may impact upon W H Smith Wholesale. The newspaper publishers are currently adopting aggressive pricing policies to increase sales of newspapers. None of these publishers can dominate the market and are reliant upon wholesalers for distribution. Potentially a price war might impact upon the profit margins of W H Smith Wholesale.

Demand side – The customers for W H Smith Wholesale are the newsagents and other retail outlets that sell newspapers. They will be relatively price conscious in view of the fact that an alternative wholesaler exists, but price is not a paramount concern, as will be seen below. Newspaper sales to the consumer have been in decline for several years. Price cuts have increased demand for newspapers considerably. W H Smith Wholesale has no control over the price the consumer pays. Demand for magazines is growing. Rates of growth and profit margins in this sector are more attractive than in newspapers.

MARKET AND INDUSTRY STRUCTURE

There are only two major national wholesalers in the newspaper and magazine market. These are W H Smith Wholesale and John Menzies. Wholesalers distribute to an estimated 70,000 retail outlets, of which 47,000 are Confectioners, Tobacconists and Newsagents (CTNs) (*Keynote,* 1991). W H Smith is the market leader, serving 24,000 of these outlets. John Menzies serves 18,000 outlets, leaving a further 200 small wholesalers with the balance. (The number of small wholesalers has fallen from 2,000 to 200 in the space of three years.) There are limited joint ventures or vertical integration. News International attempted to distribute its own titles, such as the *Sun, The Times, Today* and *News of the World,* but found this unprofitable, particularly when the market structure at the wholesaler level altered so radically. The degree of competitive balance has now moved towards the two key wholesalers. They offer limited product differentiation, but serve the suppliers of newspapers and magazines with a stable distribution system.

The focus of attention for the wholesalers has now shifted from retailers, who are numerous and offer no competitive threat, to serving the needs of the newspaper publisher (the supplier). By ensuring the best possible service and distribution of the publisher's products, that maximises sales and minimises returns, W H Smith ensures that publishers are happy to maintain the existing relationship. Multiple retailers have no power in this distribution channel compared to their power in food distribution. They are only a small player in newspaper distribution.

CONDUCT

The wholesalers exercise control over the distribution system. They control the distribution of magazines and newspapers to retail outlets based on their knowledge of the market. This relationship suits both the retailers and publishers. The retailer, because they do not need to estimate quantities themselves, and the publisher because they obtain excellent service and market information. Limited advertising is carried out by the wholesaler. Attention and time is spent ensuring that relationships with suppliers and retailers are maintained and that the needs of both are met effectively. Merchandisers will visit retailers, advising them on display and shop design.

PERFORMANCE

W H Smith and John Menzies have achieved dominance in a market that traditionally consisted of numerous small wholesalers. The power in the distribution channel has now shifted to these two key players. Their position has been achieved and is sustainable through their knowledge of the market and service to both suppliers and retailers. This ensures that efficient and effective distribution systems are in place and that all members of the channel benefit from this stability. The current supplier price wars will only be maintained while sales volumes and advertising revenue increase. It is likely that the newspaper suppliers will feel the pinch before W H Smith and John Menzies.

The above example shows clearly the relationship between the underlying structural conditions – the market structure – and the conduct and performance of the channel members.

By using market intelligence reports, such as MINTEL, you will be able to conduct a similar market analysis for any market. From these reports you can identify the relationships that exist. It is very unlikely that any market structure analysis will be the same. Each market structure will be unique and have its own dynamics influencing relationships between channel members.

The food retail scene is dominated by five major supermarkets. Food manufacturers are increasingly finding their brands under threat of being delisted. The DIY sheds, similarly, dominate their supply chains. In some markets, however, manufacturers dominate the supply chain. Car manufacturers are a good example of this. Despite increasing competitive threats from new car importers and changing market structures the traditional UK-based car manufacturers are maintaining market position and share, and a key element in their strategy is the control of their distribution channels. (No own-label threat exists in this market – yet!)

We will revisit these examples when we consider in more detail the dynamics of market structures and competitive forces.

It can be seen that the competitive dynamics of a market are influenced strongly by the underlying conditions of supply and demand. The most significant factors that will determine the nature of the relationship between supply, demand and industry structure is: the number of buyers and sellers; their relative market shares and the degree of differentiation that exists between competing firms.

1.2 Market structure and competitive forces

The number of firms that control the supply of a product on to a market will affect the nature of the relationships that exist within a market. When one or only a few firms control supply, the competitive nature of the industry will be different from when there are many suppliers. Table 1 below describes the main characteristics of the four most commonly occurring competitive structures: monopoly, oligopoly, monopolistic competition and perfect competition.

Type of Structure	Number of Competitors	Ease of Entry into Market	Product	Knowledge of market	Examples
Monopoly	One	Many barriers	Almost no substitutes	Perfect	Railways (British Rail), many government departments
Oligopoly	Few	Some barriers	Homogeneous or differentiated (real or perceived differences) products	Imperfect	Airlines, petroleum retailers, some utility providers
Monopolistic competition	Many	Few barriers	Product differentiation with many substitutes	More knowledge than oligopoly; less than monopoly	Jeans, fast food, audio-visual
Perfect competition	Unlimited	No barriers	Homogeneous products	Perfect	The London Commodity Markets, vegetable farms

Table 1: Characteristics of competitive market structures.
(Dibb, Simkin, Pride and Ferrell 1994 p53)

MONOPOLY

When one company controls the supply of products on to the market and there are no close substitutes available as alternatives, then this company is described as a monopoly. If it wants to it can adopt monopolistic market behaviour. It can restrict supply and therefore increase prices, operate at lower efficiency as no competitors threaten its position, and erect barriers to entry through its control and power in the distribution system. Barriers to entry include such factors as technological know-how, level of financial resources required to enter a market and lack of access to key distributors. Most monopolies that exist today are the public utilities, such as the gas and electricity services.

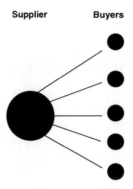

Figure 3: Monopolist market structure

ACTIVITY 2

Analyse the market behaviour of the water, gas and electricity utilities. (You can obtain information on this from the quality press including back-issues on microfiche, to be found in your university or local library.)

What behaviour is taking place? Is this consistent with an organisation that holds monopoly power in its market?

All three of these utilities exhibit evidence of monopolistic behaviour. The government has appointed watchdogs to help control excessive profits by these organisations, predominantly focusing on uncompetitive pricing and poor quality of service. Examples of such behaviour would be price increases at a time when the utilities were making record profits.

The government has also required each utility to adopt a citizens' charter in terms of performance and service standards. Limited direct competitive threat exists for these organisations. The government has recently attempted to increase each industry's competitiveness through deregulation and privatisation.

OLIGOPOLY

An oligopoly exists when a few suppliers control a large proportion of the supply of a product. Each seller must consider the reactions of other sellers when it changes its marketing mix.

The oligopolist will be able to restrict entry to its markets because of its financial and market power. There is often a degree of mutual inter-dependence between suppliers. Prices are set at a level that enables higher returns than if the market was more competitive. The products will generally be differentiated but in certain primary industries may be homogeneous. Examples of oligopoly markets are multiple retailers, petrol stations, aluminium/steel manufacturers etc.

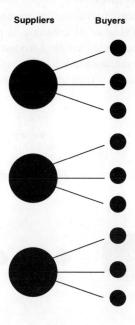

Figure 4: Oligopolist market structure

ACTIVITY 3

Analyse the behaviour of British Airways. Does this organisation operate in an oligopoly market? What evidence can you find to support this? What behaviour is taking place? Is this consistent with an oligopolist?

British Airways operates in the domestic market and also the global market. In the domestic market the airline's traditional dominance is being challenged by other airlines, such as Virgin and British Midland, who now compete directly with BA. This competitive threat is forcing BA to adopt oligopolistic behaviour. While it attempts to differentiate itself through its service, it is being threatened by its competitors in terms of negotiating flight availability and pricing. British Airways, through its dominant market position, will not willingly allow competitors to gain market access, the result being extensive negotiation and lobbying both at the level of airport authority and national government.

It is difficult, however, for any new UK airline companies to enter the market due to this competitiveness and the level of financial investment required. At a global level, BA cannot behave as an ologopolist as it is operating in a significantly more competitive market such as the one outlined below.

MONOPOLISTIC COMPETITION

This is the most common competitive market structure. In this market there are many suppliers and each is trying to differentiate its products to establish its own market share. If it can achieve this differential advantage in line with the market's needs then it will be able to increase market share and charge higher prices for its products. Examples of companies which have successfully achieved this are Levi, BMW, and Procter & Gamble.

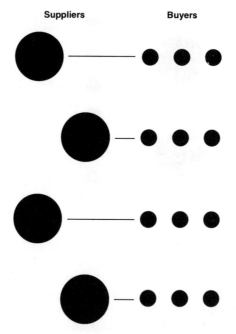

Figure 5: Monopolistic, competitive market structure.

ACTIVITY 4

Taking one of the organisations cited above, analyse its behaviour and identify evidence of monopolistic competitive behaviour. How is the company differentiating itself? Does it have many competitors?

Procter & Gamble are competing in a market in which numerous UK and overseas suppliers offer a range of brands alongside retailer own brands. Procter & Gamble adopt the traditional brand management tactics of heavy advertising and merchandising support for the brand, targeted at the retailers and wholesalers, as well as the end consumer. The markets will be heavily segmented and Procter & Gamble will supply a range of different brands of washing powders etc, targeted at these segments. Differentiation is the key aim of these tactics and this is achieved through image, performance, design and packaging etc.

PERFECT COMPETITION

In reality, the conditions in which perfect competition would be evident do not exist. However, some markets exhibit some of the elements necessary for perfect competition. In principle, a perfectly competitive market would consist of many buyers and sellers, all with perfect knowledge and no barriers to entry into the market. The product would be homogeneous; therefore no product differentiation would be possible. The market relationship between demand and supply would determine the price and behaviour of firms operating in that market. Commodity markets are often cited as examples of perfectly competitive markets. An example of a market that is beginning to exhibit some of these characteristics is the national daily newspaper market, where it is becoming increasingly difficult to differentiate the products on offer, and market forces are determining price levels.

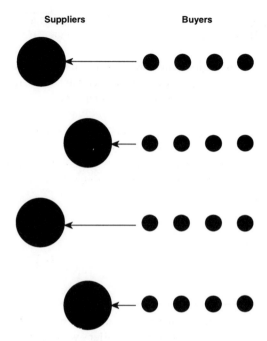

Figure 6: Perfectly competitive market

ACTIVITY 5

Analyse the national daily newspaper markets. What evidence can you find for the assertion that the market structure has some degree of perfect competition in it? Is this reflected in the behaviour of the suppliers of these newspapers? Why is this market not a true perfectly competitive structure.

It is becoming increasingly hard for newspaper publishers to differentiate their products from each other. At the same time, the market readership of newspapers is in decline. This combination has led to the market becoming increasingly competitive and price driven. A new market price for newspapers is now being determined through market forces of demand and supply. The newspaper market is not an entirely 'perfectly competitive' market. Each newspaper is not homogeneous. Publishers are still attempting to target different consumers and differentiate and position themselves against competitive papers.

From the examples that you have explored above you may have identified a range of different market behaviour caused by the competitive nature of the market structure – what was described in Unit 5 as 'adjusting the marketing mix'. Behind the front-line activities of the mix, however, there are ongoing strategies adopted by organisations to increase their power in the market place. This may be by takeover or merger, both horizontally and vertically. It may be by joint ventures or simply collusion. Alternatively, strategies may be developed to form closer relationships with channel members.

The market structure analysis you have conducted concentrates on supplier power. In many markets it is possible to see that it is the *buyer* (by which we mean the retailer) that has the power. An example already cited is the retail and DIY markets. This power of the buyers will significantly influence the strategies adopted by suppliers. This is illustrated in Figure 7.

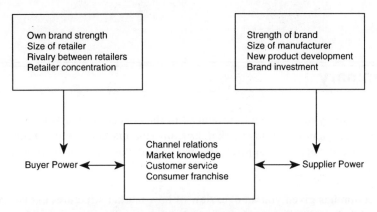

Figure 7: The power relationship between buyer and supplier

Figure 7 illustrates some of the factors that determine the extent of buyer and supplier power. Buyer power can be derived from size, level of industry concentration and the extent of competitiveness. Buyer power is derived from the level of investment in the brand, extent of new product development, the size of the manufacturer and the strength of the brand in the market. This power will, however, be influenced by other factors, such as the nature of the relationships that exist with other channel members, market knowledge, level of service and the strength of brand loyalty attained (consumer franchise). We will look at the nature of power in more detail in Section 3.

REVIEW ACTIVITY 1

For an organisation and market of your choice, consider the market structure and competitive dynamics that exist. Use the model shown in Figure 2 and the example of W H Smith Wholesale as a framework to assist you in developing your answer.

A useful source of information would be your local university business library, where you can access MINTEL reports, *Keynote* reports or *Market Assessment* reports. These will show clearly the market structure, competitive dynamics and behaviour of organisations within a market sector.

Summary

In this section you have been introduced to the concept of market structure, the competitive dynamics of this market structure, the market structure relationships that can exist between supplier and buyer and the concept of power in this relationship.

This section has given you an overview of how market structures evolve and the nature of the relationships and behaviour that develop. These issues will be explored in further detail as you continue through this unit.

You may wish to return to this section to remind yourself of the nature of the competitive dynamics that exist in any market structure. It is through understanding these dynamics that you can analyse how different market structures evolve, how organisations operate within these market structures and the relationship between market structure and organisation behaviour.

SECTION 2

Factors Influencing Market Structure

Introduction

It was stated in Section 1 that changes in market structure are caused by changes in an organisation's external environment in what are termed the macro and micro variables. In this section we will look at how changes in these variables impact upon the market structure.

The aim of this section is to help you to:

- identify the main macro-economic variables
- appreciate the effect of macro-economic changes on the structure of the market
- apply Porter's Five-Forces Model.

2.1 Macro factors

ECONOMIC

The economic factors that can impact upon market structures include the following elements:

- inflation
- unemployment
- economic growth
- interest rates
- exchange rates

The level of inflation in an economy influences the cost base of suppliers and the spending power of buyers. Traditionally, in an inflationary period wage rises in line with, or exceeding, inflation are likely to be met. It is also possible that efficiency may not be closely monitored due to buoyant market demand. UK manufacturing organisations in the 1970s, experienced declining home and export demand, and increased threats from imports as their competitiveness declined through inflation and poor efficiency. The industries where this was most apparent were those manufacturing televisions, cameras, hi-fi's and motorbikes. The impact of aggressive export strategies, particularly from Japanese manufacturers, radically changed the traditional market structures that were in place. New distribution channels were organised in advance of the market being entered. Many UK manufacturing organisations closed down.

Similarly, economic growth, interest rates and unemployment will impact upon the market behaviour of firms. In the 1990s, while economic growth of 3% is being achieved, this is being driven by UK export activity. The spending power of UK consumers is relatively low and this has affected retail spending and the level of house purchases. Estate agents have seen radical changes in market structure, with banks, building societies and solicitors all taking on estate agency functions in the boom years of the 1980s and then selling them off/closing down unprofitable agencies in the 1990s.

ACTIVITY 6

Select a current newspaper story from the quality press that indicates the link between economic change and its impact upon the structure of the market. Outline the nature of the change and the reasons why the existing market structure has changed.

Traditionally, manufacturers of branded goods used television as the main media for building brand awareness and image. In recent years television air-time for advertisers has become prohibitively expensive for all but a handful of leading brands. Heinz has recently diverted a large amount of its brand promotion from television advertising to direct mail. A major economic factor behind this decision is the effect the UK recession is having on demand for branded products. This is compounded by consumers becoming more aware and questioning traditional brand values. Budgets are being diverted to more 'cost-effective media', such as radio and posters. The market structure is changing in response to this demand, with, for example, the recent growth in radio stations. Economic pressures may yet force the BBC to accept advertising.

LEGAL
The legal and regulatory framework surrounding UK business has a significant impact upon market structure. Two examples of this are the brewery market and the ownership of media. In 1993 large brewers were forced to sell up to 50% of their tied houses because their market dominance was regarded as uncompetitive practice. This enabled smaller brewers to acquire outlets to sell their beer or deal direct with free houses. Similarly, within the media market, no company is allowed to control more than 25% of all television stations in the UK. This regulation ensures that ownership will remain competitive to the benefit of advertisers and the consumer.

ACTIVITY 7

Consider the impact of the recent legislation that allows Sunday trading. What impact has this legislation had on the structure of the retail market?

The changes in Sunday trading laws have enabled major stores to open seven days a week. The problem with the law is that many retailers in town centres are not benefiting from this. The major benefits are accruing to the out-of-town shopping centres. Many town centres remain deserted and offer no encouragement for retailers to open. The outcome of this process is that many smaller retail outlets are closing, resulting in increased retailer concentration in the hands of a few major national retailers.

TECHNOLOGICAL

The impact of technology is now regarded as one of the dominant forces creating structural change within markets. The 'information superhighway', which enables messages and transactions to be carried in minutes to virtually anywhere in the world, is expected to transform distribution systems. An obvious example of this is the development of home shopping. Consumers will be able to do their shopping globally, via modems connected to TV screens.

Wal Mart, a large American convenience store, operates its global stock control system via satellite. All stock flows are monitored and the information fed back to a central location in America. This has given Wal Mart a competitive advantage, not just at a local level, but also internationally through its efficient management of stock levels.

Manufacturing systems have also been transformed. Mass production has been replaced by flexible manufacturing systems. Customisation of products is now made possible through technological change. This will impact upon the way in which organisations service their customers needs and will increase the opportunity for marketing direct to the customer.

ACTIVITY 8

1 Why have organisations such as First Direct and Direct Line insurance been so successful?

2 What impact have these organisations had on the existing market structures for banking and insurance?

3 How have existing organisations in these markets reacted?

First Direct banking and Direct Line insurance have transformed the way in which consumers are able to bank and buy insurance. The traditional high street banks offer many outlets but limited opening hours. Compared with First Direct they employ many staff and are therefore less efficient. First Direct operate from one head office, offering 24-hour banking, and an improved and more convenient service. It is likely that many traditional high street banks will gradually disappear as competition forces closure and the adoption of similar direct-banking techniques. High-street insurance brokers are also under threat from 'direct insurance' organisations, which do not carry the overheads of the traditional insurance broker. The changes in market structure and distribution methods have been made possible through the development of new technology.

SOCIAL

Consumer spending patterns are changing as traditional values and needs change. The desire to own property and luxury goods is a direct response to the increased affluence generally felt by the population. Working patterns are changing and families are benefiting from increased leisure time. Household and family structures are changing. These forces are creating fewer mass markets and more fragmented markets. These markets require different, more precise and more flexible approaches to marketing. An example of this is in the holiday market, which has recently seen growth in specialist holiday agents and direct sellers. These new agents offer packages designed to the customer's requirements, as opposed to the traditional package holiday.

ACTIVITY 9

1 Write down what you believe to be the key social forces that are enabling large-out-of town shopping complexes to be developed.

2 What impact does this change have on town shopping centres?

ENVIRONMENTAL

Environmental issues are also impacting upon markets. New entrants who have adopted an environmental position are challenging traditional organisations and the relationship these organisations have with their consumer. Many consumers are now interested in the ethics and values of those companies from whom they buy products. This has created major new opportunities and changes in the market.

The key social forces influencing the development of out-of-town shopping complexes include such factors as the increased use of the car, a reduction in the time available time for shopping, increase in home ownership and DIY and the changing nature of food consumption (including an increase in the use of ready-made and frozen foods). Consumers in the 1990s desire convenience and speed.

2.2 Micro factors

COMPETITIVE FORCES

In considering the nature of competitiveness within a market structure, various forms of structure, from monopoly to perfect competition, were identified. These structures do not identify fully the underlying forces that create change within markets, however. Michael Porter's 'Five-Forces Model', referred to in Units 2 and 4, is helpful in this regard.

The strategies adopted by organisations operating in these markets is determined by their relative market position and the degree to which they can sustain competitive advantage in the long run. The impact of these five forces on an organisation's strategy is considerable. While Porter acknowledges that external macro factors do create change, he argues that it is the five underlying forces that are affected by these changes. It is the resultant changes in these underlying forces that will affect the competitiveness and attractiveness of a particular market.

An example of how Porter's Five-Forces Model can be used to analyse and assess market behaviour is shown below.

PHARMACEUTICAL INDUSTRY

The bargaining power of suppliers

Traditionally, drug manufacturers have been able to obtain patent protection for product innovations. As no alternatives existed for their products, the companies could obtain and maintain profit margins. The bargaining power of these suppliers was high.

The bargaining power of buyers

Buyers had a limited choice of available drugs. Buying centres were not concentrated. The negotiating power of these buyers was therefore weak.

Threat of new entrants

Because of the high investment costs involved in R&D and the patent protections held on existing drugs, new entrants were discouraged from entering this market, which further reinforced the power of suppliers.

Threat of substitute products

While there was a threat of substitute products, the time delay that was involved in developing, testing and obtaining authorisation for a new drug was so long that the costs and risks outweighed the benefits.

Level of competitor activity

The level of competitor activity was limited to that between two and three major drugs manufacturers. This ensured that their market dominance was maintained and allowed them control of the distribution channels. These companies could behave like oligopolies.

Changes to the five forces

Recently, the market structure within the drugs market has been altered by two external macro variables that have changed the nature of the five forces operating in the industry:

1   The change in law that allowed buyers to purchase generic versions of established and previously protected drugs.

2   The change in structure of the health service (the internal market), resulting in increased negotiating power, more proactive purchase behaviour and a focus on budgets.

Drugs manufacturers face a more competitive market place, with several **new entrants** supplying generic (substitute) products. New buying points, with increased **buyer negotiating power,** were established. The traditional relationships and distribution methods of the drugs manufacturers were no longer appropriate for the new market structure. In response, drugs manufacturers have had to adopt closer relationships with their customers, meet their needs more effectively through improved supply contracts, and develop keener pricing strategies, service levels and faster product development cycles.

ACTIVITY 10

Using the framework of Porter's Five Forces model adopted above, identify the changes in market structure that have occurred in the UK food retail market over the last five years. Try and answer the following questions:

1 What changes are there in the macro-environment?

2 In what ways do these changes affect the underlying five forces?

3 What is your prediction for the future market structure?

In particular, consider:

● the growth of supermarkets

● decline of corner stores

● overseas discounters

● warehouse clubs

● wholesalers.

Changes in the macro-environment have affected the five forces, as follows:

Threat of new entrants

In recent years several European and American discounters have entered the UK food retail market, resulting in a major change in the industry's market structure. These new entrants have led to increased competitive activity, reduced profit margins and loss of market share by the major multiple retailers. In response to this, the multiples are developing new strategies, including acquisition of smaller food retail chains and the introduction of loyalty schemes.

Power of buyers

Multiple retailers have, through their dominance of the food retail market, attained considerable power over suppliers. The result of this is seen in part with the growth of own-brand labels and the introduction of new products that would traditionally have been supplied by brand manufacturers. This dominance has only partially been reduced by the new entrants to the UK market. Many of these discounters sell own-brand or European branded produce and their total share of the food retail market is still low. UK multiple retailers are developing more aggressive marketing strategies to maintain/increase their market share and it is likely that their dominance of the food retail scene in terms of buying power is likely to remain strong, despite the threat of new entrants referred to above.

Power of suppliers

In contrast to the power of buyers, supplier power has been considerably reduced as reliance on the key multiple retail outlets for custom and their increasing skills in marketing their own-brand label have weakened the suppliers' position. In conjunction with this, consumer awareness of the value for money and quality of own-brands, compared with branded products, has increased. Manufacturers who do not offer strongly differentiated added-value brands that consumers still demand, face delisting. Brand manufacturers have responded by discounting their brand, investing in brand support (ie advertising) or developing closer partnerships with retailers. All of these represent a considerable risk and a challenge to suppliers whose volume sales traditionally have been achieved through access to the multiple retail outlets.

Threat of substitute products

This represents a negligible threat and is unlikely to impact upon the market structure or behaviour of organisations in the market. Substitute channels of distribution (such as home shopping) may in the future create change, as increased awareness of, access to and usage of mutimedia technology occurs.

Competitor activity

As referred to above, competitive activity in the UK food retail market has increased considerably as multiple retailers pursued major growth strategies in the 1980s and the high profit margins earned attracted overseas discounters. The result is intense competitive activity in the 1990s, and the possibility of a reduction in the number of competitors operating in this market due to poor financial returns.

REVIEW ACTIVITY 2

1 Read through the business pages of one of the quality newspapers or business magazines and pick out evidence to show how macro- and micro-environmental forces are impacting upon a market and influencing an organisation's behaviour.

2 For your chosen market, outline broadly how the five forces Porter identifies are impacting upon the market structure.

Summary

In this section it was shown that changes that occur in the external macro- and micro-environment can have a significant impact on the market structure. Changes in the macro-environment create forces that require new methods of manufacture or distribution. Examples were given of the impact of changes in the SLEPT factors.

The changes in the micro-environment were also discussed, using Michael Porter's Five-Forces Model. This model suggests that changes in market structure, and therefore the competitive nature of the industry, are a direct result of changes in any one of the five forces. These changes impact upon the market structure through new entrants coming into the market, new products being introduced or a change in the buyer-supplier relationship. Analysis of the likely changes in the five forces is important for organisations. Many organisations face the threat of closure through not monitoring this competitive environment more thoroughly.

It is important to remember how difficult, if not impossible, it is to control these external factors in an organisation's environment. The development of environmental monitoring and marketing planning are essential aspects of an organisation's operations which may limit the impact of these changes. You will have seen in this section the need for organisations continually to try and manage the process of change in order to gain some element of control over supply, distribution or negotiation of contracts.

The next section considers in more detail the changing nature of distribution and its impact on channel relationships.

SECTION 3

The Implications of a Changing Market Structure for Channel Relationships

Introduction

This section looks at the implications of the current changes in market structure on the relationships between distribution channel members. Several issues are affecting these relationships, including the impact of new technology, the growth of own-label brands and consumer and distribution trends. In response to these issues, manufacturer's are developing new strategies which will be outlined in this section.

The final part of the section will look at the whole issue of managing the supply of a product, from its beginnings as raw material, through to its purchase and use by the end consumer. This is termed supply-chain management and represents a major shift in thinking about the relationships that exists at each phase of the supply chain.

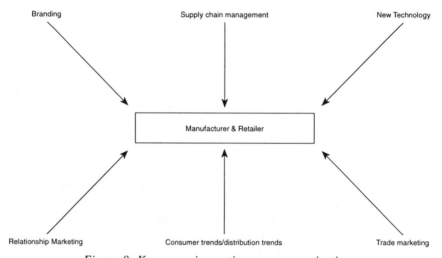

Figure 8: Key areas impacting upon organisations

Figure 8 shows the key factors and trends now impacting upon the manufacturer-retailer relationship. These factors will be outlined in this section.

> Today the product is an experience – as customers use it, they grow to trust it – and distribution represents the beginning of that evolving relationship. That's why computer companies donate their systems to junior schools. Schools are

now a distribution system for product experience.

(McKenna, 1991)

The above quotation puts the distribution system at the heart of the relationship an organisation forges with its customers. In the past the importance of distribution has not been fully recognised as a means of gaining competitive advantage. The previous sections have underlined the importance of change and its impact at all stages of the distribution process.

The impact of changes in market structure and the corresponding effects on competitiveness has now focused attention on the management of distribution channel relationships. Those companies that most successfully manage these relationships will establish competitive superiority.

The aim of this section is to help you to:

- become aware of the changes that are currently affecting the retail trade
- become aware of the developments taking place in trade marketing
- appreciate the developments in 'relationship marketing' currently taking place
- identify ways in which the new technology is likely to impact on channel relations
- appreciate the different techniques of supply-chain management.

3.1 The importance of branding

Recent years have seen an increase in the growth of own-label brands at the expense of manufacturing brands. In 1971, own-label accounted for a fifth of all UK grocery sales, whereas by 1992 it accounted for a third. (AGB Superpanel, June 1992). Five years ago retailer brands were regarded as inferior in quality to branded products. Today nobody would dispute that Marks & Spencer, Sainsbury, Tesco, Waitrose and Kwik Save have all, to varying degrees, successfully achieved brand status. Very few people subscribe to the view that own-label brands are only purchased because they are cheaper, or that consumers trade off quality for price. Some retailers are now developing brand categories within the own-label umbrella. Sainsbury's Novon was succesfully launched into the washing detergent market sector.

Manufacturers have traditionally been the 'marketing experts' when developing, launching and managing products. This mantle has now moved over to retailers, who have adopted classic marketing techniques. Quality, service and value for money are consistent throughout every location and these values are communicated clearly to the consumer.

THE MANUFACTURERS' RESPONSE
While certain brand categories have been taken over by own-brand labels, others have managed to survive. The branded washing detergent market has, in recent

years, come under increasing threat from retailer brands. The major brands have withstood this onslaught and maintained shelf presence in the major retailers. A major factor behind this success is the investment that goes into the brands. Brands are an asset and, like any asset, if investment is reduced the asset's value will depreciate. In this instance, improved product formulations, heavy television exposure and aggressive sales promotions ensured consumer loyalty.

ACTIVITY 11

While watching commercial television, note the number of adverts you see for 'fast moving consumer goods' (FMCG), as opposed to other product categories.

1   What types of brands are being advertised?

2   Are they established FMCG brands?

3   Why do you think so few branded products appear in this medium now?

Buitoni adopted an alternative strategy when launching a new brand of pasta. Instead of using traditional brand-building marketing techniques, the company developed a direct-marketing campaign targeted at specific market segments. Consumers were communicated with directly and informed of the brand, plus an opportunity to join the Buitoni pasta club. The key to this strategy lay in the company's database and knowledge of its consumers.

Evidence exists to show that consumers are still purchasing brands that offer higher quality, or which accurately meet emotional needs. The critical relationship between the brand and the consumer must be maintained through improved quality and consistent values. The brand must differentiate itself from other products, including 'me to' look-a-likes. Brands with nothing special to offer will be delisted.

While this is encouraging news for brands, it is unlikely that all but the leading brands in a category can continue to advertise 'above the line'. In recent years, media costs have risen at a faster rate than inflation and audiences are becoming difficult to reach. Better targeting and understanding of consumers, and closer relationships with distributors may be an alternative strategy.

ACTIVITY 12

Read the article on Heinz in the Resource Section (Item 9.4). What are the reasons for this brand to move its marketing spend from 'above the line' (advertising) to 'below the line' (sales promotion, direct mail)?

The reasons for Heinz' move from 'above the line' to 'below the line' activity is a strategic response to the growing power of the large supermarket groups and the need for more targeted communication techniques. Direct marketing under the current market conditions offers the most cost-effective solution for maintaining loyalty to the brand.

3.2 Trade marketing

In retail markets these days the ability of the manufacturers to differentiate brands and ensure distribution is limited by market forces, such as over-supply, technology and market saturation. Distribution is critical to a brand's success. The need for better understanding between retailers and branded manufacturers has never been so important.

Trade marketing is the development of long-term marketing strategies, that focus on delivering outstanding customer service to retailers and wholesalers in order to build and maintain strong and profitable brands.

The development of long-term strategies that focus on distribution channel intermediaries is a significant new development in the retail sector. While the consumer must still be directly communicated with if brand values are to be maintained, the increased power of intermediaries requires that their interests must also be served to avoid the question 'who needs brands?'.

Three key criteria must be met if trade marketing strategies are to work effectively:

1 The key to developing effective trade marketing strategies is to meet the needs of the trade more effectively. If the interests of the channel intermediaries can be met, even at the expense of short-term profit, then the brand's shelf-life is likely to be longer. This creates a dilemma for brand manufacturers since lower short-term profits could mean reduced marketing budgets and therefore reduced investment in the brand. This self-defeating cycle has to be avoided by manufacturers since weak brands will be increasingly delisted by multiple retailers.

2   The key to developing effective trade marketing strategies is to work in partnership with key intermediaries (such as manufacturers, wholesalers and retailers). This can involve joint product development and category management to ensure that the portfolio of brands and own brands is appropriate to a particular outlet.

3   The key to developing effective trade marketing strategies is to adopt a long-term, open and trusting relationship with the intermediaries. Short-termism usually only satisfies one party. Closed relationships suggest fear and conflicting objectives. Lack of trust will ensure traditional relationships continue to dominate the distribution channel.

Achieving effective trade marketing strategies will involve major reorganisation of the traditional marketing functions and a change in organisation culture. Trade marketing strategies represent a radical new approach to the management of brand distribution.

ACTIVITY 13

Read the article 'Managing by our Shelves' (Resource Item 9.5).

1   Identify the key issues in this article that relate to trade marketing and category management.

2   How are the brand manufacturers responding?

3   What are the key implications?

The article identifies the growing importance of trade marketing to brand manufacturers, who traditionally focused their attention on selling more product to the consumer through advertising and brand improvements/extensions. The article suggests that brand manufacturers now need to focus on the whole brand category, not just their brand, and develop marketing strategies that take into account their customer (the retailer) and not just the consumer.

The article refers to the changes occurring in the retailing sector as the 'realities of the retail environment'. Retailers are after increasing sales across a brand category, not just a manufacturer's brand. They require a range of brand choices for the consumer, offering value for money to premium brands. No single brand can now cover this range of consumer needs.

Retailers are now determining through their own research the nature of the brand categories they wish to stock. By focusing more attention on the key retail accounts, meeting their needs and servicing their needs, brand manufacturers are able to maintain their brands in these key retail outlets. If a manufacturer can develop a close long-term relationship with a retailer so that they can work together to determine how a particular product category should be developed, then it is also harder for competitors to gain entry to the customer. The outcome of this development is that the multiple retailers now have a range of different 'preferred' suppliers. The implications for the internal organisation of brand manufacturers who follow this strategy are many. The relationship between sales and account managers, marketing and finance managers, will require a change in a company's culture and philosophy to ensure the manufacturer is able to deliver the level and consistency of service required.

3.3 Relationship marketing

The focal point of marketing attention is constantly shifting, and during the early 1990s a new paradigm has emerged which suggests that traditional transactional marketing is out-dated (focusing on selling the product, but not on the ongoing relationship before and after the product has been sold) and inappropriate for the marketing environment of today. Relationship marketing is proposed as an alternative approach to meeting customer needs more effectively. (Payne & Ballantyne, 1991)

The premise upon which relationship marketing is based is that customers, at whatever point in the supply chain, will benefit from adopting strategies that focus on partnerships, customer care and two-way communication. Rather than casual, unplanned relationships, organisations are moving to casual, planned relationships. A brand manufacturer can develop relationship marketing strategies with wholesalers, retailers and the consumer.

The problems that brand manufacturers are currently facing may derive from this lack of relationship planning.

1 Retailers have achieved a position in consumers' minds of reliability, consistency, value for money and service; values which many brand manufacturers have lost.

2 Manufacturers are disadvantaged. They do not actually meet the consumer. Relationships are therefore harder to build.

3 Retailer dominance in the supply chain means that achieving meaningful relationships is more difficult than if equal power existed.

Manufacturers often pursue a brand-building exercise, when a relationship marketing strategy would be more appropriate. The improvements now available in technology mean that sophisticated database and targeting systems can be developed, thus enabling customer needs to be serviced more directly and effectively. The relationship can be managed. This provides opportunities for improved loyalty, more frequent purchasing and cross-selling of products.

ACTIVITY 14

Consider the relationship that you have with your bank.

1 What type of relationship is it?

2 How well do they know you?

3 When do they communicate with you?

4 Do you feel a high degree of loyalty to your bank?

5 What type of relationship would you like to have with your bank?

Many retail high street banks have been crtiticised in recent years because of their focus on selling their product, rather than on building relationships with their customer base. The type of relationship most customers have is a mail shot through the door, a monthly statement with which there are more mail shots. Very little two-way communication occurs, except that initiated by the customer. Despite extensive databases, banks do not know most of their customers very well. Large sums of money are spent on attracting new customers but limited time is spent on getting existing customers to purchase more of the bank's products. Banks tend to communicate with you for reasons other than to develop a better long-term relationship. Many consumers feel little loyalty to their bank, and often express dissatisfaction with the service they receive. You as an individual can answer the final question. Maybe it is one your bank should actually ask you.

ACTIVITY 15

Read the extract 'First to the phone' (Resource Item 9.6) and answer the questions below.

1 Why has First Direct as a brand been so successful?

2 Is this relationship marketing? Why?

First Direct as a brand has established itself very quickly as an alternative way of banking for many consumers. The way in which the service is delivered, the service availability, the use of information technology, the quality and level of service, all combine to create a powerful brand proposition that provides a range of benefits to the consumer. Consumers are made to feel that they are important. Staff are carefully selected and trained to ensure that the appropriate level of service is given. Many new customers come by recommendation.

First Direct is further down the road than competitive high street banks in terms of developing long-term relationships with its customers. The database lies at the heart of First Direct operations, and all customer information across product categories is held together so that an instant picture of a customer profile can be developed. The customer has indicated a high degree of satisfaction with the level of service offered. However, First Direct still needs to establish a method by which it becomes a partner and trusted adviser to the customer in controlling its financial affairs. First Direct still has further to go if it wishes to develop a fully fledged relationship with its customers.

3.4 The effect of new technology on channel relationships

The face of marketing has been changed by the advent of new technology. More information on people, multi-media applications, and improved management of marketing functions are just three areas that the IT revolution is influencing.

These technological innovations are changing the way marketers think about and deal with their customers. No longer will customers be largely unseen and unknown. At all levels in the supply chain customers will become individuals, each known by name.

The speed and effectiveness by which a customer's requirements can be serviced, is improving dramatically. The pace of change means that competitive advantage is shortlived, as other organisations introduce new technology. The use of technology is the tool by which marketers can manage the new relationships required by customers. How well that relationship is managed will be the true differentiator in the future. Those organisations that shy away from meeting the challenge of new technology may well founder.

The example of First Direct shows the impact new technology can have on existing market structures and channel relationships. Similarly, catalogue companies are able to target over 20 million consumers held on their database, and monitor purchase profiles. At a local level, home shopping is being piloted in the UK using cable technology. Complete distribution systems are able to be controlled by satellite dish, enabling more efficient and effective management of marketing logistics. The sales representative now visits the customers with a lap-top computer as the major sales aid.

Trade marketers can use new technology in order to arrive at the most profitable solutions for both manufacturer and retailer. Models of ideal store layout and location can be developed using this technology. Software packages that combine merchandising data, consumer data and financial data can plot the most effective positioning of brand categories in the store and monitor shelf performance.

Retailers now use electronic point-of-sale systems (EPOS), which enable data on sales and stock to be gathered and analysed rapidly. Stock ordering and transfer can be carried out automatically. Alongside this, some stores are now introducing scanners in store to track shopping patterns. This data can be matched with EPOS data, building an increased understanding of consumer behaviour.

New technology provides new opportunities that will transform the way in which distribution relationships are currently managed.

ACTIVITY 16

Consider the ways in which new technology might impact upon the manufacturer-distributor relationship. What implications does this have for both brand manufacturers and multiple retailers?

New technology lies at the heart of future developments in relationships between manufacturers and distributors. The major areas in which new technology will influence this relationship is in the availability of product and market information, control of the logistics of distribution, and in manufacturing processes, customer knowledge, marketing communication, sales force management and function and financial management. Data on all these areas is available, but the critical issue is how it will be used. It is probably fair to say that those companies that integrate the use of information technology most effectively into their marketing planning, implementation and control will gain a competitive advantage over other suppliers.

3.5 The development of supply-chain management

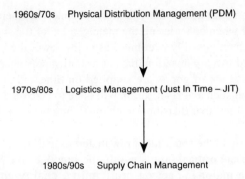

1960s/70s   Physical Distribution Management (PDM)

1970s/80s   Logistics Management (Just In Time – JIT)

1980s/90s   Supply Chain Management

Figure 9: The evolution of distribution management

The concept of supply chain management has evolved from two earlier ideas, as is demonstrated by Figure 9.

PHYSICAL DISTRIBUTION MANAGEMENT (PDM)

This term implies the physical movement of goods by treating stock management, warehousing, order processing and delivery as related rather than separate activities. It is essentially about the management of finished goods, not about the supply of raw materials prior to manufacture.

LOGISTICS MANAGEMENT

Logistics combines PDM with the allied concept of materials management. Essentially, this focuses on the process of managing the movement and storage of materials, parts and finished inventory from suppliers through the firm and on to customers. Transport and warehousing are therefore integral elements of the process. Information flows also become an important element within the system.

The Just in Time (JIT) philosophy is a relatively recent development of logistics management. It aims to make the process as efficent and flexible as possible. JIT represents the practical limits that can be achieved with current resources in terms of material supply and customer service.

SUPPLY CHAIN MANAGEMENT

Neither of the above systems looks at the management of the total supply chain. The supply chain is a shorthand term for the connected series of activities that deal with planning, coordinating and controlling materials, parts and finished goods from suppliers to customers, with payment and information as reverse flows. Effective management of the supply chain is seen as a strategy to ensure retailer custom/loyalty. The most important aspect of supply-chain management is not, however, the relationship with suppliers and buyers, although this is important, but how the end consumer is serviced by the total system. The two major principles that guide supply-chain management are:

● the reduction of total supply-chain cost

● maximising the opportunity for customer purchase.

Whether a distribution system has many or a few channel members, and is long or short, is not the issue when considering the management of the supply chain. The management of the chain possibly becomes easier the fewer the number of levels and members involved. An organisation that has a short supply chain, however, still has to ensure that its stock of goods are supplied on time and at the appropriate quality. It is likely that such an organisation will have to take on the functions that traditionally belonged to other distribution channel members.

This applies particularly to the sourcing of raw materials and stock holding, because these two areas represent critical points within the supply chain. Sourcing of raw materials can have a major impact on profitability, quality and reliability of delivery. Global sourcing of supplies and location of factories near such supplies is a key strategy for many multinational/global companies.

Stockholding is now a critical part of a company's competitiveness and profitability. JIT techniques rely on efficient and effective stockholding. The need for large stocks and lead times is diminished through the introduction of flexible manufacturing techniques. The traditional need for warehousing has now diminished.

Marks & Spencer does not own any component in its supply chain except its stores. It does, however, use legitimate and referent power in order to make the supply chain work. When buying in vegetable products for their stores, technologists visit various countries in the world and select growers and suppliers. Quality standards are strictly enforced. This ensures consistency of supply all year round.

ACTIVITY 17

From the above summary, list the key criteria that should be included in an effective supply-chain management system.

The key criteria that should be included in an effective supply-chain management system are a continuous focus on the distribution needs of each user in the supply chain and an effective planning and control and communication system that encompases the entire logistics system. Information technology is an integral part of this system because it can monitor the efficiency and effectiveness of the supply chain and be used as the central controlling mechanism of the total system.

REVIEW ACTIVITY 5

Read the article 'Time to shed a little tier or two' (Resource Item 9.4) and answer the questions below.

1 What are the key issues outlined in the article that are forcing brand manufacturers to revise their marketing strategies?

2 What responses does the article suggest manufacturers should make to ensure they maintain their presence on the shelves of the multiple retailer of the future?

(A possible answer to this activity is given at the end of the unit.)

REVIEW ACTIVITY 6

Read the article a 'Jungle Full of Strange Bedfellows' (Resource Item 9.5) and answer the questions below.

1 What does the term 'virtual company', referred to in the article, mean?

2 What are the factors identified in the article that are critical to the success of a manufacturer effectively competing in today's markets.

(A possible answer to this activity is given at the end of the unit.)

Summary

This section has outlined the development of new strategies and relationships between members of a distribution channel that have come about as a result of forces that impact upon and change the existing market structures. There is no single factor that dominates the changing nature of relationships. The issues of branding, new technology, changing market and consumer trends all impact concurrently upon the existing market structures and relationships.

The need to develop new strategies has been outlined in this section. Of equal importance is the need to manage the total supply chain to ensure that the end consumer's needs are met satisfactorily. This section has shown that major changes are occurring in many markets and that traditional relationships, organisation structures and cultures, attitudes and strategies are no longer appropriate. This trend is expected to continue as markets become more competitive and customers and consumers more demanding in the future.

Unit summary

This unit has introduced you to the types of market structures that now exist in a variety of market sectors, and the nature of the channel structures and relationships that exist within these markets. The unit has focused on the changing nature of market structures and on the impact such change is having on channel behaviour. Traditional market structures are being radically changed, particularly through new entrants into the market place changing consumer preferences and technology. Many of these forces of change were identified throughout the first part of the unit. The new market structures that have evolved from this process were then analysed, with various examples selected to demonstrate the nature and impact of the changes that have occurred.

From this, the implications for channel relationships between retailers, wholesalers and manufacturers was considered. The traditional relationships that were an established part of the traditional market structures and conditions, focused very much on conflict and mistrust. Mass advertising and brand building were the common strategies adopted by brand manufacturers. Traditionally, power lay in the hands of the manufacturer or wholesalers, and such strategies worked. As new market structures evolved, the balance of power shifted away from the manufacturer. The outcome of this change in the grocery sector was the growth of own-label brands at the expense of manufacturer brands.

The unit outlined the increasing recognition by manufacturers, wholesalers and retailers that conflict and mistrust were not the most effective way of managing channel relationships in the 1990s. Problems of oversupply, falling profit margins, increased retail competition and changing consumer preferences, all pointed to the need for a new approach. The unit assessed the implications for the new approach, based on partnership and trust. Exploitation of new technology, improved supply chain management and relationship marketing were some of the responses to the new climate that were identified and explored.

Throughout the unit, a range of unit and review activities were developed to illustrate the changes that were occurring and to reinforce your understanding of the critical issues.

References

AGB Superpanel, June 1992

Chernatony & McDonald (1993) *Creating Powerful Brands,* Butterworth-Heineman

Christopher, M (1994) 'Customer Service and Logistics Strategy', *The Marketing Book* ed M Baker, Heinemann, pp555–63

Dibb, S & Simkin, L (1994) *Marketing Concepts and Strategies,* Houghton Mifflin

Gattorna, J (1978) 'Channels of Distribution Conceptualisations: a state of the art review' *European Journal of Marketing,* vol 12, no 7, p470

Keynote (1991) Keynote Publications, Hampton Middx, 10th edn

McKenna R (1991) 'Marketing in an age of diversity', *Harvard Business Review,* no 66, pp88–94

Christopher, M, Payne, A & Ballantyne, D (1993) *Relationship Marketing: Bringing Quality, Customer Service and Marketing Together,* Butterworth-Heinemann

Porter, M (1985) *Competitive Advantage,* New York Free Press

Randall, G (1994) *The Partnership between Manufacturers, Brands and Retailers,* Marketing Series, Butterworth-Heinemann

Rosenbloom, B (1990) Marketing Channels, Drayden Press, Florida, 4th edn

Wilson, R M S, Gilligan, C & Pearson, D (1993) *Strategic Marketing Management,* Butterworth-Heinemann,

Further Reading

Randall, G (1994) *Trade Marketing Strategies,* Heinemann

Davies, G (1993) *Trade Marketing Strategy,* Paul Chapman Publishing 1993

Chernatony & Mcdonald (1993)

M Baker (ed) (1994) *The Marketing Book,* Heinemann

Christopher, M, Payne, A & Ballantyne, D (1993) *Relationship Marketing: Bringing Quality, Customer Service and Marketing Together,* Butterworth-Heinemann

Dibb, S & Simkin, L (1994) *Marketing Concepts and Strategies,* Houghton Mifflin

Doyle, P (1994) *Marketing Management Strategy,* Prentice Hall

Zikmund & d'Amico (1994) *Effective Marketing – Creating and Keeping Customers,* West Publishing, Chapters 10, 11, 12 & 13

Wilson, I (1994) *Marketing Interfaces,* Pitman

Palmer, A *Principles of Service Marketing,* McGraw Hill 1994

Wilson, R M S, Gilligan, C & Pearson, D (1993) *Strategic Marketing Management,* Butterworth-Heinemann, p84

Kotler, P (1989) *Principles of Marketing,* Prentice Hall

Porter, M (1985) *Competitive Advantage,* New York Free Press

Answers to Review Activities

Review Activity 3

1   The changes in market structure in the food retailing business include a new generation of discount stores: Costco, Cargo Club, warehouse clubs, etc. Superstore expansion is slowing down. Manufacturers are increasingly becoming multinational.

The impact on behaviour results in the following:

Supermarkets adopt 'price-busting' value range, everyday low pricing, staff reductions, brand delisting, increase in own-label exclusive brands, the introduction of copycat brands.

Manufacturers pay listing allowances, adopt product category management to maximise the 'efficiency' of their shelf space. They concentrate on product differentiation and innovation.

2   'Listing allowance' means a payment demanded by a retailer to be paid by a
     brand manufacturer as part of the negotiated agreement to stock a brand. Such
     allowances are often denied, but the article suggests that the practice is
     common. The justification for such a payment is that it shows a sign of
     commitment on the part of the manufacturer. It is also argued that the offer of
     such a payment does not guarantee a brand shelf space. The brand has to meet
     commercially based buying criteria before it will be stocked.

3   The relationship between the branded manufacturer and the major food retailers
     would appear to be one of conflict and power. The article indicates, however,
     that because of changing market structures and a recognition that manufacturers
     and major food retailers need each other, some steps towards a partnership
     approach are beginning to evolve.

4   Those brands that do not sell 'off the shelves' quickly enough are under threat
     of delisting, irrespective of the size of the brand. Product range extensions are
     more vulnerable, particularly if they do not sell more of the total product
     range as a result of the additions. Products that offer little in terms of genuine
     differentiation, such as crisps, nuts, snacks and dog food, are also under threat.
     Number three or four brands within a product category are also threatened to
     be delisted by major supermarkets.

Brand leaders within product categories such as Lever Brothers, Procter & Gamble,
Heinz and Mars are least under threat of being delisted. Products need to be
different and innovative now to secure a listing.

5   Own-label penetration – source verdict research.

Sainsbury's	65%
Tesco	50%
Asda	25%
Safeway	40%
Gateway	18%
Kwik Save	5%
Iceland	65%

This trend is likely to continue, but only marginally, particularly those stores that
already have high own-label penetration. Stores such as Asda and Kwik Save are
likely to increase penetration substantially. The key question is how far this process
will go. The article suggests a growing recognition on the part of retailers that they
need manufacturer brands that add value to the category. Also, it may not be in the
retailers' interest to weaken manufacturer brands because of the implications for
further R&D. It is probably of as much value to work more closely in developing
product categories offering manufacturer and own-label brands to maximise the
profitability within each product category.

6   Britvic confirms the point made above, that retailers may be 'biting the hand
     that feeds it'. Less product innovation and development may occur if brand
     manufacturers' marketing capabilities are weakened.

Review Activity 4

1

MACRO FACTORS
Technological change: communications, distribution and information capability
Social change: changing leisure and media consumption patterns. An increasing
need for 24-hour, up-to-the-minute broadcast news coverage.

Economic change: government philosophy of encouraging competition and market
forces, rather than directly controlling the economy.

MICRO FACTORS
Retailer outlets: high proportion of small CTNs. Limited power. No dominant
retail chains, as in the grocery market.

Newspaper publications are predominantly owned by two owners, but each
publication is targeted and positioned at specific market segments to differentiate
the product. Highly competitive market place, increasingly price driven. Two
dominant wholesalers who control the distribution channel. Newspaper sales in
decline.

2   The market structure has changed dramatically, with the number of small
    wholesalers falling from 2000 to 200 in the space of three years. There have
    been limited joint ventures or vertical integration, growth of the two major
    wholesalers occurring organically. The newspaper publishers have seen their
    power base eroded at the expense of the two major wholesales, and unlike the
    grocery retail system, no dominant retailers have emerged. The retailers
    therefore have no power over the distribution channel.

3   W H Smith Wholesale has established itself as the dominant member of this
    distribution channel. Newspaper publishers have tried to circumvent the
    wholesaler channel, but found this unprofitable. By providing an efficient and
    effective service to both newspaper publishers and retailers, W H Smith has
    been able to maintain its dominant position. By maximising sales and
    minimising returns of newspapers to the publishers, and providing market
    information and guidance to the retailers, W H Smith wholesale has secured a
    competitive advantage that benefits the total distribution channel.

4   The relationship that exists between W H Smith Wholesale and its suppliers and
    customers is one of partnership, openness and support. Their services add
    value to the total distribution channel. This relationship has replaced the
    traditional conflict relationships that exist under the former market structure.

Review Activity 5

Key issues that are forcing brand manufacturers to revise their marketing strategies are:

- changing consumer preferences
- severe over-capacity
- increasing retailer power and growth
- new competition from international players
- media inflation
- cost of maintaining brands
- dilution of brand values through too many brand extensions
- retailers' demands to add value not cost
- lack of profitability in brand extensions.

Manufacturers' responses suggested are are follows:

- Look for market gaps (niches) to exploit with high-margin products.
- Monitor closely consumer trends. Are they looking for products that satisfy emotional needs of 'community and identify'?
- Add value not cost to the retailers' shelves.
- Make direct product profitability the major criteria for brand support and management.
- Rationalise the product/brand portfolio.

Review Activity 6

1 The virtual company can be defined as a company that concentrates upon a key competence, which could be marketing, design or distribution, and then contracts suppliers to manufacture the product. The key to such an organisation is the control of information and the formation of close partnership with suppliers.

2 The factors identified in the article that are critical to the success of a manufacturer effectively competing in today's markets are the development of partnerships for mutual benefit, flexibility, quality of service, product and support activity. Such developments will require the sharing of information, exploitation of new technology, improved communication and a focus on profit margin, not volume.

RESOURCES

Approaches to the definition of marketing

1   The following definitions indicate a strong inclination that a producer is doing something which involves consumers as nothing more than pawns in a game, with profit for the producer as the end goal:

The planning and execution of all aspects and activities of a product so as to exert optimum influence on the consumer to result in maximum consumption at the optimum price and therefore producing the maximum long-term profit.

(Unilever, as quoted by J H Black in Institute of Marketing Paper, no. 128/1962)

The skill of selecting and fulfilling consumer desires so as to maximise the profitability per unit of capital employed in the enterprise.

(R Glasser: *Planned Marketing: Policy for business growth,* Business Publications, 1964)

The management function which organises and directs all those business activities involved in assessing and converting customer purchasing power into effective demand for a specific product or service and moving the product or service to the final consumer so as to achieve the profit target or other objectives set by the company.

(U.K. Institute of Marketing, 1966) (See also the definition from the same source listed under 8 below.)

Deciding what the customer wants; arranging to make it; distributing and selling it at the maximum profit.

(Durham University Careers Advisory Service, 1972)

2   The following are definitions which imply that the producer is doing something *for* consumers rather than *to* them, but still doing it to serve his own purpose.

Getting the right goods to the right people in the right places at the right time and the right place.

(Anon and almost timeless – a bland statement that reflects a widely held viewpoint.)

In a marketing company (as distinct from a company which has simply accepted the marketing concept), all activities – from finance to production to marketing – should be geared to profitable consumer satisfaction.

(R T Keith, Chairman of Pillsbury Co.,*US Journal of Marketing,* 1960)

The performance of those business activities that direct the flow of goods from producer to consumer or user.

(American Marketing Association, 1960)

The creation of time, place and possession utilities. Moving goods from place to place, storing them and effecting changes in ownership by buying and selling them. The activities of buying, selling, and transporting goods. Includes those business activities involved in the flow of goods and services between producers and consumers.

(P D Converse, H W Huegy and R V Mitchell, *Elements of Marketing,* Prentice-Hall, 1967)

The process of: a. Identifying customer needs, b. Conceptualising these needs in terms of an organisation's capacity to produce, c. Communicating that conceptualisation to the appropriate locus of power in the organisation. d. Conceptualising the consequent output in terms of the customer needs earlier identified. e. Communicating that conceptualisation to the customer.

(J A Howard, *Marketing Management, Operating, Strategic and Administrative,* Irwin, 1973, 3rd edn)

3   The following are definitions in which company-centeredness is evident, but there is a belief that marketing is a transaction of some kind

The economic process by means of which goods and services are exchanged and their values determined in terms of money prices.

(E A Duddy and D A Revzan, *Marketing,* McGraw-Hill, 1954, 2nd edition)

Selling is preoccupied with the seller's need to convert his product into cash; marketing with the idea of satisfying the needs of the customer by means of the product and the whole cluster of things associated with creating, delivering and finally consuming it.

(T Levitt, Marketing Myopia, *Harvard Business Review,* 1960)

The business activities involved in the transfer of goods or the acquisition of services.

(R Webster, *Dictionary of Marketing Terms, US usage,* Basle: Verlag fur Recht und Gesellschaft, 1962)

All activities intended to stimulate or serve demand.

(G A Fisk, *Marketing Systems: An introductory analysis,* Harper & Row, 1967)

Marketing perceives consumption as a democratic process in which consumers have the right to select their preferred candidates and elect them by casting their money votes.

(M J Baker, *Marketing: An introductory text,* Macmillan, 1971)

4   The following definitions see marketing as a process of social exchange:

The establishment of contact.

(P T Cherrington, *Elements of Marketing,* New York: Macmillan, 1920)

The delivery of a standard of living.

(P Mazur, Fortune Magazine, 1947)

The exchange taking place between consumer groups on the one hand and producer groups on the other.

(W Alderson, *Marketing Behaviour and Executive Action: A functionalist approach to marketing theory,* Irwin, 1957)

Those human activities directed towards the satisfaction of either a felt or latent demand for goods and services.

(R R Gist, *Marketing and Society: Text and cases,* Dryden, 1974)

The set of human activities directed at facilitating and consummating exchanges.

(P Kotler, *Marketing Management: Analysis, planning and control,* 1972, 2nd edn) (See also definition by Kotler under 8 below.)

5   In this definition marketing is seen as a naturally occurring social process:

The market concept of value, the emphasis on exchange value rather than use value, has led to a similar concept of value with regard to people and particularly oneself. The character orientation which is rooted in the experience of oneself as a commodity and of one's value as an exchange value I call the marketing orientation . . . It must be noted that these concepts (marketing orientation and four other character orientations) are 'ideal-types', not descriptions of the character of a given individual (which is) usually a blend of all or some of these orientations in which one, however, is dominant . . . The marketing orientation does not come out of the 18th or 19th centuries; it is a modern product . . . The whole principle of the marketing orientation implies easy contact, superficial attachment.

(E Fromm, *Man for Himself: An enquiry into the psychology of ethics,* Routledge & Kegan Paul, 1948)

6   The following definitions present marketing as a philosophy or a state of mind:

Marketing is not only much broader than selling, it is not a specialised activity at all. It encompasses the whole business. It is the whole business seen from the point of view of its final result, that is from the customer's point of view. Concern and responsibility for marketing must therefore permeate all areas of the enterprise.

(P F Drucker, *The Practice of Management,* Heinemann. 1955)

A point of view, a concept, a way of thinking.

(D S R Leighton, *International Marketing,* McGraw-Hill, 1967)

Adjusting the whole activity of a business to the needs of the customer or potential customer.

(B G S James, *Integrated Marketing,* Batsford, 1967)

As a business philosophy, marketing requires the firm to do what it has always set out to do – combine the resources at its disposal in the manner which will enable it to achieve its long-run profit goals. What distinguishes it from other business philosophies is that . . . (See quote by Baker under 3 above.)

7   In the following definitions marketing is seen to be complex, even confusing concept:

Marketing has been conceived and defined in a number of ways; as the distribution of products, as creation and satisfaction of demand, as flows of intangibles, as an institutional management process, as systems management, and as a social process. It is all of these.

(R Bartels, *Marketing Theory and Metatheory,* Irwin, 1970)

The enigma of marketing is that it is one of man's oldest activities and yet it is regarded as the most recent of the business disciplines.

(M J Baker, *Marketing : Theory and Practice,* Macmillan, 1976)

8   The following definitions are taken from a random selection of current sources:

Marketing is the management process responsible for identifying, anticipating and satisfying customers' requirements profitably.

(UK Chartered Institute of Marketing, 1990) (See also definition from same source listed under 1 above.)

Marketing is the process of planning and executing the conception, pricing, promotion and distribution of ideas, goods and services to create exchanges that satisfy individual and or organisational goals.

(American Marketing Association, 1988)

Marketing consists of individual and organisational activities that facilitate and expedite satisfying exchange relationships in a dynamic environment through the creation, distribution, promotion and pricing of goods, services and ideas.

(S Dibb, L Simkin, W M Pride and O C Ferrel, *Marketing: Concepts and strategies,* Houghton Mifflin, 1994, 2nd European edn)

Marketing as a discipline can provide few generalisations, 'principles', or 'laws'. The major contribution of the marketing discipline is in its approach to problem identification and solution.

(Y J Wind, 1982, quoted by D Mercer, *Marketing,* Blackwell, 1992, p3)

Marketing is a social and managerial process by which individuals and groups obtain what they need and want through creating, offering, and exchanging products of value with others.

(P Kotler, *Marketing Management: Analysis, planning, implementation and control,* Prentice-Hall, 1991, 7th edn) (See also definition by Kotler given under 4 above.)

Diamonds are forever?

In Japan, the matrimonial custom has survived feudal revolutions, world wars, industrialisation and even the American occupation. Until the mid 1950s, Japanese parents arranged marriages for their children through trusted intermediaries. The ceremony was then consummated by the bride and groom drinking rice wine from the same wooden bowl.

This simple arrangement had persisted for more than a millennium. There was no tradition for romance, courtship and prenuptial love in Japan; and no tradition that required the gift of a diamond engagement ring.

Then, in 1967, a South African diamond company decided to change all that. It retained J Walter Thompson, the largest advertising agency, in the world, to popularise diamond engagement rings in Japan.

The resulting advertising campaign subtly suggested that diamonds were a sign of modern western values. Colour advertisements in Japanese magazines showed very beautiful women displaying their diamond rings. The women all had western facial features and wore European clothes.

Moreover, in most of the advertisements the women were involved in some activity that defied Japanese traditions, such as bicycling, camping and mountain climbing. The message was clear: diamonds represent a sharp break with the oriental past and an entry point into modern life.

The campaign was remarkably successful. When it began in 1968 fewer than 5% of Japanese women getting married received a diamond engagement ring. By 1981 some 60% of Japanese brides wore diamonds. In a mere 13 years the 1,500-year Japanese tradition was radically revised and Japan became the second largest market for diamond engagement rings.

The sale of diamonds to the masses was a relatively recent development. Until the late nineteenth century, diamonds were a genuinely rare stone only found in a few river beds in India and the jungles of Brazil. The entire world production amounted to only a few pounds a year. In 1870, however, huge diamond mines were discovered in South Africa. Suddenly, the market was deluged by diamonds. The British financiers who had organised the South African mines quickly came to realise that their investment was endangered: diamonds had little intrinsic value, and their price depended almost entirely on their scarcity.

The Cartel's first move was to gain control over production of all the important diamond mines in the world. But this alone was not sufficient to preserve the price of diamonds. If the public's appetite for diamonds decreased precipitously, as it had with coral and pearls, the Cartel would not be able for long to keep prices from collapsing.

De Beers had to control demand as well as supply, and this required some manipulation of the psyche of the diamond buyer.

In 1938, De Beers approached one of the leading advertising agencies in the United States, NW Ayer. At that time, some three quarters of all the Cartel's diamonds were sold for engagement rings in the United States. However, American men tended to buy small, poor quality diamonds – under $80 apiece – for their loved ones and De Beers believed that they could be persuaded to buy more expensive stones through an advertising campaign.

Ayer pointed out that since 'young men buy over 90% of all engagement rings', it would be crucial to inculcate in them the idea that diamonds were a gift of love: the larger and finer the diamond, the greater the expression of love. Similarly, young women had to be encouraged to view diamonds as a integral part of courtship.

The advertising agency wasted little time in approaching the film studios in Hollywood. In its 1940 report to De Beers, it noted, 'A long series of conferences with Paramount officials, capped by your own efforts, succeeded in changing the title [of a film] from *Diamonds are Dangerous to Adventures in Diamonds.'*

It then reported that in another film it had succeeded in inserting a long scene dealing with the selection of a diamond clip and bracelet for the star, Claudette Colbert, and that in the film Merle Oberon wore $40,000 worth of diamond jewellery.

The Ayer plan also envisaged using the British royal family to help foster the romantic allure of diamonds. It observed: 'Since Great Britain has such an important interest in the diamond industry, the royal couple could be of tremendous assistance to this British industry by wearing diamonds rather than other jewels.' Subsequently, Queen Elizabeth (the Queen Mother) did go on a well-publicised trip of South African diamond mines, and she accepted a diamond from De Beers.

To further romance the romantic image of diamonds, Ayr placed lush four-colour advertisements about diamonds in magazines presumed to mould elite opinion. The ads reproduced famous paintings by such respected artists as Picasso, Berman, Derain, Dali and Dufy to convey the idea that diamonds were also unique works of art.

De Beers needed a slogan that expressed both romance and legitimacy. In 1948 Ayer came up with the caption 'A Diamond is Forever' scrawled on a picture of two young lovers on honeymoon. Even though diamonds can be in fact shattered, chipped, discoloured or incinerated to an ash, the concept of eternity perfectly captured the magical qualities that the advertising agency wanted to impute to diamonds. Within a year 'A Diamond is Forever' became the official slogan of De Beers.

Such was the campaign's success that sales of diamonds in the United States grew from a mere $23m in 1939 to more than $2.1bn, at the wholesale level, in 1979. In comparison, the expenditure on advertisements, which began at a level of only $200,000 a year and gradually increased to $10m, seemed a brilliant investment.

There was a time in the mid-1960s, however, when De Beers almost became a victim of its own success. The problem was a surfeit of minute Siberian diamonds that De Beers had undertaken to market for the Russians. Almost all of these diamonds were under half a carat in their uncut form, and there was no ready market for them. De Beers had expected the production from the Siberian mines gradually to decrease. Instead, it accelerated at an incredible pace.

Through its 20-year advertising campaign, De Beers had encouraged American women to think of the size of a diamond as a status symbol; the larger the diamond, the more status it represented. Now, however, De Beers had to reverse its theme: women were no longer to be led to equate the status and emotional commitment in an engagement with the sheer size of the diamond. Instead its advertisements stressed the importance of quality, colour and cut over size.

As an additional means of soaking up these tint diamonds, De Beers devised the 'eternity ring'. This consisted of numerous Soviet-sized diamonds and was aimed at an entirely new market of married women. The advertising campaign was based on the theme of recaptured love. Again, sentiments were born out of necessity; American wives received a snake-like ring of miniature diamonds because of the needs of a South African corporation to accommodate the Soviet Union.

Brass Bands versus Elgar

RESOURCE 1.3 ◁

The Times
3 May 1995

Which way will we really vote? Marketing experts, politicians and editors all want to know the answer.

Businesses spent an estimated £400 million on market research last year in their attempts to understand consumer desires. The colour of a soap-powder packet, for example, can have dramatic effects on consumer buying patterns. One company learnt that what it thought was the bright and cheery golds and reds of its packaging had become associated with smoky downmarket pubs and was lowering sales accordingly.

When people are asked direct questions, they often give dishonest answers. So all sorts of seemingly bizarre techniques are used these days to tease out what people really think. For example, market researchers ask members of the public to project their feelings onto other people or other situations; or they may tap into people's sense of sight, sound, smell and touch. By moving beyond the sphere of rational explanation, the researchers believe they can get a greater insight into what people really think of a brand.

One such piece of research last week into the attitudes of wavering Tories suggests that Britain is on the brink of a political sea change. Yet, tantalisingly, it also suggests that Tory supporters have not yet gone over the edge; although they are on the verge of switching, there is still hesitancy.

The research, by the advertising agency Barker and Ralston, used in-depth interviews to ask 20 once-stalwart Conservative voters in the Tory stronghold of Chorleywood in Hertfordshire to reveal what sensory images of the rival political parties create.

The sounds of Conservatism include classical music, 'posh' voices, Elgar, leather on willow, and church bells (respondents' own words). The smells encompass polish, the inside of old churches, gin and tonic, red wine, sauce and tanned leather. The

sights: country estates, City businessmen, public schools, London mews and country homes.

In stark contrast, when Tory supporters listen to Labour they hear *The Internationale,* northern accents, brass bands and heckling. They see Lowry paintings, drab women not wearing make-up and rowdy bunches of young men. They smell perspiration, stale beer, smoky pubs, cheap perfume and factory oil. Everything they love and aspire to is in the first group; everything they hate and fear is in the second.

But new images are starting to disrupt this traditional, cosy split between the desirable and the undesirable. Tory voters are glimpsing something attractive in Labour and to sense things deeply unattractive about their own party. They are hearing a new and disturbing dimension to Conservatism: harsh voices, booing and jeering, whimpering and crying. They see 'men entertaining themselves with poll-tax money', a puppet show, a rudderless boat, a grey day, a dark room with closed doors, a crack in the ozone layer.

Next to the expected feelings of luxury and tweed, they are also touching something slippery, something limp, a reptile, and over-ripe fruit. They are sensing rotten cabbage, bad eggs, over-cooked vegetables.

Labour is starting to smell of roses, as well as fresh orange, freshly-baked bread, honeysuckle, lemon and home cooking. These Tories, who have never even considered voting Labour, when they think of Tony Blair's party, are imagining spring flowers growing, sunny days and children singing.

Phil Strongman, the researcher who conducted the interviews, says that for the first time in their lives, loyal Conservatives are prepared to listen to what Labour is saying. 'They have opened Labour's book,' he says, 'and they are beginning to read it.'

Derek Ralston, the agency's managing director, is cautious: the overwhelming yearning, he says, is still for those good, old Tory values. And suspicion of Labour still runs high. The Tories may be a 'Duracell battery rabbit that's getting slower and slower' (as one participant put it) but voting Labour would still be 'like medicine. You have to take it against your will.'

Tory voters' relationship with their party is, Mr Ralston suggests, now like that of a desperate parent and a disgraceful teenage child. 'They are on the verge of kicking him out,' he explains, but they desperately do not want to. There is still an opportunity for him to apologise. But if he carries on as he has been, they are prepared to do it.'

▷ RESOURCE 2.1

(The Guardian,
24/6/95)
Nicholas Bannister,
Technology Editor

Home shopping set to mushroom

Electronic home shopping may get off to a slow start in the UK, but it will ultimately have as great an effect on British buying habits as the introduction of supermarkets in the sixties and seventies, says a report out yesterday.

Specialist research group Inteco said that by 1998 more than half the well-off households in the UK would have access to electronic catalogues either on-line or on CD-ROMs.

As a result, entrepreneurial companies, uncluttered by large investments in land, parking and staff, would use the multi-media medium to offer goods at prices which undercut the major retailers.

'The impact will be as though a bomb hit the high street,' said Graham Taylor, Inteco's survey manager. 'The basic on-line shopping services launched recently by Barclays Bank, Dixons, Tesco, Sainsbury's and other leading UK retailers, don't yet deliver the full benefits of virtual shopping.

'At present they charge full retail prices, add extra charges for home delivery and are vague about what time they will deliver.

'New home-shopping service operators, not encumbered by the cost of retail premises and telesales staff, will start a war on price and delivery, moving competition between retail and direct sale into a whole new phase.'

However, Inteco accepts that there will have to be vast improvements in home shopping services before they become popular. A main conclusion of the survey of 3,500 UK homes was that the services will have to be free. Customers were not prepared to pay phone companies for the privilege of shopping.

Companies would have to offer toll-free lines or local phone calls would have to be free. Customers were less likely to buy if they felt the range of goods offered was restricted or if they were charged a premium.

▷ RESOURCE 2.2

by Hugh Carnegy
Source: Financial
Times, 27 March
1995

Struggle to save the soul of Ikea

Hugh Carnegy on the changes at the Swedish company which ignored the rules to become a worldwide retail chain.

You cannot mistake the singular, very Swedish culture of Ikea when you visit Almhult, the little railway town in the forests of Smaland where Ingvar Kamprad founded the business 52 years ago and which remains the hub of an international retailing empire.

Distinguishing managers from 'co-workers', as Ikea employees are called, is impossible in the informal, open plan offices where suits are non-existent and ties a rarity.

A large mural on the wall in the lobby depicts a Smaland landscape with the motto 'Ikea's soul'. On a wall is pinned the 'testament of a furniture dealer' penned in 1976 by the guru-like Kamprad, who rarely shows his face to the public, but whose presence is keenly felt throughout the organisation.

Anders Moberg, chief executive of the Ikea retailing operation is an affable, self-effacing man who looks more like the coach of a schoolboy ice-hockey team than the boss of a billion-dollar business. Like everyone else at Ikea travelling on business, he flies economy class and never takes taxis when public transport is available.

'This is a company that is steered more by vision than by figures,' he says with a smile.

Ikea has certainly broken a series of conventions in building itself into a worldwide retailing chain. A privately held company still closely controlled by Kamprad, now 69 years old, Ikea largely ignored the retailing rule that international success involves tailoring product lines closely to local tastes.

Instead, it has stuck by the nostrum laid out in Kamprad's 'testament' to sell a basic product range that is 'typically Swedish' wherever it ventures in the world – underpinned by the determination to sell quality furniture at prices the majority of people can afford.

The company remains largely production-oriented: that is, it decides what it is going to sell and then presents it to the public – often with startlingly little research as to what the public wants to buy.

'We don't ask so many questions before we start up new things,' says Jan Kjellman, head of Ikea's Sweden division, whose design team – almost all Swedish – create the 12,000 items on sale in Ikea stores worldwide. 'Last year we launched the 'Swedish Cottage' range without any market research – but the customer liked it

very much.'

Financially, too, Ikea is unconventional in a business where margins are tight and overheads high. It owns almost all its 123 stores (accounting for 1.8m sq m), paid for with its own cash. Moberg says Ikea has as much capital tied up in real estate as an industrial company has in machinery.

'That is a policy we have,' he says. 'We don't like to be in the hands of the banks.'

The formula has worked: Ikea has grown in the last 20 years from a group with 10 stores in five countries, with annual turnover of $210m (£128m), to having 125 stores today in 26 countries, reaching sales in its 1993-94 financial year of $4.7bn. The company is famously reticent about figures, but does not quarrel with an assessment made last year by *Affärsvärlden*, a Swedish business magazine, that Ikea's after-tax profit margin stood at 6-7 per cent of sales.

The success has brought Kamprad a long way since 1943 when he opened a mail order business. He has long since moved his holdings out of Sweden for tax reasons. The Ikea retail operation is owned by a foundation set up in the Netherlands (which also owns the Habitat chain) and now has its legal headquarters in Denmark. The family interests also include Inter-Ikea, which owns the Ikea name and controls the franchises which run a minority of Ikea stores, and Ikano, a separate company with banking and finance interests.

No one outside the Ikea inner circle knows the real financial strength of the organisation. But *Affärsvärlden* reckoned a year ago that the Ikea retail operation had a market worth of Skr35bn (£3bn).

Not everything at Ikea is quite as serene as it appears in Almhult. In recent years, the company has had to cope with recession in some of its main markets – particularly Sweden itself, which still accounts for 11 per cent of sales. Ikea's venture into the US, launched in 1985, was beset by difficulties, and initially ran up heavy losses.

There has also been some damaging

publicity – most notably last year when the revelation that Kamprad had been involved in a Swedish pro-Nazi group during the 1940s attracted the adverse attention of influential Jewish groups in the US.

Above all, however, Ikea has been prey to structural problems stemming from its fast growth. As the organisation expands further, it has had to adjust the way it operates in ways that are likely to erode the close-knit, Swedish-driven culture of management. Coping with Ikea's evolution while maintaining its essential values and identity is a key task for Moberg.

Over the past two years, he has had to get a grip on an organisation that had become bloated. 'In all successful organisations, whether private or public, there is a risk that success will make you complacent. We had become a little bit like a stuffed tiger,' Moberg says.

Costs had risen to more that 37 per cent of sales value from levels of around 30 per cent at the end of the 1980s. This was an alarming development for an organisation which has always stressed its cost consciousness: 'An idea without a price tag is never acceptable,' wrote Kamprad in his 'testament'.

The main target was a fearsomely complex production and distribution chain, encompassing 2,300 suppliers in 76 countries, but which all too often ended with frustrated customers unable to find what they wanted in the stores.

Before the reorganisation, up to 90 per cent of goods went through Ikea's 12 distribution warehouses on the way to the stores. Today, some 30 per cent of goods go direct from the manufacturer to the store and the goal is to reach 50 per cent. Lead times for the developments of new products are being cut, the extent of the Ikea range of products is being trimmed and suppliers are being pressed for lower prices.

At the same time, a greater emphasis is being put on increasing sales volumes in existing stores rather than the rapid expansion of new outlets. After adding 18 new stores in the peak expansion year of 1992, the aim now is to average a more modest six or seven a year.

'We are not very good at space management,' admits Moberg. 'We can become more professional in that area.'

He says that Ikea's policy – again, laid down in Kamprad's 'testament' – of always offering a substantially lower price than its competitors, will help to keep in shape an organisation which does not have the pressure of shareholders scruitinising its financial performance.

'Our policy puts a lot of pressure on ourselves,' says Moberg. 'Our people cannot compensate with price increases. They have to get volume growth and better efficiency in our stores.'

But even if Ikea is overcoming these problems – Moberg says volumes are again moving up and cost ratios coming down – it still has to reconcile the structural demands of its international growth with its relaxed, but curiously rigid way of opening.

Ikea insists that all its stores, whether in the UK or the United Arab Emirates, carry the basic Ikea range as produced by the company's Swedish unit, with little room for products tailored to local tastes.

'There is always conflict between the local store and Ikea of Sweden,' admits Jan Kjellman. 'They want to follow local market trends but that is usually not in line with the Ikea identity. We have to safeguard the identity.'

Sticking too rigidly to that line has at times got Ikea into trouble – especially in the US. In what has now become part of company legend, Ikea was initially baffled by the reluctance of US customers to buy its beds and bedlinen. It eventually realised that Americans like bigger beds than Swedes and ordered larger beds and sheets from its suppliers. Sales suddenly took off. Much the same happened with kitchen units which previously did not accommodate plates large enough for pizza.

Moberg now laughs about the episode. 'We were a little bit dumb,' he says. Elsewhere, similar adjustments have been allowed – such as including leather-covered sofas in Belgian stores, and corner sofas in Austria.

And last year Ikea commissioned its first extensive market research programme in Europe to gain a sharper impression of its customers.

Although the company was reassured to find its Swedish identity was popular, a pull away from the exclusively Swedish Ikea concept seems inevitable as Ikea listens more to its customers and expands into areas such as the Far East, where it now has six stores, and, next year, even China.

'Of course when we come to China we will have to behave differently – if only because of the size of dwellings,' says Moberg.

These centrifugal forces may also be strengthened by a growing trend within Ikea towards franchising, where local partners will be the driving force in individual stores, rather than Moberg's management team. Fifteen Ikea stores are now run as franchises operated by Inter-Ikea.

But Moberg is adamant that the core Ikea culture will be maintained. He says that by remaining a private company, it will keep its commitment to long-term growth, allowing it to absorb losses such as occurred in the US without changing its basic strategy. At present, Ikea owns large banks of underdeveloped land in eastern Europe, including 180,000 sq m outside Moscow, but is content to wait for better prospects before seeking a return there.

With Ikea holding only a 5 per cent market share in its biggest single market, Germany, Moberg says the company still has 'huge' growth potential around the world. And it does not believe it should depart from Kamprad's 1976 'testament' to achieve it.

'If we had adapted to more traditional German tastes and styles we would have won a bigger share there – but we would have had a different profile,' he says. 'We believe in the long run we will win the customers over to our Swedish way of thinking on furniture and home furnishing. So we will keep our profile. Our identity is extremely important for us.'

Calf protesters win legal battle

RESOURCE 2.3

by James Erlichman, Consumer Affairs Correspondent
Source: *The Guardian,* 23 February 1995

The animal welfare group leading peaceful protests against livestock exports yesterday won the legal right to challenge flights of veal calves from Coventry airport.

The High Court victory for Compassion in World Farming (CIWF) came as William Waldegrave, the Agriculture Minister, resisted pressure from MPs for a unilateral ban on the trade, after he failed to secure an improved European welfare regime in Brussels.

Two High Court judges ruled yesterday that CIWF could intervene in a judicial review on March 20 brought by Phoenix Aviation against Coventry city council. The council voted to ban further flights of calves from its airport to Amsterdam and Rennes in France on 'public safety' grounds. The vote was taken on January 27, five days before the animal rights campaigner, Jill Phipps, aged 31, was crushed to death under the wheels of a lorry carrying calves to the airport. Phoenix has won an interim order to keep flying until the judicial review is heard.

Richard Plender, QC for the CIWF, successfully argued yesterday that High Court rules required the pressure group be heard in the judicial review – it was a 'proper person to be heard' because of its deeply held concerns about livestock welfare.

Meanwhile in the Commons, Mr Waldegrave received all party support for refusing a French plan which would still have allowed hauliers to take livestock, with the exception of pigs, on unlimited journeys to southern Italy and Greece.

A last minute deal opposed by Mr Waldegrave was almost brokered which might have forced him to accept maximum journeys for sheep of up to 68 hours including rest stops and 46 hours for calves and lambs.

But the Germans are understood to have scuppered the deal which is likely to be proposed again when EU agriculture ministers meet next month.

Labour reiterated its demands that live veal exports be banned from Britain and hauliers licensed. Mr Waldegrave repeated his claim that the move would breach single market rules and leave the Government open to lawsuits from calf producers and exporters.

● More than 150 children, in defiance of police advice, yesterday joined their parents and other adults in attempting to block lorries taking sheep from Brightlingsea, in Essex, to a ferry bound for Belgium.

▷ RESOURCE 2.4
by Martin Mulligan
Source: *Financial Times*, 9 February 1995

Asda blocked on cut-price books

The Publishers Association last night won an injunction forcing Asda, the supermarket group, to stop selling ten books at discount prices. The ten bestsellers are produced by publishers which abide by the net book agreement.

Asda immediately contacted its stores, ordering them to sell the paperback books at their list prices.

The net book agreement is the mechanism which allows publishers to fix the prices of most books sold in the UK. The Publishers Association had given Asda until 5 pm on Tuesday to stop selling the discounted books, a deadline Asda had disregarded.

Asda said the injunction was a 'slap in the face for our customers'. It said: 'We will be petitioning the Office of Fair Trading to speed up its referral of the NBA to the restrictive practices court.'

Mr Peter Kilborn, director of management services at the Publishers Association, said 'the NBA has legal force' and that an injunction was 'a routine response to any infringement' of it. Seven publishers were involved in the prospective action.

He added that about 80 per cent of books published in Britain were covered by the NBA and insisted that 'if the net book agreement did not exist, prices overall would go up'. He rejected the argument that the defence of the agreement in this instance was largely symbolic – Asda estimates that it sells about 5m books per year, a fraction of the 400m sold annually in Britain.

If the agreement disappeared, he said, 'the danger is that publishers and booksellers would concentrate on high profile titles, damaging range and availability'.

Asda's discounted bestsellers included Frederick Forsyth's *Fist of God* and Virginia Andrews' *Darkest Hour*.

Fresh ferment for the brewers

RESOURCE 2.5

by Roderick Oram
Source: Financial
Times, 9 February
1995

Government intervention continues to weigh heavily on the UK industry

In a former life, the Old Punch Bowl pub at Crawley in Sussex was a bank branch. It is within earshot of Gatwick airport but most nights it is noisier inside than out. The place is packed with young customers knocking back expensive British cask ales and premium foreign lagers.

Greene King, the brewer which spent £1m to convert it, regrets not a penny. Mr Tim Bridge, chief executive, says takings are far above plan even during the traditional post-Christmas decline in sales. One key to its success is that it appeals to local 'circuit drinkers'.

This euphemism for 'pub crawlers' speaks volumes about the migration up-market of British brewing and pub retailing. The future looks expansive and prosperous for brewers such as Greene King and Whitbread which have best responded to the trend.

But the future looks less inviting for others such as Bass and Courage, which are burdened by excess brewing capacity, a product mix of declining keg beers and standard lagers, and too many unimproved pubs.

To a great extent, the winners and losers in the industry can both cite government intervention as the cause of their present state. But what worries the industry most is that it is unlikely to be left alone to work through the changes into a modern consumer-oriented business. Only this week, the Office of Fair Trading said it would investigate the price brewers sell beer to their captive pubs.

'It is the 33rd time since 1966 the industry has been flung into apparent disarray by government intervention,' says Sir Paul Nicholson, chairman of the Brewers and Licensed Retailers Association and chairman of Vaux Group.

His message to the government is: 'You got it wrong last time and did some damage but that was controllable. Don't get it wrong again and do even more damage which might not be controllable.'

The heaviest action the government has taken in the industry in recent times was the 1989 Beer Order, made after an inquiry by the Monopolies and Mergers Commission concluded that brewers' ownership of pubs limited competition.

The main aim of the order was to weaken the hold brewers had on retailing by forcing them to sell some of the pubs they owned. The industry fiercely opposed the order, arguing the relationship helped guarantee them sales outlets, pub tenants financial support and thus consumers a choice of pubs and beers.

Sir Paul and others fear the latest OFT enquiry is a further assault on the relationship while they are still trying to come to grips with the impact of the order. This strengthened the small regional brewers and independent pub companies that have no links with brewers: they bought many of the pubs the large brewers were forced to sell. The number of pubs not tied to brewers doubled to about 25,000 out of the UK's 65,000 pubs, sparking a battle between Bass and Courage to sell their beers through them. This triggered a price war in 1992, competition that continues to undermine margins today. One consequence is that free houses can buy beer at one-third off the list price, while tied houses pay the full amount – the cause of the OFT's investigation.

Consumers have benefited from this increased competition and from a proliferation of beer varieties from brewers such as Whitbread which are trying to build new upmarket brands. But they have also faced the closure of thousands of pubs unable to justify the investment needed to modernise them. Moreover, beer prices have risen almost 50 per cent faster than inflation over the past six years, partly because of investment in new ownership or refurbishing.

The industry's ability to adjust has been hindered by an ownership logjam, with large parcels of brewing and pub assets owned by companies wanting to leave the UK industry. For example, the City believes that Foster's Brewing of Australia would like to sell Courage, Britain's second largest brewer, and its half stake in Inntrepreneur Estates Ltd, a pub-owning joint venture – but has yet to receive an acceptable offer.

The need for the industry to complete its change is ever more pressing. Beer consumption continues to decline, worsening the problem of excess capacity. There are also still an estimated 10,000 pubs in the UK that cannot justify their economic existence.

One factor behind this decline is the trend to home drinking. A decade ago 12 per cent of beer was drunk away from pubs. The share is 25 per cent and could hit 30 per cent by the late 1990s. Another is the growing incursion of cross-Channel imports and the government's unwillingness to reduce excise duties to make them less attractive.

Of the remedies to the industry's ills, the most pressing is to take out excess brewing capacity estimated at about 25 per cent. The trouble is much of the unwanted capacity is in large, relatively modern plants for keg ales owned by big national brewers. These are the mass produced beers that have lost popularity compared with rising consumption of specialist cask ales.

All the easier cuts in capacity have already been taken out: the big brewers have closed some smaller plants; a handful of medium-sized regional brewers such as Boddington and Greenalls have given up brewing to concentrate on retailing through pubs and other outlets.

The industry's ideal solution to the problem of overcapacity would be for Courage to be sold to one or more national brewers who would be willing to shoulder the cost of shutting some plants. But if there was a Courage deal in the making, as some in the City suspected, it will almost certainly have been delayed by the latest OFT enquiry. If Courage remains intact, a long period of trench warfare lies ahead for the industry.

The elimination of excess pubs will be a gradual process. If they cannot get the investment they need, they will be sold off. But this does not always remove them from the market: typically pubs sold by large brewers drop down through the ownership chain to a smaller brewer or an independent company. Only when there is no future for it as a pub does it leave the industry, normally to become a home.

A typical candidate for such a demise is an inner-city 'back-street boozer' in a large industrial town which had once lived on selling vast volumes of beer and not much in the form of food or entertainment. A pub estate manager recalls six changes in ownership of one such pub over 12 years before it was finally de-licensed and sold as a house.

For those who fear the current economics of pub owning will mean the end of their local, there is some hope. A few villages, for example, are trying co-operative ownership or doubling up the premises with other businesses, such as a hairdresser or post office. Even if the pub might be open only at the weekends, it is still there.

For the industry, however, the future lies in upgrading pubs to draw back customers. All brewers have learnt how to brand their pubs in varying formats to appeal to different customers. Scottish and Newcastle, for example, is experimenting with a chain called the Rat and Parrot, with large clear windows to encourage women customers reluctant to enter pubs they cannot see into.

Mr Peter Jarvis, chief executive of Whitbread, is not the least embarrassed to say that one of his big new pubs 'is more like Disneyworld than a boozer' or to talk of a pub visit as a 'leisure occasion'.

But all these strategies are based on developing the relationship between brewer and pub established by the Beer Orders in 1989. The fear in the industry is that this week's OFT announcement could lead to a further inquiry by the Monopolies and Mergers Commission that would change the rules again.

Ethics men at odds over Body Shop

RESOURCE 2.6 ◁

by Neasa MacErlean
Source:
The Guardian,
27 August 1994

Investors who screen their holdings on ethical grounds will have had their confidence shaken by the question marks over 'green' retailer Body Shop's commitment to environmental protection and trade aid. Managers of ethical funds are not rushing to withdraw their support, but clearly want more information.

The company's shares fell by over nine per cent last week because of concerns over the imminent publication of a highly critical article in US magazine *Business Ethics.* Investors who have money in ethical funds with holdings in Body Shop should not see the value of their investment hit dramatically because Body Shop will be mixed with other stocks.

But concerns about the allegations have created an ethical investment *cause célèbre* – sparking the biggest credibility crisis for the ethical investment industry since its first unit trusts were launched ten years ago. If the US magazine has indeed unearthed certain unethical practices, the whole British ethical investment industry will be undermined. 'If it turns out that Anita Roddick secretly tests things on rabbits in her back garden, that would be a disaster,' says Peter Webster of the Ethical Investment Research Service, the agency used by most ethical fund managers.

But neither Eiris nor the fund managers seem to expect such revelations about the Body Shop managing director or her company.

Some ethical specialists have already seen the *Business Ethics* article – due to be published on Wednesday – but are not changing their stance on the company. Last week, Friends' Provident, which manages £400 million of ethical funds, had talks with Body Shop and concluded: 'We see nothing that changes our view of Body Shop.'

But fund managers and researchers plan to discuss the allegations in detail with the company. Eiris is writing to Body Shop this week, asking it to be more open about its operations and to answer specific questions over environmental issues and the extent of its 'trade not aid' projects. NPI, another leading fund manager, is arranging a meeting with Body Shop next month.

Like Eiris, NPI still has Body Shop firmly on its approved investment list. But NPI sold its shareholding last year because it felt the shares were overpriced, a sentiment shared by other fund managers.

The *Business Ethics* article is likely to encourage investors to ask more questions of Body Shop and other companies. Fund managers hope that companies will respond by becoming more open about their practices.

Fleet Sales Drive Car Recovery

RESOURCE 3.1 ◁

by Simon Beavis,
Industrial Editor
The Guardian
7 March 1995

The new car market last month showed signs of recovering from the doldrums that have beset it since September but a rise of 4.5 per cent in sales was again largely fuelled by the fleet sector and saw imported cars grab a 60 per cent share of the market.

Figures from the Society of Motor Manufacturers and Traders showed that a total of 152,329 cars were sold in February against 145,710 in February 1994, a rise of 4.54 per cent.

But the SMMT made it clear that fleet

sales accounted for an unusually high 55 per cent of all registrations in a further sign that individual buyers are still fighting shy of the garage forecourts.

Ernie Thompson, the SMMT chief executive, said: 'This increase in registrations is encouraging but with business and fleet purchases accounting for 55 per cent of the total it is quite clear that private customers are still reluctant to come into the new car showrooms.'

Dealers said the figures demonstrated the continuing absence of private buyers from the market. Warning that the recession had dramatically slowed down replacement times for cars, they said that this was having an impact on the environment.

Importers took a 60.52 per cent share of the market, the highest figure in recent months and way above the average 57 per cent share grabbed over the last 10 months. In February last year, importers took a 57.54 per cent share.

Sales in the commercial vehicle sector were again much stronger with 20,896 trucks and vans sold in February, an increase of 28.1 on the same months last year. The continued growth of commercial vehicle sales is widely interpreted as a sign of growing business confidence in marked contrast to the attitude of consumers.

In the first two months of 1995, truck and van sales have motored ahead by 25.8 per cent.

RESOURCE 3.2

by Simon Beavis,
Industrial Editor
The Guardian
7 March 1995

Lucas wins £1bn deal to supply VW

Lucas, the automotive and aerospace engineering group has clinched its biggest ever contract with a £1 billion 10-year deal to supply an advanced electronic fuel injection system to Europe's largest carmaker, Volkswagen.

The deal will create up to 300 jobs, mostly at Lucas' Stonehouse factory in Gloucestershire, and is set to bring in £150 million a year for a minimum of six years after production starts up in 1997.

Lucas shares – battered recently by a ban on tendering for new contracts with the US Defense Department after being convicted of falsifying records on equipment supplied to the US Navy – rose 6p to 187p on news of the deal. The company refused to specify how many of the electronic unit injector (EUI) systems it will be supplying to the German giant but said that it expected total volumes to rise to 1.5 million to 2 million a year.

This type of deal is becoming increasingly the norm between carmakers and their suppliers and has become a hallmark of José Ignacio Lopéz de Arriortúa, VW's aggressive production chief.

The EUI provides greater engine efficiency by boosting injection pressure to twice the level available from mechanical systems. Lucas said that the system, which has up to now been used in trucks, would not only improve fuel economy but reduce emissions.

George Simpson, the new Lucas chief executive, said: 'The real significance of this announcement is that it not only marks a breakthrough of advanced EUI technology into the car segment of the automotive industry, but also confirms Lucas' position as a leading player in the automotive industry.'

Beating the west to the medicine cabinet

RESOURCE 3.3 ◁

Peter Montagnon
on a Bangladeshi
company's challenge

Somewhat cheekily, Mr Delwar Hossain Khan, managing director of Bangladesh's leading pharmaceutical company, says he can take on Glaxo even after its takeover of Wellcome.

His company, Beximco Pharmaceuticals, will soon be sending its first consignment of intravenous fluid to Vietnam. It wants to develop a market there before eventually building a plant in Ho Chi Minh City. This will be a test of Mr Khan's theory that pharmaceuticals companies from developing countries are better placed to tap emerging medicine than their western counterparts.

Unlike the latter, which spend heavily on research and produce sophisticated but expensive products, Beximco produces relatively simple products cheaply. It does not need to recoup the cost of research in its selling price.

A good supply of basic drugs is what markets like Vietnam require, says Mr Khan. As they grow richer, more people in developing countries will be able to afford medicines, but the market will expand horizontally with more people buying simple drugs. He believes there will be less emphasis on vertical expansion, which involves growing sales of sophisticated products to a small segment of the population at ever-increasing prices.

'Western companies have to realise they cannot pursue the same policy on profit and pricing as they do at home. In developing markets, we'll have a higher market share than Glaxo, but in similar products,' says Mr Khan.

Beximco is no stranger to exporting. It has sold antibiotics and intravenous fluids as far afield as Iran and South Korea and has even registered its products in Russia. When Bangladesh lifts foreign exchange controls on outward investment next year, Beximco plans to use the opportunity to start work on its Vietnamese plant, a joint venture with a local partner and Fresenius, a German equipment supplier.

Mr Khan believes that with the low wages and low research costs, his company can produce basic drugs cheaply. That suits his home market too. In Bangladesh the annual government spend on medicines is only $1 a head of the population, and only 40 per cent of people actually buy medicines. The scope for higher volume sales of simple drugs is large. Unlike Glaxo, Beximco is not dependent on the product cycle.

But the art is to maximise price by careful quality control and marketing. The ever-ambitious Mr Khan will fly to Washington next month to seek US Food and Drug Administration certification of a new plant he is building on the outskirts of Dhaka. The idea is not to export to the US but to use the approval to establish credibility elsewhere. Not surprisingly, Beximco has attracted the attention of investors in the stock market, where it is one of Dhaka's best-traded issues.

Not all analysts are as sanguine as Mr Khan, though. Mr Yeoh Keat Seng of Crosby Securities rates Beximco a buy largely because of its prospects in the domestic market.

But he is cautious about the speed with which exports will take off. The Vietnamese market offers good opportunities, he says, but companies in Malaysia and Singapore which are closer to it culturally may have the edge.

Tighter patent rules in the wake of the Uruguay Round may also eventually cramp Beximco's style. There is no immediate intellectual property problem in sales of intravenous fluids and antibiotics to Vietnam, but Bangladesh is now a member of the World Trade Organisation and is tightening up on the protection of patents.

Mr Khan says some of Beximco's products are copies of western products but the five-year transition period for existing drugs means his business will be little affected. By then the western drugs themselves will be out of patent.

But according to Mr Gerhard Doege of Ciba-Geigy (Bangladesh) Beximco may find it harder to launch new compounds in future. Mr Khan is unperturbed. Take China, he says. Whatever the rules on patent protection, the Chinese will quickly learn to match US products in most sectors, not just pharmaceuticals. 'The only things the US will be able to sell to them in 10 years time are movies, Coca-Cola and hamburgers.'

RESOURCE 3.4

by Lucinda Alford
The Observer
Sunday 6 June 1993
(funded by Legal and
General)

Cast-offs are back in fashion

A growing army of designers is spurning the excesses of the fashion industry to recycle old clothes and fabrics.

Of all the consumer industries, fashion is one of the most guilty of excess. No one needs the amount of new clothes the fashion industry thrives on producing. Fashion is by definition about change; what is new is fashionable and therefore desirable. A business that produces new collections twice a year, each making the last redundant, is by its very nature wasteful.

Few people go shopping to replace clothes that have worn out – they shop for new clothes to add to their existing wardrobes. But while the nature of fashion is not about to change radically, there are signs that it is waking up to the problem of waste.

Second-hand clothes have become a major fashion statement. As fashion designers look to past eras for influence, consumers have cottoned on to the fact that the originals are often better quality and cheaper than designer updates. The recent Seventies revival has been responsible for large-scale recycling of the kind of clothes which a few years ago no one would have wanted. Velvet jackets and satin bell bottoms that would have stayed on charity shops rails are now being bought by fashionable young things, instead of being overlooked or bought only as something to wear at a fancy dress party.

The focus on second-hand clothes is promoting recycling in the most basic way: the re-use of something that has been discarded as unwanted. Although the trend has been encouraged recently by the fashion press, it cannot be considered an initiative by the fashion industry to clean up its wasteful image.

The fashion industry is currently taking two quite different paths in an attempt to be more ecologically aware. High Street companies are falling over themselves in a bid to produce green ranges of clothing. While unbleached organic cotton is an attempt at cleaning up pollution caused by the industry, it feels more like a PR stunt than a true desire to be more ecologically aware. The other route is that of recycling existing fabrics and garments in an attempt to re-use what is already available rather than manufacture yet more raw material. This second route is still more of a cottage industry compared to the scale of the global fashion business, but it is a step in the right direction.

Extending the second-hand clothes market by remaking or remodelling existing materials into new garments is a relatively new concept in fashion, but one that is currently growing. Encouraged by the vogue for second-hand clothes, more and more companies are being set up by young people to produce fashionable clothing that is both desirable and ecologically sound. No Lo Go was set up in 1991 to bridge the gap between what it describes as 'fashion consumerism and green initiatives'. Working under the umbrella of Oxfam, it remakes clothes donated to the charity's chain of shops. Initially operating from one outlet, it has grown to two shops plus two concessions in Oxfam shops and has a turnover of £35,000 last year.

No Lo Go produces a range of clothing and accessories, all made from recycled materials, plus one-offs, like an evening dress made from a silk sari. Prices are kept low, as the group relies on volunteers from fashion colleges to produce the clothes, and donations of fabrics and materials that would have otherwise been wasted – some of them from established designers.

Alternative Fashion Week, held in London's Spitalfields market, recently highlighted a number of young designers working with second-hand materials. From Killergram's patchwork leather jeans made of offcuts from the leather industry, to garments made from old blankets and curtains, each is a one-off. These garments are selling alongside traditional second-hand clothes in outlets like Sign of the Times in London's Kensington Market and Souled Out in Portobello Green, and they strike a chord with a generation who are growing up more aware of green issues. Ironically, the fact that there is so much waste in the fashion business is providing a start for many young designers who could not otherwise afford to set up a business.

Lamine Kouyate Badian, a Paris-based designer born in Mali, has by necessity used second-hand clothes remodelled as the mainstay of his collection for his Xulay Bet label. He uses old sweaters and fabrics overlocked together to produce new clothes.

In his hands a baggy old pullover becomes part of a body-skimming dress. One consequence is that his clothing is not as expensive as most designer labels. Yet he shows his collections during Paris fashion week, and is now reviewed in catwalk reports alongside traditional designers.

As usual the fashion press has given a name to this new mood: recherché. The Belgian designer Martin Margiela has established a lead in this recherché movement, always including a 'found' section in his collection. Margiela scours antique markets for garments to remake; he might use four antique dresses patched together to make one new one. While he is re-using garments that may have been unwearable before, his designs are not cheap, and are produced on aesthetic grounds, rather than through a desire to be seen as green.

Alongside this 'found' section, the bulk of Margiela's collection is manufactured to look almost second-hand. His knitwear is boiled to appear old, his tailoring (produced in Italy at great expense) has a look of being around for years.

Which brings us to the latest paradox: new designer clothes that look old. The good news is that anything which makes second-hand and recycled clothes more desirable must be positive, and, as usual, what is high fashion one day will filter through to the high street the following season.

'Supermarkets get ready for a new generation of YABs'

RESOURCE 3.5

Hildegard Wiesehofer

The grocery retail industry in the UK is dominated by a small number of very large supermarket chains operating from large superstores, with the names of Sainsbury, Tesco, Asda, Gateway and Kwiksave being familiar to most shoppers. The high degree of concentration within the sector has not, however, influenced competition in any negative way as far as customers are concerned. The range of food and household items on sale has never been so varied and prices are very keen as the major players strive to capture further market share. However, consumer loyalty can never be guaranteed and an insight into the service requirements of shoppers may help the retailers to retain their relationship with customers.

A study undertaken by the Henley Centre for Forecasting on behalf of one of the large multiples illustrates how research on the future of the market can form a basis for strategic change. In this instance the research was concerned with predicting patterns of shopping behaviour in the mid 1990s and particularly with establishing a set of market segments based on behaviour patterns. The outcome of the Henley Centre's investigation was the identification of a number of different types of shopper based on a multi-variable approach which took account of demographic factors such as age, sex and income as well as lifestyle, personality and, finally, attitude to the shopping experience. As with so many of these studies, the resultant new breeds of shopper have been labelled with glib titles.

The Harried Hurrier will be the most important type of new shopper. These are typically burdened with squabbling children and crippled by a severe lack of time. Hurriers are averse to anything that eats into their precious minutes such as having too much choice. which makes them impatient. Another large group but spending less money will be the middle-aged Young-at-Heart who, in contrast to the first group have time on their hands and like to try new products. An important and growing species of grocery shopper is the Young, Affluent and Busy (or YABs) for whom money is not a major constraint in their quest for convenience and more interesting products, but they do have a low boredom threshold. Two other types who are expected to grow in importance are the Fastidious, who are attracted by in-store hygiene and tidiness, and the mainly male Begrudgers, who shop only out of obligation to others. At the same time, the Perfect Wife and Mother who is concerned with the balanced diet would appear to be on her way out. She is likely to be more than compensated for by the Obsessive Fad-Followers whose choice of food tends to be dominated by brand image and current trends.

It is expected that the new breeds will act as a catalyst for a shopping revolution. Although the already-established need for convenience will still predominate, retail analysts anticipate some significant changes such as in store traffic-routing systems, one way layouts and themed food centres by nationality. There would appear to be a considerable amount to be gained from transforming the sometimes stressful encounter with the superstore into a pleasurable leisure activity.

▷ RESOURCE 3.6 # The Complaint Letter

Most service problems are solved by direct communication between the server and the customer at the moment of service. Occasionally, however, a customer may be motivated to communicate some thoughtful and detailed feedback to a service provider after the encounter, as illustrated in the following letter:

THE COMPLAINT LETTER

123 Main Street
Boston

13 October 1995

Gail and Harvey Pearson
The Retreat House
Foliage Road
Vacationland
Hampshire

Dear Mr and Mrs Pearson

This is the first time that I have ever written a letter like this, but my wife and I are so upset by the treatment afforded by your staff that we felt compelled to let you know what happened to us. We had dinner reservations at the Retreat House for a party of four under my wife's name, Dr Elaine Loflin, for Saturday evening, 11 October. We were hosting my wife's brother and his wife, visiting from Atlanta, Georgia.

We were seated at 7 pm in the dining room to the left of the front desk. There were at least four empty tables in the room when we were seated. We were immediately given menus, a wine list, ice water, dinner rolls and butter. Then we sat for 15 minutes until the cocktail waitress asked us for our drinks orders. My sister-in-law said, after being asked what she would like, 'I'll have a vodka martini straight-up with an olive.' The cocktail waitress responded immediately, 'I'm not a stenographer.' My sister-in-law repeated her drink order.

Soon after, our waiter arrived, informing us of the specials of the evening. I don't remember his name, but he had dark hair, wore glasses, was a little stocky, and had his sleeves rolled up. He returned about 10 minutes later, our drinks still not having arrived. We had not decided upon our entrees, but requested appetisers, upon which he informed us that we could not order appetisers without ordering our entrees at the same time. We decided not to order appetisers.

Our drinks arrived and the waiter returned. We ordered our entrees at 7.30. When the waiter asked my wife for her order, he addressed her as 'young lady'. When he served her the meal, he called her 'dear'.

At ten minutes of eight we requested that our salads be brought to us as soon as possible. I then asked the waiter's assistant to bring us more rolls (each of us had been served one when we were seated). Her response was, 'Who wants a roll?' upon which, caught off guard, we went around

the table saying yes or no so she would know exactly how many 'extra' rolls to bring to our table.

Our salads were served at five past eight. At 25 minutes past the hour we requested our entrees. They were served at 8.30 – one-and-a-half hours after we were seated in a restaurant which was one-third empty. Let me also add that we had to make constant requests for water refills, butter replacement, and the like.

In fairness to the chef, the food was excellent, and as you already realise, the atmosphere was delightful. Despite this, the dinner was a disaster. We were extremely upset and very insulted by the experience. Your staff are not well trained. They were overtly rude, and displayed little etiquette or social grace. This was compounded by the atmosphere you are trying to present and the prices you charge in your dining room.

Perhaps we should have made our feelings known at the time, but our foremost desire was to leave as soon as possible. We had been looking forward to dining at the Retreat House for quite some time as part of our vacation weekend in Hampshire.

We will be hard-pressed to return to your establishment. Please be sure to know that we will share our experience at the Retreat House with our family, friends and business associates.

Yours sincerely

William E Loflin

The Restaurateur's Reply

RESOURCE 3.7 ◁

The Retreat House
Foliage Road
Vacationland
Hampshire

Dr William E Loflin   15 November 1995
123 Main Street
Boston

Dear Dr Loflin

My husband and I are naturally distressed by such a negative reaction to our restaurant, but very much appreciate your taking the time and trouble to apprise us of your recent dinner here. I perfectly understand and sympathise with your feelings and would like to tell you a little about the circumstances involved.

The Lakes Region for the past four or five years has been notorious for its extremely low unemployment rate and resulting deplorable labour pool. This year local businesses found that the situation had deteriorated to a really alarming nadir. It has been virtually impossible to get adequate help, competent or otherwise! We tried to overhire at the beginning of the season, anticipating the problems we knew would arise, but were unsuccessful. Employees in the area know the situation very well and use it to their advantage, knowing that they can get a job anywhere at any time without references, and knowing they won't be fired for incompetency because there is no one to replace them. You can imagine the prevailing attitude among workers and the frustration it causes employers, particularly those of us who try hard to maintain high standards. Unhappily, we cannot be as selective about employees as we would wish, and the turnover is high. Proper training is not only a luxury, but an impossibility at such times.

Unfortunately, the night you dined at the Retreat House, 11 October, is traditionally one of the busiest nights of the year, and though there may have been empty tables at the time you sat down, I can assure you that we served 150 people that night, despite the fact that no fewer than four members of the restaurant staff did not show up for work at the last minute, and did not notify us. Had they had the courtesy to call, we could have limited reservations, thereby mitigating the damage at least to a degree, but as it was, we, our guests, and the employees who were trying to make up the slack all had to suffer delays in service far beyond the norm!

As to the treatment you received from the waitress and waiter who attended you, neither of them is any longer in our employ, and never would have been had the labour situation not been so desperate! It would have indeed been helpful to us had you spoken up at the time – it makes a more lasting impression on the employees involved than does our discussing it with them after the fact. Now that we are in a relatively quiet period we have the time to properly train a new and, we hope, better waitstaff.

Please know that we feel as strongly as you do that the service you received that night was unacceptable, and certainly not up to our normal standards.

We hope to be able to prevent such problems from arising in the future, but realistically must acknowledge that bad nights do happen, even in the finest restaurants. Believe me, it is not because we do not care or are not paying attention!

You mentioned our prices. Let me just say that were you to make a comparative survey, you would find that our prices are about one half of what you would expect to pay in most cities and resort areas for commensurate cuisine and ambience. We set our prices in order to be competitive with other restaurants in this particular local area, in spite of the fact that most of them do not offer the same quality of food and atmosphere and certainly do not have our overheads!

I hope this explanation (which should not be misconstrued as an excuse) has shed some light, and that you will accept our deep regrets and apologies for any unpleasantness you and your party suffered. We should be very glad if someday you would pay us a return visit so that we may provide you with the happy and enjoyable dining experience that many others have come to appreciate at the Retreat House.

Sincerely
Gail Pearson

Questionnaire results from perfume survey

The Questions	The Perfumes	DUNE — Christian Dior, £30 for 50ml of eau de toilette	OPIUM — Yves St Laurent, £36 for 50ml of eau de toilette	CO — Gossip, £1 for 28ml of eau de toilette	COCO — Chanel, £30 for 75ml of eau de toilette	LE JARDIN — Max Factor, £8.50 for 22ml of eau de toilette	PANACHE — Lentheric, £6.50 for 15ml of parfum de toilette
1. What setting does this perfume bring to mind?	LC	Purple clothes	Breakfast meeting	Everyday	Evening setting	Mundane, supermarket	In a mini-cab
	RS	People standing about wanting to look like Joan Collins	Hotel	Garden Centre	Theatre foyer	Suburbs	Bathroom
	JS	Women gathered in afternoon in stripped pine house	Whiff you catch in the back of a taxi	An office	Dinner Party	Think of a man giving it to his wife in a surburban home	In someone's living room, like an air freshener
	TA	Definitely bedroom or sophisticated restaurant	Gym changing room	Shopping centre	Bedroom/spring mornings	Bedroom/seaside/country	Light jungle/flowerbed
2. Could you describe it? Do you think it is expensive, cheap, middling?	LC	Quite spicy. Expensive	Quite spicy. Expensive	Pretty flowery number. Middling	Not unlike 3 (Co) but better. Middlings	Familiar, quite floral. Could be expensive	Strong soapy smell. Cheap
	RS	Strong. Aspirational middling	Confidence about it. Expensive	Strawberry. Cheap	Too fruity, more refined version (of Co). Expensive	Flowery, perfumey. Probably expensive but shouldn't be	Like a deodorant. Cheap
	JS	Striking, you could identify it. Expensive	Understated. Expensive	Sweet. Middling	Spicy. Musky. Expensive	Classic flowery smell. Middling	Gets up your nose. Cheap
	TA	Musky, aromatic, Middling/expensive	Spicy/musky, quite sweet. Expensive	Cheap and a bit tarty, musky, nauseating. Cheap	Clean, fresh, quite subtle, hint of pepper. Expensive	Citrus, cucumber, cool green smells. Expensive	Floral, toilet water, rather worked out. Cheap/middling
3. What kind of woman do you think would wear this perfume?	LC	Wordly, not the little woman	Sure of herself, she's wearing a DKNY suit	Someone who didn't want to make a statement	Not a big statement, someone certain about herself	Someone who doesn't want to stand out at the PTA	Someone who'd had it given to them
	RS	Pushy	Confident 35-year-old	In little pink print clothes	Mature, classic	Stepford Wife	Young and hopeful
	JS	Upper middleclass	Kind of woman who thinks perfume if vulgar	Not very sure of herself	Dressed up, quite tasteful	The kind who lets her husband choose for her	Someone with no taste who wants to make an impact
	TA	Middle class, professional	Someone who's trying to impress to much	Well...	Tasteful. You'd need to be close to make the most of it	Elegant, intelligent	Tarzan's Jane
4. Is it seductive?	LC	Bit much	Dunno	Not a sexy smell	Maybe	No	No
	RS	No, I wouldn't want to give Joan Collins one either	No	No	Getting there	No	No
	JS	Not in the least	No	No	Yes	No	No
	TA	Reasonably, but I'm not sure I'd drop my boxers for it	Certainly not – too obvious	Only if you've been celibate for 15 years	Yes, but the citrus/pepper tones are a little masculine	You bet	About as seductive as cold porridge
5. Marks out of ten.	LC	7	6	5	6	5	3
	RS	5	7	4	7	5	3
	JS	6	5	4	8	4	1
	TA	6/7	4	2	7/8	8	5/6

Acme Sails Training

Strategic overview

1   Intention

It is intended to establish a company to trade primarily in training and education. Water-based activities will be the central focus.

The prime target market will be adult training and education in skills associated with management, especially leadership.

The secondary target market will be the provision of action-centred holidays.

The company will be based in England, but a substantial amount of its business will be carried out in France. It will take every advantage from the opening of European frontiers within the European Union.

The working title is Acme Sails Training (AST).

2   Keys to success

There are three keys to the success of the venture:

2.1   **Management development** is regarded as of major importance in Britain and is supported by generous funding from a variety of governmental sources. The budget for business-focused training is estimated at £50m between 1994 and 1999. This sum is only 50% of what will be spent by business on consultancy and training on sponsored schemes alone.

This is a priority area for both the EU and British government, which is unlikely to be affected by any change in political control at the next general election. In fact a Labour government is likely to fund training and education more generously than the Conservatives.

2.2   **Outdoor hobbies** are widely predicted to continue their rapid increase of recent years. In particular, the trend towards earlier retirement, on generous terms, will generate a leisured class of affluent and intelligent people. Some of these will be used to travel and will expect high-quality accommodation and service as a matter of course. Others will not have travelled as extensively but would like to if they could feel secure.

2.3   **The directors of ACME** have specialised skills and abilities which form a unique and distinct foundation upon which AST will be built.

3   The need

3.1   **A training centre** that provides stimulating and challenging outdoor opportunities for the development of decision-making and leadership skills – supported by accommo-dation, cuisine and service that is of exemplary quality.

3.2   **A holiday centre** that provides opportunities for those of mature years (45+) to learn new activities, in safety, under the guidance of qualified instructors.

4   The offering

A Management Training Centre of three-star hotel quality to accommodate 24 in en-suite rooms. Cuisine will be French, and good. Accommodation will be full board, all inclusive.

Management training will be offered throughout the winter, and both management training and sailing instruction throughout the summer.

Because the centre is located only 30 minutes from Marseilles airport the journey time will be a little over 3 hours from central London via Heathrow, by both British Airways and Air France scheduled services.

It will, by nature of its location, offer unique benefits to the British:

● the excitement of overseas travel

● excellent weather

● first-class accommodation

● french cuisine and wines

● duty free shopping.

It will offer superb instruction, from highly experienced and fully qualified instructors.

It will be possible to match UK competitors on price *and include the return air travel.* (Students have to pay their way to UK training centres.)

5 Staffing

5.1 There will be four directors:

Jason McCall is a Management & Marketing Consultant of some 30-years experience, and with excellent credentials. He is an accredited strategic management consultant with many blue chip clients.

Marge Jackson is a caterer and hotelier with 25 years experience of the trade. Trained by Marks & Spencer, she ran her own successful restaurant for 12 years before taking up the management of residential property in Nice. She is also a qualified Management Training Officer.

Peter Nicholls is a fully qualified Senior Instructor with the Royal Yacht Association. He is thus authorised to manage a RYA recognised Sailing Centre, and to issue Certificates of Competence. He has considerable experience in outdoor pursuits, notably canoeing and hiking in addition to sailing. He has represented Australia in the world sailing championships on three occasions and was part of the silver medal winning team in the Admiral's Cup of 1992.

Jeanette Davis has considerable mountaineering experience. She has been a leading climber in five Himalayan expeditions and has just left the Army where she was second in command of the Scottish adventure training centre.

5.2 Qualified instructors are not difficult to find. Many young people are anxious to take seasonal jobs, especially those that take them to interesting locations and which are helpful to their CV. The problem will not be of quantity, it will be to select only those who are of sufficient quality to match AST requirements.

5.3 There is a surfeit of hotel and catering staff in the Marseilles area.

6. Location and communication

6.1 Britain: AST will be based in Wellesley House, Redhill, Surrey. This will be an administrative centre, but will include a small training facility to provide for AST staff needs.

6.2 France: AST will be based on the coast, some 10 miles east of Marseilles. An old hotel is to be taken over and renovated to three-star standard. The property is secluded, on the water front and within easy reach of the Alps.

6.3 Directors will maintain British resident status by rotating between England and France.

6.4 Flights will be arranged through an ABTA travel agent.

6.5 Communication will be by telephone, fax and the Internet.

7 Rationale

7.1 The location was selected after exhaustive study of the southern coast from the Spanish to Italian borders. It is the only location that meets all the requirements:

- proximity to a major airport

- excellent, guaranteed weather

- excellent water, with sufficient wind at all seasons

- access to a variety of terrain (sea, lake, canal. climbing, pot holing, hiking. white water canoeing)

- variety of genuine 'tourist' attractions for spouses who accompany delegates.

7.2 **Management and plus 45s** were targeted as being:

- experienced and mature

- high spenders

- responsive to a 'quality' offering

- compatible in style and expectations.

7.3 **Outdoor pursuits, especially sailing,** were targeted because:

- there is a current and continuing demand

- the market targets can be identified and accessed

- there is flexibility to amend the offering in the light of experience.

7.4 In addition, the directors' skills and preferences match the chosen location and targets, thus maximising the probability of success.

8   Finance

All projections are in October 1994 terms, no provision for inflation has been attempted.

The main income will be generated by the two main stream activities:

8.1 **Management training** will be competitively priced, using UK competition as the benchmark. Currently, for five days in the UK, the price per delegate is £ 1,450 (plus VAT).

AST can, if it wishes, charge at the same rate, include the air fare, and show a comfortable surplus.

8.2 **Sailing instruction** will be priced using exclusive holidays as the benchmark. It is expected that a price of £750 per week, including the air fare, will be attainable.

It is expected that AST will break-even in year 2 and start to generate profits from year 3.

9. Legal

9.1 AST will be established as a British company.

9.2 Care will be taken to ensure that individual directors do not attain French resident status. Thus individual taxation will be a matter for the UK.

9.3 It will be necessary to register for VAT in the UK and for TVA in France. This will be beneficial since input taxes will be offset against output in both countries.

9.4 Double taxation shall not be paid by EU residents. Thus, once agreement is reached with both the Customs and Excise and the Douane on the proportion of business done in each country, the accounting for taxation will be a matter of routine.

10 Credibility

10.1 Management training credibility is ensured by the quality, experience and client lists of the directors.

10.2 The Royal Yacht Association will accredit the centre.

10.3 Neil Fairdown, a RYA Area Coach, will be a visiting tutor, and will be responsible to the RYA for monitoring the centre's performance to ensure that the RYA's standards are achieved and monitored.

11 Marketing

11.1 **Management training** – AST will not offer 'open' courses. The objective is to provide a venue which is fully equipped and staffed and which visiting tutors will use.

Thus the targets will be Training Managers and Training Consultants. The message will be on the lines of: 'Train in security in the warmth of France'. In this way promotional spend can be reduced and highly focused. Cost-effective results can be achieved, and monitored very closely.

11.2 **Sailing** courses will be 'open'. They will be targeted at:

- Adults buying a boat for their own personal use. They will have little or no experience of sailing, nor of the use of an outboard motor. They may wish to learn for their own enjoyment and/or to be able to teach their spouses/children.

- Adults about to hire a sailing boat/cruiser – they will only need familiarisation with the basics.

- Adults owning a boat in Britain who wish to sail in comfort in the South of France and/or improve one or more aspects of their sailing ability.

- Adults who have never sailed and who want to learn without embarrassment.

- Adults who simply want an enjoyable holiday on or near the water.

It will be necessary to provide, in this market segment, for the non-sailing spouse. Marseilles is ideally situated for excursions to places of great interest. It is planned to provide a full schedule of excursions, at no extra charge to those who do not sail.

Note: there is no sailing test similar to a car driving test. Thus, most people new to sailing learn the hard way, and many are embarrassed at their ineffectiveness. AST will offer the opportunity to learn in conditions of psychological and physical safety.

11.3 AST will not cater for children. Mature young people (18+) may be accepted, but broadly the target markets are:

- managers in post (27+)
- mature sailors (45+)

Tactical plans

The tactical planning is in outline only at this stage. It will be refined after discussion with the legal, financial and marketing advisers.

CUSTOMER CARE SURVEY

AFTER SALES

NISSAN MOTOR (GB) LIMITED

As part of our Customer Care philosophy, we at Nissan are very concerned that what you record on this questionnaire is a true representation of your experience with your Nissan dealer. If, for any question, you are unable to give an answer then please leave that question blank.

All answers to this questionnaire will be treated as completely confidential and will be used only by persons engaged in the survey or by Nissan. They will not be disclosed to others for any purpose whatsoever.

For each question please indicate your answer or answers by ticking the corresponding box(es) e.g. [✓] or by writing in the space provided.

THE DEALER WHO SERVICES YOUR VEHICLE

1. Where do you usually have your Nissan serviced or repaired?

   The Nissan dealership where I purchased my Nissan [ ] 1   (113)

   Another Nissan dealership - **Please complete the details below** [ ] 2

   NAME _____

   TOWN _____

   A non-Nissan dealership [ ] 3

   Other [ ] 4

Please complete this questionnaire for the Nissan dealer indicated above, that is the dealer you usually use for servicing and repairs. **If you do not use a Nissan dealer** (or if you use a dealer who used to be a Nissan dealer but is no longer one) write in your reasons below, do not complete the questionnaire but please do return it in the envelope provided.

(114)

2. Have you visited your Nissan dealer in the last 12 months for any of the following?

	Yes	No	
Servicing	[ ] 1	[ ] 2	(115)
Repairs	[ ] 1	[ ] 2	(116)
Warranty	[ ] 1	[ ] 2	(117)
Parts	[ ] 1	[ ] 2	(118)

   NOTE: If you have said **'No' to all of the above**, please do not complete the questionnaire but please still return it in the envelope provided.

3. When did you last visit your dealer for servicing, repair or warranty work?

Less than 3 months ago	3-6 months ago	7-9 months ago	Over 9 months ago	
[ ] 1	[ ] 2	[ ] 3	[ ] 4	(119)

BOOKING THE APPOINTMENT

4. First of all we would like you to tell us how you first made the appointment to have your vehicle serviced. Please tick the **ONE** statement that applies.

   I phoned the dealer [ ] 1   *Please answer Q.5*   (120)

   I visited the dealer [ ] 2   *Please skip to Q.6*

   The dealer contacted me [ ] 3   *Please skip to Q.6*

5. How satisfied were you with the way we handled the appointment to service your vehicle. For each of the following attributes please tick the **ONE** box that best describes your opinion.

	Completely Satisfied	Very Satisfied	Fairly Satisfied	Somewhat Dissatisfied	Very Dissatisfied	
The **speed** with which the call was answered	[ ] 1	[ ] 2	[ ] 3	[ ] 4	[ ] 5	(121)
The **manner** in which your call was answered	[ ] 1	[ ] 2	[ ] 3	[ ] 4	[ ] 5	(122)

Booking The Appointment - *Continued*

6. Were you offered a 'While-You-Wait' service, that would allow you to wait in our dealership while your vehicle was being serviced?

Yes ☐ 1 No ☐ 2 Did not require ☐ 3 (123)

OUR SERVICE RECEPTION

7. Please give us your opinion of the general appearance and facilities of our servicing department. Please tick the one box that best describes your opinion for each of these aspects.

	Completely Satisfied	Very Satisfied	Fairly Satisfied	Somewhat Dissatisfied	Very Dissatisfied	
Availability of a convenient appointment	☐ 1	☐ 2	☐ 3	☐ 4	☐ 5	(124)
Ease of finding service reception	☐ 1	☐ 2	☐ 3	☐ 4	☐ 5	(125)
Ease of parking near the service reception	☐ 1	☐ 2	☐ 3	☐ 4	☐ 5	(126)
Cleanliness of the service reception area	☐ 1	☐ 2	☐ 3	☐ 4	☐ 5	(127)
Facilities (e.g. seating and refreshments) provided for the customers in the service reception area	☐ 1	☐ 2	☐ 3	☐ 4	☐ 5	(128)
Convenience of the opening hours	☐ 1	☐ 2	☐ 3	☐ 4	☐ 5	(129)

OUR SERVICE RECEPTIONIST

8. When you first came into our service reception to deliver your vehicle, how satisfied were you with the length of time you had to wait before you were attended to?

Completely Satisfied	Very Satisfied	Fairly Satisfied	Somewhat Dissatisfied	Very Dissatisfied	
☐ 1	☐ 2	☐ 3	☐ 4	☐ 5	(130)

9. Did the Service Receptionists introduce themselves and give you their name so that you could contact them if necessary?

Yes ☐ 1 No ☐ 2 Already known ☐ 3 (131)

10. We would now like to know about the Service Receptionist with whom you dealt, so please answer by ticking one box for each of the attributes listed below.

	Completely Satisfied	Very Satisfied	Fairly Satisfied	Somewhat Dissatisfied	Very Dissatisfied	
The way you were first greeted	☐ 1	☐ 2	☐ 3	☐ 4	☐ 5	(132)
The way our Service Receptionist was dressed	☐ 1	☐ 2	☐ 3	☐ 4	☐ 5	(133)
The efficiency with which our Service Receptionist recorded all the details of the work to be done on your vehicle	☐ 1	☐ 2	☐ 3	☐ 4	☐ 5	(134)
Interest in you as a customer	☐ 1	☐ 2	☐ 3	☐ 4	☐ 5	(135)
Courtesy and friendliness to you as a customer	☐ 1	☐ 2	☐ 3	☐ 4	☐ 5	(136)
Willingness to 'put themselves out' for you	☐ 1	☐ 2	☐ 3	☐ 4	☐ 5	(137)
Ability to quote you an accurate price	☐ 1	☐ 2	☐ 3	☐ 4	☐ 5	(138)
The length of time you spent booking the vehicle in	☐ 1	☐ 2	☐ 3	☐ 4	☐ 5	(139)

11. Did our Service Receptionist advise you of the different ways you could pay for the servicing?

Yes ☐ 1 No ☐ 2

ALTERNATIVE TRANSPORT

12. Did you require any alternative transportation?

      Yes   ☐ ₁ *Please answer Q.13*   (141)

      No   ☐ ₂ *Please skip to Q.15*

13. Were you provided with...

      A loan vehicle   ☐ ₁ *Please answer Q.14*   (142)

      Collection and delivery service   ☐ ₂ *Please answer Q.14*

      Transportation to where you wanted to go   ☐ ₃ *Please answer Q.14*

      None, even though transportation was requested   ☐ ₄ *Please skip to Q.15*

      None, but I did not request any   ☐ ₅ *Please skip to Q.15*

14. Did this alternative transportation meet your expectations?

      Yes   ☐ ₁ *Please answer Q.15*   (143)

      No   ☐ ₂ *Please say why not in the box below*

(144)

YOUR OVERALL SATISFACTION WITH OUR SERVICE BOOKING-IN PROCEDURES

15. How satisfied are you, in **overall terms**, with the way our Service Receptionist handled the booking in of your vehicle for servicing?

Completely Satisfied	Very Satisfied	Fairly Satisfied	Somewhat Dissatisfied	Very Dissatisfied	
☐ ₁	☐ ₂	☐ ₃	☐ ₄	☐ ₅	(145)

VEHICLE COLLECTION

16. If unauthorised work was required on your vehicle, were you informed. . .

      Before you collected your vehicle   ☐ ₁   (146)

      When you collected your vehicle and the work was done   ☐ ₂

      When you collected your vehicle and the work was **not** done   ☐ ₃

      No unauthorised work was required   ☐ ₄

17. When you collected your vehicle how satisfied were you with. . .

	Completely Satisfied	Very Satisfied	Fairly Satisfied	Somewhat Dissatisfied	Very Dissatisfied	
The length of time you waited before you were attended to	☐ ₁	☐ ₂	☐ ₃	☐ ₄	☐ ₅	(147)
The efficiency with which our Service Receptionist handled your collection	☐ ₁	☐ ₂	☐ ₃	☐ ₄	☐ ₅	(148)

Vehicle Collection - *Continued*

	Completely Satisfied	Very Satisfied	Fairly Satisfied	Somewhat Dissatisfied	Very Dissatisfied	
Courtesy and friendliness to you as a customer	☐ 1	☐ 2	☐ 3	☐ 4	☐ 5	(149)
Explanation of the work carried out	☐ 1	☐ 2	☐ 3	☐ 4	☐ 5	(150)
Vehicle being available at the promised time	☐ 1	☐ 2	☐ 3	☐ 4	☐ 5	(151)
Explanation of any delays	☐ 1	☐ 2	☐ 3	☐ 4	☐ 5	(152)
No delays (TICK)	☐ 6					
Ability to answer your questions	☐ 1	☐ 2	☐ 3	☐ 4	☐ 5	(153)
Standard of workmanship	☐ 1	☐ 2	☐ 3	☐ 4	☐ 5	(154)
Cleanliness of the vehicle exterior when returned	☐ 1	☐ 2	☐ 3	☐ 4	☐ 5	(155)
Cleanliness of the vehicle interior when returned	☐ 1	☐ 2	☐ 3	☐ 4	☐ 5	(156)
Willingness of our Service Department to 'put themselves out' for you	☐ 1	☐ 2	☐ 3	☐ 4	☐ 5	(157)
The feeling that our Service Department cared for you as a customer	☐ 1	☐ 2	☐ 3	☐ 4	☐ 5	(158)

18. Were <u>all</u> the items of work you requested completed to your satisfaction at the first visit? (159)

Yes ☐ 1 *Please skip to Q.20*

No ☐ 2 *Please answer Q.19*

19. Why were you not satisfied? (160)

Fault not fixed ☐ 1

Parts not available ☐ 2

Other ☐ 3 _____(PLEASE WRITE IN)

20. Were you offered the opportunity to talk to the actual technician who did the work on your vehicle? (161)

Yes ☐ 1

No, but I would have liked to ☐ 2

No, and it didn't matter ☐ 3

21. When you collected your vehicle, how satisfied were you with the . . . .

	Completely Satisfied	Very Satisfied	Fairly Satisfied	Somewhat Dissatisfied	Very Dissatisfied	
Actual handover of the vehicle	☐ 1	☐ 2	☐ 3	☐ 4	☐ 5	(162)
Proximity of the vehicle	☐ 1	☐ 2	☐ 3	☐ 4	☐ 5	(163)
Actual location of the vehicle	☐ 1	☐ 2	☐ 3	☐ 4	☐ 5	(164)

22. Did the Service Receptionist fulfil all the commitments made to you when the vehicle was booked in?

Yes ☐ 1   No ☐ 2   (165)

OUR CHARGES

23. How satisfied were you with the . . . .

	Completely Satisfied	Very Satisfied	Fairly Satisfied	Somewhat Dissatisfied	Very Dissatisfied	
Itemisation of charges	☐ 1	☐ 2	☐ 3	☐ 4	☐ 5	(166)
Explanation of the invoice and charges	☐ 1	☐ 2	☐ 3	☐ 4	☐ 5	(167)
Confidence that you got what you paid for	☐ 1	☐ 2	☐ 3	☐ 4	☐ 5	(168)

OUR WARRANTY

24. Have you had any warranty repairs done on your Nissan?

Yes ☐ ₁ *Please answer Q.25* ·165·

No ☐ ₂ *Please skip to Q.26*

25. How satisfied were you with the way the warranty work was carried out?

Completely Satisfied	Very Satisfied	Fairly Satisfied	Somewhat Dissatisfied	Very Dissatisfied
☐ ₁	☐ ₂	☐ ₃	☐ ₄	☐ ₅

·170·

26. Was there any aspect of your vehicle servicing that you had to pay for that you felt should have been covered by our warranty?

Yes ☐ ₁ *Please give details in the box below* ·171·

No ☐ ₂ *Please answer Q.27*

·172·

FOLLOW UP

27. After the service were you contacted by our service staff to check all was well?

Yes ☐ ₁ *Please answer Q.28* ·173·

No ☐ ₂ *Please skip to Q.30*

28. How soon after the service were you contacted?

One - three days	Four - seven days	Eight days or longer
☐ ₁	☐ ₂	☐ ₃

·174·

29. IF THERE WERE ISSUES TO BE DEALT WITH AFTER THAT CONTACT . . .

How satisfied were you with the way these issues were dealt with?

Completely Satisfied	Very Satisfied	Fairly Satisfied	Somewhat Dissatisfied .	Very Dissatisfied
☐ ₁	☐ ₂	☐ ₃	☐ ₄	☐ ₅

No issues to be dealt with (TICK) ☐ ₆

·175·

PARTS AND ACCESSORIES

30. Have you had any reason to visit our Parts Department?

Yes ☐ ₁ *Please answer Q.31* ·176·

No ☐ ₂ *Please skip to Q.32*

31. How satisfied were you with the . . . .

	Completely Satisfied	Very Satisfied	Fairly Satisfied	Somewhat Dissatisfied	Very Dissatisfied	
Ease of finding our Parts Department	☐ ₁	☐ ₂	☐ ₃	☐ ₄	☐ ₅	·213·
Appearance of our Parts Department	☐ ₁	☐ ₂	☐ ₃	☐ ₄	☐ ₅	·214·
Way you were first greeted	☐ ₁	☐ ₂	☐ ₃	☐ ₄	☐ ₅	·215·
Product knowledge of counter staff	☐ ₁	☐ ₂	☐ ₃	☐ ₄	☐ ₅	·216·
Courtesy and friendliness to you as a customer	☐ ₁	☐ ₂	☐ ₃	☐ ₄	☐ ₅	·217·
Ability to quote an accurate price	☐ ₁	☐ ₂	☐ ₃	☐ ₄	☐ ₅	·218·
Ability to provide the correct part	☐ ₁	☐ ₂	☐ ₃	☐ ₄	☐ ₅	·219·
Length of time taken	☐ ₁	☐ ₂	☐ ₃	☐ ₄	☐ ₅	·220·
Availability of parts and accessories	☐ ₁	☐ ₂	☐ ₃	☐ ₄	☐ ₅	·221·
Time taken to supply items **not** in stock	☐ ₁	☐ ₂	☐ ₃	☐ ₄	☐ ₅	·222·

All items in stock (TICK) ☐ ₆

YOUR OVERALL SATISFACTION WITH OUR SERVICE DEPARTMENT

32. How satisfied are you, in **overall terms**, with the way we handled the servicing of your vehicle?

	Completely Satisfied	Very Satisfied	Fairly Satisfied	Somewhat Dissatisfied	Very Dissatisfied	
	☐ 1	☐ 2	☐ 3	☐ 4	☐ 5	(223)

33. If there is anything that our service department could have done to improve our service, collection or handover procedures please tell us in as much detail as possible below.

(224)

34. Based on your overall experience with our dealer's after sales support, how likely would you be to . . . .

	Definitely Would	Probably Would	Might/ Might not	Probably Would not	Definitely Would not	
Recommend this dealer to a friend as a place to have a vehicle serviced?	☐ 1	☐ 2	☐ 3	☐ 4	☐ 5	(225)
Take back your vehicle for servicing to this dealer?	☐ 1	☐ 2	☐ 3	☐ 4	☐ 5	(226)
Buy another Nissan from this dealer?	☐ 1	☐ 2	☐ 3	☐ 4	☐ 5	(227)
Buy another Nissan from any dealer?	☐ 1	☐ 2	☐ 3	☐ 4	☐ 5	(228)

YOUR SATISFACTION WITH YOUR NISSAN

35. How satisfied are you, in **overall terms**, with your Nissan?

	Completely Satisfied	Very Satisfied	Fairly Satisfied	Somewhat Dissatisfied	Very Dissatisfied	
	☐ 1	☐ 2	☐ 3	☐ 4	☐ 5	(229)

36. Has your Nissan fully met your expectations?

Yes ☐ 1 *Please skip to Q.38*   (230)

No ☐ 2 *Please answer Q.37*

37. Please tell us, in as much detail as possible, why your Nissan has not fully lived up to your expectations.

(231)

38. How many miles has your Nissan travelled in the **last twelve months?**   MILES _____   (232 234)

39. Was your previous vehicle . . .?

A Nissan vehicle ☐ 1   (235)

Another make of vehicle ☐ 2

No previous vehicle ☐ 3

A FEW DETAILS ABOUT YOU

40. The following questions are purely for statistical purposes, they tell us about the types of people who buy our vehicles.

Are you . . . ?

Male ☐ 1   Female ☐ 2   (235)

41. How old are you . . . ?

Please write in your age _____ YEARS   (237-239)

42. How many people are there in the household, including yourself and any children?

One ☐ 1   Two ☐ 2   Three ☐ 3   Four ☐ 4   Five ☐ 5   Six or more ☐ 6   (239)

43. Is your vehicle. . . . ?

A private vehicle, that is paid for entirely by you and your family ☐ 1   (240)

Or one paid for in part or in total by a company ☐ 2

HOW CAN WE DO BETTER?

If you would like to make any further comments relating to the service you have received from our dealer please use the space below.

(241)

If you are a Nissan Motor (GB) Limited employee please tick in the box provided.

NMGB employee ☐   (242)

If you have made any comments which you object to being followed up please tick in the box provided.

I object to my comments being passed on to my dealer ☐   (243)

THANK YOU VERY MUCH FOR YOUR HELP AND CO-OPERATION.
PLEASE RETURN THIS QUESTIONNAIRE IN THE REPLY-PAID ENVELOPE PROVIDED.   (244-247)

▷ RESOURCE 9.1
Source: *Marketing*,
February 1995

Heinz – direct marketing

HJ Heinz, the food manufacturer that brought the British public such memorable advertising campaigns as Beanz Meanz Heinz, is planning to create a new slogan – Heinz Meanz Direct Marketing. Mr Tony O'Reilly, the flamboyant chairman and chief executive of the Pittsburg-based international food group, is planning to end UK commercial television advertising for his products this year and instead concentrate on direct marketing. Mr O'Reilly, whose career in marketing took off after he created the Kerrygold campaign for Irish butter in his early 20s, believes the era of mass marketing is giving way to more targeted selling techniques.

The Heinz plan to give up television advertising would be one of the most radical marketing moves in recent years by a food manufacturer. It comes as manufacturers of branded food products are facing growing competition from cheaper, own-label goods produced by supermarkets. The Heinz account is one of the longest established in television advertising. Heinz has already built up a database of 5.6m homes in the UK that are heavy users of the company's products. Mr O'Reilly plans to send special discount vouchers directly to those homes, thereby bypassing conventional advertising media such as television and newspapers. The discount vouchers will be for individual Heinz products, such as baked beans, but also for groups of Heinz lines. Mr O'Reilly has decided that direct marketing is the most cost effective way of maintaining loyalty to the brands.

He sees the plan as the start of a 'guerrilla' campaign against the increasing power of the large supermarket groups, which he believes sometimes treat branded products cavalierly. If Heinz goes ahead with its plan and proves that direct marketing to its best customers works, it could be a blow to ITV, which has depended heavily for its income on the advertising of mass market products, particularly fast-moving grocery goods.

▷ RESOURCE 9.2
Source: Marketing
Week, 15 July 1994

Managing by our shelves

Coca-Cola versus Pepsi, Pepsi versus Ariel, Sindy versus Barbie. Brand wars are the heart of marketing mythology. But times are changing and brand wars are now passé as retailers become a more important focus for marketing activity than consumers.

A few years ago it would have been apostasy to admit that the centre of marketing gravity has shifted to the retailers, but last month, when a joint FT/IPA survey asked the UK's top 500 advertisers this question, 54 per cent of respondents agreed and only 30 per cent disagreed.

The survey says: 'There is a perception that trade marketing is beginning to dominate marketing activity...retailer power is taking the focus of marketing departments away from the end consumer to the intermediary channels.'

This shift is behind a radical rethink of marketing priorities sweeping a growing number of fast-moving consumer goods companies. The central idea is that brand wars are outdated because they offer few benefits to the trade. Unilever chairman Sir Michael Perry says: 'Retailers have no interest whatsoever whether they sell more of Brand A or Brand B shampoo. All they are interested in is maximising profits from that shelf.'

Consequently, manufacturers realise that driving categories, not brands, is the way forward. After years of experiments, leading-edge companies such as Colgate, Elida Gibbs, Kellogg, Lever Brothers, Mars, Pepsi and Procter and Gamble are bedding category management into their thinking and their structures. Now, the rest of the marketing fraternity is scrambling to catch up.

'Almost everyone is doing, or thinking about it,' says Lindsay Leslie-Miller of specialist executive search consultancy Hunter Miller. 'It's like a big snowball. We will see major shake-up in the way fmcg companies operate.'

Retail power is just one of the factors behind this shake-up. The establishment of regional or even global strategic brand management centres means national marketing organisations are losing their former independence and becoming implementors of strategies decided elsewhere. Meanwhile, their tactical and trade marketing role is being emphasised.

Companies are also realising the need to clear up the mess made in the Eighties when brand managers flooded the market with line extensions in a frantic quest to boost brand share. Competitors, not wanting to miss a trick, developed their own lookalike brands and it became irrelevant whether sales across the category rose. The result was cannibalisation of sales, product line proliferation, faltering profits and consumer confusion.

'Companies will spend millions researching the shape of the packaging and whether consumers prefer raspberry to strawberry, but they won't spend £100,000 on fundamentals such as consumer attitudes towards the category,' says John Brady, head of management consultancy McKinsey's consumer goods and retail practice.

Leo Burnett, head of brand consultancy Helena Rubenstein agrees: 'Brand portfolios have been getting out of control. No one is sitting down and saying 'why are we really doing this?''

It is not only the manufacturers that are suffering. Retail margins are coming under pressure. Consequently, they are looking to suppliers to help them offer the excitement and interest that drives sales and justifies price premiums. At the same time, they are getting more ruthless – Somerfield, for example, has announced plans to reduce its supplier base by a third.

Category management brings all these factors together. Retailers are increasingly running each category as a mini-business in its own right. Asda has recently reorganised on category management lines, as has Somerfield.

'Buyers have financial incentives to achieve cash profitablilty for the categories they manage. They are not constantly harassed on the performance of individual lines, allowing them to manage the mix of products that they are selling,' says Christian Rose, Somerfield trading director non-foods.

Not surprisingly, retailers welcome suppliers who can speak the same language.

'Our task is to come up with propositions, through innovation, to help retailers improve their profitability in that category and to help ourselves in the process,' says Unilever's Perry. 'Brands that drive a category, and whose brand values stand at the very heart of that category, give companies strategic advantage. By owning this brand, you own the category and everyone else will have to settle for being 'me-too'.'

Just how the category management revolution will unfold is still unclear. 'To some it is all about the retailers, to others it is about cost-cutting and others think it is about a plan for the brand in the category. It certainly hasn't settled down yet,' says Rubenstein.

Colin Buckingham, marketing director for Nielsen's European category management team adds: 'It is forcing some very fundamental changes in the way retailers and manufacturers work together.'

If manufacturers tackle this new partnership with retailers constructively and in concert, Perry told the Advertising Association recently, 'our brand can act as a coat hanger for the retailer's own brand. Instead of confrontation – synergy on the shelves.'

One of the first companies to apply category management thinking was Colgate Palmolive. Its new approach is upgrading the status of sales, bringing the skills of sales and marketing experts together. A new and higher calibre sales force was recruited and marketers were told: 'You will not be promoted without a spell on the retail negotiating front line.' The ultimate aim was not simply to sell more Colgate toothpaste, but 'to lead oral healthcare'.

A recent re-organisation at Lever also levels the status of sales and marketing and introduces a new focus on the category. Brand or consumer marketing manager jobs are rejigged so they focus on understanding local consumers. They are no longer responsible for trade promotions.

Customer development managers focus on developing relationships with key retailers. And a new breed of category managers have the task of building the company's presence in each category across all retailers.

Before, when we created brand plans or consumer-driven plans we didn't build the customer [the retailer] element into the process at an early enough stage,' says Lever Brothers homecare business manager, Jerry Wright. But last January the company restructured. 'We needed an approach that is driven by consumer wants and needs, and by the realities of the retail environment.'

'The category teams are taking the brand plans developed by the consumer marketing people and putting them into an overall category approach,' says Wright. 'We now think there are three things that are vitally important – consumers, categories and customers.' He adds that the hub of the wheel is category management, because that's where the work of the customer and consumer teams comes together.

Of course, there are those who dismiss category management as just another marketing fad. Maximising the effect across brand portfolios has been central to marketing management from the year dot, they say. The merger of sales and marketing departments is hardly new. Nor is working with retailers to mutual advantage.

Category management is not without its problems, one of which is focusing so much on the retailer that the customer gets pushed aside. One marketing director who asks not to be named, says: 'We have ended up dealing with six people in the trade who have become more important than the 50 million. We have been led by our noses. Now we have to make the 50 million more important again.'

Another pitfall is that brand culling can go too far. 'The brand garden may be overgrown, but be careful of the accountants' slash-and-burn approach,' warns Frank Milton, head of Coopers & Lybrand's marketing practice.

Yet the fact remains, it is category growth that retailers are looking for and they are favouring suppliers who can help them deliver it. 'Bad category management is suppliers trying to sell an idea for a category to retailers,' says John Maltman, group director at marketing consultancy EC Glendenning. 'Good category management is working with each other to identify the opportunities, and influencing each other so that what comes out is better than anything either of you could do alone,' he adds.

Leading manufacturers now accept this. Lever's reorganisation, says Wright, 'has given us a way to develop specific strategies in trade sectors and for customers. Our objective is for each retailer to see us as the preferred supplier.' This, he says, brings immediate tangible benefits, from having prime influence over the planning and merchandising and space allocation for the category, to having first bite at any promotional slots in the retailer's programme.

Maltman adds that once a supplier has established a joint long-term vision with a retailer for a category's development it is very difficult for other suppliers to influence it. Their marketing agenda has effectively been set by someone else. Martin Glenn, npd director at Walkers Smiths and the man behind the UK launch of Doritos, says: 'We want to be seen as the leader *vis à vis* the trade.'

This has some unsettling implications. In any one category, there's usually only enough room for one preferred supplier. Which means the rivalry between manufacturers for the first place in retailer affection is as important as brand wars in the past.

But as retailers struggle to differentiate themselves from each other, the picture becomes more complex. Alliances shift as retailer A chooses manufacturer X as its preferred supplier and retailer B responds by choosing manufacturer Y, category by category.

Balancing all this, while never losing sight of the brand and its consumer, is the new challenge. More companies are realising they have to make fundamental changes to structures, attitudes and skills. So much so that some, like Hunter Miller's Leslie-Miller, see the focus on category management merely as an intermediary step to the future.

'There are all sorts of exciting experiments, with different companies doing different things with different retailers,' she says. 'And the whole relationship between sales, national accounts, category management and marketing management is changing incredibly fast.' But into what? No one, she maintains, really knows yet.

First to the phone

RESOURCE 9.3 ◁
Source: *Marketing*,
27 October 1994

First Direct's launch shook the banking world. Five years on, Amanda Richards reports on its plans to grow the brand.

When First Direct was launched on the back of a quirky advertising campaign in 1989, the high street banks could hardly contain their mirth. Five years on, with nearly 500,000 lucrative ABC1 customers, it has firmly wiped the smiles off the big clearers' faces. First Direct has revolutionised banking: in the past 18 months, every high street bank has tried a me-too copy of the Midland offshoot.

The latest example is Bank of Scotland's Banking Direct, a 24-hour, seven-days-a-week freephone banking service. Next up, in November, will be Barclays' Barclaycall. Imitation is the sincerest form of flattery. But for First Direct, which has spent millions on start-up and educating the public about telephone banking, the challenge is to stay ahead now that the advantage of surprise has faded.

The problem, of course, is not new, especially for small companies where most real innovation takes place. According to Tim Amber, Grand Metropolitan senior research fellow at the London Business School, research on the 'first-mover advantage' shows that, on average, the share of companies second into a market is about 71% of the brand pioneer's.

'Many brand pioneers do succeed even though others wait for them to create the market, then try to go in bigger and

better themselves. The banks, however, are not very good at marketing which is why I think this is unlikely to happen to First Direct,' he says.

First Direct must continue to invest heavily in innovative products and services, he says, and 'avoid anxiety when the other banks come after them'.

Tom Blackett, deputy chairman of Interbrand, adds that First Direct has to promote the brand as the first and best. 'They've got to make sure consumers know they do it better than anyone else,' he says.

First Direct believes its ultimate USP, and the one thing which will eventually distinguish it from its rivals is its service. 'When we started out, we knew that, if we were successful, the other banks would follow,' says Kevin Newman, First Direct chief executive. 'We knew they would be able to copy our mechanics, but they would not be able to copy our culture – and that's what drives our attitude towards customers.'

Extensive research went into defining the bank's brand values, which Newman describes as 'absolute honesty, integrity, intelligence and mutuality of confidence. We have an adult-to-adult – not parental – relationship with our customers. To build that culture you have to believe it to the bottom of your soul and live it.'

'Living it' means there is no status in the organisation. There are no privileged parking slots and everyone eats in the same restaurant. There are no offices and Newman wears a name badge just like everyone else. Banking representatives, as they are called, are not chosen specifically for their banking experience, but have to undergo attitudinal tests. First Direct is looking for empathy, ability to listen, numeracy and ability to communicate. Employees are trained and empowered to solve problems and make decisions, so they have much more responsibility than front-line retail staff in most high-street banks.

A good example is when staff make mistakes. Some banks promise a £10 apology fee, but Newman believes customers would rather hear a personal 'I'm sorry'. After that, staff are left to decide how best to compensate the customer. 'For instance,' says Newman, 'when we buggered up someone's loan for a new set of golf clubs, our representative apologised by offering a free golf lesson.'

This type of service enables First Direct to boast that a third of its customers come through personal recommendation and that four out of ten applicants have to be turned away because they do not meet its credit scoring.

But a unique service or a unique product does not in itself drive profits unless it is mass marketed and that is where First Direct has had problems. Like other brand pioneers, it has suffered from one of the biggest marketing dilemmas: how to predict demand. Where there is no precedent, research is often inadequate because consumers will react one way to the theory, and do completely the opposite in practice.

For example, First Direct was forced to pull a TV advertising campaign early last year because it could not cope with the demand already created by press advertising and a mailshot. 'The response was three times better than we'd expected,' says Newman. 'It put us under immense pressure and our service deteriorated for a bit. It was a sobering experience.'

In most sectors poor projections such as these have caused many a senior marketer to lose his or her job. But not at First Direct. 'We got it wrong. Maybe we

could have projected it better. But we have learned,' he says.

Commercial director, Peter Simpson, says First Direct underestimated the response because people's experience of buying over the telephone had developed more quickly than expected (witness the impact of Direct Line).

Added to this was a growth in public contempt for mainstream banks.

It is not the first time First Direct has misjudged the effect of its advertising. Its launch campaign – probably interactive TV advertising's UK debut – failed to spell out what telephone banking actually was. 'It seemed such an obvious idea that we assumed people would understand. But, with hindsight, we should have explained it better,' says Newman.

The promotional lessons have not been lost on First Direct's competitors, most of which, to cope with the potential response, have shunned advertising initially and concentrated on targeted direct mail campaigns.

'Our system can handle about 20,000 new accounts a month so, for now, we will use direct mail to control the flow of business,' says Gordon Rankin, Barclays deputy director of personal sector marketing. He estimates four million out of seven million Barclays customers will be using its 'integrated telephone banking operation' by the year 2000.

First Direct is now working on another major integrated ad campaign which will break through Chiat Day early next year. The bank is confident it now knows how to manage the response – in part because a new second site will enable it to handle more than the current 10,000 accounts a month.

The campaign, like the bank's first TV work, will be 'innovative and interactive', but it will also try to extend the brand name to new areas, and build on the idea of communicating with your bank at a distance.

'We want people to know we're in tune with the modern world, that we're not resting on our laurels,' says Simpson, who likens First Direct's customer-first culture to that of Virgin's: slightly anti-establishment, and in touch in terms of service and price.

For First Direct, pulling last year's campaign means it will have been off-air for nearly three years when it returns – no-one will ever know what might have been achieved had it been better prepared for the initial response. The small-hours thought that must occasionally run through Newman's mind is: could we have built a bigger gap between ourselves and our rivals?

Chris Ellerton, analyst at SG Warburg, says, 'I think First Direct was taken aback by its effect on people. But research told it one thing and experience another.'

Raoul Pinnell, National Westminster marketing director, says, 'First Direct has done a wonderful job introducing marketplace innovation. But with just 500,000 customers after five years, it has not made it work on a mass-market scale. With the banks and the building societies all now offering a similar range of services, I wonder where that leaves First Direct. I think it has missed its opportunity.'

Not surprisingly, Newman takes a different view. Going for quick growth would have forced the bank to compromise on service and price, thus creating a weaker brand, he says. And rivals still cannot completely match its proposition. For example, few of them offer an automatic overdraft facility.

'First Direct has become a generic term for telephone banking and we believe we will benefit from others advertising their services,' says Newman. 'Even now, we're still spending about 50% of our marketing dollars on educating the public about telephone banking, but this will reduce with others coming into the market. First Direct's aim is to have one million customers by the end of the century, representing about 20% of the dedicated telephone-banking market.

'We're not yet a mass-market player, but who knows what will happen in the future,' says Newman.

Time to shed a little tier or two

RESOURCE 9.4
by Alan Mitchell
Source: Marketing Week, 7 October 1994

Nestlé's announcement that it is to axe a number of second tier brand names highlights the huge cost of maintaining ad spend. But while a 'great brand cull' is on the agenda, huge opportunities exist for a new range of genuine niche brands.

People have been batting on about the demise of third and fourth-line grocery brands for as long as I can remember, but there have been few examples as dramatic as last Friday's restructuring announcement by Nestlé. In one fell swoop it has exited all its canning businesses. A significant swathe of brands are being chopped, mostly from the Crosse and Blackwell range. They include tomato ketchup, salad cream, baked beans, pasta and canned soups.

Some may dismiss this decision as an isolated case. After all, few categories face the same crushing combination of adverse factors: changing consumer preferences, severe overcapacity and new competition from international players such as Italian tomato canners. But that misses the point. Every brand that's axed in the coming cull will have its special circumstances, and how many aren't competing in a context of chronic overcapacity and intensifying competition from low-cost producers from abroad?

But why should the 'great brand cull' be starting now, just when we are supposed to be leaving recession behind us? Because of a combination of factors.

First, media inflation. Almost forgotten

during the recession, it's now staging a comeback – forcing companies with bloated brand portfolios to ask hard questions about how many of their precious offspring they can really afford to keep.

Recent research by the marketing consultancy Added Value illustrates the agonies brand managers can face. It reveals that the typical marketing (advertising and below-the-line) cost of being a 'big' (top 70) brand is nearly £8m – a sum that accounts for a high proportion of lesser brands' total sales.

A company like Kellogg can afford to invest £61m in advertising its range of 16 brands – giving each one a respectable critical mass. Meanwhile, firms like Heinz, with a total advertising spend of £15m to spread across 20-plus product categories – such as baked beans, soups, baby foods, ketchups and Weight Watchers – are left panting. Its average of £800,000 a category just isn't credible, hence Heinz's celebrated decision to go below the line.

A quick glance at Nestlé's brimming UK brand portfolio (which spans the bountiful Rowntree, Findus, Nescafé, Chambourcy, Crosse and Blackwell and Carnation stables, as well as Buitoni, Dufrais, Friskies, Foxes, Libbys, Gales, Sarsons and Sun Pat) suggests it is facing similar pressures.

Secondly, a radical reassessment of the Eighties fashion for brand extensions is underway. OK, some marketers did agonise about the risk of diluting and confusing core brand values. (Until the axe fell last week Crosse and Blackwell endorsed pickles, cold sauces, ketchups, salad creams, soups and baked beans. What exactly are its brand values? What does the brand name bring to the party?) But few ever looked beyond market share arguments to the broader considerations.

Retailers, for a start, don't like cluttering their shelves with scores of me-toos. Branded goods companies should be adding value, not cost (the more stock keeping units there are, the more expensive it gets). They should be making life simpler for consumers, not confusing them with a 'plethora of product variants'. And they should help them in their choices, not trying to manipulate them, as Andrew Dixon, a Tesco marketing controller, told marketers at a Marketing Forum session last month. Me-toos (which most range extensions are), he added ominously, do have a place in retailers' minds as a 'profit opportunity' – because manufacturers are forced to offer very fat margins just to keep their product on the shelves.

Further, any analysis of the true cost of producing range extensions shows that most cost more money than they make. A recent study by PA Consulting teased out these costs by looking at such things as the time and money spent researching and developing new formulations, packaging and promotions, factory stoppage time, extra storage and distribution costs. Its conclusion? On average, among the unnamed food companies investigated about half of their products produced 150 per cent of final profits, while the other half gobbled up 50 per cent (to leave the 100 per cent final total). Simply rationalising a brand portfolio, PA concluded, could be the cleverest and quickest way to turn a quick buck.

But perhaps the most urgent pressure on brands stems from another, totally different direction – retail competition. Figures produced by Verdict managing director Richard Hyman at a Marketing Society event earlier this year sum it all up. From the Sixties onwards, he pointed out, the expansion of the grocery multiples took place at the expense of independents. Until 1980 UK grocery shopping space was actually falling. But between 1980 and 1990 it jumped from 380 million sq ft to 450 million sq ft, just when cannibalisation of sales from the corner shop was coming to an end.

The crazy rush to add excess capacity to excess capacity hasn't stopped. Instead, as discounters establish themselves (discount shopping space was up 22 per cent in 1993 alone) the pressure on retailer prices and margins is becoming acute. That pressure is being passed back up the chain to suppliers – undermining the viability of once healthy, second tier brands.

These three factors – media and marketing costs, the quest to root out expensive complexity and the developing crisis in grocery retailing – all suggest that Nestlé's announcement will be the first of many. One implication is that over the next few years the real tests of marketing skill (and the real displays of ingenuity) may not be from among the well resourced, headline grabbing 'power brands' but from smaller brands that no longer have the muscle to play the marketing game by its old rules, or which see advantages in the gaps created by big firms clearing the weak and sickly from the brand undergrowth.

Indeed, be warned. As the inexorable logic of size and power sweeps all things commercial, all the social and political trends suggest that consumers are yearning for the opposite – the warmth that local identity or cultural roots provide. Consumers may be buying 'power brands' but they are also searching for community and identity.

Of course, in the real world they'll have both. But perhaps the ironic result of a second tier brand blood-bath will be the huge opportunities it opens up for a new raft of genuine niche brands.

A jungle full of strange bedfellows

RESOURCE 9.5 ◁

by Katie Munson
Source: *Marketing,*
25 March 1993

When is a manufacturer not a manufacturer, or a retailer not a retailer? Forget the complications of factories and industrial processes. Companies like Reebok or Compaq have decided that they do not need to produce trainers or computers to remain market leaders.

The strategy of the 'virtual company' is to concentrate upon a key competence which could be marketing, design or distribution and then contract suppliers to manufacture the products. The key to such an organisation is the control of information and the formation of close partnerships with suppliers.

Traditionally, in many sectors, the supplier/buyer relationship has been hostile, or at best confrontational. In the commercial jungle, size has dictated terms and volumes have ruled the roost. But not any more. Take the food industry for example. The major food retailers have been operating as 'virtual companies' with respect to their own brands for some years now, majoring on marketing and distribution, but avoiding becoming too involved in the nitty-gritty of either production plants or the actual machinery.

For the most far-sighted companies, supplier relations go way beyond the mere physical aspects of bulk buying. Reliability and quality consistency are paramount, and often outweigh cost considerations – even in a difficult economic climate. Further, the negotiation process is working both ways. Placing big orders will not necessarily guarantee favourable terms from a supplier. Other factors, such as regularity and variability of purchasing, frequency of delivery and adherence to promotional activity in-store are gaining prominence in negotiations.

Companies are becoming more closely interwoven into partnerships based on mutual benefits and flexible arrangements. Demonstrating quality and consistency inevitably requires better communication and procedures, and the transference of information is the key to successful operation. In practice this means sharing sensitive sales information and – more importantly – sharing sales forecasts.

We have some way to go before the supply chain is so smooth that it fits perfectly with demand and operates cost-effectively and efficiently. Nevertheless, the use of techniques such as DPP and analysis of EPOS data allow distributors to fine-tune merchandise ranges at detailed level. By sharing such information, they can offer the consumer a range of products that they want to buy, and by being able to predict purchasing patterns more easily, can match demand with supply.

Of course, measuring the level of

demand will be the key to success as recovery gains momentum. One thing is sure, however, in the commercial jungle described above, it is neither the manufacturer, retailer or 'virtual company' that rules – as the ultimate controller of demand, it is the consumer who is king.